Politics in the European Union

Third Edition

Ian Bache, Stephen George & Simon Bulmer

OXFORD

UNIVERSITY PRESS

OXFORD
UNIVERSITY PRESS

Great Clarendon Street, Oxford OX2 6DP

Oxford University Press is a department of the University of Oxford.
It furthers the University's objective of excellence in research, scholarship,
and education by publishing worldwide in

Oxford New York

Auckland Cape Town Dar es Salaam Hong Kong Karachi
Kuala Lumpur Madrid Melbourne Mexico City Nairobi
New Delhi Shanghai Taipei Toronto

With offices in

Argentina Austria Brazil Chile Czech Republic France Greece
Guatemala Hungary Italy Japan Poland Portugal Singapore
South Korea Switzerland Thailand Turkey Ukraine Vietnam

Oxford is a registered trade mark of Oxford University Press
in the UK and in certain other countries

Published in the United States
by Oxford University Press Inc., New York

British Library Cataloguing in Publication Data

Data available

Library of Congress Cataloguing in Publication Data

Data available

Typeset by Techset Composition Ltd, Salisbury, UK
Printed in Italy on acid-free paper by L.E.G.O. S.p.A. Lavis (TN)

ISBN 978-0-19-954481-3

10 9 8 7 6 5 4 3 2 1

Blackburn
College

Library
01254 292120

Contents in Brief

Contents in Detail

Map of Europe

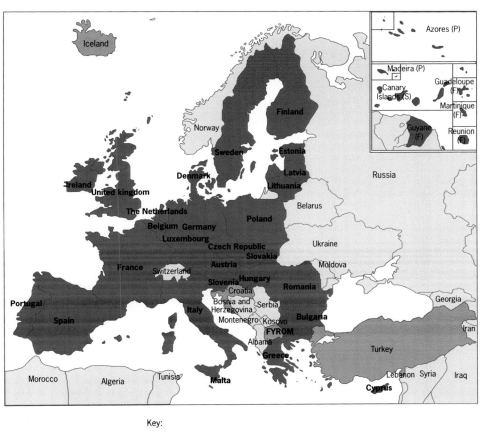

Key:

■	EU member state	(P) :	Portuguese territory
■	EU candidate country	(S):	Spanish territory
□	Non-EU country	(F):	French territory

About the Authors

Ian Bache is Professor of Politics at the University of Sheffield. He has published widely on the European Union and related issues, including: *The Politics of European Union Regional Policy*, UACES/Sheffield Academic Press, 1998; *Politics in the European Union* (with Stephen George), Oxford University Press, 1st edition 2001, 2nd edition 2006; *Multi-Level Governance* (with Matthew Flinders), Oxford University Press, 2004; *The Europeanization of British Politics* (with Andrew Jordan), Palgrave Macmillan, 2006; *Europeanization and Multilevel Governance*, Rowman and Littlefield, 2008; and *Cohesion Policy and Multi-level Governance in South East Europe* (with George Andreou), Routledge, 2011.

He has published in a range academic journals, including: the *British Journal of Politics and International Relations*; *Current Politics and Economics of Europe*; *Governance*; *Journal of Common Market Studies*; *Journal of European Public Policy*; *Journal of Public Policy*; *Journal of Southeast European and Black Sea Studies*; *Local Government Studies*; *Political Studies*; *Public Administration*; *Public Policy and Administration*; *Regional and Federal Studies*; *Scandinavian Political Studies*; and *West European Politics*. Between 2003 and 2005, he convened the UACES Study Group and ESRC Seminar Series on The Europeanization of British Politics and Policy Making.

Ian is an experienced teacher, having taught numerous undergraduate and postgraduate courses, and has supervised ten PhD students to completion. In 2008, he received a University of Sheffield Senate Award for Sustained Excellence in Teaching and Learning.

Stephen George taught in the Department of Politics at the University of Sheffield for thirty years, the last ten as Professor. During that time he authored or co-authored four major books on the European Community/European Union, two of which—*Politics and Policy in the European Union* and *An Awkward Partner: Britain in the European Union*—went into multiple editions. He also edited books on Europe, and contributed some two dozen chapters to edited books and articles to several academic journals, including *The Annals of the American Academy of Political and Social Science*, *The British Journal of International Studies*, *Contemporary Record*, *Current Politics and Economics of Europe*, *European Access*, *International Affairs*, *Journal of European Integration*, *Journal of European Public Policy*, *Millennium: Journal of International Studies*, *Modern History Review*, *West European Politics*, and *The World Today*. He has given innumerable talks, guest lectures, and conference papers throughout the world, mostly on aspects of the European Union. Between 1997 and 2000, he was Chair of the University Association for Contemporary European Studies (UACES). As a teacher he successfully supervised eight PhD students, and for undergraduate students devised innovative teaching materials on the European Union, including a simulation exercise in European decision making. Since 2003, he has been Emeritus Professor of Politics, retired from active teaching and administration, but still involved in research and writing.

Simon Bulmer has been Professor of European Politics at the University of Sheffield since September 2007. Having held prior lectureships at Heriot-Watt University and the University of Manchester Institute of Science and Technology (UMIST), he moved to the University of Manchester in 1989, was appointed Professor of Government from 1995, and served as Head of Department 2001–04. He has held a Jean Monnet *ad personam* chair since 1999 and has been an Academician of the Social Sciences since 2001. He has been a Visiting Professor at the College of Europe Bruges, the Autonomous University of Barcelona, and the Stiftung Wissenschaft und Politik (the German Institute for International and Security Affairs), Berlin. From 1991 to 1998 he co-edited the *Journal of Common Market Studies*.

Simon has written or edited thirteen books on European politics, working with a range of co-authors. His most recent monograph (with Martin Burch) is *The European-isation of Whitehall: UK Central Government and the European Union*, Manchester University Press, 2009. His most recent edited book (with Charlie Jeffery and Stephen Padgett) is *Rethinking Germany and Europe: Democracy and Diplomacy in a Semi-Sovereign State*, Palgrave, 2010. With Christian Lequesne he co-edited the textbook, *The Member States of the European Union*, Oxford University Press, 2005 (2nd edition in preparation). He has published on European politics in leading academic journals, has taught on the EU in the United Kingdom, Spain, Belgium, and the USA, and has supervised eleven PhD students to completion.

About the Book

This is a textbook on the study of the European Union (EU) within the cognate disciplines of political science and international relations. It reflects both the most significant contributions to the study of the EU within these disciplines and the gaps in existing research. It is designed to be used by students as part of a university course or module, although we hope it works well for the independent reader also.

While we would argue that there is no easy separation between economics and politics, or between law and politics, this book is explicitly concerned with politics in the EU. Thus we address some of the standard issues of the disciplines of political science and international relations. Is the EU developing into a super-state of some sort? If so, of what sort? Have national governments voluntarily surrendered sovereignty to European institutions, or are there forces at work dragging member states towards ever closer union against the will of the governments? Is the process driven by vested interests that stand to benefit from it, or by ideas that place a positive value on international integration? Does the process have legitimacy in the eyes of the people who are being brought into an ever closer union? If so, why? If not, why not?

These questions are relevant not because of their practical importance—although they do have a great deal of practical importance; nor because they figure in the coverage of the EU in the media—although because of their practical importance they do so figure. Rather, they are relevant because they are questions generated by the theories of political scientists and students of international relations about the nature of European integration and of the EU. Academic disciplines are formed when scholars are brought together by shared concerns, and they are forged by academic debates, which are fiercest when they are between advocates of different theories. That is why the textbook begins with theory. It is theory that provides our criteria of relevance. Many eclectic textbooks do exist in politics and international relations, books that never mention theory—and we are not thinking here exclusively of books on the EU. Our view is that theory is very important. It shapes what is studied and what is not, what is included and what is excluded. We see it as central to the study of the EU and not as an optional extra. However, for those who wish to know something of the EU before approaching theoretical issues, it is possible to read the 'History' section of the book first without having read the 'Theory' section: it is primarily the conclusions to the 'History' chapters that refer back to the theories in Part One.

In our final 'History' chapter of the previous edition, we suggested that the EU was at a crossroads, but that this was hardly new. Nevertheless, the crisis caused by the problems ratifying the Constitutional Treaty was perhaps as great as any in the EU's history and for some commentators threatened catastrophic consequences. We closed by saying: 'The question raised by the current crisis is not whether the EU will survive—it surely will. The question raised is "what kind of EU will emerge from the crisis?"'

We delayed writing this third edition until there was some clarity in this respect. It is now clear that the EU will proceed with most of the provisions of the Constitutional Treaty, although somewhat chastened by having to remove the more symbolic and statist aspects following its initial rejection in France and the Netherlands. The revised version, the Lisbon Treaty, brought further embarrassment with the need for Ireland to stage a second referendum before securing approval.

Change happens not only in the field of study, but also in the study of the field. Between the first and second editions of the book (2001–06), the study of the EU expanded tremendously and it continues to do so. In the area of theory, the developments have continued to be rich and varied, and this section has expanded to include new approaches or, more accurately, established approaches that have relatively recently been applied to the EU. The section on 'Institutions' has been completely overhauled to incorporate the changes brought by the Lisbon Treaty and to include the most recent academic contributions. Obviously the output did not just stop when we finished writing, so there will be more for the student to explore, but we think that this edition is as up to date on the academic literature as it could be. The strong rooting of the text in the research literature is one of the distinctive features of this book.

We have also made changes in response to the comments made to us about the second edition. In consultation with the team at Oxford University Press we have worked to make the pedagogical features more useful. In the 'Policies' section we have added two new chapters, on 'Environmental Policy' and on 'Freedom, Security, and Justice', which reflect both the EU's growing role in these areas and the increased academic attention they have received. To help us to produce this edition by our deadline, the first of these chapters was written by a guest author, Vasilis Leontitsis, although we will assume responsibility for this topic in subsequent editions.

Last but certainly not least, Ian and Stephen are delighted to welcome Simon Bulmer on board as a co-author for the third and subsequent editions of the book. Simon has taken over lead authorship on areas of the book previously led by Stephen and will take on more in the next edition as Stephen steps back further to enjoy his retirement.

New to this Edition:

- Simon Bulmer joins Ian Bache and Stephen George as a new author for the third edition.
- There is thorough consideration of the Lisbon Treaty in a new chapter, while its impact on each institution and policy area is also explored throughout the text.
- Two new chapters on environmental policy, and freedom, security, and justice provide a detailed examination of these important contemporary issues.
- The Online Resource Centre, which accompanies the text, has also been updated with new materials for students and lecturers.

Acknowledgements

This is the third edition of a textbook that first appeared in 2001 and then again in 2006. In revising it we have been helped enormously by the comments of colleagues and students who used these previous editions. We are particularly grateful to those colleagues who acted as anonymous referees for the drafts of this edition (they are identified and credited by the publisher below).

In addition to the academic reviewers credited elsewhere, we would like to thank Damian Chalmers, Tammy Hervey, Daniela Kietz, Arlene McCarthy MEP, and Roderick Parkes for their help and advice on various points. We have tried to incorporate as many of the comments received as possible, but some we have not been able to accommodate for reasons of time and space.

We would like to thank all of the production staff at Oxford University Press, and in particular Catherine Page, Joanna Hardern, Vanessa Plaister, and Mary Sheridan, for their advice, skill, and patience.

We have been tremendously encouraged by the positive feedback that we have received from users of our previous edition and from the referees on the drafts of the chapters that are new in this edition. We hope that it will continue to prove a stimulating textbook for all who use it and will lead to stimulating and critical debates in the classroom.

Ian Bache
Stephen George
Simon Bulmer
July 2010

Copyright acknowledgements

We are grateful to those listed below for permission to reproduce copyrighted material.

- The map of Europe that appears at the front of this book is adapted from the original published on <http://europa/eu> © European Union. Responsibility for the adaptation lies entirely with Oxford University Press.
- Table 2.1 is from J. Peterson (1995), 'Decision Making in the European Union: Towards a Framework for Analysis'. *Journal of European Public Policy*, 2: 69–93. Reprinted with the permission of the Taylor & Francis Group.

- Table 2.2 is from L. Hooghe and G. Marks (2004), 'Contrasting Visions of Multi-level Governance', in I. Bache and M. Flinders (eds), *Multi-level Governance*. Oxford: Oxford University Press, 15–30. Reprinted with the permission of Oxford University Press.
- Figure 3.1 is from T. Christiansen, K. Jørgensen, and A. Wiender (1999), 'The Social Construction of Europe'. *Journal of European Public Policy*, 6: 528–44. Reprinted with the permission of the Taylor & Francis Group.
- Table 4.4 is from C. Lord and P. Magnette (2004), '*E Pluribus Unum*? Creative Disagreement about Legitimacy in the EU'. *Journal of Common Market Studies*, 42: 183–202. Reprinted with the permission of John Wiley and Sons.

Every effort has been made to trace and contact copyright holders, but this has not always been possible in every case. If notified, the publisher will undertake to rectify any errors or omissions at the earliest opportunity.

Reviewers

This edition has benefited from the thoughtful criticisms and valuable insights of a range of political experts. Oxford University Press would like to acknowledge all of the reviewers for their contribution to the book, which include, but are not limited to:

Michael Burgess, University of Kent, Canterbury

Jan Erik Grindheim, University of Agder and University of Bergen

Mary Murphy, University College Cork

George Christou, University of Warwick

Fabio Franchino, University of Milan

Tim Haughton, University of Birmingham

Andrew Jordan, University of East Anglia

Elena Korosteleva-Polglase, University of Wales, Aberystwyth

Sandra Lavenex, University of Lucerne

Andrea Lenschow, University of Osnabrück

Simon Matti, Luleå University of Technology

Daniela Obradovic, University of Amsterdam

Tapio Raunio, University of Tampere

Chad Rector, George Washington University

Anna Syngellakis, University of Portsmouth

Lori Thorlakson, University of Alberta

Emek Uçarer, Bucknell University

Guided Tour of Textbook Features

This book is enriched with a number of learning tools to help you navigate the text and reinforce your knowledge of EU politics. This guided tour shows you how to get the most out of your textbook package.

Chapter overviews

Chapter 27

The Single Market

Chapter Overview

Although the European Union (EU) is much more than just a common market, the economic ideal of a common or single European market lies at its core. The aspiration to create a common market was fundamental in the decision in the mid-1950s to set up the European Economic Community (EEC). Thirty years later, the decision to institute a drive to achieve a single internal market by the end of 1992 was fundamental to the revival of European integration. It is hardly surprising, therefore, that analyses of the causes and consequences of these decisions have also been fundamental to theoretical debates about European integration.

This chapter looks at the original decision to create a common market, the patchy record of progress from the 1960s through to the 1980s, then at the moves to complete the internal market, what became known as the single-market programme, in the 1980s. It also reviews the development of internal-market policy, and the record of implementation beyond 1992.

The single market programme marked a turning point in European integration.
(Young 2005: 93)

Chapter overviews set the scene for upcoming themes and issues to be discussed, and indicate the scope of coverage within the chapter.

Insight boxes

Insight 1.1 European Integration

European integration has a number of aspects, but the main focus of Chapter 1 is on *political integration*. E. B. Haas (1968: 16) provided a definition of European political integration as a *process*, whereby:

> political actors in several distinct national settings are persuaded to shift their loyalties, expectations and political activities toward a new center, whose institutions possess or demand jurisdiction over the pre-existing national states. The end result of a process of political integration is a new political community, superimposed over the pre-existing ones.

Implicit in Haas's definition was the development of a European federal state. More cautiously, Lindberg (1963: 149) provided a definition of political integration as a process, but without reference to an end point:

> political integration is (1) the process whereby nations forego the desire and ability to conduct foreign and key domestic policies independently of each other, seeking instead to make *joint* decisions or to delegate the decision-making process to new central organs; and (2) the process whereby political actors in several distinct national settings are persuaded to shift their expectations and political activities to a new center.

The first part of this definition refers to two 'intimately related' modes of decision-making: sharing and delegating. The second part of the definition refers to 'the patterns of behaviour shown by high policy makers, civil servants, parliamentarians, interest group leaders and other élites' (Lindberg 1963: 149), who respond to the new reality of a shift in political authority to the centre by reorientating their political activities to the European level.

Throughout the book, insight boxes provide you with extra information on particular topics to complement your understanding of the main chapter text.

Glossary terms

Key terms appear emboldened in red in the text and are defined in a glossary at the end of the book to aid you in exam revision.

> **Forms of Interest Representation**
>
> Several forms of interest representation coexist in the EU:
>
> - the full institutionalization of representation through the European Economic and Social Committee (EESC)
> - the semi-institutionalized 'social dialogue'
> - a pluralist system based on competitive lobbying
> - informally institutionalized policy networks
> - legal representation.
>
> The EESC has its origins in the 'corporatist' institutions that were set up between the wars in Germany (the Economic Council) and France (the *Conseil Economique et Social*) and that were created or recreated in five of the six original member states after the war, Germany being the exception. The EESC has not proven to be a particularly effective institution (Chapter 19, pp. xxx–xx), and when new forms of institutionalized relations between government, business, and trade unions were tried in several member states during the 1970s, attempts to replicate them at the EU level did not involve this institution. Instead, the ministers of social affairs and economic and financial affairs organized a series of Tripartite Conferences bringing together European business and trade union organizations in an arrangement that is often referred to as neo–corporatism. The Tripartite Conferences met six times in 1978 to discuss issues such as employment, inflation, wage restraint, fiscal policy, vocational training, and measures to increase productivity. The business groups were reluctant participants, though, and by the end of 1978 the European Trade Union Confederation (ETUC) had withdrawn from the process because of lack of progress.

Key points

At the end of each chapter is a set of key points that summarize the most important arguments developed in each section.

> often argue that democracy cannot be established at the European level because there is no such thing as a European people: democracy can only operate within national cultures. If an attempt is made to force the diverse peoples of Europe into an artificial union, nationalism will be stirred up rather than be abolished. Here also, Europeanization processes may be crucial. However, this may be less to do with changes in formal institutions and policy through membership of the EU, and more to do with the diffusion of informal norms and values among EU citizens.
>
> **KEY POINTS**
>
> **Europeanization**
>
> - Europeanization has emerged as a key concept in EU studies and has been defined and employed in a variety of ways. For some, Europeanization is a phenomenon that is broader than or separate from the EU. However, it is predominantly used to conceptualize the changing relationship between the EU and its member (and accession) states.
> - Ladrech provided an influential early conceptualization of Europeanization. He highlighted the importance of domestic factors in mediating Europeanization effects and argued that fears of harmonization or homogenization across European states were thus unfounded.
> - Europeanization has increasingly become understood as a two-way relationship between the EU and its member states, involving both the uploading of ideas and practices from member states to the EU level as well as the downloading of ideas and practices from the EU level to member states. However, the focus of most research has been on the downloading effects.
> - The notion of *crossloading* refers to the transfer of ideas or practices from one state to another: a process in which the EU may or may not play a role.
> - *First generation* studies tended to focus on observable changes through Europeanization and explained variations in relation to the degree of fit or misfit between EU decisions and

Further reading

Take your learning further by using the reading lists at the end of chapter to fi nd the key literature in the field, or more detailed information on a specific topic.

> **FURTHER READING**
>
> For a wide-ranging review of critical perspectives on the study of the EU, see I. Manners, 'Another Europe is Possible' in K.E. Jorgensen, M. Pollack, and B. Rosamond (eds.), *Handbook of European Union Politics* (London: Sage, 2007), 77–95.
>
> On constructivism, see the influential collection in the Special Issue of the *Journal of European Public Policy*, 6, No. 4 (1999:), edited by T. Christiansen, K. Jørgensen, and A. Wiener. Other helpful contributions are: J. Checkel and A. Moravcsik, 'A Constructivist Research Programme in EU Studies?', *European Union Politics*, 2 (2001): 1–40. Key contributions on critical political economy include J. Checkel, 'Constructivism and EU Politics' in K. E. Jørgensen, M. Pollack, and B. Rosamond (eds.), *Handbook of European Union Politics* (London: Sage, 2007), 57–76; T. Risse, 'Social Constructivism and European Integration' in A. Wiener and T. Diez (eds.), *European Integration Theory*, 2nd edition, (Oxford: Oxford University Press, 2009), 144–60.
>
> For an overview of critical political economy perspectives see A. Cafruny and M. Ryner, 'Critical Political Economy' in A. Wiener and T. Diez (eds.), *European Integration Theory*, 2nd edition, (Oxford: Oxford University Press, 2009), 221–40. A clear statement of the Marxist position on European integration can be found in P. Cocks 'Towards a Marxist Theory of European Integration', *International Organization*, 31(1980): 1–40. Key contributions on critical political economy include A. Bieler, and A. Morton (eds.), *Social Forces in the Making of the New Europe: The Restructuring of European Social Relations in the Global Political Economy* (London: Palgrave, 2001); B. van Apeldoorn, *Transnational Capitalism and the Struggle over European Integration* (London: Routledge, 2002); A. Cafruny and M. Ryner (eds.), *A Ruined Fortress? Neoliberal Hegemony and Transformation in Europe* (Lanham: Rowman and Littlefield, 2003); and A. Cafruny and M. Ryner, *Europe at Bay: Neoliberal Hegemony and Transformation in Europe* (Boulder: Lynne Rienner, 2007).
>
> On gender perspectives there are a number of helpful overview pieces, including: C. Hoskyns 'Gender Perspectives' in A. Wiener and T. Diez (eds.), *European Integration Theory* (Oxford: Oxford University Press, 2004), 217–36; B. Locher, and E. Prügl, 'Gender and European Integration' in

Guided Tour of the Online Resource Centre

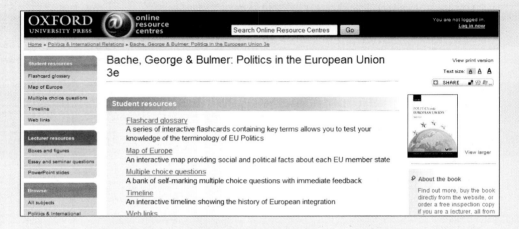

www.oxfordtextbooks.co.uk/orc/bache3e/

The Online Resource Centre that accompanies this book provides students and instructors with ready-to-use teaching and learning materials. These resources are free of charge and designed to maximize the learning experience.

The Online Resource Centre Resources have been updated by Dr. Mary Murphy of University College Cork.

For students

Interactive map of Europe

An interactive map provides a wealth of social and political facts about each EU member state. Simply click on the state you are interested in and the information appears in a separate window.

Interactive timeline

Use the interactive timeline to improve your knowledge of the history of European integration. Key events are summarized when you click on each date.

Multiple-choice questions

A bank of self-marking multiple-choice questions has been provided for each chapter of the text to reinforce your understanding, and act as an aid to revision.

Flashcard glossary

A series of interactive flashcards containing key terms allows you to test your knowledge of the terminology of EU politics.

Web links

A selection of annotated web links, which accompanies each chapter, will point you in the direction of important treaties, working papers, articles, and other relevant sources of information on EU politics.

For Registered Adopters of the Book

PowerPoint® slides

PowerPoint® slides complement each chapter of the book and are a useful resource for preparing lectures and handouts.

Essay and seminar questions

A range of essay and seminar questions have been devised to be used in assessment, or to stimulate class debate.

Boxes and figures from the text

Boxes and figures from the text have been provided in high-resolution format for downloading into presentation software or for use in assignments and exam material.

Part One
Theory

This part of the book consists of four chapters. Its purpose is twofold: first, to review the main theories used in the study of the European Union (EU); and second, to identify themes that will inform our analysis of subsequent chapters. We do not see this exercise as being an optional extra for a textbook: it is fundamental to understanding the academic study of EU.

Our understanding of the world is guided by our particular conceptual lenses or theoretical frameworks, whether we are aware of them or not. The theoretical frameworks we adopt determine the questions we ask, and so the answers that we find. As Rosamond (2003: 110) suggests: '... being conscious about the theoretical propositions chosen by authors is vital because alternative "readings" of the EU and European integration follow from alternative theoretical premises.'

There has been no shortage of theoretical models and frameworks applied to understanding EU politics and we provide an overview of what to us appear to be the most important. While doing this inevitably requires a degree of choice, there is considerable consensus among scholars about particular phases in the study of the EU, which our selection reflects.

The first phase of study, during the early stages of co-operation between western European states, was dominated by approaches from the study of international relations (IR). As the EU became more established and institutionalized, IR approaches were increasingly accompanied by insights from the study of domestic and comparative politics. The most straightforward way of understanding this theoretical shift is to see it as a move away from treating the EU as an international organization similar to others (such as the North Atlantic Treaty Organization—NATO) to seeing it as something unique, with some features more akin to those of national political systems. The approaches derived from IR are set out in Chapter 1, 'Theories of European Integration', and those based primarily on domestic and comparative politics approaches are set out in Chapter 2, 'Theories of EU Governance'.

While these approaches continue to provide important contributions to the study of the EU, they have been joined by more critical perspectives that question many of the assumptions on which these approaches are based. The range of critical perspectives now applied to the EU is vast and disparate, so we focus on three that give a flavour of the contrasting perspectives that share an emphasis on revealing the hidden sources of power. These are *social constructivism*, *critical political economy*, and *gender perspectives*.

In our final chapter in this section, we turn to attempts to theorize some of the most important implications of European integration. Specifically, Chapter 4, 'Theorizing Consequences', looks at the contribution of *Europeanization* to understanding the domestic consequences of European integration, while the second part of the chapter is devoted to approaches to understanding the challenges for *democracy*.

Chapter 1

Theories of European Integration

Chapter Overview

The dominant approaches to understanding the early phase of European integration came from international relations (IR). In particular, the study of integration was dominated by the competing approaches of neofunctionalism and intergovernmentalism. Although neofunctionalist theory neatly fitted events in the 1950s and early 1960s, subsequent events led to its demise and the rise of intergovernmentalist explanations. While theorizing European integration has moved on significantly from these early approaches, much of what followed was either framed by this debate or developed as a rejection of it. The debate about whether the EU is characterized by intergovernmentalism or supranationalism still informs much of the academic work on the subject.

'International theory' has been too readily written off by contemporary writers seeking to offer theoretical treatments of the EU ...

(Rosamond 1999: 19)

The signing of the Treaty of Paris in April 1951 by the governments of Belgium, France, Germany, Italy, Luxembourg, and the Netherlands (Chapter 6, p. 92) began the process commonly referred to as European integration (see Insight 1.1). This process has meant that the economies of participating states, and subsequently other areas, have been increasingly managed in common. Decisions previously taken by national governments alone are now taken together with other governments, and specially created European institutions. Governments have relinquished the sole right to make legislation (national sovereignty) over a range of matters, in favour of joint decision making with other governments (pooled sovereignty). Other tasks have been delegated to European institutions.

It was something of a surprise to academic theorists of IR when governments in western Europe began to surrender their national sovereignty in some policy areas. For the first half of the twentieth century, the nation state seemed assured of its place as the most important unit of political life in the western world, especially in Europe. As such, the process of European integration constituted a major challenge to existing theories and generated an academic debate about the role of the state in the process. The two competing theories that emerged from IR to dominate the debate over early

> ### Insight 1.1 European Integration
>
> European integration has a number of aspects, but the main focus of Chapter 1 is on *political* integration. Ernst Haas (1968: 16) provided a definition of European political integration as a *process*, whereby:
>
> > political actors in several distinct national settings are persuaded to shift their loyalties, expectations and political activities toward a new center, whose institutions possess or demand jurisdiction over the pre-existing national states. The end result of a process of political integration is a new political community, superimposed over the pre-existing ones.
>
> Implicit in Haas's definition was the development of a European federal state. More cautiously, Lindberg (1963: 149) provided a definition of political integration as a process, but without reference to an end point:
>
> > political integration is (1) the process whereby nations forego the desire and ability to conduct foreign and key domestic policies independently of each other, seeking instead to make *joint decisions* or to *delegate* the decision-making process to new central organs; and (2) the process whereby political actors in several distinct national settings are persuaded to shift their expectations and political activities to a new center.
>
> The first part of this definition refers to two 'intimately related' modes of decision making: sharing and delegating. The second part of the definition refers to 'the patterns of behaviour shown by high policy makers, civil servants, parliamentarians, interest group leaders and other elites' (Lindberg 1963: 149), who respond to the new reality of a shift in political authority to the centre by reorientating their political activities to the European level.

developments in European integration were neofunctionalism (Haas 1958; Lindberg 1963) and intergovernmentalism (Hoffmann 1964; 1966).

Before discussing these two main positions in the debate, it is necessary to consider the intellectual context from which the idea of European integration emerged. Below we look first at the functionalist ideas of David Mitrany on how to avoid war between nations, then at the ideas of the European federalists, and finally at the 'federal-functionalism' of Jean Monnet. We then turn to look first at neofunctionalism and then at intergovernmentalism, before looking at two later contributions to this debate: liberal intergovernmentalism and supranational governance.

The Intellectual Background

To understand the ideas that fed into the first attempts to theorize European integration, it is useful to start with one of the approaches that was influential after the Second World War about how to avoid another war. This 'functionalist' idea, which was particularly associated with the writings of David Mitrany, informed the United Nations movement. It was a theory of how to achieve world peace, rather than a theory of regional integration, and it took a very different approach to the question from the European federalists, who wanted to subordinate national governments to an overarching federal authority. The ideas of both the functionalists and the federalists were brought together in the 'functional-federalism' of Jean Monnet, which in turn provided one important source of intellectual inspiration for the neofunctionalist theory of European integration.

Mitrany and Functionalism

David Mitrany (1888–1974) was born in Romania, but spent most of his adult life in Britain and the United States. He was not a theorist of European integration. His concern was with building a *Working Peace System*, the title of his Fabian pamphlet (Mitrany 1966; first published 1943). For Mitrany, the root cause of war was nationalism. The failure of the League of Nations to prevent aggression prompted debate about a new type of international system even before the outbreak of the Second World War. For those who blamed the failure of the League on its limited powers, the response was the development of an international federation. In other words, the League had not gone far enough and the same mistake should not be repeated: henceforth, nations should be tied more closely together.

Mitrany did not agree with the idea of federation as the means of tying states together. He opposed the idea of a single world government because he believed that it would pose a threat to individual freedom. He also opposed the creation of regional federations, believing that this would simply reproduce national rivalries on a larger scale. Any political reorganization into separate units must sooner or later produce the same effects; any international system that is to usher in a new world must produce the opposite effect of subduing political division.

Instead of either of these possibilities—a world federation or regional federations—Mitrany proposed the creation of a whole series of separate international functional agencies, each having authority over one specific area of human life. His scheme was to take individual technical tasks out of the control of governments and to hand them over to these functional agencies. He believed that governments would be prepared to surrender control because they would not feel threatened by the loss of sovereignty over, say, health care or the co-ordination of railway timetables, and they would be able to appreciate the advantages of such tasks being performed at the regional or world level. As more and more areas of control were surrendered, states would become less capable of independent action. One day, the national governments would discover that they were enmeshed in a 'spreading web of international activities and agencies' (Mitrany 1966: 35).

These international agencies would operate at different levels depending on the function that they were performing. Mitrany gave the example of systems of communication. Railways would be organized on a continental basis; shipping would be organized on an intercontinental basis; aviation would be organized on a universal basis. Not only would the dependence of states on these agencies for their day-to-day functioning make it difficult for governments to break with them, but the experience of the operation of the agencies would also socialize politicians, civil servants, and the general public into adopting less nationalistic attitudes and outlook.

Spinelli and Federalism

A completely different approach to guaranteeing peace was devised during the war in the ranks of the various Resistance movements. It was a specifically European movement, and whereas Mitrany aimed explicitly to depoliticize the process of the transfer of power away from national governments, federalists sought a clear transfer of political authority.

The European Union of Federalists (EUF) was formed in December 1946 from the war-time Resistance movements. It was particularly strong in Italy, where the leading figure was Altiero Spinelli. Federalism appealed to the Resistance groups because it proposed superseding nationalism. It is important to bear in mind that whereas in Britain (and Russia) the Second World War was a nationalist war (in the former Soviet Union, it was 'the great patriotic war'), in countries such as France and Italy it was an ideological war. Resistance fighters drawn from communist, socialist, and Christian democratic groups were in many cases fighting their own countrymen—Vichy supporters in France, Italian Fascists in Italy.

While being held as political prisoners of the Fascists on the island of Ventotene, Spinelli and Ernesto Rossi (1897–1967) produced the Ventotene Manifesto (1941), calling for a 'European Federation'. It argued that, left alone, the classes 'most privileged under old national systems' would seek to reconstruct the order of nation states at the end of the war. While these states might appear democratic, it would only be a matter of time before power returned to the hands of the privileged classes. This would prompt the return of national jealousies and ultimately, to renewed war between states. To prevent this development, the Manifesto called for the abolition of the division of Europe into national, sovereign states. It urged propaganda and action to bring together the separate national Resistance movements across Europe to push for the creation of a federal European state.

The EUF adopted the Ventotene Manifesto, and began agitating for an international conference to be called that would draw up a federal constitution for Europe. This ambitious proposal was designed to build on what Milward called 'the wave of hope for a better world and a changed future for the human race which had swept across Europe' and which included an 'extraordinary wave of enthusiasm for European federation' (Milward 1984: 55).

The strategy of the EUF was to exploit the disruption caused by the war to existing political structures in order to make a new start on a radically different basis from the Europe of national states. They aimed to achieve a complete break from the old order of nation states, and to create a federal constitution for Europe. Their Congress took time to organize, though. It eventually took place in The Hague in May 1948 (see Chapter 5, p. 83). By that time, the national political systems had been re-established, and what emerged from the Congress was an intergovernmental organization, the Council of Europe, not the new federal constitutional order for which the federalists had hoped. Many federalists then turned to the gradualist approach that was successfully embodied in the European Coal and Steel Community (ECSC).

Monnet and Functional-Federalism

The plan for the ECSC was known as the Schuman Plan because it was made public by the French Foreign Minister Robert Schuman, but it is generally accepted that it was drawn up within the French Economic Planning Commission (*Commissariat du Plan*), which was headed by the technocrat Jean Monnet. It was the task of the Planning Commission to guide the post-war reconstruction and modernization of the French economy, and it was through his experiences in this task that Monnet came to appreciate the economic inadequacy of the European nation state in the modern world. He saw the need to create a 'large and dynamic **common market**', 'a huge continental market on the European scale' (Monnet 1962: 205). He aimed, though, to create more than just a common market.

Monnet was a planner: he showed no great confidence in the free-market system, which had served France rather badly in the past. He placed his faith in the development of **supranational institutions** as the basis for building a genuine economic community that would adopt common economic policies and rational planning procedures. Coal and steel were only intended as starting points. The aim was to extend integration to all aspects of the western European economy—but such a scheme would have been too ambitious to gain acceptance all at once. There had been a clear indication of this in the failure of previous efforts to integrate the economies of France, Italy, the Netherlands, Belgium, and Luxembourg.

There was also a new factor in the equation, the key factor prompting Monnet's plan: the emergence in 1949 of a West German state. For Monnet, the existence of the Federal Republic of Germany posed two problems in addition to that of how to create an integrated western European economy. The first problem was how to organize Franco–German relations in such a way that another war between the two states would become impossible. To a French mind, this meant how to control Germany. The pooling of coal and steel production would provide the basis for economic development as a first step towards a 'federation of Europe'. Stimulating the expansion of those industries for peaceful purposes would provide an economic alternative to producing war materials for those regions of Europe that had been largely dependent on providing military material. The second problem facing Monnet was the very practical one of how to ensure adequate supplies of coking coal from the Ruhr for the French steel industry. The idea of pooling Franco-German supplies of coal and steel would tie the two states into a mutual economic dependency, in addition to taking out of the immediate control of the national governments the most basic raw materials for waging another war.

Mitrany (1966) described Monnet's strategy as 'federal-functionalism'. It is not clear, though, how far Monnet was a federalist at all. He might be seen as a supreme pragmatist who proposed the ECSC as a solution to the very practical problems described above. To solve these problems, Monnet adopted a solution similar to that of Mitrany: remove control of the strategically crucial industries—coal and steel—from the governments and put it in the hands of a free-standing agency. This was the High Authority of the ECSC, and in Monnet's original plan it was the only institution proposed. The development of other supranational institutions came from other pressures (see Chapter 7). The High Authority was the prototype for the later Commission of the European Economic Community (EEC), which became central to the neofunctionalist theory of European integration.

International Relations Theories of European Integration

Realism was the dominant approach in IR in the 1950s. It assumed that sovereign states formed the fundamental units of analysis for understanding IR. The appearance of the European Community (EC) therefore provided fertile ground for those who wished to develop a critique of this dominant approach. Neofunctionalism was the name given to the first theoretical attempt to understand European integration. Its implied critique of realism led to a counter-theory from within a broadly state-centred perspective, which became known as intergovernmentalism. The debate between these two broad positions has evolved over time, but the central issues of dispute remain much the same today as they were in the 1950s.

Neofunctionalism

Starting with the analysis of the ECSC by Ernst Haas (1958), a body of theorizing about European integration known as neofunctionalism was built up in the writings of a group of US academics (see Insight 1.1, p. 4). These theorists drew on the work of Mitrany and Monnet in particular. In addition to Haas, the main figures in this school of analysis were Leon Lindberg (1963; 1966), and Philippe Schmitter (1970).

Neofunctionalism was a **pluralist** theory of international politics. In contrast to the more traditional realist theories, it did not assume that a state was a single unified actor; nor did it assume that states were the only actors on the international stage. In the concepts that it used, it anticipated later writings on global interdependence (Keohane and Nye 1977).

In the first period of European integration, neofunctionalism appeared to be winning the theoretical debate. Neofunctionalism sought to explain 'how and why they (states) voluntarily mingle, merge and mix with their neighbours so as to lose the factual attributes of sovereignty while acquiring new techniques for resolving conflict between themselves' (Haas 1970: 610). There were four key parts to the neofunctionalist argument, as follows.

(1) The concept of the 'state' is more complex than realists suggested.

(2) The activities of interest groups and bureaucratic actors are not confined to the domestic political arena.

(3) Non-state actors are important in international politics.

(4) European integration is advanced through 'spillover' pressures.

In contrast to realists, neofunctionalists argued that the international activities of states were the outcome of a pluralistic political process in which government decisions were influenced by pressures from various interest groups and bureaucratic actors. In common with the general tenor of US political science at the time, it was often assumed that these pressures constituted the complete explanation for government decisions. So, if the analyst could identify the strength and direction of the various pressures accurately, it would be possible to make predictions about government behaviour in IR.

Using the concepts that were later called 'transnationalism' and 'transgovernmentalism' (Keohane and Nye 1977: 129–30), neofunctionalists expected nationally based interest groups to make contact with similar groups in other countries (transnationalism), and departments of state to forge links with their counterparts in other states, unregulated by their respective foreign offices (transgovernmentalism).

Neofunctionalists pointed to the activities of multinational corporations to illustrate their argument that non-state actors are important in international politics. However, for neofunctionalists, the European Commission was the most important non-state international actor. The Commission was believed to be in a unique position to manipulate both domestic and international pressures on national governments to advance the process of European integration, even where governments might be reluctant. This contrasted with realist explanations of IR, which focused exclusively on the international role of states.

Neofunctionalists used the concept of spillover to explain how, once national governments took the initial steps towards integration, the process took on a life of its own and swept governments along further than they anticipated going. As Lindberg (1963: 10) put it:

> In its most general formulation, 'spillover' refers to a situation in which a given action, related to a specific goal, creates a situation in which the original goal can be assured only by taking further actions, which in turn create a further condition and a need for more action, and so forth.

Two types of spillover were important to early neofunctionalist writers: functional and political. The notion of 'cultivated spillover' was added by later theorists to explain the part played by the Commission in fostering integration (Tranholm-Mikkelsen 1991) and the concept of 'exogenous spillover' added to explain enlargement (Niemann 2006).

Functional spillover argued that modern industrial economies were made up of interconnected parts. As such, it was not possible to isolate one sector from others. Following this understanding, neofunctionalists argued that if member states integrated one functional sector of their economies, the interconnectedness between this sector and others would lead to a 'spillover' into other sectors. Technical pressures would prompt integration in those related sectors, and the integration of one sector would only work if other functionally related sectors were also integrated. For example, if a joint attempt were made to increase coal production across member states, it would prove necessary to bring other forms of energy into the scheme. Otherwise, a switch by one member state away from coal towards a reliance on oil or nuclear fuels would throw out all of the calculations for coal production. In addition, any effective planning of the total energy supply would involve gathering data about future total demand, implying the development of overall plans for industrial output across member states.

To this technical logic of functional spillover, the neofunctionalists added the idea of political spillover, and set perhaps more store by this than by functional spillover in explaining the process of integration. Political spillover involved the build-up of political pressures in favour of further integration within the states involved. Once one sector of the economy was integrated, the interest groups operating in that sector would have to exert pressure at the supranational level, on the organization charged with running their sector. So the creation of the ECSC would lead to the representatives of the coal and steel industries in all of the member states switching at least a part of their political lobbying from national governments to the new supranational agency, the High Authority. Relevant trade unions and consumer groups would follow suit.

It was argued that once these interest groups had switched the focus of their activity to the European level, they would rapidly come to appreciate the benefits available to them as a result of the integration of their sector. Further, they would also come to understand the barriers that prevented these benefits from being fully realized. As the main barrier would be that integration in one sector could not be effective without the integration of other sectors, these interest groups would become advocates of further integration and would lobby their governments to this end. At the same time, they would form a barrier themselves against governments retreating from the level of integration that had already been achieved. This was important because such a retreat would be the one alternative way in which pressures caused by functional spillover could be resolved. In addition, governments would come under pressure from other interest groups who would see the advantages accruing to their counterparts in the integrated sector and realize that they could profit similarly if their sectors of the economy were also integrated. For Haas, the driving force of political integration was the calculated self-interest of political elites:

> The 'good Europeans' are not the main creators of the regional community that is growing up; the process of community formation is dominated by nationally constituted groups with specific interests and aims, willing and able to adjust their aspirations by turning to supranational means when this course appears profitable.

(Haas 1966: xxxiv)

Neofunctionalists looked for spillover pressures to be encouraged and manipulated by the Commission. It was expected both to foster the emergence of EC-wide pressure groups and to cultivate contacts behind the scenes with national interest groups and with bureaucrats in the civil services of the member states, who were another group of potential allies against national governments (Tranholm-Mikkelsen 1991). This was the third type of spillover, which was known as cultivated spillover because it involved the Commission cultivating the contacts and the pressure on governments.

While Haas (1958) mentioned the concept of 'geographical spillover', in particular to draw attention to the external effects of integration on Britain, the main contributions to neofunctionalism paid little attention to enlargement—understandably, given that these were produced before the first enlargement in 1973 (see Chapter 10). More recently, Niemann (2006) has argued that neofunctionalism does provide tools for understanding this process: integration leads to some contradictions and demands that cannot be satisfactorily resolved by increasing the intensity or policy scope of integration, but instead requires territorial expansion (see also Niemann and Schmitter 2009: 62).

In the 1950s, neofunctionalist theory neatly fitted events, particularly in explaining the transition from the ECSC to the European Community (EC). Events in the 1960s were less supportive. The beginning of the end for neofunctionalist theory in its original manifestation came in the early 1960s and in particular the use of the veto by de Gaulle, leading to the 'empty chair' crisis of 1965–66 (see Chapter 9, pp. 128–9). National governments had power and were clearly prepared to use it to determine the nature and pace of integration:

> By 1967 Haas was already attempting to cope with the possibility that De Gaulle had 'killed the Common Market' by revising his theory to account for the prospect of 'disintegration', and by 1975 he was announcing the 'obsolescence of regional integration theory'.
>
> (Caporaso and Keeler 1995: 36–7)

Intergovernmentalism

In response to the neofunctionalist analysis of European integration, a counter-argument was put forward by Stanley Hoffmann (1964; 1966). This argument drew heavily on realist assumptions about the role of states, or more accurately, the governments of states in IR. Essentially, there were three parts to Hoffmann's criticism of neofunctionalism.

(1) European integration had to be viewed in a global context. Regional integration was only one aspect of the development of the global international system. The neofunctionalists predicted an inexorable progress to further integration—but this was all predicated on an internal dynamic, and implicitly assumed that the international background conditions would remain fixed. This criticism became particularly relevant in the light of changes in the global economic situation in the early 1970s.

(2) National governments were uniquely powerful actors in the process of European integration: they controlled the nature and pace of integration guided by their concern to protect and promote the 'national interest'.

(3) Although, where 'national interests' coincided, governments might accept closer integration in the technical functional sectors, the integration process would not spread to areas of 'high politics' such as national security and defence.

Hoffmann rejected the neofunctionalist view that governments would ultimately be overwhelmed by pressures from elite interest groups to integrate. However, his argument departed from classical realism, in which states were treated as unified rational actors, with little importance attached to domestic politics. Hoffmann's inter-governmentalist position was more sophisticated than that of realists in this respect, and his political awareness was also greater than that of the neofunctionalist writers, who tended to adopt a rather simplified pluralist view of political processes.

Hoffmann claimed the neofunctionalist argument was based on 'false arithmetic' that assumed that the power of each elite group (including national governments) was approximately equal, so that if the governments were outnumbered they would lose. In addition, he argued that government decisions could not be understood simply as a response to pressure from organized interests, but that, often, political calculations led governments to take positions to which powerful groups were hostile (Hoffmann 1964: 93). These political calculations were driven by domestic concerns, particularly in relation to the impact of integrative decisions on the national economy and on the electoral implications for the governing party.

Hoffmann acknowledged that actors other than national governments played a role in the process of integration. He recognized that in the 'low-politics' sectors (for example, social and regional policy) interest groups did influence the actions of governments—but, as he pointed out, they were not the only influence. Other influences included government officials (particularly on economic matters) and also the electoral considerations of the party or parties in office (Hoffmann 1964: 89). However, he considered national governments to be the ultimate arbiters of key decisions. The governments of states were said to be uniquely powerful for two reasons: first, because they possessed legal sovereignty; and second, because they had political legitimacy as the only democratically elected actors in the integration process. In this view, where the power of supranational institutions increased, it did so because governments believed it to be in their national interest.

In Hoffmann's picture of the process of European integration, governments had much more autonomy than in the neofunctionalist view. The integration process therefore remained essentially intergovernmental: it would go only as far as the governments were prepared to allow it to go. However, Hoffmann also pointed to the fact that European integration was only one aspect of the development of international politics. That insight led to a more restrictive view of government autonomy. In this respect, Hoffmann, like the realists, stressed the external limitations on autonomy: states were seen as independent actors, but their governments were constrained by the position of the state in the world system.

Liberal Intergovernmentalism

Building on Hoffmann's work, Andrew Moravcsik (1993) developed a subsequent version of the intergovernmental explanation of the integration process. Like Hoffmann, Moravcsik started from a critique of neofunctionalism. He restated the argument that neofunctionalism failed to explain developments in the EC itself, but he put more weight on a theoretical critique. In particular, he argued that the self-criticisms of the neofunctionalists themselves had to be taken seriously. He identified three such self-criticisms (Moravcsik 1993: 478–80), as follows.

(1) Theories of European integration had to be supplemented (or even supplanted) by more general theories of national responses to international interdependence.

(2) The development of common policy responses needed to be looked at as much as did institutional transfers of competence; the emphasis on formal transfers of authority to the EC often concealed a failure to effect a real surrender of sovereignty.

(3) Unicausal theories were inadequate to deal with the phenomenon under consideration; more than one theory was needed to grasp the complexity of EC policy making.

Instead of reviving neofunctionalism, Moravcsik argued that these criticisms should be taken seriously, and a theory constructed that took account of them. He believed that all of the points could be accounted for if the analysis of the EC was rolled into what he called 'current theories of international political economy' (Moravcsik 1993: 480).

Moravcsik's approach, like that of Hoffmann, assumed that states were rational actors, but departed from traditional realism in not treating the state as a **black box**. Instead it was assumed that the governments of states were playing what Putnam (1988) called 'two-level games'. A domestic political process determined their definition of the national interest. This constituted the first part of the analysis and determined the position that governments took with them into the international negotiation.

This approach built on the undeveloped argument of Hoffmann about the role of domestic politics, but in some ways it was less sophisticated in its account of domestic politics than Hoffmann's. Moravcsik's 'liberal' view of domestic politics was that the primary determinant of the preferences of a government was the balance between economic interests within the domestic arena—a narrow conception of domestic political process that has been frequently criticized (for example, see Wincott 1995: 601; Forster 1998: 357–9; Caporaso 1999: 162; Wallace 1999: 156–7).

The second part of the analysis was to see how conflicting national interests were reconciled in the negotiating forum of the Council of Ministers. This process was divided into two logically sequential stages. The first stage was to reach agreement on the common policy response to the problem that governments were trying to solve. The second stage was to reach agreement on the appropriate institutional arrangements. Moravcsik (1998: 21–2) gave the example of monetary union: it would be impractical to try to understand the negotiations over the constitution of a European Central Bank without first understanding the objectives that the bank was being set up to achieve.

The analytical framework of liberal intergovernmentalism was applied by Moravcsik (1998) to five key episodes in the construction of the EU:

- the negotiation of the Treaties of Rome (1955–58);
- the consolidation of the common market and the Common Agricultural Policy (CAP) (1958–83);
- the setting up of the first experiment in monetary co-operation and of the European Monetary System (EMS) (1969–83);
- the negotiation of the Single European Act (SEA) (1984–88);
- the negotiation of the Treaty on European Union (TEU) (1988–91).

On the basis of these case studies, Moravcsik came to the following conclusions.

(1) The major choices in favour of Europe were a reflection of the preferences of national governments, not of the preferences of supranational organizations.

(2) These national preferences reflected the balance of economic interests, rather than the political biases of politicians or national strategic security concerns.

(3) The outcomes of negotiations reflected the relative bargaining power of the states; the delegation of decision-making authority to supranational institutions reflected the wish of governments to ensure that the commitments of all parties to the agreement would be carried through rather than federalist ideology or a belief in the inherent efficiency of international organizations.

However, he was criticized for his choice of case studies. As Scharpf (1999a: 165) put it:

> Since only intergovernmental negotiations are being considered, why shouldn't the preferences of national governments have shaped the outcomes? Since all case studies have issues of economic integration as their focus, why shouldn't economic concerns have shaped the negotiating positions of governments? And since only decisions requiring unanimous agreement are being analysed, why shouldn't the outcomes be affected by the relative bargaining powers of the governments involved?

The alternative would have been to look at the smaller-scale day-to-day decisions that constitute the bulk of the decisions made within the EU. Here, the picture might be very different. Supranational actors might have more influence, and national preferences might be less clearly defined and less vigorously defended. We look at some of these arguments later in the book (Chapters 20–22).

A more recent contribution on liberal intergovernmentalism (LI) (Moravcsik and Schimmelfennig 2009) provided a response to criticisms, which were said to have 'small kernels' of theoretical truth, but be generally 'overstated'. Thus, while it was accepted that LI 'works best when decision-making is taking place in decentralized settings under a unanimity requirement rather than in settings of delegated or pooled sovereignty under more complex and nuanced decision rules', it was also suggested that 'the theory applies far more broadly than is commonly supposed, including much everyday EU decision-making' (Moravcsik and Schimmelfennig 2009: 74). Further, while Moravcsik and Schimmelfennig (2009) acknowledged that economic issues are not always predominant, they suggested that to read Moravcsik's earlier work as arguing this was to misunderstand it.

Supranational Governance

Starting from the intergovernmentalism versus supranationalism debate, a team of scholars claimed to offer an alternative that cut through the dichotomy (Sweet Stone and Sandholtz 1997; Sandholtz and Stone Sweet 1998; Stone Sweet, Sandholtz, and Fligstein 2001). Supranational governance was an approach that drew on the transactionalism of Karl Deutsch (1953; 1957) and on new institutionalism as applied to the EU (Chapter 2, pp. 22–7), although the authors themselves located the origins of their approach in neofunctionalism.

Fundamental to the approach was the argument that if the EU was to be analysed as an international regime, as Moravcsik insisted it could be, then it had to be seen not as a single regime but as a series of regimes for different policy sectors. The authors therefore sought to explain the different levels of supranationalism that existed in different policy sectors. The three key elements in their approach were the development of transnational society, the role of supranational organizations with meaningful autonomous capacity to pursue integrative agendas, and a focus on European rule making to resolve what they called 'international policy externalities'. By this last phrase, the authors meant the unintended effects on one country of policies being followed in another country, such as the pollution of the air in one country by smoke from factories in a neighbouring country.

Following Deutsch, Stone Sweet and Sandholtz (1997) argued that transactions across national boundaries were increasing. As they increased, so a supranational society of relevant actors would emerge. These actors would favour the construction of rules to govern their interactions at the supranational level because nationally based rules would be a hindrance to them. If companies that operated across national boundaries were to have to comply with different rules in every member state, this would impose additional costs on their activity. A good example here is merger control (Insight 1.2).

Another example of what the authors call the emergence of supranational society is provided by the case of the emergence of a supranational telecommunications regime (Insight 1.3).

The construction of rules at the supranational level would result in the 'Europeanization' of a sector: that is, the regulation of the sector would be at the EU level. Once the initial step is taken in the Europeanization of a policy sector, Stone Sweet and Sandholtz argued that the consolidation of the supranational regime would

Insight 1.2 Supranational Governance 1: The Emergence of Supranational Society—Merger Control

Two companies in the same sector operating across national borders might decide to merge so as to rationalize their operations and reduce their costs. To do so, they might have to get the approval not only of national monopoly and merger authorities in their two states of origin, but also in all of those states where either company or both combined had a significant proportion of the relevant market. To avoid this situation of 'multiple jeopardy', we would expect to see considerable support from large companies for the transfer of merger approval to the supranational level, giving them a one-stop approval procedure to negotiate, and this is what has actually happened (Cini and McGowan 1998).

Insight 1.3 Supranational Governance 2: The Emergence of Supranational Society—Telecommunications

In the 1980s, the sector was dominated by national monopoly suppliers, the nationalized post, telegraph, and telephone companies (PTTs). These national suppliers formed parts of policy communities consisting of the PTTs, the officials in the relevant national ministries, and the suppliers of switching equipment, who were also nationally based and who had a guaranteed market from the PTTs. Sandholtz (1998) showed how the domination of the sector by these national policy communities came to be challenged by a coalition of users of telecommunications who demanded cheaper and more technically advanced services than were provided by the PTTs. These users formed a supranational coalition for change, allying with the Commission and with the British government, which had liberalized its own telecommunications market and wished to extend liberalization to the other national EC markets. Gradually, the pressure from this coalition eroded the hold of the PTTs on the policy preferences of national governments and opened a window of opportunity for the Commission to get proposals through the Council of Ministers for opening up national markets to competition.

proceed through the emergence of European rules. Actors working within the new framework of European rules would start to test the limits of those rules. They would seek clarification from the adjudicators—administrators and courts. These clarifications would not only establish the precise meaning of rules, but would also, and at the same time, modify them. The actors would then face a different set of constraints, which would be tighter (and more precise) than the previous constraints, and the actors would adjust their behaviour accordingly. As rules became more precise, so they would tend to develop away from the original intentions of the member states, and would simultaneously become more difficult to modify in any different direction. This pointed to the same process as in the historical institutionalist concept of path dependence (see Chapter 2).

Branch and Øhrgaard (1999) argued that Stone Sweet and Sandholtz had not succeeded in escaping the intergovernmental–supranational dichotomy, but had instead offered a mirror image of Moravcsik's liberal intergovernmentalism. In particular, they argued that both theories privileged certain types of actor, and therefore certain types of decision, and that both theories classified actors as either intergovernmental or supranational in a way that ensured that they would oversimplify the complexity of the nature of the EU. According to Branch and Øhrgaard, Moravcsik gave a privileged role in his theoretical framework to national actors and intergovernmental bargains. He therefore concentrated on episodes, the grand bargains, which were highly likely to demonstrate the value of these concepts. On the other side of the mirror, Stone Sweet and Sandholtz gave a privileged role to transnational business actors and supranational actors, and to the operation of supranational rules of governance. They therefore concentrated on routine decision making in policy sectors that were concerned with economics and trade, which were highly likely to demonstrate the value of these concepts.

Branch and Øhrgaard also argued that both Moravcsik and Stone Sweet and Sandholtz equally made the mistake of treating evidence of influence on policy decisions by supranational actors as necessary and sufficient evidence of supranational integration, and evidence of decisions remaining in the hands of national governments as necessary and sufficient evidence of intergovernmentalism. In contrast, Branch and Øhrgaard argued that not all European integration was driven forward by transnational and supranational actors. In fields such as social policy, the process had been driven by national governments anxious to correct for the effects of the economic integration that *had* been driven by transnational and supranational actors. They further argued that European integration could not simply be equated with the influence of supranational actors. In the field of the Common Foreign and Security Policy (CFSP) (see Chapter 33), although the mechanisms remained intergovernmental and the formal power of the supranational institutions remained limited, academic experts agreed that the process involved much more than just diplomatic consultation. CFSP was a form of European integration that did not involve supranational governance.

A further criticism of Stone Sweet and Sandholtz's approach is that the framework of analysis ignored the wider context within which the process of 'Europeanization' takes place. This criticism points to an omission that is curious given the association of one of the authors, Sandholtz, with a seminal analysis of the emergence of the single market (Sandholtz and Zysman 1989) that put particular stress on the wider context of global capitalism in explaining the emergence of the policy. This study is examined in Chapter 27 (see pp. 396–7). In the empirical studies contained in the book that they edited (Sandholtz and Stone Sweet 1998), the influence of the wider capitalist system did not emerge very clearly. For example, Sandholtz (1998) explained the emergence of the supranational European society in the telecommunications sector without referring to the deregulation of US telecommunications, which both put European-based companies who were consumers of telecommunications at a disadvantage in comparison with their US competitors, and led to intense pressure from the US government for the European market to be opened to entry by US telecommunication providers (Dang-Nguyen et al. 1993; Fuchs 1994). This inadequacy in the analysis reflected the inadequacy in the theory.

A Postfunctionalist Theory of European Integration

The most recent significant contribution to this debate comes from authors closely associated with the concept of multi-level governance, which has strong antecedents in neofunctionalism (see Chapter 2). Liesbet Hooghe and Gary Marks (2008) emphasized the importance of identity in the process of European integration. They shared with intergovernmentalists and neofunctionalists the view that European integration is triggered by a mismatch between efficiency and existing structures of authority, but differed from them in believing that the outcome of this process will reflect functional pressures. Instead, they suggested that political conflict is a crucial part of the explanation and that communal identities are central to this conflict. Thus, theorizing needs to move beyond the intergovernmentalist–neofunctionalist preoccupation with economic interests. They argued that:

> Functional pressures are one thing, regime outcomes are another. Community and self governance, expressed in public opinion and mobilized by political parties, lie at the heart of jurisdictional design

(Hooghe and Marks 2008: 23)

CONCLUSION

Essentially the same 'intergovernmental–supranational debate' about the process of European integration has been going on since the very early stages of the process. Related concepts such as federalism linked to this debate have been present throughout and emerged again prominently in debates on the Constitutional Treaty and the Lisbon Treaty that replaced it (Chapters 17 and 18). Central to this continuing debate is the nature and role of the state executives in the development of the EU. In intergovernmental perspectives, European integration is a process whereby the governments of states voluntarily enter into agreements to work together to solve common problems. Some constraints operate on the autonomy of national governments, but they remain in control of the process. The alternative perspective suggests that although governments started the process, integration soon took on a life of its own that went beyond the control of the governments. This intergovernmental–supranational debate forms the first of the themes that recur throughout this book.

These questions are of more than just academic interest. Understanding the nature of the EU, and the direction in which the process of integration is heading, are important topics of political debate in the member states and beyond. However, there is some irony in how explanations of the process of integration have been used. In the 1950s and 1960s, neofunctionalist ideas were eagerly embraced by members of the Commission as a blueprint for constructing a united Europe. Today, opponents of further integration implicitly invoke the neofunctionalist idea that the process is no longer under control and threatens national identity. Conversely, intergovernmentalist arguments are more likely to be voiced by the advocates of further steps, who echo Hoffmann and Moravcsik in reassuring hesitant European public opinion that the governments of states remain in charge: that sovereignty is only 'pooled', not lost.

While, as will be discussed in subsequent chapters, theorizing about the EU has in many ways moved beyond the intergovernmental–supranational dichotomy, this debate continues to inform research. Moreover, a number of the debate's key themes—state power, the role of organized interests, the influence of supranational institutions—remain prominent in other approaches to the EU.

KEY POINTS

The Intellectual Background

- David Mitrany was not a theorist of European integration, but influenced later integration theorists. He sought to prevent war between states by taking routine functional tasks out of the hands of national governments and giving them over to international agencies.

- Mitrany argued that world government would limit freedom, and that regional federations would reproduce on a larger scale the conditions that produced wars between states.

- European federalism attracted strong support among Resistance groups in war-time Europe. The leading intellectual figure was Altiero Spinelli, who advocated a 'constitutional break' at the end of the war to supersede the system of sovereign states with a federal constitution for Europe.

- By the time the Congress aimed at adopting this new constitution had been arranged, national political elites were re-established in European states. While the (Hague) Congress did produce the Council of Europe, this was an intergovernmental body that fell far short of federalist aspirations.

- The Schuman Plan for the ECSC was devised by Jean Monnet, the head of the French Economic Planning Commission, who believed the European nation state was inadequate as an economic unit in the modern world and argued for a Europe-wide economy.

- The pooling of coal and steel resources was the first step towards a Europe-wide economic zone. It also removed strategic industries from German control and ensured adequate supplies of coal for the French steel industry: both were concerns for Monnet.

International Relations Theories of European Integration

- IR theory in the 1950s was dominated by realism. This theory treated nation states as the fundamental units of IR. It did not lead to any expectation that governments would voluntarily surrender their sovereign control over policy. As such, the first European integration theorists posed a direct challenge to realist assumptions.

- *Neofunctionalism* suggested that European integration was a process that, once started, would undermine the sovereignty of states beyond the expectations of governments.

- Neofunctionalism argued that states are not unified actors, but that national interests are determined through a pluralistic process in which governments interact with organized interests. Organized interests were also seen to be important transnational actors.

- The concept of spillover was central to the neofunctionalist theory. Functional spillover, political spillover, and cultivated spillover would lead the process of European integration to run out of the control of national governments. The concept of 'exogenous spillover' was added later to theorize enlargement.

- Hoffmann's *intergovernmentalism* argued that neofunctionalists had made three mistakes: regional integration was not a self-contained process, but was influenced by a wider international context; governments were uniquely powerful actors because they possessed formal sovereignty and democratic legitimacy; and integration in low-politics sectors would not necessarily spill over into high-politics sectors.

- Moravcsik's *liberal intergovernmentalism* incorporated the neofunctionalist insight that national interests are defined as part of a domestic pluralist political process; within this domestic process, economic interests were seen to be dominant.

- Moravcsik proposed a two-level analysis of EU bargaining, in which governments' preferences were determined at the domestic level and were then used as the basis for intergovernmental negotiations at the European level.

- Moravcsik denied the importance of supranational actors as independent actors in EU decision making and insisted that governments remained in control of the process of European integration.

- The approach of *supranational governance* was located in neofunctionalism, but also drew on transactionalism and new institutionalism. Stone Sweet and Sandholtz argued that the EU should be studied not as one international regime, but as a series of regimes for different policy sectors, and that increased transactions across national boundaries would create a supranational society that favoured the creation of supranational rules to govern its behaviour.

- Branch and Øhrgaard argued that this approach did not escape the intergovernmental–supranational dichotomy. Rather, it privileged certain types of actor and also classified actors as either intergovernmental or supranational in a way that oversimplified the complexity of the EU. The approach was further criticized for not placing the analysis in a global context.

- Hooghe and Marks emphasized the importance of identity in the process of European integration and the need to go beyond the preoccupation with economic interests and functional pressures that has characterized much of the intergovernmental–supranational debate.

FURTHER READING

The key texts on the early development of neofunctionalist theory are: **E. B. Haas**, *The Uniting of Europe: Political, Social and Economic Forces 1950–57* (London: Library of World Affairs, 1958); **E. B. Haas**, *The Uniting of Europe: Political, Social and Economic Forces, 1950–1957,* 2nd edn (Stanford, CA: Stanford University Press, 1968); and **L. Lindberg**, *The Political Dynamics of European Economic Integration* (Stanford, CA: Stanford University Press; London: Oxford University Press, 1963). On intergovernmentalism, the main early contributions are: **S. Hoffmann**, 'The European Process at Atlantic Crosspurposes', *Journal of Common Market Studies*, 3 (1964): 85–101; and **S. Hoffmann**, 'Obstinate or Obsolete? The Fate of the Nation State and the Case of Western Europe', *Daedalus*, 95 (1966): 862–915.

Neofunctionalism is elaborated, expanded, and defended in **J. Tranholm-Mikkelsen**, 'Neofunctionalism: Obstinate or Obsolete? A Reappraisal in the Light of the New Dynamism of the European Community', *Millennium*, 20 (1991): 1–22; a further development of neofunctionalism can be found in **A. Niemann,** *Explaining Decisions in the European Union* (Cambridge: Cambridge University Press, 2006). A review of the criticisms applied to neofunctionalism and subsequent revisions can be found in **A. Niemann and P. Schmitter,** 'Neofunctionalism', in **A. Wiener and T. Diez (eds)**, *European Integration Theory*, 2nd edn (Oxford: Oxford University Press, 2009). 45–66.

The earliest statement of liberal intergovernmentalism is in **A. Moravcsik,** 'Preferences and Power in the European Community: A Liberal Intergovernmentalist Approach', *Journal of Common Market Studies*, 31 (1993): 473–524. A later statement of the theory, which differs subtly, is given in **A. Moravcsik,** *The Choice for Europe: Social Purpose and State Power from Messina to Maastricht* (London: UCL Press, 1998). Of interest most recently is **A. Moravcsik and F. Schimmelfennig**, 'Liberal Intergovernmentalism', in **A. Wiener and T. Diez (eds)**, *European Integration Theory*, 2nd edn (Oxford: Oxford University Press, 2009), 67–87, which includes a response to criticisms of Moravcsik's earlier work.

Supranational governance is outlined in **Stone Sweet and W. Sandholtz**, 'European Integration and Supranational Governance', *Journal of European Public Policy*, 4 (1997): 297–317. It is developed in **W. Sandholtz and A. Stone Sweet (eds)**, *European Integration and Supranational Governance* (Oxford: Oxford University Press, 1998), and contested in **A. P. Branch and J. C. Øhrgaard**, 'Trapped in the Supranational–Intergovernmental Dichotomy: A Response to Stone Sweet and Sandholtz', *Journal of European Public Policy*, 6 (1999): 123–43.

The postfunctionalist theory of integration is set out in **L. Hooghe and G. Marks**, 'A Postfunctionalist Theory of European Integration: From Permissive Consensus to Constraining Dissensus', *British Journal of Political Science*, 39 (2008): 1–23.

 online resource centre

Visit the Online Resource Centre that accompanies this book for links to more information on theories of European integration: www.oxfordtextbooks.co.uk/orc/bache3e/

Chapter 2
Theories of EU Governance

Chapter Overview

As European integration progressed, the academic focus began to shift from explaining the integration process to understanding the European Union (EU) as a political system. As such, EU scholars increasingly drew on approaches from the study of domestic and comparative politics. While some attempts to escape the supranational–intergovernmental dichotomy have proved more successful than others, these contributions broadened the study of the EU considerably beyond the traditional international relations (IR) debate and many scholars spoke of a 'governance turn' in EU studies in the 1990s. This chapter surveys a number of approaches that focus on the EU as a political system. These approaches fall within the broad categories of 'new institutionalism' and 'governance and networks'. While they diverge in some important ways, there is also considerable overlap between the approaches.

A newer generation of scholars, uninspired by debates between intergovernmentalism and neofunctionalism ... struck out on their own ...

(Caporaso 1998: 341)

The theoretical stand-off between intergovernmental and supranational interpretations remains significant in the study of the EU. However, alongside this debate other voices have emerged that move beyond the supranational–intergovernmental dichotomy. Approaches from the study of domestic and comparative politics turn away from the focus of IR theories on the process of European integration, and instead treat the EU as a political system that is already in existence, and try to explain 'the nature of the beast'.

A shift away from the exclusive use of IR paradigms to concerns with institutional and policy analysis first appeared with Lindberg and Scheingold's book *Europe's Would-Be Polity* in 1970 (Bulmer 2009). It gathered pace with the acceleration of integration in the 1980s through the single market programme (Chapter 27), and culminated in Simon Hix's (1994) call to scholars within the discipline of comparative politics to wake up to the existence of the EU as a suitable subject for study using their established concepts. He heeded his own call a few years later, producing a textbook on the EU that took a very different approach to the subject. Instead of asking questions such as how far the EU was dominated by the member states and how far it operated as an autonomous entity, Hix (1999: 1) asked questions that derived from the study of comparative politics:

> How is governmental power exercised? Under what conditions can the Parliament influence legislation? Is the Court of Justice beyond political control? Why do some citizens support the central institutions while others oppose them? How important are political parties and elections in shaping political choices? Why are some social groups able to influence the political agenda more than others?

The approach succeeded in shifting the focus away from the study of European integration as a process to '*how the EU works today*' (Hix 1999: 1; emphasis in original).

An increasing number of concepts are applied to the EU that originated from the study of comparative and domestic politics. Here, we look at two influential sets of approaches that come under the headings of 'new institutionalism' and 'governance and networks'. While we identify these as separate approaches, and there are variants within each approach, there is also a significant overlap between the two categories, and a close relationship between these approaches and other concepts increasingly applied to the study of the EU.

New Institutionalism

One adaptation of an approach that was originally applied to the study of domestic and comparative politics that found favour among EU scholars was new institutionalism (March and Olsen 1984; 1989; 1996). This was a reaction to the behavioural approaches that had come to dominate political science in the 1960s and 1970s. Behaviouralism had been a reaction against formal institutional analyses of government and politics that had lost sight of the real political processes that lay behind the formal structures of government—in particular, the influence of societal groups. New institutionalism argued that the reaction against the old, formal institutional analyses had gone too far: that the importance of institutions in structuring political action had been lost.

Bulmer (1993) set down a marker in arguing that institutions matter in the EU context, identifying the different institutions and instruments of EU governance. This article further argued that the profile of instruments and institutions differed within discrete 'governance regimes' situated within an overarching EU structure that had pronounced regulatory characteristics (below).

From the mid-1990s, new institutionalism became more prevalent in the literature on EU governance. It not only argued that institutions matter in understanding EU politics and policy making, but also sought to explain how they matter. Moreover, one thing that was new about this reassertion of institutionalism was that institutions were not only defined as the formal organizations that the old institutionalism had recognized—such as parliaments, executives, and judicial courts—but also extended to categorize informal patterns of structured interaction between groups as institutions themselves. These structured interactions were institutions in the sense that they constrained or shaped group behaviour.

At the same time, new institutionalism argued that formal institutions were more important than behaviouralists had suggested. Behaviouralists treated formal institutions as neutral arenas within which the struggle for influence between the different societal actors was carried out. New institutionalists disagreed with this perspective in two ways. First, they argued that formal institutions were not neutral arenas, since formal institutional structures and rules biased access to the political process in favour of some societal groups over others. Second, they argued that institutions could be autonomous political actors in their own right.

While, collectively, this reassertion of institutionalist perspectives is known as new institutionalism, it is now common to distinguish between three varieties: rational choice institutionalism; historical institutionalism; and sociological institutionalism (Hall and Taylor 1996). These approaches emerged at around the same time, but in relative isolation from each other.

Rational Choice Institutionalism

Rational choice institutionalism focuses on the constraints that formal institutional structures impose on actors. It suggests that, in trying to understand the behaviour of political actors, it is important to identify the parameters that are set by the fact that they are acting within a specific framework of rules. So, for example, the activities of interest groups reflect the procedures that prevail for the passage of the legislation that affects them, the access points that are available to them in that process, and the previous relationships that they have established with key decision makers. Thus, in the case of the EU, whether interest groups choose to try to influence legislation through national governments or through the Commission and the European Parliament (EP) would reflect:

- the relative openness to those groups of the national government actors compared with the supranational actors;
- the extent to which the process is intergovernmental (for example, what decision rules applied within the Council of Ministers);
- what role the EP has in the final decision.

If national decision making were dominated by other interest groups, then 'outsider' groups trying to influence EU policy might turn to the **supranational institutions** because they would be more likely to get their voices heard there. In competition policy decisions, for example, national monopoly suppliers that have a close working relationship with national government officials would tend to work through national channels. In contrast, potential competitors, who want to see the dismantling of the advantages that the national monopoly suppliers enjoyed at the national level would be more likely to turn to the Commission because it would be difficult for them to obtain access to the national decision makers and easier for them to obtain access to the supranational institutions.

Were unanimity to apply in the Council of Ministers, it would be more important to lobby at the national level because one vote against a proposal could block it; were **qualified majority voting (QMV)** to apply, the potential influence of the Commission would be greater, making it a more attractive target for lobbying. In areas in which the powers of the EP were extended under the Single European Act (SEA), the Treaty on European Union (TEU), and the Treaty of Amsterdam (see Chapter 22), interest groups began to lobby the EP more extensively than they had previously, and to do so more than did interest groups in policy sectors in which the powers of the EP remained restricted to the consultation procedure.

Rational choice institutionalists have also made a significant contribution to understanding the ways in which supranational actors might obtain a degree of autonomy from national governments, allowing them to make their own input to the policy process (Pollack 1997). Applying what is known as **principal–agent theory**, rational choice institutionalists have highlighted the difficulties of principals (the national governments) in keeping control over the activities of their agents (the supranational institutions).

- As the range of delegated tasks has increased, so the difficulties of monitoring what the agents were doing has increased.
- As the number of principals increases with successive enlargements of membership, so the agents may play off the preferences of different coalitions of principals against the attempts of other principals to restrain them.
- As QMV has expanded, so the constraints on the Commission in constructing a winning coalition in support of its proposals have been reduced.

Mark Pollack (2003) applied rational choice theory to test hypotheses about the delegation of power by the member states to the EU's supranational organizations (mainly the Commission, the Court of Justice, and the Parliament) and the efforts of these organizations to shape the process of European integration. Pollack's first concern was with the types of function that governments delegate to supranational organizations and the conditions under which greater or less discretion is allocated to these agents. Here, principal–agent theory suggested that governments would delegate to supranational agents to reduce the transaction costs of EU policy making. The evidence suggested that this was the case with the Commission and Court of Justice, but delegation to the EP was motivated more by governments' attempts to reduce the EU's democratic deficit (Chapter 4, pp. 68–71) and was thus more effectively explained in terms of the logic of appropriate behaviour identified by sociological institutionalists (below), rather than by rational choice explanations.

The principal–agent debate extends beyond a concern with how national governments maintain control over supranational institutions to a concern with how formal institutions of government maintain control over regulatory agencies that are a key component of modern governance in the EU and beyond (see Insight 2.1). The proliferation of agencies in the EU context has been important to the development of governance approaches to understanding the EU (below) and has also raised important issues relating to the accountability of EU decision making (Chapter 4).

Historical Institutionalism

Historical institutionalists place emphasis on the argument that political relationships have to be viewed over time. Their approach argues that decisions are not made

> ## Insight 2.1 The EU as a Regulatory System
>
> The idea of the EU as a regulatory system is most closely associated with the work of Giandomenico Majone (1996). Rather than a single analytical approach, it offers a terrain of study focusing on the EU's increased use of regulatory instruments to secure policy objectives. This focus accompanied the changing character of the EU from the late 1980s, with the extensive regulatory activity aimed at completing the single market, and it continues to be important for a polity with limited budgetary policy instruments.

according to an abstract rationality, but according to perceptions and within constraints that are structured by pre-existing institutional relationships. While rational choice institutionalism focuses its analysis primarily on formal institutions, historical institutionalism takes a broader definition of institutions to incorporate also informal constraints on behaviour such as values and behavioural norms.

> They can range from the rules of a constitutional order or the standard operating procedures of a bureaucracy to the conventions governing trade union behaviour or bank-firm relations. In general, historical institutionalists associate institutions with organizations and the rules or conventions promulgated by formal organization.

(Hall and Taylor 1996: 938)

Central to historical institutionalism is the concept of 'path dependence'. This is the argument that once one decision is made, it tends to make it more likely that policy continues to develop in the same direction. Or, as Hall and Taylor (1996: 941) put it, 'forces will be mediated by the contextual features of a given situation often inherited from the past'. In extreme cases, path dependence can turn into 'lock-in' (Pierson 1996), whereby other avenues of policy are entirely blocked off by the bias towards the existing route that is built into the system. This could be one explanation of why policies such as the Common Agricultural Policy (CAP) proved so resistant to reform even after their negative effects had become obvious (see Chapter 26).

Applying historical institutionalism to the EU led to a further critique of intergovernmental analyses, and revealed further reasons for thinking that national governments might not be entirely in control of the process of integration. Intergovernmental analyses tended to focus on the historic decisions, represented mainly by revisions to the Treaties (see Chapter 1, pp. 11–14). Intergovernmentalists treated what happened between these historic decisions as simply the working through of the decisions. Historical institutionalists argued that, after the decision had been taken, it would be likely to produce unanticipated and unintended outcomes. This might be because of a simple failure to think through the implications—but it might be for one or both of two other reasons (Pierson 1998: 41).

First, the preferences of governments might change over time. For example, the preference for a Common Agricultural Policy based on price support might have been a rational response to conditions in the 1960s in Europe, when security of food supplies was a paramount concern, but no longer appropriate in the changed circumstances of the 1990s, when technological advances had removed this concern. Second, national governments might change. For example, the EC directives on social policy to which a British Labour government had agreed in the 1970s were not to the liking of the Conservative governments between 1979 and 1997. However, even where preferences change, governments would find it extremely difficult to change decisions: policy sectors became institutionalized and various incentives emerged for maintaining the status quo.

A second reason why governments find it difficult to change decisions is because the voting rules in the Council of Ministers make it difficult to get agreement to move back from a policy once it has been agreed. Where the rule is unanimity, it is impossible to retreat so long as one member state benefits from the status quo and refuses to move from it. This is sometimes referred to as 'the ratchet effect'. Even where QMV applies, in order to effect change, it is necessary to construct a coalition representing more than a simple majority of states (the exact number depending on the weighting of the votes of the members of the coalition, and therefore on the identity of the states involved: see Chapter 21).

Sociological Institutionalism

The emergence of sociological institutionalism is closely linked with the 'constructivist turn' in the study of the EU and international politics, which is dealt with in the next chapter (pp. 40–5). Like constructivism, sociological institutionalism takes as its starting point a rejection of the rationalist approach to the study of politics that characterizes rational choice institutionalism and some contributions to historical institutionalism, and places more emphasis on broadly 'cultural' practices (see Chapter 3 for more on this debate).

Hall and Taylor (1996: 947) identified three features of sociological institutionalism that distinguished it from the other new institutionalisms. First, the definition of what constitutes 'institutions' is considerably broader than in the other approaches, so that it includes not only formal rules, but also 'symbol systems, cognitive scripts, and moral templates that provide the "frames of meaning" guiding human action'. This definition blurred the lines traditionally separating the notions of 'institutions' and 'culture'.

Second, sociological institutionalism takes a distinct position on the relationship between institutions and individual action that flows from the 'cultural' approach. In particular, it suggests that institutions do not simply influence the 'strategic calculation' of actors, but have a deeper effect on their preferences and very identity. As Hall and Taylor (1996: 948) put it:

> The self images and identities of social actors are said to be constituted from the institutional forms, images and signs provided by social life.

This does not mean that actors are not 'rational' in the pursuit of the goals and objectives; rather, it means that these goals and objectives are constituted differently (that is, socially) and are more broadly defined than rationalist theory would suggest.

Finally, sociological institutionalism contrasts with rationalist explanations on how institutions are formed and developed. For rational choice institutionalists, institutions are developed by rational actors to meet particular ends efficiently, such as reducing transaction costs (see above). For sociological institutionalists, institutions are often created and developed because they contribute to social legitimacy rather than efficiency. In some cases, this may mean that the formal goals of an organization are overridden by these broader social goals. Here, a distinction is made between the rationalist 'logic of instrumentality' with the sociological 'logic of appropriateness'. Thus, in the case of delegation to supranational institutions discussed above, it may not be in the instrumental interests of national governments to enhance the EP's powers, but the need to enhance the democratic legitimacy of the EU provides a powerful logic of appropriateness.

Rosamond (2003) suggested that the application of sociological institutionalism may be particularly useful in understanding why the Commission's Directorates-General operate in very distinct ways. It may also provide insights into whether 'formally intergovernmental processes ... conform to established patterns of interstate interaction, or whether they bring about new norms of exchange between the envoys of member states' (Rosamond 2003: 117) (see Chapter 20, pp. 284–5, on socialization of national officials in COREPER). As with historical institutionalism, this variant of new institutionalism is making an important contribution to explaining the domestic mediation of Europeanization (Chapter 4).

New Institutionalism Assessed

Put concisely, new institutionalism in its three variants reveals that, respectively, rules matter to rational action (rational choice institutionalism), time matters to policy and institutional evolution (historical institutionalism), and social context matters to political behaviour within institutions (sociological institutionalism).

For Hall and Taylor (1996: 95), none of the new institutionalisms is particularly 'wrong-headed' or 'substantially untrue'; rather, 'each seems to be providing a partial account of the forces at work in a given situation or capturing different dimensions of the human action and institutional impact present there'. The three approaches rest on different assumptions about the world that led them to focus on different questions. This is illustrated in relation to EU enlargement, where sociological institutionalists have placed more emphasis on why the EU decided to enlarge and how we can account for the subsequent negotiations, while rational choice institutionalists have devoted greater attention to the impact of enlargement on the EU's institutional arrangements and historical institutionalists on the process of reform in central and eastern Europe (Pollack 2004: 151).

The various strands of new institutionalism are increasingly being refined, through both empirical research and through engagement with the other strands and with other conceptual approaches to the EU. In particular, new institutionalism has made a significant contribution to the burgeoning literature on Europeanization (see Chapter 4) by providing sensitivity to how domestic institutions (formal and informal) mediate EU pressures. The new institutionalisms link closely to research on constructivism (Chapter 3) and to governance and network approaches, to which we now turn.

Governance and Networks

While we distinguish between 'governance' and 'network' approaches here to reflect labels assigned by particular scholars, these two concepts are very closely linked.

Definitions of governance abound (for different perspectives, see Pierre 2000). Jachtenfuchs and Kohler-Koch (2004: 99) provide a broad definition of governance as 'the continuous political process of setting explicit goals for society and intervening in it in order to achieve these goals', and suggest that 'networking is the most characteristic feature of EU governance' (ibid: 100). Common to more specific definitions of governance is the view that public policy making is increasingly characterized by wide participation of public, private, and voluntary sector actors. In the context of the EU, the multi-level governance framework (below) brings together this increased 'horizontal' mix of actors from different sectors with increased 'vertical' interactions between actors organized at different territorial levels (supranational, national, and sub-national).

Policy Networks and Epistemic Communities

Richardson (1996a) took up Hix's call to approach the EU from different disciplinary directions, but instead of organizing the study around the concepts of comparative politics, he advocated organizing it around the concepts that he and others had been using for some time to study the policy-making process within member states. He argued in particular for the application of two concepts: policy networks and epistemic communities. The first of these concepts was originally developed in studies of public policy making in the United States and later became prominent in Britain, particularly through the work of Rhodes (1981; 1988). Ironically, the second concept originally arose from the study of IR and then fed back into domestic policy analysis before being applied to the EU. Both concepts are mid-range or 'meso-level', aimed at explanations of particular policy sectors or issues rather than the characteristics of the political system as a whole (the 'macro level').

According to the 'Rhodes model', a policy network is a set of resource-dependent organizations, meaning that each of the groups that makes up the policy network needs something that the others have in order to fulfil its own objectives (Rhodes 1988). The types of resource that organizations bring to a policy network to exchange in the process of bargaining include constitutional-legal, organizational, financial, political, and informational resources. These 'resource dependencies'—the extent to which organizations depend on each other for resources—are the key variable in shaping policy outcomes. As Peterson and Bomberg (1993: 28) put it: 'They set the "chessboard" where private and public interests manoeuvre for advantage.' However, interdependence between network participants is 'almost always asymmetrical' and in some cases it is possible to talk of 'unilateral leadership' within networks (Rhodes 1986: 5).

The policy-networks approach does not constitute a predictive theory of policy making, but is seen to contribute to explaining policy outputs. For Peterson and Bomberg (1993: 31):

> Policy networks are essentially descriptive theoretical tools which simply help order facts and evidence in novel ways. However, policy networks can be used to anticipate and explain policy outputs by providing insights into how and why decisions were taken which produced them.

One way in which the approach contributes to anticipating and explaining outputs is by outlining the importance of different structural characteristics of different types

---

Insight 2.2 Policy Communities and Issue Networks

A *policy community* is marked by:

- limited membership;
- stable membership over long periods of time;
- a high level of interaction between the members;
- shared values between members;
- some degree of equality in the distribution of resources;
- a relative balance of power and influence between members.

An *issue network*, in contrast, is marked by:

- large and diffuse membership;
- frequent shifts in the membership;
- fluctuating frequency of contact between members;
- lack of shared values;
- marked inequality in the distribution of resources;
- marked inequality in power and influence within the network.

---

of network. Rhodes (1988) distinguished between different types of network, ranging from highly integrated policy communities to loosely integrated issue networks (Insight 2.2). These different 'structural characteristics' of networks have different effects on both the internal dynamics of the networks and on the ability of networks to resist external pressures for change. However, policy outputs are generally not just a function of internal network characteristics, but are shaped also by changes in the broader political and economic environment (Rhodes, Bache, and George 1996). As such, the approach is often at its strongest when used in conjunction with a macro-level theory of politics or policy making that seeks to explain the broader political context within which the network is situated.

A particular strength of the policy-networks approach is its emphasis on policy implementation as an important phase in policy making: a phase in which policy 'is actually made in the course of negotiations between the (ostensible) implementers' (Rhodes 1986: 14). This aspect of the approach is particularly important in the context of the EU, in which the Commission is heavily dependent upon domestic actors for effective policy implementation.

Policy Networks and the Study of the EU

The applicability of the policy-networks framework to the analysis of the EU was questioned by Kassim (1994). He argued that EU processes were not settled enough to allow policy networks to emerge. Interest groups used different channels to influence decisions: sometimes national; sometimes EU-level. The multinational character and institutional complexity of the EU made it difficult to delimit policy networks, and particularly to identify the relevant public sector actor. Sometimes national agencies would be key; sometimes the Commission; sometimes other EU-level institutions. The institutions themselves often acted as lobbyists in the EU in pursuit of their own objectives.

One of the scholars who had advocated the use of policy networks replied to Kassim (Peterson 1995*a*). He questioned Kassim's insistence on the fluidity of EU policy-making procedures, arguing that while some sectors remained fluid, others were settling into more stable patterns. Indeed, he argued that the Commission was so under-resourced that it had to try to enter into stable relationships with partners that it could trust, which had information that it could use. While he accepted Kassim's points about the complexity of the role of institutions in the EU in comparison with national institutional arrangements, he argued that the policy-networks approach was perfectly compatible with new-institutionalist analyses of the EU, which allowed theorization of the working of institutional relations. While he accepted that the delineation of policy networks at the EU level was a difficult task, Peterson insisted that this did not make it a less important one.

Peterson's most interesting observation, though, was the need to be clear about the level of the policy-making process that was being analysed. He argued that the policy-networks model was best able to explain what he called 'the policy-shaping decisions', when proposals were being formulated and before a political decision was taken that 'set' the policy (Peterson 1995*a*: 400). In a subsequent article, the same author expanded on this argument (Peterson 1995*b*). He here identified three 'levels' of analysis in EU decision making. The highest level he termed the 'super-systemic' or 'history-making' decisions. These were mainly decisions taken by national governments in the European Council or at intergovernmental conferences (IGCs), and were most fruitfully analysed using intergovernmental ideas. The second level he termed the 'systemic' or 'policy-setting' stage. At this level, a combination of intergovernmental and inter-institutional analysis was needed to understand outcomes. The third level he called the 'sub-systemic' or 'policy-shaping' stage. At this level, policy networks were a useful concept for understanding how policy options were formulated in bargaining between the Commission Directorates-General, national civil servants, and private actors (see Table 2.1).

Subsequently, Peterson (2009: 109) put his case more strongly, suggesting that 'policy network analysis is never more powerful an analytical tool than when it is deployed at the EU level'. He set out a three-pronged argument for the applicability of the policy-networks approach to the study of the EU: first, that there is considerable variation in how different EU policy sectors operate; second, that much of the EU's policy making is highly technical; and, third, that EU policy making is 'underpinned by an extraordinarily complex labyrinth of committees that shape policy options before policies are "set" by overtly political decision makers such as the college of Commissioners, Council of Ministers, or European Parliament' (Peterson 2009: 118).

Jachtenfuchs (2001: 254) made a complementary case for the advantages of network analysis:

It appears that, on the whole, the fragmented and fluid institutional structure of the EU and the lack of a strong power centre leads to an increase of channels of access

Table 2.1 Levels of Analysis in EU Decision Making

Level	Type of decision	Dominant actors	Rationality
Super-systemic	History-making	European Council, national governments in IGCs, Court of Justice	Political, legalistic
Systemic	Policy-setting	Council of Ministers, Committee of Permanent Representatives (COREPER)	Political, technocratic, administrative
Sub-systemic/ meso-level	Policy-shaping	Commission, committees, Council groups	Technocratic, consensual, administrative

Source: Reproduced from *Journal of European Public Policy*, 2 (1995): 71

and a larger variation of participants in the policy-making process as compared to governance systems in territorial states.

Network Governance

Parallel to the Anglo-American policy-networks literature, exemplified by the work of Rhodes, is a related strand of conceptual and empirical literature on network governance that is most strongly associated with German scholars—especially Beate Kohler-Koch and her associates (see Kohler-Koch 1996; Kohler-Koch and Eising 1999). The key difference is that while the British approach is primarily an analytical model seeking to understand state–society relations in a given policy area, the German approach treats networks as an alternative form of governance to states and hierarchies (Börzel 1998). The network governance material tends to be more normative than does the Rhodes model of policy networks, and views networks as a potential solution to the co-ordination challenges posed by the increased complexity of public policy making—different actors can be mobilized, and bring different resources to the table in seeking to meet these challenges. Here, the links with multi-level governance (below) are very clear, and officials in the EU and beyond have embraced these notions of network and multi-level governance. Indeed, in 2009, the EU's Committee of the Regions (Chapter 19, pp. 235–6) launched a White Paper on multi-level governance (Committee of the Regions 2009).

However, while network governance is seen as a potential solution to co-ordination challenges in the EU, it has both strengths and weaknesses. For example, in the field of environmental policy, Jordan and Schout (2006) concluded that networked forms of governance 'while in vogue, are by no means a panacea' (Jordan and Schout 2006, 274). While network governance connects the relevant actors, who can bring different skills and resources to a specific policy challenge, it can also mean that responsibility for policy co-ordination becomes dispersed and no one takes overall responsibility.

Epistemic Communities

Whereas policy networks are held together by resource interdependence, epistemic communities are knowledge-based groups. An epistemic community was defined by Peter Haas (1992: 3) as:

> a network of professionals with recognised expertise and competence in a particular domain and an authoritative claim to policy-relevant knowledge within that domain or issue-area.

The members of an epistemic community share both normative beliefs and causal beliefs: that is, they hold a common set of values about what is right and desirable, and a common set of assumptions about how to achieve those goals. They also agree on notions of validity, so they have a common basis for settling differences of opinion between themselves, and they share a common policy enterprise, so that they are all involved in efforts to solve the same problems.

Epistemic communities are likely to exercise particular influence over policy when policy makers face conditions of uncertainty about the likely consequences of policy choice. Such uncertainty is thought to be particularly high where international co-ordination of policy is concerned. Success in such situations is heavily dependent on the actions of other states. There is also a high degree of uncertainty about the possible unforeseen consequences. In these circumstances, state actors are highly likely to turn to epistemic communities because they are not sure how to define the national interest.

> Members of transnational epistemic communities can influence state interests either by directly identifying them for decision makers or by illuminating the salient dimensions of an issue from which the decision makers may then deduce their interests. The decision makers in one state may, in turn, influence the interests and behavior of other states, thereby increasing the likelihood of convergent state behavior and international policy co-ordination, informed by the causal beliefs and policy preferences of the epistemic community.

(Haas 1992: 4)

Haas's perspective suggested that epistemic communities are useful as a means of helping governments to think their way through situations of uncertainty, and to provide a common framework of analysis that could act as a guarantee that states that try to co-ordinate policy will all work along the same lines. However, going beyond Haas's arguments, epistemic communities might also be used by supranational actors such as the European Commission as a means of furthering the Europeanization of policy. The expert analysis that they provide, and the policy prescriptions that they advocate, if they point in the desired direction, could form a powerful lever for supranational actors to move states in the direction of common European solutions to problems that confronted them.

While developed separately from the Rhodes model of policy networks, the notion of epistemic communities is a compatible approach that provides a way of understanding how professionals can come to dominate policy making. Sabatier's advocacy coalition framework, which offers an explanation for how policy change is brought about by coalitions within networks bound together by a shared belief system, has similar potential (Sabatier 1988; 1998). Moreover, Peterson (2004: 121) suggested that alliances of epistemic communities and advocacy coalitions may form to influence policy making and provides the example of the EU's 'quite radical liberalization of its agricultural sector during the Uruguay Round which gave birth to the WTO in the early 1990s'.

Multi-Level Governance (MLG)

Multi-level governance (MLG) has antecedents in neofunctionalism, but is less concerned with explaining the process of European integration and more with explaining the nature of the EU that has emerged from that process. In that respect, it is entirely in line with the approach advocated by Hix (1999).

MLG was first developed from a study of EU structural policy (Chapter 29) and was later developed and applied more widely. An early definition by Gary Marks (1993: 392) spoke of:

> the emergence of *multi-level governance*, a system of continuous negotiation among nested governments at several territorial tiers—supranational, national, regional and local.

While accepting that integration involved intergovernmental bargains, MLG theorists reasserted the neofunctionalist critique of realism that individual governments were not as firmly in control as suggested.

Marks, Hooghe, and Blank (1996) made three key points against the intergovernmental view, as follows.

(1) Collective decision making involves loss of control for the governments of individual states.

(2) Decision-making competencies in the EU are shared by actors at different levels, not monopolized by the governments of states.

(3) The political systems of member states are not separate from each other, as Moravcsik (Chapter 1, pp. 12–14) assumed, but are connected in various ways.

While Marks, Hooghe, and Blank accepted the central role of the Council of Ministers in EU decision making, they pointed to a number of constraints on the ability of individual governments to control the outcomes of such collective decision making. The use of QMV in the Council was an obvious constraint: any individual government might be outvoted. The Luxembourg Compromise (see Chapter 9, pp. 129–30) did allow a government to exercise a veto if it felt that its vital national interests were threatened, but the prevailing culture in the Council worked against frequent use of this option, making it a rather blunt instrument for maintaining national sovereignty. So, while it was true that governments might be able to attain desired objectives by pooling their sovereignty, this was not the same as arguing that their control of decision making remained intact.

Supranational institutions might be created by member governments to assist them, as Moravcsik argued, but these did not remain under close national government control. For intergovernmentalists, national governments could ultimately choose to rein in the power of these institutions. For MLG theorists, this was difficult in practice because changes to the role of supranational institutions required unanimous agreement, which was difficult to secure with so many member states.

Marks, Hooghe, and Blank criticized Moravcsik's argument that national interests were determined purely through the interplay of domestic actors (Chapter 1). Instead, they argued that component parts of national governments, and also non-state actors, could form alliances with their counterparts in other member states, which influenced national governments' negotiating positions on EU matters. These alliances would not be under the control of the core institutions of the central government, such as the Foreign Office or the Prime Minister's Office, and the Commission in particular would be able to exploit the existence of these **transgovernmental and transnational networks** of actors to promote its policy preferences within the 'domestic' politics of member states.

Rather than a coherent theory, MLG was initially an amalgamation of perspectives that were primarily directed at what its advocates saw as the misrepresentation of the nature of the EU by the intergovernmental theorists. It did contain some elements of an explanation for the development of the EU, but it was primarily concerned with the analysis of the *nature* of the EU. As such, it lacked the basis for the analysis of political dynamics that was present in neofunctionalism.

Andrew Jordan (2001) identified seven key criticisms of MLG:

- MLG was nothing new, but an amalgam of existing theories;
- it provided a description of the EU, but not a theory;
- it overstated the autonomy of sub-national authorities (SNAs);
- it adopted a 'top-down' view of SNAs;
- it focused on SNAs to the exclusion of other sub-national actors;
- it mistook evidence of SNA mobilization at European level as evidence of SNA influence;
- it ignored the international level of interaction.

Stephen George (2004) argued that Jordan's criticisms were of 'variable validity'. He agreed with the first claim, but suggested that it was 'scarcely a criticism'. More significantly, George (2004: 125) suggested that MLG went beyond description to offer a theory of what sort of organization the EU is: 'It is hypothesized to be an organization in which the central executives of states do not do all the governing but share and contest responsibility and authority with other actors, both supranational and subnational.' Of course, the validity of this theory was contested, but MLG offered counter-hypotheses to those of (liberal) intergovernmentalism.

George agreed that work adopting the MLG perspective had tended to focus on SNAs to the exclusion of other actors, but had not sufficiently addressed the question of whether the mobilization of SNAs had made a real difference to outcomes in the policy process. It had also not been applied sufficiently to the international level, where the EU itself stands in the role of potential gatekeeper between different arenas.

Table 2.2 **Types of Multi-Level Governance**

Type I	Type II
General-purpose jurisdictions	Task-specific jurisdictions
Non-intersecting memberships	Intersecting memberships
Jurisdictions at a limited number of levels	No limit to the number of jurisdictional levels
System-wide architecture	Flexible design

Source: Hooghe and Marks (2004: 17)

In a development of the approach, Hooghe and Marks (2003; 2004) developed a twofold typology of MLG to capture the EU (see Table 2.2). Type 1 MLG effectively describes the formal institutions of government at various territorial levels (supranational, national, sub-national), which have multiple tasks and responsibilities and have jurisdictions that are clearly distinct from each other. In other words, Type I MLG describes the system-wide governing architecture. Co-existing with Type I MLG, Type II describes the many smaller bodies of governance that are generally set up with a specific purpose, sometimes for a limited time period, and which are deliberately flexible in membership and organization to deal with specific public policy challenges.

Other contributions focused on the normative dimension of MLG. Peters and Pierre (2004) suggested that the flexible and informal modes of co-ordination of MLG might bring dangers. In particular, they argued that MLG could be a type of 'Faustian bargain' in which the purported advantages of MLG in terms of functional efficiency are traded for core democratic values as authority seeps away from the formal institutions in which democratic accountability is exercised, or as political actors use these informal and opaque processes to escape accountability for their decisions (see also Chapter 4).

In a similar vein, Jan Olsson (2003) considered the 'democracy paradoxes' in MLG in relation to structural policy, the policy area from which the concept first emerged. He suggested that one way in which to address the democratic challenges inherent in the partnership arrangements established to deliver structural policy (see Chapter 29, pp. 426–7) would be to allocate a greater role to the formal institutions in the region, which were directly elected. This could be done by both abolishing the institutions of MLG (multi-level and cross-sectoral partnerships) and allocating their functions to elected institutions, or, more realistically, by allowing elected institutions to play a greater role in regulating partnerships.

Building on Olsson's work, Bache and Chapman (2008) put forward three models of democracy—electoral, **pluralist**, and elite-democratic—through which to evaluate the democratic credentials of MLG. Their case study of the structural funds in South Yorkshire (UK) illustrated that among the expected complexity and technocracy at this stage of policy making, there were also experiments in local democracy that had not previously been identified in the academic literature. As such, in the context of deep MLG, there is evidence that while traditional mechanisms of accountability may be undermined, other mechanisms may provide a valuable alternative.

In summarizing the state of the debate, Bache and Flinders (2004: 197) identified four common strands in the literature on MLG that raised hypotheses for future research:

(1) that decision making at various territorial levels is characterized by the increased participation of non-state actors;

(2) that the identification of discrete or nested territorial levels of decision making is becoming more difficult in the context of complex overlapping networks;

(3) that, in this changing context, the role of the state is being transformed as state actors develop new strategies of co-ordination, steering, and networking to protect, and in some cases to enhance state autonomy;

(4) that, in this changing context, the nature of democratic accountability has been challenged.

CONCLUSION

Approaches beyond the intergovernmental–supranational debate yield a number of insights about the EU, particularly in relation to the more routine decision making. Such decisions may not be as monumental as the 'history-making decisions', but, as Richardson (1996*a*: 29) said, they constitute 'the nine-tenths of the policy iceberg that is below the water line', and 'some means has to be found of analysing it'.

If theories of EU governance were relative latecomers to the study of the EU, their proliferation has more than made up for lost time. There are a number of overlapping and related approaches competing for the same space in analysing the operation of the EU system. For organizational purposes, we have made a distinction between the categories of 'new institutionalism' and 'governance and networks'. However, the reality is less clear-cut, not only between these categories, but also within them. A key theme that cuts through these categories is the emphasis on interests versus ideas, alternatively viewed as the 'rationalist vs reflectivist' dichotomy, which has become very prominent in the study of the EU. However, as the summary of approaches provided here suggests, this dichotomy has a long lineage in theorizing on the EU and provides a thread running through both the 'newer' theories of EU governance and the long-standing theories of integration covered in the previous chapter.

The governance and networks category of approaches raises again the theme that was prominent in Chapter 1: that of the role of interest groups. In the policy-networks approach, the emphasis is squarely on the links between interest groups and policy makers and the motive force of policy making is conceived to be vested interest. This approach reproduces at the sectoral level the insight of neofunctionalists that European integration would be driven forward more by interests responding in a rational, self-serving manner to the changed circumstances produced by the existence of the EC than by an idealistic commitment such as that shown by the federalists. Liberal intergovernmentalism also emphasizes interests rather than ideas as the key to analysing the EU. However, the concept of the epistemic community (and also the advocacy coalition framework) modifies this emphasis on interest, and brings knowledge and ideas back into the analysis. Here, the key actors in networks coalesce and bring about change through shared values, ideas, and knowledge.

Sociological and historical institutionalists also bring ideas back in, while rational choice institutionalists analyse the logical responses of actors to the institutional rules that they face. Sociological and historical institutionalists put a great deal of emphasis on the values and norms that actors develop within institutionalized relationships over time. These values and norms can be interpreted as ideas that actors hold, perhaps not fully consciously, that affect and at least partially explain their behaviour. While rational choice theorists, neofunctionalists, and liberal intergovernmentalists would all tend to argue that the existence of the EU structures the responses of actors because it provides a new set of rules within which they pursue their interests, sociological and historical institutionalists would tend to argue that the existence of the EU affects the way in which the actors perceive their interests, their aims, and their objectives. The theme of the role of interests in the EU is therefore also about the role of ideas.

Moving beyond the rationalist–reflectivist dichotomy, one problem with the application to the EU of concepts that were originally derived from the study of domestic political systems is that they tend to underemphasize the influence of the wider international system. An appreciation of the impact of the wider international system is the strength of some approaches derived from IR. The absence of such a dimension was one of the most telling criticisms made by Hoffmann of neofunctionalism, although Hoffmann may himself be criticized for having under-theorized this aspect (see Chapter 1). So, approaches originating in the study of domestic politics are not alone in this failing; the point remains important though, as the effects of globalization show no signs of abating (Chapter 3, pp. 46–7). Of the theories discussed here, MLG perhaps has the greatest potential for effectively conceptualizing the relationship between developments 'internal' and 'external' to the EU. There is nothing inherent in the framework that would exclude its propositions being applied to governance beyond the EU; indeed Type 2 MLG (see Table 2.2, p. 35) appears partly designed to meet that challenge.

Finally, we should keep in mind that, MLG apart, the approaches and theories discussed in this section are primarily mid-range: they seek to explain developments at a sub-system or sectoral level and are not attempts at theorizing the EU system more broadly. Moreover, as the EU becomes more complex, there may be greater application of mid-range theories. The possibilities for applying the policy network approach to the EU are borne out by an increasing number of sectoral studies highlighted by Peterson (2004: 129–30), particularly in the domains of cohesion policy, research policy, and the CAP. Governance theories more broadly defined may become more prominent with the increased use of more informal modes of governance in the EU, such as the Open Method of Co-ordination (see Chapter 15, p. 186).

KEY POINTS

- Approaches from the study of domestic and comparative politics turn away from the focus of IR theories on the process of European integration, and instead treat the EU as a political system that is already in existence, and try to explore 'the nature of the beast'.

New Institutionalism

- New institutionalism argues that analysts have lost sight of the importance of institutions in structuring political action.
- Three varieties of new institutionalism can be distinguished: rational choice institutionalism; historical institutionalism; and sociological institutionalism.
- *Rational choice institutionalism* emphasizes the argument that the behaviour of political actors is shaped by the specific framework of rules within which they operate.
- *Historical institutionalism* emphasizes the argument that political relationships have to be viewed over time and that decisions are shaped by the nature of pre-existing institutional relationships.
- *Sociological institutionalism* emphasizes the argument that the behaviour of political actors is shaped by informal norms and values.

Governance and Networks

- Definitions of governance commonly emphasize the proliferation of non-state actors in the policy process.

- Richardson advocated the application of two concepts from the study of domestic politics: policy networks and epistemic communities.

- A *policy network* is a set of resource-dependent organizations. The approach advocates analysis of sectoral policy networks that range from tightly knit policy communities to loosely bound issue networks.

- As a 'meso-level' approach, policy-network analysis is often most effectively used in conjunction with broader theories. It places emphasis on policy implementation, which is particularly relevant in the context of the EU.

- Kassim argued that EU processes were not settled enough for policy networks to emerge. Against this, Peterson argued that while some EU policy sectors remained fluid, others had developed into policy networks. He later argued that the networks approach was particularly relevant to studying the EU.

- The literature on network governance tends to be more normative than does the Rhodes model of policy networks and views networks as a potential solution to public policy dilemmas rather than being aimed at analysing sectoral decision making.

- *Epistemic communities* are knowledge-based groups that are most likely to be influential when policy makers face uncertainty over policy choices. This approach is complementary to the policy networks approach.

Multi-Level Governance

- MLG has strong antecedents in neofunctionalism, but is a theory of the nature of the EU rather than a theory of the process of European integration.

- While accepting that integration involved intergovernmental bargains, MLG theorists argued that individual governments were not in control of the process. Actors at supranational and sub-national levels played a key role also.

- While initially established by national governments, supranational EU institutions develop a degree of autonomy from the control of governments.

- Transnational and transgovernmental alliances mean that states are open to external influences. The Commission is able to exploit this situation to promote its own agenda.

- MLG has been criticized on a number of counts, not least for its analysis of the role and significance of sub-national actors.

- Hooghe and Marks have developed a twofold typology of MLG that addresses both analytical and normative concerns.

- Peters and Pierre have warned of a 'Faustian bargain' in which the purported gains in efficiency from MLG are traded for core democratic qualities.

- Bache and Flinders identified four common strands in the literature on MLG that raised hypotheses for future research.

FURTHER READING

In relation to the adoption of governance approaches in EU studies, see **B. Kohler-Koch and B. Rittberger** 'The "Governance Turn" in EU Studies', *Journal of Common Market Studies,* Annual

Review, 44 (2006): 27–49, and **S. Bulmer,** 'Institutional and Policy Analysis in the European Union: From the Treaty of Rome to the Present', in **D. Phinnemore and A. Warleigh-Lack (eds)**, *Reflections on European Integration: 50 Years of the Treaty of Rome* (Basingstoke: Palgrave Macmillan, 2009), 109–24. A clear statement of dissatisfaction with approaches to the EU based on theories of IR is **S. Hix**, 'The Study of the European Community: The Challenge to Comparative Politics', *West European Politics*, 17 (1994): 1–30.

Significant applications of the new-institutionalist approach to the EU are to be found in: **P. Pierson**, 'The Path to European Integration: A Historical and Institutionalist Analysis', *Comparative Political Studies*, 29 (1996): 123–63; **S. Bulmer**, 'New Institutionalism and the Governance of the Single European Market', *Journal of European Public Policy*, 5 (1998): 365–86; and **M. Pollack**, *The Engines of European Integration: Delegation, Agency and Agenda Setting in the EU* (Oxford: Oxford University Press, 2003). See also **M. Pollack**. 'The New Institutionalisms and European Integration', in **A. Wiener and T. Diez (eds)**, *European Integration Theory*, 2nd edn (Oxford: Oxford University Press, 2009), 129–41, for an overview of applications of new institutionalisms to the study of the EU. For a discussion of the historical institutionalist research agenda on the EU, see **S. Bulmer** 'Politics in Time Meets the Politics of Time: Historical Institutionalism and the EU Timescape', *Journal of European Public Policy*, 16 (2009): 307–24.

Epistemic communities are explained in **P. Haas**, 'Introduction: Epistemic Communities and International Policy Coordination', *International Organization*, 46 (1992): 1–35. For an overview of the policy networks approach and its application to the EU, see **J. Peterson** 'Policy Networks', in **A. Wiener and T. Diez (eds)**, *European Integration Theory*, 2nd edn (Oxford: Oxford University Press, 2009), 105–24. On the distinction between the Anglo-American and German approaches to policy networks, see **T. Börzel**, 'Organizing Babylon: On the Different Conceptions of Policy Networks, *Public Administration*, 76 (1998): 253–73.

On network governance, see **B. Kohler-Koch and R. Eising (eds)**, *The Transformation of European Governance* (London: Routledge, 1999) and **A. Jordan and A. Schout**, *The Coordination of the European Union: Exploring the Capacities of Networked Governance* (Oxford: Oxford University Press, 2006).

On multi-level governance, arguably the classic statement is **G. Marks, L. Hooghe, and K. Blank**, 'European Integration from the 1980s: State-Centric v. Multi-Level Governance', *Journal of Common Market Studies*, 34 (1996): 341–78; the most complete statement of the approach is contained in **L. Hooghe and G. Marks**, *Multi-Level Governance and European Integration* (London: Rowman and Littlefield, 2004); the collection by **I. Bache and M. Flinders (eds)**, *Multi-Level Governance* (Oxford: Oxford University Press, 2004) undertakes a critical assessment of both the potentialities and limitations of MLG, drawing both on theoretical contributions by scholars from different academic traditions and fields, and on different policy studies. **T. Conzelmann and R. Smith (eds)**, *Multi-level Governance in the European Union: Taking Stock and Looking Ahead* (Baden-Baden: Nomos, 2008) bring together a number of case studies on the structural funds and environmental policy.

The relationship between multi-level governance and policy networks is explored in **A. Warleigh**, 'Conceptual Combinations: Multi-Level Governance and Policy Networks', in **M. Cini and A. Bourne (eds)**, *Palgrave Advances in European Union Studies* (Basingstoke: Palgrave Macmillan, 2006), 77–95, and is developed further by **I. Bache**, *Europeanization and Multilevel Governance: Cohesion Policy in the European Union and Britain* (Lanham: Rowman and Littlefield, 2008).

 online resource centre

Visit the Online Resource Centre that accompanies this book for links to more information on theories of EU governance: www.oxfordtextbooks.co.uk/orc/bache3e/

Chapter 3

Critical Perspectives

Chapter Overview

If the 'governance turn' of the 1990s heralded the arrival of significant new voices in the European Union (EU) debate (Chapter 2), there is now an even wider chorus. As with Chapter 4, the perspectives and theories covered in this chapter are long established in the study of politics, but have only relatively recently become visible in the study of the EU. Critical perspectives, although very different from each other, are united in challenging key assumptions about what should be studied in politics, how it should be studied, and what we can hope to know. They are concerned with exposing the less obvious manifestations of power that pervade both political action and political theorizing. As the critical political economist Robert Cox (1981: 128) put it: 'Theory is always for someone and for some purpose.'

The range of critical perspectives now applied to the EU is too much to cover in a single chapter (for an overview, see Manners 2007). Instead, we focus on three that give a flavour of the contrasting perspectives with a shared emphasis on revealing the hidden sources of power. *Social constructivism* stands in direct contrast to the rationalist approaches that have dominated much of the study of the EU to date (see Chapters 1 and 2). *Critical political economy* in other guises has existed at the margins of EU scholarship for at least three decades, but has received increased attention over the past decade or so. *Gender perspectives* have been even more absent from theorizing on the EU until fairly recently.

Over the past two decades critical perspectives on the study of the European Union have blossomed in ways unimaginable from within the intellectual straitjacket of traditional political science during the Cold War era.

(Manners 2007: 77)

Social Constructivism

In the late 1990s, a 'rationalist–reflectivist' debate came to prominence in EU studies and this debate remains prominent today, underpinning much of the academic exchange on the new institutionalisms (Chapter 2) and relating closely to research on Europeanization (Chapter 4). On the one side are rationalist scholars, who argue that the EU is the result of conscious action by national governments; on the other are reflectivist scholars, who highlight the extent to which national actors redefine their positions on integration through their socialization with other European actors involved in the process. In summary, rationalists on the one hand:

> tend to operate within a view of the world (an *ontology*) that sees interests as materially given. They also adhere to a positivistic conception of how knowledge should be gathered. This involves a commitment to 'scientific' method, the neutrality of facts and the existence of observable realities.

(Rosamond 2003: 121)

On the other hand, reflectivists:

> see interests as socially constructed rather than pre-given ... [and] ... are interested in how collective understandings emerge and how institutions constitute the interests and identities of actors.

(Rosamond 2003: 121)

Until the late 1990s, a rationalist **ontology** dominated the study of the EU. Social constructivism entered debate on the EU not to dispute either the intergovernmental or supranational interpretation of integration, but rather to challenge the (materialist) assumptions on which the dominant integration theories were built. As such, it should be understood as an 'ontological approach to social inquiry' (Cowles 2003: 110) rather than as a theory of EU politics or integration.

However, different constructivists would situate themselves at different points on the rationalist–reflectivist continuum, and many would see their approach as an attempt to bridge the two. Others prefer not to present these contrasting approaches as a continuum, but as two points of a triangle, with constructivism providing the third. The argument here is that this image is more adequate since, 'in general, theorists tend to position their work in-between the corners' (Christiansen, Jørgensen, and Wiener 1999: 531) (see Figure 3.1).

The social constructivist approach is closely related to sociological institutionalism (Chapter 2). Both approaches emphasize that actors' behaviour is influenced by the 'logic of appropriate behaviour' or norms, which Katzenstein (1996: 5) defined

Figure 3.1 Major Contemporary Theoretical Positions

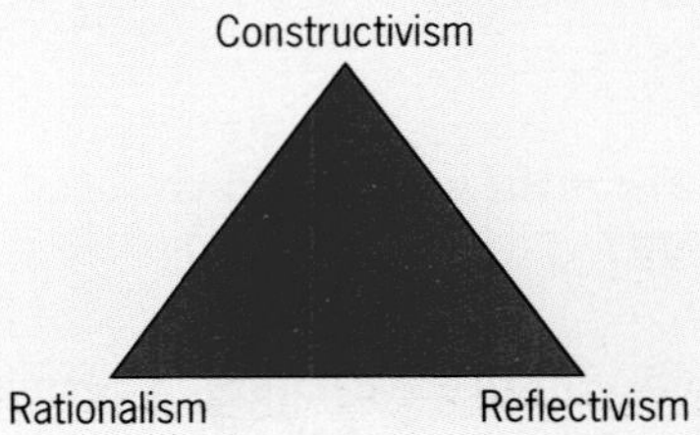

Constructivism

Rationalism   Reflectivism

Source: Christiansen, Jørgensen, and Wiener (1999: 532)

as 'collective expectations for the proper behaviour of actors with a given identity'. In this view, political actors internalize social norms, which shape their identities and thus their interests. This is what constructivists refer to as the 'constitutive effects' of norms.

The constructivist view that the actions of individuals cannot be understood in isolation from their social environment contrasts with the rationalists' emphasis on 'methodological individualism', in which the central focus is on 'individual human action' (Risse 2009: 145). However, while constructivists emphasize that individuals' interests and identities are shaped by the social environment in which they exist, equally they argue that the social environment is shaped over time by the actions of individuals. The relationship is one of two-way interaction and thus, in the words of constructivists, 'mutually constitutive'.

The essential constructivist critique of rationalist approaches is that a focus on material interests (such as economic interests or security) alone offers an inadequate explanation of key developments in European integration. Such an explanation ignores the role played by deeply embedded cultures that shape national positions, and the role of ideas and values that connect political leaders or other actors one with another.

Specifically, constructivists point to the importance of reflecting on how interaction with the EU over time may shape and redefine national positions, which places it in conflict with the 'domestic politics' assumptions of liberal intergovernmentalism (Chapter 1). As such, a constructivist history of the EU would:

> focus on the ongoing struggles, contestations, and discourses on how 'to build Europe' over the years and, thus, reject an imagery of actors including governments as calculating machines who always know what they want and are never uncertain about the future and even their own stakes and interests.

(Risse 2009: 147)

However, while the distinctions between constructivism and liberal intergovernmentalism are clear, it is less clear how neofunctionalism relates to constructivism. On the one hand, there are rationalist assumptions in neofunctionalism: for example, interest groups are seen to act rationally in shifting their political activities to a new political centre at European level to maximize their gains. On the other hand, key neofunctionalist texts also refer to interest groups' 'loyalties' moving to the new centre, which is very much the language of constructivism. Indeed, Haas (2001: 22) has stated that '[a] case can easily be made' that neofunctionalism can be seen as a precursor to constructivism.

European Identity

Risse (2004: 151) set out three main ways in which social constructivism contributes to our understanding of the EU:

- highlighting the mutually constitutive nature of agency and structure allows for a deeper understanding of the impact of the EU on its member states and particularly on statehood;

- emphasizing the constitutive effects of EU rules and policies facilitates study of the ways in which EU membership shapes the interests and identities of actors;
- focusing on communicative practices highlights both how the EU is constructed discursively and how actors come to understand the meaning of European integration.

Risse considered these arguments in relation to the development of a common European identity. For constructivists, this is a relatively neglected aspect of the study of the EU, but one that their approach places as central to an understanding of European integration. As discussed in Chapter 4, identity is seen by many as a key component to developing the legitimacy of the EU, and thus to further political integration. To date, however, a common European identity has been slow to emerge.

The constructivist approach on this suggests that there is no fixed meaning of what constitutes Europe or 'Europeanness', but different constructions that emerge from different contexts (for example, over time or in different places). This does not mean that 'anything goes' in relation to European identity, but that its meaning is not fixed, is context-dependent, and, as such, is shaped or 'constructed' over time.

Risse illustrated the importance of identity construction by arguing that the common European identity held by the then fifteen member states partly explains the EU's decision to enlarge to twenty-five members in 2004. Commission officials acted as 'norm entrepreneurs' to promote a sense of shared community values (democracy, human rights, and market economics) between the fifteen, which generated a normative obligation towards the applicant states who shared these values. In this way, '[r]hetorical commitment to community values entrapped EU member states into offering accession negotiations to the CEE [central and eastern Europe] and other Eastern European countries despite the initial preferences against enlargement' (Risse 2009: 157). It was noted, however, that once negotiations began, rationalist accounts provided a more fitting explanation of the strategic bargaining by national governments. This acceptance of the differential appropriateness of forms of explanation is evidence that constructivism does not seek to displace rationalist theories entirely, but to contribute to a more complete picture of how the EU works.

The EU as a Discursive Construct

Hay and Rosamond (2002) used constructivism to highlight how the process of globalization and European integration can be understood as 'discursive constructs'. Here, the *idea* of either European integration or globalization (or both) as external constraints on domestic action may be accepted as true by political actors (with or without evidence of the material reality) and thus influence their actions. In other words, 'it is the ideas that actors hold about the context in which they find themselves rather than the context itself which informs the way in which actors behave' (Hay and Rosamond 2002: 148).

They illustrated this argument by identifying four alternative discourses of globalization found in contemporary Europe: as external economic constraint; as the threat of homogenization; as a desirable yet contingent outcome; as a contingent and undesirable outcome. In the latter discourse, globalization is viewed as a fragile and malleable process, but not a favourable one. This discourse is used by some pro-integrationists

43

to construct a view of the EU as a 'bulwark' against the negative consequences of globalization, in particular against the threats to the notion of a European social model that places greater emphasis on welfare provision than the neo-liberal imperatives of globalization would allow (Hay and Rosamond 2002: 152–7).

While globalization discourses can be used to advance arguments for European integration, discourses of European integration are sometimes used by domestic actors to justify particular courses of domestic action or inaction. Hay and Rosamond (2002: 157) argued that:

> In a number of contemporary European contexts, it is the process of European integration (often in the immediate form of the Maastricht convergence criteria) which is (or has been) invoked as the proximate cause of often painful social and economic reforms elsewhere legitimated in terms of globalization.

The increased focus on the real or perceived constraints placed by European integration on domestic choice, and constructive arguments more generally, has been central to an upsurge in interest in the notion of Europeanization as transformation of domestic politics (Chapter 4).

Liberal and Critical Constructivism

Van Apeldoorn, Overbeek, and Ryner (2003) argued there is an important distinction between what they termed 'critical constructivism' and 'liberal constructivism'. The former, their preferred approach, suggests that an understanding of the development of ideas should be grounded in material circumstance, particularly economic interests (below). By contrast, liberal constructivism 'tends towards idealism' in that it highlights constraints, such as discourses, that are not grounded in material reality.

Thus, each of these variants of constructivism emphasizes the role of structures in shaping actor behaviour: the key point of difference between them is the nature and origins of the structures. This was illustrated in relation to a constructivist study by Risse and Wiener, who argued that it was difficult to explain agreement on European monetary union through economics-based explanations because very different views existed within the EU and within member states on the best way forward in terms of material economic interests. Instead, at a 'critical juncture', a trajectory was determined, influenced by ideas that had their origins in 'historical, religious, communal heritage (which includes liberal democracies and social markets)' (van Apeldoorn, Overbeek, and Ryner 2003: 32). Once this trajectory was taken, it was subsequently followed irrespective of how perceived material interests changed subsequently.

Van Apeldoorn, Overbeek, and Ryner (2003: 32) criticized this argument on two counts: first, on the separation between the ideas and material (economic) interests; and second, on the ground that, when material interests are discussed, they refer to the interests of national economies without any particular justification for doing this. In contrast, they argued that there can be no easy separation between ideas and material interests (below), and that the material interests that matter are best understood in relation to social classes, or perhaps particular sectors of the economy, rather than the notion of national economic interest. Thus, while van Apeldoorn, Overbeek, and Ryner (2003) agreed with the constructivist emphasis on ideas, they argued that these needed to be firmly grounded in material circumstances (below).

Constructivism Assessed

Cowles (2003: 110–11) identified three criticisms of constructivism:

- that it lacks a theory of agency and shows a tendency to overemphasize the role of structures rather than the actors who help to shape those structures;
- that much of the early constructivist literature tended to focus its analysis on public actors to the relative neglect of important non-state actors;
- that there is a tendency of some constructivists to identify the good things that have been socially constructed rather than the bad.

On the positive side, constructivism has played an important role in highlighting the importance of ideas in shaping both European integration and the more routine operation of the EU. Constructivists acknowledge that interests-based explanations continue to have validity, but that the role of ideas has been much neglected in studies of the EU to date. The source of ideas in shaping actor behaviour in the EU is now itself an important debate, which leads us neatly into the more material-based conceptions of ideas rooted in political economy.

Critical Political Economy

While the focus of this chapter is on 'critical' perspectives, it is important to note that not all approaches to political economy are critical of dominant approaches to the study of the EU; indeed, some traditionally dominant approaches covered in the previous chapters of this book are themselves informed by a political economy perspective. Verdun (2003) categorized the various political economy approaches as neo-realism, neo-liberal institutionalism, social constructivism, and critical approaches.

Neo-realism emphasizes the actions of states, who have given interests and seek to maximize these interests in an 'anarchic' international arena. This approach informed the work of intergovernmentalists, such as Hoffmann and Moravcsik (Chapter 1). Moravcsik in particular highlighted the relationship between domestic economic interests and state behaviour in international relations (IR).

Neo-liberal institutionalism accepts that states are key actors, but places greater faith in the ability of international institutions to regulate the behaviour of states on the world stage. Here, there is an emphasis on path dependence and socialization, which is highlighted in the new-institutionalist literature on the EU (Chapter 2).

Social constructivism is discussed at length above. For Verdun (2003: 92), it has three essential features: that the individual is a social creation who gains knowledge and finds identity through interaction with social processes; that an understanding of 'reality' is coloured by whoever observes or interprets it; and that social scientists studying social action are involved in the process and this involvement colours their findings.

Critical approaches to political economy are subdivided into various groups, such as the Amsterdam school, the British school, and the neo-Gramscians. They have in common the view that dominant approaches to IR and international political economy

(IPE) focus on the state and other elite actors without situating their behaviour in the context of underlying power structures (below).

These approaches all focus on issues relating to the role of the state and its relationship with the broader international economic system, but are otherwise quite distinct. The purpose in identifying these contrasting approaches is to situate what we term 'critical political economy' perspectives, which is the focus of our discussion below.

Globalization and European Integration

In critical political economy, European integration cannot be separated from the phenomenon of globalization. In this perspective, the former is often viewed as a particular regional expression of the changing nature of global capitalism.

Globalization is variously defined. On some definitions, it is no more than a contemporary term to describe a set of processes that have a long history; more commonly, globalization is taken to refer to a new phenomenon of linkages transcending territorial boundaries. Although globalization has cultural and social aspects, the view of globalization as an observable economic phenomenon is an influential one.

This economic explanation is characterized by the growth of multinational companies that operate in a number of states, and which own especial loyalty to no one state. It also highlights the emergence of global flows of capital, which increased dramatically in the last part of the twentieth century. These flows are both of **investment capital** and **liquid capital**. The rise of multinationals and the increased flows of investment capital intensify competition between states to provide the most attractive conditions for investment. If they try to impose higher taxes or more restrictive regulatory rules than their competitor states, they will lose investment to those other states.

The question of the degree of control that states have over this process is the subject of academic dispute. The term 'globalization' is often used as though it is a process beyond the control of governments, which constrains them in the policies that they can follow (see the quotation from Hay and Rosamond above). Some scholars suggest that globalization is a myth (Hirst and Thompson 1996): that it is just a new term to describe the internationalization of capitalist activity, which has been ongoing for a long time. In fact, the present 'global' economy is less open than was the international economy between 1870 and 1914. Most so-called multinational corporations are actually large national companies that trade internationally. The myth of globalization is used as an argument to prevent national governments from trying to control the forces of capitalism—but if governments were to co-ordinate their efforts, they could regulate global markets.

A third view (Amoore et al. 1997; Payne 2000) is that globalization has two aspects. On the one hand, developments that are largely independent of governments, such as technological advances, have changed the scale of operation of capitalist enterprises and made it more difficult for governments to regulate their activities. On the other hand, the responses of states to these developments have themselves fed the process. Technology makes it possible to move funds across international exchanges at speeds never envisaged in earlier periods, and this poses problems for governments in regulating the process. They could respond by investigating new, perhaps collaborative ways of regulating the exchanges—but they have mostly responded by capitulating to 'the inevitable' and lifting capital controls. This response makes a reality of the globalization of capital markets—but it could have been otherwise.

It is important in this context to see that globalization is a process, not a fixed condition. It is not the case that globalization started on a particular date; it is a name given to changes in the capitalist system that have developed in the post-war period. At each stage in this development, governments and other actors have played a role in shaping the nature of the process. Not only is the process itself fed by the actions of states and other actors, but it also affects their outlooks and arguably the institutional arrangements that govern them. Here, the EU is a case in point.

The EU and Globalization

At first sight, the emergence of the EU as a regional grouping seems to be in contradiction to the direction and thrust of globalization. It is true that, to some extent, the project of European integration, which started as a response to the problems of post-war reconstruction, became a process of responding to the evolution of the international system. However, the European project has always been one of 'open regionalism'.

Open regionalism means that policy is directed towards the elimination of obstacles to trade within a region, while at the same time doing nothing to raise external tariff barriers to the rest of the world (Gamble and Payne 1996: 251). There has been no significant voice in the debate about the nature of the EU that has advocated closing western Europe off from the global system. The central debate has been between the British position and the French position on this issue.

The British position has favoured global free trade and free movement of capital. It has seen the freeing of trade within the EU as a stepping stone to this end. The French position has seen the EU as a means of organizing European capitalism to compete more effectively on world markets. It has been a 'strategic trade' view rather than a 'free trade' view. But it has never advocated the EU being a closed trading bloc. Instead it has argued the case for the liberalization of national markets to be accompanied by the introduction of European-level industrial and technology policies to build up and promote European champions, companies that could compete effectively with US and Japanese companies on world markets.

These debates reflect differences in national approaches to the management of capitalism within Europe. French governments have generally been less willing than British ones to accept that the free market should determine the shape of the national economy, and have favoured a larger role for the state (George 1989). However, the belief that there has been a quantitative and qualitative change in the extent and nature of global economic transactions has affected the policies of individual states, and the nature of the process of European integration. This insight is central to modern critical political economy perspectives. However, these modern perspectives have firm roots in earlier contributions.

Neo-Marxism: Early Perspectives

Recent critical political economy scholarship on European integration and the EU was prefigured in the work of Peter Cocks (1980) and Stuart Holland (1980), and influenced by earlier contributions by Mandel (1968) and Poulantzas (1974). These neo-Marxist explanations of European integration focused on the close relationship

47

between economics and politics and would now be placed in the category of 'critical political economy'.

Peter Cocks (1980) argued that contemporary European integration theory was ahistorical and dealt only with the contemporary world. To understand the contemporary process of European integration, he argued, requires understanding it in the context of how capitalism shapes different phases of European and international interdependence. Understood this way, European integration is a response to problems emanating from a particular phase of capitalism. Just as political integration at the national level developed and changed in response to the need to ensure the effectiveness and legitimacy of capitalism, so European integration is explained in the same way.

Cocks (1980: 27–8) suggested that European integration offered several possibilities to political elites: ' . . . to ensure high rates of export-led economic growth . . . to provide a counterweight to American hegemony . . . [and] to perpetuate traditional relations with ex-colonies under a new guise.' The specific project of creating a **common market** would allow European states to take advantage of economies of scale comparable to those of the large scale industries existing in the United States.

In this view, there is nothing romantic or particularly radical about European integration. Politicians were not pursuing ideals, but trying to preserve existing social and economic structures by finding new means through which their economies could generate growth and stay competitive. As Cocks (1980: 39) put it:

> Regional integration was a mechanism for accommodating and reinforcing the expansion of European capital while simultaneously protecting it from the possibly excessive rigours of international competition. Ideologically, supranational ideas such as federalism and functionalism provided moral and intellectual justifications at the elite level for European regional organization.

Writing in the same period, Stuart Holland (1980) took a similarly critical position to Cocks. He took issue with the explanations of and justifications for integration offered by then contemporary economists, arguing that 'the conventional theory of economic integration largely neglects issues of social and economic class' and that this theory played a role in 'mystifying or obscuring the real power relations in capitalist society' (Holland 1980: 89). This argument that the dominant theories of integration serve to obscure deeper underlying explanations and purposes of the EU is echoed by more recent contributors to the debate (below). Holland's argument was explicitly class-based. Thus, while then contemporary 'economic' integration theorists justified their position by arguing that broader social and political issues were not the concern of economists, Holland (1980: 89) suggested that there were other reasons for their failure to incorporate social class and political power into their analysis:

> Class analysis has Marxist connotations which raise issues of exploitation and power which are inconveniently disturbing to many of the élites engaged in integration itself. Lifting the lid on class relations opens a Pandora's box of the kind which key exponents and advocates of international integration have been trying to close and bury for some time.

From this perspective, the dominant neofunctionalist theory had similar flaws to the approaches of conventional economists. It rested on **pluralist** assumptions regarding the wide dispersal of power within society, which meant that no single group would be able to dominate the integration process. Neofunctionalism identified the role of elites and interest groups in advancing integration, but did not link the role of these actors to the class structure that distributed power unevenly between them. Thus, while neofunctionalists emphasized the role of business interests in promoting integration, this would not be conceptualized in terms of 'class power'. For neofunctionalists, the main reason why business interests were more prominent in advancing integration than were labour interests was that business was better organized than labour. Holland accepted that capitalist interests were more effectively organized than labour, but suggested that this argument obscured a more important explanation for capitalist influence over the process. What was important was not an observable process of business leaders influencing state actors, but a shared world view—or, as Holland (1980: 91–2) put it, 'the combination of governmental élites and the self-electing élites of private capital, bound on a common venture in fulfilment of a common ideology'.

Developments in Neo-Marxism

A later generation of scholars built on the work of the neo-Marxists, but believed their predecessors had overestimated the existence of crisis tendencies within capitalism and had not accounted for the considerable variations in types of capitalism over time and space (Cafruny and Ryner 2009: 229). Yet the starting point for contemporary neo-Marxist scholars of the EU was essentially the same as that of Cocks and Holland, that the dominant theories of integration have basic flaws that obscure understanding of the nature of power in the EU:

> by their very design they are unable to conceptualize adequately power relations that are constitutive of capitalist market structures. In other words, these mainstream theories fail to account for the structural power that determines the particular trajectory of European integration

(van Apeldoorn, Overbeek, and Ryner 2003: 17)

In particular, 'mainstream theories' make assumptions about the inherent rationality of market forces that leave no room for alternative organizing principles. Specifically, they 'assume either explicitly or implicitly that market forces are expressions of an inner rationality of universal human nature that is held to be the essence of the realm of freedom in political affairs' (van Apeldoorn, Overbeek, and Ryner 2003: 18). Critical political economists dispute the assumption that the market is a reflection of human nature and that its operation equates with freedom in political affairs, and suggest instead that this starting point obscures the uneven distribution of power inherent in the operation of markets. The consequence is that mainstream theories define power narrowly in relation to control by political authorities and thus the empirical focus is on how this power is organized. In the critical political economy perspective, this view needs to be supplemented with a view of power derived from social forces (generally, class relations) that underpin market relations and shape formal political authority.

To understand the true nature of power in the EU, van Apeldoorn, Overbeek, and Ryner (2003) proposed a neo-Marxist approach, drawing on the work of Antonio Gramsci. This is where the 'constructivist' strand of their approach is prominent in critical political economy, with the role of ideas being central to the understanding of Gramsci's concept of 'hegemony'. Unlike liberal constructivists, though, ideas here are firmly embedded in social relations. Gramsci argued that the capitalist class does not rule by force, either exclusively or primarily, but through consent generated by the diffusion of its ideas (via state institutions and organizations in civil society). In this way, the specific interests of the capitalist class become internalized by all as the general interest and thus states only need to use force to govern as a last resort. Thus, mainstream theories of the EU not only fail to expose the underlying nature of class power that shapes its emergent political structures, but in doing so also serve to reproduce the consent that legitimizes and thus sustains this state of affairs.

Manners (2007) drew attention to an 'Open Marxism' school, including contributions such as Bonefeld (2001), Carchedi (2001), and Smith (2002). The contributions of this school differed in focus, but collectively highlighted the question: 'Who is the EU for?' There was a particular concern with the development of the single market and monetary policy and its effects on the relationship between national political elites and national working classes. As Manners (2007: 29) put it:

> The growth of anti-capitalist groups and actions since the 1990s, together with the revival of parties of the left in Europe, illustrates the extent to which the Open Marxist arguments over the role of the EU in reinforcing national class distinctions resonates with the wider European public.

The New Regionalism

While the formation of regional blocs such as the EU, particularly for trading purposes, is not particularly new, there has been a proliferation of such blocs since the mid-1980s, which is explicitly linked to globalization. They include the North American Free Trade Association (NAFTA), Asia–Pacific Economic Co-operation (APEC), and Mercusor (a Spanish acronym for the common market of countries in South America: Argentina, Bolivia, Brazil, Chile, Paraguay, and Uruguay). This proliferation of regional groupings in the context of globalization gave rise to a new group of scholars studying the phenomenon under the label of the 'new regionalism' (see Breslin et al. 2002).

The essential argument here echoes that put forward by Cocks (above) that, in the context of globalization, states in a particular 'region' pool resources to survive and compete in a more demanding economic environment. Of course, as with the EU, there is debate over the extent to which state actors are *voluntarily* pooling resources or are responding to other actors or forces shaping integration. There is a further debate about how far these regional formations promote or accelerate globalization rather than simply respond to it.

The new regionalism highlights a long-standing divide in the EU scholarly community between those who see the EU as something unique or *sui generis* and those who see it as a particular example of a wider phenomenon. The new regionalism tends to take the latter view and thus emphasizes comparing examples of regional integration.

In comparative terms, Rosamond (2003: 124) described the EU as, at most, a 'deviant case' of regional integration:

> Its longevity rules out any claim that the EU was *created* as a response to global economic upheavals in the 1970s and early 1980s. Moreover, compared to other cases of regionalism the EU is considerably more institutionalized and much more deeply integrated. Yet at the same time the acceleration of economic integration through the single market programme and progress towards monetary union has coincided with the growth of regional projects elsewhere.

Critical Political Economy Assessed

Contributions from this perspective raise important questions for 'mainstream' theorists, in particular about the assumptions that underpin dominant theories both of European integration and of the operation of the EU as a political system. In addition to highlighting the role of ideas, critical political economy contributions raise questions about the nature of power in the EU that have often been ignored entirely by mainstream theorists or dealt with in a cursory manner. In particular, 'critical political economy relates developments in the EU to the constraints and opportunities of capitalism' (Cafruny and Ryner 2009: 237).

One obvious criticism of this perspective is that a number of 'mainstream' scholars are explicitly working with mid-range theories and are not concerned with underlying processes that shape the broad contours of political power, but with how the political system works on a day-to-day basis. It is highly unlikely that scholars focusing on such matters are unaware of neo-Marxist arguments. It may be that they simply reject the neo-Marxist analysis based on class power, or it maybe that they accept the essential analysis, but feel that this is inevitable and so time should be spent on understanding (and thus improving) political processes within this context.

Gender Perspectives

Gender is taken to refer to 'the socio-cultural meanings given to masculinity and femininity and to the complex and varying relations between the two' (Hoskyns 2004: 217). Thus, the perspectives covered in this section start from the **ontological** position that gender is the main organizing principle of the social world. While gender perspectives are analytical, the feminist critique of the asymmetries associated with gender relations provides a normative dimension (Kronsell 2005: 1023). Thus gender analysis may be concerned with either understanding the EU or seeking to improve it, or indeed both. There is no single 'gender theory' or 'feminist theory' of the EU, but a broad range of perspectives (see Insight 3.1 for illustration).

While critical political economy could be described as on the margins of EU scholarship until the past decade or so, gender perspectives were even less present. Hoskyns (2004: 33) argued that 'both the core of EU policy making and many of the key concepts of theorizing European integration remain virtually untouched' by feminist and gender analysis. However, feminist and gender scholarship on the EU has grown and

> ### Insight 3.1 Varieties of Feminism
>
> Sandra Whitworth (1994) distinguished between three varieties of feminism (liberal, radical, and post-modern) and added a fourth (critical theory).
>
> - **Liberal feminism** is concerned with equality and equal representation of women.
> - **Radical feminism** foregrounds violence against women and sexual politics.
> - **Post-modern feminism** deconstructs the category 'woman' and emphasizes 'diversity'.
> - **Critical theory feminism** combines the insights of critical theory with a gendered feminist politics.
>
> *Source:* Hoskyns (2004: 217–8)

diversified in the past decade, most obviously to move beyond a focus on the EU's gender equality policies to analyse the EU more generally.

Research on EU Gender Equality Policies

Research on gender equality policies is well established in the EU literature. These policies had their origins in Article 119 of the Treaty of Rome (Hoskyns 1996) and developed through subsequent Treaty provisions, directives, Court rulings, and soft-law instruments relating to a range of policy areas including part-time work, parental leave, sexual harassment, childcare, and violence against women (see Hantrais 2000; Ellina 2003). Locher and Prügl (2009: 183–4), who described the EU gender equality regime as 'one of the more astonishing aspects of European integration', identified a three-stage development in the area—from a focus on equal rights, to positive action, to gender mainstreaming—taking into account the gender dimension in all areas and at all stages of EU policy making.

The EU's role in this area has been theorized from a range of established perspectives: intergovernmentalists have pointed to the role of particular governments in promoting particular initiatives (for example, the Nordic member states promoting mainstreaming); supranationalists have emphasized the role of the Commission in advancing equality measures—not least through building alliances with key national and transnational interest groups—and the rulings of the Court of Justice. Linked to supranationalist arguments, historical institutionalists have emphasized the path-dependent nature of developments, with incremental changes gradually taking control away from national governments (Pierson 1998). However, feminist theory has drawn on theories of social movements and advocacy networks to go beyond these explanations and highlight the role of feminist activists in promoting the agenda (Locher and Prügl 2009: 194–5).

Yet while the EU is often seen as progressive in this area compared to most national governments, its ambitions are not always realized. Mainstreaming has been seen as a mixed success, with some EU policy areas and Commission Directorates more responsive than others. Thus, Pollack and Hafner-Burton (2000: 440) found that the most receptive Commission Directorates were those that have 'historically been interventionist in character, and relatively open to consideration of social justice issues', such as those responsible for the cohesion, employment, and development policies. There is also often obstruction of EU measures at the policy implementation stage, which is the responsibility of national actors. Moreover, Hoskyns (2004) argued that despite the growth in scope of gender equality measures over time, major EU decisions continue to be taken without reference to gender or without adequate representation of women (Hoskyns 2004: 223). The Commission's 2001 Governance White Paper (see Chapter 29, p. 332) is given as an example as an important document that does not mention the word 'gender' and the Constitutional Convention (Chapter 16, pp. 195–7) as an example of an important body with a very small proportion of women members (17 per cent).

A Feminist Critique of EU Theories

Kronsell (2005) suggested that the process of European integration had, in different ways, both affirmed and challenged gender relations, but dominant integration theories had done little to develop understanding of gender dynamics. In seeking to assess the ways in which feminist analysis might contribute to theorizing about the EU, she critiqued six approaches that she saw as representing the 'state of the art' in EU studies: liberal intergovernmentalism; domestic politics approaches; neofunctionalism; multi-level governance (MLG); supranationalism; and constructivism.

At the core of *liberal intergovernmentalism* is the argument that states are the dominant actors in the EU (see Chapter 1, pp. 12–14). However, from a feminist perspective, this focus on states as the key actors rests upon a narrow conception of the relevant political space and one that excludes consideration of gender dynamics. As Kronsell (2005: 2035) put it:

> Liberal intergovernmentalism defines the place of politics as a place where women are not. Moravcsik's idea that states relate to each other and interact in the process of integration—in intergovernmental negotiations—does not take note of the fact that it is and has been almost exclusively men speaking for the state.

The *domestic politics approach* (Chapter 4, p. 61), a variant of which forms part of Moravcsik's liberal intergovernmentalism, offers more scope for incorporating analysis of gender dynamics by opening up the **'black box of the state'** to consider the complex processes at play in shaping national positions on EU issues. However, while this approach considers the role of a range of actors within and beyond the state, Kronsell (2005: 1027) suggested that the approach had been 'less prone to include gender and women's interest organizations within the overall assessment of EU integration'.

Neofunctionalism, like the domestic politics approach, placed a premium on understanding the role of interest groups, but within the transnational as well as the national context (see Chapter 1, pp. 8–11). Again, this offers the potential for understanding the contribution of organized interests representing women, but is critiqued for its liberal view of pressure group activity, which does not draw attention to asymmetries in the resources available to interest organizations of different types. Specifically, in the competition for influence between transnational interest groups, feminist organizations are not recognized to be at a distinct disadvantage in comparison to more powerful lobbies that shape a range of policies with significant gender implications

(Kronsell 2005: 1028). Hoskyns (2004: 225) added to this critique, suggesting that neofunctionalism 'has ended up explaining and thus implicitly often promoting a bureaucratic, technocratic model of policy making in the EU, which from the beginning separated the economic from the social', and thus excluded both gender concerns and democratic concerns.

Multi-level governance (Chapter 2, pp. 33–6) is seen as complementary to feminist analysis because it goes beyond a focus on the state, interest groups, and supranational norms to emphasize complex interactions involving multiple actors in which power takes multiple forms. However, like the other approaches that emphasize the plurality of actors discussed above, MLG is seen to neglect analysis of the underlying distribution of power between actors, and indeed between levels of governance. More specifically, it overlooks that the policy networks central to the notion of MLG tend to be male-dominated and difficult for women to enter. Thus, for MLG to deliver on the promise that it holds for feminist analysis, more empirical research is required on the composition and dynamics of relevant policy networks (Kronsell 2005: 1031–2).

Supranationalism focuses the EU-level of decision making and highlights how national actors learn not only how to co-operate to get deals done, but also come to appreciate the value of common norms by which decisions should be made in particular sectors (Chapter 1, pp. 14–17). Over time, these norms become institutionalized and the ways in which sectors operate constrain behaviour and shape future policy outputs. On one level, this approach is helpful for gender analysis in relation to understanding the development and evolution of the EU's gender policies. However, supranationalism ignores the history of EU institutions as shaped and governed by men, and thus its focus on norms and norm dynamics 'needs to be broadened to include also the institutionalization of the male-as-norm' that is inherent in the EU (Kronsell 2005: 1033).

Like supranationalism, *social constructivism* emphasizes the importance of norms and processes of socialization through which national preferences can be transformed. It is an approach that has an obvious appeal for feminist analysis, given its concern with the social construction of sex difference (see Insight 3.1). Indeed, Hoskyns (2004: 228) suggested that 'women academics who have been writing on gender issues in the EU context for many years are now beginning to identify themselves as social constructivists'. However, constructivism is another approach in which power is either 'downplayed or left external to construction' and thus which inadequately deals with the feminist concern that 'institutions not only delimit our world but systematically distribute privilege and thereby create patterns of subordination' (Kronsell 2005: 1035). Yet constructivist analysis is seen as having the potential to be informed by a feminist view of power.

In summarizing her critique of dominant theories, Kronsell (2005: 1035–6) highlighted two points: that they ignore the 'male-as-norm' problem; and that they are based on a simplistic view of power. Despite this, a number of the approaches are identified as being compatible with a more gender-sensitive approach and a key purpose of the critique is to promote a dialogue between established ways of theorizing the EU and feminist analysis that will highlight new or neglected aspects of EU politics. As Hoskyns (2004: 224) put it, a more gender-sensitive analysis of European integration 'brings the imbalance between the social and the economic in EU policy making into focus, puts the emphasis on democratic legitimacy and forms of participation, and prioritizes the analysis of power relations'.

Gender Perspectives Assessed

Gender perspectives draw attention to particular policy developments and raise a number of questions that are not addressed by mainstream theories of the EU. In policy terms, they reveal an EU that is, on the one hand, relatively progressive in relation to gender equality issues, but, on the other, perpetuates gender inequalities and limits the participation of women in key forums. In theory terms, gender perspectives seek to reveal hidden aspects of the EU: most particularly in this case relating to the gendered effects of EU policy making and the mechanisms through which patriarchal domination is reproduced (Locher and Prügl 2009: 181). However, many feminist scholars emphasize the potential for dialogue between gender perspectives and other theories: social constructivism in particular.

CONCLUSION

This chapter has summarized contributions that can be broadly categorized as 'critical perspectives'. As the discussion shows, these perspectives are not only critical of mainstream theories, but also of each other. Importantly, though, they share an emphasis on the 'hidden' sources of power in the realms of ideas and social forces. They are in many ways a corrective to the 'institutional bias' that has been identified as manifest in EU scholarship (Smith 2002; Manners 2007).

Yet while there has been a recent groundswell of interest in critical perspectives in the study of the EU, we should not view the application of critical perspectives as entirely new. Some of the contributions discussed above have a longer lineage in the study of the EC/EU than is at first obvious. Most notably, there are constructivist elements in neofunctionalism, and some contributions from critical political economy of recent years closely resemble the arguments of Cocks and Holland a generation earlier. Why these aspects should have been evident in earlier debates but absent for so long is an interesting question.

It is clearly the case that, particularly with the collapse of the communist regimes in the Soviet bloc in the late 1980s and early 1990s, neo-Marxist approaches fell from grace in some areas of study at least. Their revival and application to the study of the EU may be evidence of rescuing the 'baby from the bathwater' that was discarded, to highlight previously obscured aspects of European integration and the nature of political authority in the EU. Alternatively, this may be a cyclical phenomenon: there is a tendency in the academic world—and the study of the EU is no different—for theories and concepts to drift out of scholarly debate only to be revived at some later point in a revised form.

A further possible explanation is the relative isolation of academic networks. Communities of scholars, like policy communities, are often 'nested' and relatively disconnected from others. The growing application of critical perspectives to the EU suggests a greater cross-fertilization of ideas between scholarly communities than may have been the case for some time. Empirical developments, and particularly globalization, have undoubtedly stimulated this cross-fertilization of ideas, not least between EU and IR scholars.

KEY POINTS

- Critical perspectives and theories long established in the study of politics more broadly have received increasing attention in the study of EU politics in the past decade or so.

• Critical perspectives are concerned with exposing the less obvious manifestations of power that pervade both political action and political theorizing.

Social Constructivism

• Social constructivism entered debate on the EU to challenge the (materialist) assumptions on which the dominant integration theories were built. As such, it should be understood as an 'ontological approach to social inquiry' rather than as a theory of EU politics or integration.

• Social constructivism relates closely to sociological institutionalism in emphasizing the influence on actors of norms and the 'logic of appropriate behaviour'.

• In relation to the EU, social constructivism puts particular emphasis on how national positions and perceived national interests are shaped through the engagement of national actors with EU actors.

• Social constructivism emphasizes the role of identity and its fluidity.

• How constructions of Europe shape domestic politics has been important in increasing interest in the study of Europeanization.

• A distinction has been made between liberal constructivism and critical constructivism, in which the latter places greater emphasis on the material context from which ideas originate.

Critical Political Economy

• In critical political economy, European integration and globalization are inextricably linked, with the former generally viewed as a particular regional expression of the changing nature of global capitalism.

• While at first sight the EU as a regional grouping may appear in conflict with globalization, the EU's free-trade approach to the rest of the world has been characterized as 'open regionalism'.

• Recent critical political economy scholarship on European integration and the EU was prefigured in the work of Peter Cocks (1980) and Stuart Holland (1980), who argued that then-contemporary theories of integration neglected issues of social and economic class and thus obscured the underlying power relations in the EC.

• A generation later, van Apeldoorn, Overbeek, and Ryner (2003) picked up and developed the same theme, drawing more explicitly on the analysis of Antonio Gramsci.

• The proliferation of regional groupings in the context of globalization has given rise to a new group of scholars studying this phenomenon under the label of the 'new regionalism'.

Gender Perspectives

• Gender is taken to refer to 'the socio-cultural meanings given to masculinity and femininity and to the complex and varying relations between the two' (Hoskyns 2004: 217).

• There is no single 'gender theory' or 'feminist theory' of the EU, but rather a broad range of perspectives.

• Research on gender equality policies is well established in the EU literature and scholars have observed a three-stage development in the area from a focus on equal rights, to positive action, to gender mainstreaming.

• While the EU is often seen as progressive in this area compared to most national governments, its ambitions are not always realized because of constraints at both EU and national levels.

• Feminists argue that dominant integration theories have done little to develop understanding of gender dynamics in the EU. They are seen to ignore the 'male-as-norm' problem and as based on a simplistic view of power.

- However, many feminist scholars emphasize the potential for dialogue between gender perspectives and other theories: social constructivism in particular.

FURTHER READING

For a wide-ranging review of critical perspectives on the study of the EU, see **I. Manners**, 'Another Europe is Possible', in **K.E. Jorgensen, M. Pollack, and B. Rosamond (eds)**, *Handbook of European Union Politics* (London: Sage, 2007), 77–95.

On constructivism, see the influential collection in the special issue of the *Journal of European Public Policy*, 6, No. 4 (1999), edited by **T. Christiansen, K. Jørgensen, and A. Wiener**. Other helpful contributions are: **J. Checkel and A. Moravcsik**, 'A Constructivist Research Programme in EU Studies?', *European Union Politics*, 2 (2001): 219–49; **J. Checkel**, 'Constructivism and EU Politics', in **K. E. Jørgensen, M. Pollack, and B. Rosamond (eds)**, *Handbook of European Union Politics* (London: Sage, 2007), 57–76; **T. Risse**, 'Social Constructivism and European Integration', in **A. Wiener and T. Diez (eds)**, *European Integration Theory*, 2nd edn (Oxford: Oxford University Press, 2009), 144–60.

For an overview of critical political economy perspectives, see **A. Cafruny and M. Ryner**, 'Critical Political Economy', in **A. Wiener and T. Diez (eds)**, *European Integration Theory*, 2nd edn (Oxford: Oxford University Press, 2009), 221–40. A clear statement of the Marxist position on European integration can be found in **P. Cocks**, 'Towards a Marxist Theory of European Integration', *International Organization*, 31 (1980): 1–40. Key contributions on critical political economy include: **A. Bieler and A. Morton (eds)**, *Social Forces in the Making of the New Europe: The Restructuring of European Social Relations in the Global Political Economy* (London: Palgrave, 2001); **B. van Apeldoorn**, *Transnational Capitalism and the Struggle over European Integration* (London: Routledge, 2002); **A. Cafruny and M. Ryner (eds)**, *A Ruined Fortress? Neoliberal Hegemony and Transformation in Europe* (Lanham: Rowman and Littlefield, 2003); and **A. Cafruny and M. Ryner**, *Europe at Bay: Neoliberal Hegemony and Transformation in Europe* (Boulder, CO: Lynne Rienner, 2007).

On gender perspectives, there are a number of helpful overview pieces, including: **C. Hoskyns** 'Gender Perspectives', in **A. Wiener and T. Diez (eds)**, *European Integration Theory* (Oxford: Oxford University Press, 2004), 217–36; **B. Locher and E. Prügl**, 'Gender and European Integration', in **A. Wiener and T. Diez (eds)**, *European Integration Theory*, 2nd edn (Oxford: Oxford University Press, 2009), 181–98; and **E. Prügl**, 'Gender and European Union Politics', in **K. E. Jørgensen, M. Pollack, and B. Rosamond (eds)**, *Handbook of European Union Politics* (London: Sage, 2007), 433–48. For a particular focus on gender and theories of European integration, see **A. Kronsell**, 'Gender, Power and European Integration Theory', *Journal of European Public Policy*, 12 (2008): 1022–40.

 online resource centre **Visit the Online Resource Centre that accompanies this book for links to more information on critical perspectives:** **www.oxfordtextbooks.co.uk/orc/bache3e/**

Chapter 4
Theorizing Consequences

Chapter Overview

As the European Union (EU) has increasingly been understood as a political system in its own right, so academic attention has shifted to understanding the implications of this development. This chapter focuses on two sets of consequences that have prompted much scholarly interest and look set to remain at the forefront of academic debates for some time to come. The first is 'Europeanization', which is understood here as a process in which domestic politics, policies, and polities are changed through engagement with the EU system. The second concerns the consequences of the EU for democracy.

Having spent intellectual energy in seeking to understand the 'nature of the beast', that is, the nature of European integration, political scientists have now realised that a EU political system is in place, produces decisions, and impacts on domestic policies in various guises. Hence the focus has shifted to studying those impacts.

(Bulmer and Radaelli 2005: 340)

This chapter brings together what have usually been presented as separate 'consequences' of European integration: Europeanization effects, and challenges to democracy. However, there are clear links between the two, particularly when Europeanization is understood as a process through which domestic politics and polities are changed by their engagement with the EU. Most obviously, the process of Europeanization can challenge domestic democratic structures and processes by transferring responsibilities and obscuring lines of accountability. More positively, Europeanization may add to what is termed 'output democracy' by increasing the policy-making capacities of governments through collective action.

Europeanization

Over the past decade or so, Europeanization has emerged as a key theme in studies of the EU, and has become 'a staple component of European integration courses in political science and public policy degrees' (Radaelli 2004: 1). However, as is often the case with emerging concepts, its meaning is contested and leaves the field of study looking somewhat disorderly, casting doubt on the extent to which it has added value to those approaches that already existed for studying Europe. For example, some scholars refer to Europeanization as an EU-related phenomenon, while others see it as a phenomenon broader than, or largely separate from, the EU. Beyond this distinction, other definitions and usages abound. Increasingly, though, the main value of the concept appears to be in highlighting the changing nature of relations between the EU and its member (and accession) states, and this has become the primary focus of empirical studies of Europeanization. Here, we outline the range of uses before focusing on the development of Europeanization studies that relate specifically to the EU.

Meanings of 'Europeanization'

While Europeanization has become a key theme in studies of the EU in recent years, it is not a new term. Rather, its importance has grown as scholars have sought to give more precise meaning to a term that has been used loosely to indicate a range of issues and processes. In the debates over the meaning and relevance of the term, the extent to which it has been applied in different contexts with different purposes has become evident. Buller and Gamble (2002), Olsen (2002), and Bache and Jordan (2006a) have each identified five uses of Europeanization, some of which overlap, while others do not. Drawing on these contributions, we summarize the ways in which various scholars have used the term 'Europeanization', and distinguish between those uses that relate specifically to the EU and those that are not EU-specific (Table 4.1 and Table 4.2).

The Development of the Field

Attempts to give a more precise meaning to 'Europeanization' date back to the 1990s. An early and influential contribution was Robert Ladrech's study of the EU and France, in which Europeanization was defined as, 'an incremental process reorienting the direction and shape of politics to the degree that EC political and economic dynamics become part of the organizational logic of national politics and policy-making' (Ladrech 1994: 69). In other words, domestic politics was being changed by the response of domestic organizations to the changing context brought about by EU membership.

Yet while Ladrech observed Europeanization effects in France, he did not suggest that the effects of the EU would be the same across all member states. Thus, fears of harmonization or homogenization were unfounded. Instead, domestic factors played an important role in shaping the nature of the Europeanization effects in France, and would do so elsewhere. There would be 'national-specific adaptation to cross national inputs' (Ladrech 1994: 84). Ladrech's arguments about the importance of domestic mediating factors were borne out in subsequent studies.

In their study of Britain, Bulmer and Burch looked at the effects of EU membership on the machinery of central government and argued that 'while change has been substantial, it has been more or less wholly in keeping with British traditions' (Bulmer and Burch 1998: 603). At key points in Britain's relationship with the EU, the administrative response had been shaped by the way in which important political actors had perceived the integration process. So, 'the construction of the issue of integration interacts

Table 4.1 Uses of Europeanization: EU-Specific

Usage	Focus on
A top-down process of change deriving from the EU	The effects of EU membership on domestic politics, policies, and polities (Héritier et al. 2001; Buller and Gamble 2002). Later research highlighted issues of culture, discourse, identity, and norms (Bulmer and Radaelli 2005).
The creation of new EU powers	The development of EU structures of governance and the accumulation of EU competences (Risse, Cowles, and Caporaso 2001). This usage is similar to the notion of European integration.
The creation of a European lodestar of domestic politics	The idea of the EU as an increasingly important reference point for the political activities of domestic actors, such as sub-national governments and interest groups (Hanf and Soetendorp 1998; Fairbrass 2003).
An increasingly two-way interaction between states and the EU	States seeking to anticipate and ameliorate the effects of top-down Europeanization pressures by 'uploading' their preferences to the EU level. As such, the EU both affects and is affected by domestic processes (Bomberg and Peterson 2000; Börzel 2002).
Changes in external boundaries	The expansion of Europe as a political space, particularly through the process of enlargement (Grabbe 2001; 2003; Olsen 2002; 2003; Schimmelfennig and Sedelmeier 2004; 2005).
A 'smokescreen' for domestic manoeuvres	A process in which domestic actors 'hide behind' the EU to legitimize domestic action (or inaction) that may be unpopular (Dyson and Featherstone 1999; Buller and Gamble 2002; Radaelli 2004).

Table 4.2 Uses of Europeanization: Non-EU-Specific

Usage	Focus on
Horizontal transfer or 'crossloading' between states	The movement of ideas and practices between European states (whether EU members or not). The EU *may or may not* play a role in facilitating these movements. This usage is linked to ideas of policy transfer (Bomberg and Peterson 2000) and is also referred to as 'crossloading' (Burch and Gomez 2003; Howell 2003).
Exporting forms of political organization	The transfer of European political ideas and practices beyond Europe (Olsen 2002; 2003).

with the prevailing characteristics of national governmental machinery to explain the different starting points for national adaptation' (Bulmer and Burch 1998: 606). A related study by James Smith (2001: 160) on the Scottish Office came to a similar conclusion that 'while the culture has undergone subtle realignment in adapting to "European" administrative practice, the *overall* ethos and parameters of the culture have not been altered to any great extent'.

Uploading, Downloading, and Crossloading

While early studies focused on the downward flow of pressures from the EU to the national level, later studies increasingly highlighted the interactive two-way relationship between member states and the EU. As well as being 'downloaded' by the member states from the EU level, ideas and practices are also 'uploaded' from member states to the EU level. The focus on uploading had antecedents in the 'domestic politics' approach developed by Bulmer (1983), while downloading resonated with the even earlier work by Puchala (1975) on post-decisional politics: the processes and politics involved in securing compliance with European decisions. Both emphasized the importance of domestic politics in understanding the dynamics of European integration, which is central to Europeanization research. Interestingly, Puchala's (1975: 519–20) characterization of the EU (then EEC) as a system in which the European and national levels are inextricably linked resonates strongly with the notion of multi-level governance (MLG) (Chapter 2), which it prefigured by almost two decades:

> The EEC is a multilayered system arranged in political layers from the local to the supranational. Complex organizational and elite network linkages bind the national peripheries to the Brussels center; transmissions—upwards and downwards, inwards and outwards through these organizations and networks, with political bargaining at different interchanges ultimately underpin both decisionmaking and compliance in the EEC.

The incentive for states to upload is that if they can get their existing policy preferences accepted as the preferences of the EU, they will have less trouble adapting to the EU policy when it comes into force. As Mény, Muller, and Quermonne (1996: 5) noted: 'Often, the most effective results are achieved through controlling the initial stages of the development of a policy . . . The advantages accrue to those leading countries which succeed in convincing the Community institutions and public opinion that their options or solutions are the best.'

A study of environmental policy by Börzel (2002) emphasized how national executives tried to minimize the domestic implementation costs of EU environmental initiatives by seeking to upload their own preferred policy models to the EU level. Different states' executives had different uploading strategies, according to both their policy preferences and their capacity to participate at the EU level. A distinction was made between the *pace-setting* strategies of those state executives actively seeking to promote their preferences at EU level, and the *foot-dragging* strategies of those seeking to delay or block EU action so as to avoid heavy implementation costs. A third strategy of *fence-sitting* described those states that did not seek to advance or block policies, but worked opportunistically with both 'pace-setters' and 'foot-draggers' to trade their support on environmental policy for reciprocal support in other policy areas.

While this interactive dynamic of Europeanization was widely recognized, much empirical research continued to focus on downward pressures. Of particular note was a multi-state study by Cowles, Caporaso, and Risse (2001), which focused on the downward pressure from the EU-level on 'domestic structures'. The study looked at two categories of domestic structure: *policy structures*, a concern extending beyond policy content to changes in the political, legal, and administrative structures of policy; and *system-wide domestic structures*, relating to changes in the nation state, its society, and economy. The findings of this study echoed those of Ladrech (1994) on the importance of national factors in shaping outcomes. In particular, they emphasized the importance of the degree of 'fit' between EU-level changes and existing domestic structures, policies, and practices. Poor fit implies strong pressure to adapt: good fit implies weak pressure. The extent to which adaptational pressure leads to domestic change depends on five intervening factors: multiple veto points in the domestic structure; facilitating institutions; domestic organizational and policy-making cultures; the differential empowerment of domestic actors; and learning (Risse, Cowles, and Caporaso 2001: 2).

This theme of domestic adaptation was developed further by Olsen (2002: 932), who, drawing on the new-institutionalist arguments of March and Olsen (1989), argued that:

> the most standard institutional response to novelty is to find a routine in the existing repertoire of routines that can be used. External changes are interpreted and responded to through existing institutional frameworks, including existing causal and normative beliefs about legitimate institutions and the appropriate distribution, exercise and control of power.

Olsen provided two broad explanations for different patterns of Europeanization across member states. The first related to the nature of the pressures 'coming down' from the EU—specifically, that EU pressures are more likely to have an impact in the domestic arena under the following circumstances: 'the more precise their legal foundation; when they are based on hard law rather than soft law; when the affected parties (constituent units) have been involved in developing the arrangement; the greater the independence of their secretariat; if the secretariat is single-headed rather than multiple-headed; and the greater the financial autonomy of the institution or regime' (Olsen 2002: 933). The second explanation pointed to different responses to adaptive pressures across member states because 'the (West) European political order is characterized by long, strong and varied institutional histories, with different trajectories of state- and nation-building, resources and capabilities' (ibid: 934).

The studies summarized above employed different definitions of Europeanization (see Insight 4.1), but common findings emerged. Most obviously, these studies illustrated divergence in the domestic effects of EU membership across different dimensions (for example, institutions, policies). This was explained by variations in the nature of the EU initiative or decision, and in the degree of fit between this and domestic preferences and practices. Despite the focus on downward causation, there is agreement that Europeanization is a two-way process in which states also seek to upload their preferences to the EU level. However, there is a persuasive argument that, '[i]f Europeanization entails both the evolution of European integration and its domestic impact, it ceases to be a researchable subject matter' (Börzel and Risse 2007: 495). As such, most Europeanization research continues to focus on the downloading aspect

---

Insight 4.1 Definitions of Europeanization

Definitions of Europeanization abound. Perhaps the most comprehensive definition of Europeanization comes from Radaelli, who defined it as:

> ... processes of a) construction, b) diffusion, and c) institutionalization of formal and informal rules, procedures, policy paradigms, styles, 'ways of doing things', and shared beliefs and norms which are first defined and then consolidated in making of EU public policy and politics and then incorporated in the logic of domestic discourse, identities, political structures and public policies.

(Radaelli 2003: 30)

For framing empirical research with primarily a top-down focus, Bache and Jordan defined Europeanization as:

> the reorientation or reshaping of politics in the domestic arena in ways that reflect policies, practices and preferences advanced through the EU system of governance.

(Bache and Jordan 2006a: 30)

(for example, Cowles, Caporaso and Risse 2001; Dyson and Goetz 2003; Schmidt 2006; Bache 2008; Featherstone and Papadimitriou 2008).

The notion of *crossloading* adds a horizontal dimension to Europeanization mechanisms. Crossloading refers to the transfer of ideas or practices from one state to another. Such transfer may involve the EU as a facilitator, for example through funding 'twinning exercises' that promote learning between policy makers in different states or co-operation promoted through the open method of co-ordination (see Chapter 15, p. 186). Equally, transfer may be bilateral and developed through long-standing relations that may indeed pre-date EU membership or be simply the result of one state being seen to offer best practice in a particular activity that other states seek to emulate (see Harmsen 1999; Radaelli 2000; Kassim 2003; Bulmer et al. 2007).

Dyson and Goetz (2002) distinguished between first-generation and second-generation Europeanization studies to illustrate differences between those studies that emphasized the more formal, observable consequences of EU membership and those that focused on less formal and less observable changes. While first-generation Europeanization studies can be traced back to the early 1970s, the second generation emerged in the 1990s and was consistent with a broader sociological turn in EU studies around that time (see Chapters 2 and 3). In the perspective of second-generation studies, Europeanization is not limited to changes in political–administrative structures and policy content, but also focuses on the effects on ideas, discourses, and identities.

Anderson (2002: 9) captured the broader concerns of second-generation analyses through the categories of interests, institutions, and ideas (Insight 4.2). These categories are often separated for analytical purposes, but the point is to understand their relationship: that is, for example, how the motivations and values of political actors are shaped by the institutional context in which they operate; or how the ideas held by political actors shape what they perceive their interests to be. This is significant in 'isolated' domestic contexts, but in the context of EU membership, such isolation is not possible. As such, the EU 'matters' because it 'automatically entails multilayered

---

Insight 4.2 Interests, Institutions, and Ideas

- *Interests* are causally important because they directly shape policy responses by establishing a distribution of societal preferences that national officials take into account as they seek to build electoral coalitions capable of winning and then holding political power.

- *Institutions* influence what actors do or do not do by allocating power to some actors but not others, structuring the content and sequence of policy making, and providing opportunities for and constraints on the state as its officials seek societal support for their policy choices.

- *Ideas* matter because they enable actors to manage uncertainty about the expected consequences of alternative choices, and they provide actors with a symbolic and conceptual language to advance their causes. In the context of strategic interaction among numerous actors, shared ideas can bring about the convergence of expectations and strategies facilitating agreement and co-operative outcomes.

Source: Anderson (2002; 2003)

---

interactions of interests, institutions, and ideas at and across the national and supranational levels' (Anderson 2002: 10).

The key features of first-generation and second-generation Europeanization research are summarized in Table 4.3. It should be noted that while this generational division provides a useful way of distinguishing between the differing emphases of different Europeanization studies, many cover aspects contained in both categories.

Table 4.3 Summary of Dyson and Goetz (2002) on the 'Two Generations of Europeanization Research'

First generation	Second generation
• Generally top-down approaches, seeking to explain domestic change from EU 'pressures'	• Emphasizes more complex interactions (top-down, bottom-up, and horizontal)
• Assumed 'misfit' between European and domestic levels—particularly formal institutional	• Greater emphasis on the 'political' dynamics of fit: interests, beliefs, values, and ideas
• Emphasis on reactive and involuntary nature of adaptation	• Greater emphasis on voluntary adaptation through policy transfer and learning
• Focus on policy and polity dimensions	• Greater emphasis on politics, e.g. identities, electoral behaviour, parties, and party systems
• Expected increasing cross-national convergence	• Emphasizes differential impact of Europe
• Defined Europeanization in substantive terms—focus on the 'end state' effects	• Emphasizes impact of Europeanization on domestic political, institutional, and policy dynamics

Note: An earlier version of this table appeared in Bache and Marshall (2004).

Europeanization and the New Institutionalisms

As Europeanization research has become more fine-grained, it has been characterized by a new-institutionalist agenda, including the various sub-branches of that theoretical literature (see Chapter 2, pp. 22–7). However, the main variants of the new institutionalisms—rational choice, sociological, and historical—have not been utilized to the same degree, with the application of pure rational choice institutionalism limited (Bulmer 2007). The picture is blurred because authors do not always place themselves neatly in one of the categories identified above. For example, Börzel and Risse (2003), two significant contributors to this literature, have many affinities with historical institutionalism while attempting to synthesize from the other two main variants. Moreover, the choice of theoretical framework utilized in Europeanization research is inevitably influenced by the definition that is adopted (see above). Despite these caveats, the new institutionalisms retain a prominent place in the theorization of Europeanization research and it remains inconclusive which variant carries most causal weight (Börzel and Risse 2007: 493).

Europeanization Assessed

Interest in the concept of Europeanization remains central to the study of the EU, with studies being published from an increasing variety of angles. There are studies of:

- individual member states across politics, polity, and policy dimensions (for example, Dyson and Goetz 2003 on Germany; Bache and Jordan 2006*b* on Britain; and Featherstone and Papadimitriou 2008 on Greece);

- specific policy areas in a number of states (for example, Jordan and Liefferink 2004 on the environment; Faist and Ette 2007 on immigration; and Bache 2008 on cohesion policy);

- institutional effects across different states (for example, Knill 2001 on national administrations; Hughes, Sasse, and Gordon 2004 on regionalization) or within a single state (for example, Bulmer and Burch 2009 on Britain).

Other studies focus on particular parts of Europe (for example, Schimmelfennig and Sedelmeier 2005 on central and eastern Europe; O'Brennan 2008 on the western Balkans), and some studies cover a range of states and topics (for example, Cowles, Caporaso, Risse 2001; Featherstone and Radaelli 2003).

As suggested by some of the literature cited above, the scope of Europeanization research has moved beyond the boundaries of the EU membership to shed light on the dynamics of the process of enlargement both in terms of the acceptance and assimilation of the formal *acquis communautaire* by accession states, and in terms of the pressures on accession states to conform to less formal, but nonetheless important, norms of democratic behaviour—that is, acceptance of both the 'regulatory pillar' and the 'normative pillar' (Bulmer and Radaelli 2005: 340).

Given the diversity of Europeanization research to date, it is valid to ask whether the concept has been stretched too far to remain useful. In response to this question, Olsen (2003: 334) suggested that the field was still relatively new and, rather than risk abandoning a potentially useful term prematurely, the challenge was 'to explore the ways in which (or indeed whether) the term might be useful for understanding the dynamics of the evolving European polity'. Peter Mair (2004: 346) offered a more robust justification for continuing to use the term to stimulate research, and suggested that 'some of the very best and most innovative and challenging work in political science is now being carried out by scholars working in the field of European integration and Europeanization'.

Radaelli (2006) suggested that, while it was difficult to map and summarize the diverse range of empirical studies to date, a number of results stood out. In particular, the evidence for the Europeanization of public policies was more robust than the evidence for the effect of Europeanization on political competition, state structures, or the polity. Moreover, while Radaelli was clear that Europeanization did not lead to uniform convergence across Europe, there was evidence of 'clustered convergence' as states with similar characteristics or preferences in a given domain responded in similar ways to particular pressures or opportunities.

Mair (2004: 342) argued that there had been significant 'informal' Europeanization in terms of cross-cultural convergence, although this might not be directly the result of the EU. While this argument is slightly beyond our EU focus here, it is important in drawing attention to notions of 'Europeanization as convergence' that are long established in the study of comparative politics and which may have implications for the study of the EU. In this academic tradition, Europeanization is equated with the older historical process of 'nationalization': a polity-building process. The logic of this process is that:

> Through 'coercion' or through 'authoritative allocation' in the case of more formal processes, and through education, communication, and sheer imitation and diffusion in the more informal cases, certain rules, practices and forms of behaviour become increasingly standardized throughout a given political and social system. And where this once applied and led to the more or less wholesale 'nationalization' of state territories, we now appear to witness it being applied and leading to the—admittedly far more uneven—'Europeanization' of a spreading transnational territory.

(Mair 2004: 342)

Thus, debates on Europeanization look set to remain prominent for some time. Europeanization research remains a complex but important field of inquiry and one that is probably best understood in terms used by Radaelli (2006), as a challenging and exciting 'problem' rather than as a conceptual solution that provides 'off-the-shelf' explanations.

Democracy

For a long time, European integration proceeded with relatively little public or political debate on the implications for democracy and legitimacy. Decisions were taken by elites in the context of a 'permissive consensus'—the absence of public debate and protest on developments was taken as evidence of consent. European integration appeared to have low salience for most people. Economic integration was relatively

uncontroversial in the context of a globalizing marketplace, and unanimous voting procedures were in place to protect perceived national interests.

However, as the EU's reach extended into a wider range of activities, and decision-making procedures changed, reducing the use of unanimous voting, European publics increasingly signalled their objections to further integration, most obviously through negative votes in referenda on Treaty reforms. The contentious ratification of the Maastricht Treaty was a particularly significant moment (see Chapter 13, pp. 164–5). In this changing context, debates about popular control over the integration process and the accountability of EU elites have grown. These debates intensified with the fifth enlargement (see Chapter 13, pp. 164–6) and they were a prominent feature of the deliberations of the Constitutional Convention (see Chapter 16, pp. 195–7) that led to the Constitutional Treaty and ultimately to the Treaty of Lisbon. The subsequent problems in ratifying these Treaties heightened debate on the democratic dimension of the EU even further.

While public debate on democracy in the EU was limited until the 1990s, there has been a long-established academic debate over the EU's perceived 'democratic deficit'. This debate has taken a significant twist in recent years, with an increasing number of academics arguing that the democratic deficit has been overstated and, indeed, that it may not actually exist. Alongside the debate on the democratic deficit has been a related interest in the concept of legitimacy. In some cases, democracy and legitimacy are used somewhat interchangeably, although it is more usual to view legitimacy as a broader concept (see below).

Democracy and Legitimacy

Birch (2001: 72) argued that 'the term "democracy", in its modern sense, came into use during the course of the nineteenth century to describe a system of representative government in which representatives are chosen by free competitive elections and most male citizens are entitled to vote'. However, the term has been used in various ways by political theorists, leaving the concept somewhat contested. The same is true for the concept of legitimacy. In simple terms, democracy is concerned with the public control over their leaders exercised by citizens with broadly equal rights (Insight 4.3), while legitimacy is a broader concept that can be understood as the

---

Insight 4.3 Democracy

Christopher Lord (2001: 166–7) suggested that democracy, defined as 'a system of government in which the people rule themselves', can be reduced to two core attributes: 'The first is that the public must be able to control those who make decisions on its behalf, even where it does not directly assume the reins of government; and, second, citizens should exercise such control as equals, since a condition in which some decide on behalf of others is paternalism, not democracy...'

Albert Weale (1999a: 14) defined democracy as a condition in which 'important public decisions on questions of law and policy depend, directly or indirectly, upon public opinion formally expressed by citizens of the community, the vast bulk of whom have equal political rights'.

public acceptability of the exercise of power (Lord 2001: 187). Democracy is an important source of legitimacy, but not the only source.

Beetham and Lord (1998) pointed to three liberal-democratic criteria of legitimacy that are relevant to the authority of the EU. These are performance, democracy, and identity. The concept of a legitimacy deficit relates to all three, not simply the democratic dimension. *Performance*, defined as 'effectiveness in the attainment of agreed ends or purposes of government', is considered 'an important component of legitimacy' rather than as something separate from it (Beetham and Lord 1998: 25). In terms of *democracy*, EU institutions are seen to be deficient in each of the three aspects of direct democratic legitimacy: authorization; accountability; and representation. However, extending direct democratic legitimacy in the EU depends on the development of a more robust common European *identity* among the EU electorate, which is generally considered, at best, to be embryonic (Smith 1992).

The notion of a 'democratic deficit' has been the focus of much scholarly work in this area. The key concern here has been the lack of public accountability of the EU's institutions. More broadly, the concept of a 'legitimacy deficit' is used to describe the gap between the principles and practice of decision making. It is concerned with the difference between 'the moral authority or normative standing *required* by a public authority engaged in the production of binding rules and allocations, and that which it is *actually able* to command' (Beetham and Lord 1998: 126). For Beetham and Lord (1998: 3), legitimacy in the EU system 'has to be understood as a process of interaction between the EU and member state levels'. For traditional international organizations, legitimacy is secured through the recognition of their authority by other legitimate authorities (member states): an indirect rather than direct form of legitimacy, which is dependent on the pre-existing legitimacy of the member states. However, the nature of the EU is generally seen as different from other international organizations and in some respects to resemble domestic systems of governance (see Chapter 2). As such, the EU requires a legitimacy that is wider than the indirect legitimacy provided by the consent of national elites.

As will be seen below, the relationship between notions of democracy and legitimacy, and how and why they are in 'deficit' in the EU, is not always clear in the academic literature. For example, the performance dimension of legitimacy outlined by Beetham and Lord is similar to the notions of *output democracy*, while their democratic accountability dimension is echoed by the notion of *input democracy*. Thus, for Scharpf (1997: 19), democracy is a 'two-dimensional concept, relating to the *inputs* and to the *outputs* of the political system at the same time' (Insight 4.4).

The Democratic Deficit

The notion of the democratic deficit has been defined in a number of ways, but is essentially concerned with the degree to which the EU adequately represents and is accountable to European citizens (Insight 4.5).

Lord (1998: 11) referred to a number of features contributing to the perceived democratic deficit:

the unelected character of the European Commission, the alleged weakness of the European Parliament, the withdrawal of powers from national parliaments, lack of a

> ## Insight 4.4 Input–Output Democracy
>
> Scharpf (1997: 19) argued that:
>
> On the **input side**, self-determination requires that political choices should be derived, directly or indirectly, from the *authentic preferences* of citizens and that, for that reason, governments must be held accountable to the governed...
>
> On the **output side**, however, self-determination implies *effective fate control*. Democracy would be an empty ritual if the political choices of governments were not able to achieve a high degree of effectiveness in achieving the goals, and avoiding the dangers, that citizens collectively care about. Thus, input-oriented authenticity and output-oriented effectiveness are equally essential elements of democratic self-determination.

European political identity or 'demos', low voter participation in European elections, the absence of strong democratic intermediaries such as political parties, the remoteness and obscurity of the Union's decision making procedures, and doubtless much else besides . . .

A lot of the early literature on the democratic deficit focused on the relative weakness of the European Parliament (EP) within the EU's institutional balance. Strengthening the EP, the only directly elected EU body, has been widely viewed as an appropriate means through which to close the democratic deficit. To some extent, this particular deficit has been addressed, as the EP's powers have increased dramatically since direct elections were introduced in 1979 (Chapter 22, pp. 296–302). However, it remains only one of four influential organizations and, by most accounts, it is still not the most powerful. Moreover, the contribution of the EP to correcting the democratic deficit remains limited because elections tend to be fought on national rather than European issues and turnout is generally low (Chapter 22, pp. 302–3). This is because European electorates do not perceive themselves as being part of an EU-wide democratic community in the same way as they do see themselves being part of a national democratic community. So, the EU still lacks the popular authority of national assemblies. The absence of a strong common European identity, or 'demos', remains a central challenge for those seeking to address the problem of the democratic deficit by strengthening further the powers of the EP. As van der Eijk and Franklin (1996: 7) put it: 'It is true that the European Parliament lacks certain powers in comparison with modern-day national parliaments—but what it lacks most is not power but a mandate to use that power in any particular way.'

> ## Insight 4.5 The Democratic Deficit
>
> - This refers to the idea that EU decisions are 'in some ways insufficiently representative of, or accountable to, the nations and the people of Europe' (Lord 2001: 165).
> - It is said that the EU suffers from 'deficiencies in representation, representativeness, accountability and support' (Eriksen and Fossum 2002: 401).

However, some scholars have suggested that the notion of the democratic deficit is something of a 'non-problem'. Andrew Moravcsik (2002) argued that the EU has been unfairly judged in democratic terms. Specifically, it has been judged either against ideal standards of democracy or compared with national standards and practices, neither of which is appropriate:

> Comparisons are drawn between the EU and an ancient, Westminster-style, or frankly utopian form of deliberative democracy. While perhaps useful for philosophical purposes, the use of idealistic standards no modern government can meet obscures the social context of contemporary European policy-making—the real-world practices of existing governments and the multi-level political system in which they act.

(Moravcsik 2002: 605)

Moravcsik (2002: 603) argued that, rather than acting unfettered, as much of the democratic-deficit argument suggests that they do, the EU's institutions are 'tightly constrained by constitutional checks and balances: narrow mandates, fiscal limits, super-majoritarian and concurrent voting requirements and separation of powers'. Moreover, the EU's appearance of being relatively insulated from democratic accountability reflects the nature of its main functions, such as central banking, constitutional adjudication, and economic diplomacy, which are generally low-key affairs in national systems, and are often delegated to non-governmental or quasi-governmental actors. So, the EU's system should not be singled out for criticism on these grounds.

Concerns over the institutional balance, and the EU's procedures for ensuring accountability, are heightened by the perception of some scholars that the EU fails to deliver on the 'output' side of the equation. Scharpf (1999b) argued that the economic focus of the European integration project, and the relative underdevelopment of effective European social and welfare policies, provide an output imbalance that favours business and economic actors. In the context of intensified market competition, states could face a 'race to the bottom' in terms of welfare spending, which would be accelerated by the neo-liberal bias within the EU. The consequence of this is the alienation of those social groups that benefit least from the EU's system—the poor, women, and recipients of welfare benefits. Moravcsik (2002: 617) recognized Scharpf's argument as 'the most empirically and theoretically nuanced criticism of the EU's democratic deficit that currently exists', but suggested that it should be qualified on a number of grounds—in particular: that there 'is little evidence of a race to the bottom'; that 'the level of social welfare provision remains relatively stable'; and that there is 'little evidence that the EU is driving social protection downward' (Moravcsik 2002: 618).

Moravcsik's position on the democratic deficit flows logically from his argument that the EU is largely characterized by liberal intergovernmentalism (Chapter 1, pp. 12–14). In this view, national governments dominate the policy process, so the outputs of the system are legitimized primarily by the democratic accountability of those governments. Only rarely does delegation to **supranational institutions** lead to unintended consequences for national governments, and only in relatively few areas does the EU depart from national practices (the degree of independence given to the European Central Bank being the most important example). Thus, in his view, concerns arising from the lack of direct accountability of the EU's main institutions are misplaced.

Simon Hix (2006: 6) took a different view from Moravcsik, suggesting that input democracy, based on competitive elections so as to provide for the direct accountability of policy makers, brings a number of advantages. First, competitive elections ensure that decision makers respond to citizens' preferences. Second, party-political competition stimulates public debate, which forms public opinion on the EU and, in so doing, provides political elites with a mandate to undertake reform. Third, competitive elections play a role in identity formation, so rather than waiting for the emergence of a common European identity before democratizing the EU's institutions further, introducing electoral competition now could assist in the development of this identity.

Vectors of Legitimation

Lord and Magnette (2004) considered whether the existence of very different views on how the EU ought to be legitimated might in itself add to its overall legitimacy. In doing so, they identified four 'vectors of legitimation' in the EU: indirect; parliamentary; technocratic; and procedural legitimacy.

- *Indirect legitimacy* depends on the existing legitimacy of the EU's member states, on the EU's respect for the sovereignty of the member states, and on the ability of the EU to serve the purposes of the member states.

- *Parliamentary legitimacy* depends on both an elected European Parliament and the representation of the member states via the Council system. This dual legitimation reflects the co-existence of both a single people that relates to and is affected by the EU in broadly the same way, and a series of peoples with separate identities.

- *Technocratic legitimacy* depends on the ability of the EU to meet the demands and improve the quality of life of its citizens—that is, that it has problem-solving efficiency.

- *Procedural legitimacy* rests on the observance of particular procedures—such as transparency, balance of interests, proportionality, and consultation. Beyond the observance of 'due process', procedural legitimacy is also derived from the observance of given rights, and the capacity to generate new rights (Lord and Magnette 2004: 184–7).

Lord and Magnette (2004) then drew on the distinction between *input legitimacy* and *output legitimacy* to illustrate the different vectors of legitimacy evident at two broad stages of policy making (Table 4.4).

The authors pointed out that these vectors provide 'ideal types', which do not exist in pure form in the EU context, but provide the basis for analysing and understanding the nature of legitimacy and how institutions have developed to combine or manage conflicts between the different vectors. They insisted that arguments about different types of legitimacy need not be divisive, but that 'conflict about legitimacy may even stimulate acceptance' (Lord and Magnette 2004: 197) in the way that conflict between government and opposition in classic parliamentary systems has played a role in enhancing the overall acceptance of a regime.

Table 4.4 Input and Output Legitimacy under the Four Vectors of Legitimation

	Input	Output
	EU policies are legitimate to the extent that they are based on the following:	EU policies are legitimate to the extent that they deliver the following:
Indirect	authorization by states	state preferences
Parliamentary	elections	voters' preferences
Technocratic	expertise	efficiency
Procedural	due process and observance of given rights	expanded rights

Source: Lord and Magnette (2004: 188)

Academic Exchanges

In 2004, a number of leading scholars exchanged views on the state of democracy in the EU. Amitai Etzioni (2004) suggested that what he described as 'halfway integration' was a central problem for the development of democracy at the EU level. This position is characterized by advanced integration in the economic sphere, but a relative lack of political integration and weak EU institutions, in comparison to the power of national institutions within their own territories. Etzioni suggested that one solution to the democratic challenge was to increase economic integration further so that more national interest groups would shift their focus to the EU level, which would in turn 'pressure the EU to develop more EU-wide political powers to work out these differences, which in turn would build the legitimacy of an EU government' (Etzioni 2004: 3). This argument reflects early neofunctionalist thinking, as outlined in Chapter 1 (pp. 8–11), although Etzioni (2004: 3) called it 'a syndicalist integration leading to a fully-fledged supranational one', promoting political integration by stealth:

> the idea is, instead of a frontal attack and a bold attempt to jump from many nations into a United States of Europe, allow processes to unfold gradually, according people time to adjust to the new supranational realities and for their new loyalties to evolve.
>
> (Etzioni 2004: 3)

Some would argue that this is what is already happening; others would argue that it will never happen. Either way, Etzioni did not set out what a democracy in a supranational Europe would look like. His main point was that halfway integration is not politically sustainable and the EU needs either to move forwards or to step back.

Philippe Schmitter (2004) argued that there was little evidence that European citizens were unduly concerned about EU democracy, but that the 'democratic deficit' was largely a concern and construct of academics and intellectuals. He illustrated this with reference to the Constitutional Convention: 'We have just seen during the

"Convention on the Future of Europe" that ordinary citizens did not seem to be willing to devote much attention to the prospect of constitutionalizing, much less of democratizing EU institutions' (Schmitter 2004: 3).

On the surface, this is a far from persuasive argument: that a problem can only exist if it is perceived as such by mass publics. What Schmitter saw as a sign that there was no problem could just as easily be seen as a symptom of the problem for European democracy—that citizens do not engage with EU issues. This interpretation was supported by the rejection of the Constitutional Treaty in referendums in France and the Netherlands in the early summer of 2005 (Chapter 17, pp. 207–8).

However, Schmitter's argument was that the main challenges to democracy brought by European integration are challenges for national democracy rather than for the EU system. The shift of authority away from the nation state to the EU, which Schmitter suggested was 'not a practising democracy', was 'gradually diminishing the accountability of rulers to citizens acting indirectly through the competition and co-operation of their representatives' (Schmitter 2004: 3). He suggested 'two good reasons why it may be timely to begin experimenting with continental democracy sooner rather than later': the evidence that democracy in the national arena is increasingly contested (greater electoral abstention, decline of party identification, lower prestige for politicians etc.); and evidence that EU citizens increasingly find the remoteness of the EU unsatisfactory (Schmitter 2004: 3).

Vivien Schmidt (2004; 2006) argued that the starting point for discussing EU democracy was to be clear about what the EU *is*. Like Moravcsik, she suggested that comparing it to nation states is a false point of departure. Instead, the EU should be conceived as a *regional state* in which:

> the creative tension between the Union and its member-states ensures both ever-increasing regional integration and ever-continuing national differentiation. As a result, the EU will continue to be characterized by shared sovereignty, variable boundaries, a composite identity, compound governance institutions, and fragmented democracy.

(Schmidt 2004: 4)

Comparisons with democracy in member states is misleading for a number of reasons, not least that partisan politics is weak at the level of the EU and is generally submerged by an emphasis on consensus and compromise. Thus, while member states have 'government *by*, *of* and *for* the people—through political participation, electoral representation, and governing effectiveness', as well as what can be called 'government *with* the people', through interest consultation—'the EU level emphasizes governance *for* and *with* the people while leaving to the national level government *by* and *of* the people' (Schmidt 2004: 4).

Like Moravcsik, Schmidt identified a number of factors that protect democracy in the EU, but also noted that the very checks and balances that can protect democracy can also prevent changes to policies and practices that are ineffective or unpopular (that is, lacking output legitimacy). Reform of the Common Agricultural Policy is a prominent example (see Chapter 26). Moreover, this complex system of checks and balances presents other problems: not least that national politicians are often held to account over decisions that they no longer control—although it is also not unknown for national politicians to blame decisions on the EU inappropriately. However, Schmidt also emphasized the democratic challenges at the domestic level as Europeanization has affected the workings of national institutions but ideas about democracy have not changed. The situation is one in which 'policy without politics' is prevalent at the EU level, while the national level is increasingly characterized by 'politics without policy' (Schmidt 2006: 22). Thus, there is not only a need for institutional reform at the EU level to make the system work more democratically and effectively, but also for the development of discourses 'that serve to legitimate it more in the eyes of the EU citizens while encouraging them to engage more in the politics and policy-making process' (Schmidt 2009: 406).

Scharpf (1997; 2004) similarly argued that domestic control had been lost over issues that were once central to national party-political competition, such as economic management. While this might have output benefits in terms of more effective economic management, Scharpf's outstanding concern was that the viability of national welfare states was being challenged by European economic integration, thus reducing the effectiveness of democratic self-determination at the national level.

Ways Forward?

While there is disagreement over the nature and extent of the democratic challenges facing the EU, there is continued debate over how the EU's democracy and legitimacy might be enhanced (for example, Follesdal and Hix 2006; Lord and Harris 2006; DeBardeleben and Hurrelmann 2007; Kohler-Koch and Rittberger 2007; Tsakatika 2007; Ehin 2008). Chryssochoou (2007) identified five models of democracy that might aid democratization of the EU: the parliamentary; the confederal; the federal; the consociational; and the republican.

- The *parliamentary model*, as the name suggests, emphasizes the role of the elected assembly as legislator within a political system, and would democratize the EU through the enhanced role of elected representatives. However, this model would imply the extension of majority rule to all policy areas, which would be highly unlikely, and also rests on a degree of European social unity that is not yet present.

- The *confederal model* brings states together into a form of union that does not compromise their national identity or political sovereignty. It is a model that does not rest on the development of a new polity or demos, but is based on a *unity of states* rather than a *unity of peoples*. This model would democratize through national channels by 'renationalizing' some issues to provide a greater role for national parliaments, which would be unpalatable to many European and domestic actors involved in the integration process.

- The *federal model* rests on the creation of a unity of people rather than simply a union of states. This model seeks to reconcile the requirement of greater political union with the demands of the component states. In doing so, it aims to 'establish a co-operative democratic ethos in relations between the centre and the subunits' (Chryssochoou 2007: 366). The model has been criticized for its emphasis on the need for clearly demarcated competencies in an age in which more flexible forms of governance are required (on types of multi-level governance, see Chapter 2, pp. 33–6).

- The *consociational model* has generally been attempted where there are conflicting demands from different societal groups and, in particular, to prevent the abuse of minority rights. It has four features: a grand coalition (such as a council containing elites from the different groups); proportionality (representation of societal groups reflects their size); segmental autonomy (some group control in specific areas); and mutual vetoes (on important decisions). Chryssochoou (2007: 367) suggested that each of these features is evident within the EU. Its main limitation is that it is essentially an elitist approach to seeking compromise and, as it reflects much of the present EU system, it would not appear the likeliest candidate for enhancing democracy.

- The *republican model* stresses the need for greater civic participation in EU affairs in the absence of a formal European constitution and the underdeveloped European demos. Central to the republican model is the idea of 'balanced government', which is developed in two related ways: through a 'proper institutional balance'; and through promoting deliberation among different groups that make up civil society (Chryssochoou 2007: 369).

Chryssochoou (2007: 373) noted that elements of all five models were evident in the workings of the EU, although the models that most closely captured the EU's character were confederal and consociational: a state of affairs that he deemed unsatisfactory as this was likely to hinder the development of a European demos.

One explicit intention of the Lisbon Treaty, ratified in 2009, was to enhance democracy in the EU (see Chapter 18, pp. 213–14). It strengthens the powers of the EP, enshrines the republican principle of democratic equality between EU citizens, gives the national parliaments new control powers, boosts the powers of EU-level parties, and introduces a new form of participatory democracy (a petition needing a million supporters). These measures address several of the above models of democracy. Supporters and opponents of the Treaty, however, were fiercely divided about some of these measures. For supporters, democracy would be enhanced by strengthening the role of the EP in a number of policy areas, and through enhanced powers for national parliaments in relation to EU legislation. Opponents of the Treaty question the legitimacy of the EP in comparison with that of national parliaments, and suggest that the enhanced powers for national legislatures are minimal and do not allow them to reject or amend EU legislation.

However, as Warleigh (2003: 125) argued, any approach to reform of EU democracy should recognize that it is as an ongoing process rather than assume that there might be a 'once and for all' solution:

popular preferences will legitimately differ over time, according to policy issue and in each of the member states. In turn, this points towards a difficult quadruple balancing act: between various (national élite) views of the purpose of the Union; between different levels of governance (European-national-regional-local); between output and input legitimacy; and between different normative views of democracy.

CONCLUSION

This chapter has brought together what have usually been presented as separate 'consequences' of European integration: Europeanization effects and challenges to democracy. However, as noted at the outset, there are clear links between the two, particularly when Europeanization is understood as a process through which domestic politics and polities are changed by their engagement with the EU. Most obviously, the process of Europeanization may obscure lines of political accountability, so that citizens are unsure whom to hold to account on particular issues. Alternatively, political elites may use 'Europeanization' as a smokescreen that conceals their own activities and deliberately misleads voters if it is expedient for them to do so. Equally, political elites may themselves be unclear about where responsibility, and thus accountability, should lie.

On a more positive note, Europeanization effects may enhance output democracy. Common action at the level of the EU may bring 'performance' benefits to citizens: for example, through more efficient management of environmental policy. However, for this to enhance legitimacy, it is necessary that the increased efficiency is recognized and that it is recognized as an effect of membership of the EU. It is perhaps a problem for Europhiles that some of the main benefits of European integration are relatively intangible, while some of its failings are not. Moreover, the EU's supporters have the problem of proving the counterfactual: how do we know that member states and their citizens would not have fared as well, if not better, without EU membership?

According to most commentators, the outstanding problem facing democratic development in the EU is the absence of a shared identity that would produce a genuine demos. **Euro-sceptics** often argue that democracy cannot be established at the European level because there is no such thing as a European people: democracy can only operate within national cultures. If an attempt is made to force the diverse peoples of Europe into an artificial union, nationalism will be stirred up rather than be abolished. Here also, Europeanization processes may be crucial. However, this may be less to do with changes in formal institutions and policy through membership of the EU, and more to do with the diffusion of informal norms and values among EU citizens.

KEY POINTS

Europeanization

- Europeanization has emerged as a key concept in EU studies and has been defined and employed in a variety of ways. For some, Europeanization is a phenomenon that is broader than or separate from the EU. However, it is predominantly used to conceptualize the changing relationship between the EU and its member (and accession) states.

- Ladrech provided an influential early conceptualization of Europeanization. He highlighted the importance of domestic factors in mediating Europeanization effects and argued that fears of harmonization or homogenization across European states were thus unfounded.

- Europeanization has increasingly become understood as a two-way relationship between the EU and its member states, involving both the *uploading* of ideas and practices from member states to the EU level, and the *downloading* of ideas and practices from the EU level to member states. However, the focus of most research has been on the downloading effects.

- The notion of *crossloading* refers to the transfer of ideas or practices from one state to another: a process in which the EU may or may not play a role.

- *First-generation* studies tended to focus on observable changes through Europeanization and explained variations in relation to the degree of fit or misfit between EU decisions and domestic practices and preferences, while *second-generation* studies placed greater emphasis on the changes in ideas, values, and identities rather than more immediately observable effects of Europeanization.

- As Europeanization research has become more fine-grained, it has been characterized by a new-institutionalist agenda.

- Europeanization remains prominent in debates on the EU and has recently been applied to studies of the enlargement process.

Democracy

- For a long time, European integration proceeded with little public debate about the democratic dimension. This changed as the EU's competencies expanded and was given particular impetus through the controversial ratification processes of various Treaties.

- Democracy and legitimacy are contested concepts and their relationship is not always clear in the EU literature. In essence, democracy is concerned with public control over the exercise of power, while legitimacy is understood as public acceptability of the exercise of power.

- The notion of the democratic deficit has been central to much scholarly work in the area, focusing on the lack of accountability of the EU's institutions and the relatively weak position of the EP as the only directly elected body.

- Moravcsik (2002), among others, has argued that, when judged against reasonable criteria, concerns over the EU's democratic deficit are misplaced. However, Hix (2006) identified a number of advantages for the EU of competitive elections.

- Lord and Magnette (2004) identified four vectors of legitimation in the EU: indirect; parliamentary; technocratic; and procedural legitimacy. They also distinguished between *input* and *output* legitimacy to illustrate how the four vectors are evident at different policy-making stages.

- Democracy and legitimacy in Europe remain high on the academic agenda. Etzioni (2004) has characterized the present EU as 'halfway integration' that requires further integration as a precondition to democratization. Schmitter (2004), Schmidt (2004; 2006), and Scharpf (1997; 2004) have all emphasized the challenges to national democracy in the context of European integration.

- Chryssochoou (2007) identified five models of democracy that might aid democratization of the EU: the parliamentary; the confederal; the federal; the consociational; and the republican. Of these, the confederal and consociational models most closely capture the EU's character.

- An explicit aim of the Lisbon Treaty was to enhance democracy in the EU. It addressed several deficiencies according to Chryssochoou's models, although its provisions for doing this were interpreted very differently by supporters and opponents.

- Warleigh (2003) argued that any approach to the reform of EU democracy should recognize that it is an ongoing process rather than assume that there might be a 'once and for all' solution.

FURTHER READING

Europeanization

An important early contribution was **R. Ladrech**, 'Europeanization of Domestic Politics and Institutions: The Case of France', *Journal of Common Market Studies*, 32 (1994): 69–88. A more recent key reference point is **J. Olsen**, 'The Many Faces of Europeanization', *Journal of Common Market Studies*, 40 (2002): 921–52.

P. Graziano and M. Vink (eds), *Europeanization: New Research Agendas* (Basingstoke: Palgrave Macmillan, 2007) provide the most comprehensive collection on Europeanization, with twenty-five contributions from experts in their respective fields, covering theory, methods, politics, polity, and policies. **S. Bulmer and C. Lequesne (eds)**, *The Member States of the European Union* (Oxford: Oxford University Press, 2005) explore both how member states impact on the EU and how the EU impacts on them, with a final thematic section of the book that examines the impact of Europeanization on institutions, politics, policy, and political economy.

There several very good broad-ranging overviews of the topic, including: **T. Borzel and T. Risse**, 'The Domestic Impact of European Union Politics', in **K. E. Jørgensen, M. Pollack, and B. Rosamond (eds)**, *Handbook of European Union Politics*, (London: Sage, 2007), 483–504; **S. Bulmer**, 'Theorizing Europeanization', in **P. Graziano and M. Vink (eds)**, *Europeanization: New Research Agendas* (Basingstoke: Palgrave Macmillan, 2007), 46–58; and **C. Radaelli**, 'Europeanization: Solution or Problem?' in **M. Cini and A. Bourne (eds)**, *Palgrave Advances in European Studies* (Basingstoke: Palgrave Macmillan, 2006), 56–76. Most recently, a valuable book-length treatment is provided by **R. Ladrech**, *Europeanization and National Politics* (Basingstoke: Palgrave Macmillan, 2010).

Democracy

For an introduction to EU democracy and the notion of the democratic deficit, see: **D. Chryssochoou**, 'Democracy and the European Polity', in **M. Cini (ed.)**, *European Union Politics* (Oxford: Oxford University Press, 2007), 359–74; **A. Follesdal**, 'Normative Political Theory and the European Union', in **K. E. Jørgensen, M. Pollack, and B. Rosamond (eds)**, *Handbook of European Union Politics* (London: Sage, 2007), 317–35; or **C. Lord**, 'Democracy and Democratization in the European Union', in **S. Bromley (ed.)**, *Governing the European Union* (London: Sage, 2001), 165–90.

An analysis of key debates and suggested ways forward can be found in **A. Warleigh**, *Democracy in the European Union* (London: Sage, 2003). On legitimacy, see **D. Beetham and C. Lord**, *Legitimacy and the European Union* (London and New York: Longman, 1998). The most comprehensive coverage of relevant debates is the collection by **B. Kohler-Koch and B. Rittberger (eds)**, *Debating the Democratic Legitimacy of the European Union* (Lanham, MD: Rowman and Littlefield, 2007).

Other helpful book-length treatments are: **C. Lord and E. Harris**, *Democracy in the New Europe* (Basingstoke: Palgrave Macmillan, 2006); and **J. DeBardeleben and A. Hurrelmann**, *Democratic Dilemmas of Multi-level Governance: Legitimacy, Representation and Accountability in the European Union* (Basingstoke: Palgrave Macmillan, 2007). Also helpful are the two special issues published in 2007 by the *Journal of European Integration*: 'Democratic Legitimacy and the European Union' (Vol. 29, No. 3) and 'Democracy and Soft Modes of Governance in the EU' (Vol. 29, No. 5).

Europeanization and Democracy

V. Schmidt, *Democracy in Europe* (Oxford: Oxford University Press, 2006) provides an authoritative study of the relationship between Europeanization and democracy, focusing in detail on the domestic effects in Britain, France, Germany, and Italy.

 online resource centre Visit the Online Resource Centre that accompanies this book for links to more information on theorizing consequences, including papers on Europeanization: www.oxfordtextbooks.co.uk/orc/bache3e/

Part Two
History

Deciding where to begin a history is often difficult, but not really in this case. While there were attempts to integrate Europe before the twentieth century, the end of the Second World War in 1945 provided the catalyst for the phase of European integration with which we are familiar today. There is little dispute among historians that 1945 is the most appropriate starting point for discussing the events leading to the creation of what is today the European Union. Thus, while we reflect briefly on previous attempts to integrate Europe, our point of departure here is the end of the Second World War.

The history we present is largely a familiar account of developments in European integration in the second half of the twentieth century. The history of European integration often told is one that emphasizes individuals, perhaps at the expense of broader social, economic, and political forces that shape events. Our account here generally reflects this dominant approach, not least because it is the function of a textbook to cover the most recognized contributions on the field of study. However, we have sought to add to the dominant narrative in the conclusions to the chapters in this section by drawing on the themes and perspectives discussed in Part One of the book.

As with all histories, we have had to make choices about how our history is organized. Here, we follow a conventional path. In our opening chapters, we focus on the history of 'important' decisions—in particular those leading to the Treaties establishing the European Communities. Later in the section, we identify phases in the process of European integration that are distinguished by the pace of events: for example, the 'dark ages' of European integration. Towards the end, we return again to a focus on events leading to key decisions.

As time passes, it is likely that events and developments in post-war integration that seem important to observers now may seem less important to future generations. Conversely, matters less obvious at the beginning of the twenty-first century will grow in importance. Similarly, the distinct eras in the process of integration that we identify will demand redefinition at some future date. In this sense, all histories are inevitably transient and imperfect. Thus, the basis on which we organize our history is simply an informed choice in the light of current understanding and should be read as such.

We encourage a critical approach to the reading of history. In this respect, readers would be well served by reading Mark Gilbert's (2008) article, which questions many of the assumptions of the way in which the EU's history is often told as the 'progressive story of European integration'. For example, Gilbert (2008: 645) highlights rhetorical devices that are used to present this as a progressive story:

> Choice of terms: construction metaphors abound. References to Europe's 'path', 'march', 'advance', 'progress', are [...] commonplace. Moments of relative inactivity are described as 'stagnation'—the 1970s, for instance, are frequently referred to in this way. The process is always 're-launched' or 'revived' after moments of difficulty.
> Authorial judgements: the standard used to measure whether major decisions were successes or failures is almost always whether they augmented or reduced the overall degree of supranationality within the Community.

Whether we write the history in this way and, if so, how it might be written differently is something for the readers of this book to reflect upon.

Chapter 5
Europe after the War

Chapter Overview

Attempts at European integration have a long history, but most have taken the form of conquest. While the outbreak of the Second World War illustrated the force of nationalism in Europe, its aftermath provided conditions for moves towards a consensual approach to European unity. This chapter documents the moves towards European integration in the early post-war period, explaining why federalist ideas were not put into practice, and how both internal and external pressures were crucial to shaping the Europe that emerged after the war.

If Europe were once united in the sharing of its common inheritance, there would be no limit to the happiness, to the prosperity and the glory which its three or four hundred million people would enjoy.

(Winston Churchill, Zurich, 1946)

Our starting point for this discussion of European integration is the end of the Second World War—but the idea of European integration is not unique to this era. Politicians and intellectuals alike aspired to European unity over two centuries. Plans for achieving perpetual peace in Europe by overcoming the division into nation states can be traced back at least to the early eighteenth century, and the *Project for Perpetual Peace* of the Abbé de Saint Pierre (Forsyth et al. 1970: 128). At a practical level, though, moves for European unity took the form of attempts by one nation or another to dominate Europe through conquest. Both France under Napoleon and Germany under Hitler could be accused of trying to forge European unity in this way.

Whereas attempts at enforced European *political* integration foundered, the potential benefits of *economic* integration proved attractive to European political elites. Yet nineteenth-century experiments with **free trade areas** across nation states were short-lived, while early **customs unions** were specific to regions within nation states. Ultimately, these experiments in economic integration suffered the same fate as attempts at political unity.

Movements in favour of peaceful integration emerged in Europe after the First World War, but the political settlement after the war was based on the peaceful co-existence of nation states rather than integration. The failure of the League of Nations (Insight 5.1) to sustain peace was rapid and complete, with the resurgence of nationalism in the 1920s and 1930s. The pro-integration groups emerging in Europe after 1918 were unable to offer any practical solutions to this. The outbreak of the Second World War destroyed hopes of European unity. The aftermath of the war, though, provided the origins for the modern movement for European integration.

Emerging from the war physically devastated, Europe began a process of both economic and political reconstruction. The idea of European unity was present in this process from the outset, as the ideology of federalism had attracted a great deal of support during the war. However, the story cannot be told simply in terms of ideals. Although influential figures showed some degree of attachment to the concept of federalism, the steps that were taken were informed by hard-headed realism about what was necessary for reconstruction to succeed. They were also taken in the context of an emerging Cold War that divided the continent on ideological lines.

The End of the War, Federalism, and The Hague Congress

The war in Europe had extensively destroyed physical infrastructure, disrupted economic production, and caused severe social dislocation. Roads, railways, and bridges had been destroyed by Allied bombing or by the retreating German army in its attempt to slow the advance of the Allied forces. According to Laqueur (1972: 17–18): coal production at the end of the war was only 42 per cent of its pre-war level; pig iron output in 1946 was less than one-third of that in 1938; and crude steel

---

Insight 5.1 The League of Nations

- The League of Nations was inspired by the vision of US President Woodrow Wilson. Its Covenant was drawn up at the Paris Peace Conference in 1919, but the US Congress refused to ratify the Treaty, so the United States never became a member of the League.

- The League Covenant committed the states that signed to respect the sovereignty and territorial integrity of other states, and not to resort to force to resolve disputes, but to submit them to arbitration by the League.

- The League's institutional structure consisted of a General Assembly, in which all member states were represented, and a Council. The Council had four, then later six, permanent members—Britain, France, Italy, Japan; then Germany from 1926, and the USSR from 1934.

- Between 1931 and 1939, the League failed to deal effectively with aggression by Japan, Italy, Germany, and the USSR. In 1935, Japan and Germany withdrew from membership.

- Although it failed to prevent war, the League did successfully establish a number of special agencies working at a functional level to deal with matters such as health and the protection of labour. The success of these bodies may have influenced the thinking of David Mitrany (see Chapter 1, pp. 5–6).

output was about one-third of what it had been before the war. There were millions of refugees wandering around Europe trying to return to their homes, or without any homes to which to return.

Accompanying the economic and social dislocation, there was political dislocation as governments that had collaborated with the Nazis were displaced. Germany and Austria remained occupied and divided between the occupation zones of the Allies. Elsewhere, there was a mood in favour of change: a feeling that there should be no return to the pre-war elites and the pre-war ways.

This mood particularly benefited parties of the left. In Britain, a Labour government was elected in 1945 with a massive majority, despite the Conservatives being led by the war-time hero Winston Churchill. In France, the provisional government that was set up in 1945 was presided over by General de Gaulle, the conservative leader of the Free French forces, which had fought on outside of the occupied country—but the first elections favoured the parties of the internal Resistance, particularly the communists, but also the socialists and the centre-left Christian party, the *Mouvement Républicain Populaire* (MRP). In Italy, although the Catholic south ensured the emergence of a large conservative Christian Democratic Party, the communists dominated in the industrial north.

The mood for change also fed a strong popular sentiment in the countries that had suffered from Fascism, in favour of a decisive move away from nationalism in the post-war reconstruction. Ideas favouring European federalism gained support, particularly in Italy, but also in France, Germany, and elsewhere in continental Europe, although not in Britain or the Scandinavian countries.

The European Union of Federalists (EUF) was formed in 1946 from the war-time Resistance movements. It attempted to exploit the disruption caused to existing political structures by the war to make a new start on a basis radically different from the Europe of nation states, and to create a federal constitution for Europe, as part of a more distant plan for global unity. However, it took until 1947 to organize the conference that was supposed to pave the way to the new constitution, by which time national governments had already been restored to office everywhere. The conference, the European Congress, eventually took place in The Hague in May 1948.

The Congress attracted considerable attention at the time. It was attended by representatives of most of the political parties of the non-communist states of Europe, and its Honorary President was Winston Churchill, who had used a speech in Zurich in 1946 to call for a united Europe. Churchill had implied in the Zurich speech that Britain, with its Commonwealth of Nations, would remain separate from the 'United States of Europe' to which he referred. Britain, along with the United States and possibly the USSR, would be 'friends and sponsors of the new Europe'. The vital development in this project would be a 'partnership' between France and Germany. Beyond this, and the 'first step' of forming a Council of Europe (Insight 5.2), Churchill did not detail how the process towards European unity should proceed.

The Hague Congress was an occasion for fine speeches, but it gradually became apparent that the British were not interested in being part of a supranational organization that would compromise their national sovereignty. While the Congress did lead to the creation of the Council of Europe, this was so dominated by national governments that there was little realistic prospect of it developing in the federal direction that the EUF hoped.

The Council of Europe still exists today, and it has many solid achievements to its credit. In particular, it was responsible for adopting the European Convention on Human Rights in 1950, and it maintained both a Commission on Human Rights (replaced by a Commissioner in 1999) and a Court of Human Rights: the former to investigate alleged breaches of such rights by governments; and the latter to rule definitively on whether a violation of rights has occurred. It also serves useful functions as a meeting place for parliamentarians from the diverse member states and promotes Europe-wide cultural activities. This all fell far short of the hopes of the EUF.

Insight 5.2 **The Council of Europe**

Founded in 1949 as a result of the 1948 Congress of Europe in The Hague, the Council of Europe is not connected to the EU and should not be confused with the European Council, which is the name of the institutionalized summit meetings of the EU heads of state and government.

The Council of Europe is an intergovernmental organization based in the French city of Strasbourg. It originally had ten members, and by 2010 had forty-seven, covering almost all of Europe. Its main institutions are:

- the Committee of (Foreign) Ministers;
- the Parliamentary Assembly, consisting of 318 members of national parliaments, with 318 substitutes;
- the Congress of Local and Regional Authorities of Europe;
- the Secretariat;
- the European Commissioner for Human Rights;
- the European Court of Human Rights;
- the Conference of International Non-governmental Organizations of the Council of Europe.

The Council was set up to:

- defend human rights, parliamentary democracy, and the rule of law;
- develop continent-wide agreements to standardize member countries' social and legal practices;
- promote awareness of a European identity based on shared values and cutting across different cultures.

Since 1989, its main job has become:

- protecting human rights, **pluralist** democracy, and the rule of law;
- promoting awareness and encouraging the development of Europe's cultural identity and diversity;
- finding common solutions to the challenges facing European society;
- consolidating democratic stability in Europe by backing political, legislative, and constitutional reform.

Source: **http://www.coe.int/aboutCoe/**

European integration was not to be achieved in one great act of political will, because the will was not there. Some blamed the failure of the Council of Europe to develop in a federal direction on the attitude of the British—but the truth is that no national government, once installed, was willing to surrender much of its power. In 1947, the attention of governments was still focused on national economic reconstruction, not on superseding the nation state. Yet there were soon more insistent pressures on the governments to move away from national sovereignty than those that the federalists could muster.

The Cold War

To understand the origins of the EU, it is essential to see them in the context of the emerging Cold War between the capitalist West and the communist Soviet Union. Before the Second World War, advocates of a European union had assumed that it would stretch to the borders of the USSR. But as relations between the former Allies deteriorated throughout 1946 and into 1947, it became clear this would be a project confined to the western part of the continent.

Agreement was reached at an Allied summit meeting in Yalta in 1945 to divide Europe at the end of the war into 'spheres of influence'. This was intended by the western Allies to be only a temporary arrangement, but the Soviet Union soon started to make it permanent. Regimes friendly to the USSR were installed in those countries of central and eastern Europe that, at Yalta, had been assigned to the Soviet sphere. This led Churchill to make a speech in Fulton, Missouri, in March 1946 in which he talked about an 'iron curtain' descending across Europe. The speech did not receive a sympathetic hearing in Washington, where the prevailing mood was still in favour of co-operation with the USSR—but this mood changed in the course of 1946.

In September 1946, communist insurgents restarted a civil war in Greece. This was a decision that could not have been taken without the agreement of the Soviet Union. In 1945, Stalin had ordered the Greek communists, who controlled large areas of the country, not to continue with an armed insurrection against the government that the British had installed in Athens. Greece was in the British sphere of influence according to the Yalta agreement, and it seemed that whatever unwelcome moves Stalin might be making in the Soviet sphere, he was at least intent on respecting the limits set at Yalta. The recommencement of hostilities in Greece threw that interpretation into doubt. During 1946, too, the Soviet Union refused to withdraw its troops from Persia, which was also outside its sphere, and made territorial demands on Turkey.

The weather in the European winter of 1946–47 was particularly severe, and put considerable strain on the economic recovery that was under way. This had direct consequences for the emergence of the Cold War. In February 1947, London informed Washington that it could not afford to continue economic and military aid to Greece and Turkey. In response, President Truman asked Congress in March 1947 for US$400 million of economic and military aid for Greece and Turkey. To dramatize the situation, he spoke of the duty of the United States to assist 'free peoples who are resisting attempted subjugation by armed minorities or by outside pressures'. This became known as the 'Truman doctrine', and it marked a clear statement of intent by the US

Administration to remain involved in the affairs of Europe and the wider world, and not to allow isolationist sentiments within the country and within Congress to force a withdrawal from an international role.

Perhaps even more significant in converting the US Administration to Churchill's view was the collapse of the four-power Council of Foreign Ministers, a standing conference to discuss the administration and future of Germany. Soviet intransigence in that forum, and the eventual walk-out of the Soviet representative in April 1947, convinced those who were trying to negotiate on behalf of Washington that it was not possible to work with the USSR. From that point on, the emergence of separate West and East German states became gradually inevitable.

A second direct consequence of the bad winter and economic setback of early 1947 was that waves of strikes spread across France and Italy. In both cases, the strikes were supported by communists, who engaged in revolutionary anti-capitalist rhetoric. In the light of events in Greece, this was interpreted as further evidence of the Soviet Union attempting to undermine stability outside its sphere of influence, although in both cases it may have been an incorrect interpretation. Certainly in France, where the Communist Party was part of the coalition government, the strikes appeared to take them by surprise. However, it was very difficult for the French communists not to support their core electorate, and indeed not to interpret the strikes as evidence of the imminent collapse of capitalism. The other parties in the French coalition responded by expelling the communists from the government: the Truman Administration responded with the Marshall Plan.

The Marshall Plan and the OEEC

On 5 June 1947, George Marshall, the US Secretary of State, announced that the US Administration proposed to offer financial and food aid to Europe to assist in its economic recovery (Insight 5.3). Suspicious of US motives, the USSR and its allies rejected the offer. There were some grounds for this suspicion: the American gesture went far beyond simple altruism to a concern with economic self-interest.

Marshall presented the American people with a vision of Europe in crisis in 1947: people were starving; the economy had broken down. Milward (1984: 3–4) contested this orthodox view. He denied that there was a crisis, although he accepted that there was a serious problem about the ability of the western European states to build and sustain international trade because of a lack of convertible currencies to finance it. In his view, the Marshall Plan was entirely political in its conception and objectives, although its means were entirely economic. The misleading representation of the economic position in Europe was designed to get the agreement of the US Congress to the reconstruction programme.

Marshall aid offered an injection of dollars into the European economy, which would finance trade between the European states and the United States, and trade between the European states themselves. This was a policy much favoured by those sections of US industry that were involved in exporting. It was less favoured by those sections of US industry that were oriented towards the domestic market, which suspected that they would pay the bill for European reconstruction without gaining the benefits. This section of domestic opinion was strongly represented within Congress, and so it was by no means a foregone conclusion that the Administration would get its

Insight 5.3 The Marshall Plan

- The European Recovery Programme (ERP) was announced by US Secretary of State George C. Marshall in a speech at Harvard University on 5 June 1947.
- It involved the United States giving a total of US$13 billion in financial aid to the states of western Europe. The assistance was offered to the states of eastern Europe, but they declined under pressure from the Soviet Union.
- The European states that accepted held a conference in July 1947 in Paris, and set up what became the Organisation for European Economic Co-operation (OEEC) to facilitate the unified response that the United States required.

plans through Congress. Following the Soviet Union's rejection of aid, Truman and Marshall were able to justify the Plan as part of the same response to the threat of communism as was the Truman doctrine. Marshall argued that economic conditions in western Europe in 1947 were so serious that they provided a breeding ground for communism. The struggle had to be waged by economic, as well as military, means.

Whether it was motivated by genuine concern for the condition of western Europe, or by economic considerations that had more to do with lobbying by the larger US corporations, Marshall aid came with strings attached. The US Administration was committed to the idea of free trade. It was concerned to see what it described as 'European integration', meaning that national economic barriers to trade should be broken down. Both of the motives discussed above would support this position. Given that the Administration genuinely believed that free trade would strengthen the western European economies, integration was compatible with the stated aim of strengthening western Europe against communist expansion. However, it was also compatible with the aim of creating a large and exploitable market for US exports and for investments by US multinational corporations.

The United States insisted that decisions on the distribution and use of Marshall aid be taken by the European states jointly. To implement this, a body known as the Committee for European Economic Co-operation (CEEC) was set up. Despite the professed aim of allowing the Europeans to make their own decisions on the use of the aid, the United States was represented on this committee, and because it was contributing all of the funds, it clearly had some economic and political leverage. The CEEC was transformed in April 1948 into a more permanent body, the Organisation for European Economic Co-operation (OEEC). The OEEC initially had fifteen members, but was soon joined by the newly independent Federal Republic of Germany (1949), while the United States and Canada became associate members in 1950.

For Marshall and other members of the US Administration, the OEEC was to be the basis for the future supranational economic management of Europe. Nobody was quite clear what 'supranational' meant in this context, but it certainly meant breaking down national sovereignty in economic affairs. In particular, the US view was that western Europe should become a free trade area as the first step towards global free trade.

This was not a vision that particularly appealed to the governments of the European states involved. The British did not particularly want to be tied into any arrangement with the continental states. The French had already embarked on their own recovery programme, which was based on a much more restrictive view of the role of free trade and the free market. Other governments shared some of the French concern to keep as much control as possible over their own economies, giving away sovereignty neither to a supranational organization nor to the workings of the international free market.

Crucial to the economic and political stance of the European states was the position of Germany. Whether the German economy and state would be reconstituted was still an open question when the CEEC began operations. The US wanted the decisions to be made by the OEEC. Germany's neighbours were simply not prepared to see that happen. In particular, they were nervous about the extent of political leverage that the United States was able to exercise within the OEEC because of its economic influence as the sole contributor to the reconstruction funds. However, despite its economic leverage, the United States simply did not have sufficient political weight to overcome the combined opposition of Britain, France, and the smaller European states to allowing the OEEC to develop as a powerful supranational organization (Milward 1984: 168–211).

The body within the OEEC controlling policy and administration was the Council of Ministers, which consisted of one representative from each member state. Decisions taken by the Council were binding on members, but each member state retained the right of veto. While effective within its limited remit, the OEEC promised little in terms of further integration.

Despite its limitations, the OEEC continued its work for twelve years and, according to Urwin (1995: 22), 'played a major role in driving home the realization that European economies were mutually dependent, and that they prospered or failed together'. In 1961, the OEEC was superseded by the Organisation for Economic Co-operation and Development (OECD), which had a broader remit, concerned with issues of economic development both in Europe and globally, and included the USA and Canada as full members.

Germany

The German problem also dominated the debate about the future of Europe. For the United States and Britain, the future of Germany was inevitably linked to the emerging Cold War. For France and Germany's smaller neighbours, it was still a question of how to prevent the re-emergence of a threat to their sovereign independence from Germany itself.

Initially, Germany's neighbours tried to protect themselves through a traditional military alliance, in which British participation was seen as crucial. This approach produced the Treaty of Dunkirk between Britain and France in March 1947, and the Treaty of Brussels between Britain, France, and the **Benelux** states in March 1948. Both alliances were directed more at forestalling German aggression than they were at the Soviet Union.

The French government also tried to prevent the emergence of any German state. Ideally, the French Foreign Office would have liked to have kept Germany under Allied occupation. Failing that, it wanted the former German state to be divided into a large number of small separate states. By 1949, it had become apparent that this was not going to happen. Again, the crucial dynamic was the rapidly emerging Cold War.

In 1948, the Soviet Union walked out of Allied talks on the future of Germany. The United States and Britain responded by starting to prepare the Anglo-American zones for independence. The French were left in no doubt that they were expected to merge their occupation zone into the new West German state, which would be created under the plans for independence. Once the Federal Republic of Germany came into existence in 1949, the French policy had to be rethought.

CONCLUSION

Themes raised in the opening chapters are already apparent in the history this far, in particular the importance of legitimacy and identity (Chapter 4), and the importance of 'external' actors and issues (Chapter 3) in shaping the emerging contours of post-war Europe.

The governments that took office in post-war western Europe faced a series of challenges. They faced a demand from their electorates for security both from the economic problems that had afflicted pre-war Europe, and from further war. They faced a lack of popular confidence in the ability of the sovereign national state to meet these demands. They faced a challenge from federalism, which offered an alternative way of organizing Europe politically, but one that would have removed the levers of power from the hands of national governments. They faced an even more serious challenge from communism: an ideology that promised to deliver the economic security that people doubted capitalism could deliver. They faced demands from the United States that they reconstruct their economies in a way that would open them to foreign competition, which, if met, would have reduced the ability of national governments to control the impact of the market on their electorates.

The success of socialist governments in many western European states in the first post-war elections indicated the extent of the desire among the people of western Europe for a fairer and more managed economic system. It was in response to this demand that the first steps were soon taken in the construction of the welfare state systems, and an active role for the state in economic management began to be mapped out. The distinctive 'European model' of **regulated capitalism** began to emerge. Before these systems could work, though, there had to be economic recovery from the war. This proved elusive in the early years.

The United States showed itself to be willing to finance recovery through the Marshall Plan, in return for reconstruction being on the basis of liberal market economies that were open to competition. To ensure this openness, the United States insisted that recovery plans be constructed on a European basis, not a national basis. Western European governments had to cope with a demand that they surrender some of their ability to control their national economies as the price for US financial assistance.

So the first tentative steps towards some form of western European economic integration were taken in response to a combination of internal and external pressures on governments. The decisions were undoubtedly intergovernmental: there were no **supranational institutions** to push the process forward at this stage. They were taken by governments the legitimacy of which had to be established. Recourse to nationalism was not an option for gaining legitimacy because of the popular lack of confidence in the nation state following the war. On the other hand, embracing federalism implied a surrender of authority and control that most national governments were unwilling to undertake. The most efficacious way of gaining legitimacy was to provide economic growth, but this required the support of the dominant economic power in the post-war world: the United States. Support was offered on condition that the economic recovery plan would go beyond the nation state. This was not a demand for a surrender of political sovereignty, and was therefore easier for the western European states to accept than a full-blown move to a federal constitution. At the same time, the governments were able to adopt federalist rhetoric. They could appear to be moving in a popular direction while not losing control of the process.

At the same time, the insistence by the United States that the reconstruction be based on open market systems did threaten the post-war models of **regulated capitalism**. The implication of opening national economies to external competition was that jobs would be lost in some sectors. The European model of capitalism could only be reconciled with open markets if there were high rates of economic growth, so that any jobs lost to competition were replaced by new jobs generated by this growth. This was a gamble, but it was a gamble that the national governments had no choice but to make. Unless the post-war economic recovery could be got under way, there would be no jobs to be lost. In the end, the influence of the United States, exercised through the conditions attached to the Marshall Plan, was decisive.

KEY POINTS

The End of the War, Federalism, and The Hague Congress

- The Second World War caused great economic and social dislocation and created a mood for political change.
- In general, this mood favoured the left, and federalist ideas also gained support in much of continental Europe, leading to the formation of the European Union of Federalists (EUF) in 1946.
- The Hague Congress of 1948 promised much in terms of integration, but in the end delivered little beyond the Council of Europe, which was dominated by national governments.

The Cold War

- The post-war process of European integration has to be understood in the context of emerging tension between the capitalist West and the communist Soviet Union.
- As the Soviet Union began to install friendly regimes in the countries of central and eastern Europe, Churchill spoke of an 'iron curtain' descending across Europe.
- As economic and political tensions in Europe grew, the 'Truman doctrine' of 1947 declared the United States' intention to maintain an active role in world affairs.
- Following the principles of the Truman doctrine, the 1947 Marshall Plan provided US aid to assist the recovery of European economies and the CEEC was established to administer this.
- The issue of how to deal with Germany also dominated the European agenda. When the Soviet Union walked out of talks on the future of Germany in 1948, Britain and the United States advanced plans for an independent West German state.

FURTHER READING

The early post-war period is not particularly well written up, except as part of wider histories. For the whole history of European integration, **M. Dedman**, *The Origins and Development of the European Union 1945–2008: A History of European Integration*, 2nd edn (Abingdon: Routledge, 2009), and **D. W. Urwin**, *The Community of Europe: A History of European Integration since 1945*, 2nd edn (London and New York: Longman, 1995) should be treated as standard reference sources.

A particularly controversial account of the early post-war origins of European integration is given by **A. S. Milward**, *The Reconstruction of Western Europe, 1945–51* (London: Routledge, 1984).

For more information on European federalism, see **M. Burgess**, *Federalism and the European Union: The Building of Europe, 1950–2000* (Abingdon: Routledge, 2000).

 Visit the Online Resource Centre that accompanies this book for links to more information on Europe after the war:
www.oxfordtextbooks.co.uk/orc/bache3e/

Chapter 6

The Schuman Plan for Coal and Steel

Chapter Overview

The Schuman Plan to pool coal and steel production, announced in 1950, involved a considerable surrender of sovereign control over these industries for the six participating states. It would be a decisive first step towards European unity. It would make war between France and Germany not only unthinkable, but also materially impossible. It would lay the foundation for the economic unification of the participating states. This chapter examines the reasons for the participation of the six states in this Plan, and for the non-participation of Britain. It also looks at the negotiations that led from the Schuman Plan to the European Coal and Steel Community (ECSC).

> **By pooling basic production and by instituting a new High Authority, whose decisions will bind France, Germany and other member countries, this proposal will lead to the realization of the first concrete foundation of a European federation indispensable to the preservation of peace.**
>
> (Schuman Declaration)

In May 1950, the French Foreign Minister, Robert Schuman, proposed a scheme for pooling the coal and steel supplies of France and Germany, and invited other European states that wished to participate to express an interest. The idea involved a surrender of sovereignty over the coal and steel industries. It was devised by Jean Monnet, a French civil servant (Insight 6.1), and addressed practical problems for France that arose from the establishment of the Federal Republic of Germany. The first problem was how to avert the threat of future conflict between France and Germany; the second was how to ensure continuing supplies of coal for the French steel industry once the Ruhr region reverted to German sovereign control. The plan was welcomed by the German Chancellor, Konrad Adenauer, and the **Benelux** states and Italy indicated that they would wish to participate. The British government declined an invitation to take part. The negotiations between the six states that did wish to participate were marked by hard bargaining in defence of national interests, but eventually agreement was reached on what became the European Coal and Steel Community (ECSC). The six signed the Treaty of Paris in April 1951, and the ECSC came into operation in July 1952 (see Chapter 8).

National Positions and the Origins of the ECSC

In the following analysis, the positions of the six founder states are examined, and then that of Britain. The analysis starts with France, the country that proposed the scheme, then looks at Germany, without the participation of which the scheme would never have got off the ground. The Benelux states are considered together because their reasons for participation were extremely similar. Italy's reasons for joining the negotiations require a little more explanation. Britain's reasons for not joining are important for the future relationship between Britain and the EC.

France

The plan for the ECSC was known as the Schuman Plan because it was made public by the French Foreign Minister, Robert Schuman. He was born in Luxembourg, lived in Lorraine when it was part of the German empire, was conscripted into the German army in the First World War, and only became a French citizen after the war when Alsace and Lorraine reverted to French sovereignty. Thus he had a particular reason for wanting to reconcile the historic conflict between the two countries.

Milward (1984: 395–6) argued that the Foreign Ministry must have played a role in devising the plan, but the more generally accepted view is that it was drawn up within the French Economic Planning Commission (*Commissariat du Plan*—CdP), which was headed by Jean Monnet. It was the task of the CdP to guide the post-war reconstruction and modernization of the French economy, and it was through his experiences in this task that Monnet came to appreciate the economic inadequacy of the European nation state in the modern world. As he himself put it:

> For five years the whole French nation had been making efforts to recreate the bases of production, but it became evident that to go beyond recovery towards steady expansion and higher standards of life for all, the resources of a single nation were not sufficient. It was necessary to transcend the national framework.

(Monnet 1962: 205)

The wider framework that Monnet had in mind was an economically united western Europe. He saw the need to create a 'large and dynamic **common market**', 'a huge continental market on the European scale' (Monnet 1962: 205). But he aimed to create more than just a common market. Monnet was a planner: he showed no great confidence in the free-market system, which had served France badly in the past. He placed his faith in the development of **supranational institutions** as the basis for building a genuine economic community that would adopt common economic policies and rational planning procedures.

Coal and steel were only intended as starting points. The aim was to extend integration to all aspects of the western European economy—but such a scheme would have been too ambitious to gain acceptance all at once.

> Europe will not be made all at once, or according to a single plan. It will be built through concrete achievements which first create a *de facto* solidarity.

(Schuman Declaration 1950)

There had been a clear indication of this need for incrementalism in the failure of various post-war efforts to integrate the economies of France, Italy, The Netherlands, Belgium, and Luxembourg. Although negotiations for an organization to be known as 'Finebel' had proceeded for some time, they were on the verge of collapse in 1950. Besides, the new factor in the equation, and the key factor prompting Monnet's plan, was the emergence in April 1949 of a sovereign West German state.

For Monnet, the existence of the Federal Republic of Germany posed two problems in addition to that of how to create an integrated western European economy. The first was how to organize Franco–German relations in such a way that another war between the two states would become impossible. To a French mind, this meant how to control Germany. The pooling of coal and steel production would provide the basis for economic development as a first step towards a 'federation of Europe', and would change the future of those regions devoted to producing munitions, which had also been 'the most constant victims' of war.

> The solidarity in production thus established will make it plain that any war between France and Germany becomes not merely unthinkable, but materially impossible.

(Schuman Declaration 1950)

The problem of how to control Germany remained at the heart of the process of European integration throughout the early post-war period.

The second problem facing Monnet was the very practical one of how to ensure continuing adequate supplies of coking coal from the Ruhr for the French steel industry. The idea of pooling Franco-German supplies of coal and steel was not new: similar schemes had been proposed on many occasions previously (Gillingham 1991*b*: 135; Duchêne 1994: 202). In fact, the idea of pooling coal and steel supplies had featured in two recent publications: one from the Assembly of the Council of Europe and the other from the UN Economic Commission for Europe (Urwin 1995: 44). These reports were concerned with the very practical problems affecting the coal and steel industries of Europe. There was excess capacity in steel, and a shortage of coal. This combination was of particular concern to Monnet, whose recovery plan for France involved expanding steel-producing capacity. The French steel industry was heavily dependent on supplies of coking coal from the Ruhr.

At the end of the war, the Ruhr region of Germany had been placed under joint Allied control. Its supplies of coal had been allocated between the various competing users by the International Authority for the Ruhr (IAR), which had been established in April 1945. It seemed unlikely that this arrangement could be long continued once the Federal Republic was constituted, which raised the question of how France could ensure that it continued to get access to the supply of scarce Ruhr coal that its steel industry needed. The coal and steel pool had the potential to achieve this.

In summary, Monnet's reasons for proposing the plan to pool Franco-German supplies of coal and steel were a combination of taking a first step on the road to complete integration of the western European economy, finding a way in which to organize Franco–German relations that would eliminate the prospect of a further war between the two states, and solving the problem of how to ensure continued access for the French steel industry to supplies of coking coal from the Ruhr. That Schuman essentially accepted this thinking informs the standard explanation for France's participation in the Schuman Plan.

Germany

Chancellor Adenauer accepted the Schuman Plan with alacrity. Yet if the proposal had been made to serve French interests, why was the German Chancellor so keen on it?

As with Schuman, one of the factors was a commitment on the part of Adenauer to the ideal of European integration. Like Schuman, Adenauer came from a border region: in his case, the Rhineland. Like Schuman, he was a Roman Catholic and a Christian Democrat. In accepting the Schuman Plan, Adenauer committed himself to Franco–German reconciliation and to European integration. This does not mean, though, that he acted only for idealistic reasons. There were also very practical reasons for Adenauer's acceptance of the Schuman Plan: the Federal Republic needed to gain international acceptance; Adenauer wanted to make a strong commitment to the capitalist West; and the new German government was looking for a way of getting rid of the IAR.

The legacy of the Nazi era and of the war had left Germany a pariah nation. It had also left it divided into two separate states: the Federal Republic in the west and the Democratic Republic in the east. Adenauer wanted to establish the Federal Republic as the legitimate successor to the pre-war German state, but also as a peace-loving state that would be accepted as a full participant in European and international affairs. Adenauer also wanted to establish the western and capitalist orientation of the Federal Republic beyond question or reversal. This was important to Adenauer because the Social Democratic Party (*Sozialdemokratische Partei Deutschlands*—SPD) was arguing for the Federal Republic to declare itself neutral in the emerging Cold War, in the hope that this would facilitate reunification of the country. As well as being strongly anti-communist, Adenauer believed that the Democratic Republic was dominated by the Soviet Union, and he feared the cultural influence of Russia would be damaging to the vitality of German culture and to the process of moral renewal in the aftermath of Nazism, which, as a devout Catholic, he believed to be essential (Milward 1992: 329–30).

The importance for Adenauer of getting rid of the IAR was both political and economic. Politically, it was important to him that the region be integrated into the Federal Republic. Economically, the Ruhr had always been one of the powerhouses of the German industrial economy, so it was important to the prospects of economic recovery that it be unchained from the restrictions that the IAR placed on its industrialists. There was a risk that, in accepting the Schuman Plan, Adenauer would commit his country to a relationship from which French industry would gain at the expense of German industry. However, Adenauer was confident that German industrialists could stand up for their interests within a coal and steel pool (Gillingham 1991*a*: 233).

The Benelux States

The reason why the Benelux states agreed to enter the negotiations for the ECSC was the same in each case: they could not afford to stay out of any agreement between France and Germany on coal and steel. These commodities were essential to the economies of the three states, and there was a high degree of interdependence between the industries in the border regions of France and Germany, and those in Belgium and Luxembourg particularly. There was also support in all three states for any moves that promised to reduce the risk of war between their two larger neighbours.

Italy

Italian reasons for joining in the negotiations require a little more explanation than the reasons for Benelux participation. Italy is not geographically part of the same industrial region as the other participants, so there was not the same inevitability about its involvement. In many ways, the reasons for Italian participation in the negotiations resembled those of Germany more closely than those of the Benelux states.

Like Germany, Italy was governed by Christian Democrats; as in the case of Adenauer (and of Schuman), the individual who dominated the government was also a Roman Catholic and someone who originated in a border region. Alcide de Gasperi came from the Alto Adige region of Italy, which had been part of the Austro-Hungarian Empire before the First World War. Like Germany, Italy had to rebuild its international reputation after the war. Mussolini had been Hitler's ally and had ended up as his puppet. Like Germany, Italy was on the front line in the emerging Cold War. Geographically, it had a land frontier with the communist state of Yugoslavia, and only the Adriatic Sea separated it from Albania. At the end of the war, there had been a serious risk that the Italian Communist Party would take over the country in democratic elections, and it remained the largest single party in terms of support. De Gasperi therefore had a similar need to that of Adenauer in Germany to enmesh his country in a complex of institutional interdependencies with the capitalist west, to establish its western and capitalist identity politically, economically, and in the minds of its own people.

Britain

The other state that was invited to participate in the conference that followed the Schuman Plan was Britain. The negative attitude of the British government has been extensively analysed (J. W. Young 1993: 28–35; Dell 1995; George 1998: 19–22; H. Young 1998).

All accounts accept that there were certain peculiarities of the British position that made it highly unlikely that its government would welcome the proposal. Whereas in continental Europe, nationalism had been discredited through its association with Fascism, in Britain, Fascism had never succeeded, and the war had been fought as a national war. Unlike the other states, Britain had neither been defeated nor occupied in the war. There was not the same sense in Britain of discontinuity with the past. The attitude of the British governing elite was that Britain was not just another European state: it was a world power with global responsibilities. Although this attitude has been described as a 'delusion of grandeur' (Porter 1987), it had some basis in reality: Britain still had a considerable empire; British companies had interests in all parts of the world; and British armed forces were globally deployed in keeping the peace, or acting as a bulwark against communist encroachment.

The perception at the time was that Britain was economically far stronger than the other western European states, and that tying the future of the British economy to that of the German and French economies was dangerous. Britain had adequate indigenous supplies of coal, and the Labour government had just completed the nationalization of the coal and steel industries. Having campaigned over many years for nationalization, the Labour Party was unlikely to surrender control once it had been achieved. Also, European integration was at this time particularly associated with the leader of the Conservative Party, Winston Churchill. Although there were some Labour Party members who participated in the Hague Congress and remained supporters of a united Europe, the idea was associated with the opposition, not the government.

To add to these general factors, Ernest Bevin, the Foreign Secretary, was personally upset that he had no forewarning of Schuman's announcement. Dean Acheson, the US Secretary of State, was told about the Plan in advance by the French Prime Minister, Georges Bidault, and Acheson subsequently met Bevin, but did not mention the Plan. As Acheson had been given the information in confidence, this was reasonable enough—but it led Bevin to see a Franco-American plot to seize the initiative away from Britain in the formulation of plans for western Europe (Young 1998: 52). Bevin's annoyance was increased when the French government insisted that all of those who wished to participate in the scheme must accept the principle of supranationalism. This condition was pressed by Monnet, who was concerned that otherwise the outcome would be another intergovernmental organization. He must have known that it would be an impossible condition for the British government to accept, given the strong attachment of the Labour Party to national sovereignty, and perhaps he did not really want British participation at the outset. It was, after all, the British who had been primarily responsible for the watering down of the commitment to supranational institutions in the Council of Europe.

The British government did not immediately reject the demand for a commitment to supranationalism. Instead, the French were asked to specify exactly what they meant by the phrase, to spell out the full extent of the surrender of sovereignty that was envisaged and its effects. After some three weeks of inconclusive discussions of the implications of supranationalism, Schuman announced on 1 June 1950 that the principle was non-negotiable, and that any state that wanted to be involved in the negotiations must accept it by 8.00 p.m. on 2 June. The British Cabinet immediately rejected this condition.

From the Schuman Plan to the Treaty of Paris

Negotiations between the six began on 20 June, with all delegations supposedly committed to the principle of supranationalism. However, both the Belgians and the Dutch had reservations, as became apparent once the opening session was completed and the substantive negotiations began on 22 June (Duchêne 1994: 209).

Monnet insisted that the French delegation should be hand-picked by himself, and he rigorously excluded representatives of the French coal and steel industries from influence in the process. This was not the case with the other delegations, which consisted of diplomats and officials from the national Energy Ministries, who were open to influence from the affected industries.

There followed months of hard bargaining during which various departures were made from the original principles set out in Monnet's working document (Insight 6.2). These concessions were necessary to make a success of the negotiations. That they had to be made reinforces the view that most participants were concerned to use the ECSC

Insight 6.2 Bargaining Concessions in the ECSC Negotiations

- At the insistence of the Dutch, supported by the Germans, a Council of Ministers, consisting of representatives of national governments, was added to the institutional structure to curtail the supranationalism of the High Authority.

- At the insistence of the Belgians, a special 'equalization tax' on efficient coal producers was agreed, which would be used to subsidize the modernization of inefficient mines. In practice, this amounted to a subsidy from Germany to Belgium.

- At the insistence of the Italians, the Italian steel industry was allowed to maintain tariffs against the rest of the participants for five years, and to continue to import cheap coking coal and scrap metal from outside the ECSC. As with the Belgian coal mines, there was to be an equalization fund to finance the modernization of inefficient Italian steel plant, although this was much smaller than the coal equalization tax.

to further their own national interests. The biggest concessions were made by the German government, for whom the main potential advantage of the Schuman Plan was the opportunity it offered to get the removal of the constraints imposed by the IAR.

At the end of the war, the Allies had forced the deconcentration of the coal and steel industries in Germany, and the break-up of the cartels that had restricted competition. From the German point of view, this only served to give an artificial advantage to their French competitors. The IAR acted to prevent reconcentration and re-emergence of cartels, so the German industrialists wanted to get rid of it. But they did not want the High Authority of the ECSC to take over those functions from the IAR, whereas Monnet was determined that the High Authority would do exactly that.

From the French point of view, concentration was dangerous because it gave too much political influence to the large industrial concerns. The support of the Ruhr industrialists for Hitler had contributed to the Nazis coming to power. Cartelization was a device that, in Monnet's eyes, acted as a restraint on competition. In this view, he was strongly supported by the United States.

The role of the US Administration in the negotiations was vital. Not officially represented at the talks, the United States nevertheless exerted a tremendous influence behind the scenes. A special committee was set up in the US Embassy in Paris to monitor progress, and it acted as a sort of additional secretariat for Monnet. For the United States, the cartel arrangements were an outrageous interference with the operation of market forces, and could not be tolerated. There was initially less concern about the concentration issue because the size of the units involved would still be much smaller than those in the United States. However, after the outbreak of the Korean War in June 1950, the US Administration came to the reluctant conclusion that Germany would have to be rearmed. In this context, the issue of not allowing the emergence of the industrial conglomerates that had supported the previous militaristic German regime became more significant in US minds.

After months of hard negotiation, the United States cut through the arguments and forced a settlement. On 3 March 1951, Adenauer was summoned to see John J. McCloy, the US High Commissioner in Bonn, who told him that the delays caused by the Germans were unacceptable, and that 'France and the United States had no choice but to impose their own decartelization scheme' (Gillingham 1991a: 280). Despite vigorous protests from the Ruhr producers, Adenauer accepted the ultimatum because for him the political gains of the ECSC were paramount, and he could not afford to allow the process to collapse.

It appeared, then, that although Monnet's concept had been severely modified, the essential purpose had been achieved of creating a supranational body that could exercise some control over the coal and steel producers in the interests of promoting efficiency and competition (see Insight 6.3).

The High Authority was funded through a direct levy on Europe's coal and steel firms and had a wide brief on taxes, production, and restrictive practices. Alongside it were established a Council of Ministers consisting of national government representatives, and a Common Assembly. In addition, a Consultative Committee to the High Authority was established to represent producers, employers, and consumers. More significantly in terms of future integration, a Court of Justice was set up, with judges drawn from the national judiciaries to rule on the legality of the High Authority's actions.

Insight 6.3 Extracts from the Treaty Establishing the European Coal and Steel Community

Article 2

The ECSC shall have as its task to contribute, in harmony with the general economy of the Member States and through the establishment of a common market as provided in Article 4, to economic expansion, growth of employment and a rising standard of living in the Member States.

The Community shall progressively bring about conditions which will of themselves ensure the most rational distribution of production at the highest possible level of productivity, while safeguarding continuity of employment and taking care not to provoke fundamental and persistent disturbances in the economies of Member States.

Article 3

The institutions of the Community shall, within the limits of their respective powers, in the common interest:

(a) ensure an orderly supply to the common market, taking into account the needs of third countries;

(b) ensure that all comparably placed consumers in the common market have equal access to the sources of production;

(c) ensure the establishment of the lowest prices under such conditions that these prices do not result in higher prices charged by the same undertakings in other transactions or in a higher general price level at another time, while allowing necessary amortization and normal return on invested capital;

(d) ensure the maintenance of conditions which will encourage undertakings to expand and improve their production potential and to promote a policy of using natural resources rationally and avoiding their unconsidered exhaustion;

(e) promote improved working conditions and an improved standard of living for the workers in each of the industries for which it is responsible, so as to make possible their harmonization while the improvement is being maintained;

(f) promote the growth of international trade and ensure that equitable limits are observed in export pricing;

(g) promote the orderly expansion and modernization of production, and the improvement of quality, with no protection against competing industries that is not justified by improper action on their part or in their favour.

Article 4

The following are recognized as incompatible with the common market for coal and steel and shall accordingly be abolished and prohibited within the Community, as provided in this Treaty:

(a) import and export duties, or charges having equivalent effect, and quantitative restrictions on the movement of products;

(b) measures or practices which discriminate between producers, between purchasers or between consumers, especially in prices and delivery terms or transport rates and conditions, and measures or practices which interfere with the purchaser's free choice of supplier;

(c) subsidies or aids granted by States, or special charges imposed by States, in any form whatsoever;

(d) restrictive practices which tend towards the sharing or exploiting of markets.

Article 5

The Community shall carry out its task in accordance with this Treaty, with a limited measure of intervention.

To this end the Community shall:

- provide guidance and assistance for the parties concerned, by obtaining information, organizing consultations, and laying down general objectives;

- place financial resources at the disposal of undertakings for their investment and bear part of the cost of readaptation;

- ensure the establishment, maintenance, and observance of normal competitive conditions and exert direct influence upon production or upon the market only when circumstances so require;

- publish the reasons for its actions and take the necessary measures to ensure the observance of the rules laid down in this Treaty.

The institutions of the Community shall carry out these activities with a minimum of administrative machinery and in close co-operation with the parties concerned.

CONCLUSION

The first steps in the process of European integration were taken not primarily because of any commitment to the ideas of the federalists, but in response to practical problems. Schuman, Adenauer, and de Gasperi may have had personal reasons for wanting to see a move away from nationalism, but the architect of the ECSC, Jean Monnet, was concerned with solving immediate and longer-term problems. The two immediate problems were, first, the reconstruction of the two industries that were central to the European economies of the day, coal and steel, and second, how to accommodate West Germany within the system of capitalist European states without reviving the risk of war, and without serious damage to the French steel industry. In the longer term, he was looking at how to ensure that Europe would be competitive in comparison with the United States. The way in which solutions to practical problems became the basis for advances in European integration recurs throughout the story of the founding and evolution of the European communities.

Another consistent theme of the story of European integration is the tension between free-market capitalism and planned capitalism. The system of planned capitalism, or managed markets, is sometimes known by the French word *dirigisme*. Monnet saw very clearly the economic necessity for western Europe to move away from the fragmentation of national markets to form a single large market. He did not consider that the way in which to achieve this was through the immediate creation of a free market. He wanted the process to be controlled by planners, such as himself, and to proceed economic sector by economic sector. The end result, though, would be a managed European market rather than managed national markets. This theme is returned to in the conclusion to Chapter 8 (pp. 101–2).

The importance of the background of the Cold War was again evident in the launch of the ECSC. The breakdown of co-operation between the Soviet Union and the western Allies led to the creation of a West German state, posing the problems of how to handle Germany and how to ensure adequate coking coal for French steel manufacturers. It coloured the reaction of the governments to the Schuman Plan, particularly in Germany and Italy where the theme of the search for a new national identity was particularly prominent. In both states, the governments wanted to find a way of consolidating their position in the western capitalist camp. The ECSC offered a way of embedding their states into the capitalist west, and they could appeal to the idea of European federalism as a way of convincing their electorates that the move was a good one.

This did not mean that the governments of any of the states that agreed to take part in the ECSC were prepared to sell short their national interests as they perceived them. A consistent theme of the history of European integration is that advances are made only after hard bargaining between governments. This bargaining tends to produce package deals that give something to everyone. E. B. Haas (1968: 155) said of the Treaty of Paris that set up the ECSC:

> The very ambiguity of the Treaty ... made this pattern of convergence possible. Something seemed to be 'in it' for everybody and a large enough body of otherwise quarrelling politicians was persuaded to launch the first experiment in deliberate integration.

In this process of bargaining, the United States was a central actor. Although not having a formal seat at the negotiating table, the US Administration exerted influence on the negotiations and imposed its position on the maintenance of the cartels. Many episodes in the process of European integration can only be fully understood with reference to the position of the United States, which was often either directly involved with, or was a factor in the reckoning of, the participants.

Finally, the analysis that has been presented here focuses on the interests of states as interpreted by their governments, not on the activities of interest groups. In Chapter 1 (pp. 8–11), a distinction was drawn between realist and **pluralist** theories of international relations. For realists, states are the only significant actors in the international arena. For pluralists, other actors such as interest groups are also significant. In the case of neofunctionalism, a key role was allocated to organized interests. However, even Haas, the founding father of neofunctionalism, could not tell the story of the foundation of the ECSC in terms of interest-group pressures. He examined the positions of all of the key interest groups in the various states, and was able to show that they affected the detail of the positions taken up by national governments—but in the end the agreement to the ECSC was based on an independent interpretation of the national interests of the participating states taken by the governments of those states. However, this should not be so surprising, because neofunctionalism was essentially a theory about how the interests would react to the first steps in the process of European integration. ECSC *was* the first step. The time for neofunctionalist analysis had not yet arrived.

KEY POINTS

National Positions and the Origins of the ECSC

- The reactions to the proposal for coal and steel, known as the Schuman Plan, and the reasons for accepting it varied from state to state.
- The French government saw the coal and steel pool as a way to solve its problem with the emergence of a West German state, and as a way to guarantee supplies of coal from the Ruhr.

- The German government saw participation in the scheme as a route back to international respectability, and Adenauer saw in it a means of consolidating West Germany's capitalist identity.
- For the governments of the Benelux states, there was no choice but to participate in a coal and steel pool that involved France and Germany, so interdependent were their economies.
- The Italian government saw the scheme as a potential protection against a communist takeover.
- The British Labour government was unsympathetic to involvement in any **economic union** with other European states, and coal and steel had just been nationalized, so the sectors could not have been less well chosen to encourage British participation.

From the Schuman Plan to the Treaty of Paris

- Negotiations over the Schuman Plan led to significant changes to reflect national interests.
- Ultimately, however, the United States played an important 'behind the scenes' role in shaping an agreement that angered German steel producers, but which Adenauer accepted because, for him, the political gains from the ECSC were paramount.
- While Monnet's initial concept was modified, the agreement still created a supranational body, the High Authority, with some control over domestic coal and steel producers.
- Established alongside the High Authority were a Council of Ministers, a Common Assembly, and a Court of Justice to rule on the legality of the High Authority's actions.

FURTHER READING

There is a considerable literature on the Schuman Plan. The outline of the negotiations is ably recounted by **D. W. Urwin**, *The Community of Europe: A History of European Integration since 1945*, 2nd edn (London and New York: Longman, 1995), but for a detailed insight into the process the account given by **F. Duchêne**, *Jean Monnet: The First Statesman of Interdependence* (New York and London: W. W. Norton and Co., 1994) is indispensable. Most of **J. Gillingham**, *Coal, Steel, and the Rebirth of Europe, 1945–1955* (Cambridge: Cambridge University Press, 1991) is devoted to the build-up to the negotiations and the negotiations themselves, and **E. B. Haas**, *The Uniting of Europe: Political, Social and Economic Forces, 1950–1957* (Stanford, CA: Stanford University Press, 1968) contains information on the positions of all of the main actors, scattered through a book that is organized thematically rather than chronologically.

For the revisionist view that the ECSC was not a move away from state autonomy but a means of protecting it, the reader should turn to **A. Milward**, *The European Rescue of the Nation State* (London: Routledge, 1992).

The British failure to take the Schuman Plan seriously is recounted in **E. Dell**, *The Schuman Plan and the British Abdication of Leadership in Europe* (Oxford: Clarendon Press, 1995).

 online resource centre Visit the Online Resource Centre that accompanies this book for links to more information on the Schuman Plan:
www.oxfordtextbooks.co.uk/orc/bache3e/

Chapter 7

The European Defence Community, the European Political Community, and the Road to the Rome Treaties

Chapter Overview

Negotiations over a plan for a European Defence Community (EDC) ran parallel to those over the European Coal and Steel Community (ECSC), which were discussed in the previous chapter. Connected with the EDC was a proposal to create a European Political Community (EPC) to provide democratic European structures for co-ordinating foreign policies. This provided federalists with another opportunity to pursue their strategy of 'the constitutional break', moving directly from a Europe of nation states to a federal constitution for Europe. However, the feasibility of doing this was no greater in 1953 than it had been in 1948, and for the same reason: governments were not prepared to surrender their sovereignty. With the collapse of the EDC and EPC, the radical federalist strategy of a direct attack on the system of nation states disappeared from this story. This chapter looks at the development of the EDC/EPC plan and the ultimate failure to reach agreement on this in 1954, before looking at the relaunch of the integration project in 1955, leading in 1957 to the Treaties of Rome that established the European Economic Community (EEC) and the European Atomic Energy Community (Euratom).

In the autumn of 1952, there were not one but three prospective Communities, two pillars and the roof of a potential European union. Covering coal, steel, defence, arms production and perhaps elements of foreign policy—that is, economic and political functions close to the core of the state—they provided the outline of a federation in the classic style. To achieve so much would be extraordinary three or four years from a standing start and less than a decade after the war. On the other hand, there were disturbing signs that all this might be a house of cards resting on the fate of the European Army.

(Duchêne 1994: 234–5)

While the development of the ECSC (Chapter 6) set much of the tone and framework for future developments in European integration, it was largely overshadowed at the time by parallel negotiations on another plan devised by Monnet: the Pleven Plan for a

European Defence Community (EDC). The failure of this proposal was perhaps as much responsible as the successes and failures of the ECSC in explaining the initiatives that led to the Treaties of Rome.

The Pleven Plan

Following the collapse of the four-power administration of Germany (Chapter 5, p. 86), the Cold War developed rapidly. In April 1949, a mutual defence pact, the North Atlantic Treaty, was signed in Washington between the United States, Canada, and ten western European states (Britain, France, the **Benelux** states, Denmark, Iceland, Italy, Norway, and Portugal). This set up the North Atlantic Treaty Organization (NATO). In the same month, the Federal Republic of Germany came into existence. In June 1950, communist North Korea invaded capitalist South Korea. The ensuing civil war involved the United States, acting under the auspices of the United Nations, on the side of the South, and the Soviet Union and communist China on the side of the North. It had a profound impact on western thinking about security.

Like Korea, Germany was divided into capitalist and communist states. While Korea was at that time geographically peripheral to the main global balance of power, Germany was not. The fear in the West was that the Korean invasion was a precursor to an invasion of West Germany from East Germany. In this context, and because the United States was committing troops to the Korean conflict, the US Administration decided that the Europeans had to make a bigger contribution to their own defence. In particular, it reluctantly decided that there was no alternative to reconstituting a German army.

This idea alarmed the French. For them, it was unthinkable that a German army should come back into existence. Monnet tried to solve the problem with a proposal based on the same principles as his plan for ECSC. Under his scheme for a European Defence Community, instead of having a German army, he proposed to pool the military resources of France and Germany into a European army. There would be German soldiers, but they would not wear German uniforms, and they would not be under German command. The corollary, of course, was that the French army would at least partially disappear into the same European force. Monnet's proposal did, however, allow France and the other participants, except Germany, to have their own national armies alongside the European army.

The plan proposed the creation of a European army consisting of fourteen French divisions, twelve German, eleven Italian, and three from the Benelux states. The command of the army would be integrated, but there would be no divisions of mixed nationality. The EDC would have had a similar institutional structure to the ECSC: a Council representing the member states, with votes weighted according to each state's contribution to the European army, alongside a Commission and an Assembly.

As with the pooling of coal and steel, a European army was not a new idea. A similar proposal had been made by the French representatives in the Consultative Assembly of the Council of Europe in August 1950, and had received the support of the Assembly, but had been blocked in the Council of Ministers. Monnet now formalized the idea, making an explicit link to the ECSC. The plan was publicly launched by the French Prime Minister, René Pleven, an old collaborator of Monnet, on 24 October 1950.

Despite the election in Britain in October 1951 of a Conservative government under Churchill, who professed to be a supporter of European integration, the British were unwilling to become involved in plans for the EDC. The US Administration was initially cautious, but Monnet talked round the new NATO Supreme Allied Commander in Europe, Dwight D. Eisenhower, and his support swung the Administration behind the scheme (Duchêne 1994: 231). Adenauer welcomed the idea, seeing in it a way of finally ending the Allied occupation of West Germany. The other four states that had joined in the Schuman Plan signed up to talks for essentially the same reasons as they had joined ECSC: the Benelux states did not feel that they could stand aside from such an initiative between their two larger neighbours, and Italy continued to seek acceptance into the European states system.

The EDC, the ECSC, and the EPC

At Monnet's prompting, Pleven made it a condition of progress on the EDC that the ECSC Treaty be signed first. This was particularly resented in Germany, because Monnet had accompanied preparation of the Pleven Plan with a hardening of his attitude towards the position of the German steel cartels in the talks on the Schuman Plan. This had stalled the talks: Adenauer and the German negotiator, Hallstein, felt that they were being railroaded into accepting an unfavourable agreement on the ECSC in order to secure negotiations on the EDC. They were not mistaken. Gillingham (1991b: 146) was clear that these two developments were linked in Monnet's mind. Indeed, the same author (1991a: 264) went so far as to suggest that the Pleven Plan 'saved the Schuman Plan'. This sort of cross-bargaining worked both ways, however. Duchêne (1994: 250) believed that one explanation for Monnet's failure to press home the Treaty provisions against the Ruhr cartels when he became President of the ECSC High Authority was that Adenauer warned him that any premature action on this front would jeopardize the ratification of the EDC Treaty in the German Parliament.

A problem with the proposed EDC was the plan for a common European army without a common foreign policy. The proposed institutions of the EDC would not be able to provide this. At the insistence of Italy, a clause was inserted into the draft Treaty linking the EDC with the creation of a EPC to provide a democratic dimension to the project. Plans were to be drawn up by the Common Assembly of the EDC, but as delays in ratifying the Treaty stretched out the process, Paul-Henri Spaak, the Belgian Premier, suggested that the Common Assembly of the ECSC, enlarged in membership so as to resemble the proposed EDC Assembly, should prepare the EPC proposal.

The opportunity to draft a Treaty for a EPC was seized on by federalists within the Assembly. In the course of its work, the ECSC Assembly was supplemented by members of the Parliamentary Assembly of the Council of Europe (see Chapter 5, Insight 5.2). The draft Treaty was adopted by this ad hoc Assembly on 10 March 1953. It proposed: a two-chamber European Parliament consisting of a People's Chamber that would be directly elected every five years, and a Senate of indirectly elected members from national parliaments; a European Executive Council that would have to be approved by both chambers of the Parliament, but once in office would have the power to dissolve the People's Chamber and call new elections; a Council of National Ministers; and a Court of Justice. The EPC would not be only a third community, 'but nothing less than the beginning of a comprehensive federation to which the ECSC and EDC would be subordinated' (Urwin 1995: 64).

The Fate of the EDC and EPC

The fate of the EPC was inevitably linked to the fate of the EDC. The EDC Treaty had been signed in May 1952, but it had not been ratified by any of the signatories when the EPC proposals emerged. In fact, the EDC Treaty was 'rotting before the ink was dry' (Duchêne 1994: 233). Its prospects were crucially dependent on French support, but the French government only signed it on the 'tacit condition that no immediate attempt should be made to ratify it' (Duchêne 1994: 233). German rearmament, even as part of a European army, was unpopular in France. Pleven only managed to get approval for his proposal from the National Assembly by 343 votes to 220. By the time that the intergovernmental negotiations were completed, there had been elections in France and the parliamentary arithmetic did not indicate a clear majority for ratification. In consequence, successive prime ministers refused to bring the Treaty to the Assembly for ratification, fearing that its failure would bring down their government.

This prevarication, which went on for almost two years, caused exasperation in the United States, and led Secretary of State John Foster Dulles in December 1953 to threaten an 'agonizing reappraisal' of policy. Eventually, the Treaty was submitted to the National Assembly by the government of Pierre Mendès-France at the end of August 1954, but the government gave it no support, and indicated that it would not resign if the Assembly were to vote against ratification. The EDC Treaty was not ratified and the demise of the EDC was accompanied by the collapse of the EPC.

The Aftermath of the EDC and EPC

The issue of European defence was eventually solved according to a formula proposed by the British government. The Brussels Treaty of 1948 was extended to Germany and Italy; a loose organization called the Western European Union (WEU) was set up to co-ordinate the alliance; an organic link was made with NATO, to which Germany and Italy were admitted. Adenauer achieved his aim of bringing to an end the Allies' occupation of West Germany (although not Berlin), and a German army was formed, although it was hedged around with legal restrictions on operating beyond the borders of the Federal Republic. The WEU appeared to contemporary observers to be an organization of no particular importance because it was overshadowed by NATO. However, like other organizations that were set up in the post-war period, it was later to acquire functions that had not been envisaged at the time when it was formed (Insight 7.1).

The other practical significance of the EDC episode, or rather of the related EPC initiative, was that it kept the federalist idea alive. As Gillingham (1991a: 349) put it, it 'kept the cadres in being, dialogue moving, and served as a learning experience'. The importance of this became clear with the 'relaunching of Europe' that followed the collapse of EDC.

Defence was not an obvious next step after coal and steel in the process of building mutual trust through practical co-operation. It was not an issue with a low political profile, but a sensitive issue that struck to the heart of national sovereignty. Had it not been for the international crisis of the Korean War, it would surely not have surfaced

---

Insight 7.1 The Western European Union

Following the collapse of the EDC, the British government proposed an alternative security structure for western Europe. This involved Italy and Germany becoming signatories to the Brussels Treaty of 1948, by which Britain, France, and the Benelux states had committed themselves to treat any act of aggression against one as an act of aggression against all.

The Western European Union (WEU) that resulted began work on 6 May 1955. Its headquarters were in London. Its institutions consisted of:

- a Council of Foreign and Defence Ministers;
- a Secretariat, headed by a Secretary-General;
- an Assembly (based in Paris), made up of the member states' representatives in the Parliamentary Assembly of the Council of Europe.

In the 1980s, the WEU took on a new role as a bridge between the EC and NATO in the context of efforts to forge a European security and defence identity. The Treaty on European Union (signed February 1992) contained as an annex a Declaration on WEU, which said: 'WEU will be developed as the defence component of the European Union and as a means to strengthen the European pillar of the Atlantic Alliance.' The WEU's operational activities were transferred to the EU in 2000. The Lisbon Treaty took over the WEU's mutual defence clause. The WEU Treaty was terminated in March 2010, and the organization was to be wound up over the following year.

---

at this stage. Monnet himself may have been of this view. Duchêne (1994: 229) reports that several people who were working close to Monnet at the time had the impression that he regarded the EDC scheme as premature. After winning over Eisenhower, Monnet took no further part in the negotiations on the plan, suggesting a lack of further commitment to the project.

Messina

In November 1954, Monnet announced that when his first term as President of the High Authority of the ECSC ended in February 1955, he would not seek a second term. Citing the collapse of the EDC, he said that he wanted to free his hands to work for European unity. He then formed an organization called the Action Committee for the United States of Europe, consisting of leading political and trade union figures from the member states of the ECSC, but also from Britain and other states.

The main proposal to come from the Action Committee was for a European Atomic Energy Community (Euratom). It was accompanied by a plan to extend the sectoral responsibilities of the ECSC to cover all forms of energy, and transport. Nothing came of these latter proposals, although transport was given a special place in the Treaty of Rome (EEC). The member governments were simply not interested in extending the remit of the ECSC.

Also accompanying the proposals from the Action Committee was a proposal from Beyen, the Dutch Foreign Minister, for a general **common market**. Richard Mayne

(1991: 115) maintained that this scheme also originated with Monnet, but he offered no evidence for this, and it is a view that is flatly rejected by other writers. Duchêne (1994: 269–72) provided evidence that Monnet actually rejected the idea of a general common market, believing that it was too ambitious, and might produce another EDC debacle.

There was no great enthusiasm for further sectoral integration. In so far as business interests expressed support for further integration, it was for an extension of the market aspect of the ECSC, not for the centralized regulatory functions of the High Authority. The lesson that was learned from ECSC was the limitations of sectoral integration. As *The Economist* (11 August 1956) reported:

> In the last four years the Coal and Steel Community has proved that the common market is not only feasible but, on balance, advantageous for all concerned. But it has also shown that 'integration by sector' raises its own problems of distortion and discrimination. The Six have therefore chosen to create a common market for all products rather than continuing to experiment with the sector approach.

On 4 April 1955, Spaak circulated a memorandum to the governments of the six states of the ECSC proposing that negotiations begin on the extension of sectoral integration to other forms of energy than coal, particularly nuclear energy, and to transport. The proposal met with a cool response: only the French government supported it. Beyen then pressed the case for a relaunch based on the idea of a general common market.

The Federal German government reacted very positively to Beyen's proposal, but in France, the idea of a general common market was strongly rejected by industry, which argued that it would not be able to compete with German industry. French politicians had generally accepted this argument, but there was a growing belief that the excuse could not be used forever, and that French industry would never be competitive until it had to compete. At this stage, though, the mood in France was not conducive to taking such a step, which may explain why Monnet was reluctant to advocate it.

Spaak subsequently met with the Prime Minister of Luxembourg, Joseph Bech, and, as a result of that meeting, a formal Benelux initiative was launched combining Monnet's ideas for further sectoral integration with Beyen's idea of a general common market. This proposal was circulated in late April 1955, and was discussed at the beginning of June in Messina in Italy at a meeting of the heads of government of the six, which had originally been called to decide on a successor to Monnet as President of the High Authority of the ECSC.

Agreement was reached at Messina to set up a committee under the chairmanship of Spaak to study the ideas in the Benelux memorandum. The French government was not enthusiastic, and appeared not to expect anything to come of the talks, but it was difficult for France to block them so soon after its rejection of the EDC. Because the agreement to hold talks was reached in Messina, the negotiations took that name. In fact, most of the meetings were held in Brussels. Their success was unexpected, except perhaps by optimistic partisans of integration such as Spaak. In fact, the success of the Spaak Committee, which met in Brussels between July 1955 and March 1956, owed a great deal to his energetic and skilful chairing of the proceedings. Also very important, though, were the changed circumstances between the original Messina meeting and the actual negotiations.

France and the Suez Crisis

One very important change was in the government of France: Guy Mollet, the leader of the Socialist Party, became Prime Minister in 1956. Having originally been sceptical about European integration, Mollet had become convinced that French industry needed to be opened up to competition if it was ever to achieve the sort of productivity gains that lay behind the remarkable German economic recovery. He had also become a member of Monnet's Action Committee, and Duchêne (1994: 287) maintained that a relationship developed between Monnet and Mollet similar to the earlier relationship between Monnet and Schuman.

Mollet was brought to office by the deteriorating situation in Algeria, where French settlers were under attack by the National Liberation Front (FLN) of Algeria. The war that developed there was traumatic for the French, and dominated the nation's attention so that the negotiations in Brussels were able to proceed without attracting much notice from critics. But Algeria was only one of the international events of 1956 that had an effect on the outcome of the Messina negotiations. In October, the Soviet Union invaded Hungary to suppress an anti-communist national movement that had the sympathy of the Hungarian army. Hungary brought home to western Europeans once again the reality of the Cold War that divided their continent. More directly, the Suez Canal crisis also blew up in October.

The nationalization of the Suez Canal by Egyptian President Gamal Abdel Nasser not only caused outrage in France, as it did in Britain, but it also offered the French a possible excuse to topple Nasser, whose pan-Arab rhetoric inflamed the situation in Algeria, and whose regime was suspected of sheltering and arming the Algerian rebels. However, once the nationalization had been effected, Nasser gave no further cause for outside intervention. The canal was kept open to international shipping; it was business as usual under new ownership. To foment an excuse to invade, the French government colluded with the Israeli government and hatched a scheme that was subsequently sold to the British government of Anthony Eden. Israel would invade the canal zone; the French and British governments would demand an immediate withdrawal from the canal by the armed forces of both sides. Egypt would certainly refuse, and the combined Franco-British force would then move in to occupy the canal zone and reclaim the canal. The fall of Nasser was confidently expected to follow.

However, the invasion failed because, in the face of opposition from the Soviet Union and, more significantly, from the United States, the British government decided to pull out. France could not carry through the operation alone. The episode was perceived in France as a national humiliation at the hands of the Americans, but also as a betrayal by the British who were believed to be too subservient to US wishes. It fed support for the nationalist position of Charles de Gaulle, who subsequently came to office as first President of the new Fifth Republic in May 1958. It also fed into the Messina negotiations, helping them to reach a speedy and successful conclusion.

Directly, Suez underlined much more than events in Hungary the impotence of France in the post-war world of superpowers. It gave support to the concept of France acting together with other European states. Indirectly, the clear signs that this episode marked the beginning of the end for the government of Mollet, and the strong indications that he would be succeeded by de Gaulle, who had always opposed European integration, accelerated the efforts to reach agreement. A 'rush to Rome' began in an effort to get the Treaties signed before de Gaulle came to office and aborted the whole experiment.

The Road to the Rome Treaties

The agreements reached in the Spaak Committee were a series of compromises between different national positions, particularly those of France and Germany. Central to the agreement detailed in the Spaak Report of March 1956 was the creation of the general common market favoured by the German government. Although Mollet believed that this step would be good for France as well as for Germany, he had to negotiate concessions that would allow him to get the Treaty ratified in the French National Assembly. There were three main areas in which the French government extracted concessions: Euratom; agriculture; and relations with France's overseas territories and dependencies.

Euratom was attractive for many French politicians because they saw it as a means of obtaining a subsidy from Germany for the expensive process of developing nuclear energy, which in turn was linked to the development of nuclear weapons. Although Mollet personally believed that France should confine itself to the peaceful use of nuclear energy, the sentiment in the National Assembly in the aftermath of Hungary and Suez was very much in favour of an independent French nuclear deterrent. Euratom offered the opportunity to devote more national resources to the weapons programme, while depriving Germany of a national nuclear capability, and guaranteeing French access to uranium from the Belgian Congo.

Agriculture was given a separate chapter in the EEC Treaty. Its inclusion, not as part of the general common market, but as, in effect, a further extension of sectoral integration was another factor that was important in ensuring French ratification of the Treaty.

For the French governments of the Fourth Republic, agriculture was both politically and economically important. Politically, small farmers had a disproportionate electoral importance under the voting system that was used in the Fourth Republic. The small farmers were inefficient producers, but were determined to retain their independence, which in effect meant that they had to be subsidized by the state through a national system of price support. By transferring this cost to the common EEC budget, the French state again obtained a subsidy from the more prosperous Germans. Economically, France also had an efficient agricultural sector, and actually produced a considerable surplus of food, so the guarantee of a protected market for French agricultural exports was another concession that helped to sell the EEC Treaty within France.

In the context of decolonization and the war in Algeria, it was very important for all French governments to ensure that the special links with the former colonies were maintained. There were considerable French economic interests that were dependent on trade with these overseas dependencies and territories, and there was a general sentiment in France in favour of the link. The continuation of this special relationship, by guaranteeing preferential access to the common market for the products of the former colonies, was the third important factor to allow the Treaty to obtain ratification in France.

On each of these points, the German government made considerable concessions: there was no sympathy for Euratom in German industrial or government circles; the

Germans would have preferred to leave agriculture to national management, and to continue to allow food to be imported as cheaply as possible from the rest of the world; and there was no enthusiasm for supporting the last vestiges of French colonialism. However, in order to obtain the considerable prize of the common market in industrial goods, the German government was prepared to make these concessions to France.

The other major bargaining concession was made to Italy in the form of the inclusion in the Treaty of a commitment to reducing the differences between prosperous and poor regions. This was the Italian government's attempt to claim a subsidy from Germany, given that the problems of the south of Italy represented the main regional disparity within the original six member states.

Insight 7.2 Extracts from the Treaty Establishing the European Atomic Energy Community

Article 1

By this Treaty the HIGH CONTRACTING PARTIES establish among themselves a EUROPEAN ATOMIC ENERGY COMMUNITY (EURATOM).

It shall be the task of the Community to contribute to the raising of the standard of living in the Member States and to the development of relations with the other countries by creating the conditions necessary for the speedy establishment and growth of nuclear industries.

Article 2

In order to perform its task, the Community shall, as provided in this Treaty:

(a) promote research and ensure the dissemination of technical information;

(b) establish uniform safety standards to protect the health of workers and of the general public and ensure that they are applied;

(c) facilitate investment and ensure, particularly by encouraging ventures on the part of undertakings, the establishment of the basic installations necessary for the development of nuclear energy in the Community;

(d) ensure that all users in the Community receive a regular and equitable supply of ores and nuclear fuels;

(e) make certain, by appropriate supervision, that nuclear materials are not diverted to purposes other than those for which they are intended;

(f) exercise the right of ownership conferred upon it with respect to special fissile materials;

(g) ensure wide commercial outlets and access to the best technical facilities by the creation of a common market in specialized materials and equipment, by the free movement of capital for investment in the field of nuclear energy and by freedom of employment for specialists within the Community;

(h) establish with other countries and international organizations such relations as will foster progress in the peaceful uses of nuclear energy.

The Spaak Report was agreed by the governments of the six member states in May 1956. The Spaak Committee was transformed into a conference with responsibility for drafting the necessary Treaties. In March 1957, two Treaties emerged: one for the EEC; the other for Euratom. The Treaties were signed by national governments in Rome in the same month, prior to being passed on for domestic ratification. If the failure of the EDC had meant several steps backwards in the process of integration, the Treaties of Rome (Insights 7.2 and 7.3) promised a major leap forward.

Insight 7.3 Extracts from the Treaty Establishing the European Economic Community

Article 2

The Community shall have as its task, by establishing a common market and progressively approximating the economic policies of Member States, to promote through the Community a harmonious development of economic activities, a continuous and balanced expansion, an increase in stability, an accelerated raising of the standard of living and closer relations between the States belonging to it.

Article 3

For the purposes set out in Article 2, the activities of the Community shall include, as provided in this Treaty and in accordance with the timetable set out therein:

(a) the elimination, as between Member States, of customs duties and quantitative restrictions on the import and export of goods, and of all other measures having equivalent effect;

(b) the establishment of a common customs tariff and of common commercial policy towards third countries;

(c) the abolition, as between Member States, of obstacles to the free movement of goods, persons, services and capital;

(d) the adoption of a common policy in the sphere of agriculture;

(e) the adoption of a common policy in the sphere of transport;

(f) the institution of a system ensuring that competition in the common market is not distorted;

(g) the application of procedures by which the economic policies of Member States can be co-ordinated and disequilibria in their balances of payments remedied;

(h) the approximation of the laws of Member States to the extent required for the proper functioning of the common market;

(i) the creation of a European Social Fund in order to improve employment opportunities for workers and to contribute to the raising of their standard of living;

(j) the establishment of a European Investment Bank to facilitate the economic expansion of the Community by opening fresh resources;

(k) the association of the overseas countries and territories in order to increase trade and to promote jointly economic and social development.

CONCLUSION

Several of the persistent themes of this story emerge once more in this chapter. The influence of the Cold War on the whole EDC episode is clear, as is the role of the United States in the affairs of western Europe during this period of its hegemony of the capitalist world. However, the fate of the EDC is vindication of the functionalist analysis that a head-on attack on sovereignty would be resisted, whereas gradual steps to tie states together might succeed.

It is contestable whether the opening of negotiations on the EEC is vindication of the neofunctionalist argument that spillover would operate to move integration forward once the first steps had been taken (Chapter 1). The line of spillover from ECSC to Euratom is clearer, and was the line of progression favoured by Monnet. However, the proposal for Euratom was countered, rather than complemented, by the proposal from the Benelux states for a general common market. In this can be seen the tension between *dirigisme* and free-market approaches to integration. The general common market was designed to open national markets by removing tariffs, at that time the main barrier to free trade. It stood in marked distinction to the Euratom proposal to extend the system of planning of the 'commanding heights' of the economy from coal and steel to what was expected to be the new main source of energy.

Monnet's scheme also reflected the need to gain the acceptance of the French political elite. France was developing nuclear energy as a priority project, so it could be expected to support Euratom, which offered France the prospect of a subsidy from the other member states for its research and development costs. A free market in industrial goods was less likely to find favour in a country where there was less industrial efficiency than in West Germany. However, things were changing in France. There was a growing awareness among the political elite that if France were to keep up with its German neighbour, it would have to modernize its economy. Euratom, and concessions on agriculture and overseas territories, were necessary sweeteners to sell the package to the French National Assembly—but the assertion, often made, that the EEC was a deal between German industry and French agriculture hides the truth, that for certain sections of the French political elite the common market was a useful tool to sweep away the protectionism that was stifling French economic growth. Another theme that reappears later in the story emerges here: this is the argument that 'Europe' is used as a smokescreen by governments to hide behind when pursuing domestically unpopular measures (see Chapter 4).

There is no strong evidence that a commitment to maintaining the momentum of integration was a motive for the acceptance of the EEC by the political elite in any of the member states. Events in Algeria, Suez, and Hungary did, though, bring home to them the weakness of European states in an era of superpowers, and made clinging together more attractive. These dramatic incidents also impacted on public opinion, and reinforced a general sentiment in favour of federalist ideas. Suez and Algeria in particular caused a crisis of identity among the French public that allowed their government to push through the Treaties of Rome behind a rhetoric of maintaining the momentum of integration. At the same time, the account given here shows that the Messina negotiations were no exception to the rule that national interests will be strongly defended in all moves in the direction of integration.

KEY POINTS

The Pleven Plan

- While the ECSC is often seen as the first step on the road to the EU, negotiations over the Pleven Plan for a European Defence Community were considered more important at the time.

- The EDC would place German troops under European command, thus heading off US demands for German rearmament following the outbreak of the Korean War. Adenauer reacted positively because it offered a means of ending the Allied occupation of West Germany.
- The Pleven Plan became linked with a proposal for a European Political Community.
- Both projects collapsed when the French National Assembly refused to ratify the EDC Treaty.

Messina

- Following the collapse of EDC/EPC, Monnet launched initiatives based on extending the ECSC model to other forms of energy, especially atomic energy, and to transport.
- The Benelux states supported a general common market for industrial goods.
- The two sets of proposals were discussed together in the Messina negotiations.
- The negotiations were given impetus by international events in 1956: the war in Algeria; the invasion of Hungary by the USSR; and the Suez crisis.

The Road to the Rome Treaties

- The Treaties of Rome involved compromises between France and Germany.
- The French price for accepting the general common market in industrial goods was German agreement on Euratom, the Common Agricultural Policy, and a preferential relationship with the EEC for the former French colonies.
- Italy was allowed to have a commitment in the EEC Treaty to create a regional policy.

FURTHER READING

The Pleven Plan and the abortive attempt to create a European Defence Community is less written about than the Schuman Plan, but it is the subject of **E. Fursdon**, *The European Defence Community: A History* (London: Macmillan, 1980), and **K. Ruane**, *The Rise and Fall of the European Defence Community: Anglo-American Relations and the Crisis of European Defence* (Basingstoke: Palgrave Macmillan, 2000). As with the Schuman Plan, **F. Duchêne**, *Jean Monnet: The First Statesman of Interdependence* (New York and London: W. W. Norton and Co., 1994), 229–32, provides an insider account.

 online resource centre **Visit the Online Resource Centre that accompanies this book for links to more information on the European Defence Community: www.oxfordtextbooks.co.uk/orc/bache3e/**

Chapter 8

The European Coal and Steel Community and Euratom

Chapter Overview

This chapter examines the independent existence of both the European Coal and Steel Community (ECSC) and Euratom up to the merger of the High Authority and Euratom Commission with the Commission of the European Economic Community (EEC) in July 1967. In this period, both the High Authority and the Euratom Commission ran into conflicts with the governments of member states, who were reluctant to relinquish actual control over the two key industries—particularly with the French government after de Gaulle became President of France in 1958. Their difficulties had several parallels, and could lead to the conclusion that they were failed experiments. However, Monnet himself claimed that the ECSC at least contributed to changing perceptions of what was necessary to make European integration work. This chapter asks what lessons can be learned from the experience of these two 'failed' attempts at supranational regulation, and identifies issues that can be later applied to the EEC.

> In itself, this was a technical step, but its new procedures, under common institutions, created a silent revolution in men's minds.
>
> (Monnet 1962: 208)

The European Coal and Steel Community

The ECSC survived the European Defence Community debacle and began operation in July 1952 under the presidency of Jean Monnet. Although it had considerable powers at its disposal (Insight 8.1), it proceeded cautiously in using them, but still found itself in conflict with national governments.

In the original plan for the ECSC, there was only one central institution: the High Authority. During the negotiations, a Council of Ministers and a European Parliamentary Assembly (EPA) were added to the institutional structure. This reflected concern about the power and possible *dirigiste* nature of the High Authority, but did not allay that concern.

While coal producers were ambiguous about supranational *dirigisme*, most of them hoping for some degree of support for their troubled industry, steel producers were generally hostile to this aspect of the Schuman Plan. German industrialists in particular opposed the *dirigiste* element to the Plan, and the Federal German government supported them. The governments of the **Benelux** countries also had severe doubts about the role of the High Authority. It was at the insistence of these governments that a Council of Ministers was included in the institutional structure of the ECSC, alongside the High Authority.

Although its independence was reduced from Monnet's original proposal, the High Authority was still given considerable formal powers. Diebold (1959: 78–9) considered that:

> It was truly to be an imperium in imperio, wielding powers previously held by national governments and having some functions not previously exercised by governments.

Despite these powers, in practice, the High Authority proceeded very cautiously. It was in a constant state of tension with member state governments, who did not take easily to having their sovereignty circumscribed by a supranational body. The Council regularly rejected proposals of the High Authority that conflicted with national interests. For this reason, the High Authority needed a strong President who could impose his authority. In their comprehensive history of the ECSC, Spierenburg and Poidevin (1994: 649) argued that the first two Presidents, Monnet and René Mayer, fitted this description, as did the last President, Del Bo, although by the time he took office in 1963 the High Authority was already in its twilight years. The two intervening Presidents, Finet and Malvestiti, did not carry the same weight (Insight 8.1).

Insight 8.1 The High Authority

The High Authority of the ECSC had nine members, two each from France and Germany, and one from each of the other member states, the ninth member to be co-opted by the other eight; its seat was in Luxembourg. It had five Presidents, as follows.

- Jean Monnet (1952–55)
- Rene Mayer (1955–57)
- Paul Finet (1958–59)
- Piero Malvestiti (1959–63)
- Rinaldo Del Bo (1963–67)

It had the power under the Treaty of Paris to obtain from firms in the coal and steel sectors the information that it required to oversee the industries, and to fine firms that would not provide the information or evaded their obligations (Article 47).

It could impose levies on production, and contract loans to raise finance to back investment projects of which it approved (Articles 49–51), and it could guarantee loans to coal and steel concerns from independent sources of finance (Article 54). It could also require undertakings to inform it in advance of investment programmes, and if it disapproved of the plans could prevent the concern from using resources other than its own funds to carry out the programme (Article 54).

Even taking account of this difficult relationship with the Council, Haas (1968: 459) considered that, 'in all matters relating to the routine regulation of the **Common Market**, the High Authority is independent of member governments'. Because of this independence, those governments that were concerned about the possible *dirigisme* of the High Authority took care to nominate as their members people who were not themselves committed to this outlook. For Milward (1992: 105), the most notable feature of the members of the High Authority was that they never liberated themselves from their national governments. Monnet became the first President of the High Authority, but found himself at the head of a group of people who were not in sympathy with his own view on its role. Haas (1968: 459) argued that, in 'the ideology of the High Authority, the free enterprise and anti-*dirigiste* viewpoint ... definitely carried the day'.

This way of presenting the issue is perhaps a little misleading. It suggests that Monnet was in favour of intrusive public-sector intervention and was opposed by other members who favoured free competition. In fact, one of the things that Monnet wanted the High Authority to do was to prevent the reformation of the coal and steel cartels: organizations of producers that regulated the industries through their collaboration on prices and output. Monnet wanted such regulation as there was to be carried out by the High Authority—but he was also committed to preserving competition between producers. The other members of the High Authority were committed to preventing it from interfering with self-regulation of the markets, not to competition. Perhaps this is what Haas meant by a 'free enterprise' viewpoint, but the terminology tends to suggest that less-regulated markets were the objective. In any case, Monnet was frustrated in his policy objectives for the High Authority.

He was also frustrated in his organizational objectives. Mazey (1992: 40–1) argued that Monnet wanted a small, supranational, non-hierarchical, and informal organization, but that internal divisions, bureaucratization, and pressures from **corporatist** and national interests foiled him in this. Internal divisions between members of the High Authority itself were reproduced within the administration, and when combined with the non-hierarchical structure that Monnet adopted, these led to increasing problems of administrative co-ordination, delays, and duplication of effort because of overlapping competencies.

However, as the demands for administering the common market for coal and steel grew, so did the bureaucratic nature of the High Authority. Problems of co-ordination increased as the different Directorates of the ECSC developed different links with interests and producers in the member states. The consequence was that, in the first three years of its operation, 'the administrative services of the High Authority were ... transformed from an informal grouping of sympathetic individuals into a professional bureaucracy which, in terms of its structure and "technocratic" character, resembled the French administration' (Mazey 1992: 43).

When the ECSC was proposed, coal was in short supply; by 1959, the increasing use of oil had led to overcapacity in the industry. This became a crisis in 1958 when a mild winter and an economic downturn produced a serious fall in demand. Although economic growth picked up in the second quarter of 1959, stocks of coal at the pithead continued to accumulate because of a second mild winter, low transatlantic freight costs, which allowed cheap imports of US coal, and an acceleration of the switch from coal to oil. The High Authority diagnosed a manifest crisis and, in March 1959, asked the Council of Ministers for emergency powers under Article 58 of the Treaty. However, this request failed to achieve the qualified majority necessary, primarily because neither France nor Germany was prepared to grant the extra powers to the High Authority that it requested.

This was one of a series of crises in the history of the European Communities that shook the collective morale of the central bureaucratic actors. The immediate effect was to make it very difficult for the High Authority to respond to the crisis. It had to resort to palliative measures such as social assistance, and a restructuring plan for the Belgian industry, which was hardest hit by the crisis. More fundamentally:

> The High Authority's powerlessness revealed the inadequacy of sectoral integration for which it was responsible and which did not cover competing energy sources—oil and nuclear energy.

(Spierenburg and Poidevin 1994: 652)

The realization that the attempt to integrate in one sector could not be successful unless integration were extended to other sectors might have led to an increase in the competencies of the High Authority. The Council of Ministers did ask the High Authority to undertake the co-ordination of energy supplies and to draw up plans for a common energy policy, but by this time, the Treaties of Rome had come into effect, creating the two new communities, the EEC and Euratom, each with its own Commission.

The decision to make a new start with new institutions, rather than to extend the competencies of the High Authority, inevitably produced a conflict between the established bureaucratic actor and the newcomers. Although the High Authority helped the two Commissions to get started by seconding many of its experienced staff, 'there were undeniable jealousies that precluded closer union between the three executive bodies' (Spierenburg and Poidevin 1994: 652).

Finet complained about the 'poaching' of High Authority staff by the Commissions of Euratom and the EEC (Spierenburg and Poidevin 1994: 381), and there were tensions both over issues of responsibility and budgetary matters. The Commissions, one headed by a Frenchman and the other by a German, had the support of the French and German governments on these matters. More generally, governments were content to see responsibilities of the High Authority transferred to the less supranational new Commissions.

Yet the ECSC could claim partial success for its activities, for example in limiting restrictive practices in the coal and steel sectors. More importantly, for Monnet, the creation of the ECSC laid vital foundations for further European integration:

> It proved decisive in persuading businessmen, civil servants, politicians and trade unionists that such an approach could work and that the economic and political advantages of unity over division were immense. Once they were convinced, they were ready to take further steps forward.

(Monnet 1962: 208)

While the supranational instincts of the High Authority were kept under control by national governments, it was significant for future developments in European integration that both the Assembly and the Court of Justice were supportive of its supranational efforts. The Court in particular 'stamped its imprint on the ECSC, and in doing so built up a body of case law, an authority, and legitimacy that could serve as foundations for the future' (Urwin 1995: 56).

Six years after signing the Treaty of Paris establishing the ECSC, the six parliaments ratified the Treaty of Rome establishing the Economic Community, taking the major step towards the creation of a common market for all goods and services. Monnet (1962: 211) spoke of a 'new method of action' in Europe, replacing the efforts at domination by the nation states 'by a constant process of collective adaptation to new conditions, a chain reaction, a ferment where one change induces another'.

In 2002, the Treaty of Paris expired. The strategic importance of these two sectors had declined, and the rationale for the ECSC had disappeared.

Euratom

The Euratom Commission had similar powers and responsibilities to those of its sister institution, the EEC Commission (Insight 8.2). While the EEC Commission made skilful use of these powers during its first decade to push forward the process of integration, the Euratom Commission failed to make any significant progress. Illness forced the resignation of its first President, Louis Armand, in the first year. Armand was replaced in February 1959 by Etienne Hirsch, a former colleague of Monnet's at the CdP (Chapter 6, p. 93). Delays over recruitment and establishing priorities meant that by the time the Euratom Commission really began work in 1960, the context in which it had been created had changed. In particular, the easing of the coal shortage and reduced concern about dependence on oil from the Middle East in the post-Suez period removed some of the urgency on the development of nuclear energy.

Insight 8.2 The Euratom Commission

The Euratom Commission consisted of five members, one from each member state except Luxembourg, which had no national nuclear-power programme. During its time, it had three Presidents, as follows.

- Louis Armand (1958–59)
- Etienne Hirsch (1959–62)
- Michel Chatenet (1963–67)

It was charged to ensure that the member states fulfilled the terms of the Treaty:

- it had the sole right to propose measures to this end to the Council of Ministers;
- it had a duty to oversee the implementation of agreements;
- it represented the Community in the negotiation of agreements with the outside world;
- it was answerable to the European Parliamentary Assembly (EPA) for the activities of the Community.

The delay in the start of Euratom operations also allowed national rivalries to become embedded. France, with the largest nuclear research programme, had expected the bulk of the subsidies available, but Italy and West Germany rapidly developed their programmes following agreement on Euratom. After 1959, France, which was then under the leadership of de Gaulle, was less enthusiastic about Euratom than it had been. The Hirsch Euratom Commission clashed with the French government over both the right of the Commission to inspect French plutonium facilities and the Commission's decision to divert funds to a joint programme of reactor development with the United States. On the first, Hirsch found no support in the Council of Ministers. On the second, however, the Commission won a majority vote in the Council. Yet even this victory was hollow, as the French government subsequently insisted that budgetary decisions be taken on the basis of unanimity. Thus, in both instances of conflict with the French government, the Commission's position was ultimately weakened. Further, de Gaulle refused to renominate Hirsch as President and his successor, Michel Chatenet, was less assertive in his leadership of the Commission.

From 1962 onwards, Euratom drifted into deeper crisis. In 1964, there was deadlock over the size of the budget, which was eventually resolved only at the cost of the Commission having to make massive cutbacks in the already modest remaining research programme. A second crisis in 1966 meant that Euratom went into the merger year of 1967 having to survive on the system of 'provisional twelfths' which allowed no more than one-twelfth of the previous year's budget to be spent each month until agreement was reached on the new budget.

A number of explanations have been offered for the failure of Euratom (Scheinmann 1967). First, because it dealt with a single functional sector, the Commission was unable to offer national governments trade-offs in other policy areas to secure deals on nuclear power. Second, the external environment that favoured the creation of Euratom had changed by the time it became operative. Moreover, internal rivalry between member states increased and was consolidated with the election of de Gaulle. France was particularly important here because the matter of nuclear power development was a key issue for the French government that was closely linked to the high politics issue of nuclear weapons. Perhaps the key weakness of the Euratom Commission was that it failed to develop a **transnational network** of interests around the nuclear energy issue that could create a momentum that would overcome national rivalries. In sum, while the Euratom Commission faced inevitable constraints, it also failed to deploy tactics that were important to the relative success of the EEC commission.

CONCLUSION

In the history of the ECSC and Euratom, we can see the struggle between *dirigisme* and free-market economics, the fragmentation of the supranational executives that was later to afflict the EC Commission, and the assertion of national control over supranational institutions, but also the first stirrings of independence among the **supranational institutions**.

The story of *dirigisme* versus free-market economics that is told here offers a warning against a simple assumption that the former is about unwarranted interference in the beneficent workings of the market, while the latter is about competition from which the consumer will benefit. In fact it was Monnet, the champion of a *dirigiste* approach, who wanted to create genuine competition in the market for steel by breaking up the German cartels, which were clearly organizations in restraint of trade. Among business elites, advocates of market economics are sometimes motivated more by a desire to avoid state regulation so as to leave them free to adopt collusive practices than they are by an abstract commitment to the public good. In the EC/EU, competition policy has proved to be an important supranational power (see Chapter 25).

The bureaucratization of the High Authority prefigured the bureaucratization of the EC Commission, which was to prove one of its weaknesses in the 1970s. Bureaucratization involved, among other things, the fragmentation of the High Authority into Directorates that operated in relative isolation from each other and formed tightly integrated 'policy communities' with key interest groups. This phenomenon is central to understanding the later history of the EC, and especially the operation of the Common Agricultural Policy (see Chapter 26).

Finally, the assertion of national control over the supranationalism of the High Authority and the Euratom Commission is clear. If we were to focus only on these forerunners of the EC Commission, the lesson to be drawn would have to be that the member states were suspicious of supranational tendencies in the institutions they had created, and were capable of restraining them. But the first stirrings of the supranational European Court of Justice (ECJ) offered a different lesson for the future. The body of case law that the ECJ began to build up was not particularly controversial, and was not widely noted at the time; it was, however, laying the basis for an independent supranational institution of the future (see Chapter 23).

KEY POINTS

The European Coal and Steel Community

- The High Authority was not as powerful as originally planned, but still had considerable formal independence.
- There was considerable suspicion of Monnet's *dirigiste* tendencies among national governments, which consequently nominated members to the High Authority who were mostly not sympathetic to Monnet's aims.
- Monnet tried to run the High Authority on informal lines, but it became internally divided and increasingly bureaucratized.
- Excess supply of coal led to a crisis in 1959. The Council of Ministers refused the High Authority emergency powers to deal with the crisis. This precipitated a collapse of morale in the High Authority.
- Despite its shortcomings, Monnet believed that the ECSC pioneered the development of a **Community method** of working.

Euratom

- By the time that Euratom began operation, the energy crisis that existed when it was negotiated had disappeared. Instead of a shortage of coal, there was a glut.
- Whereas France had the only developed programme of research on nuclear energy in the mid-1950s, by the end of the decade, Germany and Italy also had independent programmes in competition with that of France.
- The French government did not fully co-operate with the Euratom Commission and the Commission never managed to build a supportive network of industry groups or technical experts to help it to counter French obstructionism.

FURTHER READING

Several books are devoted to, or contain extensive sections on, the experience of the early communities: **W. Diebold Jr**, *The Schuman Plan: A Study in Economic Cooperation, 1950–1959* (New York: Praeger, 1962); **J. Gillingham**, *Coal, Steel, and the Rebirth of Europe, 1945–1955* (Cambridge: Cambridge University Press, 1991); **E. B. Haas**, *The Uniting of Europe: Political, Social and Economic Forces, 1950–1957* (Stanford, CA: Stanford University Press, 1968).

There is one indispensable work on the ECSC: **D. Spierenburg and R. Poidevin**, *The History of the High Authority of the European Coal and Steel Community: Supranationality in Action* (London: Weidenfeld, 1994).

On the Euratom, there is less. The most revealing piece is **L. Scheinmann**, 'Euratom: Nuclear Integration in Europe', *International Conciliation*, 563 (1967). There is also a discussion of the adoption of Euratom in **A. Milward**, *The European Rescue of the Nation State* (London: Routledge, 1992), 200–11.

 online resource centre **Visit the Online Resource Centre that accompanies this book for links to more information on the European Coal and Steel Community and Euratom: www.oxfordtextbooks.co.uk/orc/bache3e/**

Chapter 9

The European Economic Community: 1958–67

Chapter Overview

Soon after its creation, the European Economic Community (EEC) emerged as the most important of the three Communities. This chapter takes the story to the 1967 merger of the three Communities, which was effectively a takeover of Euratom and the European Coal and Steel Community (ECSC) by the EEC. In this time, the EEC's successful start in creating a **customs union** between the six member states was followed by setbacks in 1963 and 1965: the first when de Gaulle unilaterally rejected the British application for membership, and the second and more serious setback when he withdraw his ministers from Council of Ministers meetings. The eventual compromise on the second crisis damaged the morale of the Commission and undermined the prospects for further integration. The destiny of the project remained firmly in the hands of individual governments and not with **supranational institutions**, which was what de Gaulle had wanted.

... to lay the foundations for an ever closer union among the peoples of Europe.

(Preamble to the Treaty of Rome establishing the European Economic Community)

It was not obvious in 1957 which of the two new communities, the EEC or Euratom, would become the more important. Within a few years, though, Euratom had lost all momentum. Driven by the vigorous leadership of Commission President Walter Hallstein, the EEC made a successful start and achieved most of its objectives over most of the first decade of its existence. If attempts to create a European Political Community had been ambitious, the development of the EEC was no less so, although the political implications were less obvious. The explicit task was to create a **common market** within fifteen years. Nonetheless, the Treaty of Rome establishing the EEC implied political integration.

The institutional arrangements of the EEC followed those of the ECSC, with a supranational Commission as the equivalent of the High Authority, a Council of Ministers, and a Parliamentary Assembly. In addition, an Economic and Social Committee played an advisory role. Finally, the European Court of Justice (ECJ) was

---

Insight 9.1 The Institutional Arrangements of the EEC

The Commission consisted of nine Commissioners appointed by national governments: two each from France, Germany, and Italy; one each for Belgium, Luxembourg, and the Netherlands. While national appointees, Commissioners were not supposed to advocate national interests but to protect the European ideal. The Commission's primary tasks were to make proposals to the Council of Ministers and to implement the Treaty of Rome. (On the Commission, see Chapter 20.)

The Council of Ministers consisted of one representative from each member state. Provision was made for it to vote on proposals from the Commission by qualified majority vote (QMV). For these purposes, seventeen votes were allocated among the six member states: four each to France, Germany and Italy; two each for Belgium and the Netherlands; and one vote for Luxembourg. A qualified majority required twelve votes, ensuring that a decision required the support of at least four states. However, in the first stage, prior to the completion of the common market, it was agreed that all decisions would be taken by unanimity. (On the Council, see Chapter 21.)

The European Parliamentary Assembly (EPA) of 142 members was a purely consultative body. Although provision was made in the Treaty for direct election, initially the members were nominated by national parliaments from among their own members. (On the European Parliament, see Chapter 22.)

The ECJ was made up of seven judges: one from each member state, plus one appointed by the Council. (On the ECJ, see Chapter 23.)

---

established to interpret the provisions of the Treaty of Rome and to act as arbiter in disputes on Community decisions (Insight 9.1).

The Early Years: 1958–63

For the whole of its separate existence, the Commission of the EEC had only one President. Walter Hallstein had been the State Secretary in the Foreign Office of the Federal Republic of Germany, and had been in charge of the German team during the negotiation of the EEC. Hallstein's appointment was accepted unanimously, a remarkable development only twelve years after the war.

> The very lack of a sense of drama in the choice of a German for the most important of the new posts was not only a tribute to Hallstein's achievements and reputation but proof of giant progress since the Schuman plan.
>
> (Duchêne 1994: 309)

Close to Chancellor Adenauer in his views on western European integration, Hallstein was in no doubt about the political nature of the Commission. In a book published in 1962, he made clear that, in his view, the logic of economic integration not only leads on toward political unity, but it also involves political action itself.

We are not integrating economics, we are integrating policies ... 'Political integration' is not too bold and too grandiose a term to describe this process.

(Hallstein 1962: 66–7)

Hallstein was backed in this view of the role of the Commission by the energetic
Dutch Vice-President and Commissioner for Agriculture, Sicco Mansholt. Between
them, Hallstein and Mansholt gave vigorous leadership to the Commission, which,
according to one observer, constituted 'a relatively united, committed partisan organisation' (Coombes 1970: 259).

The morale of the Commission was increased by its success in getting the Council
of Ministers to agree to an acceleration of the timetable for the achievement of a customs union in 1962. It went on to broker agreement on the level of the common
external tariff (CET), and at the same time to negotiate acceptance of a Common
Agricultural Policy (CAP).

The EEC Treaty (Article 14; now removed) specified a precise timetable for the progressive reduction of internal tariffs. On the original schedule, it would have taken at
least eight years to get rid of all such tariffs. This rather leisurely rate of progress
reflected the concerns of specific industrial groups about the problems of adjustment
involved in the ending of national protection. However, once the Treaty was signed
and it became obvious that the common market was to become a reality, those same
industrial interests responded to the changed situation facing them. Even before the
Treaty came into operation on 1 January 1958, companies had begun to conclude
cross-border agreements on co-operation, or to acquire franchised retail outlets for
their products in other member states. Just as the neofunctionalists had predicted,
changing circumstances led to changed behaviour.

So rapid was the adjustment of corporate behaviour to the prospect of the common
market that impatience to see the benefits of the deals that were being concluded and of
the new investments that were being made soon led to pressure on national governments to accelerate the timetable. Remarkably, the strongest pressure came from French
industrial interests, which had opposed the original scheme for a common market.

On 12 May 1960, the Council of Ministers agreed to a proposal from the Commission
to accelerate progress on the removal of internal barriers to trade and the erection of a
common external tariff, and on the creation of the CAP. Pressure had come only for
the first of these to be accelerated. Progress was slow on agriculture, the negotiations
having been dogged by disagreements over the level of support that ought to be given
to farmers for different commodities. But the issues were clearly linked: progress on
the CAP to accompany progress on the industrial common market had been part of
the original deal embodied in the EEC Treaty.

It seemed that in keeping the linkage between the two issues in the forefront of all
of their proposals to the Council of Ministers, the Commission had played a manipulative role that coincided with the view of neofunctionalism about the importance of
central leadership. Indeed, it is possibly from the performance of the Commission in
this period that the importance of leadership from the centre was first theorized and
added to the emerging corpus of neofunctionalist concepts. As described by Lindberg
(1963: 167–205), the progress of the EEC between 1958 and 1965 involved the
Commission utilizing a favourable situation to promote integration. Governments
found themselves trapped between the growing demand from national interest groups

that they carry through as rapidly as possible their commitment to create a common market, and the insistence of the Commission that this could only happen if the governments were prepared to reach agreement on the setting of common minimum prices for agricultural products.

These agreements were engineered by the skilful use of the 'package deal': linking the two issues together, and not allowing progress on one without commensurate progress on the other. In that way, each member state would agree to things in which it was less interested in order to get those things in which it was more interested. It was just such a package deal that the French President Charles de Gaulle was to reject in spectacular fashion in 1965, plunging the EEC into crisis. However, before that, in 1963, there was a warning of the problems that lay ahead.

The 1963 Crisis

As Urwin (1995: 103) noted:

> To some extent, the Commission could be so active because the national governments, through the Council of Ministers had been content to allow it to be so. Even President de Gaulle had on the whole been quite circumspect about the Commission.

However, the Commission's influence and the apparent smooth progress of the EEC received a setback in January 1963 when President de Gaulle unilaterally vetoed the British government's application for membership. The most comprehensive history of this episode is Ludlow (1997), on which the following account is largely based.

Having declined the invitation to be present at the creation, Harold Macmillan announced in the House of Commons in July 1961 that the British government had decided to apply for membership of the EEC. The development was not welcomed by Walter Hallstein, who saw it as potentially disruptive to the smooth progress of integration among the six. It was also unwelcome to de Gaulle, who had ambitions to use the EEC as a platform for the reassertion of French greatness in international affairs.

To this end, de Gaulle tried to get agreement between the six on co-operation in foreign policy, which he believed that France would be able to dominate. From 1960, it was agreed that the Foreign Ministers of the member states would meet four times yearly. De Gaulle also developed a special relationship with the German Chancellor, Konrad Adenauer. This relationship was important in securing support for de Gaulle's plans to extend political co-operation between the six. The matter was subsequently considered by a committee chaired by the French official, Christian Fouchet (Insight 9.2). The Fouchet negotiations on political co-operation were taking place in 1961 when the British application was lodged, but they had already run into some difficulties over proposals for foreign and defence policy.

British entry did not fit de Gaulle's plans: it would have provided an alternative leadership for the four other member states, the governments of which were suspicious of him and wished to resist French domination. Technically, de Gaulle could have vetoed the application, but politically he was in no position to do so. In addition to Fouchet, there were negotiations proceeding in 1961 on two issues that were of crucial importance to France: the CAP, and new association terms for Africa. Also, de

---

Insight 9.2 The Fouchet Plan

In 1961, President de Gaulle proposed to the other members of the Communities that they consider forming what he called a Union of States. This would be an intergovernmental organization in which the institutions of the existing three Communities would play no role. It would involve the member states in pursuing closer co-operation on cultural, scientific, and educational matters, and, most significantly, in the co-ordination of their foreign and defence policies.

At summit meetings in 1961, it was agreed to set up a committee under the chairmanship of the French Ambassador to Denmark, Christian Fouchet, and subsequently to ask the committee to prepare a detailed plan for such co-operation.

This 'Fouchet Plan' proposed a confederation of states with a Council of Ministers, a Consultative Assembly of seconded national parliamentarians, and a Commission. However, unlike the Commissions of the EEC and Euratom, this Commission would not be a supranational body with independent powers, but would consist of officials from national Foreign Ministries.

Gaulle did not want to make it more difficult for the pro-French position of his ally Adenauer to prevail in Bonn.

The approach that de Gaulle chose to adopt was to allow negotiations on enlargement to open, but to instruct the French delegation to set the price high in the hope that the terms would prove unacceptable to the British government. The French position was presented as defending the Treaty of Rome and the *acquis communautaire*. Both had been so strongly influenced by French demands that their defence was almost the same as the defence of the French national interest. Because the French demands were couched in *communautaire* language, it was very difficult for the other member states to resist them. They were torn between support for British membership and a desire not to dilute the achievements of the EEC to date.

The negotiations did not collapse, but they went on for so long that de Gaulle was eventually presented with the excuse that he needed to issue his unilateral veto: the deal on nuclear weapons that was reached between Macmillan and US President John Kennedy at Nassau in December 1962. Macmillan persuaded Kennedy to sell Britain Polaris missiles to carry Britain's independent nuclear weapons. This was presented by de Gaulle as clear evidence that the British were not yet ready to accept a European vocation, and used as justification for ending negotiations that had stalled in late 1962 anyway.

The other member states reacted angrily to the veto. Given that the negotiations had run into difficulties, the anger was directed less at their enforced ending than at the way in which de Gaulle had undermined the system of collaborative working that had emerged in the six, and within which the others had operated throughout the negotiations.

The 1965 Crisis

A more fundamental and considerably more serious crisis began in July 1965, when de Gaulle withdrew France from participation in the work of the Council of Ministers in protest at a proposal from the Commission concerning the financing of the Community's budget.

Once agreement had been reached on the details of the CAP, the question arose of how the policy would be funded. For the first time, the EEC would have a budget that went beyond the salaries and administrative costs of the central institutions. The Commission proposed that instead of the cumbersome method of annual contributions negotiated between the member states, the Community should have its 'own resources'. These would be the revenue from the CET on industrial goods and the levies on agricultural goods entering the Community from outside, which would be collected by national customs officials at their point of entry into the EEC, and then handed over to Brussels, after the deduction of 10 per cent as a service charge. The justification was that the goods might be intended for consumption in any part of the Community, and it was therefore unreasonable that the revenue should accrue to the state through which the goods happened to enter the common market.

However, the French President questioned another aspect of the proposal. Using the method of the package deal, the Commission linked the idea of having its own resources with a proposal for an increase in the powers of the European Parliamentary Assembly (EPA), giving it the right to approve the budget. The argument for this was that if the revenues passed directly to the EEC without having to be approved by national parliaments, there would be a lack of democratic scrutiny, which could only be corrected by giving that right to the EPA.

President de Gaulle objected to this increase in the powers of a supranational institution, and when discussion became deadlocked, he showed how important he held the issue to be by imposing a French boycott of all Council of Ministers meetings from June 1965. This action was subsequently termed the 'empty chair crisis'. In essence, the dispute was about the very nature of the Europe that the six were hoping to build. For de Gaulle, primacy had to be given to the interests of national governments.

The Luxembourg Compromise

After six months, an agreement was reached between France and the other five member states in Luxembourg. The so-called 'Luxembourg Compromise' of January 1966 represented a considerable blow to the process of European integration. First, there was agreement not to proceed with the Commission's proposals: funding of the budget would continue to be by national contributions. Second, France demanded that there be no transition to majority voting in the Council of Ministers. This move had been envisaged in the original Treaties once the customs union was complete, and completion was on schedule for January 1966. Under the terms of the Luxembourg Compromise, governments would retain their right to veto proposals where they deemed a vital national interest to be at stake. This agreement was a serious blow to the hope of the Commission that brokering agreement on further integrative moves would be easier in the future.

Third, France made four other demands: that the President of the Commission should no longer receive the credentials of ambassadors to the EEC; that the information services be taken out of the hands of the Commission; that members of the Commission should be debarred from making political attacks on the attitudes of member states; and that the Commission should not reveal its proposals to the EPA before they were presented to the Council of Ministers, as it had with the controversial package on the budget.

The terms of the deal precipitated a collapse of morale in the Commission. In particular, the authority of Hallstein and Mansholt was undermined by the episode. Some Commissioners had warned against a confrontation with de Gaulle on supranationality, but Hallstein and Mansholt had overruled them (Camps 1967: 47). Neither was to regain the air of invincibility that he had acquired in the past. Hallstein withdrew his name from the list of nominations for the presidency of the new combined Commission of the ECSC, EEC, and Euratom that was due to take office on 1 July 1967, and simply served out the remainder of his term. Mansholt stayed on as a Commissioner, but did not put his name forward for the presidency.

CONCLUSION

The struggle between supranationalism and intergovernmentalism is the clear theme of this chapter. The neofunctionalist interpretation of the history of European integration seems to get both its strongest support and its greatest challenge from the period under consideration. The support comes from the story of the acceleration agreement as told by neofunctionalists (Chapter 1). Lindberg (1963) took the role of the Commission in the success of the EEC in the 1960s as clear evidence of its centrality to the process. The setback came from the actions of de Gaulle in vetoing British entry in 1963 and in boycotting the Council of Ministers in 1965.

The acceleration agreement resulted from pressure from business interests for an acceleration of the original timetable for the creation of the common market. This vindicates the neofunctionalist argument that changed circumstances change attitudes and behaviour. The exploitation of this demand by the Commission to lever the member states into accepting a general acceleration of their timetable, for the agricultural negotiations as well as for the reduction of industrial tariffs, vindicates the argument that the central supranational actor can act in conjunction with interest groups to push governments into taking further integrative steps.

However, it should be noted that this interpretation has been strongly contradicted in the intergovernmentalist tradition, notably by Andrew Moravcsik (1998: 159–237; see Chapter 1). It is also incontestable that the pressure came not from transnational interest groups, as neofunctionalist theory predicted that it would, but from national groups, especially French business interests. The linkage to agriculture was hardly a surprise given that the two issues had been linked in the original package, and the French government itself could not simply bow to the wishes of French business and ignore the wishes of French farmers.

Moravcsik's research indicated that the deals were not cut by the Commission but by the governments of other member states. He argued that 'the Commission was ineffective and repeatedly sidelined' (Moravcsik 1998: 233). Its proposals were often ignored, and were only successful when they paralleled proposals made by key member states. Although the Commission made the final proposal on which agreement was reached (as it had to under the rules of the EEC), this was often the opposite of what the Commission had originally proposed.

The 1965 dispute over the funding of the budget certainly illustrated the continued ability of national governments, even of a single national government, to stop the process of European integration in its tracks. It also prefigures, though, another theme that becomes more prominent later in the story. The Dutch government insisted that, if the budget was to be funded from the EC's own resources, the EPA must be given some control over the budget. The Dutch argument was that national parliaments would lose their ability to exercise democratic scrutiny and control of the budget once the own-resources system of financing was introduced, so to ensure that there was some democratic oversight, the EPA would have to be given some control. There is an aspect of spillover here. If the success of a policy is defined not only as the instrumental 'does it work', but also in terms of the extent to which it can be seen as an example of democratic decision making, there is spillover from the removal of decisions from national parliamentary control to the increase in the powers of the EPA, or later the European Parliament (EP). When this did not take place, there emerged a democratic deficit within the EC. Governments did not worry too much about the democratic deficit until it began to undermine the legitimacy of the EC in the eyes of their electorates. This was an early indication of the potential for such a democratic deficit to open up.

KEY POINTS

The Early Years: 1958–63

- The EEC Commission, under the presidency of Walter Hallstein, was very proactive in promoting integration.
- Its apparent successes included getting agreement from the member states to accelerate progress on creating the common market and the CAP.

The 1963 Crisis

- In 1961, President de Gaulle proposed intergovernmental political co-operation. Negotiations on the 'Fouchet Plan' were ongoing when Britain applied for EC membership.
- De Gaulle did not want to see Britain become a member, but rather than risk collapsing the Fouchet negotiations, he allowed negotiations on membership to begin while trying to ensure that French demands would make the terms of entry unacceptable to Britain.
- When the Fouchet negotiations came near to collapse, and the entry negotiations did not, de Gaulle unilaterally vetoed British entry.

The 1965 Crisis

- In 1965, the Commission proposed a system of financing the CAP that would have given the EEC its own financial resources. This was linked to a proposal to increase the budgetary powers of the EPA.
- De Gaulle rejected the increase in the powers of the EPA, and when agreement could not be reached, he withdrew France from participation in the work of the Council of Ministers.
- In January 1966, France resumed its place in the Council in exchange for the planned move to QMV be abandoned. This was accepted in the so-called 'Luxembourg Compromise'.
- The 'empty chair crisis' caused a crisis in the Commission.

FURTHER READING

When we get to the establishment of the EEC the range of reading extends considerably. For studies by historians, see **A. Milward**, *The European Rescue of the Nation State* (London: Routledge, 1992) and **A. Milward and A. Deighton (eds)**, *Widening, Deepening and Acceleration: The European Economic Community 1957–63* (Baden-Baden: Nomos, 1999). Also useful is the official history by **M. Dumoulin and M.-T. Bitsch**, *The European Commission, 1958–72: History* *and Memories* (Luxembourg: Office for Official Publications of the European Communities, 2007).

The standard political-science account of the early years of the EEC is **L. Lindberg**, *The Political Dynamics of European Economic Integration* (Stanford, CA: Stanford University Press; London: Oxford University Press, 1963); but this is rejected by **A. Moravcsik**, *The Choice for Europe: Social Purpose and State Power from Messina to Maastricht* (Ithaca, NY: Cornell University Press; London: UCL Press, 1998), 158–237.

On the British application in 1961, see **P. Ludlow**, *Dealing with Britain: The Six and the First UK Application to the EEC* (Cambridge: Cambridge University Press, 1997).

 online resource centre

Visit the Online Resource Centre that accompanies this book for links to more information on the European Economic Community:
www.oxfordtextbooks.co.uk/orc/bache3e/

Chapter 10

After Luxembourg: The 'Dark Ages' of European Integration?

Chapter Overview

If the period up to the 'empty chair' crisis was characterized by steady progress on integration, the decade following the Luxembourg Compromise began with limited expectations. Signs of a revival began with the Hague Conference in 1969, but the revival was limited by a downturn in economic circumstances. In addition, the accession of three new member states, two of which were opposed to supranationalism, made the prospects for further integration bleak. Although there were some achievements, scholars generally saw this period as a low point for European integration.

The period from the early 1970s to the early 1980s has often been characterized as the doldrums era or the 'Dark Ages' for the Community.

(Caporaso and Keeler 1995: 37)

Whereas the 1960s had been an era of high rates of economic growth within a reasonably stable (if militarily threatening) international environment, the 1970s were times of turbulence and flux in the international economic system. Three factors were particularly important: the collapse of the international monetary system in 1971 (Insight 10.1); the oil crisis in 1973; and the concurrence of low growth and high inflation (**stagflation**) producing economic divergence in the European Community (EC).

The economic recession that started in 1971 really began to bite after the December 1973 decision of the **Organization of the Petroleum Exporting Countries (OPEC)** to force a quadrupling in the price of oil. This context made governments more defensive and less inclined to agree to integrative measures that would weaken their ability to preserve domestic markets for domestic producers. As the economic context changed, the pace of European economic integration slowed and there was no advance towards political union. Uncertainty within member states restricted the scope for Commission activism. The Hallstein Commission was initially given tremendous credit for promoting integration in the period following the signing of the Treaties of Rome. However, subsequent reassessments suggested that in fact it had done little

Insight 10.1 The Collapse of the International Monetary System

The key aspects of the international monetary system were agreed at a conference at **Bretton Woods** in New Hampshire in 1944. These were the **International Monetary Fund (IMF)** and the International Bank for Reconstruction and Development (the '**World Bank**'). The **General Agreement on Tariffs and Trade (GATT)** was added later. The system worked with the United States playing a leading and directive role and provided a stability that was central to the prosperity of western European economies. However, the gradual erosion of US economic dominance in this period, culminating with the ending of the convertibility of US dollars to gold in 1971, marked the collapse of the Bretton Woods international system and a less secure international economic context.

beyond fill out the details of agreements that had been made between the member states in the Treaty of Rome.

If this view is correct, then for the Commission to play an active role required a new mandate from the member states. During this period, the Commission had four Presidents (Table 10.1). Neither Jean Rey nor Franco Malfatti had that mandate, and besides they were both preoccupied with the difficult issues involved in combining the three executive bodies of the European Coal and Steel Community (ECSC), European Economic Community (EEC), and Euratom into a single Commission.

When a new mandate was given, at a summit meeting in The Hague in December 1969, it involved completion of the financing arrangements for the EC budget, enlargement to take in Britain and the other applicant states, progress to economic and monetary union, and trying to develop a common foreign policy. The first of these was easily accomplished. The second was successfully carried through for three of the four applicants, but at considerable cost in terms of time and resources for the Commission. Economic and monetary union might have been the mandate that the Commission needed to produce a new impetus to integration, but as Tsoukalis (1977) argued, this decision was more akin to the decision to negotiate on the EEC than it was to the Treaty of Rome itself. As we shall see, this proved to be an intractable issue. Progress on co-ordination of foreign policy was made in a purely intergovernmental framework.

Not only were these issues more difficult in themselves, but also the overall context of the period was unfavourable to further integration. The Luxembourg agreement that ended the French boycott in January 1966 (Chapter 9, pp. 129–30) effectively meant

Table 10.1 Presidents of the Commission, 1967–77

1967–70	Jean Rey (Belgium)
1970–72	Franco Maria Malfatti (Italy)
1972	Sicco Mansholt (the Netherlands)
1973–77	François-Xavier Ortoli (France)

that the national veto was retained on all matters that came before the Council of Ministers. Although the Commission had operated with a veto system in the 1960s, the further integration progressed, the more likely it was that particular vested interests would come under challenge, and that individual states would try to block measures. The problem was exacerbated by enlargement, which brought into membership two more states, Britain and Denmark, which were opposed to supranationalism. The cumulative effect of these developments was to ensure that the second decade of the EEC was not marked by the rapid progress on integration that had marked the first decade.

This chapter examines in more detail the Hague Summit and its attempt to relaunch the European project; it assesses the degree of success achieved in each of the four main objectives. It also looks briefly at the origins of one of the major institutional innovations of the period: the formalization of the periodic summit meetings of heads of government as the European Council.

The Hague Summit

The resignation of President de Gaulle in April 1969 appeared to free the way to further integration. De Gaulle was succeeded by his former Prime Minister, Georges Pompidou, who soon let it be known that he did not object in principle to British membership.

Also in 1969, there was a change of government in Germany. The SPD, which had been the junior coalition partner to the Christian Democrats for the previous three years, became the larger partner in a coalition with the Free Democrat Party (FDP). Willy Brandt, the new Chancellor, intended to pursue an active policy of improving relations with the communist bloc, but was anxious to demonstrate that this *Ostpolitik* did not imply any weakening of German commitment to the EC.

As a result of these two changes, a summit meeting of heads of government was convened in The Hague in December 1969 with the explicit aim of relaunching European integration. This Hague Summit declared the objectives of completion, widening, and deepening. Completion meant tidying up the outstanding business from the 1965 crisis: moving the EC budget from dependence on national contributions to a system of financing from its own resources. Widening meant opening accession negotiations with Britain and other likely applicants. Deepening meant taking the next steps in the process of European integration, specifically in the direction of economic and monetary union and closer political co-operation. The objectives of completion and widening were successfully met; less so the objective of deepening.

Completion

Completion was achieved relatively easily. A system was agreed for the EC to have as its own resources the levies on agricultural products entering the EC under the Common Agricultural Policy (CAP), and the revenues from the common customs tariff on imports of non-agricultural products from outside of the EC.

There were the usual compromises, but France did accept some budgetary role for the European Parliament (EP), giving it the right to propose amendments to those parts of the budget that were not classified as 'compulsory expenditure' under the Treaties, and to propose modifications to the items of 'compulsory' expenditure. The Council of Ministers, acting by qualified majority, could amend the amendments, and could refuse to agree to the modifications, so in effect it retained the final say on the budget. The distinction between compulsory and non-compulsory expenditure defined expenditure under the CAP as compulsory, so making the bulk of the budget difficult for the EP to amend. Nevertheless, there was an acknowledgement that the EP should have some role in scrutinizing the budget, and there was the prospect that deepening would lead to a larger budget in which agriculture was not so dominant, so there would be more areas of non-compulsory expenditure.

Widening

Negotiations with four applicant states—Britain, Ireland, Denmark, and Norway—opened in June 1970, and were successfully completed by January 1972. Referendums were then held on membership in Ireland, Denmark, and Norway. The first two produced clear majorities in favour of entry, but in September 1972, the Norwegian people, not for the last time, rejected membership. In Britain, the Conservative government of Edward Heath refused to hold a referendum, arguing that it was not a British constitutional instrument—but parliamentary ratification was successfully completed. So on 1 January 1973, the six became nine.

While enlargement achieved the objective of widening the membership of the EC, it was to cause problems as well. The new member states entered at a time when the economic growth of the 1960s had already started to slow and was about to receive a further setback when OPEC quadrupled the price of oil in December 1973 (above, p. 133). Not having experienced the positive benefits of membership, neither the governments nor the peoples of these new member states had the same degree of psychological commitment to the idea of European integration as had those of the original six members. In addition, in Britain in particular there was considerable scepticism about the merits of the EC. Edward Heath was personally strongly committed to membership, but he never managed entirely to convince his own Conservative Party; Heath was soon displaced as Prime Minister when he lost the general election early in 1974, and Harold Wilson once again formed a Labour government.

While in opposition, the Labour Party had been riven with dissension, and membership of the EC had been a central issue. Several of Wilson's cabinet ministers from 1964 to 1970 were committed to British membership. Wilson himself was also convinced of the necessity of membership. But a majority in the party was still opposed, and the pressure from this majority meant that Wilson could not give unqualified approval to entry when Heath negotiated it. On the other hand, his own certainty that membership was necessary, and the importance of the pro-membership minority within the leadership of the party, made it impossible for him to oppose entry. The result was an ingenious compromise of opposition to entry on the terms negotiated by the Conservative government. Labour went into the 1974 election committed to a full renegotiation of the terms of entry, with a threat (or promise) of withdrawal if 'satisfactory' terms could not be agreed.

The renegotiation involved serious disruption to other business in the EC, at a time when there were several important issues on the agenda. It also involved a great deal of posturing and nationalist rhetoric from the British government. What it did not involve was any fundamental change in the terms of entry. Nevertheless, the renegotiated terms were put to the British people in a referendum in June 1975, with a recommendation from the government that they be accepted, which they were.

The two-to-one vote in the referendum in favour of Community membership was a passing moment of public favour. Soon the opinion polls were again showing majorities against membership. Britain had joined at a bad time, and the continuing economic difficulties of the country could conveniently be blamed on the EC. Although the Labour opponents of membership had to accept, for the time being, the verdict of the referendum, they lost no opportunity to attack the EC, and Wilson was prepared to accept this if it diverted attention away from his failure to solve the economic difficulties of Britain. He himself continued to take a strongly nationalistic line in EC negotiations, as did his Foreign Secretary, James Callaghan, who succeeded him as Prime Minister in March 1976.

By succeeding in widening its membership, the EC placed another barrier in the way of further integration. Yet it is a mistake to blame Britain alone for blocking further integration. Certainly, Britain became an awkward partner—but as Buller (1995: 36) argued: '[E]verybody consciously attempts to be obstructive every now and again in European negotiations. It is all part and parcel of politics in this kind of environment.' The degree of awkwardness of all member states increased during this period of economic problems.

Deepening

Attempts at deepening co-operation between member states met with limited success. The two main objectives agreed at The Hague were 'economic and monetary union by 1980' and the creation of a common foreign policy.

Economic and Monetary Union (EMU)

This was the logical next step in the building of the EC. **Economic union** meant that the member states would, at most, cease to follow independent economic policies, and at least would follow co-ordinated policies. This would remove distortions to free competition and would help to make a reality of the **common market**. Monetary union meant, at most, the adoption of a single Community currency; at least, the maintenance of fixed exchange rates between the currencies of the member states.

In 1969, there were the first major realignments of member states' currencies since the EC had started, and the prospect of monetary instability threatened to hinder trade within the common market by introducing an element of uncertainty into import and export deals. In this context, monetary union was seen as a means of making the common market effective.

Following the Hague Summit, a Committee was set up under the chairmanship of Pierre Werner, the Prime Minister of Luxembourg, to produce concrete proposals on EMU. It reported within a few months, and in February 1971, the Council of Ministers adopted a programme for the achievement of EMU in stages between 1971 and 1980. The institutional centrepiece of the scheme was the 'snake in the tunnel': an arrangement for approximating the exchange rates of member currencies one to another while holding their value jointly in relation to the US dollar. It was to be accompanied by more determined efforts to bring national economic policies into line, with Finance Ministers meeting at least three times per year to try to co-ordinate policies. Thus there would be progress on both monetary and economic union, the two running in parallel.

The 'snake' did not last long in its original form. It was destroyed by the international monetary crisis that followed the ending of the convertibility of the dollar in August 1971. Only after the **Smithsonian agreements** of late 1971 had restored some semblance of order to the world monetary system was it possible to attempt once again a joint Community currency arrangement, this time with the participation of the four states that had just completed the negotiation of their entry to the EC. That was in April 1972—but it took under two months for this second snake to break apart. In June, the British government had to remove sterling from the system and float it on the international monetary markets. Italy was forced to leave in February 1973. France followed in January 1974, rejoined in July 1975, but was forced to leave again in the spring of 1976. In every case, the currency had come under so much speculative pressure that it had proved impossible to maintain its value against the other currencies in the system.

By 1977, the snake had become a very different creature from that which had been envisaged. Of the nine members of the EC, only West Germany, the **Benelux** states, and Denmark were still members (Ireland had left with Britain, the Irish punt being tied to the pound sterling at that time). In addition, two non-member states, Norway and Sweden, had joined. Yet during 1977, even this snake was under strain, and Sweden was forced to withdraw the krona.

European Political Co-operation (EPC)

This was the more successful attempt at deepening, ironically since it was only included in the Hague objectives as a concession to France. President Pompidou was dependent for his majority in the French National Assembly on the votes of the Gaullist Party of which he was himself a member. De Gaulle had opposed giving budgetary powers to the EP, and Pompidou agreed to this at The Hague. De Gaulle had also opposed British entry to the EC. He had made it clear when a second British application was tabled in May 1967 that there was no point in entering into negotiations, because he would veto British membership. Pompidou had made it equally clear that he was prepared to enter into negotiations, and perhaps even to accept British membership if satisfactory terms could be agreed. Both of these departures from Gaullist orthodoxy were controversial in his own party, and he needed concessions at The Hague in order to be able to sell the package to this domestic constituency.

One of de Gaulle's pet projects had been to set up a system of intergovernmental political co-operation between the member states of the EC. This was the basis of the Fouchet Plan, which had been under discussion at the same time as the first British application, and had finally collapsed as a result of the French veto on British entry (Chapter 9, p. 127). It was therefore unsurprising that Pompidou should look for a commitment to revive this project as part of the price for his co-operation on completion and widening. It was agreed at The Hague to set up a committee under the chairmanship of Viscount Etienne Davignon, a senior official in the Belgian Foreign Ministry, to devise machinery for co-operation between the member states on foreign policy issues. This committee reported in October 1970, and the system that it recommended became the basis for some successful diplomatic initiatives. Indeed, EPC came to be seen as one of the few achievements in the 1970s.

One of the successes was the formulation of a common position on the Middle East, which allowed the EC to pursue its clear interest in improving trade with the Arab OPEC states in the 1970s, through the Euro–Arab dialogue. In 1980, this common policy culminated in the Venice Declaration, which went further than the United States was prepared to go in recognizing the right of the Palestinians to a homeland. The nine member states were also extremely successful in formulating a common position at the Conference on Security and Co-operation in Europe (CSCE) in Helsinki in 1975, and at the follow-up conferences in Belgrade in 1977, and Madrid in 1982–83. Again, the common position adopted by the EC ran somewhat contrary to the position of the United States, which regarded the Helsinki process with some suspicion as running the risk of legitimating communist rule in eastern Europe. Third, the Community states achieved a high degree of unity in the United Nations, voting together on a majority of resolutions in the General Assembly, and developing a reputation for being the most cohesive group there at a time when group diplomacy was becoming much more common.

Admittedly there were also failures for the policy of EPC. On balance, though, there were more substantive successes than there were failures. However, all of this remained officially intergovernmental, rather than being rolled up into the more supranational procedures of the EC, so there was a question mark over whether it could be considered to be an advance for the process of European integration. On the other hand, the actual working of the system was less strictly intergovernmental than the formal procedures, a point that is explored further in Chapter 33 (see pp. 510–12).

The European Council

Mid-way through this period, there were again coinciding changes of government in both France and Germany, which strengthened the Franco–German relationship. Georges Pompidou died in office in 1974, and was succeeded by Valéry Giscard d'Estaing, who was not a Gaullist, although he was dependent on the Gaullist Party for a majority in the National Assembly. In Germany, Brandt resigned following the discovery that an East German spy had been part of his personal staff, and was succeeded by his former Finance Minister, Helmut Schmidt.

These changes brought to office two strong national leaders who had an excellent *rapport*, and who dominated the EC for the next six years. They were not, though, particularly committed to reviving the process of supranational integration. Their approach was pragmatic rather than ideological, and they were prepared to use any instruments that presented themselves to deal with the problems that their countries faced.

In 1974, Giscard called a summit meeting to discuss his proposal that the EC should institutionalize summit meetings. The smaller member states were suspicious of this proposal, which sounded very Gaullist, but Giscard got strong backing from Schmidt, and it was agreed to hold meetings of the heads of state and government three times every year under the title the 'European Council'. At the same time, as a concession to the fears of those governments who saw in this a weakening of the supranational element of the EC, agreement was reached to hold direct elections to the EP in 1978. The British government was reconciled to this by concessions on the renegotiation of its terms of entry that was taking place at the same time.

Direct elections were not actually held until 1979 because the British government was unable to pass the necessary domestic legislation in time to hold the election in 1978. In the long run, the decision to hold direct elections was far from insignificant. In the short to medium term, though, the creation of the European Council was much the more significant outcome of Paris, 1974.

The European Council was, from the outset, an intergovernmental body. It had no basis in the Treaties until the Single European Act came into force in July 1987. It became the overarching institution of the EU in the 1992 Maastricht Treaty. In the 1970s, it was symbolic of a profoundly intergovernmental era in the history of the EU. However, it later presided over a set of major Treaty reforms and policy initiatives (Chapter 21, pp. 274–80).

CONCLUSION

In this period, when US hegemony began to falter, the EC had to deal with an increasingly turbulent international environment. The theme of the impact of the wider system on developments within the EC (Chapter 3) is clearly illustrated here, particularly trends in international political economy. The retreat into covert national protectionism, to preserve jobs for nationals, was a direct consequence of the shadow that recession cast over the process of European integration. The sceptical attitudes of the British and Danish people to the advantages of European integration were not produced by the recession, but the failure of membership of the EC to produce tangible economic benefits reinforced their prejudices.

The other part of the explanation for developments in this period is provided by the continuing importance of domestic politics. In the original six member states, the compromise on the principle of an ever closer union of the peoples of Europe reflected both the shallowness of that commitment among the political elites, and the fact that, to retain office, they needed to win votes among their own electorate. One of the consistent paradoxes of European integration has been an increasing divorce between politics and policy in the EC. Politics has remained firmly national, while policy has become increasingly Europeanized. This tension existed even in the early stages of the process, and the adverse economic conditions of the 1970s exposed it graphically.

Domestic politics can also be seen at work in the attitude of the British Labour government to the renegotiation of Britain's terms of entry to the EC. The objectives of the renegotiation could have been achieved—perhaps could have more easily been achieved—through the normal process of intergovernmental negotiations within the context of the EC. That the demands were made into a high-profile renegotiation was primarily due to the need of the Prime Minister, Harold Wilson, to satisfy the critics of EC membership within his own party, and to convince the British people that he had won a series of 'victories' on their behalf in the negotiations. The disruption that this approach caused to the functioning of the EC was a high price to pay, but the tension between domestic politics and European integration is again very apparent, as in this case is the primacy of domestic politics.

The impact of international economic factors and domestic politics was to apply the brakes to supranationalism. The main innovations of the period were the creation of the European Council, which to a large extent was an attempt to reclaim leadership of the EC for national heads of government, and the beginning of EPC, an intergovernmental process of co-ordinating foreign policy. The main integrative initiative, the 'snake in the tunnel' system designed to move the EC towards monetary union, collapsed in the face of the global turbulence in currency markets. There was little in the period onto which the neofunctionalists could cling as evidence of their theory being vindicated.

KEY POINTS

The Hague Summit

- Changes of leadership in France and Germany in 1969 appeared to free the way for further European integration. The result was the Hague Summit, which declared the objectives of completion, deepening, and widening.

- *Completion* was achieved through allowing the EC to have its own resources for the first time. The EP was also given some budgetary powers.

- *Widening* was achieved through the entry of Britain, Denmark, and Ireland into the EC in 1973.

- *Deepening* of co-operation on foreign policy through EPC had some success; less so co-operation on monetary union.

The European Council

- In 1974, Giscard d'Estaing called for the institutionalization of summit meetings of EC heads of state and government. He received support for this from Helmut Schmidt.

- It was agreed that these meetings be institutionalized under the auspices of the European Council and would be held three times each year.

- The creation of the European Council symbolized a profoundly intergovernmental period in the history of European integration.

FURTHER READING

This whole period is dealt with extensively by **D. W. Urwin**, *The Community of Europe: A History of European Integration since 1945*, 2nd edn (London and New York: Longman, 1995), 146–79. **K. Middlemass**, *Orchestrating Europe: The Informal Politics of European Union, 1973–1995* (London: Fontana, 1995), 73–110, calls the years between 1973 and 1983 'The Stagnant Decade'. **A. Moravcsik**, *The Choice for Europe: Social Purpose and State Power from Messina to Maastricht* (London: UCL Press, 1998), 238–313, focuses on monetary co-operation and the European Monetary System. The official history of British negotiations for entry is available in **C. O'Neill**, *Britain's Entry into the European Community: Report by Sir Con O'Neill on the Negotiations of 1970–72* (London: Frank Cass, 2000). For the 1973 enlargement in broader context, see **W. Kaiser and J. Elvert (eds)**, *European Union Enlargement: A Comparative History* (London: Routledge, 2004).

 online resource centre **Visit the Online Resource Centre that accompanies this book for links to more information on European integration after the Luxembourg Compromise: www.oxfordtextbooks.co.uk/orc/bache3e/**

Chapter 11

The European Community into the 1980s

Chapter Overview

The early 1970s marked a low point in European integration, but signs emerged in the late 1970s of the European Community (EC) turning a corner. A revived Commission, led by Roy Jenkins, secured agreement to be involved in international economic summits; the European Monetary System (EMS) was set up; and membership applications from Greece, Portugal, and Spain reflected positively on the external reputation of the EC. However, new problems also surfaced in this period: most notably the British government's claim for a rebate on its contributions to the EC budget. By the mid-1980s, though, important domestic political changes and the resolution of the British rebate claim had provided a platform for the relaunch of European integration.

European integration was considered dead in the water in the 1970s and barely ten years later the European Community was being hailed as the new superpower for the twenty-first century.

(Mutimer 1994: 42)

Institutional Developments

The authority of the European Commission was strengthened by the presidency of Roy Jenkins between 1977 and 1981. Jenkins was an established political figure with considerable experience in government. He had held all of the major posts in the British cabinet other than Prime Minister. As such, his appointment raised great expectations amongst those who regretted the decline in the authority of the Commission. Perhaps not all of those expectations were fulfilled. However, Jenkins did enhance the position of the President, and therefore of the Commission, by securing agreement from the heads of state and government that he should be present at meetings of the international economic summits, which had previously been restricted to the leaders of the major industrial nations. This development was strongly resisted by French President

Giscard d'Estaing, but was strongly supported by the smaller member states, who felt excluded from an important economic decision-making forum, and who therefore wished to see the President of the Commission present acting as a spokesperson for the EC as a whole (Jenkins 1989: 20–2).

Jenkins also undertook a fundamental reform of the internal structure of the Commission, attempting, against considerable opposition from vested interests, to remove some of the causes of the bureaucratization that had been identified as one of the reasons for its decline in influence (Jenkins 1989: 310, 376). Although he was not completely successful, he did have some impact, and the strong leadership he demonstrated in tackling this problem was probably responsible for earning him the nickname 'Roi Jean Quinze', although this was also suggestive of his grand manner.

The other significant institutional development in this period was the introduction of direct elections to the European Parliament (EP) in 1979. Until this point, the demands of the EP for greater powers had always been countered by the argument that it lacked democratic legitimacy because it was only an indirectly elected body. After it became directly elected, the EP was in a much stronger position to extract new powers from the member states. The decision to move to direct elections was made at the Rome European Council in December 1975 (Chapter 22, p. 297). Further controversy had followed when the first elections were delayed for a year because of the failure of the British Parliament to pass the necessary enabling legislation in time for the May/June 1978 date agreed at Rome. However, the elections in June 1979 were relatively low-key affairs within the member states, with national parties taking a prominent role in the selection of candidates and campaign organization.

The European Monetary System

In the policy field, there was one very significant development in the late 1970s. The decision taken at the Brussels European Council in December 1978 to create the European Monetary System (EMS) did not exactly constitute a revival of EMU, but it did provide a basis for a future step in that direction.

As explained in the previous chapter, the 'snake' had, by 1977, become a system that embraced only five member states of the EC, together with two non-members. During 1977, even this truncated snake was under pressure from international speculation, and Sweden was forced to withdraw. In this far-from-promising context, Jenkins launched an initiative that met with a certain amount of initial scepticism about its feasibility even from colleagues within the Commission. In a lecture at the European University Institute in Florence, in October 1977, he called for a new attempt to start the EMU experiment (Jenkins 1977).

The following year, Helmut Schmidt and Giscard d'Estaing came up with a joint proposal for what became the EMS. In July 1978, the European Council meeting in Bremen agreed to pursue the idea, and in December 1978, meeting in Brussels, agreed to create what looked remarkably like another snake. It would be more flexible than its predecessor, allowing wider margins of fluctuation for individual currencies, and it would be accompanied by the creation of a new European currency unit (ecu). The ecu would take its value from a basket of the national currencies of the member states, and it would be used in transactions within the EMS. A stock of ecus would be created by each member state depositing 20 per cent of its gold and 20 per cent of its foreign currency reserves with a European Monetary Fund (EMF). If a government was having difficulty in holding the value of its currency in relation to the other currencies in the system, it could apply to the EMF for short-term loans, and later if necessary for medium-term loans, up to a predetermined limit, from the central reserve. The loans would be denominated in ecus. It was hoped that ecus would gradually become the normal means of settlement of international debts between EMS members, thus forming the basis of a common Community currency.

In addition to France and West Germany, the **Benelux** states and Denmark supported the EMS. After initial hesitation, Italy and Ireland agreed to become full participants. But Britain declined to put sterling into the joint float against the dollar, although it was included in the basket from which the value of the ecu was calculated. Despite the scepticism that had greeted Jenkins's initiative, the EMS did get off the ground, and this time the system did hold together, so that the scheme must be judged a relative success in the context of the overall history of attempts to move towards EMU (see also Chapter 28, pp. 403–4).

The Southern Enlargements

In 1974, two significant events took place in southern Europe: Turkey invaded Cyprus, and a revolution in Portugal overthrew the right-wing Caetano government. Each led to an application for membership of the EC. Subsequently, political developments in Spain led to a Spanish application.

Greece had concluded an Association Agreement with the EC in 1964. This had envisaged eventual membership, but in 1967, Greece entered a period of military dictatorship that precluded an application. The inability of the Greek military to prevent the Turkish occupation of Cyprus precipitated the collapse of the dictatorship, and in June 1975, the new democratic Greek government sought membership of the EC as a means of consolidating democracy. In January 1976, the Commission issued a very cautious Opinion on the ability of Greece to adapt to membership, but political and strategic considerations led the Council of Ministers to accept the application and order the opening of negotiations. Democracy had to be shored up—but also Greece had to be prevented from swinging to the far left and reorienting itself towards the communist bloc. The negotiation of terms of entry for Greece was not easy, and it took up a great deal of the time of the Commission between July 1976 and May 1979, when the Accession Treaty was signed (membership began in January 1981). Nevertheless, the launching of the negotiations gave a new role to the Commission and put it back at the centre of the EC.

An application from Portugal followed the Greek application in March 1977. Again, there were political and strategic reasons for accepting it. The Portuguese revolution threatened to run out of the control of the pro-capitalist forces, and to fall into the hands of extreme left-wing groups that would have emphasized relations with the Third World. The Socialist International, with the German Social Democratic Party (SPD) taking a lead, provided support to the Portuguese Socialist Party (PSP), and so when the PSP was elected to government in 1976, there was not much doubt that it would apply for EC membership, nor that the application would be accepted.

Similar political and strategic considerations applied in July 1977 to the acceptance of an application from Spain following the death of the dictator Franco and the restoration of democracy there. In the Spanish case, membership of the EC was held out as a bonus if it decided also to join the NATO alliance. Given Spain's strategic position in the Mediterranean, this was a vital interest of the western alliance.

Whereas the first of these applications stimulated a revival of the role of the Commission, handling three sets of difficult negotiations became a problem, and the Portuguese and Spanish Accession Treaties were not signed until 1985 (membership began in January 1986).

The British Budget Rebate

Another issue that caused problems for the EC in the 1980s was the British budgetary rebate. Although budget contributions had been central to the renegotiation, already by 1976, while transitional arrangements still limited the extent of its contributions, Britain was the third biggest net contributor to the EC budget, behind Germany and Belgium. In 1977, still under transitional arrangements, the British net contribution was the second highest to that of Germany. By mid-1978, it was becoming apparent that, once the transitional period of membership ended in 1980, Britain would become the largest net contributor to the budget.

This situation arose for the following reasons.

(1) Britain imported more goods, especially foodstuffs, from outside the EC than did other member states, and therefore paid more in import levies.

(2) Low direct taxes meant that British consumers spent more in proportion to the relative wealth of the country, and Britain therefore contributed more to the budget in VAT receipts.

(3) Payments out of the budget were dominated by the Common Agricultural Policy (CAP), and Britain had a small and efficient farming sector that meant that it received less than states with larger agricultural economies.

The developing position was unacceptable to the Labour government. The Foreign Secretary, David Owen, told the House of Commons that the situation whereby 'the United Kingdom has the third lowest per capita gross domestic product in the Community' yet was already the second highest net contributor to the budget, 'cannot be good for the Community any more than it is for the United Kingdom', and promised that the government would 'be working to achieve a better balance, especially in relation to agricultural expenditure, to curb the excessive United Kingdom contribution' (Hansard, 14 November 1978, col. 214).

In fact, the Labour government never had the opportunity to work for a better balance because it lost office in the June 1979 election to the Conservatives under Margaret Thatcher. The new government soon took up the same theme concerning the budget. Shortly after coming into office, Sir Geoffrey Howe, the Chancellor of the Exchequer, announced that the size of the problem was far greater than the Conservatives had realized while in opposition, and something would have to be done about it urgently.

Margaret Thatcher and the Battle for a Rebate

Margaret Thatcher raised the issue at her first European Council in Strasbourg in June 1979, soon after her election victory. Her presentation there was moderate and reasonable, and the complaint was offset by an announcement on the first day of the meeting that Britain would deposit its share of gold and foreign currency reserves with the European Monetary Co-operation Fund that had been set up to administer the EMS. The move was widely interpreted as a sign that sterling would soon join the exchange rate mechanism of the EMS. Discussion of the budgetary issue at Strasbourg was brief and limited to agreeing a procedure for analysing the problem. The Commission was asked to prepare a report by September; this would be discussed by Finance Ministers, then revised in time for the next European Council in Dublin in late November.

At that November 1979 Dublin European Council, Thatcher adopted an entirely different tone. She insisted that the Commission proposal of a rebate of £350 million was unacceptable, and that she would not accept less than £1 billion. The French said that they would not agree to more than £350 million, which the British would have to accept as full and final settlement of their claim. This provoked an argument that lasted ten hours, in the course of which Thatcher upset her partners by her uncompromising demands for what she insensitively described as Britain's 'own money back'.

This was the tone that Thatcher persistently adopted in negotiations for the next four-and-a-half years. During that time, several temporary abatements of the British contributions were agreed, but a permanent settlement eluded all efforts to bridge the gap between what the British Prime Minister demanded and what the other member states were prepared to pay. British tactics became increasingly obstructionist on other issues, and relations with the other states became increasingly strained.

Relations reached their nadir in May 1982. Britain was blocking agreement on agricultural price increases for 1982–83, linking agreement to a permanent settlement of the budgetary dispute. Finally, the Belgian presidency called a majority vote on the agricultural prices. Britain protested that this breached the Luxembourg Compromise, but the vote went ahead and was passed. Several of the other states, though, appeared shocked at their own behaviour. It seemed apparent that a settlement of the British dispute was necessary before progress could be made in other areas.

Leadership Changes

The confluence of challenges facing the EC at the beginning of the 1980s coincided with the appointment of Gaston Thorn to the Commission presidency in 1981. Member States generally welcomed Thorn's appointment. Although he took over at a difficult time, there was a feeling that he was uniquely well qualified for the job, as few people had a wider experience of the EC. Early in his presidency, there were two significant changes among the national leaderships with which Thorn would have to work.

In May 1981, François Mitterrand defeated Giscard d'Estaing in the French presidential election. This result was consolidated a month later by a victory for Mitterrand's Socialist Party in elections to the National Assembly. The change broke apart the Franco-German axis because Helmut Schmidt had less in common with the Socialist President than he had with the conservative Giscard. In particular, the Socialist government came into office committed to tackling unemployment rather than emphasizing low inflation as its predecessor government had done. However, a U-turn in economic policy in 1983 brought France more into line with the neo-liberal and deregulationist tendencies already evident in West Germany and Britain.

The second change in political leadership came in West Germany itself. Although the SPD/Free Democrat Party (FDP) won the 1980 Federal election, dissension within the coalition was increasing in the face of the economic problems the country was facing. Within the SPD, the left-wing and the trade unionist membership were demanding some measures of reflation to relieve unemployment, which in 1981 stood at one-and-a-quarter million. But at the same time, the FDP was returning to its basic principles of economic liberalism, represented most strikingly by the Economics Minister, Count Otto Lambsdorff. The clash between the two parties over economic affairs led to the eventual breakdown of the coalition. The FDP changed partners and allowed the Christian Democratic Union (CDU)/Christian Social Union (CSU) into office, with Helmut Kohl, the CDU leader, as Chancellor.

Moves to Revive the EC

By the start of the 1980s, there was an acceptance within both national governments and the Commission that the response to challenges facing the EC required, in part at least, institutional reform to facilitate easier and more effective decision making.

The first response came in September 1981 from the foreign ministers of Germany and Italy, and was known as the Genscher–Colombo Plan. This plan called for a new European Charter that would supersede the Treaties of Paris and Rome as the basic constitutional document of the Communities, and would bring European political co-operation, together with the EC, under the joint direction of the European Council. This would only be a formalization of the existing situation, although Genscher and Colombo also wished to improve the decision-making ability of the Council of Ministers by increasing the use of majority voting, to expand the functions of the European Parliament, and to intensify foreign policy co-operation in security matters.

The plan received a cool response in the Council, as had an earlier proposal led by Altiero Spinelli—now a senior figure in the European Parliament—that sought to diminish the institutional position of the Council in favour of the Parliament and Commission. Yet while these two sets of proposals made no immediate impact on integration, they contributed to the European Council beginning a new round of negotiations on the question of political union and possible revision of the Treaties.

On the economic front, attempts by Thorn and his Vice-President and Commissioner for the Internal Market, Karl-Heinz Narjes, to highlight the problems faced by industrialists in trading across national borders within the EC met with little response from national governments. Governments were determined to reserve jobs for their own nationals (read 'voters') by tolerating, or even themselves erecting, non-tariff barriers to trade, and by giving public contracts exclusively to national companies. Yet Thorn, Narjes, and particularly Vice-President Etienne Davignon, the Commissioner for Industrial Policy, laid the groundwork for the agreement that was concluded under the following Delors presidency to free the internal market of all of these obstacles by the end of 1992 (see Chapter 12, p.155).

Thorn and Narjes maintained a constant propaganda campaign against barriers to a genuine internal market. This campaign had an effect in raising awareness of the issue, especially when it was taken up by a group of members of the European Parliament (MEPs) who called themselves the Kangaroo Group because they wanted to facilitate trade that would 'hop over' national boundaries. The work of Davignon was less public, but possibly more influential in persuading governments to accept change. He called into existence a network of leading industrialists involved in the European electrical and electronics industries to discuss their common problems in the face of US and Japanese competition. Out of these discussions came the ESPRIT programme of collaborative research in advanced technologies—but more significantly there also arose the European Round Table of Industrialists, which was to become an influential pressure group pushing governments into taking measures to liberalize the internal market of the EC (Chapter 12, p. 155).

Fontainebleau

The European Council meeting at Fontainebleau in June 1984 marked a turning point in European integration. First of all, the summit resolved the British budgetary question, in the context of an agreement at Fontainebleau to cut back on CAP expenditure and to increase the Community's own resources through an increase in VAT contributions by member states. The agreement settled five years of dispute and opened the door for reform of the CAP.

The meeting also agreed to set up an ad hoc committee on institutional affairs, which came to be known by the name of its chair, James Dooge of Ireland. The report of this committee became the basis for the institutional changes that were later to be made, alongside the fundamental policy commitment to completion of the internal market.

CONCLUSION

The first signs of the revival of the EC were ambiguous. The initiative to launch the EMS did not mark a new commitment to further European integration. Whatever Jenkins's motives for proposing a revival of monetary union, the EMS fell well short of being that. It was actually a response by West Germany to the threat posed to German exports by the US policy of benign neglect of the external value of the dollar. The themes that are relevant here are the impact of the international economic system on developments in the EC, and the defence of national interest by the larger member states. Later, the EMS was to form the basis on which a new attempt at monetary union could be built (Chapter 28, p. 404), but this illustrates another consistent theme of the story: that steps taken in pursuit of national interest can often have unintended consequences that favour further European integration.

The continued decline of US hegemony drew the EC into playing a larger international role, and this was the main motive behind the Southern enlargements of the EC in this period. The development of the EC was still being played out against the background of the Cold War, and it was a fear that political instability might open the way for communist influence that inspired the leading states of the EC to push for the membership of Greece, Portugal, and Spain despite the obvious economic weaknesses of these states. Again, the unintended consequences of these decisions were arguably to advance European integration, because the new member states became a powerful lobby for the extension of the structural funds of the EC, which eventually accounted for one-third of the EC budget, second only to the CAP.

The influence of domestic politics came through again in the British dispute over the budget rebate. Margaret Thatcher used the technique that Harold Wilson had adopted very successfully in the renegotiation of British terms of entry. She adopted a confrontational and nationalistic tone, which played well to a domestic audience, but caused disruption to the smooth operation of the EC.

The introduction of direct elections to the EP enhanced the legitimacy of the EU decision-making process and provided a boost both to federalist aspirations and supranational interpretations of integration. At the same time, there were the first stirrings of a more active role for the Commission in this period. The agreement to allow the President of the Commission to attend meetings of the economic summits reflected the concerns of smaller member states that the era of summitry might become the era of large states dominating smaller states. Again, a step that was negotiated from a viewpoint of defending national interest had positive implications for the strength of supranationalism.

On the other hand, the internal reforms by Jenkins indicated the problem of bureaucratization of the Commission, a problem that Jenkins did not manage to solve. Nevertheless, the increasing activism of the Thorn Commission, which is often unfairly treated as ineffective, showed the extent to which the presidency of Jenkins had marked a turning point in the self-confidence of the Commission, and paved the way for Delors (see next chapter).

KEY POINTS

Institutional Developments

- As Commission President, Roy Jenkins managed to secure a place at international economic summits for the Commission for the first time.

The European Monetary System

- Following a call from Jenkins to renew attempts at monetary union, the European Council passed a proposal by Schmidt and Giscard for a European Monetary System (EMS) in 1978.
- The new EMS would be more flexible than its predecessor, but Britain declined to put sterling in the exchange rate mechanism and play a full role.

The Southern Enlargements

- Following a difficult period of negotiations, the accession of Greece to the Community was agreed in 1979. Portugal and Spain, which applied later, were eventually accepted into the EC in 1985.

The British Budget Rebate

- Britain was set to be the largest net contributor to the Community budget by 1980. The tactics of the Thatcher government over the issue jeopardized progress in other areas until a satisfactory solution was found in 1984.

Leadership Changes

- The appointment of Gaston Thorn to the Commission presidency in 1981 coincided with important leadership changes in France and Germany.

Moves to Revive the EC

- The challenges facing the EC in the early 1980s demanded a response. The Genscher–Colombo plan proposed institutional reforms that received a cool response from the Council. However, Commission plans for freeing the internal market began to win over national governments.

Fontainebleau

- The resolution of the British budgetary question at Fontainebleau allowed for progress on both the internal market and institutional reform.

FURTHER READING

For an insider account of the early part of this period, see **R. Jenkins**, *European Diary, 1977–1981* (London: Collins, 1989). The British budget rebate issue is explained more fully in **S. George**, *An Awkward Partner: Britain in the European Community*, 3rd edn (Oxford: Oxford University Press, 1998), 137–65. For general accounts, see **D. W. Urwin**, *The Community of Europe: A History of European Integration since 1945*, 2nd edn (London and New York: Longman, 1995), and **M. Dedman**, *The Origins and Development of the European Union 1945–2008: A History of European Integration*, 2nd edn (Abingdon: Routledge, 2009).

 online resource centre

Visit the Online Resource Centre that accompanies this book for links to more information on the European Community in the 1980s: www.oxfordtextbooks.co.uk/orc/bache3e/

Chapter 12
The Single European Act

Chapter Overview

If the platform for the revival of European integration was laid in the early 1980s, the mid-1980s marked a turning point. The Commission under Jacques Delors, which assumed office in 1985, championed the scheme for a new integrative push starting with an ambitious project to free the internal market of the European Community (EC) of non-tariff barriers. This push led to the Single European Act (SEA), which marked a key moment in the history of European integration. It was the collective response of EC states to the global economic challenges of the late twentieth century and marked a new phase in European integration. By the end of the decade, the EC had cast off the image of 'Eurosclerosis' and was demonstrating a dynamism that had hardly seemed possible five years earlier. This chapter examines the initiative taken by Delors, and the SEA itself. It looks at the provisions of the SEA, particularly the institutional reforms that it introduced, and then briefly at the debate over the role of the Commission in getting it accepted and problems of implementing what had been agreed.

[T]he SEA ... had potential for revolution, suggesting a shift in the existing balance of power away from the member states towards the Community institutions.

(Urwin 1995: 231)

When a new Commission assumed office in 1985 under the presidency of Jacques Delors (Insight 12.1), it offered a visible symbol of a new start under dynamic leadership. Delors proposed that the EC should set itself the target of removing a whole series of barriers to free trade and free movement of capital and labour that had grown up during the 1970s. This project would be pursued with a target date for completion of the end of 1992, and became known as the '1992 Programme'. This economic project was linked to a programme of institutional reform that would have far-reaching implications for the way in which the EC made decisions, although those implications were not all immediately apparent.

From the outset, the single-market project was linked to certain institutional reforms, particularly the introduction of **qualified majority voting (QMV)** into the proceedings of the Council of Ministers, thus overcoming the blockage to progress imposed by the system that allowed individual governments to veto proposals. It was also intended to revive the momentum of integration, because Delors believed that

> **Insight 12.1 Jacques Delors**
>
> Jacques Delors was born in Paris in 1925. His father was a middle-ranking employee of the Bank of France, and the son went to work for the bank straight from school. The young Delors was active in Catholic social movements, and became a devotee of the doctrine of 'personalism', a form of Christian socialism associated with the philosopher Emmanuel Mounier. Delors was also an active trade unionist.
>
> In the 1960s, he moved from the bank to a senior position in the French Planning Commission, which had been created by Jean Monnet. Although he was an adviser to the Gaullist Prime Minister Jacques Chaban-Delmas at the end of the 1960s and in the early 1970s, he subsequently joined the reformed Socialist Party of François Mitterrand, and was elected to the European Parliament in 1979 as a Socialist. When Mitterrand became President of France in 1981, Delors became Finance Minister in the Socialist government. He was instrumental in moving the government away from policies of economic expansion that were not working and were undermining the value of the currency. He played a crucial role in the negotiation of the 1983 realignment of currencies within the exchange rate mechanism of the EMS, and won the respect of the German government in the process.
>
> In 1985, with strong support from Chancellor Kohl of Germany as well as from Mitterrand, he became President of the European Commission, a post that he retained for ten years.

the freeing of the internal market would lead to spillover into other policy sectors. In particular, he believed that it would not be feasible to have the single market without strengthening the degree of social protection available to workers at the EC level, and that the single market would set up a momentum towards monetary union.

Despite British reluctance to see these related aspects, the Thatcher government wanted to see the single-market programme itself put into place. Subsequently, the British Prime Minister tried to block these aspects, but in the meantime, the success of Delors's initiative revived the self-confidence of the Commission, which had already begun to recover under Jenkins and Thorn (see previous chapter). It also led to a revival of theoretical interpretations of the EC that emphasized the role of the Commission and other supranational actors, thus rekindling the supranational–intergovernmental debate about the nature of the EC, which had lain dormant during the 'doldrums years' of the 1970s and early 1980s (see also Chapter 27, pp. 396–8).

1985: A Watershed Year

Delors had been Finance Minister in the 1981–83 French Socialist governments, which had tried to tackle the problem of unemployment in France by reflating the economy. The result had been a serious balance of payments crisis as the reflation did little to restore full employment, but did suck in imports. There had been two views on how to respond to this. One had been to withdraw from the European Monetary System (EMS), and to impose import controls, in contravention of France's EC obligations; the other, of which Delors had been the strongest advocate, had been to revert to national policies of balancing the budget by cutting public expenditure, and to develop a European solution to the problem of unemployment. That view had prevailed, and

Delors's advocacy of it made him acceptable to both Germany and Britain as a nominee for the Commission presidency. It had been tacitly accepted that the presidency of the Commission would be given to a German candidate if the Federal government were to wish to take it up—but Kohl chose to throw his weight behind Delors.

The Brussels European Council of February 1985 instructed the Commission to draw up a timetable for the completion of the single market. Within a few months of taking office, the British Commissioner for Trade and Industry, Lord Cockfield, produced a White Paper listing the barriers that needed to be removed for there to be a genuine single market inside the EC. This listed some 300 separate measures, later reduced to 279, covering the harmonization of technical standards, opening up **public procurement** to intra-EC competition, freeing capital movements, removing barriers to free trade in services, harmonizing rates of indirect taxation and excise duties, and removing physical frontier controls between member states. The list was accompanied by a timetable for completion, with a final target date of the end of 1992.

At the Milan European Council in June 1985, heads of government agreed the objectives of the White Paper and the timetable for its completion by the end of 1992. A massive publicity campaign would be organized to promote the project. It was also agreed, against the protests of the British Prime Minister, to set up an intergovernmental conference (IGC) to consider what changes were necessary to the original Treaties in order to achieve the single market, and to consider other changes to the institutional structure that had been recommended by an ad hoc committee under James Dooge, which had been set up at the Fontainebleau European Council a year earlier (Chapter 11, p. 148). This IGC drew up what became the SEA, which was agreed by the heads of government at the Luxembourg European Council in December 1985, and eventually ratified by national parliaments to come into effect in July 1987. Thus was born the 1992 Programme, which did more than any initiative since the Treaties of Rome to revitalize the process of European integration.

The Single European Act

Although modest in the changes that it introduced in comparison with the hopes of federalists in the European Parliament (EP) and within some member states (particularly Italy), the SEA rejuvenated the process of European integration. The intention of the SEA appeared relatively modest, seeking to complete the objective of a **common market** set out in the Treaty of Rome. By the early 1980s, the need for member states to compete in world markets, especially against the United States and Japan, was an overriding concern. A single European market would increase the specialization of production at company level and allow greater economies of scale, leading to more competitive firms. The issue of monetary union as an accompaniment to the single market was not addressed at this stage of developments.

While ostensibly an economic project, the SEA had implications for a range of policy areas such as social protection and the environment (see Chapters 25 and 30). More broadly, in its proposals for institutional change, the SEA:

had potential for revolution, suggesting a shift in the existing balance of power away from the member states towards the Community institutions. The radical political implications of the economic target of a common market—the single internal market—were there for all to read in the document ... while the issues of political and economic integration are closely interlinked, the parallel debates tended to muddy the waters of each.

(Urwin 1995: 231)

In retrospect at least, the political implications of the SEA are clear (Insight 12.2). At the time, though, the SEA was largely seen as a mechanism for implementing the commitment made at Milan to achieve the single market. This goal was not contested by member states. Moreover, the Commission was concerned with emphasizing the practical rather than the political implications of aspects of the reform. Only in the final section of the White Paper did the Commission refer to the wider implications of the internal-market project, acknowledging that '[j]ust as the **Customs Union** had to precede Economic Integration, so Economic Integration has to precede European Unity' (European Commission 1985: 55). Despite the political implications of the single market being deliberately understated by the Commission, the proposed institutional reforms proved the most controversial aspect of the project.

Institutional Reforms

While ostensibly a project to complete the single market, the institutional reforms of the SEA were to be of lasting significance for European integration: in particular the introduction of QMV in the Council of Ministers. QMV was designed to speed up decision making by reducing substantially the number of areas in which individual states could reject progress by use of their veto. QMV would apply to measures related to the freeing of the internal market, although certain measures, including the harmonization of indirect taxes and the removal of physical controls at borders, were excluded at British insistence. Without the extension of QMV, the internal market project was likely to be delayed and possibly lost through intergovernmental disputes.

The codification of the commitment to QMV as a formal amendment of the founding Treaties, and as part of a potentially wider reform of the institutional procedures for making decisions, was resisted strongly by Prime Minister Thatcher. The whole

---

Insight 12.2 The Political Provisions of the SEA

- It introduced qualified majority voting (QMV) for single-market measures.
- It increased the legislative powers of the European Parliament in areas in which QMV applied.
- It incorporated European political co-operation (EPC) into a Treaty text for the first time.
- It incorporated in the Preamble a reiteration of the objective of an economic and monetary union.
- It incorporated in the Preamble a commitment by the member states to 'transform relations as a whole among their States into a European Union'.

issue of institutional reform was one of several regarding which the British government differed from most of its continental European partners. Mrs Thatcher insisted at Milan that no institutional reform, and so no IGC, was necessary. However, it seems that she was persuaded by her Foreign Secretary, Sir Geoffrey Howe, and her adviser on European affairs, David Williamson, that unless a legally binding commitment were made to an element of majority voting in the Council of Ministers, the measures necessary to implement the Cockfield White Paper would never be agreed.

The freeing of the internal market was supported by all of the member states, and it coincided with the belief of the British Prime Minister in universal free trade. On the other hand, it was also an excellent issue for the new Commission to make into the centrepiece of its programme. As Helen Wallace (1986: 590) explained:

> The internal market is important not only for its own sake, but because it is the first core Community issue for over a decade ... which has caught the imagination of British policy-makers and which is echoed by their counterparts elsewhere ... The pursuit of a thoroughly liberalized domestic European market has several great advantages: it fits Community philosophy, it suits the doctrinal preferences of the current British Conservative government, and it would draw in its train a mass of interconnections with other fields of action.

Whereas doctrinal preferences may be sufficient explanation for British support of the internal market project, the support of other member states needs further explanation.

One important factor was the support given to the freeing of the market by European business leaders, some of whom formed the European Round Table of Industrialists in 1983 to press for the removal of the barriers to trade that had developed. This pressure occurred in the context of a generalized concern among governments about the sluggish recovery of the European economies from the post-1979 recession in comparison with the vigorous growth of the US and Japanese economies. In particular, the turning of the tide of foreign direct investment, so that by the mid-1980s there was a net flow of investment funds from western Europe to the United States, augured badly both for the employment situation in Europe in the future, and for the ability of European industry to keep abreast of the technological developments that were revolutionizing production processes.

It was in response to the worry that Europe would become permanently technologically dependent on the United States and Japan that President Mitterrand proposed his EUREKA initiative for promoting pan-European research and development in the advanced technology industries. This concern also lay behind the promotion by the new Commission of framework programmes for research and development in such fields as information technology, bio-technology, and telecommunications (Sharp and Shearman 1987). But when European industrialists were asked what would encourage them to invest in Europe, they replied that the most important factor for them would be the creation of a genuine continental market such as that which they experienced in the United States.

It was therefore in an attempt to revive investment and economic growth that governments other than Britain embraced the free-market programme. The pressure to break out of the short-termism that had prevented the EC from making progress in

155

the 1970s and early 1980s came partly from interest groups, but also from the economic situation that faced governments. The EC, as only one part of the global capitalist economy, was seeing investment flow away from it to other parts of the global economy, and was already being left behind in rates of economic growth and in technological advance by rival core areas within the system. It was a calculation of the common national interests of the member states that led them to agree a new contract, in the form of a White Paper and the Single European Act.

Beyond these economic interests, other member states were happy to see the SEA's introduction of institutional reforms, and the strengthening of other Treaty provisions: notably on social policy, the environment, the structural funds, research and technology policy, and economic and social cohesion. The SEA therefore created a much wider package deal beyond the immediate confines of the single-market programme.

The Role of the Delors Commission

The emphasis that Delors put on the single market was part of a carefully considered strategy. During the autumn of 1984, he considered a variety of candidates for the role of the 'Big Idea' that would relaunch European integration (Grant 1994: 66). Initially attracted to completion of economic and monetary union, following the relative success of the EMS, Delors ultimately decided that the idea of completing the internal market was the best starting point. This project was firmly within the boundaries of integration established by the Treaty of Rome. Even more important, perhaps, with policies of market liberalization adopted by key member states, the single-market project stood the best chance of winning the support of even the most **Euro-sceptic** governments: Britain's in particular. Moreover, successful completion of the 1992 Project had implications for a wide range of Community policies. Most notably, the project would inevitably prompt reconsideration of the advantages of monetary union as a complement to the single market and would also lead to demands for strengthening EC social and regional policies from the member states most likely to be adversely affected by the internal market.

Few dispute that the Delors Commission played a pivotal role in developing and pushing forward the single-market programme as a means to the end of ever closer union. The emergence of the programme, and eventually the drive towards full monetary union and the adoption of a social charter, all bore the hallmarks of a plan devised in Paris in the light of the failures of the 1981–84 French economic experiment. Delors and the British Commissioner Cockfield worked together closely on developing and promoting the project. Cockfield faced accusations from the British Prime Minister that he had 'gone native' in his support for wide-ranging European integration, and it was no great surprise when Thatcher chose not to renominate him to the Commission in 1988.

Under Delors, the Commission regained the high profile that it had under Hallstein, and, irrespective of whether the Hallstein Commission had been the genuine motor of integration, the Delors Commission certainly appeared to play that role by the 1980s. But it was only able to play that role because of the support that Delors received from Mitterrand, and because of the diplomatic skill of Mitterrand himself in ensuring that other member states—Germany above all—were carried along with the plan.

Implementing the SEA

While national governments were initially slow to implement the measures detailed in the SEA, businesses began to take advantage of the emerging opportunities offered by the 1992 Project. Company mergers accelerated to take advantage of EC-wide economies of scale. In 1988, the business publication *The Economist* noted that, in 1987, there were 300 major mergers compared with only sixty-eight in the previous year. In comparison, by November 1987, the Council of Ministers had adopted only sixty-four of the measures set out in the White Paper (Dinan 1994: 150).

The core problem of implementation related to accompanying measures to the SEA: in particular, the demands of southern member states for adequate compensatory mechanisms to balance the adverse effects of market liberalization. While a number of member states were reluctant to commit greater resources to Community regional aid, ultimately these demands had to be satisfied to protect the 1992 Programme. Subsequently, at the Brussels European Council of February 1988, heads of government agreed to a doubling in the allocations to the structural funds to promote greater cohesion as a complement to the internal market.

CONCLUSION

This was the period in which the EC was revitalized, and with it the theory of neofunctionalism. The debates surrounding the origins of the single-market programme are considered further in Chapter 27 (see pp. 396–8). Interpretations of the relevant importance of different factors certainly vary, but there is a considerable body of analysis that attributes a central role to the European Commission under Jacques Delors, and to the European Round Table of Industrialists. Two of the actors that neofunctionalists had predicted would be influential appeared to be influential in this landmark decision: the Commission and transnational business interests. Neofunctionalism also received support from another development: the speed with which businesses responded to the announcement of the 1992 Programme to conclude mergers and announce new investment plans vindicated the argument that changed circumstances would lead to changed attitudes and behaviour.

However, the interpretations that emphasized the role of supranational actors did not go along with neofunctionalism in seeing spillover as the dynamic force that produced the 1992 Programme. There is general agreement that global economic developments were the catalyst for the acceptance of the single market. The remarkable economic recovery of the United States and Japan from the second oil crisis contrasted starkly with the sluggishness of the western European economies. Not only was there a marked difference in performance, but also the success of the United States and Japan was based on the adoption of new technologies into their production processes that threatened to leave western Europe with an obsolete industrial base unless investment could be revived.

In exploiting the problems that the changed global economic environment posed for national governments, Delors acted as a **policy entrepreneur**. However, he did not mobilize the Commission to support this role by carrying through the reforms that had eluded Jenkins. It remained a bureaucratized and fragmented body. Rather than reform its procedures, Delors chose to short-circuit them, using an informal network centred on his personal *cabinet* as the agents for pushing through the necessary initiatives. This was to store up problems for the future that would lead directly to a substantial crisis in the late 1990s.

KEY POINTS

1985: A Watershed Year

- In February 1985, the European Council instructed the Delors Commission to draw up a timetable for the completion of the single market. In June 1985, the Council agreed to the Commission's proposals and the 1992 timetable for completion.
- An IGC on institutional reform drew up what became the Single European Act.

The Single European Act

- The SEA rejuvenated the process of European integration, but the broad political significance of the institutional reforms of the SEA only became clear later.
- The British government was instinctively averse to QMV, but accepted it as necessary to achieve the completion of the single market by 1992.
- On the whole, governments were persuaded of the need of the SEA by the desire to compete with Japan and the United States.
- For Delors, the single-market programme was the 'Big Idea' that would relaunch European integration, but the support of key member governments was essential to its ultimate success.
- Companies were quick to take advantage of the opportunities provided by the single-market project, but implementation of SEA measures varied across member states.

FURTHER READING

C. Grant, *Delors: Inside the House that Jacques Built* (London: Nicolas Brealey Publishing, 1994) and **G. Ross**, *Jacques Delors and European Integration* (Cambridge: Polity Press, 1995) both give accounts of what went on within the Delors Commission. For the analysis of the SEA, begin with **D. R. Cameron**, 'The 1992 Initiative: Causes and Consequences', in **A. Sbragia (ed.)**, *Euro-Politics: Institutions and Policymaking in the 'New' European Community* (Washington, DC: Brookings Institution, 1992), 23–74, continue with **W. Sandholtz and J. Zysman**, '1992: Recasting the European Bargain', *World Politics*, 45 (1989): 95–128, and then read **A. Moravcsik**, *The Choice for Europe: Social Purpose and State Power from Messina to Maastricht* (London: UCL Press, 1998), 314–78, or his chapter 'Negotiating the Single European Act', in **R. O. Keohane and S. Hoffmann (eds)**, *The New European Community: Decision-Making and Institutional Change* (Boulder, CO, San Francisco, CA, and Oxford: Westview Press, 1991), 41–84. For an institutionalist account, read **K. Armstrong and S. Bulmer**, *The Governance of the Single European Market* (Manchester: Manchester University Press, 1998), ch. 1.

online resource centre   Visit the Online Resource Centre that accompanies this book for links to more information on the Single European Act: www.oxfordtextbooks.co.uk/orc/bache3e/

Chapter 13

Maastricht: The Treaty on European Union

Chapter Overview

The success of the 1992 Project revived European integration, although the difficult issue of monetary union had yet to be addressed. Following the collapse of communism in eastern Europe and the reunification of Germany, the future of European integration was once again brought into focus. The result was the Treaty on European Union (TEU), signed in Maastricht in December 1991, which brought agreement on moves towards a single currency and further institutional reforms. This chapter examines the moves towards monetary union, the impact of the collapse of communism on the European Community (EC), the terms of the TEU, and the aftermath of its signing, when public opinion began to turn away from support for European integration.

More than the SEA, the Maastricht treaty helps to clarify the rules of the game and the international *compétences* of the emergent Euro-polity.

(Schmitter 1996: 1)

The 1992 Project was a tremendous success for the EC. It led to a revival of investment in Europe, which had been stagnating. Companies anticipated the arrival of the single market by engaging in cross-border mergers and joint production arrangements. The EC experienced a wave of business euphoria, which ensured that the work of public officials in actually agreeing the necessary measures did not waver. By the target date of the end of 1992, 260 out of the consolidated list of 279 measures that had been identified in the White Paper had been agreed in the Council of Ministers: a staggering 95 per cent success rate (Pelkmans 1994: 103).

However, the freeing of the market was not the end of the project so far as Delors was concerned. He saw it as a first step that implied further extensions of integration. In particular, he argued for a social dimension to the project, and for its completion by agreement on monetary union. On both of these issues, he had the support of a majority of the governments of the other member states, but was implacably opposed by the British Prime Minister, Margaret Thatcher.

The British government rejected the proposed Social Charter, which Mrs Thatcher described as 'Marxist' (Urwin 1995: 231). The proposal for worker representatives on

> **Insight 13.1 Objectives of the Social Protocol Annexed to the Treaty on European Union**
>
> - Promotion of employment
> - Improvement of living and working conditions
> - Adequate social protection
> - Social dialogue
> - The development of human resources to ensure a high and sustainable level of employment
> - The integration of persons excluded from the labour market

company boards was a particular problem for the Thatcher government. Despite subsequent revisions to the proposed Social Charter, the UK government refused to sign, leaving the remaining eleven governments to sign a Protocol on social policy outside of the Treaty (Insight 13.1).

Towards Maastricht

Monetary policy had been largely absent from the SEA (Chapter 12), but the logic of the internal market suggested at least some harmonization of taxation policies. Following the SEA there had been growing support for a single currency controlled by a European central bank, but the British government rejected this concept. Despite British opposition, the heads of government agreed in Hanover in June 1988 to set up a committee of central bankers and technical experts, under the chairmanship of Delors, to prepare a report on the steps that needed to be taken to strengthen monetary co-operation. The subsequent 'Delors Report' proposed a three-stage progress to monetary union leading to a single currency by 1999. The report was presented to the June 1989 meeting of the European Council in Madrid, which, on a majority vote of eleven to one (Thatcher voting against), agreed to convene an intergovernmental conference (IGC) to prepare proposals for changes to the Treaties to allow movement to a monetary union.

The dramatic collapse of communism in the Soviet Union and other central and eastern European countries in the course of 1989 and 1990 added to the complexity of the situation. This forced a serious reconsideration of the political aspects of the European Community (EC). The immediate impact was the destabilization of the geographical area immediately to the east of the EC and, more positively for the EC, the opening up of potential new markets and new sites for investment for west European capital. In addition, the collapse of communism raised the prospect of German reunification.

This 'acceleration of history' as Delors called it had an impact on the EC and on Delors's plans for its development. In particular, the prospect of a reunified Germany caused alarm in the neighbouring states, particularly over a possible resurgence of German nationalism. A more immediate concern was that the new Germany would turn its attention more to the east and become less concerned with its obligations to western Europe.

Chancellor Kohl of Germany shared these concerns. Kohl had not hitherto been noted for providing strong or dynamic leadership, but he seized the opportunity to go down in the history books as the person who reunified his country. At the same time, however, he did not want to be remembered as the Frankenstein who created a new monster in the centre of Europe. Such concerns led directly to the convening of a second IGC on political union to run alongside the one that had already been called on monetary union. Although Delors supported the move, it was not part of his plan. The IGC on political union, together with that on monetary union, meant that the Maastricht Treaty became a very high-profile issue: 'a treaty too far', as Lady Thatcher later described it.

The two IGCs met throughout 1991, and their proposals were incorporated into the TEU, which was agreed in Maastricht in December of that year, and which created the European Union (EU). Britain, under the new premiership of John Major, agreed to the TEU only when a chapter on social policy had been removed from the main text, and only when it was agreed that Britain could opt out of the final stage of monetary union if its Parliament so decided.

The Treaty on European Union

Intergovernmental negotiations leading up to the Maastricht Summit of December 1991 were tough and much of what was agreed reflected the lowest-common-denominator bargaining position of governments. The Treaty on European Union was signed in February 1992 and entered into force in November 1993. It marked a further big step on the road to European integration, with important implications for both internal and external activities (Insight 13.2). The TEU has been revised subsequently, and the Insights in this chapter utilize the original 'Maastricht' text.

The name of the 'European Economic Community' was changed to the 'European Community', and there were important new areas of co-operation in the fields of Common Foreign and Security Policy (CFSP) (Insight 13.3) and Justice and Home Affairs (JHA) (Insight 13.4). The EC, CFSP, and JHA became part of a three-pillar structure known as the 'European Union' (see Chapter 19, Fig. 19.1, p. 227). While the first pillar remained an area of pooled sovereignty in which the **Community method** of decision making would continue to predominate, the second and third pillars were explicitly areas of intergovernmental co-operation depending largely on unanimous decisions taken by the member governments.

Monetary union was the biggest single policy initiative in the TEU (see below, and Chapter 28, pp. 404–5), but in addition, the Treaty contained a number of other important provisions. In institutional terms, it strengthened the power of the European Parliament (EP) through the extension of the co-decision procedure, which gave the Parliament greater legislative power in a range of policy areas (Chapter 19, pp. 240–1), and it created a Committee of the Regions and Local Authorities, in

Insight 13.2 Extract from Treaty on European Union: Common Provisions

Article B

The Union shall set itself the following objectives:

- to promote economic and social progress which is balanced and sustainable, in particular through the creation of an area without internal frontiers, through the strengthening of economic and social cohesion and through the establishment of economic and monetary union, ultimately including a single currency in accordance with the provisions of this Treaty;
- to assert its identity on the international scene, in particular through the implementation of a common foreign and security policy including the eventual framing of a common defence policy, which might in time lead to a common defence;
- to strengthen the protection of the rights and interests of the nationals of its Member States through the introduction of a citizenship of the Union;
- to develop close cooperation on justice and home affairs;
- to maintain in full the *acquis communautaire* and build on it with a view to considering, through the procedure referred to in Article N(2), to what extent the policies and forms of cooperation introduced by this Treaty may need to be revised with the aim of ensuring the effectiveness of the mechanisms and the institutions of the Community.

The objectives of the Union shall be achieved as provided in this Treaty and in accordance with the conditions and the timetable set out therein while respecting the principle of subsidiarity as defined in Article 3b of the Treaty establishing the European Community.

Insight 13.3 Extract from Treaty on European Union: Provisions on a Common Foreign and Security Policy

Article J.1

(1) The Union and its Member States shall define and implement a common foreign and security policy, governed by the provisions of this Title and covering all areas of foreign and security policy.

(2) The objectives of the common foreign and security policy shall be:

- to safeguard the common values, fundamental interests, and independence of the Union;
- to strengthen the security of the Union and its Member States in all ways;
- to preserve peace and strengthen international security, in accordance with the principles of the United Nations Charter as well as the principles of the Helsinki Final Act and the objectives of the Paris Charter;
- to promote international co-operation;
- to develop and consolidate democracy and the rule of law, and respect for human rights and fundamental freedoms.

(3) The Union shall pursue these objectives:

- by establishing systematic co-operation between Member States in the conduct of policy, in accordance with Article J.2;
- by gradually implementing, in accordance with Article J.3, joint action in the areas in which the Member States have important interests in common.

(4) The Member States shall support the Union's external and security policy actively and unreservedly in a spirit of loyalty and mutual solidarity. They shall refrain from any action which is contrary to the interests of the Union or likely to impair its effectiveness as a cohesive force in international relations. The Council shall ensure that these principles are complied with.

Insight 13.4 Extract from Treaty on European Union: Provisions on Co-operation in the Fields of Justice and Home Affairs

Article K.1

For the purposes of achieving the objectives of the Union, in particular the free movement of persons, and without prejudice to the powers of the European Community, Member States shall regard the following areas as matters of common interest:

- asylum policy;
- rules governing the crossing by persons of the external borders of the Member States and the exercise of controls thereon;
- immigration policy and policy regarding nationals of third countries:
  — conditions of entry and movement by nationals of third countries on the territory of Member States;
  — conditions of residence by nationals of third countries on the territory of Member States, including family reunion and access to employment;
  — combating unauthorized immigration, residence, and work by nationals of third countries on the territory of Member States;
  — combating drug addiction in so far as this is not covered by (7) to (9);
  — combating fraud on an international scale in so far as this is not covered by (7) to (9);
  — judicial co-operation in civil matters;
  — judicial co-operation in criminal matters;
  — customs co-operation;
  — police co-operation for the purposes of preventing and combating terrorism, unlawful drug-trafficking, and other serious forms of international crime, including if necessary certain aspects of customs co-operation, in connection with the organization of a Union-wide system for exchanging information within a European Police Office (Europol).

163

recognition of the growing role of sub-national government in EC affairs, and in line with the principle of **subsidiarity** (see Chapter 19, pp. 235–6). The principle of subsidiarity was itself established as a general rule of the Community by the Treaty, having only applied to the field of environmental policy in the SEA (see Insight 23.2 for the current Treaty text).

The Treaty also introduced the concept of European citizenship, and gave the European citizen the rights: to circulate and reside freely in the Community; to vote and stand as a candidate for European and municipal elections in the State in which he or she resides; to receive protection while in a non-EU country from diplomatic or consular authorities of a member state other than that of his or her state of origin; and to petition the EP or submit a complaint to the Ombudsman (European Union 2005).

In sum, these measures provided a strong political dimension to the economic imperatives that had dominated the integration process to date. More generally, EC competencies were established or extended in a number of areas including education and training, environment, health, and industry. Built on compromise, the TEU included something positive for the EC institutions and for each of the member states involved.

After Maastricht

Although agreed by the heads of governments, the decision to move to a single currency raised concerns within member states. Notably, this decision caused a collapse of support for the EU in Germany itself, where the Deutschmark was held in high regard as the factor that had facilitated post-war prosperity. Problems were made worse when the German currency union took effect, following the decision to convert East German Ostmarks at an artificially high rate into Deutschmarks. This led to inflationary tendencies in the unified Germany, which were suppressed by the Bundesbank (the German central bank) raising interest rates. This in turn solidified resistance within Germany to European monetary union, and therefore to Maastricht. It also pushed the buoyant European economies into recession, which made it more difficult to sell Maastricht to European citizens, who were already rather alarmed by the pace of change that was being proposed.

It was against this background that the Danish referendum in June 1992 rejected the Treaty by 50.7 per cent to 49.3 per cent. In Denmark, farmers and fishermen had usually been strong supporters of the EC. Danish opposition to membership had been concentrated in Copenhagen and the other urban areas. In 1992, concern about the reforms of the Common Agricultural Policy (CAP) (see Chapter 26, pp. 372–3) and the Common Fisheries Policy reduced the 'yes' vote in rural areas, and may have been sufficient to make the difference between a narrow 'yes' and a narrow 'no'. It was only when concessions were made on monetary union—giving Denmark similar opt-out rights to those of Britain—and on some other issues of concern that it was narrowly accepted in a second referendum in May 1993.

Perhaps even more significantly, the Treaty was only accepted by the French public by the narrowest of margins (50.3 to 49.7 per cent) in September 1992. Guyomarch, Machin, and Ritchie (1998: 97–8) identified six factors that shaped this outcome: high unemployment and the argument of the 'No' campaign that, under the TEU, the government would no longer be able to take effective action to create jobs; concern that further integration would lead to a weakening of the level of social security; hostility to the MacSharry reforms of the CAP (see Chapter 26, pp. 372–3); concern at the effects on previously protected sectors of the economy of the opening of the domestic market; concern at what was seen as interference by Brussels with aspects of the traditional French way of life, including the right to produce and eat unpasteurized cheese, and to shoot migrating birds; and splits in all of the main parties on their attitude to the TEU, which deprived the electorate of clear leadership. The same authors pointed to the fact that the controversy generated by the referendum led to an increase in interest in the EU. This meant that, in the 1994 elections to the EP, the turnout in France increased against the EU-wide trend, from 50.4 per cent in 1989 to 55 per cent (Guyomarch, Machin, and Ritchie 1998: 101).

In Germany, there was no referendum, but the strength of public concern about monetary union was such that the Bundestag secured the right to vote on the issue again before any automatic abandonment of the Deutschmark in favour of a common European currency. There was clear evidence of serious public discontent with the Treaty in other member states, not least in Britain.

The Commission after Maastricht

The Commission became caught in this wave of popular discontent about the pace of integration. Delors was personally associated with the proposals on monetary union, which were what caused the greatest concern in Britain and Germany. He had also adopted a very high profile in the run-up to the ratification debacles. In particular, his ill-timed statement shortly before the Danish referendum, to the effect that small states might have to surrender their right to hold the presidency of the Council of Ministers in a future enlarged EC, was seen as a contributory factor in the negative vote in Denmark.

Delors's comments about small states were actually made in the context of an entirely different debate about enlargement of the EC. The success of the 1992 Programme had led to concern among the members of the European Free Trade Association (EFTA) that they were not sharing in the investment boom that 1992 precipitated. Led by Sweden, these states began to broach the question of membership of the EC. Delors was against this because he believed that further enlargement would dilute the degree of unity that could be achieved, and he proposed instead a way in which the EFTA states could become part of the single market without becoming full members of the EC. Membership of the European Economic Area (EEA) would involve the EFTA states adopting all of the relevant commercial legislation of the EC, without having any say in its formulation. It was never likely to be a satisfactory agreement for the governments of those states, which would thereby be surrendering sovereignty over large areas of their economies; more significantly, it did not convince the businesses that were already diverting their investments from EFTA to inside the EC. In addition, these states had also pursued foreign policies of neutrality, but the end of the Cold War meant that their policies were no longer incompatible with full membership. Consequently, a group of EFTA states decided to press ahead with membership applications, but Switzerland withdrew its application after the Swiss people rejected the EEA in a referendum in December 1992; the Norwegians again rejected membership in a referendum in November 1994.

Sweden, Finland, and Austria became members of the EU on 1 January 1995 (Chapter 34, p. 352). The EU that they joined was not the self-confident one that they had applied to join. As well as disagreement about the future direction, and signs of public disaffection with the whole exercise, the European Monetary System (EMS) had effectively collapsed during the ratification problems. Britain had withdrawn and floated sterling, and other states had only been able to remain inside because the bands of permitted fluctuation had been widened from 2.25 per cent either side of parity to 15 per cent.

Delors had started his long period as President of the Commission with a considerable triumph in the single-market programme. He ended it with that achievement somewhat overshadowed by the hostile reaction of public opinion in much of the EU to the Maastricht Treaty. Yet whether it was reasonable to blame the Commission for this debacle is very doubtful. Delors had been upset at the extent to which the Commission had been ignored during the IGCs that prepared the TEU, and had opposed several of the provisions of the Treaty. However, he had adopted such a high profile during his period as President that it was easy for the governments of the member states to pass the blame onto him personally and the institution of which he had been President for ten years.

CONCLUSION

Delors approached the single-market programme as the first step in a wider programme of integration. There is no doubt that he was familiar with the central concepts of neofunctionalist theory himself, as evidenced in his inaugural address to the sixth annual conference of the Centre for European Policy Studies (CEPS) in 1989 (CEPS 1990: 9–18). Delors expected and intended that the economic liberalization programme would be followed by both monetary union and an extension and deepening of social policy. Here, the theme of the tension between contrasting types of capitalism re-enters the story, because the British Prime Minister, Margaret Thatcher, objected strongly to the idea that either of these things was entailed by the 1992 Programme. While her objection to monetary union can be interpreted as a reflection of her commitment to an intergovernmental view of the EC, her objection to the social dimension of the single-market programme was clearly a reflection of her adherence to a different concept of how capitalism should be organized in the late twentieth century. That particular debate was to continue after her political demise.

While personal convictions cannot be written out of the explanation for Margaret Thatcher's opposition to both monetary union and an EC social policy, the question of the personal position of her successor, John Major, is less important. Major had little choice but to negotiate opt-outs for Britain on both issues at Maastricht, because of the domestic political constraints that he faced, which were in turn the legacy of the Thatcher years. The primacy of domestic politics, a consistent theme of these chapters, re-emerges here.

The crisis in the exchange rate mechanism of the EMS gives strong support to the argument that the evolution of the EC can only be understood against the background of an understanding of global economic forces. The globalization of money markets, and the increase in the quantity of **liquid capital** traded across the international exchanges, made it impossible for the system to be maintained in the form that had functioned for years to stabilize European exchange rates, and gave added force to the argument that only a single currency would provide the stability that was necessary to ensure the smooth and complete functioning of the single market, even though the British government chose to interpret the episode as evidence that the infrastructure was not yet in place for a single currency.

Neofunctionalism received some additional support from the applications for membership by the EFTA states. The idea of spillover was extended to cover the idea of geographical spillover, and this appeared to cover the case of the EFTAns. Once the single market was a reality, the attitude and behaviour of businesses changed—and not only of businesses based inside the EC, but also of businesses based in the rest of western Europe. The result was an inflow of investment to the single-market zone, and an imperative for those states that remained outside to join. When the halfway house of the EEA failed to convince businesses that it would constitute full membership of the single market, the EFTA states were forced to reconsider their position on full membership. Again, the relative impotence of the governments of individual states in the face of the forces of contemporary capitalism was illustrated.

It was in this period that the Cold War finally came to an end, although the impact of the uncertainty that this change in the background conditions of the EC produced was only fully felt in the next period, after Maastricht. The collapse of communism may have given additional momentum to a process that was already under way, in the same way that Algeria, Hungary, and Suez gave additional momentum to the Messina negotiations in the late 1950s, but the 'acceleration of history' did not dramatically change the agenda of the IGCs that were already scheduled.

The TEU focused on strengthening the legitimacy and effectiveness of the institutions and brought new areas of co-operation that marked a key stage in the process of European integration. The creation of the second and third pillars in particular marked a significant step forward, but these were explicitly intergovernmental. Yet the very formalization of co-operation in these areas may suggest a neofunctionalist logic at work, for example in the pressures to develop more systematic ways of dealing with effects of greater flows of people across borders caused by the single-market programme.

Finally, the developments after Maastricht illustrate a theme that had been largely neglected by governments and analysts until then: the importance of legitimacy for the process of European integration. In a majority of member states, the EC had an independent legitimacy of its own because it represented European integration, which was perceived as a 'good thing'. The aftermath of Maastricht raised questions about whether this was still the case. At the same time, governments did not hesitate to undermine further the legitimacy of the EC/EU by blaming it for unpopular measures that they felt needed to be taken, but for which they were reluctant to accept the responsibility themselves, for fear of weakening their electoral position.

KEY POINTS

Towards Maastricht

- In June 1989, the European Council agreed to Delors's three-stage plan for monetary union by 1999, despite British opposition.
- The collapse of communism in central and eastern Europe and the prospect of a reunified Germany focused minds on the political aspects of European integration.
- In 1991, IGCs were held on both monetary union and political union. The proposals of these IGCs were incorporated into the TEU, agreed at Maastricht in December 1991.

The Treaty on European Union

- The TEU marked a major step on the road to European integration. It committed most of the member states to adopting a single currency, extended EC competencies in a range of areas, strengthened the powers of the European Parliament, created a Committee of the Regions, and introduced the concept of European citizenship.
- The Treaty created a three-pillar structure known as the European Union, consisting of the EC pillar and the intergovernmental pillars of the CFSP and JHA.

After Maastricht

- The decision to move to a single currency caused concern within member states, not least Germany, which had a strong attachment to the Deutschmark.
- The TEU was rejected by the Danish following a referendum in 1992 and was only accepted in 1993 following major concessions. A referendum in France (1992) was only narrowly in favour.
- By the time Austria, Finland, and Sweden became members in 1995, the EU was not the confident one that they had applied to join.
- The Commission became caught up in the wave of unpopularity affecting the EU. Delors' high-profile presidency ensured that he was the focal point of much criticism.

FURTHER READING

The negotiation of the Treaty is analysed by **M. Baun**, 'The Maastricht Treaty as High Politics: Germany, France and European Integration', *Political Science Quarterly*, 110 (1996): 605–24, and **A. Moravcsik**, *The Choice for Europe: Social Purpose and State Power from Messina to Maastricht* (London: UCL Press, 1998), 379–471. Also see **M. Baun**, *An Imperfect Union: The Maastricht Treaty and the New Politics of European Integration* (Boulder, CO: Westview, 1996).

The aftermath of the signing of the Treaty is analysed in: **B. Criddle**, 'The French Referendum on the Maastricht Treaty, September 1992', *Parliamentary Affairs*, 46 (1993): 228–38; **D. Baker, A. Gamble, and S. Ludlam**, '1846–1906–1996? Conservative Splits and European Integration', *Political Quarterly*, 64 (1993): 420–34, and 'The Parliamentary Siege of Maastricht 1993: Conservative Divisions and British Ratification of the Treaty of European Union', *Parliamentary Affairs*, 47 (1994): 37–60; and **H. Rattinger**, 'Public Attitudes towards European Integration in Germany and Maastricht: Inventory and Typology', *Journal of Common Market Studies*, 32 (1994): 525–40.

 online resource centre **Visit the Online Resource Centre that accompanies this book for links to more information on Maastricht and the Treaty on European Union: www.oxfordtextbooks.co.uk/orc/bache3e/**

Chapter 14

The Road to Amsterdam: A Flexible Europe?

Chapter Overview

By the mid-1990s, the prospect of 'flexible integration' was clearly on the agenda. A majority of member states signalled their support for a single currency by 1999, but others were reluctant. As an alternative to making no progress until everyone was prepared to proceed, the idea of flexible integration—of allowing those states that wished to go ahead to do so—began to be discussed. The proposed enlargement to include states of central and eastern Europe was the other major issue of the period. Enlargement would bring with it a much greater variety of member states, which raised the prospect of even more issues on which there would be no unanimous agreement, thus providing another argument for allowing greater flexibility. Before looking at the debate over flexible integration, this chapter first examines the debates over monetary union, particularly over what form it would take, and reviews key changes in domestic politics. It then turns to the Treaty of Amsterdam, which contained procedures for flexible integration and attempted to prepare the ground for further enlargement.

... flexibility, according to its proponents, promised a new principle and a new tool for responding to differences in the enthusiasms and capabilities of the member states of the EU to take on new tasks of policy integration. In the period following Maastricht, it had become evident that subsidiarity was both a contested concept and a muddled guide for practice.

(Wallace 2000*b*: 175)

As the European Union (EU) expanded to fifteen states on 1 January 1995 (see Chapter 13), Jacques Santer became president of the European Commission for a five-year term. He inherited an agenda that included further enlargement, an intergovernmental conference (IGC) to review the Treaty on European Union (TEU), and monetary union. He also inherited the legacy of the concerns and suspicions that had arisen over the TEU, and the role of the Commission in promoting integration. This led him to adopt as an unofficial mission statement a formula that had already been advocated by the British Foreign Secretary, Douglas Hurd: 'do less, but do it better'. However, not everyone in the EU wanted to do less. Despite the unfavourable move in public opinion, voices in both France and Germany were raised in favour of an arrangement that would allow those member states that wished to do so to forge ahead with closer integration, and not be held back by those states that were more hesitant. The field of monetary union was central to this issue.

Monetary Union

The agreement on monetary union that had been reached at Maastricht represented a compromise between the positions of states with very different perspectives on the issue. Those compromises had to be sorted out in order for the programme for a single currency to go ahead. During 1995, the decisions on the detail of the monetary union began to be settled, generally in favour of German views. These included agreement that the location of the European Central Bank (ECB) would be in Frankfurt, and that the new currency would be called the euro, not the ecu as the French wished, because that name was not liked by the German public. More significantly, during 1996, it was agreed that the convergence criteria set out in the TEU (Chapter 28, p. 405) would have to be met precisely, with no fudging of the issue, and that there would continue to be a stability pact after the single currency came into existence. French hopes for more political control over the monetary policy of the ECB were also dashed (Chapter 28, p. 406).

Continuing economic recession in Europe hindered the efforts of those member states that wished to participate in the single currency to meet the convergence criteria. During 1995, it was decided to abandon the earlier of the two possible starting dates for the single currency—that is, 1997—because it was obvious that not enough states, if any, would fully meet the convergence criteria by then. There was also doubt about how many would achieve the targets by 1999, the second of the two possible starting dates. In France and Belgium, the efforts of the governments to reduce the level of their budget deficits to the target of 3 per cent led to strikes and disruption. The imposition of lower public spending on economies that already had high levels of unemployment was a sure recipe for political problems.

However, in the course of 1996 and 1997, a surprising number of states did manage either to achieve or to approach the targets. This caused concern in Germany, because the idea that Italy in particular could possibly observe the conditions of the stability pact in perpetuity was not considered credible. There was a fear that the German public might reject a euro of which Italy was a part. As the trend in the Italian economy moved in the direction of the targets, so the insistence of the Germans that the targets be treated as absolutes grew. On the budget deficit, which was treated as the most important criterion, the German Finance Minister, Theo Waigel, and the President of the Bundesbank, Hans Tietmeyer, insisted that 3 per cent meant exactly 3 per cent or less, not even 3.1 per cent. This was clearly an attempt to set the target at a level that Italy would not be able to reach. The irony was that Germany missed the deficit target of 3 per cent in 1996, and looked like missing it again in 1997. A single currency without German participation was inconceivable, yet the continuing problems posed for the German economy by the absorption of East Germany threatened to disqualify it from membership on its own criteria.

All of this caused some glee within the British Conservative government, which found the whole project of monetary union extremely difficult. For domestic political reasons, the government could not join the single currency, even if it met the convergence criteria—but if the project went ahead without it, there was a risk that British economic interests would be damaged, and that British political influence within the EU would be permanently diminished. So it was with a certain air of wishing rather than predicting that Prime Minister John Major had said in an article in 1993 that 'economic and monetary union is not realisable in present circumstances' (*The Economist*, 25 September 1993). While there might have been some justification for this view in 1993, by the end of 1997, it was apparent that the single currency would start on schedule in 1999, and although it was not clear which member states would be members, it began to look as though all of those that wished to join, except Greece, would be in a position to do so.

Domestic Politics

There were significant domestic political developments during this period that affected the position of key member states on the EU. In Germany, the government of Chancellor Kohl continued uninterrupted, but the authority of the Chancellor was called into question by a number of difficulties on policy and a number of electoral setbacks. In Britain, the Conservative government of John Major experienced a series of defeats in parliamentary by-elections, which reduced its majority. This, combined with the increasingly militant anti-EU position of a significant number of its own members of Parliament (MPs), left the government with little room for manoeuvre, and its discourse on the EU became increasingly negative. Just prior to the Amsterdam European Council in June 1997, at which the Treaty of Amsterdam was agreed, the Conservative government lost office in a general election and was replaced by a Labour government under Tony Blair.

In France, there were two changes of government. In May 1995, the Gaullist Jacques Chirac was elected President in succession to the Socialist François Mitterrand. There was already a conservative majority in the National Assembly, from which Chirac nominated Alain Juppé as his Prime Minister. However, when the two rounds of parliamentary elections were held in May/June 1997, the Socialist Party won the largest share of seats, and formed a coalition with the Communists.

Chirac's initial actions as president were viewed with some concern in Germany. His decision to permit the testing of nuclear weapons in the Pacific met with protests throughout the EU, including in Germany. Only the British government supported Chirac on this. Together with the common experience of working together in Bosnia, this incident led to a measure of agreement between France and Britain. Chirac at one stage suggested that France might learn something from the British approach to the EU. However, he gradually came back into line with the position of his predecessor.

Flexible Integration

During 1994, the joint parliamentary group of the German Christian Democratic Union (CDU) and the Christian Social Union (CSU) produced a paper, authored by Karl Lamers and Wolfgang Schäuble, which suggested that a hard core of member states that wished to go ahead with closer integration should do so. A similar approach, envisaging a 'Europe of concentric circles' with France and Germany at its centre, had been outlined by the French Prime Minister, Edouard Balladur, in an interview published two days before the German paper.

These ideas were prompted primarily by the increasingly obstructionist stand taken by the British Prime Minister, John Major, on all suggestions for further integration. Shackled by a small parliamentary majority and with a significant number of his back-bench MPs hostile to further integration of Britain with the rest of the EU, Major had become an increasingly unco-operative partner. Faced with the apparent determination of the French and German governments to push ahead with monetary union, and with other measures that would be unacceptable to the parliamentary Conservative Party, Major himself had begun to contemplate the possibility of extending the arrangements that had been agreed at Maastricht for Britain to opt out of both monetary union and an integrated social policy.

In September 1994, Major gave the William and Mary Lecture at the University of Leiden. He used it as an opportunity to expound the idea of flexible integration. On the basis that trying to force all of the member states into the same mould would crack that mould, he called for an agreement that if some states wanted to integrate more closely, or more rapidly than others, they should be allowed to do so. On the other hand, it was important that no state should be excluded from participation in closer integration in any policy sector if it was willing and able to participate. This principle led Major to reject the idea of a 'hard core' Europe, although he did advocate a hard core of basic policies from which no state could opt out. These were international trade obligations, the single market, and environmental protection. Looking ahead, Major argued that bringing prosperity and stability to the states of central and eastern Europe was a historic task that required the enlargement of the EU. That enlargement would produce such a variety of member states in size, shape, economic and industrial profile, philosophy, history, and culture that it would require the introduction of the flexibility that he was advocating.

In January 1995, the former French President Valéry Giscard d'Estaing published two articles in the daily *Le Figaro* in which he went further and argued for a new Treaty with an explicitly federal aim. He suggested that, since British membership, the EU had lost sight of that ultimate objective and that it would be impossible to get back on course for a federal Europe while the British government could block every step. The new Treaty would be separate from the EU Treaties, and would exclude Britain and other countries that were reluctant to embrace the federal vocation of European integration. In common with the previous contributors to this debate, Giscard also mentioned the impending enlargement of the EU to the east. This he considered inevitable— but in common with John Major, he believed that it would be impossible to proceed down a federal road with so many and so diverse a range of members. So as well as British obstructionism, the proposed enlargement figured prominently in this debate about the need for flexibility.

Enlargement

All member states paid lip service to the principle of enlargement of the EU to the east, but some states were keener than others. For Germany, the enlargement was an absolute priority; it was also strongly supported by Britain and the Scandinavian countries. However, France, Italy, and Spain had reservations. When the shift was made from the general issue of supporting enlargement to the discussion of the detailed steps that were needed to make a reality of the aspiration, even the strongest supporters were not necessarily prepared to accept the full implications.

Germany's commitment to enlargement was based largely on security considerations. Following reunification, Germany was once again a central European state, having borders with Poland and the Czech Republic. Instability in the region would be right on Germany's doorstep, and admitting its nearest neighbours to the EU was seen as a way of guaranteeing their stability. There were also economic considerations. Before the First World War, German companies and banks had been the leading foreign investors in central Europe, and soon after the collapse of communism, German investment began to flow into the area. Guaranteeing the security of those investments was another reason for the German government's support of membership for the central European states.

British motives for welcoming enlargement were less immediately obvious, but reflected a combination of security, economic, and political considerations. In terms of security, British governments since the war had continued to support the principle of global stabilization even where British investments were not immediately involved. This was a habit of statecraft that dated back to the period before the First World War when Britain was the hegemonic power in the world and shouldered responsibility for policing the international capitalist system. That responsibility had largely passed to the United States in the period since the Second World War, but British governments had consistently supported such efforts at global stabilization. In the situation after the end of the Cold War, the US Administrations of both Bush and Clinton made it clear that they expected the EU states to play a leading role in stabilizing central and eastern Europe, and membership of the EU was specifically pressed by the Clinton administration as a means of achieving this.

In economic terms, British support for further enlargement reflected the hope that British business would be able to profit from access to a larger market. Politically, however, this enlargement would also imply a looser EU less likely to move in a federal direction. Thus in both economic and political terms, eastern enlargement suited the Conservative government of John Major.

Concerns of Member States about Enlargement

While the governments of France and the Mediterranean member states could see the arguments for enlargement to the east, and even accepted them, they were apprehensive about the effect that such an enlargement would have on the EU. First, they were concerned that an eastern enlargement would shift the balance of power in the EU decisively to the north, especially coming immediately after the accession of Austria, Finland, and Sweden. Second, and related to the first point, they were concerned that the problems of the Mediterranean, which affected them more than instability in the east, would be relegated to a secondary issue. Instability in North Africa—particularly civil war in Algeria—was already having an impact on them in the form of refugees, and threats to their companies' investments in the region. Third, they feared that EU funds that came to them through the Common

Agricultural Policy (CAP) and the structural funds would be diverted to central and eastern European economies.

The concern that attention would be diverted from the problems of the Mediterranean was recognized by the German government when it held the presidency of the EU in the second half of 1994. Agreement was reached at the Essen European Council in December 1994 to launch an initiative on North Africa and the Middle East. This assumed more tangible form during 1995 under the successive French and Spanish presidencies, culminating in a major conference in Barcelona from 23 to 29 November 1995 involving the EU member states, the Maghreb states (Algeria, Morocco, and Tunisia), Israel, Jordan, Lebanon, Syria, Turkey, Cyprus, and Malta. The central and eastern European states were also represented. The conference agreed on a stability pact for the Middle East on the model of the Conference on Security and Co-operation in Europe (CSCE) and the EU agreed to contribute US$6 billion in aid and US$6 billion in **European Investment Bank (EIB)** loans to the economic development of the region.

The problem of accepting the implications of a commitment to enlargement to the east were apparent in November 1995 when the Commission proposed that agricultural imports from six central and eastern European states (Bulgaria, the Czech Republic, Hungary, Poland, Romania, and Slovakia) be increased by 10 per cent a year. Britain, Denmark, The Netherlands, and Sweden supported the proposal. France and the Mediterranean member states opposed it, indicating that they would only be prepared to accept an increase of 5 per cent a year. Germany, which was ostensibly the strongest supporter of enlargement, joined the Mediterranean states in opposing the Commission's proposal. This indicated the strength of the farming lobby in Germany, and the fragmented nature of decision making in the country, which allowed the Agriculture Ministry to adopt a line so clearly incompatible with the official policy as enunciated by the Chancellor's office.

The same contradiction in policy emerged after July 1997 when the Commission published its *Agenda 2000* report on the future direction of the EU in the likely context of enlargement. The German Farm Minister, Ignaz Kiechle, publicly stated that the proposed reforms of the CAP were unnecessary. He received no reprimand for this from Chancellor Kohl. In addition to the reform of key policies, the eastern enlargement had implications for the decision-making procedures of the EU. This came to be one of the key issues in the IGC that led up to the Treaty of Amsterdam. (On enlargement, see also Chapter 34.)

The 1996 IGC

Originally, the 1996 IGC was intended to review the working of the TEU (Chapter 13, pp. 161–4). Provision for such a review was written into the agreements that were reached at Maastricht in December 1991. However, nobody expected the ratification of the TEU to take as long as it did, with the result that the review started after only two-and-a-half years of experience of the new arrangements. The difficulties in ratifying the TEU (Chapter 13, pp. 164–5) also meant that there was little appetite for further fundamental change. Increasingly, the IGC came to be seen as primarily about preparing the ground for the Eastern enlargement. There were several institutional issues that needed to be addressed if the EU were to enlarge to over twenty members: the size of the Commission and the European Parliament (EP); the rotation of the presidency of the Council; the extent of **qualified majority voting (QMV)**; and the weighting of votes under QMV.

The Commission had twenty members in 1995, and that was already too many for the number of portfolios available, as Jacques Santer found out when he tried to allocate responsibilities without upsetting either national sensibilities or the *amour propre* of his colleagues in the College of Commissioners. Enlargement threatened to produce an unwieldy organization. The British government offered to relinquish its second Commissioner if the other large states would agree to do so, but this was not an easy concession for the others. For Italy and Spain in particular, having two Commissioners was a matter of national pride, singling out their countries as larger member states on a par with Germany, France, and Britain. Even if there were to have been unanimous agreement to dispense with the second Commissioners, the problem of too many Commissioners would have remained.

The EP would also become unwieldy if the same rough formula that had been used up to the 1995 enlargement were applied to further member states. Clearly, there had to be some limit put on the numbers—but that had implications for the existing distribution of seats.

With twelve member states, and with the presidency of the Council changing every six months, there were six years between presidencies for any one state (see Chapter 21, pp. 286–8). This meant that all of the expertise that had been acquired for one presidency was lost by the time the next one came round. There was also concern that the next enlargement would involve mostly small states, as had the 1995 enlargement. Small states often had problems with servicing the presidency. The problems had been eased since the Troika system had come into operation, whereby the present, previous, and immediate future presidents co-operated. However, the impending enlargement heralded a situation in which there might not be a large state in the Troika for much of the time.

On QMV, the German and French governments wanted to see an extension to cover areas under the Justice and Home Affairs (JHA) pillar of the TEU, but the British Conservative government was adamantly opposed to any extension of QMV. The British government was also, along with Spain, one of the strongest advocates of a reweighting of the votes under QMV.

Because the number of votes allocated to a state was not directly proportional to its population, the increase in the number of small member states had produced a situation in which measures could be passed under QMV with the support of the representatives of a decreasing proportion of the total population of the EU. In the original European Community (EC) of six states, votes representing 70 per cent of the population were needed to pass a measure. By 1995, this had been reduced to 58.3 per cent and, on the basis of some reasonable assumptions about the allocation of votes to future members, the proportion required could be as low as 50.3 per cent with an EU of 26 states. The French government supported the idea of a reweighting of votes, but the German Chancellor was hesitant because of the concern expressed by the smaller member states that this would be yet another step towards downgrading their role.

Beyond these specific institutional issues, each member state went to the IGC with particular issues that it wished to push. Sweden, Denmark, and the Netherlands were concerned to increase the accountability and transparency of Council business, and proposed that a freedom of information clause be written into the Treaty. Sweden was also a leading mover in pressing for a chapter on employment policy to be added to the Treaty.

In March 1996, the Swedish government called a meeting in Oslo to build support for this proposal; France, Germany, Britain, and Italy were not invited. Britain wanted reform to the working of the European Court of Justice (ECJ), having suffered several adverse judgments at its hands. Britain and France both pressed for an enhanced role for national parliaments in the policy-making process. France and Germany pressed the flexibility issue hard; they also co-operated in putting forward proposals to move towards incorporating the Western European Union (WEU) (see Chapter 7, Insight 7.1, p. 108) into the EU, something that was strongly opposed by the neutral member states (Austria, Ireland, and Sweden) and by Britain.

The IGC was preceded by a 'Reflection Group', which met in the second half of 1995 under the Spanish presidency. This consisted of representatives of the Foreign Ministers and two members of the EP. It had a remit to seek the views of other institutions on progress towards European union, and possible amendments to the TEU, and to prepare a report on the issues that should form the agenda of the IGC.

When he reported on the work of the Group in December 1995, the Spanish Foreign Minister Carlos Westendorp said that there was agreement that the IGC should not aim at fundamental reform, but be about necessary changes: in particular it should be seen as one part of the process of Eastern enlargement. Werner Hoyer, the German representative on the Reflection Group, indicated publicly that the work of the Group had soon deteriorated into an exchange of national positions, and warned that there was a risk of the IGC turning into a confrontation between integrationists and intergovernmentalists.

The IGC and the British Beef Dispute

The IGC opened officially in Turin on 29 March 1996. The special European Council that was called to inaugurate it was dominated, though, by the ban on exports of British beef. This had been imposed in the aftermath of the announcement that bovine spongiform encephalopathy (BSE) in cattle, with which British herds were particularly infected, could be the cause of Creutzfeldt–Jakob disease (CJD) in humans. As British efforts to get the ban lifted made little progress over the coming weeks, John Major threatened to block progress in the IGC, and to refuse to sign any Treaty that emerged from it until the ban was lifted. His government did in fact veto just about every item of EU business over which it could exercise a veto until an agreement was reached on a phased lifting of the ban.

This incident marked a new low in relations between the British Conservative government and the rest of the EU. Patience was already exhausted before Major threatened to block agreement on a new Treaty unless two changes were made to the existing one. First, he demanded agreement to allow the reversal of a decision of the ECJ that a directive on a 48-hour maximum working week must apply to Britain, despite the

British government's opt-out from the social protocol, because it was a health and safety issue and so covered by the Single European Act (SEA). Second, he demanded that changes were made to the Common Fisheries Policy, to prevent fishing boats from other member states buying quotas from British fishermen.

There were some indications that the IGC was deliberately prolonged into 1997 in the hope that the British general election would produce a change of government, which it did. The Labour government under Tony Blair indicated immediately that while its priorities would remain largely those of its predecessor, it would not block a Treaty over any issue other than that Britain must be allowed to retain its border controls. The way was thus cleared for agreement on the text of a new Treaty at the European Council in Amsterdam in June 1997.

The Treaty of Amsterdam

Agreement was reached at Amsterdam on a rather modest Treaty. In particular, no agreement could be reached on the institutional reforms that were believed to be essential to pave the way for enlargement. Also, there was little extension of QMV because Chancellor Kohl retreated from his earlier advocacy of the principle, and actually blocked its extension to cover industrial policy, social policy, and certain aspects of the free movement of labour.

As a result of what may have been an oversight, the failure to extend QMV to these three areas did not lead to withdrawal of the linked proposal to increase the powers of the EP in the same areas. So when the EP was given the right to amend or reject proposed legislation in two dozen areas that were brought under co-decision for the first time, these areas were still included.

Dutch plans to extend QMV into eleven policy areas, ranging from cultural activities to industrial policy, ran into German resistance. Kohl insisted that these extensions would undermine the position of the German Länder. The only two extensions of QMV that were agreed were for research programmes and compensatory aid for imports of raw materials. In addition, new areas were agreed in which QMV would apply from the start—namely: countering fraud; encouraging customs co-operation; collating statistics; and laying down rules for the free movement of personal data.

On the number of Commissioners, a compromise was reached that if more than two and fewer than six new members were to join the EU, the Commission would continue to have one representative from each member state. However, Spain insisted that it would only surrender its second Commissioner in return for changes in the weighting of votes in the Council, which could not be agreed.

Rules on allowing flexible integration were agreed. In the first pillar, if a group of member states were to want to proceed with closer integration in a sector, but others did not, those who wanted to go ahead could do so provided that the Council of Ministers agreed to such a proposal by QMV. However, if any member state were to insist that the development would jeopardize its vital national interests, it could veto the move.

In the second pillar—Common Foreign and Security Policy (CFSP)—the system would be 'constructive abstention'. This would allow a group of member states to undertake a joint action in the name of the EU, if those member states that did not feel that they could take part were prepared not to vote against but to abstain, on the understanding that they would not then be required to contribute to the action (see Chapter 33, p. 514).

In the third pillar, complete freedom of movement was pledged for all individuals within the EU, but the UK and Ireland were allowed to retain border controls. Decisions on immigration, visas, and asylum were to be subject to unanimity for at least five years, and then reviewed with a view to introducing more flexible arrangements, but with any member state being allowed to apply a veto on changing the procedure.

On CFSP, it was agreed that the Council Secretary-General would represent the EU to the outside world. QMV would be used on implementing foreign policy measures, but any state that believed that its vital national interests were at stake could exercise a veto. The WEU might be incorporated into the EU in the future, but NATO was reaffirmed as central to Europe's defence. The Amsterdam Treaty also amended the TEU to distinguish between, on the one hand, deciding the principles and general guidelines of the CFSP, and common strategies in pursuit of these, and, on the other, the adoption of joint actions, common positions, and implementing decisions (Chapter 33).

Finally, it was agreed that an area of freedom, security, and justice (AFSJ) for EU citizens would come into force within five years of ratification. This was the big policy idea of the Amsterdam Treaty and communitarized some of the EU's policy on JHA (see Chapter 31, pp. 471–2).

CONCLUSION

The post-Maastricht period prepared the ground for flexible integration as the EU entered a period of tremendous uncertainty in both its global context and its internal functioning. Ironically, the provisions for flexible integration were scarcely used. They had been designed with the obstructionism of the Major government in mind, but it was replaced by the more constructive government of Tony Blair.

Enlargement to eastern Europe was the biggest item on the post-Maastricht agenda, and promised to transform the EU itself beyond all recognition. A definite tension developed between the will of all member states to consolidate democracy and capitalism in eastern and central Europe and the willingness of any member state to accept economic sacrifices to allow that enlargement to happen. Willing the end did not appear to mean necessarily willing the means. Domestic politics often assumed priority when it came to trying to agree the details of reforms to the common policies and to the central institutions that everyone agreed were necessary to facilitate the enlargement.

As with the EC and the Mediterranean enlargements in the 1970s, eastern enlargement in the forthcoming twenty-first century was part of the enhanced security role for the EU in the world after the decline of US hegemony; so was the need to make progress on the CFSP, which had been incorporated into the TEU. Here, immediate national economic interests were less directly involved, so there was the prospect of progress—but national cultural differences emerged, as did differing national security interests. The CFSP forum also provided Britain with an opportunity to be more centrally involved with the EU, alongside France, as the two states with the most efficient professional armies. Germany remained hampered by a suspicion throughout central

Europe of Germans in uniforms, and reluctance among the German people themselves to see their forces committed to military operations in other countries.

The attitudes of the publics of France and Britain were different, being accustomed to their national forces forming part of UN peacekeeping operations. The legitimacy of the EU in Germany was shaken by the decision to adopt the single currency, and by what appeared to be the centralization of functions that had previously been the responsibility of the Länder. It was this last concern that caused Helmut Kohl to backtrack at Amsterdam from his previous insistence that there should be more QMV.

Concern to prevent further slippage of powers from the national or sub-national level to the supranational level was apparent throughout the EU by the time of Amsterdam, indicating the increasing emphasis on intergovernmentalism. There were the first indications that a new form of co-operation was emerging, one that cast the Commission in a different role as an impartial arbiter and referee of agreements for co-ordinated national action rather than as enforcer of legally binding commitments, a development that would also have implications for the role of the ECJ.

KEY POINTS

Monetary Union

- In 1995, details of monetary union began to emerge. The ECB would be located in Frankfurt and the single currency would be called the 'euro'.

- Although recession hindered attempts by some states to meet the convergence criteria, the single currency stayed on course for a 1999 launch.

Domestic Politics

- Significant domestic political developments during this period affected the position of key member states on the EU and shaped the prospects for flexible integration.

Flexible Integration

- In 1994, the idea of flexible integration became widespread. This was the notion that some member states might integrate further and faster than others.

Enlargement

- While member states were generally supportive of further enlargement to include countries of central and eastern Europe, there were a number of concerns over the impact this would have on key policies, such as agriculture and the structural funds, and also on decision-making procedures.

The 1996 IGC

- The 1996 IGC focused on the institutional changes necessary to prepare for further enlargement. This IGC was also marked by conflict over the British 'beef' crisis, which resulted in the Major government blocking agreement on a range of issues.

The Treaty of Amsterdam

- Resulting from the 1996 IGC, this Treaty was relatively modest in scope. In particular, it did not contain the decision-making reforms that most thought were necessary for incorporating several new member states.

179

FURTHER READING

Useful guides to the Treaty of Amsterdam are **European Commission**, *The Amsterdam Treaty: A Comprehensive Guide* (1999) and **A. Duff**, *The Treaty of Amsterdam: Text and Commentary* (London: Federal Trust/Sweet and Maxwell, 1997). On the politics that led up to the Treaty, see **G. Edwards and A. Pijpers**, *The Politics of European Treaty Reform: The 1996 Intergovernmental Conference and Beyond* (London, and Washington, DC: Pinter, 1997).

A reaction to Amsterdam from an intergovernmentalist perspective is given in **A. Moravcsik and K. Nicolaïdes**, 'Explaining the Treaty of Amsterdam: Interests, Influences, Institutions', *Journal of Common Market Studies*, 37 (1999): 59–85. Other analyses are offered by **E. Philippart and G. Edwards**, 'The Provisions on Closer Co-operation in the Treaty of Amsterdam', *Journal of Common Market Studies*, 37 (1999): 87–108, and **Y. Devuyst**, 'The Community-Method after Amsterdam', *Journal of Common Market Studies*, 37 (1999): 109–20.

online resource centre

Visit the Online Resource Centre that accompanies this book for links to more information on flexible integration and the Treaty of Amsterdam: www.oxfordtextbooks.co.uk/orc/bache3e/

Chapter 15

From Amsterdam to Nice: Preparing for Enlargement

Chapter Overview

Following the agreement of the Amsterdam Treaty, the agenda of the European Union (EU) was initially dominated by the opening of enlargement negotiations. However, the post-Amsterdam period began with both a symbolic milestone and an embarrassing setback. The milestone was the start of monetary union, thirty years after it had first been declared an objective of the European Community (EC) at the Hague Summit in 1969. The embarrassment was a crisis that led to the resignation of the European Commission. The period also saw significant steps taken in the formulation of a European Security and Defence Policy, and the declaration of a new approach to increasing the economic competitiveness of the EU. The period concluded with the longest European Council in history, which led to the Treaty of Nice. In these negotiations, concerns with flexible integration were soon overtaken by more traditional battles over institutional reform.

The Treaty of Nice may have paved the way for enlargement, but to many it provided sub-optimal solutions to the institutional challenges posed by a significantly larger EU.

(Phinnemore 2003: 58)

Following the Amsterdam European Council, momentum quickly began to build towards enlargement. Soon after the European Council meeting, in July 1997, the Commission produced a report entitled *Agenda 2000*, which outlined the internal reforms that would be needed to prepare the EU for enlargement, and the Commission's formal Opinions on the preparedness of the applicant states. However, before the enlargement process took its next significant step at the Helsinki European Council in December 1999, the EU achieved a major milestone in the field of monetary union and experienced a major setback in credibility through a crisis in the Commission.

The Euro

In January 1999, the euro came into operation for eleven member states: Austria, Belgium, Finland, France, Germany, Ireland, Italy, Luxembourg, The Netherlands,

Portugal, and Spain. This meant that the euro became the official currency of these states, although national notes and coins continued in circulation until 2002. Greece was initially excluded from the eurozone by failing to meet the convergence criteria, but its application to join was approved by the European Council in Santa Maria de Feira (Portugal) in June 2000, and it became a full member in January 2001. Britain, Denmark, and Sweden chose not to join the single currency. Britain and Denmark had negotiated opt-outs, while Sweden excluded itself on the technicality that it had not been a member of the exchange rate mechanism (ERM) for two years and as such was not eligible. There were concerns over Italy's use of a one-off 'euro-tax' to ensure that it met the budget-deficit criterion in the qualifying financial year; both Belgium and Italy had debt ratios that appeared to go beyond the criteria (see Chapter 28, pp. 405–8). Despite all of this, the completion of monetary union, almost thirty years after the Hague Summit had made it an explicit objective, was a considerable achievement.

Although the single currency came into existence more smoothly than many economists predicted, it soon ran into difficulties. The external value of the euro fell steadily against the US dollar, and the 'eurozone' itself began to exhibit some of the problems of having a single interest rate for such a diverse economic area. National economies on the fringes of the zone, particularly those of Spain and Ireland, began to experience the symptoms of repressed inflation, with rapidly rising property prices and shortages of labour. At the same time, the core economies of Germany and France were experiencing sluggish growth.

It was in this context that, as soon as the new currency came into existence, Oskar Lafontaine and Dominique Strauss-Kahn, Finance Ministers of Germany and France respectively, pressed the European Central Bank (ECB) to lower interest rates to stimulate growth. The ECB and its President Wim Duisenberg vigorously resisted such interference, though, and the pressure was reduced after Lafontaine resigned in March 1999. Nevertheless, a majority of states within the eurozone continued to experience lower rates of growth and higher unemployment than the economies of those EU member states—Britain, Denmark, and Sweden—that remained outside the single currency. Against such a background, it was perhaps unsurprising that the Danish people rejected membership of the euro in a referendum in September 2000. The Swedes would follow suit three years later and the British government deferred holding a referendum on joining (see Chapter 16).

The Commission in Crisis

If the Amsterdam Treaty (Chapter 14) represented little advance on key areas of institutional reform, the Commission crisis of 1999 put the transparency and accountability of EU institutions under severe scrutiny. The report of the Court of Auditors on the 1996 budget had led the European Parliament's (EP) Budget Committee in March 1998 to refuse to recommend discharge of the budget by the whole EP (the process of discharging the budget is explained in Chapter 19, p. 239). The Committee was particularly concerned about alleged mismanagement of the Humanitarian Aid budget, which at that time had been under the control of Commissioner Manuel Marin, who was by 1998 a Vice-President of the Commission.

In October 1998, President Santer, together with Emma Bonino, who was by then in charge of the European Community Humanitarian Aid Office (ECHO), appeared before the Budget Committee to admit that an investigation by the Commission's internal fraud unit had indeed revealed irregularities in the expenditure of funds allocated to ECHO. In fact, ECHO had apparently not audited any of its external contracts until 1995, and the Commission therefore had no guarantees of how money had been spent between 1993 and 1995. The internal fraud unit had discovered that at least two contracts, for personnel and equipment for operations in Bosnia and in Africa, had been completely fictitious, and that most of the money appeared to have been spent on extra administrative staff for the Brussels office. However, some 400,000–600,000 ecus of the money had proved untraceable.

Despite an offer from Santer to recreate the fraud office as a separate agency outside of the Commission, the EP in December 1998 refused discharge of the 1996 budget. It expressed concern about the ECHO affair, and also about what appeared to be impropriety in making appointments under the LEONARDO Youth Training Programme, which was the responsibility of the French Commissioner, Edith Cresson. In the meantime, the Court of Auditor's report on the 1997 budget had appeared, and indicated that some 5 per cent of total EC expenditure could not adequately be accounted for.

The EP laid down a motion of censure on the Commission, which did not achieve the two-thirds majority required to remove the Commission from office, but which did achieve the largest vote for a motion of censure since the EC began: 232, with 293 against and 27 abstentions. This result was despite the Socialist Group, the largest single party group in the EP, officially deciding to vote against the motion. In an attempt to head off the censure, Santer produced a plan of action, which he put to the EP on 11 January 1999. This involved:

- new codes of conduct for Commissioners, their *cabinets*, and all Commission staff;
- the setting up of an independent fraud unit outside of the Commission itself;
- an audit of all of the Commission's activities and departments, leading to proposals for restructuring;
- a promise of proposals to modernize the administration of the Commission;
- a review of budgetary management and of appointments to senior positions;
- the negotiation of an agreement with the EP on how members of the European Parliament (MEPs) would be kept informed on financial expenditure, and how to ensure effective EP scrutiny of spending.

This compromise at first seemed to have averted a crisis, but in March 1999, a committee of five independent experts that had been set up to look into the internal management of the Commission issued a damaging report, which suggested widespread malfunctioning of the system. Santer and his whole College of Commissioners then resigned, just after midnight on 15–16 March. The EP claimed this as a great victory for its persistence in scrutinizing the activities of the Commission.

The European Council's preferred candidate to succeed Santer was the former Prime Minister of Italy, Romano Prodi, whose candidature was approved by the EP in May

1999 by a majority of 392 to 72. Prodi's appointment was delayed by a case in the Italian courts over what proved to be false accusations of corruption relating to the Italian privatization programme. He came to the job in September 1999 committed to cleaning up the Commission's image and made clear his intention to discipline errant Commissioners. Prodi stated that his own staff would be multinational, to avoid claims of national 'cronyism'.

Enlargement

In December 1999, the Helsinki European Council agreed to open accession negotiations with Bulgaria, Latvia, Lithuania, Malta, Romania, and Slovakia, and also recognized Turkey as an applicant country (see Chapter 34, p. 534). In January 2000, accession negotiations with these states opened in Brussels. The key issues outlined by the EU delegation were the importance of: formal transposal and implementation of Community law; ensuring effective functioning of the single market and EU policies; and alignment with EU policies on relations with third countries and international organizations. Later that year, in October, the Commission provided the Council with its report on enlargement, which consisted of progress reports on the preparations of each country and outlined the requirements for Turkey to begin accession negotiations. The Gothenburg European Council of June 2001 agreed the framework for the successful completion of the enlargement negotiations, and in December of the same year, the Council signalled its intention to conclude negotiations with the candidate countries by the end of 2002 so that they could participate in the 2004 EP elections.

In order to be ready to take as many as twelve new members, the EU had to deal with some difficult issues requiring reforms of both policies and institutions. Two policy issues were particularly crucial to the prospects for enlargement: agriculture and the structural funds. The institutional questions were those that were already apparent at the time of the European Free Trade Association (EFTA) enlargement: the weighting of votes under **qualified majority voting (QMV)**, and the size of the blocking minority; the abandonment of the national veto in more policy sectors; and the size of the Commission.

Agriculture accounted for 25 per cent of the gross domestic product (GDP) of the applicant states, with production concentrated in the products that were already the most problematic for the EU: meat; dairy products; and cereals. Productivity within the applicant states varied considerably, but was generally lower than in the EU. Application of the Common Agriculture Policy (CAP) directly to the new entrants would be likely to encourage higher output. It would have an unsustainable impact on the cost of the CAP, and would generate increased surpluses in the products that were already most of a problem. At the same time, the higher cost of food to the consumer would have an inflationary effect in the new entrants, for which expenditure on food accounted for a higher proportion of total household expenditure than it did in the west. The struggle to get the existing member states to accept the sort of far-reaching reform of the CAP that was necessary to pave the way for enlargement is told in Chapter 26.

The reform of the structural funds was similarly dogged by the refusal of existing beneficiaries to accept that they would have to give up much of their funding in order to allow enlargement to take place within existing budgetary ceilings. The Commission's proposals, unveiled in March 1998, would result in no state losing more than one-third of its eligibility for Objective 2 aid (for regions suffering industrial decline). Long and generous transitional arrangements were made for regions that would lose Objective 1 status (for least developed regions). Even so, it proved difficult to get agreement, leading the Commissioner, Monika Wulf-Mathies, to warn a Council of Ministers meeting in Glasgow in June 1998 that governments had to stop pretending that enlargement would be possible without making sacrifices on structural funding (see also Chapter 29 on 'Cohesion Policy').

Difficulties in getting agreement on policy issues were paralleled by problems in getting agreement on the institutional reforms that would also be necessary to facilitate enlargement. The Amsterdam European Council of June 1997 (Chapter 14, pp. 177–8) ended one intergovernmental conference (IGC) that was supposed to resolve these issues, but without agreement on them. A new IGC was convened in February 2000, and met throughout the year, but it also had produced no agreement on the most controversial issues by the time of the Nice European Council in December.

Other Developments

There were significant policy developments in this period in the areas of economic and social policy (with the agreement on 'the Lisbon Strategy'), the Common Foreign and Security Policy (CFSP), and Justice and Home Affairs (JHA).

The Lisbon Strategy

In March 2000, a special European Council held in Lisbon agreed to a new EU strategy on employment, economic reform, and social cohesion, with the goal of making the EU 'the most competitive and dynamic knowledge-based economy in the world' by 2010. Its adoption was justified with reference to the challenge of globalization:

> The European Union is confronted with a quantum shift resulting from globalization and the challenges of a new knowledge-driven economy. These challenges are affecting every aspect of people's lives and require a radical transformation of the European economy.

> (Presidential Conclusions, Lisbon Special European Council, 23–4 March, para. 1)

The outcome subsequently became known variously as the 'Lisbon Strategy', the 'Lisbon Process', or the 'Lisbon Agenda'. Success of the strategy depended on strengthening investment in research and development, reducing bureaucracy to stimulate innovation and entrepreneurship, and improving the employment rate to 70 per cent overall, including a minimum of 60 per cent for women.

Two features of the strategy were particularly significant. First, economic competitiveness and social cohesion were placed side by side as objectives. Critics of the strategy from the left maintained that the economic competitiveness elements represented a victory for the advocates of an Anglo-Saxon model of capitalism, while critics from the right argued that the social cohesion elements represented a victory for the advocates of a 'social Europe'. It seems more likely that the new approach represented less the victory of one model of capitalism over the other than a political compromise between the positions of the left and right.

Second, the Lisbon Strategy was to be pursued through what the Presidential Conclusions to the summit described as the 'open method of co-ordination' (OMC). The OMC is described in more detail in Chapter 25 (pp. 363–4). Its main features, as delineated at Lisbon, were common guidelines to be translated into national policies, combined with periodic monitoring, evaluation, and peer review organized as mutual learning processes, and accompanied by indicators and benchmarks as means of comparing best practice. In essence, this was an extension of the approach already adopted 'in the procedures for coordinating national economic policies under the Economic and Monetary Union (EMU) established in the Maastricht Treaty, and in the employment chapter of the Amsterdam Treaty' (Borras and Jacobsson 2004: 187–8). As such, it was a departure from the 'Community method' of decision making, whereby the Commission makes proposals for legislation and the Council of Ministers (increasingly in conjunction with the EP) adopts the legislation, which then supersedes national legislation (subsequently the Union method). Most significantly, it was a departure in the direction of a more intergovernmental process, where policy competences would not be transferred to the EU, but would be retained at the national level, the Commission would play a less prominent role as the facilitator of intergovernmental co-ordination, and the EP and European Court of Justice would have no real role at all. To strengthen this impression of firm national control over the process, it was agreed that one European Council out of three each year—the spring meeting—would be devoted to reviewing progress.

Common Foreign and Security Policy (CFSP)

In the immediate aftermath of agreement at Amsterdam to extend the scope of CFSP, the EU was once again embarrassed in the course of 1998 by its inability to take decisive action in former Yugoslavia. Attacks by Serb forces on ethnic Albanians in the province of Kosovo had to be countered by NATO, which launched a bombing campaign against the Serbs. Although EU member states participated in this, the lead came from the United States, which flew 60 per cent of all sorties, 80 per cent of strike sorties, and provided the crucial intelligence, communications, and logistical capabilities (Cornish and Edwards 2001: 588).

Kosovo provided the stimulus to a further push on the CFSP front. In December 1998, the French President, Jacques Chirac, and the British Prime Minister, Tony Blair, held a bilateral summit at St Malo in France, at the end of which they declared their joint support for a European Security and Defence Policy (ESDP); a year later, the Helsinki European Council announced the creation of a European Rapid Reaction Force. These moves served the interests of both Chirac and Blair. For Chirac, they were a further step towards a long-standing French goal, which was in line with the Gaullist aspiration for an EU that was capable of acting independently of the United States. For Blair, ESDP marked a new leading project for the EU in which British participation would be central, in marked contrast to the marginalization of Britain in the previous leading sector of monetary union.

Although Blair had an interest in seeing security and defence take the centre of the EU stage, there was no wish on the part of the British government to weaken the NATO alliance. For this reason, the appointment in November 1999 of Javier Solana, the then NATO Secretary-General, as the first EU High Representative for Foreign Affairs was an important decision. Solana was acceptable to the United States, and in moving directly from the NATO post to the EU post, he was in a strong position to ensure compatibility between the actions of the two organizations.

So, by the end of the decade, CFSP/ESDP looked as though it was about to become a significant new direction of advance for the EU. That it was not just a Franco-British enthusiasm was indicated by the fact that all fifteen of the then member states agreed to participate in the Kosovo Force (KFOR), which moved in to preserve the peace and assist in the reconstruction of the province after the end of the bombing campaign. It was widely noted at the time, though, that in this traditionally most intergovernmental of policy sectors, the member states had ignored a strong suggestion from the Commission that the office of the High Representative should be located within the Commission, and had instead opted to make it a position within the Secretariat of the Council. This was in line with the same mood for inter-governmental approaches that was evident in the adoption of the OMC as the basis for the Lisbon Strategy. Also, seasoned observers of the CFSP, and its predecessor European Political Co-operation (EPC), might have wondered what would happen to the new spirit of EU co-ordination should another crisis like the Gulf War erupt, in which the United States opted for military intervention and demanded that its NATO allies follow its lead. Would European unity hold, or would the old differences of opinion on how to respond to US unilateralism re-emerge? (see also Chapter 33, pp. 512–5).

Justice and Home Affairs (JHA)

Following agreement at Amsterdam that an area of freedom, security, and justice for EU citizens would come into force within five years of ratification, the Tampere European Council (October 1999) agreed a programme of action to address the problems raised by the free movement of people across its internal borders. This involved some sixty steps to be taken by 2004 relating largely to issues of asylum and immigration, and combating crime. The Commission was charged with the task of monitoring the progress towards the completion of these steps (see also Chapter 31, p. 472).

The Nice European Council

The Treaty of Amsterdam made institutional reform a precondition of enlargement and contained a Protocol anticipating further discussions on reform. The Cologne European Council of 1999 referred to this Protocol in agreeing to set up an IGC to discuss the outstanding institutional issues that had not been resolved at Amsterdam: particularly in relation to the weighting of votes in the Council, the size and composition of the Commission, and the possible extension of QMV. The Commission was charged with putting forward options for change.

The IGC opened in February 2000, under the Portuguese presidency, and continued into the French presidency in the second half of the year. At the Biarritz European Council in October 2000, a number of points of contention remained. There were different political positions on the weighting of votes within the Council, with Germany arguing that its voting weight should reflect its size and population. France, however, was keen to retain the same voting weight as Germany. On the Commission, the larger member states joined forces to argue for a smaller Commission based on a rotation system, while smaller member states were critical of a proposed reduction in the number of Commissioners. On QMV, there were clear and distinct positions. For example, Britain in particular was keen to prevent QMV from spreading to areas of taxation, Germany was keen to protect unanimity over asylum and immigration policies, and France was keen to prevent QMV from being applied to certain external issues in the area of trade in services.

Nice turned out to be the longest European Council in the history of the EC/EU. For four days, the heads of government haggled over the areas that would become subject to QMV, and over the weighting of votes. Membership of the Commission proved less difficult, although really tough decisions were deferred by allowing the size of the College of Commissioners to grow to twenty-seven before there would be a move to having fewer than one Commissioner per member state—but in return for giving up their second Commissioner, the large member states fought even harder on the weighting of votes in the Council. In the end, an agreement was reached that just about opened up the prospect of the EU being ready for enlargement.

The Outcome

The veto was removed from twenty-nine of the seventy Treaty Articles to which it still applied—but in important areas, national interests prevented movement. Britain would not agree to the removal of the veto on tax or social security harmonization. Although QMV for trade negotiations was extended to services, at French insistence, exceptions were made for audiovisual services, education, and health. Maritime transport was exempted from QMV at the insistence of Denmark and Greece. Many aspects of immigration and asylum policy were not transferred to QMV at German and French insistence. Perhaps most significantly, though, Spain, with the support of Portugal and Greece, retained the right to veto changes to the cohesion funds until after the conclusion of the negotiations on the 2007–12 Financial Perspective. This cast further doubt on the possibility of keeping the cost of enlargement to the common budget within limits acceptable to the net contributors.

On the weighting of votes under QMV, the large member states seemed to gain an advantage over the small. The reweighting, which would apply from 1 January 2005, left the small and medium-sized states with a smaller percentage of the total vote relative to the larger states than under the previous system. There was also the insertion of a clause requiring any measure agreed by QMV to comprise the votes of governments representing at least 62 per cent of the population of the EU. The effect was to put Germany, France, and Britain, or any two of these three plus Italy, in a position in which they could effectively block progress on any measure on which they agreed to co-operate. In compensation, the small states were allowed a clause that a measure agreed under QMV would also have to have the support of a majority of the member states. The cumulative effect of these two concessions to different coalitions of 'bigs' and 'smalls' was to make the decision-making system much more complex, and also to make it more difficult than previously to achieve a qualified majority, which now required a 'triple majority': a majority of weighted votes; a majority of member states; and a 62 per cent or higher majority of the population.

The Treaty of Nice was formally signed in the following February, following eleven months of negotiation. The Treaty redistributed votes in the Council in favour of the more populous member states and also introduced the complex 'triple majority' voting procedure that would be in place from 2005 and which looked certain to slow down decision making in an enlarged EU. It also extended the use of QMV into around thirty new areas, but retained the veto in areas such as social policy and taxation. The Treaty strengthened the powers of the President of the Commission and provided for one Commissioner per member state from 2005, with the proviso that the maximum number in future should be twenty-six, and from that point onwards a rotation system would ensure parity among states. In relation to the EP, the Treaty extended the co-decision procedure and also changed the allocation of seats between states and set a maximum of 732 MEPs.

Commentators were critical of the achievements of Nice. Phinnemore (2003: 58) described the outcome as 'sub-optimal' in relation to enlargement, while Dinan (2004: 288) suggested that 'rarely did an intergovernmental conference devote so much time to so few issues with so few consequential results'. It undoubtedly made decision making more complex by increasing the number of thresholds for agreement in the Council, and deferred decisions in other areas. Moreover, the negotiations raised tensions between big states and small states that would reappear when the outstanding issues were tackled in the negotiations over the Draft Constitutional Treaty (Chapter 16).

The Charter of Fundamental Rights

In a parallel initiative, also confirmed at Nice in December 2000, the EU set out its commitment to citizens' rights in the Charter of Fundamental Rights of the European Union. This Charter was drawn up by a Convention established by the Cologne European Council in June 1999 and set out a range of civil, economic, political, and social rights of European citizens for the first time in a single text. The fifty-six Articles of the Charter fell under six headings—namely: Dignity; Freedoms; Equality; Solidarity; Citizens' Rights; and Justice. The Charter was agreed by the Biarritz Council in October 2000 before being approved by the Commission and EP. The formal signing of this Charter by the Presidents of the Council, the EP, and the Commission at Nice was a political declaration that was not legally binding on member states. Its significance would have to await future events and, not least, the deliberations and outcome of the Lisbon Treaty (Chapter 18).

CONCLUSION

This period highlights a number of the themes that were set out in the opening chapters of the book. The most prominent is perhaps that of intergovernmentalism (Chapter 1), which had by this time become the dominant tone of the EU. Although governments sought enlargement, in the negotiations over both the policy reforms and the institutional reforms that were necessary to assimilate the new member states, the protection and projection of national interests were never far from the surface. Developments in CFSP/ESDP pointed to the influence of external factors on internal EU relations, but the decision to locate the High Representative for Foreign Affairs within the Council Secretariat rather than the Commission again indicated the intergovernmental nature of this area of policy. Intergovernmentalism may also be seen as a prominent explanation of the move away from the traditional Community method of decision making with the introduction of the OMC—but this development highlights as well the growing relevance of theories emphasizing new forms of governance in the EU (Chapter 2).

The Commission crisis raised questions about the legitimacy of the EU and its institutions (Chapter 4). As an unelected body, the Commission draws much of its legitimacy through its contribution to efficient and effective decision making—the 'performance' dimension of legitimacy. In this case, the Commission's failings in one particular area cast a shadow over its legitimacy more generally and, in doing so, added to wider concerns over the legitimacy of the EU as a whole. On a more positive note, the decisive response of the EP did something to redeem perceptions of the EU and added weight to arguments for its role to grow further for the sake of greater accountability.

If in some respects this was a period in which governments were assertive, it was also one in which developments were linked by the need for the EU to compete economically in a rapidly globalizing marketplace. Monetary union and the Lisbon Strategy have a clear and explicit link to European competitiveness, and there is also a strong economic dimension to enlargement. Not surprisingly, then, this period was marked by a resurgence of academic interest in the links between economics and politics in explaining European integration (see Chapter 3). Critical political economists highlight the importance of structural power in shaping the trajectory of European integration and, in particular, how in this period the contours of integration should be understood in relation to the needs of European capitalism in the context of globalization.

KEY POINTS

The Euro

- In 1999, the euro came into operation in eleven member states, although national currencies continued in circulation until 2002. In 2000, Greece was included, but Britain, Denmark, and Sweden remained outside the eurozone.

The Commission in Crisis

- In 1999, the Santer Commission resigned following investigations into claims of fraud and mismanagement.
- The new President, Romano Prodi, came to office with a commitment to 'clean up' the Commission's image.

Enlargement

- Accession negotiations opened with several states in 2000.
- Enlargement required difficult policy revisions (particularly in relation to agriculture and structural funds), and significant institutional reforms.

Other Developments

- The Lisbon Strategy responded to the challenges of globalization by aiming to make the EU 'the most competitive and dynamic knowledge-based economy in the world' by 2010. The Strategy was to be pursued using OMC, which was a departure from the established 'Community method' of decision making.
- The EU's inability to respond decisively to the Kosovo conflict provided a push towards further co-operation on CFSP.
- The Tampere European Council (October 1999) agreed a sixty-step programme of action to address the problems raised by the free movement of people across its internal borders.

The Nice European Council

- Nice became the longest European Council in the history of the EC/EU as leaders negotiated over institutional changes in preparation for enlargement. There was particular tension between large and small states over voting weights under QMV, and more widespread disagreement about the extension of QMV to new areas of policy.
- Reform of voting weights led to a complex 'triple majority' system, which seemed to advantage the larger member states against the smaller.
- QMV was extended into around thirty new areas, but the veto remained in others.
- In a parallel initiative, also confirmed at Nice in December 2000, the EU set out its commitment to citizens' rights in the Charter of Fundamental Rights of the European Union.

FURTHER READING

A distinctive interpretation of the enlargement negotiations is provided by **A. Moravscik and M. A. Vachudova**, 'Bargaining Among Unequals: Enlargement and the Future of European Integration', *EUSA Review*, 15 (2002): 1–3. Two articles on the OMC contain a great deal of information on the whole Lisbon Strategy: **D. Hodson and I. Maher**, 'The Open Method as a New Method of Governance: The Case of Soft Economic Policy Co-ordination' *Journal of Common Market Studies*, 39 (2001): 719–46; and **S. Borras and K. Jacobsson**, 'The Open Method of Co-ordination and New Governance Patterns in the EU', *Journal of European Public Policy*, 11 (2004): 185–208.

On the Treaty of Nice, see **M. Gray and A. Stubb**, 'Keynote Article: The Treaty of Nice—Negotiating a Poisoned Chalice?', in **G. Edwards and G. Wiessala (eds)**, *The European Union: Annual Review of the EU 2000/2001* (Oxford: Blackwell, 2001), 5–24, and **K. Feus (ed.)**, *The Treaty of Nice Explained* (London: Federal Trust for Education and Research, 2001).

 online resource centre **Visit the Online Resource Centre that accompanies this book for links to more information on the Treaty of Nice: www.oxfordtextbooks.co.uk/orc/bache3e/**

Chapter 16

After Nice: Enlargement Overshadowed

Chapter Overview

Enlargement was the major ongoing concern of the European Union (EU) after the Treaty of Nice, but events in the United States on 11 September 2001 overshadowed enlargement and put security and defence at the top of the agenda. A desire to facilitate progress on this front, together with an awareness that Nice had probably not gone far enough to simplify decision making in an enlarged EU, led to the creation of a Constitutional Convention at the end of 2001. This seemed to mark a concerted effort to ensure the effectiveness of the EU, but the subsequent invasion of Iraq by the United States and an ad hoc coalition, in which Britain was a prominent participant, led to sharp disagreements between EU member states. This chapter covers these issues through to the successful enlargement in May 2004. It also tells the story of the undermining of the stability and growth pact, which had seemed to be one of the cornerstones of monetary union, but which was weakened in the face of the unwillingness of France and Germany to accept the fiscal discipline that it imposed.

Less than a year after the Nice summit, the terrorist attacks of 11 September 2001 rocked the world ... international politics came to be dominated by their aftermath.

(Menon 2004: 225)

The Al-Qaeda terrorist atrocities in the United States on 11 September 2001 shocked the world and had a profound effect on international politics. The political climate in which the EU operated changed immediately, with implications for a range of internal policies—most obviously those concerned with security and defence.

European Security and Defence Policy (ESDP)

Up to September 2001, steady progress was being made on security and defence policy. The smooth progress ran into choppy waters, though, following the terrorist attacks in the United States (see also Chapter 31, p. 470 on the implications for EU co-operation on internal security matters, and Chapter 33, pp. 516–17 on external security and defence).

The initial response from the EU was to declare solidarity with the United States, and this support was maintained during the subsequent US campaign in Afghanistan to unseat the Taliban government, which had harboured and supported the Al-Qaeda terrorists. Nevertheless, the effect of the united EU response was somewhat spoiled by Britain, France, and Germany trying to act independently of the EU as a whole. In October 2001, their respective leaders—Blair, Chirac, and Schröder—met outside of the EU forum to discuss their responses to September 11, and intended to do so again in London in early November. However, on the second occasion, vigorous protests by other member states led to the invitation to participate being thrown open to other states and to the EU High Representative, Javier Solana (Chapter 33, p. 516).

The most serious problems for the EU resulted from the determination of the Bush Administration to make Iraq the next target after Afghanistan. There was no evidence that the secular Ba'ath regime of Saddam Hussein supported Islamic terrorism, or had any involvement in the September terrorist attacks. Similarly there was no more than circumstantial evidence, which subsequently proved to be totally inaccurate, that Iraq possessed weapons of mass destruction with which it could attack the United States or its allies.

In the build-up to the eventual invasion of Iraq, the EU split over how to react to the US initiative. France and Germany led a group of states that opposed any military action; Britain, Spain, and Italy were the leading supporters of a group that backed the US action.

Europe Split

In January 2003, in response to French and German statements implying that the EU was opposed to the US attitude towards Iraq, eight European states signed a letter indicating their support for the United States. Five of the eight were existing members of the EU—Britain, Denmark, Italy, Portugal, and Spain. The other three were prospective members—the Czech Republic, Hungary, and Poland. On 22 January, Donald Rumsfeld, the US Secretary for Defense, told a press conference that France and Germany posed 'a problem', but that they did not speak for Europe. They were, he said, 'old' Europe. The new Europe, of states to the east that had recently become members of NATO, was supportive.

Both the letter and Rumsfeld's undiplomatic comments infuriated the French. When ten former communist states, seven of them EU applicants, jointly expressed their support for the US position in February, President Chirac publicly rebuked them, saying that they had shown bad manners, and had 'missed a good opportunity to keep quiet'. He pointedly went on to remind the prospective members who had already negotiated entry that the decision to admit them to the EU on 1 May 2004 had yet to be ratified by national parliaments; he indicated that Bulgaria and Romania, which were still in the early stages of negotiating membership, had been particularly foolish to associate themselves with the statement.

In March 2003, France publicly declared that it would veto any resolution in support of military action against Iraq that might be presented by the United States and Britain to the United Nations Security Council. This caused a serious division between the two member states that had been in the forefront of efforts to create the European Security and Defence Policy (ESDP).

On 18 March, Blair made a strong attack in the House of Commons on the French position. Following the invasion of Iraq in March 2003, Franco–British relations were at a very low ebb, and the prospects for an ESDP looked poor. Yet by the end of the year, there were signs of improvement, particularly following Blair's agreement in principle that the EU should have the joint planning capacity to conduct operations without the involvement of NATO, a concession that appeared to alarm the United States. So, the signs were that the British wanted to facilitate the relaunch of the ESDP.

One other interesting phenomenon came out of this episode. On 15 February 2003, there were mass public demonstrations across Europe against the prospect of an invasion. These protests took place both in countries the governments of which opposed the invasion, and in many of the states the governments of which supported the United States.

Enlargement: Towards an EU of 25

As international events unfolded, the momentum of the enlargement process continued despite the difficulties in achieving the desired institutional and policy changes (Chapter 15, pp. 172–4). In October 2002, the Commission declared that the applicant states—Cyprus, the Czech Republic, Estonia, Hungary, Latvia, Lithuania, Malta, Poland, the Slovak Republic, and Slovenia—were in a position to conclude negotiations successfully by the end of that year and would be ready for membership in 2004. In April 2003, the European Parliament (EP) gave its assent to the accession of these states.

Two applications from central and eastern European countries remained outstanding in 2004: Bulgaria and Romania, neither of which was deemed ready for membership.

Negotiations opened with Croatia in 2004, and an application was accepted from the former Yugoslav Republic of Macedonia. Other Yugoslav successor states were expected to apply, and several Soviet successor states expressed an interest in joining, but were ruled out by the EU (Chapter 34, pp. 533–4). However, the major outstanding issue at this stage was the question of Turkey.

Turkey had had an Association Agreement envisaging membership since 1963. It was excluded from the enlargement process in 1997, largely through opposition from Greece and Germany. However, it was offered the prospect of future negotiations in 1999 following a change of government in Germany in 1998 and a dramatic improvement in Greek–Turkish relations in 1999. Further, a decision by the EU in 1999 to allow states to negotiate entry at their own pace made it easier to open negotiations with Turkey, and more difficult not to do so. A change of government in Turkey in 2002 produced rapid progress to meeting the Copenhagen criteria. Moreover, the international climate meant that geo-strategic factors were increasingly in Turkey's favour, although opposition to its accession remained strong in some states in 2004, particularly in France (Chapter 34, pp. 544–8).

The Constitutional Treaty

Alongside progress on enlargement were further moves to overhaul the EU's decision-making system. But these moves were not only linked to enlargement. They were also explicitly related to two other factors: the need to connect the EU more closely with its citizens; and the wish to put in place machinery to allow the EU to speak with one voice on international issues.

Existing concerns over the low level of public support for the EU were raised further when the Irish people rejected the Nice Treaty by a vote of 53.87 per cent to 46.13 per cent in a referendum in June 2001, with a turnout of only 32.9 per cent. Although this decision was reversed in a second referendum in October 2001, and the Treaty of Nice entered into force in February 2003, the Irish episode reflected the serious challenges facing the EU on the road to further deepening and widening.

In December 2001, the heads of government, meeting in Laeken (Belgium), agreed to move beyond the modest institutional changes agreed in the Nice Treaty. The adoption of the *Declaration on the Future of the European Union* committed the EU to transforming its decision-making procedures to make them more democratic and transparent and to preparing the ground for a European Constitution. The vehicle for moving forward reform was a Constitutional Convention, which brought together representatives of national governments and parliaments from both the member and accession states with representatives of the EU institutions (Insight 16.1), and which was chaired by the former French President, Valéry Giscard d'Estaing. It would be a unique forum in both its role and composition, designed to secure legitimacy for the reforms by incorporating the views of a broad range of actors. In addition to the formal members of the Convention and observers, various business representatives, non-governmental organizations, academics, and other interested parties would be consulted on specific topics. The Convention's Chair would report on progress at each European Council meeting and receive the views of the heads of government, and the Convention's final report would provide the starting point for discussions and decisions at an intergovernmental conference (IGC) scheduled for 2004.

The proposals of the Convention for a Constitution for Europe were submitted by Giscard d'Estaing to the Thessaloniki European Council in June 2003. There followed a formal IGC, at which some of the proposals were amended, but the Treaty establishing a Constitution for Europe was signed by the heads of government and the EU Foreign Ministers in October 2004. Once ratified within member states, it would replace the existing Treaties.

The Treaty agreed had a four-part structure (Insight 16.2) and had implications for the founding principles of the EU, the institutions, the decision-making process, and its policies. The Treaty also specified for the first time the areas that would be the exclusive competence of the EU (Article I-13), and those areas that would be shared between the EU and the member states (Article I-14). Both of these were long-standing federalist demands, although national governments had become increasingly aware of the possible protection that a clear demarcation of spheres of competence would offer against the creeping extension of competencies that had sometimes occurred as a result of the Commission's **policy entrepreneurship** (Chapter 19, pp. 263–4).

Insight 16.1 Composition of the Constitutional Convention

In addition to its Chairman (Valéry Giscard d'Estaing) and two Vice-Chairmen (Giuliano Amato and Jean-Luc Dehaene), the Convention was composed of:

- fifteen representatives of the heads of state or government of the member states (one from each member state);
- thirteen representatives of the heads of state or government of the candidate states (one per candidate state);
- thirty representatives of the national parliaments of the member states (two from each member state);
- twenty-six representatives of the national parliaments of the candidate states (two from each candidate state);
- sixteen members of the EP;
- two representatives of the European Commission.

There were alternates for each full member.

Observers were invited to attend from the Economic and Social Committee (three representatives), the Committee of the Regions (six representatives), the social partners (three representatives), and the European Ombudsman.

The Laeken Declaration provided for the candidate states to take a full part in the proceedings without, however, being able to prevent any consensus emerging among the member states.

Source: http://european-convention.eu.int/organisation.asp?lang=EN

Insight 16.2 Structure of the Constitutional Treaty

The Treaty was divided into four main parts, each of equal rank.

- **Part I** was devoted to the principles, objectives, and institutional provisions governing the new European Union and was divided into nine Titles: the definition and objectives of the Union; fundamental rights and citizenship of the Union; Union competencies; the Union's institutions; the exercise of Union competence; the democratic life of the Union; the Union's finances; the Union and its neighbours; and Union membership.

- **Part II** comprised the European Charter of Fundamental Rights. It contained seven Titles, preceded by a Preamble: dignity; freedoms; equality; solidarity; citizens' rights; justice; general provisions.

- **Part III** comprised the provisions governing the policies and functioning of the Union. The internal and external policies of the Union were laid down, including provisions on the internal market, economic and monetary union (EMU), the area of freedom, security and justice (AFSJ), the common foreign and security policy (CFSP), and the functioning of the institutions. It contained seven Titles: provisions of general application; non-discrimination and citizenship; internal policies and action; association of the overseas countries and territories; the Union's external action; the functioning of the Union; and common provisions.

- **Part IV** grouped together the general and final provisions of the Constitution, including entry into force, the procedure for revising the Constitution, and the repeal of earlier Treaties.

A certain number of Protocols were annexed to the Treaty establishing the Constitution, in particular the: Protocol on the role of national parliaments in the European Union; Protocol on the application of the principles of **subsidiarity** and proportionality; Protocol on the Euro Group; Protocol amending the Euratom Treaty; Protocol on the transitional provisions relating to the institutions and bodies of the Union.

Source: **http://www.europa.eu.int/scadplus/constitution/introduction_en.htm**

At the time, there was divergent opinion on the significance of the Treaty. On content, some viewed it as a little more than a 'Nice II' or a 'tidying-up' exercise that mainly brought together existing rules and agreements into a single, more comprehensible Treaty. More sceptical observers viewed it as a major step away from the sovereignty of nation states and towards the creation of a European super-state. However, since the Treaty failed to be ratified, the divisions over the Lisbon Treaty took on more relevance (see Chapter 18).

In terms of process, the Convention was, for its advocates, a new model created to go beyond what had been and what might be achieved through IGCs: one that promoted deliberation, broad participation, and consensus-based politics. For others, it was dominated by hard bargaining, corridor politics, and political horse-trading. There was evidence of both sets of characteristics in practice. While the Convention's activities were clearly elite-led, the range of actors from civil society that were involved in the process was unusual, and the style of proceedings sought to promote deliberation and consensus. However, there were inevitable tensions between pro-integrationists and intergovernmentalists, and, as in the run-up to the Nice Treaty, serious tensions emerged between large and small states.

There was also disagreement on how far the Convention really extended consultation beyond the limits of official government positions. Moravscik (2004: 15) suggested that the negotiations were dominated by the member states. This view was rejected by Lord Kerr (2004: 17), the Secretary General of the Convention, who pointed out that, in the Presidium, the member states' representatives were in a minority. Moreover, there was a sense in which Convention members listened to each other and worked in a spirit of solidarity. However, he also suggested that the final months of the Convention did begin to resemble an IGC.

As with the earlier Treaties, the Constitutional Treaty had to be ratified by the member states before entering into force. Some states chose to ratify through parliament; others by referendum. The ratification process was expected to last for two years and the Constitution expected to come into force on 1 November 2006 (see Chapter 17, pp. 207–8).

Monetary Union

If the symbolic importance of the Constitutional Treaty was uncertain during this period, there was no doubting the symbolic importance of the appearance of a European currency. In January 2002, euro notes and coins came into circulation for

197

the first time in the twelve participating states and became the sole currency in these states the next month, following a short change-over period. Britain, Denmark, and Sweden were the non-participants (Chapter 28, p. 411). Following the Danish precedent in 2000, the Swedish people voted against membership of the eurozone in September 2003. The British government concluded in June 2003 that the time was not right to make an application to join, and the issue gradually disappeared from the British political agenda. For the citizens of the participating states, the circulation of euros was an important symbol of European integration.

However, the new currency was soon at the centre of disputes between member states. The stability and growth pact, which effectively made the Maastricht criteria on debt and budget deficits permanent requirements for the participating states (Chapter 28, pp. 406–7), was proving difficult for some states to adhere to. In particular, the requirement that states keep their budget deficits below 3 per cent of GDP brought difficulties initially for Portugal and Ireland, and subsequently for France and Germany. How these difficulties were handled again brought out tensions between small and large states. While Portugal and Ireland were reprimanded for exceeding the budget-deficit target, France and Germany resisted criticism, and were viewed by the smaller states as abusing the conditions of the pact.

Initial Commission threats of sanctions against France and Germany were followed up by a formal proposal in November 2003 to impose sanctions unless France and Germany took steps to reduce their budget deficit for 2004 below the 3 per cent limit. However, it became clear that there was no majority among the member states for the Commission proposal and the sanctions were suspended, henceforth effectively making the stability pact requirements mere guidelines for national policy rather than mandatory rules for fiscal discipline (Chapter 28, pp. 409–11). Despite this, both France and Germany did make efforts to meet the conditions of the pact, which raised the question of how much the issue was one of fiscal discipline and how much it was an issue of who was in charge—national governments or the Commission.

The European Central Bank (ECB)—now under the presidency of a Frenchman, Jean-Claude Trichet—was very critical of the Council and expressed support for the stability pact. The pact was reformed in 2005 and made more flexible. The consequences of this relaxation of rules were to become clear with the eurozone crisis in 2010 (see Chapter 28, pp. 411–12).

CONCLUSION

Enlargement dominated concerns at the beginning of this period, and with the exception of Turkey, the process continued smoothly through this period. However, enlargement and the EU's internal developments were soon overshadowed by the threats to global security evident in the terrorist attacks on the United States. In the EU, these attacks highlighted long-standing differences in the foreign-policy outlooks of key member states. Most obviously, Britain's support for the United States over Iraq highlighted Atlanticist tendencies that were at odds with France in particular. However, while there may have been immediate problems for EU co-operation on ESDP, for some commentators this episode highlighted the need for such co-operation in the longer term.

On 31 May 2003, the German philosopher Jürgen Habermas and the French philosopher Jacques Derrida published a joint plea for a common foreign policy for Europe. Their joint essay was published in German in the *Frankfurter Allgemeine Zeitung*, and in French in *Libération*. They argued that demonstrations on 15 February showed the existence of a European public opinion that supported a European foreign policy independent of the United States—but that such an independent policy, which would throw the weight of Europe into the scales against US global hegemony, could only be devised and led by France and Germany, together with those EU states that supported their position. Perhaps it was to head off the possibility of such a policy in opposition to the United States that Blair was so eager to get ESDP with British involvement back on track after the end of the Iraq war.

The decision to create a Constitutional Convention to make proposals for a Constitutional Treaty was in part a response to ongoing concerns over the EU's legitimacy (Chapter 4), and the Convention model itself was seen as a step in the direction of more open and inclusive decision making at the EU level. However, the operation of the Convention was subject to contrasting interpretations. Intergovernmentalists emphasized the dominance of national governments and the hard-bargaining approach to negotiations, while others emphasized the supranational dimension and a process characterized largely by problem-solving rationality (Chapter 2), rather than bargaining.

The draft Treaty that emerged was viewed differently in different member states. For example, the right in Britain saw the Treaty as a major step towards a federal Europe and the loss of national sovereignty. By contrast, many on the left in France saw the Treaty as dominated by the Anglo-Saxon model of capitalism and a threat to French models of social welfare (see also Chapter 17, pp. 207–8).

The circulation of euro notes and coins in the member states that were participating in the single currency was a step of both practical and symbolic significance. For the citizens of the participating states, the euro was physical evidence of a closer Europe. From a social constructivist perspective (Chapter 3), this physical manifestation of European integration would serve to enhance citizens' attachment to and identification with Europe.

KEY POINTS

European Security and Defence Policy (ESDP)

- EU progress on ESDP co-operation was stalled by the September 11 attacks in the United States, with splits emerging between key member states on how to respond, in particular to the subsequent US decision to take military action against Iraq.

Enlargement: Towards an EU of 25

- In April 2003, the EP assented to the accession of ten new member states in 2004. Turkey's application remained the major outstanding issue at this stage.

The Constitutional Treaty

- The Constitutional Convention prepared the ground for a European Constitution. It was unique in its composition and purpose.

- The Convention's proposals were presented in June 2003 and, following some amendments, the Treaty establishing a Constitution for Europe was signed by the EU heads of government and the their Foreign Ministers in October 2004.

Monetary Union

- In January 2002, euro notes and coins came into circulation in the twelve participating states. However, the stability and growth pact underpinning the new currency became difficult for some states to adhere to and led to a number of disputes.

FURTHER READING

Detailed analysis of the Constitutional Convention's process, and of the emergence of the resultant Treaty, is available in **P. Norman**, *The Accidental Constitution: The Making of Europe's Constitutional Treaty* (Brussels: EuroComment, 2003).

The essay by **Habermas and Derrida** is reproduced, together with a wide range of responses to their proposals, in **D. Levy, M. Pensky, and J. Torpey (eds)**, *Old Europe, New Europe: Transatlantic Relations After the Iraq War* (London: Verso, 2005).

online resource centre

Visit the Online Resource Centre that accompanies this book for links to more information on the Constitutional Convention and Draft Constitutional Treaty: www.oxfordtextbooks.co.uk/orc/bache3e/

Chapter 17
The European Union at a Crossroads

Chapter Overview

The period began with the 2004 enlargement, an ambitious expansion creating a union of twenty-five states. However, it closed with perhaps the biggest crisis in its history, leaving the European Union (EU) at a crossroads. The rejection of the Constitutional Treaty in France and the Netherlands created uncertainty about the legitimacy and future direction of the European project. But the problems ratifying the Treaty were not the only significant problems in this period. This chapter looks at the first year of membership for the new member states, which raised issues that challenged the public enthusiasm for membership in some states, but also illustrated some of the advantages. It then turns to the EU elections and the difficult approval process for the new Commission. It reflects on the progress towards the objectives set out at Lisbon, before considering the ratification crisis.

The danger is obvious. Locked between a rock of an unratifiable treaty and a hard place of dysfunctional institutions, the EU can only become more discredited in a vicious circle of decline, ever more obvious impotence and growing illegitimacy ... Europeans have to think straight, to talk honestly and recognise their commonality.

(Hutton 2005: 18)

On 1 May 2004, the EU's biggest enlargement brought in ten new member states, taking the size of the Union to 25 states and increasing its population by almost 75 million to 450 million. The date for the enlargement had been set to allow the new member states to take part in elections to the European Parliament (EP) that were scheduled for June 2004. This in turn was the first stage in a new constitutional timetable, which had applied for the first time in 1995, whereby the election of the new EP was followed by the nomination of the new Commission.

The New Member States

Accession to the EU was never going to be a painless process for the applicant states. The negotiations took four years, even though the earlier negotiations on the Europe agreements had already dealt with the removal of an array of trade restrictions. The *acquis communautaire* to which the applicants had to adjust their domestic legislation consisted of some 80,000 pages of EC law. Yet the difficult negotiations did not seem to have any significant effect on public support for entry in the applicant states, as reflected in the opinion polls. Support generally held steady, albeit at different levels in different states, and it actually increased in the run-up to the referendums in 2003 to accept the terms of entry. After that, though, it sank quite markedly as the euphoria cleared and the full implications of the terms began to sink in. Some issues rankled, particularly:

- the determination of almost all of the existing member states to restrict the free movement of workers from the new entrants for up to seven years after entry;
- the refusal of the EU to allow the new members permanently to restrict the right of citizens of other member states to purchase property and agricultural land, which the applicants feared would lead to their homes and farms being bought up by rich Austrians and Germans;
- the parsimony of the existing members over payments from the agricultural and regional funds to the new members, which, for example, would result in farmers in the new member states receiving only 25 per cent of the subsidies that went to their much wealthier counterparts in the older member states.

This disillusionment seemed to be reflected in the low turnout for the EP elections in June 2004. Although the turnout was low everywhere (see below), in some of the new member states, it was only around 20 per cent.

Yet, within a year, sentiment had turned around. The Eurobarometer poll in autumn 2004 showed increases in the percentage of respondents who considered membership a good thing in almost all of the new member states when compared with the previous poll six months earlier (Eurobarometer 2004*a*; 2004*b*). Wagstyl (2005) attributed this change of sentiment largely to two developments: the first economic; the second political.

At a time when the core economies of the eurozone were still performing badly, economic growth in the new members reached 5 per cent in 2004, partly as a result of a 20 per cent increase in exports, mainly to the old EU. Agricultural exports grew particularly vigorously, with the Czech Republic and Poland benefiting considerably. Even though the subsidies to their farmers were capped at a low level in comparison with those paid to farmers in the older member states, the first payments, combined with the increased exports, led to an increase in farm incomes in the new members estimated by the European Commission at 50 per cent overall, at 108 per cent for the Czech Republic, and at 73 per cent for Poland.

The second development was the attitude of President Putin's Russia to the presidential elections in Ukraine in November 2004. The Russians were widely suspected to have been involved in blatant attempts to rig the Ukrainian election to hand victory to Russia's favoured candidate, the Prime Minister, Viktor Yanukovich. When that result was announced, Putin immediately congratulated the 'winner'—but tens of thousands of Ukrainians turned out in the streets of the capital, Kiev, in bitter winter weather, and maintained their vigil until the authorities agreed to a rerun of the poll, which was won by the pro-western Viktor Yuschenko. The role played by Russia underlined concerns in central and eastern Europe about the growing authoritarianism and aggressive nationalism of the Putin administration. Also, the role played by mediators from two of the new EU member states—the President of Poland, Aleksander Kwasniewski, and the President of Latvia, Valdas Adamkus—underlined that membership of the EU conferred a weight and importance in international affairs that these small states could not hope to attain separately.

Elections to the European Parliament

There was hope among EU leaders that the publicity that enlargement had generated would result in an increased turnout for the elections to the EP in June 2004. In fact, turnout, which had fallen in every election since 1979, declined further to a record low of 45.6 per cent. As noted above, in the new member states, it was much lower. It was unclear at this stage what conclusions should be drawn from this. Pat Cox, the President of the EP, expressed the view that the low turnouts in the new member states reflected the fact that the citizens felt that they had already shown their support for the EU in the referendums on accession in 2003.

The New Member States

In the new member states, the campaigns tended to be dominated by national political debates, and the results reflected these debates rather than attitudes to the EU. So although Euro-sceptic parties did well in the Czech Republic and Poland, this was more because they were the opposition parties to which voters naturally turned in order to express discontent with the incumbent government than because they were Euro-sceptic. In Slovakia, which had the lowest turnout in the EU at just 17 per cent, no nationalists or extreme Euro-sceptics were elected.

The 'Pre-2004' Member States

Among, the 'pre-2004' member states, there was no consistent pattern. In Germany, the election was fought almost entirely on domestic issues, with the attempts of the Federal government to introduce structural economic reforms at the forefront of the debate. The big story of the results was that Gerhard Schröder's Social Democratic Party (SPD) recorded its lowest ever vote in any election that spanned the whole of the Federal Republic; moreover, the turnout of 43 per cent was very low by German standards, perhaps indicating disillusionment with the EU. In France, the debate had an unusually strong focus on European issues, and particularly the question of what sort of EU the French people wanted to see. The big winners, with 28.9 per cent of the vote, were the Socialists, who campaigned in favour of a social Europe and against what they presented as the collaboration of the ruling Gaullists with the swing towards a liberal 'Anglo-Saxon' vision of the EU (Chapter 16, p. 199). Turnout was again disappointing, though, at only 42.7 per cent: the lowest ever recorded in a European election in France.

Denmark and Sweden showed contrasting trends. In Denmark, the rejection of membership of the euro in the referendum of 2000 suggested a hardening of Euro-sceptic sentiment. However, the EP election campaign was marked by an aggressive pro-EU stance from the opposition Social Democrats, who were the big winners with 32.6 per cent, and turnout went up to 47.9 per cent, which was above the EU average. In Sweden, on the other hand, the turnout was very low—at 37.9 per cent, it was the lowest of the pre-2004 members and lower than five of the new members—and the most notable trend was an increase in support for Euro-sceptic lists and candidates.

Britain, which was also a traditionally Euro-sceptic state with low turnouts in EP elections, saw an increase in turnout for the first time since 1979, up from 24 per cent to 38.4 per cent, the highest level ever recorded in a European election in Britain. However, this result was undoubtedly influenced in part by the coincidence of local elections in many parts of the country, and by the experimental adoption of postal ballots in some areas. Most of the significance of the results was purely domestic, but the United Kingdom Independence Party (UKIP), a hard Euro-sceptic party, secured a surprisingly high 16.2 per cent of the vote.

From these diverse experiences—and the experiences of other member states were equally as diverse—the only strong trend was for the elections to be used as a chance to register a protest against the incumbent government. However, even this did not apply everywhere: in Spain, the Spanish Socialist Workers' Party (PSOE), which had won a general election three months earlier, emerged as the clear winner in the European election, with 43.3 per cent of the vote. Nevertheless, the general trend to vote against incumbent national governments resulted in a centre-right majority in the new EP.

The New Commission

In line with the new constitutional timetable, the EP elections were followed by the nomination of the new Commission. In June 2004, the European Council nominated Portuguese Prime Minister José Manuel Durao Barroso as the next Commission President. Formerly a Maoist revolutionary, the conservative Barroso was appointed after some dispute within the Council over Romano Prodi's successor. The French and German governments had sought to install the Belgian Prime Minister Guy Verhofstadt, while Britain had backed Barroso. In the end, Barroso's appointment was not only seen as a compromise between federalists and Atlanticists, but also reassured the concerns of smaller states. It was also in line with the expectation of the EP that the nominee would be drawn from the same political 'family' as the majority that had been returned in the elections. This, combined with Barroso's competent and convincing manner in his own confirmation hearing before the EP, resulted in a comfortable majority in favour of his nomination.

Trouble really began for Barroso with the confirmation hearings for the proposed members of his Commission. The President had no choice in the nominations of the individuals, which were made by the governments of the member states, but he was responsible for the allocation of portfolios. At first, his decisions were welcomed, particularly because he refused to bow to pressure from large member states to give the most central portfolios to their nominees. France's Jacques Barrot, for example, was allocated the transport portfolio—hardly the most important responsibility. However, during the parliamentary confirmation hearings, doubts arose about the suitability of several of the individuals for the posts for which they had been proposed. They included: Mariann Fischer Boel of Denmark, who was criticized for a lack of rigour in answering questions about agricultural policy; Neelie Kroes of the Netherlands, whose nomination for the competition portfolio was criticized because her past involvement on the boards of several leading Dutch and international companies might lay her open to suspicion of conflicts of interest; Laszlo Kovacs of Hungary, who was nominated Commissioner for energy policy, and whose technical competence in the energy field was questioned; and Ingrida Udre of Latvia, nominated for the taxation and **customs union** portfolio, who was criticized for her negative view of the EU and for her reluctance to answer questions about an investigation into allegations of impropriety in the funding of her political party in Latvia.

The Buttiglione Affair

The biggest furore, though, arose over the hearing of Rocco Buttiglione, the Italian nominee for the justice, freedom, and security portfolio. Buttiglione was a devout Roman Catholic, and in response to questions from MEPs, he expressed the conventional Catholic views that homosexuality was a sin, and that the purpose of marriage was to allow women to have children and be cared for by their husbands. Socialist, Green, and Liberal MEPs felt that these were inappropriate sentiments for a Commissioner whose duties would include the protection of human rights and civil liberties. They threatened to vote down the whole Commission unless something was done about Buttiglione's nomination.

Barroso tried to reach agreement with the party groups, first on removing the sensitive parts of the justice, freedom, and security portfolio from the responsibility of Buttiglione, and exercising them himself. Even that did not satisfy the MEPs, though, and despite pressure from national governments on their own parties to vote to confirm the Commission, it looked as though the vote would be lost. On 27 October, just days away from the scheduled transfer of responsibilities to the new Commission on 1 November, Barroso told the EP that he would not be presenting his team for the vote, but would instead look again at all of the portfolios. By this time, the MEPs scented blood, and it seemed unlikely that they would accept anything less than the replacement of Buttiglione. This was seriously embarrassing for Barroso, because he had no right to demand that the Italian government get him off the hook. He was saved by Buttiglione's decision to resign and so walk away from what he had insisted was systematic persecution of him for his religious beliefs.

The Final Outcome

Eventually, the EP approved the Barroso Commission in a vote of confidence on 18 November, but not before Barroso had persuaded the Latvian government also to replace Udre, and then moved Kovacs from energy to taxation. The new Latvian nominee, Andris Piebalgs, was given the energy portfolio, and the new Italian nominee, former Foreign Minister Franco Frattini, was allocated the justice, freedom, and security portfolio. Frattini performed well at his hastily arranged confirmation. Barroso did not make changes to the responsibilities of Boel or Kroes, but overall the whole incident was seen as a clear victory for the EP in its struggle to extend its influence over individual Commissioners.

Progress on the Lisbon Strategy

In March 2004, the European Council appointed the former Dutch Prime Minister, Wim Kok, to convene a committee of experts that would carry out a mid-term review of progress towards the commitment made in Lisbon in 2000 to make the EU by 2010, 'the most dynamic and competitive knowledge-based economy in the world' (Chapter 15, pp. 185–6). The Kok Report, *Facing the Challenge*, was presented to the European Commission on 3 November 2004, and to the European Council the following day.

The report confirmed what everyone knew already: that delivery on the process of reform had been 'disappointing'. There had been some progress. Employment rates in the fifteen older member states had increased from 62.5 per cent in 1999 to 64.3 per cent in 2003. There had been a particularly good improvement in the rate of female employment. The use of information technology and the Internet had increased, and twelve member states had met their target for household Internet penetration. Against that, though, net job creation had stopped, probably making the target of 70 per cent participation by 2010 already beyond reach, only two states were meeting their targets on research and development, only five were above target for transposing single market directives into national law, and environmental targets were being missed by some way. The report also noted that the EU was already facing new challenges: increased economic competition from China, India, and a revitalized United States; the problems of an ageing population; enlargement, which had brought in ten new member states that were even further from achieving the Lisbon targets; low investment; low rates of utilization of labour, with hours worked being well below the levels in the United States; and the weak fiscal position of many member states.

Blame for the relative failure of the process was partly attributed to unfavourable conjunctural factors. The collapse of the bubble in technology stocks and shares in 2000 had discouraged investment in the industries that were central to the Lisbon agenda. Two years of low growth in the United States and Europe had followed the September 2001 terrorist attacks. Business confidence had been hit not only by terrorism, but also by trade disputes, environmental problems, and rising oil prices. However, the report also pointed to an overloaded agenda, poor co-ordination of the process, and conflicting priorities. The biggest culprits were identified as the member states, which had shown a collective lack of political will in pursuit of the objectives.

Although it was already too late to meet some of the targets that had been set for 2010, the report argued that the date should not be abandoned, as there was a need to instil a sense of urgency into the process, and the embarrassment of reaching 2010 with results that were so bad that Lisbon would become 'a synonym for missed objectives and failed promises' might impart some momentum.

Beyond that, the report pointed to the need to focus on core objectives and to allocate responsibilities more precisely. So long as the Lisbon agenda remained so broad, it ran the risk of being about everything, and therefore about nothing. The number of key indicators should be reduced from over a hundred to just fourteen, and the emphasis should be placed clearly on growth and employment, because they were essential to underpin the social and environmental objectives. While the governments of the member states had to accept the main responsibility for the relative failure to date, the Commission ought to be made the unambiguous co-ordinator of the process. It needed to be prepared to name and shame those member states that were simply not doing enough. To be able to do this without fear, it needed to monitor the process closely, and the report recommended that the next President of the Commission should make driving the Lisbon Agenda forward the main mandate for his period in office. This is exactly what Barroso sought to do.

Ratifying the Constitutional Treaty

Initially, members of the Constitutional Convention (Chapter 16, pp. 195–7) had proposed that the Treaty be voted on in simultaneous referendums Europe-wide on the same date as the EP elections in June 2004. This proposal was rejected as being too federalist, and the decision on how to ratify was left to individual member states. Subsequently, some states chose to hold public referendums, while others chose to ratify through parliamentary procedures.

The ratification process began successfully with parliamentary ratification in Hungary, Latvia, and Slovenia; the Treaty overcame its first referendum hurdle with the endorsement of the Spanish people in February 2005. The vote was 77 per cent in favour. While this was a decisive vote in favour, the low turnout was a cause for concern. Only 42 per cent of eligible voters took part: particularly low in a country that was generally supportive of European integration, and one chosen to be the first to stage a referendum in the expectation of an outcome that would build momentum elsewhere.

The worst fears of the Treaty's supporters were realized in May 2005 when the French referendum returned a 55 per cent vote against. This was followed shortly afterwards by a negative vote in the Netherlands of almost 62 per cent. The French vote in particular was significant, not only as the first major 'no' vote over the constitution, but because it came from a country at the heart of Europe, and one, perhaps more than any other, associated with driving integration forward. The vote prompted arguably the biggest crisis in the EU's history.

A range of factors contributed to the French 'no' vote. These included domestic factors such as the unpopularity of the Chirac presidency and the state of the French economy. Related to this last point was a growing resentment about the influx of cheap labour following the Eastern enlargement at a time of rising unemployment. This resentment linked to concerns over the potential implications for immigration in France of the putative Turkish accession to the EU.

There was also a distinct strain of debate in France that linked the Constitutional Treaty to Britain and British preferences. It was widely portrayed as an Anglo-Saxon Treaty and one that would undermine the French social model. Ironically, in Britain, the Treaty was opposed by the Euro-sceptic right for not being Anglo-Saxon enough and threatening to institutionalize EU involvement in new areas of social policy. Less contentious was the view that the French vote almost certainly let the Blair government off the hook, faced as it had been with holding a referendum that most commentators believed it could not win. Although there had been a clear prior agreement by the heads of government that *all* member states would attempt to ratify the Treaty before the position was reassessed, the British government maintained that there was no point in it proceeding to a referendum after the French and Dutch 'no' votes, and unilaterally announced an indefinite postponement.

CONCLUSION

To suggest that the EU was 'at a crossroads' is hardly controversial. However, in this period, the crisis caused by the problems ratifying the Constitutional Treaty was perhaps as great as any in the EU's history. One commentator suggested that, '[i]f mishandled, the crisis may even lead to closure, protection, recession and the disintegration of the euro—and the balkanisation of Europe into mutually suspicious and hostile camps ... the entire EU edifice, and all the benefits it has brought in terms of trade, stability and peace, is at risk' (Hutton 2005: 18).

In relation to the conceptual themes that were identified in the opening part of this book, the period highlighted above all the issue of the EU's legitimacy. Turnout for the EP elections in 2004 reached a record low. As suggested in Chapter 4, low turnouts can be read in more than one way. A low turnout may be seen as tacit support by the public for the process of European integration—the notion of the permissive consensus (Chapter 4, pp. 66–7). Alternatively, it may be viewed as apathy or disenchantment with the political system. In most cases, the decline in participation in EU elections has been seen as the latter. Put together with the evidence from the ratification process for the Constitutional Treaty, this would seem to be the more persuasive argument.

At the same time, it should be noted that while we are concerned with the legitimacy problems facing the EU here, the trends in relation to voting in EP elections are broadly consistent with those for national elections. So while there are arguments that suggest that it is unfair to make comparisons between democracy at EU level and that in established political systems (Chapter 4), on this occasion it does the EU no harm: liberal democracy as a whole faces a growing problem of legitimacy.

The problems around the approval of the Barroso Commission can also be read in more ways than one in relation to democracy and legitimacy. One the one hand, the proposed appointment of certain individuals to particular portfolios can be viewed as clumsy, insensitive, and wholly avoidable, thus casting further public doubt over the efficiency of the EU system. On the other hand, the firm response of the EP on this issue and the way in which it was ultimately resolved may be taken as evidence of the growing maturity and effectiveness of the EU system, and, more specifically, of the growing influence of the most democratic body within that system.

The fourth enlargement demanded a more effective decision-making system than the EU had yet delivered. As such, the larger EU brought a focus on the conflicting interests of large and small states and between richer and poorer states that promised continuing challenges to legitimacy. The fourth enlargement was in many ways a remarkable achievement, but already some were beginning to show signs of regret at the nature and scale of this enlargement, as was expressed in the French debates over the Constitutional Treaty. However, further expansion of the EU still remained on the agenda (Chapter 34).

Finally, we turn specifically to the Constitutional Treaty itself. It was in large part an attempt to bring the EU closer to its citizens, but it was seen to have the opposite effect. At the same time, it did galvanize a widespread public debate on the EU in those states where a referendum took place.

In the French debate in particular, a key issue was the type of Europe that was being developed. French critics of the Treaty portrayed it as 'Anglo-Saxon', one shaped by the British to take the EU closer to American-style capitalism. This interpretation of British motivations was seen as a distortion of the Blair government by many British commentators, who pointed to the Scandinavian influence on the government's social policies, such as tax credits for the poorest families, a national minimum wage, and increased investment in public services. Collectively, these policies were seen to justify a new 'Anglo-social label' (Pearce and Paxton 2005).

Faced with the need to reform its institutions to reflect its enlarged membership and to be able to respond to new external and internal security challenges, it fell to the European Council to work out whether the Constitutional Treaty could be salvaged and if so, how. The outcome of this reflection is considered in the next chapter.

KEY POINTS

The New Member States

- Soon after entry, public support for the EU fell in a number of new member states. This was reflected in particularly low turnouts for the EP elections in these states.
- Public opinion soon began to turn around as economic and political benefits were realized.

Elections to the European Parliament

- Turnout at EP elections fell to a record low in 2004, and national issues remained prominent in the election campaigns in most member states.

The New Commission

- Barroso's appointment was a compromise between federalists and Atlanticists, and also appeased smaller member states.
- The proposed Commission hit problems over a number of nominees, but particularly Rocco Buttiglione, whose views were deemed inappropriate by the EP.
- The strength of reaction against Buttiglione ultimately forced his resignation. The incident was seen as a victory for the EP.

Progress on the Lisbon Strategy

- The Kok Report described progress on the Strategy as 'disappointing', although there had been some achievements.
- There were several explanations for the disappointing progress, but the failure of member states to drive the Strategy forward was prominent among them.
- The 2010 targets were not abandoned, although some had already become unrealizable, and Commission President Barroso made the Strategy a priority of his term in office.

Ratifying the Constitutional Treaty

- The ratification process began successfully with parliamentary ratification in Hungary, Latvia, and Slovenia, and a 'yes' vote in the Spanish referendum of February 2005.
- The worst fears of the Treaty's supporters were realized in May 2005 when the French referendum returned a 55 per cent vote against. The vote prompted arguably the biggest crisis in the EU's history.

FURTHER READING

Assessments of the 2004 European elections are contained in **J. Lodge (ed.)**, *The 2004 Elections to the European Parliament* (Basingstoke: Palgrave Macmillan, 2005). For analyses of the European Constitution, see **C. Church and D. Phinnemore**, *Understanding the European Constitution: An Introduction to the EU Constitutional Treaty* (London: Routledge, 2006), and **G. Amato and J. Ziller (eds)**, *The European Constitution: Cases and Materials in EU Member States' Law* (Cheltenham: Edward Elgar, 2007). For analysis of the impact of the EU on candidate states in the 2004 enlargement, see **H. Grabbe**, *The EU's Transformative Power: Europeanization through Conditionality in Central and Eastern Europe* (Basingstoke: Palgrave Macmillan, 2006).

online resource centre

Visit the Online Resource Centre that accompanies this book for links to more information on the European Constitution, including updates on the ratification process: www.oxfordtextbooks.co.uk/orc/bache3e/

Chapter 18

From a European Constitution to the Lisbon Treaty

Chapter Overview

This chapter looks at how the European Union (EU) responded to the rejection of the Constitutional Treaty in France and the Netherlands, taking the story up to and beyond the ratification of the Lisbon Treaty. Alongside this, we consider the global financial crisis that engulfed the EU and its member states, as well as key developments in a number of policy areas, before discussing the most recent European Parliament (EP) elections and appointments to the Commission. We conclude by reflecting on the implications of this period for the legitimacy of the EU.

> By raising expectations and, for some, fears of the future ambitions of the European Union, popular debate and therefore popular opposition were invited. The 'permissive consensus', in any case fragile since the early 1990s, was put to the test—a test it did not quite pass.
>
> (Christiansen 2010: 17)

The Lisbon Treaty

The Road to the Lisbon Treaty

The rejection of the Constitutional Treaty in France and the Netherlands in 2005 prompted what was arguably the biggest crisis in the EU's history and increased uncertainty over its legitimacy and future trajectory. It was a period of flux, with the accommodation of ten new member states also taking place, the imminent arrival of two more, and waning public enthusiasm evidenced by record low turnouts at EP elections (see Chapter 17). Against this difficult background, EU officials and their allies sought a resolution to the crisis engendered by the Treaty's rejection.

In the wake of the French and Dutch 'no' votes, the European Council of June 2005 called for a period of reflection. The passage of time would allow for the depoliticization of some of the more sensitive issues raised in the referendum campaigns and held the prospect of a change of government in some key states: France and the Netherlands in particular (Christiansen 2010: 24).

For a while, the Treaty fell from public view. Indeed, at one point, Commission President Barroso declared that the Treaty would not come back for several years (Church and Phinnemore 2010: 61). However, in June 2006, the European Council asked the incoming German presidency to present a report on how to end the constitutional impasse.

Reflection brought the conclusion that what was needed was separation of the more controversial symbolic (constitutional) aspects of the Treaty from the practical requirements of institutional reform. In January 2007, the new German presidency announced plans to revive the constitution and began a series of bilateral and multilateral meetings with national leaders to discuss ways forward. The tone of domestic politics revealed in these meetings signalled to the German negotiators that the EU needed to step back from its initial ambitions (Carbone 2010: 222).

A number of governments raised important issues. The UK government placed a number of 'red lines' around policy areas such as taxation and social security, and wanted there to be no legal status for the Charter of Fundamental Rights, no single legal personality for the EU, and no reference to the primacy of EU law over national law. The Polish and Czech governments wanted to reopen negotiations on voting weights in the Council of Minsters and, along with the Dutch government, wanted a mechanism through which national parliaments could block legislation at EU level (*European Voice*, 24–30 May 2007: 13).

In short, the task facing the German presidency was one of reconciling the demands of the maximalist eighteen states that had ratified the Constitutional Treaty and wanted to retain as much of it as possible, with those of the minimalists that wanted simply to amend the EU's rules (Dedman 2010: 176). EU leaders meeting in Berlin in March 2007 used the opportunity of the fiftieth anniversary of the Treaties of Rome to emphasize the symbolic aspects of European integration in a less controversial manner—the non-binding Berlin Declaration on the Union's aims and values—while also calling for a new Treaty to be in place by 2009. A new intergovernmental conference (IGC) was called for the summer of that year.

On 19 June, the German presidency presented its 'draft mandate'. It proposed that instead of consolidating and replacing the existing treaties—the Treaty on European Union (TEU) and the Treaty establishing the European Community (TEC)—these should be amended to incorporate most of the provisions of the Constitutional Treaty. However, the more controversial aspects of the Constitutional Treaty would be dropped—the term 'constitution', an article referring to symbols of the Union (including the EU anthem and the Union flag) and references to an 'EU Minister' for foreign affairs. The EU's legal instruments would remain as regulations, directives, and decisions, and not be replaced by the terms 'law' and 'framework law'. In short, the text would be 'changed significantly in order to remove the kind of language that could be seen as an indication of statist aspirations' (Christiansen 2010: 25–6).

The mandate for the IGC to finalize a 'reform Treaty' was soon agreed by the European Council and subsequently by the European Parliament, the Commission, and the European Central Bank (ECB). The IGC was launched on 23 July 2007 and negotiations over the content of the new Treaty continued into the autumn. Sticking points included the Polish government's position over various institutional changes (in particular relating to blocking minorities in the Council of Ministers) and UK and Irish opt-outs in justice and home affairs. The text of the new Treaty was finally agreed in Lisbon in October 2007 and signed by heads of state and government in the same city in December. However, before the Lisbon Treaty could come into force, it had to be ratified by each of the twenty-seven member states.

The Main Provisions

While some of the more controversial aspects of the Constitutional Treaty were removed, the vast majority of provisions were retained in the Lisbon Treaty. Over sixty revisions were made to the TEU and nearly 300 changes were made to the TEC —or 'Treaty on the Functioning of the European Union' (TFEU) as it would be renamed.

The Lisbon Treaty would fundamentally restructure the EU's governing architecture by removing the three-pillar structure that had been established by the Maastricht Treaty (see Chapter 13, p. 161). This would make Common Foreign and Security Policy (CFSP) a more integral part of the EU (see Chapter 33, p. 514) and also mean that aspects of Justice and Home Affairs (JHA) policy that had remained in the intergovernmental 'third pillar' of the old architecture would become subject to the **Union method** of decision making. JHA policy, already partially recast by the Amsterdam Treaty around creating an area of freedom, security, and justice in the EU, was consolidated and enhanced around that goal by the Lisbon Treaty (see Chapter 31). The Treaty also clarified the role of the European Council, gave it full status as an EU institution, and signalled that it would oversee the new procedure by which any state that wanted to could withdraw from the EU (Chapter 21, pp. 276–8).

Two new high-profile positions would be created: a 'permanent' President of the European Council and a High Representative of the Union for Foreign Affairs and Security Policy. The President would serve a two-and-a-half-year term (renewable once) and this post would in some respects replace the six-month rotating presidency (although this would stay in place for the Council of Ministers).

The High Representative post was essentially a renaming of the proposed 'Foreign Minister' that was among the statist symbols culled from the Constitutional Treaty. This position involved merging the Foreign Affairs portfolio for External Relations and the High Representative for CFSP, thus creating a unique role that would straddle two of the major institutions. The post-holder would be both chair of the Foreign Affairs Council and also a Vice-President of the European Commission (in charge of external relations). The High Representative would be assisted by a European External Action Service (EEAS), also newly created by the Treaty.

The procedure of **qualified majority voting (QMV)** would be extended into new policy areas. Its rules would be changed from 2014 to create a 'double majority' system in which, for a decision to be approved by QMV, the support of at least 55 per cent of national governments representing at least 65 per cent of the EU's population (see Chapter 19, p. 233) would be required.

The Treaty would strengthen the powers of the EP in relation to the budgetary process and also through expansion of its co-decision powers in areas such as agricultural policy, transport, and asylum and immigration (see Chapter 19, p. 234). The number of members of the European Parliament (MEPs) was capped at 751 (750 plus the EP President).

The size of the European Commission would be reduced so that only two-thirds of member states would have a Commissioner at any given time. Previously, each member state had nominated a Commissioner: a principle that had worked well with an EU of fifteen, but which, with an EU of twenty-seven, was deemed unwieldy.

The Treaty also sought to enhance the powers of the European Court of Justice (ECJ) to rule on cases relating to areas of JHA that had been transferred from the third pillar (above). In addition, the Charter of Fundamental Rights would become 'solemnly binding' and would be used for the interpretation and implementation of EU law. However, the UK and Poland negotiated an opt-out that meant that this would not confer any new rights in national law (see Chapter 15, p. 189).

A greater role was allotted to national parliaments in responding to Commission proposals and, if a third of national parliaments were in agreement, the Commission could be asked to redraft a proposal. The Treaty would also introduce an 'emergency brake' procedure in a small number of policy areas, which allowed a member government to suspend the **ordinary legislative procedure** and appeal to the European Council where the government deemed its national sovereignty to be threatened.

In addition to the institutional changes relating to specific policy areas set out above, the Treaty provided additional policy competencies for the EU relating to civil protection, tourism, and sport. Competencies in other areas of policy were recast (including energy and environment), while the Treaty also set out the formal balance of competencies between the EU and the member states (see Chapter 25, pp. 352–3).

For some, the Lisbon Treaty was a serious dilution of the intentions of the Constitutional Treaty, particularly through the removal of reference to the term 'constitution' and the symbols that would have given the EU a stronger identity. For others, the substance of the original remained and the revisions were seen as mainly cosmetic. How much had actually changed was a very sensitive issue politically, but one that was not always handled sensitively. Dedman (2010: 177) commented that:

> Lisbon contained 95 per cent of what was in the Constitutional Treaty as its Chief Architect, Valéry Giscard d'Estaing was keen to announce in successive interviews, undermining governments' cases against referendums that they had originally promised but now insisted were not necessary.

Ultimately though, rebadging the Treaty as a more technical 'reform Treaty' allowed a number of governments—such as France, the Netherlands, and the UK—to avoid ratification via referendum (Sedelmeier and Young 2008: 2). EU leaders stated at Lisbon that there would be no further institutional reform for at least a decade.

The Ratification Process

While there was political pressure in some states to hold a referendum on the Lisbon Treaty, only Ireland was committed to a popular vote. This was in sharp contrast to the ten states who had decided to do this for the Constitutional Treaty.

Despite the revisions that the Treaty contained, on 12 June 2008, the Irish people rejected it with a vote of 53.4 per cent against (from a turnout of 53.1 per cent). The vote shook EU leaders, while giving succour to those who had viewed the revised Treaty as simply a cynical attempt to repackage a Treaty once rejected. As Copsey and Haughton (2009: 2) noted:

> The very fact that Ireland was the only Member State to ask its citizens to pass judgement on the treaty only fuelled the fires of critics of the EU such as Czech President Vaclav Klaus, for example, who could not contain his glee when the result was announced, claiming he could write a better treaty from his hospital bed.

Opinions varied on the reasons for the vote against. Those disappointed by the outcome spoke of misinformation being spread about the purposes of the Treaty in relation to issues such as abortion, euthanasia, and defence policy. Domestic politics also played a role, not least the unpopularity of Prime Minister Bertie Ahern, who was in favour of a 'yes' vote. There was also wide recognition that the 'yes' campaign had been lacklustre. The bottom line, though, was that the Irish people were not persuaded of the case for the Treaty, despite the fact that the EU remained broadly popular in Ireland: a Eurobarometer poll taken soon after the referendum that showed that 87 per cent of Irish people thought that Ireland benefited from EU membership—a higher percentage than for any other state (Dedman 2010: 178).

Despite the Irish vote and the soul searching that this caused, EU leaders urged other member states to continue with the ratification process: eighteen had already done so and these were joined by another five by the end of 2008. The four countries that had not ratified by this point were Ireland, the Czech Republic, Germany, and Poland.

At the European Council of December 2008, Ireland was given reassurances in relation to areas of concern raised in the referendum campaign, including taxation policy, family and social issues, and foreign policy. In exchange, the Irish government agreed to hold a new referendum by the end of 2009 (Carbone 2010: 224–5). The European Council also reversed its decision on reducing the number of Commissioners, so that all states retained one each. While some claimed that this had been an issue in the Irish referendum—not least the Irish Commissioner Charlie McCreevy and former Commissioner Ray MacSharry—there was general recognition among EU leaders that this move was neither necessary nor desirable, particularly for smaller states.

That absence of referendums in other member states did not mean the absence of controversy. In Germany, the Federal Constitutional Court had been asked to rule on the compatibility of the Lisbon Treaty with the German Constitution (the Basic Law). Its 2009 judgment ruled that the Treaty was compatible, but placed domestic conditions on further transfers of power: conditions that have been interpreted as likely to contribute to a decline in Germany's support for integration in the future (Bulmer and Paterson 2010). The presidents of both the Czech Republic and Poland refused to sign the ratification instruments and there were splits between political elites in a number of member states.

However, the fate of the Treaty ultimately rested on a positive vote in the second Irish referendum. The fact that this was secured in October 2009 with a clear majority in favour (67.13 per cent of a 59 per cent turnout) was largely explained by deteriorating economic circumstances, although this time the 'yes' campaign was far more effective and the negative consequences for Ireland of a 'no' vote emphasized more (van der Veen 2010). The second Irish referendum cleared the way for the Treaty to come into effect on 1 December 2009.

New Appointees

With the second Irish referendum out of the way, attention focused on who would be appointed to the two senior posts created by the Lisbon Treaty. In the months leading up to the decision, speculation surrounded a number of high-profile figures—former British Prime Minister Tony Blair being prominent among them. Thus, there was some surprise when the Brussels European Council in November 2009 announced that the first President of the European Council would be Herman Van Rompuy and the first High Representative designate would be Baroness Catherine Ashton. Neither individual had a particularly high profile.

Van Rompuy, a Christian Democrat, had been Prime Minister of Belgium for less than a year, while Baroness Ashton (British Labour Party) had been Commissioner for Trade for just over a year and was largely unknown within her own country. As such, Ashton in particular appeared to be underqualified, although she had impressed during her brief spell as a Commissioner.

There was a widely held view that low-profile and less-powerful individuals were appointed to limit the prospects for challenges to the authority of national governments within the EU system. However, in the case of both appointments, there was a high degree of pragmatism and compromise involved in finding candidates suitable to a wide range of opinion. This meant avoiding not only the more powerful names mentioned, but also the more controversial. One or two potential candidates, including Tony Blair, fell into both categories and were to be avoided by some governments at all costs. There was also an element of a political fix to ensure that both of the EU's major political families secured a post.

The reaction was generally one of disappointment. Simon Hix (quoted in Traynor 2009) suggested that '[t]he EU is losing influence rapidly and these appointments make that worse ... The rest of the world was expecting big figures. But Europe has shown it would rather be a super-sized Switzerland'. Quoted in the same article, the Swedish Foreign Minister, Carl Bildt, spoke of the appointments as 'an historic missed opportunity', and Daniel Cohn-Bendit, the leader of the Green Party group in the EP, suggested that 'Europe is sinking to a new low' (Traynor 2009).

Other Developments

The Financial Crisis

The financial crisis that struck the global economy late in 2008 brought into question the effectiveness of the eurozone as states struggled to find the appropriate economic and monetary tools with which to respond (see Chapter 28, pp. 411–12). In response, EU leaders came together in European Council and eurozone meetings to co-ordinate fiscal and other measures to address the crisis and to underline their commitment to the single market. The initial response was characterized by a commitment to maintaining levels of public spending to stimulate recovery.

In October 2008, European leaders called for an overhaul of the global financial system and were part of **G20** meetings that agreed a common approach to the financial crisis. In April 2009, the G20 agreed to transfer €832 billion into the **International Monetary Fund (IMF)** and other financial institutions to assist states struggling to respond to the crisis (Europa 2010).

While states both within and outside the eurozone faced similar problems, the scale of the problems faced by some of the weaker economies brought challenges to the stability and credibility of the euro. Greece faced particularly acute challenges in dealing with the global downturn. The extent of the problem in Greece was revealed following a change of government in October 2009 (see Chapter 28, p. 411). The proposed solutions led to a series of street protests. More generally, the crisis also had the effect of undermining support for integration in many of the newer member states, which had believed that membership would provide greater protection against such challenges (Copsey and Haughton 2009: 3).

In response to the Greek situation, in May 2010, the EU and IMF agreed financial assistance of €110 billion over three years, in exchange for a programme of public sector reform leading to cuts in public spending and increases in tax revenue. This deal did little to quell the protests, in which the EU and the IMF joined the Greek political establishment as targets for protestors.

While there was some reluctance to 'bail out' Greece in some of the member states that had managed their public finances more prudently (see Chapter 28, p. 411), EU leaders argued that if the EU did not act to bolster the Greek economy, there could be a domino effect that would threaten other weak eurozone economies (the so-called 'Piigs'—Portugal, Ireland, Italy, and Spain, in addition to Greece). Moreover, the EU did not want to countenance Greece being forced out of the eurozone and thus undermining the credibility of the currency. EU and IMF funding was also set aside to aid eurozone states during the crisis. Following criticisms that the EU had 'done too little, too late' in response to the crisis, it established an economic task force shortly after its agreement with Greece.

While the Greek situation stood out as a particularly acute case, 'austerity' quickly become the watchword of the day across the EU and public expenditure cuts commonplace. This marked a reversal of the initial European response to the global downturn, which had been to stimulate economic recovery. There remained disagreement within both national and international arenas about how best to respond to the crisis, with the US government critical of the Europe's apparent volte-face (*The Observer*, 13 June 2010).

The preoccupation with the financial crisis overshadowed the Lisbon Strategy for European competitiveness, which was supposed to have produced its headline goals by 2010 (see Chapter 17, pp. 206–7). Instead of demonstrating the EU as 'the most competitive and dynamic knowledge-based economy in the world', the global economic situation and the eurozone crisis demonstrated that a lot more work was needed. Accordingly, in June 2010, the European Council adopted 'Europe 2020', a new ten-year strategy for jobs and growth to promote the delivery of structural reforms.

Enlargement

In 2005, the EU opened accession negotiations with both Croatia and Turkey and gave the former Yugoslav Republic of Macedonia candidate status. Following the 'big bang' of the 2004 enlargement, the EU prepared for a quieter period in this sphere. The unfinished business of the Eastern enlargement saw Bulgaria and Romania accede to the Union in January 2007: a controversial feature of which was the number of states placing work-permit restrictions on workers from these countries until 2014 (the maximum time allowed under the Treaty). This was a reaction to the effects of the large number of incoming workers experienced by some states after the 2004 enlargement.

There were claims within Turkey that the prospects for Turkish accession had not been helped by the appointment of Herman Van Rompuy as first permanent President of the European Council. Van Rompuy was on record as stating (in 2004): 'An expansion of the EU to include Turkey cannot be considered as just another expansion as in the past. The universal values which are in force in Europe, and which are also fundamental values of Christianity, will lose vigour with the entry of a large Islamic country such as Turkey' (quoted in Tait 2009). Among the 'big three' governments, France and Germany were seen as responsible for slow progress on Turkish accession, while Britain remained an advocate.

In July 2009, Iceland's Parliament voted to apply to join the EU by a majority of thirty-two to twenty-eight. It had been an associate member of the European Economic Area (EAA) since 1994, so was already in line with many EU requirements. However, three obstacles were identified in the path of speedy accession: the EU's Common Fisheries Policy, which would give other member states access to Iceland's fish; the weakness of the Icelandic economy in the wake of the global financial crisis; and that popular support in a referendum could not be guaranteed (*The Economist*, 25 July 2009: 24). Iceland was given official candidate status in June 2010.

External Relations

In terms of external relations, the period was marked by important developments in relation to the EU's eastern neighbours. Relations with Russia were tense for most of the period, and when hostilities broke out between Georgia and Russia in August 2008, the EU condemned Russia's behaviour as a 'disproportionate reaction'. The EU presidency was subsequently involved in negotiating a ceasefire and the EU provided a mission to monitor the ceasefire. The conflict was said to have 'brought into sharp relief the debates about further enlargement . . . and the kind of policies that are needed for the EU's neighbourhood. It also highlighted the very different attitudes towards Russia that exist in the EU-27' (Copsey and Haughton 2009: 2–3).

Following on from this conflict, in September 2008, the European Council requested that the Commission bring forward its proposals for enhanced co-operation with its eastern neighbours. In December 2008, the EU announced the creation of an 'eastern partnership' with six former Soviet states (Armenia, Azerbaijan, Belarus, Georgia, Moldova, and Ukraine). The partnership sought to develop relations with these states through a range of measures aimed at promoting their economic, social, and political development. However, there was no offer of membership in sight for these states.

Beyond Europe, the EU was involved in a number of security operations in a wide range of conflicts including parts of Africa, Kosovo, the Palestinian territories, and Afghanistan (see Chapter 33, pp. 518–19). However, the EU's relative weakness in foreign affairs was recognized by key provisions of the Lisbon Treaty that were aimed at strengthening its capacity to act. In addition to the creation of the two senior posts and the EEAS discussed above, no fewer than twenty-five of the Treaty's sixty-two amendments to the Treaty on European Union related to its provisions on CFSP and European Security and Defence Policy (ESDP) (Menon 2010: 2).

History suggested that member states would still want to remain in the driving seat on important foreign policy issues and this was indicated by the fact that foreign policy would not be part of the Union method under the Lisbon Treaty. As such, the Lisbon changes alone were not expected to transform the EU's foreign policy potential: 'After all, even if the Union enjoyed sufficient military capabilities, consensus between member states would be required before these could be deployed' (Menon 2010: 3).

Other Policy Developments

While policies are treated in detail in the final section of this book, decisions taken in some policy areas in this period may well prove to be of historical note. On the environment, in December 2008, the EU agreed to cut greenhouse gas emissions by 20 per cent by 2020 (compared with 1990 levels) through national reduction targets and an EU-wide carbon emissions trading scheme (see Chapter 30, Insight 30.1, p. 457). In December 2007, the Schengen area (for elimination of internal border controls) was extended to include the Czech Republic, Estonia, Hungary, Latvia, Lithuania, Malta, Poland, Slovakia, and Slovenia (see Chapter 31, pp. 474–6). In relation to monetary policy, both Cyprus and Malta adopted the euro in January 2008 and Slovakia did so in January 2009.

Elections and Appointments

Elections to the EP took place in June 2009. Due to the delay with the ratification of the Lisbon Treaty, the elections took place under the existing rules, meaning that 736 MEPs were elected rather than the 750 provided for in the new Treaty (for the distribution of seats, see Table 22.1). The main feature of these elections was that turnout was again down—from 45.6 per cent in 2004 to 43.2 per cent in 2009. This was the lowest turnout since direct elections began thirty years earlier and added further weight to concerns about the contribution of the EP to the Union's democratic legitimacy.

In 2010, José Manuel Barroso secured a second five-year term as President of the Commission. His reappointment had faced some opposition within the EP, most notably from the Greens and some MEPs on the left, but his case was helped by a strengthening of centre-right parties in the EP elections of June 2009 (see Chapter 22, Table 22.3). The new Commission as a whole was approved by a vote in the EP on 9 February 2010, but the process had not been without incident.

The proposal of Michel Barnier, a former French Foreign Minister and ally of President Sarkozy, as Internal Market Commissioner was controversial in some circles because it promised stricter regulation of financial services. In particular, the UK government had concerns that this might undermine the City of London as a financial centre. The deal struck involved a British official becoming the leading civil servant in the Directorate (Traynor 2009). Another proposed Commissioner, the Bulgarian Rumiana Jeleva (International Co-operation, Humanitarian Aid, and Crisis Response) performed poorly during the hearings and was subsequently replaced as the Bulgarian nominee.

CONCLUSION

In a period dominated by attempts to secure institutional changes to make the EU more effective and more accountable, our primary analytical theme here is that of legitimacy—a recurring theme since the Maastricht Treaty (see Chapter 13, p. 167). Scholars have identified a gap between elites and public opinion in relation to integration, and domestic political audiences have become more difficult to ignore. In the words of Carbone (2010: 230), 'the "permissive consensus" that characterized the early years of the European Union has increasingly turned into a "constraining dissensus"'.

The EU's action in pushing for a second referendum in Ireland was viewed with cynicism in many quarters. Dedman (2010: 175) claimed that the first vote was treated by EU leaders as a 'mistake' and that 'this contempt for popular opinion actually confirms Eurosceptics' charge that the EU is elitist and undemocratic'. In reality, the biggest mistake was the one made by EU leaders in misreading the public mood in a number of member states when seeking to advance an EU constitution. Moreover, the process of repackaging the Constitutional Treaty to make it more acceptable to publics that had been given scant regard in the first instance was unseemly and damaged the EU's legitimacy.

But what of the Treaty itself? Commission President Barroso (2009: 13) argued that it 'does a great deal to enhance accountability and transparency', pointing to the increased scrutiny rights of national parliaments, minutes of the Council of Ministers going on the record, and the right of European citizens to ask the Commission to table legislation over which it has jurisdiction if a million signatures can be mustered. Others were more critical. Börzel (2010: 5) pointed to key areas remaining out of supranational competence, such as macroeconomic stability and redistribution, and suggested that the Treaty's reforms were 'not sufficient to remedy the declining problem-solving capacity of the EU nor do they provide an adequate response to the increasing politicization'. Wyles (2007: 11) added that 'it takes a real stretch of the imagination to believe that three presidencies and a high representative are going to deliver the coherence and singleness of purpose that is needed'.

In terms of other debates, the strengthening of the European Council through its formalization as an EU institution with a 'permanent' president can be viewed as a shift towards intergovernmentalism at the expense of **supranational institutions**: the Commission in particular. The European Council presidency was intended to provide greater continuity of purpose and be better placed to promote a more consistent agenda.

However, writing so close to events, it is sensible not to draw too many conclusions about the implications of the Lisbon Treaty. Moreover, it appears likely that there will be plenty of time to reflect on these implications, there being little appetite among either political elites or publics for major reform in the near future.

KEY POINTS

The Lisbon Treaty

The Road to the Lisbon Treaty

- The rejection of the Constitutional Treaty in France and the Netherlands in 2005 increased uncertainty over the EU's legitimacy and future trajectory.
- After a period of reflection, some of the more controversial aspects of the Treaty were removed. References to 'constitution' and key symbols were dropped.
- The revised 'Lisbon Treaty' was signed in the Portuguese capital in December 2009.

The Main Provisions

- The Treaty proposed restructuring the EU's governing architecture to make CFSP a more integral part of the EU, and JHA subject to the **Community method**.
- It clarified the role of the European Council and gave it full status as an EU institution.
- It created two new high-profile posts: a 'permanent' President of the European Council, and a High Representative of the Union for Foreign Affairs and Security Policy,
- QMV was extended into new policy areas and a new 'double majority' voting system was agreed for 2014 onwards.
- The EP's powers were to be enhanced in relation to the budgetary process and also through expansion of its co-decision powers.
- The Charter of Fundamental Rights became solemnly binding and would be used for the interpretation and implementation of EU law.
- For some, the Lisbon Treaty was a serious dilution of the intentions of the Constitutional Treaty; for others, the substance of the original remained and the revisions were seen as mainly cosmetic.

The Ratification Process

- In Ireland, the only state to hold a referendum, 53.4 per cent of the public voted against ratifying the Treaty in June 2008.
- Although there were no other referendums, ratification proved controversial in other member states: most notably Poland and the Czech Republic.
- Following assurances in relation to areas of concern, including taxation policy, family and social issues, and foreign policy, a second Irish referendum in October 2009 produced a vote of 67.13 per cent in favour of ratifying the Treaty.

New Appointees

- In November 2009, Herman Van Rompuy became the first President of the European Council. Baroness Catherine Ashton became the first High Representative of the Union for Foreign Affairs and Security Policy. Both were relatively low-profile figures.

Other Developments

- The financial crisis that struck the global economy late in 2008 brought into question the effectiveness of the eurozone and caused acute problems in Greece. While there was some reluctance in some of the member states to 'bail out' Greece, a package of aid was finally agreed in May 2010.
- In 2005, the EU opened accession negotiations with both Croatia and Turkey and gave the former Yugoslav Republic of Macedonia candidate status.
- In January 2007, the unfinished business of the 2004 enlargement was completed with the accession of Bulgaria and Romania.
- In July 2009, Iceland applied for membership, followed by Serbia in December of the same year.
- The EU was involved in mediating a ceasefire between Georgia and Russia and subsequently created an 'eastern partnership' agreement with six former soviet states.
- There were other important agreements in relation to the environment, the Schengen area and monetary policy.

221

- The EP elections of June 2009 showed another fall in voter turnout to the lowest since direct elections began in 1979.
- A new Commission took office in February 2010, with José Manuel Barroso beginning a second five-year term as its President.

FURTHER READING

The earlier part of the period discussed here (before the second Irish referendum) is covered by both **M. Dedman**, *The Origins and Development of the European Union, 1945–2008*, 2nd edn (London: Routledge, 2010) and **R. McAllister**, *European Union: An Historical and Political Survey*, 2nd edn (London: Routledge, 2010). Covering a similar period, **M. Carbone (ed.)**, *National Politics and European Integration: From the Constitution to the Lisbon Treaty* (Cheltenham, UK; Northampton, MA: Edward Elgar, 2010) covers the domestic politics of treaty reform. More recent, but briefer reflections on the Lisbon Treaty can be found in *EUSA Review*, 23(1), (European Union Studies Association, USA), Winter 2010 (**http://www.eustudies.org/publications_review_winter10.php**).

 online resource centre

Visit the Online Resource Centre that accompanies this book for links to more information on the Lisbon Treaty:
www.oxfordtextbooks.co.uk/orc/bache3e/

Part Three
Institutions

Theories derived both from international relations (IR) and from the analysis of domestic policy making include positions that emphasize the importance of institutions. In the IR literature on international regimes, there is an emphasis on institutions as 'persistent and connected sets of rules (formal and informal) that prescribe behavioral roles, constrain states, and shape expectations' (Keohane 1989: 3). In the 'new institutionalist' approaches to the study of domestic policy making, there is a similar emphasis on the importance of institutions, broadly defined. In short, *institutions matter*, although not only institutions matter, nor is it only formal institutions that matter. However, to understand the politics of the European Union it is necessary to know something about the nature of the formal institutions and the relationships between them. The long-standing debate between intergovernmentalist and neofunctionalist accounts of integration is reflected in assessments concerning which of the institutions are most influential.

There are six chapters in this part of the book. The opening chapter on 'The Institutional Architecture' provides essential introductory information on the institutions, the Treaties, the legislative and budgetary processes, and other broad features. It presents the context within which the institutions operate, and provides background to understanding the debates that are presented in later chapters. The content of the chapter has been updated to take account of the Lisbon Treaty, which was implemented on 1 December 2009.

For most of the rest of this part of the book, the choice of which subjects to include was straightforward. Traditionally, the EU has had four 'main' institutions: the Commission; the Council of Ministers; the European Parliament; and the European Court of Justice. The Lisbon Treaty gave the *European Council* separate status from the *Council of Ministers*. The European Council is now considered more fully, but, because of the similarities in its make-up, it is considered within the same chapter as the Council of Ministers. All five of the main institutions are therefore treated in detail. The final chapter in this part deals with 'Organized Interests', the interaction of which with the formal institutions is a central component of the EU's decision-making process.

Chapter 19
The Institutional Architecture

Chapter Overview

Up to now, this book has introduced the institutions of the European Union (EU) only as part of the history of European integration, and their powers have only been briefly outlined. To understand the debates that surround the institutions themselves, though, it is necessary to understand in more detail their powers and their roles in relationship to one another. The same material is needed to understand the debates around the various policies of the EU, which are the subject of Part Four of the book.

This chapter examines the pattern of institutions and the formal rules that govern them. It also gives information on the composition of the less-important institutions, although for the main institutions—the Commission, the Council of Ministers (or 'Council'), the European Parliament (EP), and the Court of Justice of the European Union (CJEU)—that information is provided in the separate chapters devoted to them.

The chapter starts with a review of the Treaties that form the founding 'constitutional' documents of the EU. The main institutions involved in the processes of decision making are then introduced. Decision making is examined, covering both the budgetary and legislative procedures. Brief consideration is also given to the different decision-making process on foreign and security policy. The chapter then looks at the implementation of decisions once they have been made. Finally, the chapter returns to some broader considerations relating to the post-Lisbon institutional architecture.

The institutional design is not stable, but subject to periodic debate, argument and revision ...
(Wallace 2005: 50)

The Treaties

The EU is governed by Treaty. Specifically, since the implementation of the Lisbon Treaty in December 2009, it has been governed by two Treaties: the Treaty on European Union (TEU) and the Treaty on the Functioning of the European Union

(TFEU). In order to understand the current arrangements, it is necessary to look at the evolution of Treaty provision.

There were three 'founding Treaties'—the Treaty of Paris (1951) and the two Treaties of Rome (1957) (see Chapters 5 and 8). They were supplemented in ways that affected the powers of the institutions by three further Treaties in the 1960s and early 1970s. One merged the Councils and the Commissions of the three Communities, while the other two were concerned with budgetary provisions. After the last of these, in 1975, there were no further major revisions of the Treaties for another decade, but then there were four new Treaties in the next fifteen years: the Single European Act (SEA); the Maastricht Treaty; the Amsterdam Treaty; and the Nice Treaty (Table 19.1). Leaving aside the Treaty of Paris, which expired in 2002, and the Euratom Treaty, which maintains its separate status, by 1997, the Treaties had been consolidated into two: the TEU, and the Treaty establishing the European Community (TEC). The Constitutional Treaty, agreed at the Brussels European Council on 18 June 2004, was designed to consolidate the existing Treaties into one. However, following its abandonment in 2005, the somewhat more modest Lisbon Treaty made revisions to the existing Treaties (see Chapter 18, pp. 213–14). However, it also renamed the TEC the TFEU. Although more modest than the Constitutional Treaty that was originally planned, the Lisbon Treaty is very important. First of all, it changed the general organization (or architecture) of the EU in a way comparable with the earlier Maastricht Treaty. Second, it included many amendments to the existing Treaties.

The Maastricht Treaty had introduced a structure consisting of three 'pillars': the EC pillar, governed by the TEC; and two intergovernmental pillars, covering the Common Foreign and Security Policy (CFSP) and Justice and Home Affairs (JHA)

Table 19.1 The Treaties

- The Treaty of Paris (signed 1951; took effect 1952) created the European Coal and Steel Community (ECSC)
- The two Treaties of Rome (signed 1957; took effect 1958): the first created the European Atomic Energy Community (Euratom); the second created the European Economic Community (EEC)
- The Treaty Establishing a Single Council and a Single Commission of the European Communities, also known as the Merger Treaty (signed 1965; took effect 1967)
- The Treaty Amending Certain Budgetary Provisions of the Treaties (1970)
- The Treaty Amending Certain Financial Provisions of the Treaty (1975)
- The Single European Act (signed 1986; took effect July 1987)
- The Maastricht Treaty (signed 1992; took effect November 1993), which introduced the Treaty on European Union (TEU)
- The Treaty of Amsterdam (signed 1997; took effect 1999)
- The Treaty of Nice (signed 2001; took effect 2003)
- The Lisbon Treaty (signed 2007; took effect December 2009)

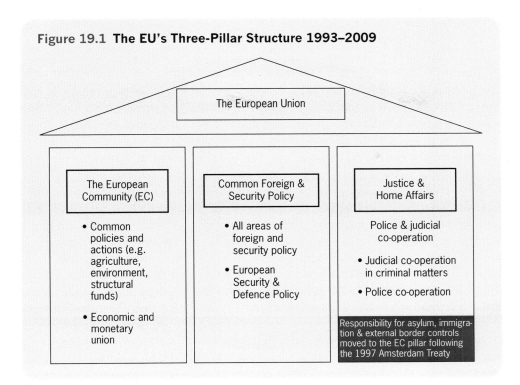

Figure 19.1 **The EU's Three-Pillar Structure 1993–2009**

The European Union

| The European Community (EC) | Common Foreign & Security Policy | Justice & Home Affairs |

- Common policies and actions (e.g. agriculture, environment, structural funds)
- Economic and monetary union

- All areas of foreign and security policy
- European Security & Defence Policy

Police & judicial co-operation

- Judicial co-operation in criminal matters
- Police co-operation

Responsibility for asylum, immigration & external border controls moved to the EC pillar following the 1997 Amsterdam Treaty

(Figure 19.1), governed by the TEU. Subsequent amendments, made by the Treaties of Amsterdam and Nice, scaled back the policies covered by the JHA pillar by moving some to the EC pillar. However, the CFSP remained distinctively intergovernmental. This three-pillar structure was an important part of the EU's functioning from 1993 to 2009. However, it was abolished as of December 2009. The CFSP remains distinctively intergovernmental, but all other policies are consolidated into a single order governed by the TFEU.

The staff of the EU institutions constantly refer to the Treaties. They are always careful to check the Treaty base of any action that they take. In the Preamble of any legislative proposal, the Commission is formally obliged to state under which Article of the Treaties it is making the proposal. This incessant engagement with the text of the Treaties has led to the internal discourse of the institutions being peppered with references to Articles of the Treaties, usually just citing them by number.

However, as the founding Treaties were amended and added to by the later ones, the numbering grew more and more complex, with letters having to be used in addition to numbers. Finally, at Amsterdam in June 1997, the heads of government agreed to renumber the Articles and consolidate all revisions to the original Rome Treaty on the European Economic Community (EEC) in the TEC. The other Treaties, including the TEU, were kept separate. The Lisbon Treaty repeated this renumbering exercise. Consequently, in this book, the new number of a Treaty Article is given, followed by the old one in brackets, except where the reference is purely historical, when the numbering current at the time is given first followed by the current, 'post-Lisbon' numbering in brackets. In all cases, the reference is to what is now called the TFEU (previously the TEC), unless it is indicated that it is to the TEU.

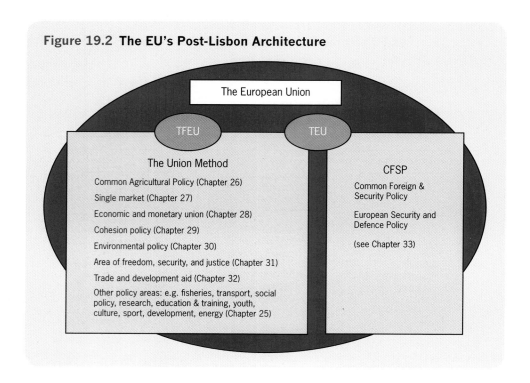

Figure 19.2 The EU's Post-Lisbon Architecture

The European Union

TFEU

TEU

The Union Method

Common Agricultural Policy (Chapter 26)

Single market (Chapter 27)

Economic and monetary union (Chapter 28)

Cohesion policy (Chapter 29)

Environmental policy (Chapter 30)

Area of freedom, security, and justice (Chapter 31)

Trade and development aid (Chapter 32)

Other policy areas: e.g. fisheries, transport, social policy, research, education & training, youth, culture, sport, development, energy (Chapter 25)

CFSP

Common Foreign & Security Policy

European Security and Defence Policy

(see Chapter 33)

The key distinction between these two Treaties is as follows. The TEU sets out:

- the broad principles governing the EU, such as its commitment to democracy;
- the general role of the institutions;
- the principles governing who may apply to join the EU;
- how a member state may leave the EU (a provision that is new in the Lisbon Treaty).

It also sets out the details of the operation of the CFSP, making clear that its location in this Treaty designates it as not subject to the full authority of the Court of Justice. The TFEU, by contrast, sets out the detailed operation of the institutions and of all other policy areas. In what follows, the arrangements covered by the TFEU will be termed the **Union method**. As an indication of the scale of the revisions made by the Lisbon Treaty, over sixty revisions were made to the TEU and nearly 300 were made to the TEC in addition to renaming it the TFEU (Figure 19.2).

The Decision-Making Institutions (the Union Method)

Following ratification of the Lisbon Treaty, the most logical way in which to understand the decision-making institutions is to consider first of all the Union method.

Later in the chapter, we consider the arrangements for CFSP. With one exception, the main decision-making institutions of the EU central to the Union method are those that were set up in the Treaty of Rome (EEC):

- the Commission;
- the Council of Ministers;
- the European Parliament (EP).

The exception is the European Council. This body was set up in 1974 and has grown in importance, but the Treaties did not spell out its operation in detail until the Lisbon Treaty.

In addition, to the main institutions there are also two consultative committees:

- the Economic and Social Committee, which was in the original Treaty of Rome (EEC), and which in 2002 became the European Economic and Social Committee (EESC) following the incorporation within it of the formerly independent Consultative Committee of the European Coal and Steel Community (ECSC);
- the Committee of the Regions and Local Authorities (CoR), which was established in 1994 under provisions in the Maastricht Treaty.

Under the Union method, just as in CFSP, the European Council should be seen as the main agenda-setter of the EU. Either through overseeing Treaty reform or through identifying policy strategy, it steers the broad direction of integration as a whole and is able to use its political authority to guide the broad direction of individual policies. However, it does not legislate. In legislation, it is the European Commission that plays the initial role. It is the proposer of legislation, and the Council of Ministers and the EP are the joint legislative decision makers. The EESC and the CoR also have a right to be consulted on legislative proposals. Implementation of legislation once it has been passed is partly a responsibility of the Commission, but mostly it is the responsibility of the member states. The Commission and the Court of Justice act as watchdogs to ensure that the member states fulfil their obligations.

A similar division of functions exists for budgetary decision making. The European Council agrees the multi-annual financial perspectives, setting the EU's financial envelope for a seven-year period. The Commission proposes the annual budget; the Council of Ministers and EP jointly decide on the annual budget. The Court of Justice and the Court of Auditors perform the watchdog role.

The European Council

The important agenda-setting role of the European Council has already been identified, as well as its oversight of all EU activity including CFSP. Article 15 TEU states:

> The European Council shall provide the Union with the necessary impetus for its development and shall define the general political directions and priorities thereof. It shall not exercise legislative functions.

This latter sentence is important, since it makes a clear delineation of responsibilities between the European Council and the Council of Ministers. Whilst this is a functional distinction—the European Council plays a political role while the Council of Ministers plays a legislative one—the other essential difference is of composition. The European Council is comprised of the EU's top political figures: the heads of state and government of the twenty-seven member states; the President of the European Council; the President of the European Commission; and the EU's High Representative for Foreign Affairs and Security Policy. By contrast, the Council of Ministers comprises regular Ministers. Fuller discussion of the membership of both bodies is undertaken in Chapter 21, but the key point here is that the European Council represents the EU's summit of member-government power and has the political clout to drive forward the EU's agenda. The European Council has effectively positioned itself at the apex of the European Union, guiding the direction of all pillars of the EU during the period 1993–2009, and, from December 2009, of all EU policies, whether under the Union method or not. In practical terms, this situation means that legislation and other decision making typically takes place in a context that the European Council may have already shaped.

The Commission

In the formal decision-making system of the EU, the Commission has two important roles (Figure 19.3). It submits legislative proposals to the Council of Ministers, and it draws up the draft annual EU budget for agreement by the Council of Ministers and the EP.

The Commission is formally the sole institution with the right to propose legislation. In the view of the Commission, it is only its monopoly of the right of initiative that allows a coherent agenda to emerge for the EU as a whole. However, even leaving aside its limited authority in CFSP (below), there are several qualifications to its exclusive right to initiate proposals. First, as noted the European Council—the EU summit meetings—sets out the EU's strategy and *may* therefore set the agenda that the Commission then follows in terms of specific legislation. Second, as a legacy of the

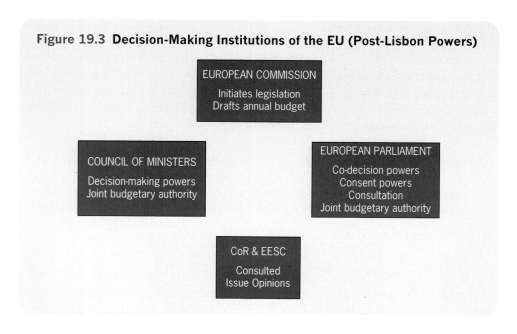

Figure 19.3 Decision-Making Institutions of the EU (Post-Lisbon Powers)

situation relating to JHA under the three-pillar EU structure from 1993 to 2009, the Commission has to share the right of initiative in measures relating to creating an area of freedom, security, and justice (AFSJ) (see Chapter 31). Either the Commission or a quarter of the member states may propose initiatives in this policy area.

The Commission's exclusive right to initiate legislation was also somewhat undermined by an amendment made under the Maastricht Treaty. Under Article 225 TFEU, the EP 'may, acting by a majority of its component Members, request the Commission to submit any appropriate proposal on matters on which it considers that a Union act is required for the purpose of implementing the Treaties'. Given that the democratic legitimacy of the EP has been increasingly emphasized, it would be difficult for the Commission to ignore such a request. Mirroring this power, the 'Council acting by a simple majority may request the Commission to undertake any studies the Council considers desirable for the attainment of the common objectives, and to submit to it any appropriate proposals' (Article 241 TFEU). Finally, even in the areas in which it retains the full right of initiative, to say that the Commission is the sole proposer of legislation should not be taken to imply that it works on legislative proposals in isolation. In practice, it has always consulted widely with interest groups, committees of technical experts, and civil servants from the member states. Nevertheless, despite the qualifications to its right of initiative, the standard practice is that the Commission initiates legislation and this is a powerful role in the legislative process.

The Commission's legislative proposals can only be amended by the Council of Ministers if the latter acts unanimously, and the Commission may withdraw or amend its own proposals at any stage as long as the Council has not acted on them. However, where the EP has the right of co-decision with the Council, and where the Council and the EP cannot agree on the text presented by the Commission, they may agree an alternative in a Conciliation Committee that can be passed without unanimity in the Council (see below, pp. 240–1). The alternative does not have to be proposed by the Commission.

The Council of Ministers (the Council)

The Council of Ministers consists of representatives of the member states. Most meetings in the Council structure are not of Ministers themselves, but of various committees of member state officials (see Chapter 21, pp. 283–6). Nearly all business for the meetings of Ministers is filtered through such committees, and then through the Committee of Permanent Representatives (COREPER), which consists of the ambassadors from the member states to the EU (see Chapter 21, pp. 283–5).

The Council makes decisions on proposals from the Commission either unanimously or through **qualified majority voting (QMV)** depending on the Treaty provision. As was explained in Chapter 9 (pp. 128–30), in 1965, de Gaulle blocked the formal transition to QMV, but the SEA introduced it for legislative acts related to the single-market programme, and it has been extended at every subsequent Treaty reform to cover a range of other policies. The TEU's Article 16(3), as revised by the Lisbon Treaty, presented QMV as the default provision for decision making: 'The Council shall act by a qualified majority except where the Treaties provide otherwise.' There were quite a large number of new provisions for QMV in the Lisbon Treaty but quite a lot of them are limited in scope. The key moves to QMV were on energy security, emergency humanitarian aid, intellectual property, social security for migrant workers, and judicial co-operation (the last after a five-year transition period) (see Table 19.2). The key areas that remain subject to unanimity are: tax; social security; foreign policy; common defence; operational police co-operation; language rules; and the location of the EU's institutions.

Two additional points are worth noting about the extension of QMV in the Lisbon Treaty. First, the Treaty provided for some institutional matters to be decided by QMV in the European Council—for instance when deciding its own President or in proposing to the EP a candidate for the President of the European Commission. These changes were an important innovation for the summit meetings, which have traditionally reached decisions by unanimous consent. Second, the Lisbon Treaty introduced potentially significant provisions for further moves to QMV without the need for treaty revision. By including so-called *passerelle* clauses, it is possible to move some policy areas to QMV, notably on CFSP (but not defence-related matters), the multi-annual financial framework, employment law, environmental taxation, and judicial co-operation on family law. In each case the European Council has to agree to the step by unanimity, and then in most cases has to get agreement from all national parliaments

---

Table 19.2 Policy Areas Covered by Qualified Majority Voting

The Maastricht Treaty extended QMV to:

- environment
- development co-operation
- the free movement of workers

In the Treaty of Amsterdam, QMV was extended to:

- freedom of establishment
- equal pay and treatment of men and women
- mutual recognition of qualifications
- the framework programmes for research and development
- the internal market
- public health
- access to official documents
- consumer protection
- combating fraud
- co-ordination of national provisions on the treatment of foreign nationals
- customs co-operation

The Lisbon Treaty extended QMV to:

- energy security
- emergency humanitarian aid
- social security for migrant workers
- intellectual property
- specific areas of judicial and police co-operation (with effect from 2014)

QMV also applies to the implementation of a range of policy areas.

(Dougan 2008: 642). Amongst those issues regarding which unaimity remains with no prospect of change under a *passerelle* clause are taxation, social security, citizens' rights, the location of the EU institutions, and languages.

The weighting of votes applicable (until 2014) is indicated in Table 19.3. These were agreed at the Nice European Council in December 2000, and incorporated into the Nice Treaty to take into account the planned enlargement of the EU later in that decade. During the lengthy negotiations on constitutional revision, the requirement for a qualified majority would have been changed to a population-based system. This was eventually agreed to in the Lisbon Treaty, but, in a complicated arrangement, it was agreed that the new rules would only be introduced in 2014. From that date, a qualified majority will require support from 55 per cent of the members of the Council, representing at least 65 per cent of the population of the EU. A blocking minority will have to include at least four member states, thereby limiting the ability of the biggest states to block measures. The figures were varied for votes on proposals that were not tabled by the Commission or the new EU Minister for Foreign Affairs. In that case, the qualified majority would be 72 per cent of the member states representing at least 65 per cent of the population of the EU. The current weighting of votes as set out in Table 19.3 will be abandoned completely from 2014 in favour of this new system. However, to add further confusion, during the period 2014–2017, a state can ask for the voting rules established in the Nice Treaty to be applied if it feels disadvantaged by the new system.

Table 19.3 Weighting of National Votes under Qualified Majority Voting (until 2014)

Austria	10	Hungary	12	Slovakia	7
Belgium	12	Ireland	7	Slovenia	4
Bulgaria	10	Italy	29	Spain	27
Cyprus	4	Latvia	4	Sweden	10
Czech Republic	12	Lithuania	7	United Kingdom	29
Denmark	7	Luxembourg	4		
Estonia	4	Malta	3		
Finland	7	Netherlands	13		
France	29	Poland	27		
Germany	29	Portugal	12		
Greece	12	Romania	14	**TOTAL**	**345**

Note: When a vote is called, a qualified majority comes about in the Council of Ministers under the following circumstances:

• if a minimum of 255 votes is cast in favour—which is 73.9 per cent of the total; and

• if a two-thirds majority of member states approve.

In addition, a member state may insist on confirmation that the votes in favour represent at least 62 per cent of the total population of the Union. From 2014 a new system (already set down in the Lisbon Treaty) will come into operation.

One important qualification concerning QMV has to be entered at this point. According to research by Mattila (2008: 27), approximately 90 per cent of votes in the Council are uncontested. Hence the heated Treaty-reform debates related only to the principle and not necessarily to the practice of QMV.

The European Parliament (EP)

In the original blueprint for the ECSC, Jean Monnet did not include any parliamentary body—but in an attempt to make the new community more democratic, a European Parliamentary Assembly was added to the Treaty of Paris (Diebold 1959: 62). This body was carried over into the Treaties of Rome.

The EP has consistently tried to insert itself more effectively into the decision-making process of the EU, especially since 1979 when it became a directly elected body. Under the original process, the Council of Ministers was obliged to consult the EP before deciding on legislative proposals made by the Commission, but it could ignore the EP's opinion if it wished. This remains the case in a very few policy areas. In most, however, the so-called **ordinary legislative procedure** (OLP) applies. Under the OLP, the EP, taking its decision by simple majority, co-legislates with the Council, which decides by QMV. Under the OLP, the EP is able to block legislation altogether, an ultimate power that makes it difficult for the Council to ignore amendments proposed by the EP lest the legislation as a whole be lost. These powers are outlined under the heading 'Decision-Making Procedures' below.

The EP is formally a co-decision maker with the Council on the annual budget, and its approval is necessary for the budget to be given effect (see below). The other areas in which the EP has gained influence are in holding the Commission and the Council of Ministers to account, and these are examined in Chapter 22.

The European Economic and Social Committee (EESC)

The EESC consists of representatives of producers, farmers, workers, professionals, and of the general public. It is divided into three groups representing employers, workers, and 'various interests', although members are not obliged to join any of the groups. The 'various interests' group includes farmers, the professions, the self-employed, consumers, and environmental groups. Its 344 members are proposed by national governments and formally appointed by the Council of Ministers. They sit on the EESC in a personal capacity and formally may not be bound by any mandate or instructions from their organizations.

The main work of the EESC is carried out by its six sections, which are the equivalent of the committees in the EP. They are:

- Agriculture, Rural Development, and the Environment;
- Economic and Monetary Union and Economic and Social Cohesion;
- Employment, Social Affairs, and Citizenship;
- External Relations;
- the Single Market, Production, and Consumption;
- Transport, Energy, Infrastructure, and the Information Society.

A secretariat-general is responsible for the EESC's administration.

The EESC is consulted on a range of issues including agricultural matters, freedom of movement for workers, the right of establishment of companies, social policy, internal market issues, measures of economic and social cohesion, and environmental policy. In addition, the Commission may consult it on any matter that it thinks appropriate; the EESC has the right to issue opinions on any matter on its own initiative.

In practice, the EESC is not particularly influential. It has become overshadowed by the EP, which has increased its legitimacy and powers significantly over the last decades as a result of direct elections and, more recently, with the growth of co-decision powers. By contrast, the EESC's powers have remained consultative and its influence has declined in comparative terms. Under the Lisbon Treaty, the EESC's term of office was extended from four to five years.

The Committee of the Regions and Local Authorities (CoR)

The CoR was created by the Maastricht Treaty, and was given the right to be consulted on proposals that affected regional and local interests, and the right to issue opinions on its own initiative. Its members are chosen by the member states and officially appointed by the Council of Ministers. As with the EESC, they moved to a five-year, renewable term with implementation of the Lisbon Treaty (Table 19.4). A maximum of 350 members has been set for membership of the CoR to take account of possible future enlargements of the EU: a rule also applicable to the EESC.

The members, collectively known as the Assembly, participate in the work of seven specialized commissions that are responsible for drafting the CoR's opinions. The Bureau, which organizes the work of the Committee and its commissions, includes the chair, a first vice-chair, plus one vice-chair from each of the member states, elected

Table 19.4 **Membership of the Committee of the Regions and Local Authorities**

Austria	12	Latvia	7
Belgium	12	Lithuania	9
Cyprus	6	Luxembourg	6
Czech Republic	12	Malta	5
Denmark	9	Netherlands	12
Estonia	7	Poland	21
Finland	9	Portugal	12
France	24	Slovakia	9
Germany	24	Slovenia	7
Greece	12	Spain	21
Hungary	12	Sweden	12
Ireland	9	United Kingdom	24
Italy	24	**TOTAL**	**317**

by the members of the Assembly. They also include the chairs of the political groups. A secretariat-general is responsible for the Committee's administration.

At first sight, the CoR appears to be another incarnation of the EESC, with which it originally shared a meeting chamber and support staff. However, there is an important difference: the CoR is strongly backed by political actors of considerable influence. It was put into the TEU at the insistence of the German Federal government under pressure from the Länder, the regional states that make up the German federation. With the political weight and the resources of these significant political actors behind it, the CoR has become an influential institution on those policies of the EU that have a regional focus. The Commission therefore has every incentive to work closely with the Committee, particularly because the Commission itself has tended to favour the emergence of a 'Europe of the regions' that would break down the domination of all decision making by the central governments of the member states. So, as well as being another constraint on the freedom of action of the Commission, the CoR provides it with a potential ally against national governments.

In 2009, and linked to the momentum associated with the Lisbon Treaty, the Committee proposed a political project to 'build Europe in partnership' through its White Paper on multi-level governance (MLG) (CoR 2009). The Committee explicitly took on the role of advocate of MLG and undertook consultation on how to embed it more strongly in its programme of work. This step bears some resemblance to the way in which the European Commission has been seen to encourage more integration through cultivated spillover (see Chapter 1, p. 10). In this case, the CoR has explicitly embraced and sought to promote the body of academic work on MLG (see Chapter 2).

Decision-Making Procedures

There are two types of decision-making procedure within the Union method: that for adopting the annual budget of the EU—the budgetary procedure—and the various legislative procedures. The precise workings of both procedures are usually facilitated by inter-institutional agreements.

The Budgetary Procedure

The budget demonstrates the importance of the European Council as agenda-setter. This is because the annual budget negotiations take place within a multi-annual budgetary envelope that will have been agreed politically in the European Council. Under the Lisbon Treaty, the multi-annual financial perspective must also then be formally signed off by the Council of Ministers, deciding—like the European Council—by unanimity. The EP's involvement is limited to giving its consent to the Council's agreement. The Commission tends to play a key role in proposing the multi-annual financial perspective. The first of these covered the years 1988–92. At its meeting in December 2005, the European Council agreed the fourth financial perspective, for the seven-year period 2007–13.

The annual budgetary negotiations thus take place within limits strongly influenced by the European Council, which plays no formal role in the annual process. The annual budgetary procedure was amended by the Lisbon Treaty and is now set down in Article

314 TFEU. Happily, this is a change arising from the Lisbon Treaty that brings simplification, abolishing a previous distinction between different categories of spending (see Bache and George 2006: 238–40 for the pre-Lisbon process).

The budgetary procedure begins with the Commission drawing up a preliminary draft budget, which it has to do under the Treaty by 1 September of each year, but which it normally completes by June (see Figure 19.4). The work is performed by the Budget Directorate-General in consultation with the other services of the Commission and under the supervision of the Budget Commissioner. In preparing this document, the Commission is constrained by the multi-annual budgetary framework agreements.

Once the preliminary draft budget is prepared, and agreed by the Commissioners as a whole, it is sent to the Council of Ministers, which formally has until 1 October to adopt a draft budget. Often, however, the draft budget has been adopted earlier than this. Most of the detailed work at this stage is done by the Budget Committee, a specialist body responsible to the Council. The Budget Committee is 'composed of senior officials (the "tough guys") from the national finance ministries' (Hayes-Renshaw and Wallace 2006: 43). The Council acts by QMV to adopt its position.

The draft budget is then sent to the EP, which has forty-two days either to approve the Council's position (or to take no decision), in which case the budget is approved, or to amend the Council's position, for which an absolute majority of members of the European Parliament (MEPs) is required. The Budgetary Committee of the EP takes the lead, co-ordinating with the other specialized committees as necessary, and then reports to the plenary for the vote. Typically in the past (and under the pre-Lisbon rules), the EP has proposed a lot of amendments to the preliminary draft budget, most of which increase expenditure to the maximum permissible level. If this pattern were to be practised under the new rules, utilized for the first time in autumn 2010 for the 2011 budget, the draft budget would go back to the Council. The Council would then have ten days to consider its response to the amendments proposed by the EP. It would either accept the EP's amendments (by QMV), thereby adopting the budget, or reject them, which would lead to the convening of the Conciliation Committee.

The Conciliation Committee comprises an equal number of representatives of the Council and of the EP. The Commission is also present and attempts to broker an agreement. An agreed position at this stage requires both a qualified majority on the part of the Council representatives and a majority on the part of the EP representatives. If no agreement is reached, the Commission has to present a new budget. However, if agreement is reached in the Conciliation Committee, the draft budget as amended is set for the final stage of the process.

This stage is arguably the most complex. There are fourteen days for the EP and Council to act. If they both approve (or fail to act), the budget law is approved. If the EP adopts the budget but the Council rejects it (by QMV), the EP may decide to restore some or all of its amendments. If it can secure an absolute majority and three-fifths of the votes, the amendments are restored and the budget law is approved. If the three-fifths threshold is not met, the amendments fall and the 'conciliated' budget is passed. Symbolically, the President of the EP declares the budget to be adopted when that stage is reached. In all other circumstances, which includes the Council adopting the budget by QMV but the EP rejecting by absolute majority, the budget falls and the Commission has to present a new proposal.

If no budget has been agreed by the 1 January start of the financial year, the EU has to operate on a system known as 'provisional twelfths'. This means that, each month,

Figure 19.4 The Annual Budgetary Process

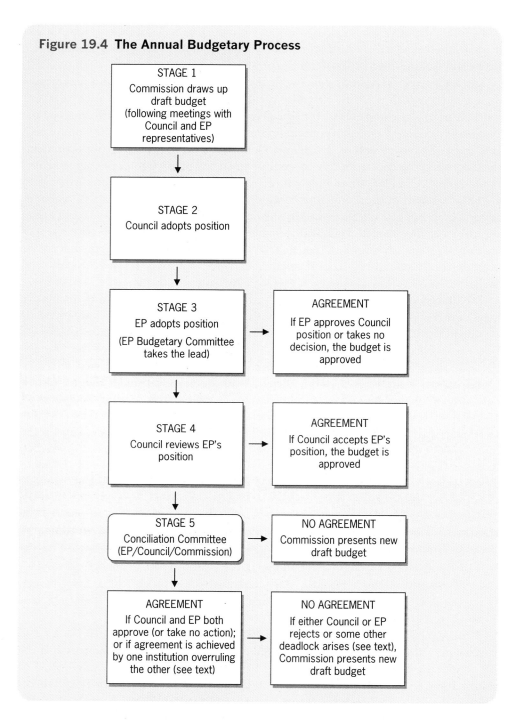

STAGE 1
Commission draws up draft budget (following meetings with Council and EP representatives)

STAGE 2
Council adopts position

STAGE 3
EP adopts position
(EP Budgetary Committee takes the lead)

AGREEMENT
If EP approves Council position or takes no decision, the budget is approved

STAGE 4
Council reviews EP's position

AGREEMENT
If Council accepts EP's position, the budget is approved

STAGE 5
Conciliation Committee (EP/Council/Commission)

NO AGREEMENT
Commission presents new draft budget

AGREEMENT
If Council and EP both approve (or take no action); or if agreement is achieved by one institution overruling the other (see text)

NO AGREEMENT
If either Council or EP rejects or some other deadlock arises (see text), Commission presents new draft budget

one-twelfth of the previous year's budget total is released to cover expenditure. This will obviously prove cumulatively more restrictive as the year progresses, and in particular it will mean that new programmes, which had no budget line the previous year, will not be able to begin operation.

As revised in the Lisbon Treaty, the budget process has given more powers to the EP. In addition, detailed parts of the process were revised, including the functioning

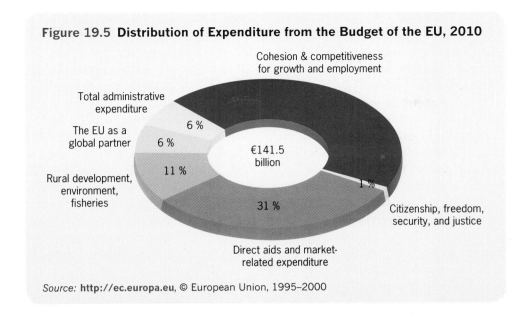

Figure 19.5 Distribution of Expenditure from the Budget of the EU, 2010

Cohesion & competitiveness for growth and employment

Total administrative expenditure — 6 %

The EU as a global partner — 6 %

Rural development, environment, fisheries — 11 %

€141.5 billion

1 %

Citizenship, freedom, security, and justice

Direct aids and market-related expenditure — 31 %

Source: **http://ec.europa.eu**, © European Union, 1995–2000

of the Conciliation Committee. The new arrangements draw on experience with the co-decision process for legislation (see below). The annual process has also depended on some ground rules. These have taken the form of an inter-institutional agreement. A new such agreement was under discussion in 2010 following the implementation of the Lisbon Treaty. These agreements govern how the three institutions (Commission, Council, and EP) work together as well as a wide range of technical issues. The pattern of EU budgetary expenditure can be seen in Figure 19.5, which shows the planned budget for 2010.

There is one other part to the budgetary process. Every year, the Commission is required to submit to the Council and the EP the accounts of the previous financial year. These are considered by both institutions in the light of the annual report from the Court of Auditors. The EP receives a recommendation from the Council, and in the light of this and its own deliberations, gives discharge to the Commission in respect to implementation of the budget. This means that the EP formally acknowledges that the Commission has implemented the budget properly and efficiently.

Legislative Procedures

The Lisbon Treaty provided some significant simplification of the legislative procedures that were applicable prior to 2010. It reduced the number of procedures from four to three. It also created the OLP as a default pattern. All other arrangements are termed 'special legislative procedures' but there is quite some variation between them, so the term is not of much use in this outline. The process becomes 'special' if the Council decides by unanimity and/or the EP uses the consultation or consent procedures.

The three main procedures are:

- the ordinary legislative procedure (or co-decision) (Figure 19.6);
- consultation (Figure 19.7);
- consent.

239

The Ordinary Legislative Procedure (Co-decision)

Until the reforms introduced by the 1986 SEA, the EP had not really functioned as a legislative body. In other words, it had not gone through a process of scrutinizing legislation and then tabling amendments, which the Council in turn had to consider and take into account. Previously, the EP's role was restricted to giving Opinions, which the Council could simply ignore (the consultation procedure—see below). The first step away from this, introduced in the SEA, was the co-operation procedure. It entailed two readings of legislation, each followed by the Council taking a decision. The second step, one of the key changes introduced by the Maastricht Treaty into the EU's legislative process, was the co-decision procedure. Unlike the co-operation procedure, co-decision did not leave the Council with the last word, but introduced a Conciliation Committee to try to reconcile differences at the end of the process. The co-operation procedure had more or less disappeared as a result of amendments in the Amsterdam Treaty, but was formally abandoned by the Lisbon Treaty, and so is not considered in detail here (see Bache and George 2006: 242–3 for information on its operation in the past). However, the Lisbon Treaty made a further change by using the terminology of the OLP to designate what is now the norm in EU law making: namely, the provision for QMV in the Council combined with co-decision between the Council and the EP.

Co-decision is based on the principle of parity between the EP and the Council: neither institution may adopt legislation without the other's agreement. The procedure starts informally with the Commission consulting interest groups, civil servants from the member states, and MEPs in order to gather expertise and gain feedback on its initial ideas. The Commission then formally publishes a proposal after securing internal agreement.

This step commences the first stage of the formal process as provided for in Article 294 TFEU (see Figure 19.6: boxes 1–10). In the first phase, national governments and the EP examine the proposal in their respective working groups and committees. Where provided for in the TFEU, the EESC and the CoR examine the proposal and seek to influence the Council and the EP. This role is also played through lobbying by the various interest groups that are potentially affected. Indeed, interest groups typically lobby the EP and the Council (or the individual member governments) throughout all stages of this process.

Also participating at this stage, and formalized for the first time by the Lisbon Treaty, are the national parliaments. Their specific role, under a process set out in Protocols 1 and 2 of the TEU, is to scrutinize whether the Commission's proposal breaches the principle of subsidiarity. In other words, national parliaments are required to check that action at EU level is appropriate and can better achieve results than action taken at the member-state level. If enough national parliaments deem within an eight-week period that the subsidiarity principle is being breached, they can play the 'yellow card' and oblige the Commission to review the proposal and decide to maintain, amend, or withdraw it, with supporting justification. This practice applies to all legislation. However, in the case of the OLP, if a simple majority of national parliaments continues to challenge the proposal's compliance with the subsidiarity principle, the 'orange card' can be played as a further challenge against the proposal. Their challenge is upheld if either the Council (with a majority of 55 per cent of the votes) or the EP (with a simple majority) agrees with the breach of subsidiarity, and the proposed legislation falls. The yellow and orange cards were untested at the time of writing, and require a form of co-operation between national parliaments that may take time to organize.

Assuming—as is likely to be the case in the vast majority of instances—that the orange card has not been played successfully, the first stage is characterized by the EP holding its first reading, and deciding to approve the proposal or suggest amendments. In the latter case, the Commission may amend its proposal if it considers the EP amendments to have improved it. If the Commission reissues the proposal, the Council may decide by QMV when it holds its first reading. If the Commission has not revised its proposal, the EP's amendments are only passed if unanimity is secured in the Council. If the EP and Council are of the same view, the legislation is adopted. Duff (2009: 52) reports that, in the legislative period 2004–09, this had become the predominant pattern. Where no agreement has been reached, the Commission is given the opportunity to offer its opinion, including whether it supports the Council's common position.

This opinion commences the second phase (see Figure 19.6: boxes 11–20) comprising scrutiny by first the EP and then the Council, working on the basis of the Council's common position. Once again, it is quite likely that legislation will be agreed at this stage. However, if the EP rejects the common position, or the Council does not approve the EP's amendments, then a Conciliation Committee is set up: the third phase (Figure 19.6: boxes 22–28). The Committee consists of representatives of the twenty-seven members of the Council, and an equal number of representatives of the EP. With the help of the Commission, which acts in the role of a facilitator, the Conciliation Committee tries to negotiate a mutually acceptable compromise text, which can then be recommended to both institutions. The Committee has six weeks in which to do so, operating on the basis of QMV for the Council members and simple majority voting for the EP members. Provided that they can agree a joint text, the legislation goes back to the Council and EP for final adoption, for which a six-week period is available. The Council is likely to adopt since its delegation will have comprised a representative of each member state. However, it is more difficult to ensure that the EP delegation to the Conciliation Committee represents the whole of the EP. Hence a very small number of instances have arisen in which the EP has not approved the Committee's joint text. Along with a different scenario—namely, the failure on the part of the Committee to reach an agreement—these two sets of circumstance result in no legislation being adopted.

The Lisbon Treaty brought in several changes, which are worth reiterating here. First, national parliaments have been given powers in the early stages of the process. Second, co-decision between the Council and the EP has become the predominant pattern of work between the two institutions. Third, it is important to note the very close alignment of co-decision with the provision for QMV in the Council as the new normal pattern of the OLP. The second and third changes suggest a more supranational legislative process, while the first change offers the opportunity for national parliaments to intervene in the process and in rare cases (in which the requirements of the orange card can be met) to stop more legislation at EU level.

The Consultation Procedure

The original 'consultation procedure' for deciding on EU legislation involved the Commission submitting a proposal to the Council of Ministers, which was then obliged to seek the opinion of the EP, and, where required by the Treaty, of the EESC. In the

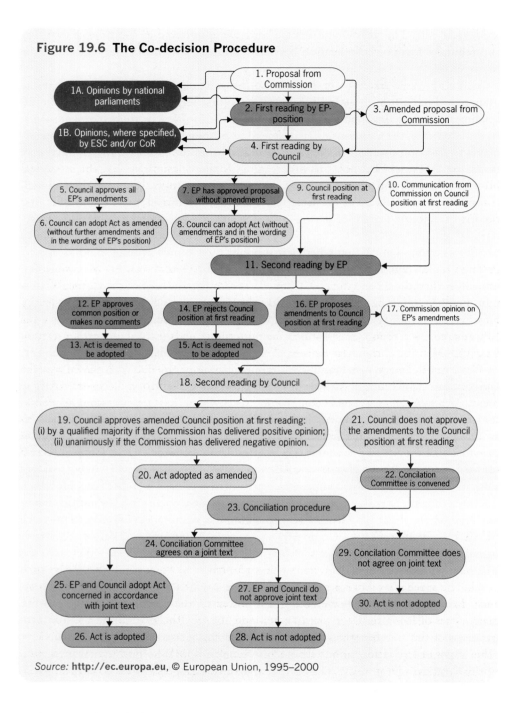

Figure 19.6 The Co-decision Procedure

Source: **http://ec.europa.eu**, © European Union, 1995–2000

Isoglucose case (1980), the European Court of Justice (ECJ) ruled that the Council could not act legally in deciding on a proposal from the Commission without receiving the opinion of the EP. However, having received that opinion, the Council could if it so wished simply ignore it and agree to the proposal, or reject it. Amendments could only be made by unanimity in the Council. This procedure still exists, but the Lisbon Treaty has further reduced the circumstances under which it can be used to about

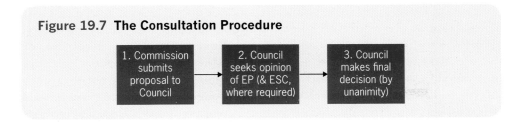

Figure 19.7 The Consultation Procedure

1. Commission submits proposal to Council → 2. Council seeks opinion of EP (& ESC, where required) → 3. Council makes final decision (by unanimity)

twenty (see Figure 19.7). For example, agricultural policy, transport, the structural funds, and asylum and immigration were amongst the prominent policy areas in which consultation was replaced by co-decision through the revisions, thereby strengthening the EP's powers.

Consent

Prior to the Lisbon Treaty, the EP was able to block decisions under what was then known as the assent procedure. This was originally introduced for agreements with non-member states, but was extended to other policy areas through different Treaty reforms. Some policy areas assigned to the assent procedure were subsequently re-allocated to co-decision, for instance the structural funds (as a result of the Lisbon Treaty), and citizens' rights (as a result of the Amsterdam Treaty).

The Lisbon Treaty introduced the renamed consent procedure. Its main area of application is agreements with non-member states (including to accession of new members). New areas added include some aspects of judicial co-operation as well as the multi-annual financial framework for the EU budget. Consent requires the EP's agreement for a measure to be adopted. There is no provision for the EP to amend proposals. However, the fact that its consent is required does give it considerable influence at the stage when proposals are being prepared.

Implementation

The policy process does not end once agreement has been reached on a legislative proposal. The agreement still has to be implemented before the policy has any real existence. In other words, implementation is an integral part of the policy process. For many types of legislation, the primary implementers are the governments and administrations of the member states. The Commission itself has a central role in the case of other types of legislation, and is charged by Article 17 TEU to 'ensure the application of the Treaties, and of measures adopted by the institutions pursuant to them'. In performing this latter task, the Commission has recourse to judicial authority through the referral of cases to the ECJ. Finally, the implementation of all financial instruments is subject to scrutiny by the Court of Auditors.

National Authorities and Implementation

There are three main types of EU instrument that are legally binding: decisions, directives, and regulations. Alongside these are recommendations and Opinions. They do not have legal status; they are of political significance only. The legal instruments may be legislative or non-legislative: a new distinction introduced by the Lisbon Treaty. Hitherto, attention has focused on legislative instruments as part of an exploration of the role of the institutions in law making through the ordinary and special legislative procedures. However, non-legislative instruments (that is, those that do not go through the whole legislative process) such as European Commission rulings on competition policy do have legal force, perhaps requiring a company to pay a large fine for anti-competitive behaviour. The focus here is on legislative instruments.

Decisions are addressed to particular individual legal actors such as companies or individual states. Directives are the most common form of general legislation agreed in the Council of Ministers; it is left to individual member states to decide how they are incorporated into national law. Regulations are directly applicable in all member states.

Where directives are concerned, there are two stages to implementation by national authorities. First, the directives have to be transposed into national law through appropriate national legal instruments. Second, they have to be implemented on the ground—that is, they have to be applied by national administrative authorities. Regulations do not need the extra stage of being transposed into national law through national legal instruments since they are directly applicable. However, it is still the responsibility of national administrative authorities to ensure that they are applied.

In the case of both aspects of implementation, the record of member states in actually doing what they have agreed to do varies considerably. This means that the outcomes of EU decisions are not always the same as the intention. The Commission monitors the record of member states in implementing EU law in specific areas. For example, the varying record of member states in implementing single-market legislation was recorded in the successive reports on the implementation of the Internal Market Strategy (European Commission 2004a; 2005a).

The Commission and Implementation

Formally, the Commission has overall responsibility for the implementation of EU decisions. There are several processes of implementation in the EU, in each of which the Commission has a role. First, there is the implementation of common policies that are centrally administered by the Commission itself. These are few, but some of the powers of the Commission—notably competition policy, including the control of large-scale mergers—fall under this heading. A slightly different area is the administration of international policies such as the provision of food aid, where again the Commission is the sole responsible EU body, although it has to work in conjunction with other organizations. Second, there is the implementation of common policies, which takes place partly at the European level and partly at the national level: the administration of the Common Agricultural Policy (CAP) and the structural funds come under this heading. Third, there is the implementation of Council directives, where the Commission has a dual role as guardian of the Treaties: to ensure that directives are promptly and accurately incorporated into national law in the member states, and to ensure that they are actually implemented on the ground.

Under Article 258 TFEU, if the Commission considers that a member state has failed to fulfil its obligations, it is required to deliver a reasoned Opinion on the matter after giving the government of the member state concerned the opportunity to submit its own observations. If the state does not comply with the reasoned Opinion, the matter may be brought before the ECJ. Another member state may also bring an alleged infringement of obligations to the attention of the Commission, which is required to act on the matter within three months, or the case automatically goes to the ECJ.

The European Court of Justice (ECJ)

Article 19 TEU charges the ECJ to ensure that European law is observed. It is the final arbiter on the interpretation of the Treaties and the application of EU law. As such, it is a referee in disputes between institutions and member states.

Where the ECJ is asked to rule on whether a member state has fulfilled its obligations under EU law, its decision is final. Originally there was no penalty other than moral pressure if a member state still failed to fulfil its obligations after an adverse ruling by the Court. However, the Maastricht Treaty amended Article 171 EEC (now Article 260 TFEU), to allow the Commission to return to the ECJ if it felt that a state was not complying with a ruling, and to request that a financial penalty be levied against the state.

The Court of Auditors

In 1975, the Treaty Amending Certain Financial Provisions of the EEC created a new institution: the European Court of Auditors. The Treaty confers upon the Court of Auditors the main task of auditing the accounts and the implementation of the budget of the European Union with the dual aim of improving financial management and the reporting to the citizens of Europe on the use made of public funds by the authorities responsible for their management.

The Court of Auditors is based in Luxembourg, and consists of one member from each member state appointed for a renewable six-year period. Members must have belonged to national audit offices, or be especially qualified for the office, and their independence must be beyond doubt. The members of the Court themselves elect a President from among their number for a period of three years. The court has some 850 staff, of whom about one-third are auditors.

This Court examines the accounts of all revenue and expenditure of the EU to determine whether the revenue has been received and the expenditure incurred in a lawful and regular manner. It provides the EP and the Council with a statement on the reliability of the accounts, and publishes an annual report. It also prepares special reports on aspects of the audit, either on its own initiative or at the request of another institution; it also delivers opinions on request from the other institutions concerning the financial implications of proposed legislation.

The Decision-Making Institutions (CFSP)

The 1992 Maastricht Treaty introduced a three-pillar structure. As already noted, this structure was abolished as a result of the Lisbon Treaty and the 'Union method' became the predominant character. The principal practical consequence of this step was to transfer police and judicial co-operation from an intergovernmental 'third pillar' to the Union method, albeit with some transitional arrangements (see Chapter 31 on AFSJ). Nevertheless, some EU activity remains subject to different arrangements: namely, the CFSP, which used to be the second pillar of the EU. Reflecting this situation, the CFSP is governed by the TEU, whereas the TFEU addresses those policy areas governed by the Union method.

The CFSP is concerned with a range of activities, such as:

- safeguarding the common values, fundamental interests, independence, and integrity of the Union in conformity with the principles of the United Nations Charter;
- strengthening the security of the Union;
- preserving peace and strengthening international security;
- promoting international co-operation;
- developing and consolidating democracy and the rule of law, and respect for human rights and fundamental freedoms.

With the passage of the Lisbon Treaty, these objectives are now absorbed into a wider set of goals relating to the EU's external action, including trade and aid policy, which are governed by the Union method.

The Lisbon Treaty introduced the new position of High Representative of the Union for Foreign Affairs and Security Policy, a position to which (Baroness) Catherine Ashton was appointed in January 2010. The post is combined with that of Vice-President of the European Commission. The High Representative might be considered as a kind of EU Foreign Minister. Indeed, under the failed Constitutional Treaty, the position was to be called 'Union Minister for Foreign Affairs', but this terminology was abandoned in the Lisbon Treaty. The High Representative is able to draw on the expertise of the Commission, which has the right of initiative on external economic policy, and on the Council and the member states for CFSP, regarding which she makes proposals. The High Representative thus pulls together two strands of external action that are subject to different decision-making rules. Here, the concern is with the rules concerning foreign and security policy, but not trade, aid, enlargement, or other provisions covered by the TFEU.

CFSP is almost exclusively intergovernmental in character. In consequence, the ECJ, the Commission, and the EP are either absent or have very limited powers. The principal actors are the European Council, the Council of Ministers (meeting as the Foreign Affairs Council), and the High Representative.

The key characteristics of decision making on the CFSP are as follows.

- The European Council is responsible for the strategic interests and objectives of the Union.
- The European Council acts unanimously on the basis of recommendations from the Council of Ministers.
- The High Representative may submit proposals to the Foreign Affairs Council on CFSP matters (and chairs this formation of the Council as well).

- The decisions under CFSP are non-legislative in nature. This makes clear that the legislative procedures considered above under the Union method are not applicable.

The CFSP is put into effect by the High Representative, who acts as an international envoy and negotiator, and by the member governments, using national and Union resources. These resources refer to the diplomatic networks of the member states, the Commission, and the Council. These networks were brought together following the passage of the Lisbon Treaty to form the European External Action Service (EEAS).

- The work of the Foreign Affairs Council is prepared by a committee of diplomats known as the Political and Security Committee.
- The High Representative consults regularly with the EP on policies under the CFSP and shall 'ensure that the views of the European Parliament are duly taken into consideration' (Article 36 TEU).

The character of the CFSP is overwhelmingly intergovernmental, requiring unanimous decisions. Because the member states were not ready to risk any surrender of control over foreign and security policy, CFSP is not subject to the Union method. Nevertheless, there are some departures from this intergovernmental pattern. First, the already-accepted practice of 'constructive abstention' may be utilized. Under this arrangement, a member government may abstain from a decision—as opposed to voting against it—and is consequently not bound by it. However, it is expected that any government in this situation will act in a spirit of solidarity and not work against the interests of the majority (Article 31 TEU). Further, there are some specific circumstances in which decision making may be by QMV. Essentially, these circumstances relate to the operationalization of decisions already reached by unanimity, or to the appointment of special representatives. If this provision sounds like a shift towards supranationalism, it is worth bearing in mind the following safeguard clause:

> If a member of the Council declares that, for vital and stated reasons of national policy, it intends to oppose the adoption of a decision to be taken by qualified majority, a vote shall not be taken. The High Representative will, in close consultation with the Member State involved, search for a solution acceptable to it. If he [sic] does not succeed, the Council may, acting by a qualified majority, request that the matter be referred to the European Council for a decision by unanimity.

(Article 31(2) TEU)

This provision bears some relationship to the Luxembourg Compromise of 1966 (see Chapter 9, pp. 129–30), except that it only applies to the CFSP.

Decision making under CFSP remains largely intergovernmental in character, as national governments are concerned to retain their full authority. However, the creation of the EEAS raises the possibility that diplomats across the EU and the EU institutions will, by virtue of their networked relations, develop shared understandings that may transcend the purely national perspectives that have predominated hitherto.

The Post-Lisbon Architecture of the EU

Hitherto, this chapter has been concerned with the decision-making arrangements and the key institutional players under the Union method and for CFSP. There are some other architectural considerations that need to be taken into account. These address four features that have an overarching character and impact on the EU. The first is the creation of a catalogue of competencies that sets out the balance of authority between the EU and the member states. The second relates to differentiated integration: the situation whereby not all member states participate in all of the EU's activities, such as the single currency. The third concerns the somewhat haphazard emergence of a set of 'emergency brake' procedures. The fourth is slightly different, but also relates to scattered provisions across the Lisbon Treaty, known as *passerelle* clauses, which permit future procedural changes to take place on specific matters without the need to go through the whole process of Treaty reform (see above). Taken together, they comprise an important set of considerations, which can bear upon the decision-making process.

Catalogue of Competencies

Behind this legal terminology is a rather simple matter: what the EU can or cannot do. This issue was shaped by the debate at the time of the Maastricht Treaty concerning subsidiarity (see above). The basic principle of subsidiarity is that decisions should be taken as closely as possible to citizens. Or put another way, the EU should demonstrate that it can deliver policy more effectively than the member governments (or even sub-national governments). This concern has chimed with British governments, which have consistently revealed a concern about the loss of national sovereignty. However, it has also been supported by sub-national governments, notably the German Länder, which became concerned in the run-up to the Maastricht Treaty that their national government was giving up sub-national law-making powers to the EU, thus reshaping the balance of domestic power in the German federation. This concern has never really gone away, and a catalogue of competencies was a German demand in the constitutional debate so that there could be some demarcation of what the EU can or cannot do (Bulmer 2010). Accordingly, the Lisbon Treaty spells out four types of EU competence: exclusive; shared; co-ordination; and supporting, co-ordinating, and supplementary action (see Insight 19.1). The CFSP provisions are not included in the detailed catalogue of competencies in the TFEU because they are outside the Union method and therefore contained in the TEU.

Exclusive competencies represent the core business of the EU or what Duff (2009: 32) terms the 'lynch-pins of the *acquis communautaire*'. Most of these powers are longstanding. Two innovations were embodied in the Lisbon Treaty. First, marine conservation was made an exclusive competence of the EU, on the basis that preservation of fishing stocks would only be effective if responsibility were to lie at Union level. Second, the Lisbon Treaty slightly strengthened the competencies of the EU in external relations. The wording relating to the external authority of the EU that derives from its internal competencies was strengthened, and intellectual property and foreign direct investment were added to powers in commercial policy.

Insight 19.1 The EU's Catalogue of Competencies

Areas of exclusive competence

- **Customs union**
- Competition rules for the internal market
- Monetary policy for those states in the eurozone
- Conservation of marine biological resources under the Common Fisheries Policy
- Common commercial policy
- Where an international agreement is necessary to enable the Union to exercise its internal competence

Areas of shared competence

- Internal market
- Aspects of social policy
- Economic, social, and territorial cohesion
- Agriculture and fisheries (except marine conservation—see above)
- Environment
- Consumer protection
- Transport
- Trans-European networks
- Energy
- Area of freedom, security, and justice
- Aspects of public health safety
- Research, technological development, and space
- Development and humanitarian aid

Areas of policy co-ordination

- Member states' economic policies
- Member states' employment policies
- Member states' social policies

Areas of supporting, co-ordinating or supplementary action

- Protection and improvement of human health
- Industry
- Culture
- Tourism
- Education, vocational training, youth, and sport
- Civil protection
- Administrative co-operation

The Common Foreign and Security Policy

The Union shall have competence ... to define and implement a common foreign and security policy, including the progressive framing of a common defence policy.

Source: Summarized from Articles 3–6 TFEU. The CFSP provisions derive from Article 2 TEU.

As regards areas of shared competencies, the list again mainly codifies the existing balance of authority. The main exceptions were the addition of space policy and some shifts within the environmental and energy provisions to include climate change and energy security respectively. In areas of supporting action, there were some small additions: namely, administrative co-operation, civil protection, tourism, and sport. In sum, the catalogue of competencies forms an important component of the EU's post-Lisbon architecture.

Differentiated Integration

Differentiated integration allows for permanent or temporary arrangements whereby not all member states proceed at the same pace in all policy areas. Differentiated integration has been practised within the EU since the 1970s, notably in monetary policy. As noted already, the Maastricht Treaty provided opt-outs for the UK regarding monetary union and the social chapter, although the Labour government of Tony Blair opted into the latter in 1997 at the time of the Amsterdam Treaty. Under the Amsterdam Treaty, the UK and Ireland exercised opt-outs thereby retaining passport controls and not participating in the practices of the Schengen area (see Chapter 31). By early 2010, only sixteen of the twenty-seven member states had joined the single currency. These examples of differentiated integration developed in an ad hoc manner. However, from the Amsterdam Treaty onwards, member governments started to make general provision for core groups to proceed more quickly with integration, should they wish to do so. The official terminology for this practice is 'enhanced co-operation'.

Enhanced co-operation was introduced in the Amsterdam Treaty largely as a response to the obstructionist European diplomacy of the British Conservative government of John Major, which had a small parliamentary majority during the period 1992–97. German Chancellor Helmut Kohl was concerned at integration having to proceed at the pace of the slowest ship in the convoy. The provisions of the Amsterdam Treaty were designed to circumvent such a situation, but were quite tightly drawn and had negligible practical impact on the EU. Their basic principles were that enhanced co-operation could be used only as a last resort, needed a majority of the member states as participants, and had to allow other member states to join at a later stage. The safeguards were so tightly drawn that, according to David Phinnemore (2010: 39), it was not until 2008 that the first formal proposal was made to use these provisions.

The Lisbon Treaty has relaxed the requirements for enhanced co-operation in a number of ways, with potentially significant ramifications over the period from 2010. They are now governed by Article 20 TEU and Articles 326–34 TFEU. The basic principles are set out in Insight 19.2. The conditions are less onerous than before, so resort to them can be expected to be greater. In particular, it is possible for the core group to decide that it wishes to take decisions by QMV within enhanced co-operation even in a policy area in which the Treaties provide for unanimous voting for the twenty-seven states. Potentially, such a decision could then bypass provisions for an emergency brake (see below).

Had they been in existence at the time, these provisions for enhanced co-operation might well have been used in the mid-1990s to bypass the obstructionism of the then British government; it is perhaps worth bearing in mind that a **Euro-sceptic** government—from whichever member state—might in future find itself marginalized,

---

Insight 19.2 Enhanced Co-operation in the EU

- Enhanced co-operation may only be practised in the EU's non-exclusive competencies (see Insight 19.1) and must follow detailed provisions in Articles 326–334 TFEU.

- Enhanced co-operation shall aim to advance the EU's objectives, protect its interests and reinforce its integration process.

- A minimum of nine member states is needed to launch enhanced co-operation.

- Enhanced co-operation shall be open at any time to all member states.

- 'The decision authorising enhanced cooperation shall be adopted by the Council as a last resort, when it has established that the objectives of such cooperation cannot be attained within a reasonable period by the Union as a whole, and provided that at least nine Member States participate in it.' (Article 20(1) TEU)

- All members of the Council may participate in its deliberations, but voting is confined to those member states participating in enhanced co-operation following rules set out in Article 330 TFEU.

- Only participating member states are bound by the resultant acts in the framework of enhanced co-operation. These acts do not form part of the *acquis communautaire*, which accession states must accept prior to membership.

- Enhanced co-operation must not undermine the internal market or economic, social, and territorial cohesion.

- Requests to move to enhanced co-operation are addressed to the Commission in the case of the Union method and to the High Representative of the Union for Foreign Affairs and Security Policy in the case of CFSP. The Commission and High Representative give their opinion. The decision to proceed is taken by the Council of Ministers acting unanimously.

- Procedures are spelt out in the TFEU for any state wishing to join an existing group of states undertaking enhanced co-operation. In the Union method, the Commission takes a decision within four months. In CFSP, unanimous agreement is needed by the Council of Foreign Affairs, but with only the core group voting.

---

rather than being able to hold up policy making. Indeed, given the difficulty experienced with moving towards further integration in the period between the Nice and Lisbon Treaties, it is open to question whether states wishing closer political integration might not find this route an easier one to take than Treaty reform (see Duff 2009: 106).

Emergency Brakes

In a very small number of policy areas, the Lisbon Treaty introduces an emergency brake. The principle is that a member government can suspend the OLP (in which it could be overruled by a QMV decision) and appeal to the European Council (Dougan 2008: 643–4). The details differ between the policy areas, but apply to the co-ordination of social security systems and judicial co-operation. An emergency brake may also be invoked in the CFSP to stop an operational decision being taken by QMV. In short, the emergency brake has emerged as a device that was built into the Lisbon Treaty where one or a small number of governments had concerns about sovereignty, but were prepared to recognize that QMV was likely to make decision making more effective in principle.

Passerelle Clauses

The idea behind a *passerelle* clause is that it provides the possibility of changing at a later stage the procedure applicable to decision making, without the need for Treaty reform. For example, in a range of policy areas, it is possible to move to the OLP from one of the special legislative procedures, thereby adding either QMV in the Council or co-decision with the EP, or both, to what the current rules specify. In all cases, the shift would be towards a more supranational set of decision-making rules. However, the *passerelle* clause requires approval by a 'super-majority': namely, the agreement of all member states in the European Council, and approval by the EP under the consent procedure. In addition, in most cases, national parliaments have six months in which to lodge an objection, otherwise the change to QMV is deemed to be approved. There are also some special cases in which a move to QMV in the Council could occur, but not to the OLP because the EP's powers remain under the consent procedure, for instance in connection with the EU's multi-annual financial framework (see Dougan 2008: 642).

The basic principle of these clauses is to enable a more efficient decision-making method to be introduced if this is an uncontroversial step, and provided that the super-majority can be achieved. The need for Treaty reform in order to make such changes is side-stepped, although the super-majority offers some comparison to the requirements of Treaty ratification.

CONCLUSION

The Lisbon Treaty made some fundamental changes to the EU's architecture. The abolition of the three-pillar system introduced in the Maastricht Treaty provided some simplification. The creation of the default pattern of the OLP under the Union method should also help students to find their way out of what had become a procedural maze. Alas, the potential for greater use of enhanced co-operation or *passerelle* clauses does risk restoring some complexity, but it remains to be seen whether these provisions are actually utilized.

So, the decision-making procedures of the EU are complex, but have generally been tidied up somewhat by the Lisbon Treaty. In theory, this tidying should lead to greater clarity over the legislative procedures to be followed on particular policy issues. In the past, the procedure to be followed was by no means immediately apparent. In such cases, the Commission could exercise some discretion in deciding under which Articles of the Treaties it would bring forward its proposals. Sometimes this was challenged. For example, in 1990, the Commission brought forward proposals on maternity rights under what was then the new Article 118A of the EEC Treaty (now Article 153 TFEU), which the SEA had introduced. This meant that the measure was subject to QMV in the Council, rather than unanimity. The British government objected to the Treaty base, and threatened to refer the matter to the ECJ, before eventually accepting a compromise solution.

Whatever Treaty base is chosen, the main actors remain the same; only the relative balance of influence is shifted. The Commission, the Council of Ministers, and the EP are the dominant institutional actors. Behind the scenes of the formal constitutional arrangements, interest groups always exercise a considerable influence on both the content of proposals and the outcome of the decision-making process. At the implementation stage, the Commission and the ECJ are particularly important in the Union method, but national governments are often the key to how policies are implemented.

The formal relationships outlined in this chapter are only one part, although an important part, of the analysis of the role of the EU institutions. The informal relationships between the institutions themselves, and between the institutions and the member states, are the part not covered here. In the chapters that follow, these informal relationships become central to the discussion, and attention focuses on the academic debates that have been generated about these relationships and their implications.

KEY POINTS

The Treaties

- The EU was founded by the Treaty of Paris (1951) and the two Treaties of Rome (1957), which were amended and supplemented by later Treaties.
- The Maastricht Treaty (1992) created the three-pillar EU.
- In 1997 the various Treaties were codified into two: the Treaty on the European Community (TEC) and the Treaty on European Union (TEU).
- The Lisbon Treaty, implemented in December 2009, abolished the EU's 'pillar' architecture dating from 1993 and created the 'Union method', which applies to all policy areas except the CFSP. The TEC was renamed the Treaty on the Functioning of the EU (TFEU).

The Decision-Making Institutions (the Union Method)

- The European Council sets the EU's broad policy agenda and the general direction of integration.
- The Commission has the sole formal right to initiate legislation, although this has been undermined in practice.
- The Council of Ministers has to agree to proposals for them to become law. Originally, it had to agree unanimously, but there has been a steady move towards the adoption of QMV.
- Since it became directly elected in 1979, the powers of the EP have grown, particularly in relation to the legislative process, until today it is effectively the co-legislator with the Council of Ministers in most policy areas.
- The EP is co-equal decision maker with the Council on the annual budget.
- The EESC consists of representatives of producer and consumer groups, and has to be consulted before certain categories of legislation can be adopted, but its opinions are not often influential.
- The CoR consists of representatives of regional and local authorities, and represents an advocate for MLG in the EU's territorially organized policies.

Decision-Making Procedures

- There are two main types of decision-making procedure in the EU: budgetary and legislative.
- The EU annual budget passes through a complex process, which involves the Commission, the Council, and the EP.
- The Lisbon Treaty creates the OLP as the norm: QMV in the Council and co-decision with the EP. Consultation and consent remain for a reduced set of circumstances.

253

Implementation

- Implementation is an integral part of the policy-making process.
- Three main types of EU legislative instrument are legally binding: decisions; directives; and regulations.
- While the Commission has formal responsibility for implementation, in practice, national authorities play an important role.
- The ECJ has the power to interpret EU law, and its decisions are final.
- The Court of Auditors checks the legality and regularity of EU expenditure.

The Decision-Making Institutions (CFSP)

- In CFSP, the Commission, the EP, and the ECJ have less authority than under the EU pillar.
- The High Representative of the Union for Foreign Affairs and Security Policy plays a key role in CFSP decisions and in co-ordinating a new External Action Service.

The Post-Lisbon Architecture of the EU

- The EU's powers are set out in a catalogue of competencies.
- In a small range of policies, the Lisbon Treaty built in a number of 'emergency brakes' to ensure that the member states can appeal if supranationalism threatens their sovereign interests.
- The Lisbon Treaty has increased the prospects for the emergence of further core groups in specific policy areas. It also introduced possibilities to move to more supranational decision-making on specific policies under *passerelle* clauses.

FURTHER READING

The changes introduced by the Lisbon Treaty have been significant, but the academic literature has not yet caught up with the changes. One exception is the standard work on the institutional structure of the EU: namely, **N. Nugent**, *The Government and Politics of the European Union*, 7th edn (Basingstoke: Palgrave Macmillan, 2010). Commentaries on the Lisbon Treaty are offered by **Andrew Duff**, *Saving the European Union: The Logic of the Lisbon Treaty* (London: Shoehorn Books, 2009) and, from a more legal perspective, by **Michael Dougan**, 'The Treaty of Lisbon 2007: Winning Minds not Hearts', *Common Market Law Review*, 45 (2008): 617–701. Students are advised to exercise considerable caution in using earlier publications owing to their potential to confuse or mislead. The websites of the European Union's institutions are an important resource on post-Lisbon arrangements.

 online resource centre

Visit the Online Resource Centre that accompanies this book for links to more information on the institutional architecture, including the text of the Treaties: www.oxfordtextbooks.co.uk/orc/bache3e/

Chapter 20
The European Commission

Chapter Overview

When the European Economic Community (EEC) was established, the European Commission was expected to be the motor of European integration. Because of this, it attracted considerable academic attention, becoming a focal point for the theoretical disputes between intergovernmentalists and supranationalists (Chapter 1). This chapter sets out the Commission's functions and its structure, before detailing its role in policy making. It reviews the debate on the extent to which the Commission is an autonomous political actor or simply an agent of the member states. It then turns to the increasing challenges faced by the Commission in securing effective implementation of European Union (EU) policies and its response to concerns over its financial management of EU programmes.

To many observers, the Commission is a unique institution. It is much more than an international secretariat, but not quite a government, [al]though it has many governmental characteristics.

(Egeberg 2010: 126)

Functions

The Commission has several key functions in the political system of the European Union. It is the formal initiator of legislative drafts and of the budget (see Chapter 19). It may act as a mediator during the legislative process, for instance in helping find agreement between the member governments or between the Council of Ministers and the European Parliament (EP). It has an important role in managing certain Commission policies, such as competition policy, where executive powers are at the EU level. It is the 'guardian of the Treaties' in that it is entrusted with ensuring, in those areas in which policy is implemented by member states' authorities, that they are correctly putting EU legislation into effect. It has traditionally held an important role in external economic relations, such as trade negotiations. Finally, it is the 'conscience of the European Union'. Traditionally seen as *the* supranational voice of the collective interest in EU legislation, the Commission has found competitors for this role in recent decades: notably the EP, in which the EU's elected representatives develop their own positions. The European Council, as the institution in which heads of government set the EU's strategic direction, has become the intergovernmental voice of the collective interest. As noted in Chapter 19, these Commission functions relate to the **Union method** and not to the Common Foreign and Security Policy (CFSP), regarding which its functions are very limited.

Composition and Appointment

In an echo of debates between intergovernmentalists and supranationalists, the Commission has been pilloried by **Euro-sceptics** as a bureaucratic monster that is out of control and usurping the rights of the member states. In fact, it is a relatively small organization in comparison not just with national civil services, but even with individual departments of state in national governments.

The European Commission consists of a College of Commissioners and a permanent civil service. In 2009, the Commission employed some 34,000 staff in total. However, a more typical figure of 25,000 is quoted when a host of auxiliary staff and service providers is excluded. Of this smaller figure, around 19,000 are permanent or temporary administrators, the rest being employed either in scientific research, as translators and interpreters, or in the Commission delegations around the world. This is the 'Brussels bureaucracy' that is frequently attacked or ridiculed by critics of the EU. 'The Commission' in fact refers both to the Services of the Commission and to the College of Commissioners. However, these should be clearly distinguished, not least because, as Cram (2001: 776) pointed out, 'the members of each may have very different perspectives and, most importantly, very different interests or preferences'.

The Services are divided into twenty-nine Directorates-General (DGs), plus a number of special services. They are listed in Table 20.1. The DGs are the equivalent of national civil service departments of state. Originally, they were known by their number only (for example, DG IV for the Competition Directorate-General), but this system was abolished under Romano Prodi's presidency of the Commission (1999–2004) as part of a reform designed to bring the structure of the DGs more into line with the designation of portfolios within the College. Instead a set of acronyms is now utilized (see Table 20.1).

The permanent senior administrators (in the so-called AD category) number about 12,500; additionally, about 1,000 'Detached National Experts' are seconded from the member states. Recruitment to the permanent posts is on the basis of merit, although a loose quota system is utilized to ensure an approximate balance of nationalities.

Political direction is given by the College of Commissioners. Since the Maastricht Treaty, Commissioners have been appointed for five-year terms (previously four-year) in order to achieve an alignment with the five-year terms of the EP. The pattern of the appointment process was adjusted in the Lisbon Treaty. Starting with the 2010–14 Commission, the process is as follows.

- 'Taking into account the elections to the European Parliament', as Article 17 TEU puts what is now recognized to be a politicized process, the European Council proposes a candidate for President of the Commission. He or she must be approved

Table 20.1 The Directorates-General and Services of the Commission (March 2010)

Policies	External Relations	General Services	Internal Services
DG Agriculture and Rural Development (AGRI)	DG Development (DEV)	DG Communication (COMM)	DG Budget (BUDG)
DG Climate Action (CLIMA)	DG Enlargement (ELARG)	European Anti-Fraud Office (OLAF)	Bureau of European Policy Advisers (BEPA)
DG Competition (COMP)	Europe Aid—Co-operation Office (AIDCO)	Eurostat (ESTAT)	European Commission Data Protection Officer
DG Economic and Financial Affairs (ECFIN)	DG External Relations (RELEX)	Joint Research Centre (JRC)	DG Human Resources and Security (HR)
DG Education and Culture (EAC)	DG Humanitarian Aid (ECHO)	Publications Office (OP)	DG Informatics (DIGIT)
DG Employment, Social Affairs and Equal Opportunities (EMPL)	DG Trade (TRADE)	Secretariat General (SG)	Infrastructures and Logistics—Brussels (OIB)
DG Energy (ENER)			Infrastructures and Logistics—Luxembourg (OIL)
DG Enterprise and Industry (ENTR)			Internal Audit Service (IAS)
DG Environment (ENV)			DG Interpretation (SCIC)
Executive Agencies			Legal Service (SJ)
DG Maritime Affairs and Fisheries (MARE)			Office for Administration and Payment of Individual Entitlements (PMO)
DG Mobility and Transport (MOVE)			DG Translation (DGT)
DG Health and Consumers (SANCO)			
DG Information Society and Media (INFSO)			

(Continued)

Table 20.1 (Continued)			
Policies	**External Relations**	**General Services**	**Internal Services**
DG Internal Market and Services (MARKT)			
DG Justice, Freedom and Security (JLS)			
DG Regional Policy (REGIO)			
DG Research (RTD)			
DG Taxation and Customs Union (TAXUD)			

In parentheses are the acronyms utilized within the European Commission and elsewhere. Directorates-General are denoted DG; others are Services.

by a majority of members of the European Parliament (MEPs); if not, the European Council must propose a new candidate.

- The member states put forward candidates for the post of Commissioners. The President-Elect of the Commission then selects a team and assigns portfolios before submitting the line-up to the Council of Ministers for approval by qualified majority vote (QMV). One of the Commissioners is the High Representative of the Union for Foreign Affairs and Security Policy (HRUFASP; see Chapter 21, p. 287).

- The EP, acting by the consent procedure (see Chapter 19, p. 243), must then approve the Commission team, following individual hearings of the candidates.

- Finally, after this investiture by the EP, the Council of Ministers formally appoints the Commissioners (again with QMV available).

The number of Commissioners has increased over the years as a result of enlargements. Until 2005, each state had one Commissioner, and the larger member states (France, Germany, Italy, Britain, and Spain) had two each. In the Treaty of Nice (Chapter 15, pp. 188–9), it was agreed that, starting with the Commission that took office on 1 January 2005, the number of Commissioners would be limited to one per member state. The Lisbon Treaty (Article 17 TEU) made provision for the number of Commissioners to be reduced further with effect from the College to be nominated in November 2014. Its size would correspond to two-thirds of the number of member states, and be selected on a basis of equal rotation between the member states. When the Irish people rejected the Lisbon Treaty in the June 2008 referendum, the possibility of there not being an Irish Commissioner after 2014 was an issue that came to the fore. Consequently, at its December 2008 meeting, the European Council made the following statement:

The European Council agrees that provided the Treaty of Lisbon enters into force, a decision will be taken, in accordance with the necessary legal procedures, to the effect that the Commission shall continue to include one national of each Member State.

Consequently, one Commissioner will continue to be appointed for each member state. This arrangement satisfied Irish concerns, but means that it is increasingly difficult to find meaningful responsibilities for each Commissioner, especially in the event of future enlargement.

The 2010–14 College of twenty-seven Commissioners, with their portfolios, is listed in Table 20.2. Commissioners are sworn to abandon all national allegiances during their tenure of office, and they are bound by the principle of collegiality, so all actions are the responsibility of the Commission as a whole.

The term of the Commission President is renewable and José Manuel Barroso's term was renewed in 2009 for five more years. Perhaps the most prominent President of recent decades, Jacques Delors, held the office for two full terms (then of four years each), plus an interim two-year period to bring the period of office of the Commission into line with that of the EP under provisions in the Maastricht Treaty. A list of Presidents of the Commission is given in Table 20.3. There are also five vice-presidents, one of whom—as High Representative, a joint appointment with the Council of Ministers—has the potential to be a prominent figure, representing the EU on the world stage.

Each Commissioner has a team of policy advisers, typically seven. Collectively, the advisers are known by the French word *cabinet* (pronounced 'cab-ee-nay'). The President's *cabinet* is larger, approximately double the size of the others. The members of the *cabinet* act as the eyes and ears of the Commissioner within the organization, and perform a valuable co-ordination function—particularly valuable because the structure of the Commission tends to produce fragmentation of the policy-making process between the DGs. It is widely accepted that the dynamism of Jacques Delors' presidencies would not have been possible without the sheer energy and effectiveness of the President's *cabinet* under the leadership of Pascal Lamy, who later went on to become a Commissioner himself.

Each member of the *cabinet* will have responsibility for monitoring one or more areas of policy, and there are weekly meetings of these specialists, chaired by the relevant member of the President's *cabinet*, to discuss issues that are current and to monitor the progress of draft legislation. The heads of the units—*chefs de cabinet*—also meet weekly, two days prior to the weekly meetings of the College of Commissioners. All draft legislation that has been prepared within the DGs has to go to the College for final approval, in keeping with the principle of collegiality. Before it gets there, it is considered by the *chefs*, and if difficulties that can be resolved are spotted at that stage, the draft will be referred back for amendment or further consideration. Where differences are highly politicized, the matter will be allowed to go through to the College for discussion.

The Commission in the Policy-Making Process

There is considerable academic debate around the role of the European Commission in the policy-making process. There is no doubt about its formal role: it has the sole right

Table 20.2 Commissioners and their Portfolios (2010–14)

Name	Portfolio	Nationality
José Manuel Barroso	President	Portuguese
Catherine Ashton	Vice President; High Representative of the Union for Foreign Affairs and Security Policy	British
Viviane Reding	Vice-President; Justice, Fundamental Rights and Citizenship	Luxembourgish
Joaquin Almunia	Vice-President; Competition	Spanish
Siim Kallas	Vice-President; Transport	Estonian
Neelie Kroes	Vice-President; Digital Agenda	Dutch
Antonio Tajani	Industry and Entrepreneurship	Italian
Maroš Šefčovič	Inter-Institutional Relations and Administration	Slovakian
Janez Potočnik	Environment	Slovenian
Olli Rehn	Economic and Monetary Affairs	Finnish
Andris Piebalgs	Development	Latvian
Michel Barnier	Internal Market and Services	French
Androulla Vassiliou	Science and Research	Cypriot
Algirdas Šemeta	Taxation and Customs Union, Audit and Anti-Fraud	Lithuanian
Karel De Gucht	Trade	Belgian
John Dalli	Health and Consumer Policy	Maltese
Máire Geoghegan-Quinn	Research and Innovation	Irish
Janusz Lewandowski	Financial Programming and Budget	Polish
Maria Damanaki	Fisheries and Maritime Affairs	Greek
Kristalina Georgieva	International Co-operation, Humanitarian Aid and Crisis Response	Bulgarian
Günther Oettinger	Energy	German
Johannes Hahn	Regional Policy	Austrian
Connie Hedegaard	Climate Action	Danish
Štefan Füle	Enlargement and European Neighbourhood Policy	Czech
László Andor	Employment, Social Affairs and Equal Opportunities	Hungarian
Cecilia Malmström	Home Affairs	Swedish
Dacian Cioloş	Agriculture and Rural Development	Romanian

to initiate proposals for legislation in all policy areas under the Union method, with the exception of the area of freedom, security, and justice (AFSJ), for which this power is shared (see Chapter 31). Thus, without a proposal from the Commission, neither the Council of Ministers nor the EP can legislate. However, the debate centres on whether

Table 20.3 Presidents of the European Commission

Walter Hallstein (West Germany)	1958–67
Jean Rey (Belgium)	1967–70
Franco Maria Malfatti (Italy)	1970–72
Sicco Mansholt (Netherlands)	1972
François-Xavier Ortoli (France)	1973–76
Roy Jenkins (UK)	1977–80
Gaston Thorn (Luxembourg)	1981–84
Jacques Delors (France)	1985–94
Jacques Santer (Luxembourg)	1995–99
Romano Prodi (Italy)	1999–2004
José Manuel Barroso (Portugal)	2004–

the Commission actually determines the direction in which the EU moves, particularly given the European Council's similar aspirations as well as those of the EP (see Chapter 21, pp. 274–80). Pessimistically, De Gucht (2003: 165) argued that the Commission faced extinction as an independent political entity. As an unusual twist, Karel De Gucht, Professor of Law at the Vrije Universiteit Brussels and a former MEP, was appointed Commissioner for Trade in 2010, so perhaps he has the opportunity to prevent the extinction of which he warned!

The Commission and the Member States

The story of the decline and revival in the fortunes of the Commission has been told in Chapters 10–18 (pp. 133–222). Theorizations of the role of the Commission moved from the neofunctionalist view of it as the 'motor of integration' to the intergovernmental view of it as no more than the servant of the member states. This balance of opinion swung back after the launch of the single-market programme in the mid-1980s. After this development, it rapidly became a widely accepted view that:

> The renewed drive for market unification can be explained only if theory takes into account the policy leadership of the Commission.

(Sandholtz and Zysman 1989: 96)

This view did not go unchallenged, though (Chapter 27, pp. 396–8). The disagreements over the role of the Commission in the single-market programme represented fundamental disagreements about the nature of the Commission in more general terms. Is it simply an agent of the member states, acting at their behest and under their control, or is it an autonomous actor in its own right, capable of playing a leadership role in the EU?

If the argument that the EU is an intergovernmental organization is to hold, then those who defend the position have to confront the assertion that the Commission is the prime mover of the process of European integration. This assertion was made from the early days of the EEC by Lindberg (1963) and other neofunctionalists (Chapter 1). The counter-argument is that the Commission is simply an international secretariat like many others that help the member states of international organizations to achieve their collective aims. It simply acts on behalf of the member states and in accordance with their will. This view has been strongly argued by intergovernmentalists, notably Andrew Moravcsik (Chapter 1).

The Commission as an Agent of the Member States

The intergovernmentalist view of the Commission is that it is only an agent of the member states. Its function is to make it easier for governments to find agreement on the details of co-operation with each other. Where there is agreement on the broad agenda for co-operation, it is convenient for member states to delegate some control over the detailed agenda to the Commission. They see it as a reliable source of independent proposals because it has technical information, and is a neutral arbiter between conflicting national interests. Delegating the making of proposals to the Commission in this way reduces the costs of co-operation by reducing the risk that 'decisions will be delayed by an inconclusive struggle among competing proposals, or that the final decision will be grossly unfair' (Moravcsik 1993: 512). Where there are alternative proposals that might win majority support, the choice is often decided by which proposal is backed by the Commission. Although this delegation of the right to make detailed proposals gives the Commission a certain formal power to set the agenda, in the intergovernmentalist view, the Commission does not determine the direction in which the EU moves. It is only helping the member states to agree on the details of what they have decided, they want to do anyway.

This intergovernmental interpretation also coincides with a principal–agent interpretation of delegation to the Commission that draws on work from comparative politics rather than integration theory (see Chapter 2). Majone (2001) argued that there are two reasons for delegating to agencies such as the Commission: for reasons of efficiency and credibility. The efficiency argument is that the agency—in this case, the European Commission—is endowed with better information and expertise than the individual member governments or the EP. The credibility argument is that it may be less exposed to being captured by powerful groups, such as the corporate lobby or, indeed, a powerful member state. The Commission's function of 'guardian of the treaties' is an important aspect of this credibility argument, since member states seeking to undermine EU legislation can ultimately be brought before the Court. These interpretations have generated significant debate and empirical testing (see, for instance, Franchino 2007).

The concern of Euro-sceptic politicians and the critique offered from neofunctionalists is that the Commission may use the margin of discretion that the member states have delegated to it to try to manoeuvre the member states towards objectives that they had not anticipated. It is difficult for the states to keep a check on exactly what the Commission is doing because it is in possession of more information than they are. Nevertheless, there are ways in which the member states can keep a check on the Commission (Pollack 1997; 2003). First, they have set up a whole complex of implementation committees of national experts to monitor the actions of the Commission.

There are approximately 250 of these committees—collectively known as comitology—but grouped into three categories. Advisory Committees give the Commission the greatest discretion; Management Committees make their decisions subject to being overruled by a QMV decision in the Council of Ministers; Regulatory Committees are a potential veto point for the Commission's decisions or the proposed measure is referred to the Council of Ministers for review. The Lisbon Treaty sought to tidy up this comitology system, which had developed in a rather ad hoc manner, as well as to ensure that the EP has proper oversight of it (Article 291 TFEU). Second, Article 263 TFEU allows challenges through the European Court of Justice (ECJ) to the actions of the Commission should any individual member state, or any directly affected individual or company, believe that it has overstepped its mandate. Other EU institutions, such as the EP and the Court of Auditors, also monitor the activities of the Commission, providing member states with the information that they need to keep a check on it.

The Commission as an Autonomous Actor

The alternative to the view that the Commission is no more than an agent of the member states is that it can and does act autonomously to provide policy leadership to the EU. Defenders of this view point to key resources that allow it to do so: its sole right of initiative in the legislative process of the EC; its ability to locate allies among influential interest groups; and its powers under the competition clauses of the Treaties to act against monopolies. (For a fuller list, see Nugent 1995: 605–13; also see Beach 2005.)

The Commission does not have to wait passively for the member states to ask it to bring forward proposals. It can identify a problem that has already started to concern governments, and propose a European solution. It can use its sole right of initiative to package issues in the form least likely to engender opposition in the Council of Ministers or the EP. Where there is opposition from member states to the full-blown development of a policy, the Commission may propose instead a limited small-scale programme; where there is resistance to a directive or regulation, the Commission may propose a less threatening recommendation or Opinion. In each case, the limited step establishes a precedent for action in the policy sector and can be followed up later with further steps if and when the environment in the Council of Ministers is more conducive (Cram 1997: 162–3).

The Commission can also act to put the Europeanization of a policy sector onto the agenda (cultivated spillover—see Chapter 1). By involving domestic interests at the EU level, through instruments such as advisory committees, the Commission seeks to win converts to the idea that an issue can best be handled at the European level. In the aftermath of the 2007 financial crisis, it actively advocated the strengthening of EU regulation of hedge funds and other financial instruments, aware that it had support in the EP and that the member governments were on relatively weak ground since the failure of domestic regulation was part of the explanation for the crisis.

Similarly, the Commission can utilize, and if necessary create, **transnational networks** of producers who will be its allies in the private sector and bring pressure to bear on governments to transfer competence in a sector to the EU level. It was most successful at this approach in the 1980s and 1990s: in the cases of technology policy (Sharp and Shearman 1987; Sharp 1989; Peterson 1991), telecommunications

(Dang-Nguyen et al. 1993; Fuchs 1994), and energy (Matlary 1993). In each of these last two sectors, it encouraged industrial users to press governments to move away from national monopolies to create a European market under European regulation.

Once governments have become aware of a problem, and faced up to the possibility of a European solution, the Commission can use technical experts to increase the pressure on governments, as it did with the Cecchini report of economists for the single market (see Chapter 27, p. 397), or for monetary union, the Delors Committee, which consisted mainly of central bankers (see Chapter 28, p. 404).

Nevertheless, any move to develop a European competence in a policy sector will produce counter-pressures from groups that benefit from the status quo. The Commission can break down this opposition by threatening the use of its existing powers under the competition clauses of the Treaties if actors in the sector will not co-operate to find a negotiated way forward. Again, it did this to achieve the opening up of national monopolies in telecommunications and energy supply and liberalizing the air-transport sector (Bulmer et al. 2007). In each case, the Directorate-General for Competition (then DG IV) threatened to use its powers under what was then Article 90 of the Treaty (now Article 106 TFEU). This Article specifically said that national public monopolies were subject to the rules prohibiting the prevention of competition within the **common market**. The vested interests against change were therefore faced with the alternative of either reaching an agreement with the relevant Commission DG to allow phased and regulated competition, or facing legal proceedings. In many cases, these Article 90 challenges were linked to proposed legislation on liberalization going through the Council of Ministers. In all three cases cited, the alternative of having some say in *how* the transition from national monopoly to European market was carried out proved more attractive than the uncertainty of the alternative of legal proceedings, and the resistance to the Commission's proposals was seriously weakened as a result (Chapter 27, pp. 390–2 and 398–9).

This pattern of Commission activism has been less evident in the last decade or so. Greater concern for **subsidiarity** from the mid-1990s, checks on the regulatory burden of Commission action, and the changed EU agenda have been major contributors. A key emphasis of the Commission from 2005 to 2009 was the competitiveness of the European economy, but the Lisbon Strategy was much more one of policy co-ordination via the Open Method of Co-ordination (see Chapter 25) and therefore not amenable to Commission activism.

The Commission and the European Parliament

While most attention has been paid to the relationship between the Commission and the member states, sympathetic practitioners have recently expressed concern about the erosion of the autonomy of the Commission resulting from the extension of the powers of the EP (De Gucht 2003). Several academic observers have identified an erosion of the Commission's powers and independence within the decision-making process (Tsebelis and Garrett 2000; 2001; Majone 2002; Burns 2004). Four main ways in which this has happened are identified.

(1) Although the Commission and the EP have traditionally been allies in attempting to wrest powers away from the member states, the Commission resisted

suggestions that the EP be given an equal right of legislative initiative. The Commission argued that sharing the right of initiative would weaken its ability to give coherence and strategy to European legislation. Formally, the Commission has maintained its monopoly of initiative. Yet, since Maastricht, the EP has the right to request that the Commission 'submit any appropriate proposal on matters on which it considers that a Community act is required for the purpose of implementing this Treaty' (Article 225 TFEU). Majone (2002: 376) considered that this 'comes close to a true right of legislative initiative'.

(2) The introduction of co-decision (Chapter 19, pp. 240–1) has made it more difficult for the Commission to play the role of motor of integration because its proposals have to satisfy a larger number of actors. Specifically, co-decision requires the Commission to satisfy a majority in the EP as well as in the Council of Ministers (hereafter abbreviated to the Council). The more actors that have to be brought into agreement, the more the proposals are likely to become compromises rather than reflect the autonomous preferences of the Commission.

(3) Co-decision also opens the possibility of the Council and the EP agreeing an entirely different legislative text from that put forward by the Commission. If the Council and the EP cannot reach agreement on an amended version of the original Commission proposal, a Conciliation Committee is convened, in which the representatives of the two legislative institutions seek to reach agreement directly with one another. This may mean agreement on an entirely different text. The compromise text then has to be agreed in the Council by QMV, and by the EP by a simple majority. Thus, the original centrality of the Commission's proposal, which could only be amended by unanimity in the Council, is circumvented, thereby eroding the Commission's autonomy.

(4) The changes made to co-decision in the Treaty of Amsterdam further eroded the Commission's influence. Because the Council and the EP can reach agreement at first reading under the revised procedure, there is an incentive for them to open direct informal contacts at a much earlier stage than under the original co-decision procedure. This may deprive the Commission of the pivotal role in the negotiations around the legislation. However, claims that it rendered the Commission irrelevant were rebutted by Burns (2004: 6), who pointed out that the Commission can still affect the chances of the EP's amendments being accepted by the Council. It should be pointed out that agreement between Council and EP at first-reading stage did become the predominant pattern in the 2004–09 EP legislative period (Duff 2009: 52).

The Commission and Managing Implementation

Up to this point we have focused on the role of the Commission in policy making. However, the Commission also has to be an effective manager of EU business if it is to play its part in putting policy into practice. Concern at its effectiveness initially emerged at the start of the 1990s. In 1991, the then Secretary General of the Commission, David Williamson, admitted to the failings of the Commission when it came to implementing the growing body of EC legislation. This analysis was echoed by Metcalfe (1992) and other academic observers, who had noted that the Commission was better adapted to proposing policies and legislation than to implementing them once they were agreed. Metcalfe went so far as to argue (1992: 118) that: 'The EC has a management deficit at least as significant for its future effectiveness as its more widely recognised democratic deficit.'

It had long been argued that the two functions of initiation and implementation require different types of organizational structure, which Coombes (1970) identified as *organic* and *mechanistic* organizations. He described the Commission as an organic organization, well equipped to generate proposals, but lacking sufficient of the qualities of a classical mechanistic bureaucracy to implement them effectively. Others have seen this bias against implementation as embodied in the culture of the Commission.

> There has always been a bias within the Commission in favour of policy formulation as opposed to policy execution.
>
> (Ludlow 1991: 107)

During the 1990s, the implementation problems of the Commission increased as a result of several factors.

(1) The success of the 1992 Programme and other policy initiatives taken under Delors' presidency left the Commission with a much larger body of legislation to implement.

(2) The extension of EU competences into new policy sectors, such as social and environmental policy, raised different problems of implementation from those that the Commission had previously encountered (Peters 1997: 191).

(3) The question of consistent implementation of single-market rules became an issue because of the wide disparities between member states that were shown up by Commission monitoring reports. The states with the better records felt that they were being placed at a competitive disadvantage in comparison with states that were less meticulous about applying the rules.

(4) The crisis over the ratification of the Maastricht Treaty (Chapter 13, pp. 164–5), and the subsequent renewed emphasis on the principle of subsidiarity, further complicated the relationship between the Commission and the member states (Laffan 1997b: 425).

(5) The internal Commission crisis that culminated in the resignation of the Santer Commission in 1999 (Chapter 15, pp. 182–4) revealed poor management and accountability structures within the Commission.

In consequence, the incoming Commission of Romano Prodi initiated a major programme of reform, for which the British Vice-President of the Commission, Neil Kinnock, took responsibility (Metcalfe 2000). It entailed changes to the structure, organization, and management of the Commission. Changes were introduced to terms of appointment of both Commissioners and personnel in the Services. Codes of conduct were introduced relating to their practices. As Metcalfe wrote at the time (2000: 819): 'The management deficit is not just about the inadequacies within the Commission—it is a structural problem that threatens the performance of the whole system.' A decade later, it became possible to evaluate the reforms. Hussein Kassim (2008: 548) offered the following verdict: 'When crisis forced member governments to intervene, the Commission in a case of self-reform under delegation seized the "once-in-a-generation" opportunity to implement an internal reform agenda.'

The Commission as Implementer

The Commission operates in two modes as implementer. First, there are a very few policy sectors in which the Commission has direct implementation powers. The most notable is competition policy, which has been called 'the first supranational policy' (McGowan and Wilks 1995). Others are fisheries and some of the programmes involved in the external relations of the EU, such as the Humanitarian Aid Programme. Second, for most internal policies, the Commission sits at the apex of a multi-level system of implementation that extends down to the central authorities of the member states, then below them to sub-national authorities and agencies. Morten Egeberg has argued that this multi-level EU administration represents a 'transformation of executive politics in Europe' (Egeberg 2006). In this second mode, the Commission acts as the agent of the member states; national and sub-national actors are the agents of the Commission. The problem for the Commission is ensuring that these agents do not pursue their own agendas.

This problem is compounded by two circumstances. First, the Commission has scarce personnel resources and lacks independent information. Second, the number of agents that it has to monitor has been increased by the fragmentation of public administration that has taken place in many member states under the banner of the 'New Public Management' (Peters 1997: 198). In consequence, the Commission has had to operate as the manager of European networks of member-state administrators. The latter may take on a 'double-hatted' role as both domestic policy managers and as part of an EU-centred administration co-ordinated by the Commission (see Egeberg 2006 for illustrations). Indeed, it is quite possible that the European External Action Service (Chapter 33, p. 515), although headed by both the Commission and Council of Ministers, may have the same effect amongst European diplomats.

Majone (2002) argued, in similar vein, that the transfer of new competences to the EU had not involved increasing the exclusive competences of the EU, but had involved the extension of the number of areas in which the EU and the member states shared competence, or in which competences were dispersed to new institutional actors, such as the European Central Bank (Majone 2002: 376). The reluctance of member states to transfer further exclusive competences to EU institutions reflected their concern about the loss of control that earlier transfers had involved. However, it also reflected a realization that the implementation role of the Commission could not be increased further without an increase in its size and resources that the member states were unwilling to sanction (Majone 2002: 382). In the view of Majone (2002: 382–3), this situation obliged the Commission to share responsibility with national administrative authorities, even though it was difficult to do so because of differing national regulatory philosophies and differing levels of national administrative competence.

Table 20.4 Independent Agencies

EU Agencies

Community Fisheries Control Agency (CFCA)

Community Plant Variety Office (CPVO)

European Agency for Safety and Health at Work (EU-OSHA)

European Agency for the Management of Operational Co-operation at the External Borders (FRONTEX)

European Aviation Safety Agency (EASA)

European Centre for Disease Prevention and Control (ECDC)

European Centre for the Development of Vocational Training (Cedefop)

European Chemicals Agency (ECHA)

European Environment Agency (EEA)

European Food Safety Authority (EFSA)

European Foundation for the Improvement of Living and Working Conditions (EUROFOUND)

European Global Navigation Satellite Systems Supervisory Authority (GSA)

European Institute for Gender Equality

European Maritime Safety Agency (EMSA)

European Medicines Agency (EMEA)

European Monitoring Centre for Drugs and Drug Addiction (EMCDDA)

European Network and Information Security Agency (ENISA)

European Police College (CEPOL)

European Police Office (EUROPOL)

European Railway Agency (ERA)

European Training Foundation (ETF)

European Union Agency for Fundamental Rights (FRA)

Office for Harmonization in the Internal Market (Trade Marks and Designs) (OHIM)

The European Union's Judicial Co-operation Unit (EUROJUST)

Translation Centre for the Bodies of the European Union (CdT)

CFSP Agencies

European Defence Agency (EDA)

European Union Institute for Security Studies (ISS)

European Union Satellite Centre (EUSC)

Note: Excludes Euratom agencies as well as executive agencies established to administer individual EU programmes.

Source: **http://europa.eu/agencies/index_en.htm**, March 2010

At the same time, the Commission faced the prospect of becoming increasingly subject to political interference with performance of its implementation function because of the reform measures taken to deal with the democratic deficit. The Lisbon Treaty reinforced this trend by stating in Article 17 TEU that the nomination of the Commission President must take into account the elections to the European Parliament. The danger of such politicization is that it risks adversely affecting the credibility principle that lies behind delegation to the Commission in the first place.

Majone (2002: 387) argued that there was a case for a 'fourth branch of government' on the model of US federal regulatory agencies. In fact, some further independent agencies were created in connection with the transfer of new competences, but they were not given regulatory powers, being mainly charged to collect and collate information. A list of these agencies is given in Table 20.4. Their numbers have increased in recent years, and have even been extended into CFSP activity. In short, they have become an important facet of executive governance at EU level. Indeed, the Commission now has a DG responsible for overseeing these executive agencies. Agencies have also been brought under more systematic control, including accountability to the Court and the EP, through provisions incorporated across the Lisbon Treaty.

Financial Management

Alongside the Commission's burgeoning implementation problems, concern grew about effective financial management of EU programmes. As Laffan (1997b: 427) noted, for many years, the annual reports of the Court of Auditors highlighted weaknesses in the Commission's financial management. As one response, the Maastricht Treaty upgraded the status of the Court of Auditors to that of a full EC institution, and raised the status of budgetary discipline and sound financial management to central principles (Laffan 1997b: 429).

The resignation of the Santer Commission in 1999 was partly due to problems of financial mismanagement, so it came as no surprise that the Commission's reform White Paper of 2000 included, as one of four key components, reform of the system of financial control and management (Hussein 2008: 659). Internal accountability was overhauled, with financial responsibility de-centralized to Director-Generals, and the creation of an Internal Audit Service (see Table 20.1). More broadly, the Commission has to make sure that fraud is not taking place using EU funds, but in this case including through malpractice at member state level. The main weapon to this end is the European Anti-Fraud Office, known by its French acronym, OLAF (see Table 20.1).

CONCLUSION

The debate over the role of the Commission remains central to explanations about the nature and pace of European integration. It is clearly central to one of the themes of this book: the debate about the nature of the EU itself. If the Commission can be shown to be an autonomous actor, the argument that the EU is an intergovernmental organization is severely weakened. Up to now, the debate has been inconclusive, although the supranational challenge was greatest under the Delors Commissions (1985–95).

The Commission has been fiercely criticized in its role as manager of EU policies and finances. It was forced to put its house in order following the crisis in 1998–99. Oversight of policy implementation remains a concern. While implementation is never straightforward for domestic legislation within member states, it becomes even more difficult in a union of twenty-seven member states, in which the Commission is dependent on national governments and national administrations for effective compliance. Added to this, the proliferation of actors involved in the policy process nationally and the increased role of 'agency government' at member-state level, has made the Commission's task even more difficult. Such developments have been central to the increased interest in the application of the concepts of governance and policy networks to the EU (Chapter 2) and of multi-level administration. The significant growth of agencies at the EU level merely adds to the complexity. Executive governance in the EU has become increasingly complex as the integration process has developed over the decades. However, there has been one constant: the Commission has proved to be very resilient in maintaining a central role in administering EU policy, as well as in its formulation.

KEY POINTS

Functions
- The Commission initiates legislation, may act as a mediator, and manages some policy areas, and is guardian of the Treaties, a key actor in international relations, and the 'conscience of the EU'.

Composition and Appointment
- The Commission consists of a College of Commissioners and the Services.
- The Services are the bureaucracy—the permanent civil service—of the EU.
- The Commission President is a particularly influential figure, and is nominated by the European Council and then approved by the EP.
- The Commissioners are appointed by the European Council, subject to approval by the EP.
- There is one Commissioner per member state. They are sworn to abandon national allegiances.

The Commission in the Policy-Making Process
- Formally, the Commission has the sole right to propose EU legislation.
- There is debate about how much autonomy it actually has.
- The intergovernmentalist view is that the Commission is merely the agent of the member states; the supranationalist view is that the Commission can and does achieve a degree of autonomy from the member states to pursue its own agenda.
- Treaty changes designed to deal with the democratic deficit have reduced the autonomy of the Commission by increasing the control over it by the EP.

The Commission and Implementation
- The Commission has always been more active as a proposer than as an implementer of legislation.

- In most areas, the Commission has to work alongside the national administrations of the member states, leading to suggestions that it should evolve as a manager of European networks of implementation agents.

- Increasing politicization of the Commission because of its subjection to closer control by the EP threatens its perceived independence, and also points to the need for the emergence of transnational regulatory networks.

Financial Management

- The 1999, the Commission crisis triggered a root-and-branch reform of the Commission's financial management.

FURTHER READING

N. Nugent, *The European Commission* (Basingstoke: Palgrave Macmillan, 2000) is the most comprehensive introduction to the institution. **D. Dimitrakopoulos (ed.)**, *The Changing European Commission* (Manchester: Manchester University Press, 2004) offers a useful collection of chapters on the European Commission, as does a special edition of the *Journal of European Public Policy*, 15(8) (2008). Still useful is **N. Nugent (ed.)**, *At the Heart of the Union: Studies of the European Commission* (Basingstoke and London: Macmillan, 1997). For the European Commission as a bureaucracy, see **A. Stevens and H. Stevens**, *Brussels Bureaucrats? The Administration of the European Union* (Basingstoke: Palgrave Macmillan, 2001).

 online resource centre **Visit the Online Resource Centre that accompanies this book for links to more information on the European Commission, including the European Commission's own website: www.oxfordtextbooks.co.uk/orc/bache3e/**

Chapter 21

The European Council and the Council of Ministers

Chapter Overview

This chapter examines those institutions principally composed of government representatives. Prior to the Lisbon Treaty coming into effect, these institutions could all be seen as part of a single 'Council' system. With its entry into force, the European Council became an institution in its own right, and the chapter title reflects this change. Even so, by virtue of their composition of government representatives (government heads, ministers, and civil servants), the two institutions remain part of a hierarchy of institutions (see Insight 21.1). The European Council is the name for the periodic summit meetings of heads of state and government that are largely responsible for determining the direction of the integration process. The Council of Ministers (officially known as the 'Council of the European Union' and in shorthand as the 'Council') is a multi-faceted and multi-tiered institution that does not have a constant membership, but involves different ministers depending on the policy under consideration. Even that, though, is not the full extent of the complexity of the Council. The work of the meetings of ministers is prepared by a myriad of committees, consisting primarily of national officials, that are brought together by the Committee of Permanent Representatives (COREPER) and a large number of preparatory committees at technical level. Each of these is considered in what follows.

The whole European Union system revolves round the European Council.

(Peter Ludlow, quoted in de Schoutheete 2002: 44)

The Council of Ministers ... is one of the EU's most powerful institutions and its primary decision-making body.

(Bomberg, Martin, and Cram 2003: 49)

It is important at the outset of this chapter to be clear about terminology. The subject matter of the chapter is those European Union (EU) institutions composed of representatives of national governments. Both are important, as the quotes above indicate, but in different ways. The European Council is at the top of this hierarchy and is the institution that brings together the EU's heads of government (or, in the French case, the head of state). As will be seen, it is a relatively recent body, having been set up in 1974, and since implementation of the Lisbon Treaty (in December 2009) is a formal

EU institution. It is not to be confused with the Council of Europe (Chapter 5, Insight 5.2) —as it sometimes is in student essays—as this is a completely separate international organization from the EU. The other institution to be considered in this chapter is the Council of the European Union or, as it is usually termed the Council of Ministers. It is the Council of Ministers that is referred to with the shorthand term 'the Council'. The so-called Council hierarchy comprises the Council of Ministers, as well as other preparatory bodies arranged beneath it (see Insight 21.1). It is attended by ambassadors and civil servants of the member states.

The Council of Ministers was first set up as part of the European Coal and Steel Community (see Chapter 6, pp. 92–103). Over six decades later, its activities span the full range of public policy. Two things have remained constant, however. First, it is the institution that enshrines the importance of member governments in the EU. Second, it remains the focal point of the making of EU legislation, but has been joined increasingly over recent years by the European Parliament as a co-legislator. Its principal functions are decision making and legislating. The European Council was created in 1974 as part of an effort to re-energize the integration process in a more intergovernmental way, given the setback suffered by the supranational method in the aftermath of the 1965 crisis (Chapter 19, pp. 128–9). The European Council has become the motor of European integration in the subsequent period. These two institutions may grab the headlines, but a large majority of decisions are made before they reach them: at the level of COREPER or the preparatory technical committees.

As with the previous chapter, a key theme in this one is the relationship between the intergovernmental and supranational interpretations. On the face of it, both the European Council and the Council of Ministers, comprised as they are of member governments and their officials, represent intergovernmentalism 'writ large'. The top layers of the hierarchy bring together 'the core executive' of the EU member states: the Prime Ministers, Foreign Ministers, and other departmental ministers, together with their officials. However, in their comprehensive study of the Council of Ministers, Hayes-Renshaw and Wallace (2006: 321) put paid to this simplistic analysis:

> to view the importance of the Council as the victory of intergovernmentalism over supranationalism, or to expect the Council to be able to 'run' the EU, is to misunderstand the institutional constellation of the EU. The Council shares and diffuses power between countries, between different kinds of interests and constituencies, and between national and EU levels of governance. The Council cannot act alone, but is dependent on intricate relationships with other EU institutions.

The supranational argument is less easy to present, but revolves around several points of departure from intergovernmentalism:

- that ministers and officials from the member states are partners who may work together frequently and will have regard to collective solutions as well as the national interest;
- that the provision for **qualified majority voting (QMV)** changes the calculation of ministers away from 'hard bargaining' based exclusively on the national interest, even if they prefer not to vote but to decide by consensus;
- that the Council increasingly needs to work with the European Parliament (EP) in the 'ordinary legislative procedure' (co-decision);

> ### Insight 21.1 The EU's Intergovernmental Institutions
>
> #### The European Council
> Summit meetings of the heads of government (France sends the head of state), held four times per year, with provision for additional meetings.
>
> #### The Council of Ministers
> Consists of a representative of each member state 'at ministerial level', authorized to commit the government of the member state. It meets (as of 2010) in ten different formations depending on the subject matter under consideration.
>
> #### The Committee of Permanent Representatives (COREPER)
> The Permanent Representatives are the ambassadors of the member states to the EU. Their deputies meet as COREPER I and the Representatives themselves as COREPER II. They prepare business for the meetings of ministers.
>
> #### High-Level Preparatory Bodies and the Working Parties
> COREPER itself is prepared by a small number of specialized committees, such as on agriculture or trade policy. At the lowest level are Council working parties, which deal with most specialist policy issues. According to Hayes-Renshaw and Wallace (2006: 70), there were 162 of these in 2005, with a further 121 sub-groups.
>
> #### The Presidency
> Prior to the Lisbon Treaty, the presidency was held for six months by one member state as determined by a rota. A representative of this state would chair all meetings of the Council and, indeed, of meetings in the Council hierarchy. The Lisbon Treaty ended the simplicity of this set-up by turning the presidency into a 'trio' of three states playing the above role across an eighteen-month period. However, separate arrangements were introduced for the Presidency of the European Council, the Presidency of the Council of Foreign Affairs, and the Presidency of the Euro Group.
>
> #### The Secretariat
> The state holding the presidency is assisted by a Council Secretariat of over 3,000 staff, about a tenth of whom are senior administrators.

- that there is some evidence of socialization into shared values amongst participants at all levels in the hierarchy of intergovernmental institutions.

The European Council

Over the years, the European Council has held meetings at least twice a year and generally three or four times. The Lisbon Treaty states that it shall meet 'twice every six months' (Article 15(3), TEU). Additional informal meetings are also called in response to urgent matters. The origins of the European Council were in the summit meetings that started with the 'relaunching of Europe' at The Hague in 1969

The first formal meeting of the European Council was in Dublin in March 1975.

The Rationale for the European Council

After de Gaulle's resignation in 1969, there was a wish by the national governments to re-start the development of the European Community (EC), but in the direction that they, not the Commission, decided; hence the Hague Summit of that year. The 1965 crisis had led to a loss of confidence inside the Commission. If the Commission was not going to drive the EC forward, another motor would be needed. The agreement to formalize summits in the form of the European Council was an indication that the governments were determined to play a continuing role. Despite the European Council taking on a fundamental role in steering the course of integration from the mid-1970s, its elusive and under-institutionalized nature led to a lamentable neglect in the academic literature.

The origins of the European Council stemmed from the French President, Valéry Giscard d'Estaing, and the German Chancellor, Helmut Schmidt, who both came to office in 1974. Both had been Finance Ministers and had participated in numerous meetings on the international monetary system. They both strongly valued the opportunity to sit with their counterparts and hold informal discussions in confidence without the requirement to take formal decisions (Bulmer and Wessels 1997: 76). This 'Library Group' approach, which was quite informal, was important at the outset, but the Lisbon Treaty can be seen as its abandonment. Characteristic of the earlier 'Library Group' approach was a strong effort to keep the European Council outside of the Treaties in order to allow it as much flexibility as possible in its political actions. This informality eventually became unsustainable, not least with twenty-seven participating states.

The existence of the European Council was first acknowledged in the 1986 Single European Act (SEA), albeit in just three sentences. The Maastricht Treaty formalized the European Council but did not cite it as being one of the EU's institutions. It gave the European Council a very small number of specific tasks: notably in economic and mone-tary policy, and in setting the direction of the Common Foreign and Security Policy (CFSP). However, the Lisbon Treaty set out much more explicitly the role of the European Council and unambiguously refers to it as an institution of the EU (see Insight 21.2).

A further explanation for the establishment of the European Council was to 'orches-trate' the EC. The 1969 Hague Summit had demonstrated that the heads of govern-ment could set the direction of integration: both broadly through authorizing enlargement negotiations and specifically through triggering particular policy initia-tives, such as foreign policy co-operation. The European Council could also overcome the risk of policy segmentation, which arose because no single body could take an overview of policy. The General Affairs Council (see below) was supposed to act as policy co-ordinator, but the heads of government had more authority to play that role. Finally, the European Council was also an attempt to present a united front to the out-side world and its role in this respect has expanded, to some extent usurping the role of the Council of Foreign Ministers.

Composition and Organization

Although the European Council is comprised of the heads of government, they are not the only participants. Traditionally, the Foreign Ministers of the member states have also participated, as has the Commission President and one Vice-President. The Lisbon Treaty made some subtle changes. Membership was redefined as follows (Article 15 TEU):

- the heads of state (France) or government of the member states, together with the President of the European Council and the President of the Commission;
- the High Representative of the Union for Foreign Affairs and Security Policy (HRUFASP);
- as necessitated by its agenda, heads of government may each be assisted by a minister and, in the case of the President of the Commission, by a member of the Commission.

As noted in Insight 21.1, the Presidency of the European Council became a separate appointment for two-and-a-half years (from January 2010, Herman Van Rompuy, the former Belgian Prime Minister) and no longer follows the previous system whereby meetings were chaired by the head of government from the presidency country. This change was introduced to ensure continuity in the European Council's work and to give an external face to the institution, for instance in reporting to the EP on its work. The second change is the close involvement of the High Representative: a step that reflects the importance of foreign and security policy to the European Council's work. Third, the previous default situation whereby heads of government were accompanied by their foreign ministers has been amended. In reality, some changes had already occurred, notably with Economics or Finance Ministers attending the annual spring European Council meeting on the European economy.

The European Council's organization was undefined until the Lisbon Treaty. Again, significant changes took place. The Treaty provides for qualified or simple majority voting in the European Council, for instance in appointing its President, although the standard practice is decision making by consensus. In any event, neither the President nor the Commission President may vote. Having studiously avoided any internal regulation of its activities under the 'Library Group' model, the European Council took the radical step of agreeing rules of procedure, something already well established for the other institutions (European Council 2009). Herman Van Rompuy's selection as the first President of the European Council was widely interpreted as an attempt to ensure the office did not have too high a profile and did not challenge the authority of national leaders in the way that a better-known politician might. Another candidate had been Tony Blair, the former British Prime Minister, who was seen as having given the position a higher profile as a 'traffic stopper' when representing the EU abroad. One consequence of the new position has been a possible confusion of roles with those of the Commission President, the High Representative—not to mention the country holding the presidency of the sectoral Councils of Ministers. Another consequence of the new position looks set to be an expansion of the European Council's activities. Kietz and von Ondarza (2010: 4) report Van Rompuy as planning smaller, more frequent (six to eight per annum), and thematically organized sessions of the European Council, building on the pattern established by the annual spring session on the European economy. Another development worthy of note is that the government heads from the eurozone states have held

Insight 21.2 The European Council's Post-Lisbon Functions

(1) **General political guidance and momentum**

- 'The European Council shall provide the Union with the necessary impetus for its development and shall define the general political directions and priorities thereof. It shall not exercise legislative functions.' (Article 15 TEU)

(2) **Oversight of Treaty reform and enlargement**

- Any proposals to revise the Treaties through the 'ordinary revision procedure' will be decided on by the European Council, which will consult the EP and the Commission and may decide by a simple majority to either convene a Convention or an intergovernmental conference (IGC) to consider the proposals. (Article 48 TEU)

- Under 'simplified revision procedures', the European Council can agree less significant changes that nevertheless affect the character of the EU: for instance, to change decision-making rules to the ordinary legislative procedure (QMV in the Council and co-decision with the EP)—see Chapter 18 on the *passerelle* **clauses.**

- The European Council sets the eligibility conditions for accession states (Article 49 TEU).

- The European Council sets the guidelines for the process should a member state wish to withdraw from the EU (Article 50 TEU).

(3) **Foreign policy making**

- The 'European Council shall identify the strategic interests and objectives of the Union.... [in relation] ... to the common foreign and security policy and to other areas of the external action of the Union' (Article 22 TEU).

- 'If international developments so require, the President of the European Council shall convene an extraordinary meeting of the European Council in order to define the strategic lines of the Union's policy in the face of such developments.' (Article 26 TEU)

(4) **Decision maker of last resort**

- Nominates the Commission President and appoints the Commission after the EP's consent (Article 17 TEU).

- Appoints the High Representative (HRUFASP) (Article 18 TEU).

- Decides on Council formations and presidency rota (Article 236 TFEU).

- Decides on number of Commissioners (Article 127 TEU and 244 TFEU).

- Decides on size of the EP (Article 14 TEU).

- Acts as court of appeal if a member state invokes the 'emergency brake' arrangements (scattered across the TFEU, but see Articles 48, 82, and 83 as examples).

(5) **Policy monitoring**

- 'The European Council shall define the strategic guidelines for legislative and operational planning within the area of freedom, security and justice.' (Article 68 TFEU)

- The European Council 'shall, acting on the basis of the report from the Council, discuss a conclusion on the broad guidelines of the economic policies of the Member States and of the Union' (Article 121 TFEU).

meetings during both the financial crisis that started in 2008 and also in the context of the eurozone crisis triggered by the parlous state of Greece's public finances. In connection with the latter, the President of the European Council was tasked in May 2010 with developing reforms for the functioning of the eurozone. The President's functions are to: convene meetings; prepare sessions; maintain continuity of work; represent the European Council in inter-institutional discussions (for instance, reporting to the EP); and draw up conclusions from its meetings.

Functions and Dysfunctions

The European Council has five main functions (see also Insight 21.2), as follows.

- *General political guidance and momentum*   To this end, the European Council is like a 'board of directors' giving general guidance to the EU on its future direction. Although the details have to be filled out by interaction between the Commission, the Council of Ministers, and the EP, if the European Council gives a lead, the presumption is that the Commission will make proposals and the Council and EP will try to reach agreement on policy.

- *Oversight of Treaty reform and enlargement*   The European Council has been closely involved in authorizing and then finalizing all Treaty reforms from the 1986 SEA through to the 2007 Lisbon Treaty. Of course, the European Council does not tie up twenty-seven government heads in detailed negotiations; those are conducted by officials and ministers. But without its initial agreement to start the process, and its consent at the end of it, Treaty reform would not be possible. Ever since the Hague Summit in 1969, summit meetings have taken key decisions on enlargement. For instance, the Copenhagen criteria of 1993 specified the requirements expected of all accession states and were defined at a European Council meeting in the Danish capital.

- *Foreign policy making*   Over the years, the European Council has issued many foreign policy declarations. These range from the 1980 Venice Declaration, in which it set out key principles on the Middle East, such as recognizing the Palestinian right to self-determination and to a homeland, to its December 2003 approval of a European Security Strategy. These powers were further developed by the Lisbon Treaty.

- *Decision maker of last resort*   From its very first meeting, the European Council has been called on to tackle problems that could not be resolved lower down the system. For many sessions from 1979 to 1984, the British Conservative government's efforts to secure a rebate on its budgetary contributions were on the European Council's agenda. However, it is not just a court of appeal, but is also brought in where decisions require its authority. It has had to thrash out agreement on the multi-annual financial perspective (see Chapter 19, p. 236). The Lisbon Treaty added specific provisions for the European Council to act as court of appeal if a member state wishes to use the 'emergency brake' because an exceptionally important interest is at risk of being overruled in the Council by a QMV decision (see Dougan 2008: 643–4). Finally, the European Council makes a number of key appointments as well as is able to take decisions on the size of some of the institutions (see Insight 21.2).

- *Policy monitoring*   Increasingly, the heads of government have sought to monitor the subsequent development of their own policy initiatives, in part to ensure policy delivery. For instance, the 2000–10 Lisbon Strategy on enhancing European competitiveness resulted in monitoring at the annual spring session of the European Council. Starting with the Tampere Programme of 2000, the European Council agreed a five-year programme for developing the area of freedom, security, and justice (AFSJ). This role has become firmly established through five-yearly programmes, typically with the Commission providing a mid-term review on progress (see Chapter 31).

The European Council can still function as a forum for personal contact between heads of government. While the meetings have become more formal as the number of member states has increased, opportunities for informal conversations still exist—for instance, during meals.

In carrying out these functions, the European Council faces some serious problems. These can be considered the *dysfunctions* of the European Council. They can be summarized as problems of overload, over-optimism, overcautiousness, and over-expectation.

- *Overload*   During the late 1970s and into the 1980s, there was a tendency for more and more problems to be referred up from the Council of Ministers to the European Council, so that it often found itself considering quite detailed and technical issues. However, since the introduction in the SEA and the Treaty on European Union (TEU) of QMV into the work of the Council of Ministers, the tendency for matters not to be resolved at lower levels has receded. European Council business can still be considerable for meetings lasting only five or six working days in a year.

- *Over-optimism*   Sometimes, the atmosphere of mutual co-operation that can be generated, together with the expectation that something will come out of every European Council, can lead to commitments being made that subsequently prove difficult to honour. When they go home after the meeting, heads of government may not be able to get the agreement of their own political parties or their cabinets/councils of ministers to carry through the commitment.

- *Overcautiousness*   The publicity can make it more difficult for heads of government to make concessions that might be made in a less exposed bargaining context.

- *Over-expectation*   If the meetings do not produce dramatic results, this can cause disillusionment amongst the European public because the media has built up expectations.

Intergovernmentalism and Informality in the European Council

Although the European Council 'is the body universally recognized as the ultimate intergovernmental protectorate in the EU', it is also 'one which has paradoxically increased the supranational character of the EU over its three decades of operation' (Lewis 2003*a*: 1006). It has increased the supranational character of the EU because it provides the political framework for supranational legislation and other agreements. Although the heads of government do not themselves formally agree legislation, if they say that something should happen, it will be acted upon by the Commission and the Council of Ministers. Thus, the European Council gives legitimacy to supranational actions that might otherwise be contested at the level of the Council of Ministers.

Although its functions are now more specified, the European Council is still a forum for informal contact between heads of government, and this can increase the degree of collegiality of the institution. In the past, it was particularly important where French and German leaders had a close relationship—Giscard d'Estaing and Schmidt in the second half of the 1970s; Kohl and Mitterrand in the 1980s—since the Franco-German relationship had in some senses become the motor of integration. If leading members of the European Council remain in post for several years, they can become socialized into more co-operative working with the other heads of government. This effect is never likely to work as strongly for the heads of government as it does for other levels of the Council hierarchy (see below), because the frequency of interaction is lower and the level of politicization of the heads of government is higher—but in reading the analyses that follow of the Council and its committees as supranational phenomena, it should be borne in mind that some of the same effects may operate even at the highest level of the European Council.

The Council of Ministers

The Council of Ministers is not an institution with a constant membership. It meets in a variety of formations depending on the subject under discussion (see Table 21.1). It should be noted that all formations act in the name of 'the Council of Ministers' and may decide on any business. Formally, there is no hierarchy between different Councils. However, the General Affairs Council (GAC), normally attended by Foreign Ministers, has a co-ordination function between the various technical councils and a relationship to the European Council, which implies that it has additional authority over the technical expertise possessed by the other formations.

The GAC was re-established as a separate formation after passage of the Lisbon Treaty, having previously been known as the General Affairs and External Relations Council (GAERC). GAERC was by far the busiest Council formation and a very important one as well, meeting on twenty-two occasions in 2006. However, following the Lisbon Treaty, the GAERC was split into the GAC and the Foreign Affairs Council. The latter is chaired by the High Representative, Catherine Ashton (a Briton who had previously been European Commissioner for Trade).

Apart from the GAC and the Foreign Affairs Council, the other key formations are: the Council of Economic and Finance Ministers (ECOFIN), which normally meets every month; and the Agriculture and Fisheries Council (Agfish), which also normally meets monthly. In the past, other formations have been important: for instance, the then Council of Internal Market Ministers (now the Competitiveness Council) during the single-market programme in the late 1980s and early 1990s (see Chapter 27, p. 386).

Table 21.1 Formations of the Council of Ministers, 2010

(Includes areas of responsibility where these are not clear from the title)

- **General Affairs**: cross-cutting issues such as enlargement and multi-annual financing, plus preparation for, and follow-up of, European Council meetings
- **Foreign Affairs**: CFSP and ESDP, trade policy, development co-operation
- **Economic and Financial Affairs**: economic policy co-ordination, monitoring of member states' budgetary policy and public finances, financial markets and capital movements, and economic relations with third countries
- **Justice and Home Affairs**: the area of freedom, security, and justice (AFSJ)
- **Employment, Social Policy, Health and Consumer Affairs**: also includes equal opportunities
- **Competitiveness**: internal market, industry, and research
- **Transport, Telecommunications, and Energy**
- **Agriculture and Fisheries**
- **Environment**
- **Education, Youth, and Culture**

ECOFIN meetings are important in the Council's informal 'pecking order' because of the importance and centrality of their subject matter. This position was enhanced in the late 1990s because the issue of monetary union dominated the agenda of the EU. The start of the single currency (the euro) on 1 January 1999 complicated the institutional position because, since then, the Finance Ministers from those member states that are also members of the eurozone have met prior to the full meetings of ECOFIN to discuss single-currency matters. The existence of this Euro Group was formally recognized in a Protocol attached to the Lisbon Treaty. It is chaired by its own President, elected for a two-and-a-half year term from amongst the national Economic and Finance Ministers. Meetings of ECOFIN are prepared by three specialist groups—the Economic and Financial Committee; the Economic Policy Committee; and the Budget Committee—depending on the agenda issues.

The Agfish Council also has a privileged status because of the importance of agriculture to the EU, although this position has been scaled back in relative terms due to the rise of other policy areas. Agfish business is prepared by the Special Committee on Agriculture (SCA), the work of which becomes especially intensive at the time of the annual fixing of agricultural prices in the first half of each year.

The importance of the other Councils can be regarded as a function of two factors: first, the extent of EU competence (see Insight 19.1); and second, the intensity of policy activity. Thus a Council formation such as Education, Youth, and Culture, in which the EU has only supporting competences, does not carry the 'clout' of the Competitiveness Council, which covers important economic issues over which the EU has greater authority. The frequency of meetings varies considerably, although most of the sectoral councils meet between twice and four or five times a year (Hayes-Renshaw and Wallace 2006: 38–9; Bulmer and Burch 2009: 55–6).

The functions of the Council are characterized by Hayes-Renshaw and Wallace (2006: 323–7) as being legislature, executive, setter of guidelines, and forum. The Council's role as legislature was set out in Chapter 18. The Lisbon Treaty formalized a practice whereby the Council meets in public when voting on a legislative act (Article 15 TFEU). The executive function relates to where the Council takes decisions that are not legislative in character. This is most obviously the case in CFSP, but is also applicable, for instance, in some of the work of ECOFIN and the Euro Group. Although the European Council has tended to set policy guidelines, there are some policy areas in which the Council steers the course of policy, such as overseeing the details of enlargement negotiations. This function is particularly associated with the GAC. Finally, the Council serves as a forum in those policy areas in which member state policy is being co-ordinated. The growth of this pattern of governance—known as the Open Method of Co-ordination (OMC)—in the last decade or so has increased this 'forum' function for the Council (on the OMC, see Chapter 25, pp. 363–4).

Voting rules were discussed in Chapter 19. As noted there, the practice of QMV is much less than the formal provision for it. Even though one of the rationales for making greater provision for QMV was in order that an enlarged EU of twenty-seven would still be able to take decisions efficiently, initial findings were rather ambiguous as to whether the 2004 enlargement had affected the decision-making efficiency of the Council of Ministers (Hagemann and De Clerck-Sachsse 2007).

A Purely Intergovernmental Institution?

Fritz Scharpf (1989) contrasted 'problem solving' and 'bargaining' as modes of negotiation within the EC. His distinction at least partly corresponds to the differences between theorists about how to understand the operation of the Council. For intergovernmentalists, the Council is simply 'a forum for hard bargaining' (Lewis 1998: 479; 2000: 261). For those who adopt a more supranational perspective, combined with a social constructivist theoretical position (see Chapter 3, pp. 40–2), bargaining takes place between actors whose positions are influenced, at least partially, by their social interaction with their ministerial colleagues from other member states; 'communicative rationality' is at least as important as 'instrumental rationality', which means that the discussion is about how to find a solution to common problems rather than just playing a negotiating game to win, and there is an instinct to proceed consensually (Lewis 1998: 480–81).

The hypotheses that these theories generate are fairly clear. If the supranational theorists are correct, one would expect to find more collegiality, and a discourse more oriented to joint problem solving, in Councils that meet more frequently than in those that meet less frequently, and also in the more technical Councils rather than in the more political Councils (although deciding what is technical and what is political is notoriously difficult).

The extent to which ministers meeting in the different Councils engage in hard-headed intergovernmental bargaining, or adopt a more supranational approach, is difficult to research. Perhaps the requirement for legislative decisions to be taken in public will enable observation of ministers' behaviour, but much of the Council's work—not to mention the work of its preparatory bodies—continues to be held in private.

One particularly interesting research finding in this respect is that very few issues are actually decided by the ministers themselves. Taking data from 2004, Hayes-Renshaw and Wallace (2006: 53) calculated that 78 per cent of all Council decisions were A-points: that is, where ministers rubber-stamp decisions taken lower down the Council hierarchy. (B-points are those in which ministers themselves need to reach political agreement, but which issue may then be referred back to the preparatory bodies for the details to be negotiated.)

COREPER and other Preparatory Bodies

There are three levels of committee considered in this section: COREPER, which is the formal filter beneath the Council; a group of high-level preparatory bodies, such as the Political and Security Committee (PSC), which is responsible for CFSP and European Security and Defence Policy (ESDP) co-ordination; and, beneath them, over 150 Council working parties, some with sub-committees (see Council of the EU 2009a).

Although it formally only prepares the agenda and meetings of the Council, COREPER has a great deal of discretion about what it classifies as A-points or B-points on the agenda. So although COREPER and the working groups formally prepare the meetings of the ministers, in one sense the ministers can be said to set the agenda for the meetings of the committees. This is the case where an issue has been discussed at ministerial level, and broad consensus has been reached, but the issue is then referred back down the hierarchy for the detail to be filled in.

COREPER

The Permanent Representatives are the ambassadors from the member states to the EU. Each heads up what is officially an embassy to the EU. They perform some formal functions in Brussels, but their main task is to co-ordinate the work of the various committees that meet under the banner of the Council of Ministers. Where possible, they negotiate an agreement arising from the work undertaken by the committees ahead of a meeting of the Council of Ministers. This they do in the context of COREPER.

COREPER meets at least weekly at ambassador level as COREPER II, and at deputy level as COREPER I. Both prepare the agendas of meetings of the Councils of Ministers. COREPER II is responsible for the agendas for meetings of the GAC, the Foreign Affairs Council, and ECOFIN. COREPER I is responsible for the agendas of all other Councils. It is worth noting that two bodies, the SCA and the PSC, more or less substitute for the role of COREPER in the specific domains of agriculture and CFSP/ESDP respectively. The Antici Group of officials, named after the Italian official who was the chair of the first such group, assists COREPER and the GAC in preparing the European Council.

All studies of COREPER indicate that its members consider themselves to have a dual role. According to Hayes-Renshaw et al. (1989: 136), while the Permanent Representatives 'are the trustworthy executors of the instructions from their respective capitals', they also have strong ties of solidarity with their colleagues in COREPER.

These ties are developed as a result of intensive social interaction in Brussels. Committee members eat, drink, and breathe EU issues seven days a week. Lewis (1998: 487) argued that this constant interaction between the same individuals built up a considerable legacy of 'social capital', meaning that the individuals concerned trust one another, and understand and have sympathy for each other's points of view.

The ties are also the result of all of the Permanent Representatives being in the same position vis-à-vis their national governments. All of them will have sympathy with one of their number who is bound by a tight mandate on a particular issue, because they are sometimes placed in that position themselves. In such a situation, they will try to help each other out, perhaps by persuading their own government to make concessions if they feel that the issue is not so important for them. The attitude of the Permanent Representatives to a negotiation is ambivalent: they all want their government's position to prevail; they also want to reach agreement even at the cost of not achieving all of their own government's objectives in the negotiation (Hayes-Renshaw et al. 1989: 136).

One explanation of this approach is based on rational choice and game theory. It is also compatible with an intergovernmental-bargaining image of the committee. On this view, when Permanent Representatives make concessions, or urge their governments to make concessions, it is not just because they feel a sense of social solidarity with their counterparts from other member states. It is also indicative of the strong sense that they have of being involved in a continuous process of bargaining with the same partners. In the language of game theory, they are involved in *iterated* games (that is, the same game is repeated several times with the same participants). This changes the calculation of what is rational as compared with isolated games. In a one-off game, it is rational to take any step to damage your opponent's position and to further your own, even so far as cheating on the rules if you can get away with it. In iterated games, the use of such tactics is likely to backfire during a subsequent round. If you have reneged on a deal in one round of negotiations, it will be difficult to get anyone to conclude a deal with you in subsequent rounds.

This logic of iterated games in EU bargaining is more apparent to Permanent Representatives than it sometimes is to ministers, who have many other concerns, such as accounting for their Brussels diplomacy to their national parliaments and cabinet colleagues, and are less intensively socialized into the **Union method** of bargaining. It means that Permanent Representatives are often involved in trying to educate their governments about the nature of the EU bargaining process. The German Permanent Representative is sometimes jokingly referred to in the national capital as the *ständiger Verräter* (permanent traitor) rather than the official designation as *ständiger Vertreter* (Permanent Representative) (see Barber 1995: I; Lewis 1998: 483). Although this sort of suspicion may occasionally exist in national capitals, it would be a foolish government that did not listen seriously to the advice of the Permanent Representative when deciding on its national negotiating position. This could be taken as evidence that the intergovernmentalist view, that national preferences are formulated independently of influence from the EU level, is false.

Another explanation of the approach of COREPER, which also challenges the intergovernmentalist view, is based on social constructivism. Lewis (2000) identified five main features of the operation of COREPER that resulted from the circumstances and socialization processes identified above. He labelled these: diffuse reciprocity; thick trust; mutual responsiveness; a consensus-reflex; and a culture of compromise.

- *Diffuse reciprocity* means that the Permanent Representatives will support one of their number on an issue that is important to that individual's member state but less important to their own, and in return will expect to receive such support when they themselves have a problem. This is not the same as the sort of formal agreement that is allowed for in rational-choice bargains, in which deals are done that A will support B on issue C in return for the support of B on issue D. The reciprocity is diffuse, not specific. It relates to the collectivity of COREPER across the whole range of issues.

- *Thick trust*—as opposed to 'thin trust'—means that the Permanent Representatives feel that they can be honest and open with one another without anything that they say being reported back to other governments. In restricted sessions, they feel that they speak freely, knowing that what they say will not come out.

- *Mutual responsiveness* means that the Permanent Representatives, because they work together so closely, come to understand one another's perspectives and problems, and will try not to approach an issue in a way that they know will cause problems for other members of COREPER.

- The *consensus-reflex* is deeply embedded in the culture of COREPER. Although there is provision for QMV where the Treaty specifies, it is not used extensively, and is always the last resort. COREPER will continue to seek a consensus long after it is apparent that a qualified majority could be mustered if a vote were called.

- The *culture of compromise* arises from a spirit of accommodation that brings together the previous features. Lewis (2000: 271) refers to the permanent representatives spending extra time to 'bring everyone on board' even if one member state is being inflexible in its position.

High-Level Preparatory Bodies

There are several of these high-level preparatory bodies. Some have been mentioned already: the three that prepare ECOFIN; the SCA in agricultural policy; and the PSC as one of the preparatory bodies for the Foreign Affairs Council. Two other bodies prepare the Foreign Affairs Council: the Article 207 Committee, which deals with the common commercial policy, and the EU Military Committee, which is responsible for ESDP and which may be attended by the chiefs of military staff of the member states, but is more likely to be attended by Brussels-based military attachés.

Lewis (2000) went on to ask whether the pattern of socialization applied to these bodies as with COREPER. He surveyed six of these preparatory bodies, which correspond to the present-day SCA, Article 207 Committee, the Budget Committee, the Economic and Finance Committee (EFC), the PSC, and the K-4 Committee (a co-ordinating body for Justice and Home Affairs that was later split up). The conclusion of this investigation (Lewis 2000: 282) was that only the EFC came close to exhibiting the five features to anything like the same extent as COREPER. This weakened somewhat the thrust of the supranationalist argument, but not the validity of the social constructivist approach, because the empirical findings underlined the need to investigate the 'sociality and normative environment in which interests are defined and defended' (Lewis 2003*b*: 262). Lewis's research was pioneering in highlighting the socialization effects, but the data are now from over a decade ago and a re-examination of these findings is overdue.

The Working Parties

Moving further down the hierarchy, the working parties that prepare recommendations for the Permanent Representatives involve intensive interaction between national and Commission officials. The processes of socialization that Lewis and others argued apply to COREPER also apply here. Although the people who sit on these committees are national representatives, research by Beyers and Dierickx (1998: 307–8) showed that members of working groups soon started to judge other members on the basis of the level of expertise that they showed in the committee rather than on nationality. Ludlow (1991: 103) went further to argue that 'Commission officials act as thirteenth members of the Council machinery', implying that the distinction between national and Commission representatives was almost meaningless in the work of these groups.

The thrust of all of these arguments is that the members of the working parties develop a sense of collegiality and engagement in a joint enterprise that makes it more sensible to see them as individuals participating in a team effort than as representatives of individual states. Here, we are operating very much at the 'problem-solving' end of Scharpf's spectrum of types of negotiation. Agreements are reached largely on the basis of convincing arguments, not political weight or bargaining skill.

The Council Presidency

Under the original Treaty provisions, a different member state assumed the presidency of the Council every six months. During its period of office, that member state had responsibility for preparing and chairing meetings of the European Council, the Council of Ministers and its various committees, as well as for some functions of representing the EU externally. In the course of its six months in charge, the presidency arranged and chaired from seventy to ninety meetings of ministers, and many more times that of committees. In addition, at least one European Council meeting fell during the six months' presidency. Although assisted in this considerable task by the Council Secretariat (see Insight 21.3), the civil service of the state holding the presidency carried much of the burden of this work. Some authors, for instance Tallberg (2003), argued that states holding the presidency were able to advance their interests during their term in charge of the EU's agenda.

This system was subject to two main criticisms: that six months was too brief a period for the tenure of the presidency; and that the scale of demands on the country holding the presidency had outstripped the capacity of all but the largest member states to cope (for analysis of the old system, see Hayes-Renshaw and Wallace 2006: 154–7). The increasing range of policy areas from the 1980s simply added additional activities

Insight 21.3 The Council General Secretariat

- According to Lewis (2010), the Council Secretariat employs about 3,300 people. A tenth of these are at the senior A grade. It is the 'institutional memory' of the Council of Ministers and assists with the organization of meetings, and can help with mediating between national delegations. It is based in Brussels in the Justus Lipsius building.

- The two most senior positions were, until recently, the post of Secretary-General and High Representative and the Deputy Secretary-General. The former position was held by Javier Solana from 1999 to 2009. The appointment of Catherine Ashton to an enhanced position that straddles both the Commission and the Council resulted in change at the top of the Council Secretariat.

- The Council Secretariat has a Legal Service as well as over 1,000 translators. Interpreters are drawn from the European Commission's staff. There are currently eight Directorates-General (DGs). The DG for External and Political-Military Affairs will become integrated into the new European External Action Service, which will also encompass staff from DG RELEX in the Commission.

- Also situated under the auspices of the Council Secretariat is the EU's Military Staff (EUMS), which oversees ESDP activities, and is headed by a three-star general. Within the EUMS, there are several Directorates responsible for such functions as intelligence, operations and logistics. The operations function includes provision of a Council facility, the EU Operations Centre, which can command small operations of up to 2,000 troops anywhere in the world. Twenty-four military or civilian operations had been conducted (or were under way) under the auspices of the ESDP by February 2010, so the role of the EUMS is very important.

for the presidency to prepare. The enlargements of 2004 and 2007 added medium-sized states, small states, and micro-states to the EU, and new arrangements were deemed necessary, although the protracted period of constitutional reform meant that some of the new states had held the presidency under the old rules before the new ones came into effect.

The new, post-Lisbon system comprises four different presidencies:

- the European Council—an appointment for two-and-a-half years, this arrangement is consistent with the European Council being designated a separate institution;

- the Council of Foreign Affairs, chaired by the High Representative for Foreign Affairs and Security Policy (a five-year appointment) (from January 2010 Catherine Ashton);

- the Euro Group, which comprises only states in the eurozone, elects its own president to a two-and-a-half-year term; already serving in this position since 2005, Jean-Claude Juncker was re-elected under the new arrangements in January 2010;

- a 'trio presidency' of three member states, which spans an eighteen-month period, and is responsible for other sectoral Councils and their preparatory bodies.

The trio system had, in fact, commenced in 2007 after reform to the Council's rules of procedure. The Lisbon Treaty merely formalized this change, and there was no obvious change after the Treaty's implementation apart from the change in countries involved. The first post-Lisbon trio presidency consisted of Spain, Belgium, and Hungary, with Spain taking the lead for the first six months of 2010. However, there had already been co-operation between the preceding three presidencies under the old system (France, the Czech Republic, and Sweden), such co-operation having been first established in 2003 (Hayes-Renshaw and Wallace 2006: 16).

CONCLUSION

The European Council and the Council of Ministers are quite different institutions and with different paths of development. The European Council is of central importance to the 'high politics' of the EU, while the Council of Ministers is central to decision making and legislation. The European Council has moved from the informality of the 'Library Group' to an institution in its own right. The Council of Ministers has gradually become more of a co-legislator as the powers of the EP have increased (see Chapter 22). Like the Council of Ministers, the European Council holds occasional informal sessions to try to attain some of the advantages of the less-structured organization of the past. The Spanish presidency programme for the first half of 2010 had scheduled no fewer than twenty informal meetings of the Council of Ministers! Formal sessions of the Council of Ministers are reported as having to take place with camera and screen facilities so that the speakers can be identified in a chamber comprising twenty-seven delegations (plus the presidency, the Commission, the Council Secretariat, and interpreters), each being permitted a minister and at least one official. In other words, meetings are typically attended by over a hundred participants. Indeed, the increased size of the Council may reduce the socialization effects reported in earlier research. It may also be that the Lisbon Treaty's strengthened provisions for enhanced co-operation will lead to greater use of pioneer groups of like-minded states (see Chapter 19, pp. 250–1). These are amongst the research agendas for the future.

At first sight, it would appear obvious that the Council of Ministers is an intergovernmental organization. However, this is a simplification of a complex situation. First, it is clear that the Council of Ministers as a collective entity is a **supranational institution**, because it can and does agree to legislation that is then binding on all of the member states. Second, it is not clear that the Council of Ministers, in all of its manifestations, operates simply as an intergovernmental bargaining forum. Wessels (1991: 136) insisted that 'the Council is not an "interstate body"... but a body at the supranational level'. Hayes-Renshaw and Wallace (1997: 278) were less sure of that, but were clear that it was 'not a wholly "intergovernmental" institution'. As they put it:

> For the analyst the Council and its processes embody the recurrent tension in the construction of the EC between the 'supranationalists' and the 'intergovernmentalists'.

(Hayes-Renshaw and Wallace 2006: 2–3)

To try to analyse the role of the Council of Ministers as a whole would be a mistake. It is important to disaggregate its component parts in order to understand at exactly which point in the machinery issues are dealt with. Only with this knowledge can an informed judgement be made concerning the key actors involved and their motivations. Even then, the task is complicated by the secrecy that surrounds the activity of the Council in virtually all of its manifestations. The holding of open sessions when passing legislative acts—as formalized in the Lisbon Treaty—may simply transfer the secrecy to other venues or to other parts of Council sessions.

Here it is worth noting the provisions in Article 16 TEU, that 'each Council meeting shall be divided into two parts, dealing respectively with deliberations on Union legislative acts and non-legislative activities'.

The most informed research suggests that a high proportion of Council of Ministers', decisions are taken relatively low down in the decisional hierarchy. It is here, within COREPER and the preparatory bodies, that observers have found the greatest departure from intergovernmentalism in Council activities. At the ministerial level, decisions tend to be more politicized and national positions less open to negotiation. However, to complicate matters further, anecdotal evidence suggests that, even at the ministerial level, some formations of the Council are more collegial than others. Lewis (2000) also concluded that there is considerable variation in the degree of collegiality exhibited by the senior preparatory committees. The conclusion must be, therefore, that the argument between intergovernmental and supranational theorists cannot be settled finally so far as the Council is concerned, but that there are some grounds for not assuming too readily that because the Council is the institution in which the governments of member states are most directly represented, it is necessarily an intergovernmental body. The increasing provision for decision making in the Council of Ministers by QMV is a further dimension to any departure from pure intergovernmentalism, since even the provision—if not the practice—can result in a shift in the calculation of national interests.

The other theoretical debate around the Council of Ministers concerns whether to approach it using the techniques of rational choice institutionalism and game theory, or whether to understand it as a case study in social constructivism. To some extent, this division corresponds with the division between intergovernmental and supranational theories of the nature of the Council of Ministers. Intergovernmentalists tend to favour rationalist approaches to understanding its workings because they see it as a forum for hard bargaining around national interests, and it is in understanding the operation of such forums that rational choice and game theory have made some of their biggest contributions. Supranationalists tend to rest their arguments on evidence that the representatives of the member states on the various committees and Council of Ministers formations become socialized into a different construction of what they are trying to achieve from a simple defence of national interests, and into informally institutionalized procedures that emphasize consensus and co-operation rather than instrumental bargaining. However, it is possible to accept a social constructivist **epistemology** and still come to the conclusion on the basis of empirical evidence that the socialization process does not operate very effectively in some of the committees and some of the manifestations of the Council.

KEY POINTS

The European Council

- The European Council was established in the 1970s to provide a collective response to the challenges of economic interdependence, to allow national governments collectively to control the direction of the EC, to avoid policy segmentation, and to present a united front to the outside world.

- The functions of the European Council now include: to provide general direction to the EU; to oversee Treaty reform and enlargement; to make key foreign policy decisions; to act as policy maker of last resort; and to monitor the development of certain policies.

- The European Council faces problems of overload, over-optimism, overcautiousness, and over-expectation.

- The European Council's work has arguably resulted in it increasing the supranational character of the EU.

The Council of Ministers

- The Council of Ministers meets in a variety of formations depending on the subject under consideration.
- Although there is no formal hierarchy of Council meetings, informally the GAC and those sectoral Councils concerning foreign affairs, finance, and agriculture have the highest status.
- The frequency with which ministers meet in sectoral Councils can lead to the emergence of a sense of collective enterprise, marked by communicative rationality rather than instrumental rationality.
- Because of the secrecy in which the Council of Ministers meets, it is difficult to research the degree to which individual Councils engage in problem solving rather than bargaining around national interests.

COREPER and other Preparatory Bodies

- A large proportion of 'Council' decisions are actually taken lower down the decisional hierarchy. Arguments that the Council is a supranational entity are strongest at this level.
- The Permanent Representatives of member governments interact regularly and develop trust and solidarity, which makes agreement between them easier than between politicians who are less regularly engaged and who have broader concerns.
- The operation of COREPER can be explained either from a rational choice bargaining perspective as the behaviour appropriate to actors involved in iterated games, or from a social constructivist perspective as the building of a new sense of identity among the Permanent Representatives.
- Other senior preparatory bodies have not achieved the same degree of trust and solidarity as COREPER, with the exception of the Economic and Financial Committee.
- National representatives on working parties also undergo a process of socialization that produces a problem-solving approach in which decisions are taken more on the strength of evidence than of political considerations.

The Council Presidency

- Originally, the Council presidency applied to all levels of the hierarchy and rotated between member states every six months. This system was criticized on the grounds of brevity of tenure and for the scale of the demands that it placed on smaller member states.
- Following the Lisbon Treaty's implementation, the European Council has its own President, as does the Council of Foreign Affairs and the Euro Group. All other business is run by 'trio presidencies' comprising three states over a period of eighteen months.

FURTHER READING

Caution has to be exercised with recommending further reading because of the important changes brought about by the Lisbon Treaty, and which are scarcely covered beyond the EU institutions' websites as yet. An extremely comprehensive treatment of the functioning of the Council, which remains a standard work on the subject, is **F. Hayes-Renshaw and H. Wallace**, *The Council of Ministers*, 2nd edn (Basingstoke: Palgrave Macmillan, 2006). **M. Westlake and D. Galloway (eds)**, *The Council of the European Union*, 3rd edn (London: John Harper Publishing, 2004) is a less academic guide, written by knowledgeable Brussels insiders. Also recommended is **J. Lewis**, 'Institutional Environments and Everyday EU Decision Making: Rationalist or Constructivist?' *Comparative Political Studies*, 36 (2003): 97–124.

An early assessment of the strengths and weaknesses of the institutionalized summit meetings, which remains relevant, is in **S. Bulmer and W. Wessels**, *The European Council: Decision-Making in European Politics* (Basingstoke and London: Macmillan, 1987). A more recent study is that by **J. Werts**, *The European Council* (London: John Harper, 2008).

Finally, the European Council (by **de Schoutheete**), the Council of Ministers (by **Hayes-Renshaw**) and COREPER (by **Lewis**) are each given chapter-length consideration in **J. Peterson and M. Shackleton (eds)**, *The Institutions of the European Union*, 2nd edn (Oxford: Oxford University Press, 2006).

 online resource centre   **Visit the Online Resource Centre that accompanies this book for links to more information on the Council: www.oxfordtextbooks.co.uk/orc/bache3e/**

Chapter 22

The European Parliament

Chapter Overview

The European Parliament (EP) is the one directly elected institution of the European Union (EU). The members of the EP (MEPs) are elected once every five years, and since the first direct elections in 1979, the EP has campaigned for more power and influence. Over the subsequent period, there has been a considerable increase in its powers, including through the Lisbon Treaty. The struggle for increased powers is discussed in more detail below, after the basic structure and functions of the EP have been summarized. The chapter then turns to look at debates and research on the EP. One theme of the academic debate is the extent to which the EP has become an effective independent actor in the affairs of the EU, and how far it will continue to move in that direction in the future. This clearly parallels the discussion in the previous two chapters, on the Commission and the Council.

... of all the EU's institutions, the EP has come furthest and fastest in the enhancement of its role and powers since what was, in many respects, a 'standing start' after the first direct European elections in 1979.

(Judge and Earnshaw 2008: 1)

Composition and Functions

The EP, as elected in 2009, consisted of 736 MEPs, divided between the member states on a basis that is approximately proportionate to size of population, although the small countries are somewhat over-represented to strengthen their voice. The distribution of the 736 seats following the 2009 election is shown in Table 22.1. Confusingly, the Lisbon Treaty provided for 751 MEPs. This confusion came about because the Lisbon Treaty was originally expected to be in force before the 2009 elections. Moreover, as Germany would lose three seats in the new share-out, it was agreed that its members could continue to serve the current term, thereby creating an EP of 754 members until the next elections in 2014. In the meantime, the institutions were elaborating a process to introduce the additional eighteen MEPs in the middle of a parliamentary term.

Table 22.1 Distribution of Seats in the European Parliament

Austria	17 (19)	Germany	99 (96)	Netherlands	25 (26)
Belgium	22	Greece	22	Poland	50 (51)
Bulgaria	17 (18)	Hungary	22	Portugal	22
Cyprus	6	Ireland	12	Romania	33
Czech Republic	22	Italy	72 (73)	Slovakia	13
Denmark	13	Latvia	8 (9)	Slovenia	7 (8)
Estonia	6	Lithuania	12	Spain	50 (54)
Finland	13	Luxembourg	6	Sweden	18 (20)
France	72 (74)	Malta	5 (6)	United Kingdom	72 (73)
TOTAL (2009)	**736**	**TOTAL LISBON TREATY**	**751**	**COMPROMISE TOTAL UNTIL 2014**	**754**

Note: Figures in parentheses indicate the revised distribution provided for under the Lisbon Treaty. Eighteen additional MEPs are to be elected under a procedure being discussed in 2010. The reduction in number of German MEPs will not take effect until the 2014 elections.

The EP meets in plenary session in Strasbourg for three or four days every month, except August, and additional plenaries are held in Brussels. However, most of its work is channelled through twenty standing committees (Table 22.2). It can also establish temporary committees (a special committee on the Financial, Economic, and Social Crisis was meeting in 2009–10) and committees of enquiry. Committee meetings are normally held in Brussels.

The EP has a President, a Bureau, a Conference of Presidents, and a Secretariat. The President is elected by the MEPs from among their number for a two-and-a-half-year renewable term. The President represents the EP on official occasions, and in relations with other institutions, presides over debates during plenary sessions, and chairs meetings of the Bureau and the Conference of Presidents. The Bureau consists of the President, the fourteen Vice-Presidents, and five 'quaestors' who deal with administrative and financial matters relating to MEPs. The members are elected by the MEPs for a term of two-and-a-half years. The Conference of Presidents consists of the President and the Chairs of the Political Groups. It draws up the agenda for plenary sessions, fixes the timetable for the work of parliamentary bodies, and establishes the terms of reference and size of parliamentary committees and delegations. The Secretariat consists of over 5,000 administrative and clerical staff, headed by the Secretary-General (Judge and Earnshaw 2008: 166). Around one-third of the staff are in the language service, concerned with translation and interpretation. In addition to the Secretariat, the political groups have their own administrative support.

The powers of the EP are summarized in Insight 22.1. It has legislative, budgetary, and supervisory functions. In the legislative field, it has emerged as a co-legislator with the Council of Ministers in most areas of EU legislation primarily via the ordinary legislative procedure (co-decision), which applies to over eighty specific provisions in the Treaty on the Functioning of the European Union (TFEU). The various legislative procedures, and the powers of the EP in each of them, are discussed in Chapter 19,

Table 22.2 Committees of the European Parliament (as of 2010)

- Foreign Affairs Committee
  — Security and Defence Sub-Committee
  — Human Rights Sub-Committee
- Budgets Committee
- Budgetary Control Committee
- Civil Liberties, Justice and Home Affairs Committee
- Economic and Monetary Affairs Committee
- Legal Affairs Committee
- Internal Market and Consumer Protection Committee
- International Trade Committee
- Industry, Research and Energy Committee
- Employment and Social Affairs Committee
- Environment, Public Health and Food Safety Committee
- Agriculture and Rural Development Committee
- Fisheries Committee
- Regional Development Committee
- Transport and Tourism Committee
- Culture and Education Committee
- Development Committee
- Constitutional Affairs Committee
- Women's Rights and Gender Equality Committee
- Petitions Committee

pp. 239–43. The EP and the Council of Ministers are the joint budgetary authorities of the EU. The budgetary procedure, and the role of the EP in it, is described in Chapter 19, pp. 236–9.

The supervisory functions of the EP relate to both the Commission and the Council. Under the Maastricht Treaty, the EP was given the right to approve appointment of the President and members of the Commission. The Treaty of Amsterdam strengthened the power relating to the President, who needed specific approval by the EP. Under the Lisbon Treaty, the candidate for the presidency has to be chosen taking into account the results of the most recent EP elections. The EP has the power to dismiss the whole of the Commission on a vote of censure—but in neither case can it target individual Commissioners. A motion of censure requires a positive vote from an absolute majority of MEPs and two-thirds of the votes cast. The EP also has the right to ask the Commission written and oral questions.

In respect to the European Council and the Council of Ministers, the powers of the EP are more limited. It can table written and oral questions about the activities of the

Insight 22.1 The Powers of the European Parliament

Legislative

- Under the ordinary legislative procedure, the EP shares final decision on most proposals with the Council (co-decision procedure).
- Consent is required for the enlargement of the European Union, agreements with third countries, and a range of other decisions.
- It delivers opinions on Commission proposals under the consultation procedure in a limited number of policy areas.

Budgetary

- Its approval is required for the annual budget.
- Its Budgetary Control Committee checks expenditure (together with the Court of Auditors).

Supervisory

- It approves the appointment of Commission President.
- It approves the appointment of the Commission after public hearings.
- It questions the Council and Commission.
- It can censure and dismiss the whole Commission.

Council of Ministers, and the Foreign Minister of the state holding the presidency of the Council reports to the EP at the beginning and end of the presidency. For the European Council, the Lisbon Treaty (Article 15 TEU) formalized the practice whereby the EP is given a report following each European Council meeting. This report is given by the President of the European Council. Since the Lisbon Treaty came into effect, this report has been given by Mr Van Rompuy, who was appointed to the post for two-and-a-half years from the start of 2010, but, prior to that, was given by the head of government of the state holding the six-month presidency. The President of the EP is invited to the start of European Council sessions 'to be heard' (Article 235 TFEU) but does not participate in its meetings after this opening opportunity to make a contribution.

Outside the 'Union method', the EP is to be kept informed of developments relating to the Common Foreign and Security Policy (CFSP) and the Parliament's views are to be taken into consideration. With the implementation of the Lisbon Treaty, the responsibility for relations with the EP moved from the Foreign Minister of the state holding the presidency to the new position of High Representative of the Union for Foreign Affairs and Security Policy (HRUFASP). As this position is a joint one of the Council and Commission, the EP may have slightly more leverage, since it had to approve Catherine Ashton's appointment as HRUFASP as part of the investiture of the Commission.

The Struggle for Power

In the original Treaties, the forerunner of the present EP was neither directly elected nor endowed with significant powers. Members of the European Parliamentary Assembly (EPA) were members of national parliaments who were seconded to the EPA. They were full-time national MPs and part-time European MPs. The EPA had the right to be consulted by the Council of Ministers before legislation was agreed, but its opinion could be, and frequently was ignored; it could dismiss the Commission as a whole on a vote of censure, but only if it could achieve the difficult degree of unity needed to reach the double majority requirement (two-thirds of those voting, constituting an absolute majority of members). From the outset, though, the EPA set about trying to extract the right to be directly elected, and to have stronger powers.

The main steps in the transformation of the weak EPA into the much stronger EP were listed by Corbett, Jacobs, and Shackleton (2003: 354) as:

> the budget Treaties of 1970 and 1975; the introduction of direct elections by universal suffrage in 1979; the 1980 *Isoglucose* ruling of the European Court of Justice, giving Parliament a *de facto* delaying power; the Single European Act in 1987, introducing the co-operation procedure and the assent procedure; the Treaty of Maastricht in 1993, bringing in the co-decision procedure, and giving Parliament the right to allow (or not) the Commission as a whole to take office through a vote of confidence; and the Treaty of Amsterdam, which greatly extended the scope of co-decision, modified it to Parliament's advantage, and gave Parliament the right to confirm or reject a designated President of the Commission.

To this list must now be added the further reforms introduced by the Lisbon Treaty, which greatly extended the scope of co-decision, while renaming assent as the consent procedure (see Chapter 19, pp. 239–43).

In achieving these gains, the EP has used a number of tactical devices. First, most of its members have acted as an interest group pressing for increased powers for the EP within their national parties. Here, the most significant step forward was the introduction of direct elections. Direct elections 'created a new class of elected representatives in Europe ... whose career depended on making something of the European dimension' (Corbett, Jacobs, and Shackleton 2003: 356). Second, the argument that the powers of the EP needed to be increased in order to close the 'democratic deficit' has been consistently used by the EP. The academic debate about the democratic and legitimacy deficits is reviewed in Chapter 4 (pp. 66–75). Third, it has made the most extensive use possible of its existing powers, and tried to stretch the definition of those powers. In this, the EP sometimes found an ally in the European Court of Justice (ECJ). A number of judgments of the ECJ, on cases brought to it by the EP, have given a more far-reaching interpretation of the constitutional powers of the EP than the member states had foreseen, starting with the 1980 *Isoglucose* judgment. These judgments are examined in Chapter 23 (pp. 317–20). Alongside this 'minimalist' approach, the EP has also pursued a 'maximalist' approach. In 1984, the EP, under the leadership of the Italian federalist MEP Altiero Spinelli, produced its draft Treaty Establishing the European Union. It had little influence on the shape of the EU at the time, but set out the EP's maximalist approach and provided inspiration for some of the changes introduced by the member states in later Treaty reforms. During the Constitutional Convention of 2002–03, sixteen MEPs participated in the drafting of what became the Constitutional Treaty (see Chapter 17, pp. 195–7).

In what follows, the powers of EP and how they were gained are discussed in more or less the order that they were granted. The grant of additional budgetary powers came before direct elections, but so fundamental were direct elections to the use that could be made of those powers that direct elections are discussed first, then the budgetary powers. Then the increased legislative and scrutiny powers are considered. The discussion of the rulings of the ECJ comes in the next chapter (pp. 317–20).

Direct Elections

Agreement to replace the EPA with a directly elected body was reached at the Rome meeting of the European Council in December 1975. Why was this decision taken— and what were its consequences?

The decision took place in a less-than-transparent deal amongst the heads of government in the European Council. Germany, Italy, and the **Benelux** countries had long favoured a directly elected EP. The governments of these states were convinced by the argument that transferring competences to the EC would lead to a democratic deficit unless there were a directly elected parliament at that level that could take over the role of scrutiny that would be lost to national parliaments. The crucial shift was on the part of France, probably for domestic political reasons, under the presidency of Valéry Giscard d'Estaing, the first President of the Fifth Republic not to belong to the Gaullist Party (Bache and George 2006: 299).

This shift in position placed Britain, which was even more reluctant, in a more isolated position. Having agreed to the elections, the Labour government, which was contending with divisions in its own party and was reliant on support from the Liberal Party to stay in office, caused delay to the implementation arrangements (Bache and George 2006: 299–300). Consequently, the first elections were put back a year, until June 1979. The first directly elected Parliament sought to exploit its new democratic credentials by several routes. It challenged the Council of Ministers over the annual budget. It was also emboldened to demand more powers of decision making and control over the Commission.

Budgetary Powers

The first grant of additional powers to the EP came in the Treaty of Luxembourg in 1970, when it was given the right to amend 'non-compulsory' items of expenditure in the budget. This agreement was the outcome of an intergovernmental negotiation about the settlement of the long-running budgetary dispute that had led to the 1965 crisis (Chapter 9, pp. 128–9). France continued to be reluctant to grant any budgetary powers to the still indirectly elected EPA at that time, but President Pompidou was anxious to get the system of 'own resources' agreed prior to the opening of entry negotiations with Britain. For France, the goal was to set up a budgetary system to fund the Common Agricultural Policy (CAP) in a way that would leave France a large net beneficiary from the system. As Britain would inevitably lose out from such a system, agreement could not be left until after British entry because the British government would block any such settlement. However, the other five member states insisted that the loss of parliamentary control over national budgetary contributions must be redressed by an increase in the control of the EPA. As with all such inter-governmental negotiations, the outcome was a compromise.

> A distinction introduced by the French between expenditure items that followed directly from Community legal acts (compulsory expenditure) and expenditure that did not, such as administrative expenses (non-compulsory expenditure), was accepted, albeit grudgingly by some delegations (the Dutch delegation most notably) as it gave the EP a final say over only about 4–5 per cent of the entire Community expenditure (that is, non-compulsory expenditure).

(Rittberger 2003: 217)

Subsequently, in the 1975 Budget Treaty, the EP was granted the formal right to reject the budget as a whole. Working with these limited powers, the EP pushed its budgetary role to the maximum, especially after the first direct elections in 1979, so that '[i]n the early 1980s the annual budgetary cycle was punctuated with unending disputes between the institutions on what were relatively small amounts of money' (Laffan 1997a: 77).

In December 1979, the first directly elected EP blocked the passing of the budget for 1980 in a test of strength against the Council. For several months, the EC had to survive on the system of 'provisional twelfths', whereby it is allowed to spend each month an amount equivalent to one-twelfth of the previous year's budget. Eventually, the MEPs came under tremendous pressure from their national parties to lift their veto, which they did without winning any further concessions on the substance of the budget from the Council—but a marker had been put down that the Council should not Treat the directly elected EP with disdain. An informal agreement was reached on resolving such disputes should they arise in the future, although this did not prevent another crisis the following year, when the EP passed a budget that exceeded the maximum rate of increase. The EP was taken to the Court of Justice by the Council, but an out-of-court agreement was reached in June 1982. Again the EP gave way on the substance of the dispute, but in return got agreement on a joint declaration on the definitions of compulsory and non-compulsory expenditure, and on the respective roles of the two institutions in the budgetary process (Laffan 1997a: 82).

After further acrimonious exchanges in each of the next two years, in 1985, another serious crisis erupted. The EP was becoming increasingly agitated at the failure of the member states to provide adequate funds for new common policies that had been agreed. The main reason for this failure was an inability to bring under control expenditure on the CAP, over which the EP did not have the power of amendment. At first reading on the 1986 budget, the EP inserted amendments to reduce agricultural expenditure, which it had no right to do. The Council removed the amendments, but the EP restored them, and declared the budget passed. The case went to the Court again, where the budget was declared illegal, but the ECJ also banged heads together, telling the Council and the EP that they were joint budgetary authorities, that neither could act unilaterally, and that they had to find means of reaching agreement (Laffan 1997a: 82; Corbett, Jacobs, and Shackleton 2003: 360–2).

It was clear that the disputes and delays in agreeing the annual budgets could not go on indefinitely. Out of this awareness arose the 1988 Inter-Institutional Agreement on Budgetary Discipline. After this, the budget ceased to be at the forefront of the EP's struggle for power. Finally, as a result of reforms in the Lisbon Treaty, the distinction between compulsory and non-compulsory expenditure was abolished. Consequently, the EP and the Council are co-equal budgetary authorities and follow procedures set out in Chapter 19 (pp. 236–9).

Influence in the Legislative Process

The EP from the outset argued the case for it to be an effective co-legislator with the Council of Ministers. This was gradually introduced, first through the now-abolished co-operation procedure, and then through the co-decision procedure (Chapter 19, pp. 240–1). The crucial breakthrough was the introduction of the co-operation procedure in the Single European Act (SEA), which came into effect in 1987. This was insisted upon by the governments of those states—especially Germany and Italy—that were most convinced by the federalist arguments and the arguments about widening the democratic deficit (Rittberger 2003: 220). Consensus gradually emerged between the governments that, for the single market to be created, they would have to accept **qualified majority voting (QMV)**, otherwise every individual measure would be vetoed by the government of the state that stood to be most adversely affected. This implied, though, that national parliaments would no longer be able to reject a proposed measure by instructing their government's representative to veto it in the Council. The democratic deficit argument implied that the loss of control by the national parliaments should be made up by an increase in the role of the EP.

Once the principle of a larger role for the EP in the legislative process had been established, the extension of that role followed as experience of operating the new system made it clear that co-operation was a clumsy procedure, and that the EP would use its powers to improve legislation, not just to be obstructive. Subsequent Treaty reform has increased the number of policy issues on which co-decision applies and the co-operation procedure was abolished under the Lisbon Treaty. The move to the co-decision process provoked an academic debate as to whether it did increase the effective influence of the EP in the legislative process. This is reviewed at length in the next main section of this chapter, on 'Debates and Research'. Practitioners, though, have no doubt that co-decision has increased the influence of the EP.

The EP and the Commission

There are two main aspects of the ability of the EP to exercise control over the Commission. The first is in its powers over the appointment of the College of Commissioners. The second is in its power to dismiss the College if it disapproves of their conduct.

The power of the EP in the appointment of a new Commission was originally zero. This is an area, however, in which the maximalist strategy produced results: Treaty amendments gave the EP limited powers that were then exploited fully under the minimalist strategy. The interaction between the maximalist strategy (formal rule change) and the minimalist one (informal rule changes) has been charted well in an institutionalist analysis undertaken by Adrienne Héritier (2007: 139–59). At Maastricht, the heads of government agreed to consult the EP on the choice of the President of the Commission and to give it the right to consent (or not consent) to the appointment of the College of Commissioners as a whole. They also agreed to bring the term of office of the Commissioners into line with that of the EP, so that the newly elected Parliament would be asked as one of its first acts to approve the proposed new Commission. In 1994, the EP introduced hearings of Commissioners-Designate. In the Amsterdam Treaty, there was a further extension of powers, when the EP was given a formal right of approval of the European Council's nominee for President. These changes were made with an eye on the need to address the democratic deficit. It was hoped that the new powers would persuade voters that the EP was an institution that had the characteristics of a real parliament, and thereby contribute to increased interest in the European parliamentary elections (Smith 1999: 68).

Having gained the right to approve the appointment of the President, and separately of the other Commissioners as a whole, the EP reverted to its minimalist strategy of making the most extensive use possible of its powers. It adapted its internal rules of procedure so that the approval or rejection of the Commission President required only a simple majority, and if the nomination was rejected, the member states would be asked to make a new nomination. It also adopted a rule of procedure that the approval of the Commission as a whole would follow parliamentary hearings in which each of the Commissioners would be subjected to cross-examination *in public* by the members of the relevant specialist committee of the EP (Judge and Earnshaw 2002: 355). These procedural adaptations increased the leverage of the modest extra powers granted in the Maastricht Treaty in ways that will be explored below.

The other aspect of parliamentary control over the Commission is in its power to dismiss Commissioners. Here, the Treaty gives the EP what at first sight is a powerful weapon. If a motion of censure on the Commission is passed by a two-thirds majority of the votes cast, representing a majority of MEPs, then the Commission must resign as a body (Article 234, TFEU). However, this right is less powerful than it seems for at least two reasons. First, the majority required is very difficult to attain. Of nine such motions tabled prior to 1998, none came close to achieving the double majority required. Second, the most likely reason for a censure is because of the behaviour of an individual Commissioner or a small number of Commissioners, yet the censure motion can only target the College as a whole.

Despite these problems, at the end of the 1990s, the EP managed to use the blunt instrument given it by the Treaty to effect a shift in its influence. In 1998, its Budgetary Affairs Committee postponed a decision on whether to discharge the 1996 budget because it was unhappy with the response of the Commission to certain charges of lax financial administration. Although the Committee subsequently decided by one vote to recommend the grant of discharge, the EP meeting in plenary rejected the recommendation. Jacques Santer, the President of the Commission, then made the issue one of confidence by challenging the EP either to give discharge to the budget or to lay down a motion of censure on the whole Commission. This the EP did, although when it was voted on in January 1999, it failed to get even a majority, let alone the two-thirds majority that was required. However, the vote of 232 for and 293 against was the biggest vote ever for a motion of censure, and prompted the Commission to agree to set up a committee of independent experts to report to the EP on fraud, mismanagement, and nepotism in the Commission. When the report appeared in March 1999, it was so damning of the level of mismanagement by some Commissioners that the whole Commission resigned. Although the EP had not managed to summon the substantial majority needed to censure the Commission formally, it had managed to raise the public awareness of the issues identified by the Court of Auditors to the point at which the position of the Commission became untenable. By adept use of its limited powers, the EP achieved a considerable victory (see Chapter 15, pp. 182–4).

At this point, the powers of the EP to approve the new Commission President and College of Commissioners took centre stage. The new nominee for President was Romano Prodi. He anticipated that the EP would want to seek some assurance that, in future, it would not need to attack the whole Commission if, as had been the case with the Santer Commission, the problem lay with certain individuals. In fact, the Santer Commission probably could have survived had one individual Commissioner agreed to resign, but her refusal to do so left the Commission with no option but to resign as a whole. Prodi therefore told the EP at his own confirmation hearing that he would require every individual Commissioner to promise to resign if asked by the President to do so. The promise was repeated by Prodi's successor, José Manuel Barroso. Although it did not give the EP the right to dismiss individual Commissioners, it did mark a further advance towards that goal. The EP then underlined the importance that it set on this development by requiring each of the proposed new Commissioners to make a public declaration at their confirmation hearing that they would resign if asked by the President to do so. In July 2000, a new Framework Agreement on Relations between the European Parliament and the Commission was adopted by the EP. In it, the commitment of Prodi to hold Commissioners individually responsible was strengthened by a commitment that if the EP were to express a lack of confidence in an individual Commissioner, the President would consider whether to ask that individual to resign.

Five years later, the EP again flexed its muscles during the confirmation hearings for the incoming Barroso Commission, when the EP expressed an unwillingness to confirm the new Commission in office if the Italian nominee Rocco Buttiglione was a member of the team, and expressed doubts about the competence of other nominees (Chapter 17, p. 205). After something of a stand-off, Barroso agreed to rethink the position. Buttiglione's nomination was withdrawn and the Italian government put forward another Italian nominee, and two other changes were made to national nominations. This outcome was achieved because of the impressive degree of independence demonstrated by MEPs in the Socialist and Liberal groups, in the face of intense pressure from national governments to allow the contested nominations.

Ratification of the Lisbon Treaty did not bring about such major changes. The Treaty itself mainly introduced nuances into the provisions for approval of the Commission President. As noted already, the nomination—once again of Barroso—had to take into account the elections to the EP, as newly provided for under Article 17 TEU. He was then 'elected', as the new terminology terms this process. During the hearings, Bulgarian Commissioner-Designate Rumiana Jeleva (International Co-operation, Humanitarian Aid, and Crisis Response), a former MEP, performed poorly and failed to allay concerns that she had conflicts of interest. She resigned as Commissioner-Designate on 19 January 2010. The Bulgarian Prime Minister then nominated Kristalina Georgieva, and she 'passed' her hearing in early February. Following this change of line-up, the Commission was approved on 9 February 2010 by a 'vote of consent' (as it is now termed) under Article 17 TEU. With the new post of High Representative overseeing the EU's emerging External Action Service, a joint Commission/Council appointment, the EP attempted to extend its powers to the right to a hearing on the appointment of EU ambassadors (Kietz and von Ondarza 2010: 7). This attempt was resisted, but it indicates that the EP is likely to seek to develop its checks on the Commission still further.

Debates and Research

Debate and research on the EP have been far-reaching and diverse. In a very useful summary, Hix, Raunio, and Scully (2003: 193–6) classified contemporary research on the EP into four areas:

- work on the general development and functioning of the EP;
- research on political behaviour and EP elections;
- research on the internal politics and organization of the EP;
- examinations of inter-institutional bargaining between the EP, the Council, and the Commission.

The first of these has been dealt with already in this chapter. In this section of the chapter, each of the other three categories of research will be briefly reviewed to indicate the main academic concerns. Related debates on the EU's democracy and legitimacy are considered in Chapter 4.

Political Behaviour and EP Elections

The strongest argument for the direct election of the EP was that it would increase the legitimacy of the institution and thereby of the EU as a whole—yet turnout in European elections has gradually fallen. Overall turnout declined from 63 per cent (1979) to 49 per cent (1999), to 46 per cent (2004), and 43 per cent (2009). It has varied between member states, but the more significant fact is that, in every state, the turnout is much lower than for national elections.

Successive European elections studies have examined this phenomenon (Reif and Schmitt 1980; van der Eijk and Franklin 1996; Schmitt and Thomasen 1999). The thrust of the argument of these studies is that European elections are treated by the electorate as 'second-order national elections', which means that they are seen as secondary to national elections, while being conducted as national rather than European contests. The electorate behaves in this way as it considers European elections not to affect which party or coalition governs the EU. The outcome is perceived to affect neither the composition of the Commission, nor that of the Council of Ministers, the two most powerful institutions in the system. So, the campaigns are fought predominantly on domestic issues rather than European ones. Most of the actual campaigning centres on the record of the national government rather than on the differences between the parties on European issues. This held true in 2009 as much as in earlier elections.

There are, in fact, two different competing interpretations of the pattern of results in EP elections, which typically result in setbacks for the incumbent governments. These are the 'punishment' and 'protest' explanations, and they have been examined by Simon Hix and Michael Marsh (2007). The punishment thesis is that EP elections function as mid-term elections in which incumbent national governments are punished by their voters. The competing thesis holds that the support for protest parties, such as the United Kingdom Independence Party (UKIP), together with the falling turnout at European elections, reflect specific protest against the EU. Of these two explanations, the punishment thesis is more closely in line with the 'second-order national elections' interpretation. By contrast, the protest thesis assumes that the EU does matter in voters' thinking, and that it is the source of the protest. Hix and Marsh (2007) examined the results for all EP elections 1979–2004. Their findings showed that the punishment thesis better explains the results. Nevertheless, smaller parties tend to perform better than larger ones, and anti-European parties (where they exist) do better, as do Green parties. However, protest against the EU remained 'at best a minor element in these elections in most cases' (Hix and Marsh 2007: 506).

Internal Politics and Organization of the EP

Hix, Raunio, and Scully (2003: 194–5) divided research under this heading into three categories: analysis of the committee work in the EP; analysis of party groups; and 'other aspects of political behaviour inside the EP', by which is meant the issue of the independence of MEPs as demonstrated by their behaviour in the EP.

Committee Work in the EP

For many years, this was a neglected area of research, although one early piece of research found that beyond the requirements that proportionality was respected in the composition of committees (in terms of both nationality and party group) scope had emerged for 'specialized membership and recruitment' (Bowler and Farrell 1995: 254). In the last decade, this research area has developed strongly, building upon research questions and methods that have been applied to committee work in the US Congress. Other analysts have explored the mechanisms through which party groups, while respecting the requirements of proportionality, have tried to influence the allocation of committee chairs, membership, and the important task of selecting a rapporteur, the MEP charged with producing a committee report on a piece of legislation and with speaking on the committee's behalf when full debate takes place in the EP. Mamadouh and Raunio (2003) showed that the allocation of all of these positions tended to be influenced by national delegations within the EP's transnational party groups (see below). A burgeoning literature has by now emerged on the politics of EP committee work (for a fuller review, see Judge and Earnshaw 2008: 167–78).

The Party Groups

Just as the EP cannot expect to extend its power and influence unless MEPs show themselves to be competent, so it cannot do so by definition if it lacks independence and autonomy. The main constraint on MEPs acting autonomously is the influence of national political parties. Unless the party groups in the EP can establish their autonomy from national parties, the EP will be constrained.

MEPs do not sit in the EP in national delegations, but in transnational party groups. Since the 2009 election, a party group may be established by twenty-five MEPs from at least seven member states. These rules have fluctuated over time in line with the accession of new member states and changes to the size of the EP. The aim has remained constant: to promote groupings that have a truly transnational character. Each party group has its own administrative and support staff, paid for out of the central budget of the EP. Groups are co-ordinated by a Bureau, consisting of a Chair, a Vice-Chair, and a Treasurer as a minimum. The groups play an important role: for instance, in setting the agenda of the EP and allocating speaking time in plenary sessions. A full list of the groups, and their level of representation in the 2009–14 Parliament is given in Table 22.3.

There are definite advantages to being a member of one of the party groups. The groups receive funding from the EP to cover their administrative costs. Memberships of committees, and their chairs and rapporteurs, are allocated to groups in proportion to their size. (For a list of EP committees, see Table 22.2, pp. 294.) It is not surprising, therefore, that there are strong incentives for national parties and individual MEPs to form a group. The Rainbow Group in the 1984–89 Parliament consisted of members of environmentalist parties, regionalist parties, and anti-EC Danish MEPs; the only thing that they had in common was a wish to draw down the funding and other advantages that would be denied them if they did not join a group. The current rules set a somewhat higher hurdle for the formation of groups, such that the smallest in the 2009 EP—the Europe of Freedom and Democracy Group (thirty-one MEPs)—brings together **Euro-sceptic** MEPs around the common theme of co-operation among sovereign European states and opposition to a 'European superstate'. As Table 22.3 indicates, in the summer of 2010, twenty-seven MEPs were not located within a political group.

Even the largest groups may be subject to change, highlighting the way in which the EP's party system is weak even if its committees are quite powerful: a characteristic that makes it comparable to the US Congress. Following the 2009 election to the EP, the

Table 22.3 **Membership Numbers of Political Groups in the European Parliament (as at June 2010)**

Group	MEPs
European People's Party	265
Progressive Alliance of Socialists and Democrats	184
Alliance of Liberals and Democrats for Europe	85
Greens/European Free Alliance	55
European Conservatives and Reformists	54
European United Left/Nordic Green Left	35
Europe of Freedom and Democracy	31
Non-attached	27
Total	**736**

Source: European Parliament website, June 2010.

British Conservative Party formed the cornerstone of a new group, the European Conservatives and Reformists. Previously, it had been in a grouping known as the European People's Party and European Democrats (EPP-ED). However, when David Cameron campaigned for the leadership of the Conservative Party, he made a commitment to withdraw from this grouping on the grounds that is was too pro-European, thus tapping into the Euro-scepticism of his party's backbenchers in the national parliament. The EPP-ED thus became the EPP from 2009. On the centre left of the political spectrum, the Socialist Group adopted a broader title after the 2009 elections—the Progressive Alliance of Socialists and Democrats—to accommodate the Italian Democratic Party, which had only been established in 2007 as an amalgamation of several parties. (For a short profile of each parliamentary group, see Insight 22.2.)

These shifting formations also hint at the fact that cohesion of transnational parties is less than the norm in national parliaments. Not only can genuine differences of national perspective lead to divergence in voting behaviour, but the MEPs in the party groups are also subject to pressure from their national parties. In many, although not all member states, the proportional representation (PR) electoral systems that operate make it easier for national party leaders to put pressure on their MEPs, because European elections are held on the basis of closed party lists—that is, the voter is presented with a list of the candidates for that party in the order of preference decided by the party, and is unable to change the order. The chances for an individual of being elected on any particular level of vote for the party depend on where he or she is placed on the list. As the lists are drawn up by the national party organizations, the MEPs face the prospect of being dropped down the list, and of their seats being jeopardized, if they offend the national party leadership too much.

Despite the relative weakness of the transnational party groups, research indicates that their internal cohesion has generally increased over time. For instance, Hix, Kreppel, and Noury (2003; see also Hix, Noury, and Roland 2005) undertook an analysis of **roll-call voting** over the period from 1979 and concluded that the party system in the EP had become more consolidated over time. Kreppel (2002; 2003) correlated the increasing group cohesion with the increased power of the EP. As the powers of the EP were increased under successive revisions of the Treaties, so the party groups tended to become more cohesive in order to be more effective.

Where the parties have similar policies (on EU integration and external trade) they tend to vote together, and where they have differing positions (on environmental, agriculture, economic and social issues) they tend to vote on opposite sides.

(Hix, Kreppel, and Noury 2003: 327)

A test of the strength of group cohesion in the face of pressure from national governments occurred with the confirmation of the Commission in 2004. Despite pressure from several national governments on the MEPs from their own parties to break ranks and vote for the confirmation of the Barroso Commission as a whole, the groups generally held firm, forcing the withdrawal of the most controversial nominee, the Italian Rocco Buttiglione (see above). President-elect Barroso was consequently forced to reshuffle his College. This incident underlined one of the arguments of Kreppel (2002): namely, that MEPs were always likely to unite around the drive to secure more influence for the EP within EU decision making.

305

Insight 22.2 Transnational Political Groups in the 2009 EP

Group of the European People's Party (EPP)

Centre-right grouping based on Christian Democracy parties, with German and Italian parties forming the largest national delegations.

Group of the Progressive Alliance of Socialists and Democrats (S & D)

Formerly known as the Socialist Group, but renamed after the 2009 elections. Comprises members from all twenty-seven member states and includes socialists, social democrats, and other centre-left parties. German, Spanish, and Italian delegations are the largest. British Labour MEPs are also members.

Group of the Alliance of Liberals and Democrats for Europe (ALDE)

Usually the third largest group in the EP, it comprises centrist liberals and democrats as well as more right-wing economic liberals. Largest national delegations are the Free Democrats from Germany and the Liberal Democrats from the UK.

Group of the Greens/European Free Alliance (Greens/EFA)

Established in 1999, the party started off as a marriage of convenience, combining greens and regionalist/nationalist parties. German Greens and French ecologists are the main delegations. UK members come from the Green Party, Plaid Cymru, and the Scottish National Party.

European Conservatives and Reformists' Group

Newly formed after the 2009 elections after the British Conservatives abandoned their previous alliance with the Christian Democrats, whose pro-European stance was disliked. Principal delegations are British Conservatives plus the Polish Law and Justice Party. It is a centre-right grouping that is opposed to federalism in the EU.

Confederal Group of the European United Left/Nordic Green Left (GUE/NGL)

Largely comprises members from left-wing and former communist parties. The group is loosely organized and favours policies tackling unemployment and the environment.

Europe of Freedom and Democracy Group (EFD)

Created in 2004, this group comprises Euro-sceptic parties. The largest delegation is made up of UKIP MEPs from Britain.

One important point provides context to this pattern of growing cohesion: namely, the striking number of near unanimous votes in the EP. For instance, Hix, Kreppel, and Noury (2003: 318) reviewed roll-call votes over the period 1979–2001 and found that the two largest party groupings, the socialists and the European People's Party (Christian Democrats), voted together in a minimum of 61–71 per cent of cases depending on the parliamentary term. In national parliaments, party cohesion and competition arise because of the government's wish to secure its legislative programme and the opposition's wish either to obstruct or to modify the legislation. This situation finds no parallel in the EP because there is no EU government based on a majority of MEPs.

A number of explanations have been offered for the high number of near-unanimous votes (Hix, Kreppel, and Noury 2003: 319–20). First, it has been argued that, on issues relating to European integration, both major party groupings share a pro-European position. Hence where issues relating to EU reform arise in the EP, these two groups hold quite similar positions and are likely to vote together. A related explanation is that MEPs of both groups share a common interest in increasing the powers of the EP, resulting in a strategic calculation in favour of voting together in the later stages of the legislative process (see Kreppel 2000). Another explanation that has been offered is that the rules in the legislative procedure act as an incentive for the two main blocs to vote together, assuming that they can reach agreement. Specifically, where co-decision (or budgetary) voting rules require an absolute majority (that is, at least 369 of the EP's 736 MEPs), the two main blocs' support is going to be necessary in view of the attendance rate of 65–75 per cent (Hix, Kreppel, and Noury 2003: 319).

There are, therefore, some distinctive features of the EP that encourage the two main party groups to vote with each other, while a left–right competition is also emerging. In this way, research on the party groups has opened up a debate about whether behaviour in the EP reflects 'party politics as usual' or whether the distinctive character of the EU's institutions prevents the patterns of behaviour that we would recognize from national parliaments (Lindberg, Rasmussen, and Warntjen 2008). As most commentators agree, the terrain of party politics in the EP has begun to change markedly over the past decade or so (on this, see Hix 2008). Alongside this, the debate concerning the behaviour of party groups in the EP has advanced considerably and attention has now begun to explore partisan voting in other institutions: notably, the Council of Ministers and the European Council, in which the focus has traditionally been upon governments voting along national lines (Hagemann and Hoyland 2008; Tallberg and Johansson 2008).

The Independence of MEPs

One of the peculiarities of the relationship between voters and the EP is that the electorate may be completely unfamiliar with the political group for which they are effectively voting in the European elections. Moreover, the party groups in the EP add to the allegiances that MEPs already have to their home party, their constituents, and their nation.

As suggested above, one of the factors that affects the ability of the EP to extend its power and influence further is the independence of MEPs from national party influence. Because candidate selection is undertaken by political parties at member-state level, independence from this level is seen as being the appropriate measure of MEPs adopting a role defined by the EP. In the early years of the EP, few MEPs had any real incentive to assert their independence from their national parties. Some MEPs were senior politicians who served out the latter years of their political career at EU level, while younger members often saw the EP as the first step prior to taking up a career in national politics.

What was less evident was an obvious career route at the European level. National MPs can aspire to enter government, or at least to become an official spokesperson for their party if it is in opposition. At the European level, the executive is not drawn from the EP, which means that there is little obvious career progression. Nevertheless, it is not unusual to find some former MEPs amongst the European Commissioners. Hix and Lord (1997: 117) pointed out that eleven of the twenty members of the Santer Commission had been MEPs. However, Commissioners may just as easily be nominated from the national level of politics.

Comparison with the United States is of some help in explaining what has developed over the years, since the executive in Washington is also not chosen from members of the legislature. Nevertheless, that has not prevented the emergence of professional members of Congress who aspire to occupy senior committee chairs. As the powers and influence of the EP have grown, so a similar career route has come to be followed by some MEPs, as suggested by Bowler and Farrell (1995) (see also Westlake 1994). These findings were supported in a later study by Scarrow (1997), who saw the proportion of European career politicians steadily increasing, and similarly predicted that MEPs would become increasingly independent of national parties.

A number of studies have explored the relationship between MEPs and their national parties in the subsequent period. Tapio Raunio (2007: 255) stated that 'national party delegations are the cornerstones upon which the EP groups are based'. Yet, while most national party delegations have their own staff and hold meetings before participating in the transnational parliamentary groups, the scope for national parties to 'control' their MEPs is limited (see Scully 2001). Indeed, 'MEPs often perceive themselves to be rather peripheral actors in their parties, complaining that their work is not taken seriously enough' (Raunio 2007: 257). And yet, as Raunio also notes (2007: 256), another slightly contradictory finding has been that national political parties are increasingly paying attention to their MEPs. This finding is attributed to research on British Labour MEPs, in which a 'link system' was established to maintain co-operation with the party leadership and the Labour government. It might be an early sign of a new trend or it might be a development arising from the 'logic' of British politics.

The EP and Inter-Institutional Bargaining

This is an area that has attracted a lot of academic attention, which has centred on the extent to which the effective influence of the EP over the legislative process has really increased. The general view of the progression from consultation through the now-abolished co-operation procedure to co-decision was that 'the consecutive institutional reforms are moving the EU towards a genuinely bicameral system' (Crombez 2000: 366). On the face of it, each step represented an increase in both the power and influence of the EP. However, some analysts have challenged this automatic growth of power.

In order to give a flavour of the debates amongst exponents of formal modelling, we examine the changes to the EP's powers over time. Under its original power—the *consultation* procedure—its opinion could be ignored whether the voting rule was unanimity or QMV. However, the SEA also introduced the *co-operation* procedure (for more discussion, see Bache and George 2006: 242–3). Under this procedure, the Commission and the EP shared the power to determine the final form of the legislation. This was because of the combination of QMV in the Council, and the introduction of a second reading with a conditional power of veto for the EP. At the second reading, if the EP was unhappy with the version of the draft legislation that had been adopted by the Council as its 'common position' (which, in effect, meant if the EP's proposed amendments had largely been ignored), the EP could reject the common position by an absolute majority of its members. This constituted a veto, but the Council could override it if it acted by unanimity. A key element in the balance of influence here was the attitude of the Commission to the EP's proposed amendments at second reading. If the Commission accepted the amendments, the Council had to act by unanimity to overturn them—but the Council could accept the amended proposal by QMV. This meant that if the EP and the Commission could agree on a proposal that was acceptable to a coalition in the Council that constituted a qualified majority, they together had the decisive influence on the form of the legislation. The co-operation procedure was largely replaced by the Amsterdam Treaty and finally abolished by the Lisbon Treaty.

The *co-decision* procedure, introduced by the Maastricht Treaty changed the inter-institutional balance again. As introduced at that stage (termed Co-decision 1), it gave the EP:

- three readings of legislation;
- the right to negotiate directly with the Council via a Conciliation Committee on any amendments for which there was an absolute majority in the EP, but with which the Council did not agree;
- an absolute right of veto.

Some analysts offered a counter-intuitive argument that the EP had less effective influence on legislation under the co-decision procedure than it had under co-operation (Garrett and Tsebelis 1996; Tsebelis and Garrett 1996). Under their interpretation, the formal power to determine the final wording of the legislation passed to the Council of Ministers. The reasoning of Tsebelis and Garrett was as follows.

(1) The position of the Commission was fatally weakened because, after the second reading, the Council and the EP could convene a Conciliation Committee and negotiate a text bilaterally, which could overrule the Commission text.

(2) On the assumption that the EP would normally prefer to see some legislation rather than no legislation, it was engaged in an uneven negotiation with the Council. If agreement could not be reached in the Conciliation Committee, the Council could either allow the proposal to drop by simply not acting on it, or could adopt the original common position. In the latter case, the EP could reject the common position by an absolute majority, but the effect was to revert to the status quo.

These conclusions were strongly contested by several writers (Crombez 1996; 1997; 2000; Moser 1996; 1997; Scully 1997a; 1997b). They accepted the general framework of the model put forward by Tsebelis and Garrett, but pointed to flaws in the argument. In particular, the role of the Commission was underestimated. For example, it still had the sole right of initiative for legislative proposals, and drafted the initial text. If it worked in conjunction with the EP at this stage, and if the two institutions acted strategically to agree proposals that could command a qualified majority in the

Council, then they had the same joint influence as under the co-operation procedure. At the same time as academics were engaged in this debate, Richard Corbett, a former EP official and a leading empirical analyst of the institutions (also an MEP 1996–2009) argued that Tsebelis and Garrett's argument was 'the opposite of the opinion of almost every practitioner' (Corbett 2000: 373).

In practice, much of Tsebelis and Garrett's analysis was based on ignoring the informal aspects of the inter-institutional bargaining process. This failing is perhaps related to the rational choice framework of analysis that they adopted, which does not place much emphasis on empirical research. Scholars whose approach involved intensive research 'in the field' were clear that 'the informal dimensions of inter-institutional relations are of major significance in understanding policy-making in the EC' (Judge, Earnshaw, and Cowan 1994: 45).

The importance of the informal aspect is related to the EP's vigorous pursuit of the minimalist strategy of making the greatest possible use of its formal powers. This first emerged with reference to the consultation procedure in the aftermath of the *Isoglucose* judgment (Chapter 23, p. 318). As a result of the judgment, the EP was able to force the Commission to interact more intensively with it to try to ensure that it would not delay legislation. Under the *renvoi* procedure, the EP refused to deliver a formal opinion until it had received some indication from the Commission of how it proposed to react to the amendments that the EP was suggesting. The level of informal interaction in particular increased, and in 1990, the Commission offered a code of conduct that committed it to keeping the EP informed. In a similar way, the formal changes to the rules made under the Maastricht Treaty led to the emergence of informal institutional changes.

Initially, the Council attempted to minimize the impact of the changes on the way in which legislation was dealt with. However, the determination of the EP to make the maximum use of its new powers soon convinced the Council that it could not carry on as before. The EP showed itself willing to take even relatively uncontroversial legislation to conciliation unless its positions were taken seriously. As a backlog of legislation began to mount, the Council agreed to institute informal 'trialogues' with the Commission and EP in an attempt to ease the passage of important measures.

Subsequently, the experience of trying to make the system introduced at Maastricht operate effectively led to further changes to the formal rules at Amsterdam: the creation of what is called Co-decision 2. These changes allowed the Council and EP to conclude the process at first reading if they could reach agreement, and changed the rules of conciliation so that there was no longer the possibility of legislation that had been rejected by the EP being passed if the Conciliation Committee failed to reach agreement. The decision to allow agreement after the first reading reflected the concern of the Council Secretariat that, with the transfer of even more areas to co-decision, the system needed to be streamlined. However, the new rule implied a further extension of informal discussion, effectively involving the EP in the formulation of legislative proposals at the same early stage as the Commission consulted with the Council.

The change of rule on what happened after an unsuccessful conciliation simply reflected acceptance that the EP would never accept the reinstatement of a Council common position, as it had demonstrated in 1994. According to Shackleton and

Raunio (2003: 173), in an assessment that is given authority by the fact that Shackleton was the Head of the Conciliations Secretariat of the EP at the time:

> Co-decision is now seen as an interlinked, continuous procedure where it is essential and normal that there be intensive contacts throughout the procedure from before first reading onwards. Such contacts offer the opportunity of coming to agreements without having recourse to the time-consuming procedure of conciliation.

The other change—to the rules governing the final stage of the process—led Tsebelis and Garrett (2000) to conclude that equality had been reached at last because the Council could no longer carry its common position if conciliation failed. However, empirical analysis of Co-decision 2 has revealed a growing trend towards early agreements, thereby rendering the formal rules at the conciliation stage of less practical relevance. In the 2004–09 Parliament, Judge and Earnshaw (2008: 233) note that two-thirds of legislative dossiers were agreed in the first reading. In addition, as they also note, informal agreements at the start of the second reading accounted for a further 15 per cent of measures. In this way, norms of early agreement, along with 'trialogues' between the three institutions, were being practised in order to minimize resort to the conciliation stage.

What emerges from practice on the ground and academic analysis is that, through Treaty reform and informal agreements, the EP has become a co-legislator with the Council. Moreover, the analysis of the EP's power cannot simply rely on interpretation of formal rules, because informal rules and conventions are also important factors.

CONCLUSION

The themes of the book that are brought out in this chapter are particularly those concerned with the supranational or intergovernmental nature of the EU, and with the democratic and legitimacy deficits of the EU. The debate between rational choice and social constructivist approaches to the analysis of the EU also emerges when the process by which the EP has extended its influence is analysed.

The issue of the nature of the EU as an organization is clearly affected by the view that is taken of the effective influence of the EP. If it is accepted that the successive changes in the EP's formal role have made it a co-legislator with the Council of Ministers, then the view that the EU is no more than an intergovernmental organization cannot be sustained. There is no other such organization in which the member governments have to share decision making with a directly elected institution. This is true whether or not the EP's formal role translates into effective influence. However, if there is no real power attached to the EP's role, it can be dismissed as no more than an appearance of supranationalism. With the further extension of its powers under the Lisbon Treaty, this analysis of the EP is no longer tenable.

On legitimacy, the main reason why the powers of the EP have been extended has been in response to the argument that this would help to close the democratic deficit, and therefore the legitimacy deficit of the EU. The evidence does not indicate that much has been achieved in that direction, in particular because there are limits to the legitimacy of the EP's democratic mandate that may only be eased with the development of a stronger sense of European identity among EU citizens. The Lisbon Treaty arguably recognized this situation by giving new powers to the national parliaments (see Chapter 19, pp. 240–1).

In other respects, though, the EP may be helping to close the legitimacy deficit identified in Chapter 4. Its scrutiny of the Commission—notably in forcing the resignation of the Santer Commission in 1999—may help to convince European publics that the efficiency issue is being addressed. Also the role of the EP as an alternative point of access to the policy-making process for interests that feel excluded elsewhere by the domination of business interests could help to build a sense of European identity among such groups in the longer term.

The debate between rational choice and social constructivist approaches to the analysis of the EU is apparent in the explanations that each side offers for the way in which the EP has extended its powers and influence. The social constructivist position is apparent in the argument of Pollack (2003), which is examined in Chapter 2 (p. 24), that the governments of the member states have largely extended the formal powers of the EP in response to arguments about the need to address the 'democratic deficit' rather than in an attempt to reduce transaction costs. However, the process whereby formal rule changes led to informal changes that were subsequently formalized, was analysed by Farrell and Héritier (2003) using a game-theoretical approach. Although the insight that informal procedures are central to the operation of inter-institutional relationships is usually associated with historical institutionalists and constructivists, the adoption of the idea of *iterated games*, instead of treating each round of bargaining as a 'one-off shot', allows the rational choice models to be adapted to take account of the informal developments. So, there is no definitive judgement that can be made between the explanatory power of the two approaches.

KEY POINTS

Composition and Functions

- The EP elected in June 2009 had 736 seats, which were distributed between the member states approximately in proportion to population.
- It meets monthly in plenary sessions in Strasbourg, but most of its work is done in Committee in Brussels.
- Organizationally, it has a President, a Bureau, a Conference of Presidents, and a Secretariat.

The Struggle for Power

- The forerunner of the EP (the EPA) was not directly elected and had limited powers.
- The EP has steadily increased its powers by putting pressure on national parties and governments, arguing that it needed increased powers to close the EU's democratic deficit.
- The first direct elections to the EP took place in June 1979. Direct election emboldened MEPs to challenge the member states over the budget and to demand more powers.
- In 1970, the power of the EP over the budget was increased when it was given the power to amend 'non-compulsory expenditure', which excluded the CAP. In 1975, it was given the power to reject the budget as a whole. As a result of the Lisbon Treaty, the EP and the Council of Ministers are co-equal budgetary authorities.
- The EP can force the Commission as a whole to resign by a motion of censure, but to do so requires a positive vote from an absolute majority of MEPs and two-thirds of the votes cast. It cannot dismiss individual Commissioners.
- Originally, the EP had no say in the appointment of the Commission. Under successive Treaty amendments, it gained the right to elect the governments' nomination for President and subsequently hold a vote of consent for the new College of Commissioners.

Debates and Research

- The electorate in all member states treats European elections as less important than national elections. They are fought primarily on domestic issues, and turnout is lower than for national elections.

- MEPs sit in transnational party groups, which can contain within them a wide variety of ideological positions, but research indicates that the degree of group cohesion has increased as the powers of the EP have increased.

- In the early years, no obvious career path existed, but research has indicated that being an MEP is increasingly attractive to ambitious politicians.

- The role of the EP in the legislative process has moved from the weak position in the consultation procedure, through successively stronger positions under co-operation and co-decision.

- Academic debate over the power of the EP in the legislative process has been contested from different perspectives. A concentration on formal rules by some analysts has been criticized by others who hold that informal rules can be as important.

FURTHER READING

A very good review of the emergence of the EP, although not covering the most recent developments, is offered by **B. Rittberger**, *Building Europe's Parliament: Democratic Representation Beyond the Nation State* (Oxford: Oxford University Press, 2005). For general guides to the EP, see **R. Corbett, F. Jacobs, and M. Shackleton**, *The European Parliament*, 7th edn (London: John Harper Publishing, 2007), and **D. Judge and D. Earnshaw**, *The European Parliament*, 2nd edn (London: Palgrave Macmillan, 2008). For a study of the politics within the EP from a comparative-politics standpoint, see **S. Hix, A. Noury, and G. Roland**, *Democratic Politics in the European Parliament* (Cambridge: Cambridge University Press, 2007). Another detailed analysis is offered by **N. Ringe**, *Who Decides, and How? Preferences, Uncertainty, and Policy Choice in the European Parliament* (Oxford: Oxford University Press, 2009).

For an analysis that argues that the EP's representative role is being undermined by the electoral systems utilized at member-state level, see **D. Farrell and R. Scully**, *Representing Europe's Citizens? Electoral Institutions and the Failure of Parliamentary Representation* (Oxford: Oxford University Press, 2007). **Juliet Lodge** has edited several books on European elections, including *The 2004 Elections to the European Parliament* (Basingstoke and New York: Palgrave, 2005), and *The 2009 Elections to the European Parliament* (Basingstoke and New York: Palgrave, 2010). On the party system in the EP, see **A. Kreppel**, *The European Parliament and Supranational Party System: A Study in Institutional Development* (Cambridge: Cambridge University Press, 2002).

online resource centre

Visit the Online Resource Centre that accompanies this book for links to more information on the European Parliament, including the EP's own website: www.oxfordtextbooks.co.uk/orc/bache3e/

Chapter 23
The European Court of Justice

Chapter Overview

Unlike international organizations more broadly, much of the work of the European Union (EU) is undertaken through legislation and other legal acts. It therefore follows that its legal system is an important feature. At the apex of that system sits what is formally known as the 'Court of Justice of the European Union' (CJEU). It in fact comprises three courts: the Court of Justice; the General Court; and the EU Civil Service Tribunal. The first of these, commonly referred to as the European Court of Justice (ECJ), is the most important one. It makes binding decisions on disputes over Treaty provisions or secondary legislation. It therefore plays an essential role in the developing EU.

This chapter looks first at the structure and functions of the Courts, and then at some of the ECJ's main rulings and their significance. It considers rulings on the powers of the institutions, some key legal judgments made in response to questions referred to the ECJ by national courts, and some illustrations of the impact of ECJ rulings on EU policy. The chapter then turns to look first at the political reactions to the judgments of the Court, and then at the debate over whether the member states have lost control of the process of European integration because of the radical jurisprudence of the ECJ.

Tucked away in the fairyland Duchy of Luxembourg and blessed, until recently, with benign neglect by the powers that be and the mass media, the Court of Justice of the European Communities has fashioned a constitutional framework for a federal-type structure in Europe.... Proceeding from its fragile jurisdictional base, the Court has arrogated to itself the ultimate authority to draw the line between Community law and national law. Moreover, it has established and obtained acceptance of the broad principle of direct integration of Community law into the national legal orders of the member states and of the supremacy of Community law within its limited but expanding area of competence over any conflicting national law.

(Stein 1981: 1)

There is consensus on the need for a European judicial order to exist with an authoritative interpreter of both the Treaties and the secondary legislation (directives, regulations) put in place by member states. This task falls to the ECJ. As sometimes occurs with courts more generally, especially constitutional courts such as the US Supreme Court or the German Federal Constitutional Court, the ECJ has been criticized for stepping beyond its legal role into the realm of politics. However, unlike controversies in other political systems, the ECJ not only has to tread the line between law and politics, but it also polices the boundary between EU and national law and politics. This is important because 'there is joint responsibility between national courts and the Union courts for the interpretation and maintenance of EU law' (Chalmers, Davies, and Monti 2010: 142).

The ECJ has been accused in the past of ruling in favour of integrationist solutions to disputes. This has provoked hostility from member states that see their powers or sovereignty being undermined by Court rulings. In the period after the Maastricht ratification crisis, the ECJ was subjected to increased criticism from member states for its radical jurisprudence, known as judicial activism. However, while the 1990s witnessed questions concerning the ECJ's growing influence, 'in recent years ... its level of activism has fallen' (Kapsis 2010: 187).

Structure

The Court of Justice of the EU comprises three courts:

- the European Court of Justice (ECJ);
- the General Court;
- the European Union Civil Service Tribunal.

It is the ECJ that is of greatest interest in this chapter, but it is worth briefly discussing the other two courts beforehand.

The EU Civil Service Tribunal, established in 2005, is a very specialized court the responsibility of which is for hearing disputes between employees of the EU institutions and the institutions themselves, and not of political significance. The General Court has a rather wider remit. It was established in 1989 as the Court of First Instance, but gained its new name with implementation of the Lisbon Treaty in 2009. It was created to help the ECJ with the sheer volume of business that it had to get through. It comprises twenty-seven judges, with one from each member state. The General Court is effectively the central administrative court of the EU. The General Court can act in a range of circumstances, but it plays a particularly important role in hearing 'challenges by private parties adversely affected by EU measures': notably, in competition law or external trade law (Chalmers, Davies, and Monti 2010: 147). The most important cases, including those of political significance, are the responsibility of the ECJ.

Like the General Court, the ECJ meets in Luxembourg, which is a legacy of its origins dating from its creation as part of the European Coal and Steel Community (see Chapter 6, p. 99), the institutions of which were all located in the Grand Duchy. It comprises twenty-seven judges and eight advocates-general, who are appointed by common accord of the governments of the member states and hold office for a renewable term of six years (Article 19 TEU). The judges are chosen from persons whose independence is beyond doubt and who are of recognized competence. Approximately half of the judges and advocates-general are replaced every three years. With implementation of the Lisbon Treaty, candidates for the positions of judge or advocate-general are to be scrutinized by a panel of seven people, comprising former EU judges, national Supreme Court judges, and a nominee of the European Parliament (EP). The panel's Opinion will be offered to the Council on candidates' suitability, although it is not binding in its effect.

The judges select one of their number to be President of the Court for a renewable term of three years. The President directs the work of the Court and presides at hearings and deliberations. The advocates-general assist the Court in its task. They deliver legal opinions on cases before the Court at a stage before the ECJ issues its own judgment.

The ECJ's work is primarily conducted in chambers of three or five judges; important matters can, upon request, come before a Grand Chamber of thirteen judges and exceptionally important ones come before the Court as a whole (Chalmers, Davies, and Monti 2010: 145). The ECJ's authority is confined to 'Union business'. It therefore has no jurisdiction on Common Foreign and Security Policy. The ECJ's remit was expanded following implementation of the Lisbon Treaty by the transfer of remaining areas of Justice and Home Affairs co-operation to the '**Union method**' as part of the Area of Freedom, Security and Justice, but only after a five-year transition period (see Chapter 31). Like the General Court, the ECJ has problems keeping up with the volume of cases referred to it.

Functions

It is the responsibility of the ECJ to ensure that the law is observed in the interpretation and application of the EU Treaties with the exception of the provisions relating to foreign and security policy. To enable it to carry out that task, the Court has wide jurisdiction to hear various types of action and to give preliminary rulings.

The Court may hear several different categories of proceeding, as follows.

(1) Failure to fulfil an obligation (TFEU Articles 258, 259, and 260)

A member state may be taken to the Court by the Commission or by another member state for failing to act to meet its obligations under the Treaties or EU secondary legislation. If the Court finds against the state so charged, it must comply without delay. If it fails to do so, the Commission may go back to the Court and ask, under Article 260 TFEU, for a fine to be imposed on the state.

(2) Application for annulment (TFEU Articles 263 and 264)

This judicial review power allows a member state, the Council, the Commission, the EP, the Court of Auditors, the European Central Bank, and the Committee of the Regions to apply to the ECJ as plaintiffs for the annulment of EU acts or legislative acts. Individuals may, via the national court system, seek the annulment of a legal measure that is of direct concern to them. The annulment may be sought and granted on grounds of lack of competence, infringement of an essential procedural requirement, infringement of the Treaty, or misuse of powers. Expansion of the scope of Article 263 under the Lisbon Treaty has extended judicial review beyond acts of the Commission, the Council, and the EP to include such acts of the European Council, the European Central Bank, and EU agencies as have legal effects (Dougan 2008: 676).

(3) Failure to act (TFEU Articles 265 and 266)

The Court may review the legality of a failure to act by a Community institution (the EP, the European Council, the Council, the Commission, or the European Central Bank), and penalize silence or inaction.

(4) Actions to establish liability (TFEU Article 268)

In an action for damages, the Court rules on the liability of the EU for damage caused by its institutions or servants in the performance of their duties.

(5) Appeals (TFEU Article 256)

The Court may hear appeals, on points of law only, against judgments given by the General Court in cases within its jurisdiction.

(6) Reference for a preliminary ruling (TFEU Article 267)

Preliminary rulings are judgments by the Court on the interpretation of the Treaties or secondary legislation arising under the Treaties. Under Article 267, national courts that are hearing cases involving EU law may request a ruling from the ECJ on the interpretation of the law, and where the issue is raised before a national court against the judgment of which there is no appeal in domestic law, that court must seek a preliminary ruling from the ECJ. The ECJ cannot deliver a preliminary ruling unless it is asked to do so by a national court.

Although judges are usually thought of as conservative, that cannot be said of the ECJ judges. It has been argued that the ECJ has done more than any other institution to advance European integration (Freestone 1983: 43). Its approach has been heavily criticized by some commentators as stepping beyond the bounds of legal interpretation to become political (Ramussen 1986). Perhaps this lack of conservatism is because some of the members of the ECJ are not judges by profession. Many of the appointees have been academics rather than professional lawyers. Whatever the reasons, the ECJ pursued a form of judicial activism that created a supranational legal order in the mid-1960s. This development came at the time when the empty chair crisis brought political integration to a halt and entrenched an intergovernmental political order, thus demonstrating why the legal dimension of integration must be kept in view. The Court's judicial activism was to be found both in judgments on the powers of the institutions arising from actions brought under the Articles listed above, and in Article 267 referrals from national courts seeking clarification of points of EU law.

ECJ Rulings on the Powers of the Institutions

The biggest beneficiary of the ECJ's distinctive approach to institutional relations has been the EP. In a series of judgments, the ECJ has interpreted the powers of the EP in an expansive manner. Key cases, which are considered here, were:

- *Roquette* v. *Council* (1980) (the *Isoglucose* case) Case 138/79;
- *Parti Écologiste, 'Les Verts'* v. *Parliament* (1986) Case 294/83;

- *European Parliament* v. *Council* (1988) (the *Comitology* case) Case 302/87;
- *European Parliament* v. *Council* (1990) (the *Chernobyl* case) Case C-70/88.

The *Isoglucose* Case (1980)

In March 1979, the Commission submitted to the EP a draft regulation on fixing quotas for the production of isoglucose—a food sweetener produced from cereals—to take effect from the beginning of July. The draft regulation went to the EP's Committee on Agriculture, which reported to the May plenary session of the EP. However, the plenary rejected the report of the Committee containing an opinion on the regulation. This effectively meant that the quotas could not be introduced at the beginning of July (1979 was an election year for the EP, so there was no June plenary). In the meantime, the Council had considered the draft regulation and agreed to adopt it. Faced with a possible delay of four months or more, the Commission acted on the approval of the Council and published the directive in the Official Journal.

Subsequently, an individual who was directly affected by the directive brought a case to the ECJ under Article 173 of the EEC Treaty (now Article 263 TFEU), claiming that the Council and Commission had acted beyond their powers by adopting the directive without having received the Opinion of the EP. The Court could have decided that the EP had been consulted, and had failed to deliver an opinion in time. Instead, it upheld the complaint, choosing to interpret 'consult' to mean that the formal Opinion of the EP had to be delivered before the Council could act.

In its judgment, the Court insisted that the EP had a duty to give an Opinion within a reasonable length of time, without defining what would be considered reasonable. Thus, the judgment did not give the EP an effective power to veto legislation under the consultation procedure, but it did give it a significant power to delay legislation by holding back on formally delivering its opinion.

Les Verts v. *European Parliament* (1986)

In 1984, the French Green Party (*Les Verts*) stood candidates for election to the EP for the first time. In doing so, it discovered that those of its opponents that had been represented in the previous Parliament had been voted funds by the EP to defray their election expenses. Subsequently the Greens brought a case to the ECJ under Article 173 EEC (now Article 263 TFEU) claiming that the EP had acted beyond its powers in effectively supporting the election of existing parties at the expense of new parties.

The immediate issue here was whether any such case could be brought to the Court. Article 173 explicitly said: 'The Court of Justice shall review the legality of acts of the Council and the Commission.' There was no mention of the ECJ reviewing the legality of acts of the EP. The Court nevertheless accepted the case on the grounds that, although the Treaty did not explicitly make the actions of the EP subject to judicial review, this omission was not in keeping with the spirit of the Treaty.

The Court argued that the EP must have been omitted from Article 173, because when the Treaty was signed, the EP had no real powers. Subsequently, it had acquired powers that would normally be subject to judicial review. These included the powers that were contested in this case, and as these *should* be subject to judicial review, the Court would review them.

In this judgment, the ECJ increased its own powers by a unilateral reinterpretation of the Treaty. Although apparently acting in a way that would restrict the powers of the EP, the judgment also took the first step towards giving the EP a legal personality that it had not been granted by the member states when they signed the Treaty. Once it had been decided that the EP could be a defendant in such a hearing, it seemed logical that it should also be accorded the right to be a plaintiff—that is, that it be allowed to bring cases to the Court under the same Article. The Court was given the opportunity to take this step in the next case reviewed below.

European Parliament v. Council (the Comitology Case) (1990)

This case was brought by the EP under Article 175 EEC (now revised as TFEU Article 265), which said:

> Should the Council or the Commission, in infringement of this Treaty, fail to act, the Member States, and the other institutions of the Community may bring an action before the Court of Justice to have the infringement established.

The EP argued successfully that it was allowed to bring a case under this Article because it was one of the 'other institutions of the Community'. But it also argued that it should be allowed to bring a case under Article 173 if the issue was one of another institution acting beyond its powers, rather than of not acting at all. The EP argued that it was illogical for it to be allowed to bring a case under Article 175, but not under Article 173. It also quoted the Court's judgment in *Les Verts* that the EP could be a defendant under Article 173, and argued that if it could be a defendant, it was illogical that it should not be allowed to be a plaintiff.

The Court rejected the EP's arguments. It said that: there was no logical link between the circumstances outlined; the EP could normally rely on the Commission to take up a case under Article 173 on its behalf; and the member states had recently had the specific opportunity to grant this right explicitly to the EP in the Single European Act and had declined to do so. However, within a short period of time, the Court appeared to have a change of heart on the issue.

European Parliament v. Council (the Chernobyl Case) (1990)

In this case, the EP applied to the Court for a review of the procedure adopted for agreeing a public health regulation on the permissible radioactive contamination of food that could be sold for public consumption following the Chernobyl disaster (Insight 23.1). The Commission proposed the regulation under Article 31 of the Euratom Treaty, which dealt with basic standards for the protection of the health of the general public arising from radiation. Proposed legislation under this Article was subject to the consultation procedure. The EP maintained that the matter was a single-market issue, and therefore should have been introduced under (the then) Article 100A of the EEC Treaty (now TFEU Article 114). This would have brought it under the co-operation procedure, and given the EP a second reading. The EP wished to challenge the treaty base under which the regulation was adopted, but first

---

Insight 23.1 Chernobyl

On 26 April 1986, a major accident occurred at the Chernobyl nuclear power station in Ukraine. Radioactive pollution extended over a vast geographical area. Contamination was detected in the food chain as far west as Ireland. The EU introduced standardized rules on the permissible levels of radioactive contamination, and provided financial support for the farmers worst affected.

---

had to establish that its case was admissible because it was invoking Article 173 EEC (now Article 263 TFEU).

Despite the Court's decision in the *Comitology* case, its decision in this one, coming soon after, was even more surprising. Here, the Court decided that the EP could bring the case after all, despite its reasoning in the *Comitology* judgment, because the ECJ's role was to preserve the institutional balance. In the *Comitology* judgment, the Court had asserted that the Commission could normally be relied upon to protect the prerogatives of the EP where Parliament required an Article 173 case to be brought. However, in this instance, the dispute over the treaty base pitted the Commission against the EP. Therefore in these and similarly limited circumstances, the EP had to be granted the right to be a plaintiff in an Article 173 case. The other argument that had appeared in the *Comitology* judgment, that the member states had only recently declined to grant this power explicitly to the EP, now disappeared from view.

ECJ Rulings on the Nature of EC Law

If the jurisprudence of the ECJ has pushed back the limits of the Treaty in judgments based on judicial review cases, it has been even more radical in its judgments on references for preliminary rulings. In a number of judgments, the Court laid out principles that expanded the EU's legal order. The following cases were particularly important:

- *Van Gend en Loos* (1963) Case 26/62;
- *Costa* v. *ENEL* (1964) Case 6/64;
- *Van Duyn* v. *Home Office* (1974) Case 41/74;
- *R.* v. *Secretary of State for Transport, ex parte Factortame* (1990) Case 213/89;
- *R.* v. *Secretary of State for Transport, ex parte Factortame* (1991) Case C-221/89;
- *Francovich* v. *Italy* (1991) Cases C-6 and 9/90.

Van Gend en Loos (1963)

In this early case, the Court first asserted the principle that EU law confers rights on individuals as well as on member states. This was the principle of 'direct effect', which had no explicit authority in the Treaties, and represented a dramatic departure from international law. Under international law, treaties are held to impose obligations on the states that sign and ratify them, but neither to confer rights nor impose obligations directly on individual citizens.

A Dutch company claimed that its rights had been breached by the Dutch government, which had levied a higher rate of duty on formaldehyde—a chemical used as a disinfectant and preservative, and in the manufacture of synthetic resins—after the date on which it was agreed in the EEC Treaty that there would be no increase in internal tariffs. The Dutch government maintained that the company had no power to claim a right deriving from an international treaty. The Court disagreed. It maintained that a new legal order had come into existence with the signing of the Treaty, in which citizens could claim rights against their governments. The ruling of the Court contained the following famous phrase:

> the Community constitutes a new legal order of international law for the benefit of which the states have limited their sovereign rights, albeit within limited fields, and the subjects of which comprise not only member states but also their nationals. Community law therefore not only imposes obligations on individuals but is also intended to confer upon them rights that become part of their legal heritage.

(Quoted in Kuper 1998: 5)

As a result of this judgment, 'in individuals and in the national courts, the ECJ found two powerful allies in efforts to force national governments to comply with European law' (Kapsis 2010: 183).

Costa v. ENEL (1964)

In this case, the Court first asserted the supremacy of EU law over national law. Again, there was no explicit authority for this in the Treaty. An Italian court referred the case to the ECJ, requesting whether an Act of the Italian Parliament, passed later in time than the Act that embodied an EU directive into Italian law, took precedence. The Court said that it did not, making clear that national law cannot take precedence over EU law. This was a perfectly logical position, but it had particular consequences for those states—in this case Italy, but after its accession in 1973, also the UK—in which Parliament holds sovereignty. In such systems, the principle that prevails is *lex posterior priori derogat*: 'the later law overrides the earlier'. The *Costa* v. *ENEL* judgment struck at the heart of the principle of parliamentary sovereignty.

Van Duyn v. Home Office (1974)

A Dutch national who had been debarred from entering Britain because she was a member of the Church of Scientology, which the British Home Office considered to be a socially undesirable organization, brought a case in the English courts challenging the ruling. This case was brought on the grounds that Article 48 of the EEC Treaty (now TFEU Article 45) committed the member states to allow free movement of workers, and that the British government had accepted Directive 64/221 which implemented this Treaty provision as part of the *acquis communautaire* when it joined the EC. The Court was asked to decide whether rights could be acquired directly in this way from a directive that had not yet been incorporated into national law.

321

The Court decided that the directive did, in fact, have direct effect. Although the relevant directive had not yet been explicitly incorporated into English law, the Court maintained that the defendant could still quote it as grounds for her opposition to the British government's position. This ruling had wide implications since a member state's failure to transpose a directive could not prevent citizens from invoking it in the national courts.

The *Factortame Cases* (1990; 1991)

These cases arose because Spanish fishermen had been purchasing British fishing vessels, and with them the quotas that the boats had been allocated to catch fish under the EU's Common Fisheries Policy. In effect, the Spanish fishermen had been catching fish on the British quota and landing it in Spain. The British government had responded by passing the Merchant Shipping Act 1988, which required 75 per cent of the shareholders and directors of a company to be British in order for the company to be able to register as British. The Spanish fishermen claimed that this was a breach of their rights under European law.

In its 1990 judgment, the ECJ underlined the supremacy of European law, but also empowered the House of Lords to overturn British legislation: the first time that British courts had been allowed to set aside an Act of Parliament. The ruling had major constitutional implications in Britain. In its 1991 ruling, the ECJ subsequently agreed with the Spanish fishermen that the Merchant Shipping Act was in breach of European law because of its discriminatory nationality rules on ownership. Each of these steps caused a furore in the British Parliament, both because of what was seen as the manifest unfairness of allowing Spanish fishermen to take fish on the British quota, but also because of the domestic constitutional implications. The full impact of the ECJ's judicial activism only really came home to many British parliamentarians with these cases.

Francovich v. *Italy* (1991)

Before this case arose, the Italian government had already been taken to the ECJ by the Commission and charged with not incorporating into Italian law a directive that gave redundant workers the right to compensation, and made such compensation the first claim against the assets of a bankrupt employer. It had still not been incorporated when workers for a bankrupt Italian company took a case to court in Italy because they had received no compensation for redundancy. The Court's ruling established the principle of state liability—that is, that any government that did not properly implement European law was liable to damages claims by its own citizens.

Subsequently, the Court used the same principle, that a government that did not properly implement EC law was liable to damages claims, to decide that the Spanish fishermen in the *Factortame* case were eligible for compensation from the British government for loss of earnings during the period when they were prevented from catching fish on the British quota. It also decided, in another case—*Brasserie du Pêcheur* (1996)—that a French brewery could claim damages from the German government for the period when the German government enforced its beer purity laws, which the Court had subsequently ruled to be an illegal barrier to trade. So in these two cases, the liability of a government that had not properly applied a directive to be sued for damages was extended beyond its own citizens to cover other citizens of the EU.

ECJ Rulings and Policy Impact

The ECJ has made many important rulings that have not only defined the shape of the legal order (see the last section) or, as discussed earlier, by clarifying the powers of the institutions, its rulings have also been influential for EU policies. The single market will serve as illustration.

The original route to creating a **common market** was based upon agreeing harmonized regulations. This method proved unwieldy, since it could be highly contentious as to what should be the ingredients of, say, beer. As unanimity was needed in the Council, progress was going to be very slow. However, in 1979, the ECJ made a ruling known as *Cassis de Dijon* (Case 120/78), which centred on Germany's discriminatory alcohol legislation. The ECJ ruled that if cassis (a French blackcurrant liqueur) was acceptable under French legislation, then it should be acceptable in Germany as well unless some pressing public health argument could be mounted. The *Cassis de Dijon* ruling set an important principle: namely, that of mutual recognition. In other words, if goods lawfully met the standards of one member state, they should be accepted for sale in another member state. This principle was fundamental to the achievement of the single market, since it made clear that it was not necessary to harmonize legislation for every product. Instead, mutual recognition combined with a much more limited legislative package would accomplish the single market (see Chapter 27).

A second example relates to air transport liberalization. Prior to the 1990s, air transport was highly regulated and dominated by national flag carriers (British Airways, Air France, Lufthansa, and others), which were typically state-owned. Routes across Europe were regulated between pairs of governments and pairs of airlines. Intra-EU competition was very limited, because all routes were duopolies between flag carriers, which shared revenues on individual routes. The European Commission, with support from the British and Dutch governments, was trying to liberalize the market, but progress was slow because of the vested interests of the airlines, governments, and other actors. In 1986, the ECJ issued its *Nouvelles Frontières* judgment (Joined Cases 209–213/84). The ruling effectively declared the current bilateral air transport regime to be contrary to the EU's competition rules. With the authority of this ruling behind it, the Commission could apply more pressure with its liberalization legislation, which was later to usher in the era of low-cost air travel associated with easyJet and Ryanair (Armstrong and Bulmer 1998: 177–8).

It is important to point out that many of the ECJ's rulings are not as significant as these cases. Nevertheless, a proper understanding of the dynamics of those policy areas falling under the 'Union method' is usually facilitated by grasping a set of court judgments. Since the EU is distinctively characterized by its legislation and its supranational body of law, these features tend to be integral to policy dynamics. It is also worth underlining that the Commission has an important role in ensuring that agreed legislation is put into effect. Under Articles 258–260 TFEU, it proceeds through a set of stages that may ultimately lead to the ECJ. The ultimate sanction, introduced by the Maastricht Treaty, is for the ECJ to impose a penalty where a state has not complied with an earlier judgment. This power was first used as a result of a ruling by the ECJ in 2000 (*Commission* v. *Greece*, Case C-387/97), when the Greek government was fined for failure to comply with a 1992 ECJ ruling concerning the closure of a toxic waste tip on the island of Crete. The fine was €20,000 for each day of delay beyond the original 1992 ruling. Although a lengthy process, this case showed that a member state could receive a substantial fine for flouting an ECJ ruling.

Political Reactions to the Radical Jurisprudence of the ECJ

After a long period during which the pro-integration stance of the ECJ was tolerated by the governments of the member states, there was something of a backlash against the process of European integration generally, and against the ECJ more particularly, in the 1990s. The difficulties that were encountered in several member states in getting ratification of the TEU reinforced a tendency that had already been apparent in the inclusion in that Treaty of clauses on **subsidiarity** (Insight 23.2). The desire to limit the transfer of competences from member states to the EU institutions came from different quarters: John Major's government in Britain; some subnational governments (notably the German *Länder*); and the French government, which pressed for the *acquis communautaire* to be reviewed in the light of subsidiarity.

> The formal introduction by the Maastricht Treaty (TEU) of subsidiarity as a general principle into EC . . . law both symbolized and contributed to a gradual change in the political and legal culture of the European Community. If much of the Community's legal activity before the 1990s reflected a self-conscious teleology of integration, the teleology of subsidiarity suggests a rather different future.
>
> (De Búrca 1998: 218)

Insight 23.2 Subsidiarity Articles of the TEU and TFEU

Article 1 of the TEU

This Treaty marks a new stage in the process of creating an ever closer union among the peoples of Europe, in which decisions are taken as openly as possible and *as closely as possible to the citizen.* [Our italics]

Article 5 of the TFEU

In areas which do not fall within its exclusive competence, the Community shall take action, in accordance with the principle of subsidiarity, only if and insofar as the objectives of the proposed action cannot be sufficiently achieved by the Member States and can therefore, by reason of the scale or effects of the proposed action, be better achieved by the Community.

As well as the general change of mood away from pro-integration sentiments, the implications of the Court's judgments in the *Francovich*, *Factortame*, and *Brasserie du Pêcheur* cases led the British and German governments to sponsor a proposal to the 1996 intergovernmental conference that the right to damages should only apply where there was 'grave and manifest disregard of their obligations' by governments—that is, not where governments believed in good faith that they were abiding by EU law and applying the relevant directives. The Court, not surprisingly, did not want to get into having to make these decisions, which are far from clear-cut.

It should be noted at this point, though, that it was John Major's Conservative government that, in the negotiations leading to the Maastricht Treaty, had successfully proposed that the ECJ should have the power to fine a member state if it flouted an ECJ ruling on 'a failure to act' (see above). Similarly, the Major government expressed its underlying support for the ECJ in its 1996 White Paper (Foreign and Commonwealth Office 1996):

> The Government is committed to a strong, independent Court without which it would be impossible to ensure even application of Community law, and to prevent the abuse of power by the Community institutions. . . . The ECJ safeguards all Member States by ensuring that partners meet their Community obligations.

In more recent years, the ECJ's judicial activism has declined, probably reflecting the greater attentiveness to subsidiarity in the post-Maastricht period.

Is the ECJ out of the Control of the Member States?

The evidence that the ECJ has been instrumental in considerably advancing the cause of European integration is convincing. However, the question then arises of how the Court was able to get away with its radical jurisprudence. In the 1990s, an academic debate emerged on this question that paralleled the intergovernmental vs neofunctionalist debate of the 1960s (Chapter 1). The intergovernmental case is considered first, and then the 'legal neofunctionalist' argument.

The Intergovernmental Case

Geoffrey Garrett and his collaborators (Garrett 1992; 1995; Garrett and Weingast 1993; Garrett, Keleman, and Schultz 1998) put the intergovernmental case. Their argument was summarized by another contributor to the debate (Carrubba 2003: 78), that 'the ECJ helped to facilitate integration, but only to the degree that member state governments desired it'. Although governments did sometimes contest cases brought to the ECJ, they often accepted and applied the judgment after it was handed down. This reflected the fact that governments were under pressure from domestic interests that would be adversely affected by a particular interpretation of EC law, and so argued against it. However, member states all accepted that they would be better off in the long term if the rules of the single market were implemented by everyone, and for that to happen required an independent and impartial referee to adjudicate on disputed interpretations of the rules, which is the role of the ECJ. To refuse to accept an adverse ruling would weaken the legitimacy of the impartial referee, and that was a cost that member states would be loath to pay.

In some cases, Garrett (1995) argued, the strength of a domestic interest that was adversely affected by a ruling of the ECJ would be sufficiently great that the government of a member state would attempt to placate it by unilaterally, but covertly, not implementing the ruling. In that way, it could avoid weakening the legitimacy of the independent arbitrator, while possibly avoiding the political costs of not doing so. Whether this course was followed would depend on the relative gains to the member state from the existence of an efficiently functioning internal market when set against the political cost of upsetting a powerful interest group. The states that stood to gain the most from the single market—generally the more northern member states—would be most reluctant to risk damaging the legitimacy of the ECJ even by covert non-compliance. Those that stood to gain less—mainly the southern member states—might be more inclined to engage in unilateral non-compliance to try to evade the political costs of displeasing a powerful domestic vested interest. Even then, the government would try to conceal evasion, and would plead implementation problems if caught.

On its part, the ECJ was very aware that its legitimacy was dependent on the behaviour of the member states. If governments were openly to flout its decisions, its legitimacy would be seriously damaged, and pressure might build for its powers to be weakened by revision of the Treaties. As a result, according to this intergovernmentalist interpretation, the ECJ avoided making decisions that would place powerful governments in a difficult position. It was able to do this because although the Treaty prohibited restrictions on internal trade, exceptions were allowed if 'justified on grounds of public morality, public policy or public security; the protection of health and life of humans, animals or plants; the protection of national treasures possessing artistic, historic or archaeological value; or the protection of industrial and commercial property' (Article 36 TFEU). According to Garrett (1995: 178), this gave the ECJ plenty of scope to find a reason for allowing an exception if it would be politically uncomfortable not to do so.

The Neofunctionalist Case

Burley and Mattli (1993) and Mattli and Slaughter (1995) argued that the ECJ had been the prime mover in European integration, and that the governments of the member states had passively accepted this lead. The ECJ had used European law as a 'mask' to cover its integrationist agenda, wrapping its promotion of integration in the discourse of legal logic and necessity. It had also used the law as a 'shield' to protect itself from political attack. If the governments of the member states did not like the activism of the ECJ, they had the means available to counter it, either by non-compliance with the rulings or by amendment of the Treaties. Yet the first had not been done to any significant degree, and the second had not been done at all. Burley and Mattli (1993) used the example of the famous *Cassis de Dijon* case to illustrate their argument, and were subsequently challenged specifically on their interpretation of this case by Garrett (1995).

The 'mask and shield' part of the argument was frequently quoted in later contributions to the debate (Garrett 1995: 171–2; Garrett, Keleman, and Schultz 1998: 149–50).

However, it was never a particularly strong element in the neofunctionalist argument. As Carrubba (2003: 78) pointed out:

> First, to assume that law 'masks' the political ramifications of a decision is to suggest that governments are incapable of evaluating what outcome would serve their purposes best. Since governments make observations on ECJ cases on a regular basis, it seems demonstrably implausible that the governments do not have well-formed preferences over outcomes. Further, to say that the legal venue 'shields' decisions from political interference, owing to the domestic norms of the rule of law, is to assume that governments will obey court rulings because governments have been observed doing so in the past. There are a number of reasons why governments may obey court rulings in one situation and not in another.

The threat of Treaty revisions could also 'be dismissed fairly easily' (Carrubba 2003: 76) because it required the unanimous consent of all member states' governments, which was unlikely to be achievable given the commitment of some states to the enforcement of the single market, and of others to the enhancement of integration.

The second part of the legal neofunctionalist argument was stronger. It started with the observation that, for the legal doctrines of the ECJ to be effective, they had to be accepted by national courts. This seemed to have happened. By making Article 267 references for a preliminary ruling, national courts had been the main accomplices of the ECJ in its 'constitutionalization' of the Treaties. Why had this collaboration taken place? Burley and Mattli (1993) suggested that a legal version of neofunctionalism was at work. Spillover was implicit in the concept of EC law itself, but it was cultivated by the ECJ to give the most integrationist interpretation possible to the existing laws. Other actors—national courts, private individuals—fed the process simply by pursuing their own self-interest in a rational manner within the changed context: for example, individuals did so by bringing cases against their own governments under European law when they felt that their rights had been breached.

Alter (1996; 1998; 2001) went further, arguing that the Article 267 procedure (previously the Article 177 procedure) actually empowered lower national courts. They were used to having their judgments overturned on appeal by higher national courts, but by making Article 267 references, they could directly influence the evolution of national legal principles. Higher courts might be able to overturn the substance of their judgments, but they were unable to challenge the points of European law on which they were based.

The ECJ has also been careful always to get the national courts on its side by proceeding in what another advocate of this theory, Mancini (1991: 185), described as a 'courteously didactic' manner. The judges:

> developed a style that may be drab and repetitive but explains as well as declares the law, and they showed unlimited patience vis-à-vis the national judges, reformulating questions couched in imprecise terms or extracting from the documents concerning the main proceedings the elements of Community law that needed to be interpreted with regard to the subject matter of the dispute.

(Mancini 1991: 185)

In this way, the European judges won the confidence of their national colleagues. Those who presided over even the lowest courts knew that they would receive sympathetic treatment if they were to make an Article 267 referral, and were therefore more inclined to do so.

This co-opting of national courts raised the stakes for national governments that might be inclined to defy the jurisprudence of the ECJ, for it would also be defying the jurisprudence of its own domestic courts. The indirect political costs of undermining the legitimacy of the rule of law in the domestic arena were considerably higher than the costs of undermining the ECJ. Research reported by Carrubba (2003: 95) indicated that European publics would be inclined to support their own government if it were in dispute with the ECJ, but not if it were in dispute with national courts.

A criticism of this analysis is that the alliance forged between the ECJ and lower national courts is not the whole of the story. The reception of the jurisprudence of the ECJ by national supreme courts has been less enthusiastic. Problems have arisen with the reception of the judgments of the ECJ by the Italian, French, British, and German supreme courts (Kuper 1998: 19–27). In no case has a national Supreme Court attempted to negate a decision of the ECJ: were one to do so, it would cause a constitutional crisis. In several cases, though, the national Supreme Court has disagreed with the reasoning of the ECJ, while finding alternative lines of legal reasoning to arrive at the same substantive decision. In particular, the doctrine of the supremacy of EU law over national law has not been universally accepted by member states. However, this is compatible with the argument that lower courts were prepared to collaborate with the ECJ on preliminary rulings because that increased their influence within their national legal hierarchies. The corollary of that argument is that higher courts would see their influence weakened, and so would be expected to resist the jurisprudence of the ECJ.

CONCLUSION

This review of the role of the ECJ particularly raises two of the themes that run through the book. The first is the theme that has been most prominent in the chapters on the institutions: the intergovernmental–supranational debate about the nature of the EU. A second theme is that of legitimacy.

If the role of the ECJ is approached in the same way as was the discussion about role of the Commission in Chapter 20 (see pp. 262–4)—that is, whether it is an agent of the member states or an autonomous actor in its own right—there is little doubt that the judgments of the Court have gone beyond what the governments of the member states were expecting. The radical jurisprudence of the Court may represent the logical consequences of the actions of the member states, but it is not a logic that was thought through by their governments, nor is it always welcome to them. In this sense, the ECJ has proved itself to be an autonomous, supranational actor in the process of European integration.

As intergovernmentalists would point out, the member states can rescind those powers that they have given to the Court—but this is not easy, because without an independent and authoritative interpreter of the law, all of the rules put in place by the Treaties and by EU secondary legislation would be subject to different interpretation by different parties. There has to be an authoritative source of interpretation, and it has to be unquestionably independent. Some parties to any dispute will not like some of the decisions of the independent arbitrator, but they will abide by them rather than see the collapse of the system from which they benefit generally. The result is to make it difficult to recall powers once delegated. Treaty changes require unanimity, and if even one member state is happy with the thrust of the ECJ's decisions, it will not be possible to reduce its powers because its one supporter has a veto on any attempt to do so.

There is no doubt that the ECJ has the formal right to reach the decisions that it does. Whether those decisions are accepted as legitimate is another matter. Most decisions of the Court have not impinged on the consciousness of national politicians or members of the public. They have received legitimacy through being accepted by national courts, especially those lower down the legal hierarchy. When ECJ judgments have come to the attention of national politicians, there has sometimes been a strong negative reaction, suggesting that the legitimacy of the Court's doctrines does not extend beyond the national courts and professional judges. The strength of reaction in Britain to the *Factortame* judgment is indicative of this. As Carrubba (2003: 96–7) noted, 'public perceptions of institutional legitimacy are critical to the EU legal system being able to act as an effective democratic check', but 'the ECJ remains woefully short on public legitimacy today'.

The highest courts in the member states have been less comfortable than have lower courts with the judgments of the ECJ. In consequence, difficult domestic constitutional issues have been raised intermittently. Essentially the ECJ has, in effect, 'constitutionalized' the EU from the raw material of the Treaties (Weiler 1999: 19–29). It has had plenty of scope to impose its own interpretation of what that constitution should look like, because Treaties are not carefully crafted legal documents; rather, they are the outcome of diplomatic negotiations and compromises. These far-from-watertight documents leave judges plenty of space to fill in the gaps. In doing so, the ECJ has enunciated principles that conflict with some fundamental national constitutional principles. The legal conflict shows the impossibility of taking several different national constitutions and reconciling them with one overarching European constitution. The political reaction raises again the issue of identity, which appears in the discussion of the legitimacy of the EP in Chapter 4 (p. 69). National politicians and publics find it difficult to accept that decisions made by their democratically elected national institutions can be overruled by an organization that has far less legitimacy in their eyes.

While this chapter has necessarily been selective in the material covered, it should be clear that the ECJ's impact through its rulings has been felt widely: across the EU institutions; across the EU's policies; and across the member states. Integration has not only been economic and political, as charted elsewhere in this book, but it has also had an important legal dimension. Moreover, the legal and political dimensions are often closely intertwined.

KEY POINTS

Structure and Functions

- The Court consists of twenty-seven judges and eight advocates-general.
- It is charged to ensure that EU law is observed.
- It has wide-ranging powers to hear various types of action and to give preliminary rulings.

ECJ Rulings on the Powers of the Institutions

- The EP has been a major beneficiary of the Court's radical jurisprudence.
- Although on occasions the Court has found against an extension of the EP's legal position, it also reversed this in subsequent judgments.

ECJ Rulings on the Nature of EC law

- The ECJ has been most radical in cases referred by national courts under Article 267.

- In early rulings, the Court stated the principles of 'direct effect'—that EU law confers rights on individuals—and the supremacy of EU over national law. Subsequent rulings confirmed these principles.

- A series of later cases also produced rulings that surprised the governments of the member states, because they placed upon them obligations to which they did not think that they had agreed.

Political Reactions to the Radical Jurisprudence of the ECJ

- The ECJ has been criticized for stepping beyond its legal role and behaving politically in favouring judgments that advance European integration.

- Partly because of a general anti-integrationist mood in the 1990s, the ECJ was subjected to increased criticism by member governments for its perceived political activism.

- The ECJ's judicial activism has declined in more recent years.

Is the ECJ out of the Control of the Member States?

- Both intergovernmental and neofunctionalist explanations have been offered of why member states have accepted the radical jurisprudence of the ECJ.

- The intergovernmental argument is that member states have tolerated the rulings of the ECJ because it is important to them to have an independent arbitrator that can enforce the single-market contract between them, and they do not want to undermine the legitimacy of the arbitrator by defying its rulings.

- The neofunctionalist case is that the ECJ had used the legal system as a 'mask' and a 'shield' to advance integration further than the member states have wanted, and that it has recruited national courts to assist it in this process.

FURTHER READING

For a useful review of scholarship on the EU's judicial system, see **A. Arnull**, 'European Union Law: A Tale of Microscopes and Telescopes', in **M. Egan, N. Nugent, and W. Paterson (eds)**, *Research Agendas in European Union Studies: Stalking the Elephant* (Basingstoke: Palgrave Macmillan, 2010), 168–88. Two very good non-technical introductions to the role of the ECJ are available, but are no longer up to date on detail: **R. Kuper**, *The Politics of the European Court of Justice* (London: Kogan Page, 1998); and **R. Dehousse**, *The European Court of Justice: The Politics of Judicial Integration* (Basingstoke and London: Macmillan, 1998). It is therefore important to check the details with an authoritative textbook on EU law, such as **D. Chalmers, G. Davies, and G. Monti**, *European Union Law*, 2nd edn (Cambridge: Cambridge University Press, 2010).

A view of the relationship between the ECJ and both national courts and national governments that is in line with what has here been described as the 'legal neofunctionalism' perspective is presented in **K. J. Alter**, *Establishing the Supremacy of European Law: The Making of an International Rule of Law in Europe* (Oxford: Oxford University Press, 2001). A collection of very good essays on legal integration is available in **J. Weiler**, *The Constitution of Europe: 'Do the New Clothes Have an Emperor?' and Other Essays on European Integration* (Cambridge: Cambridge University Press, 1999).

online resource centre

Visit the Online Resource Centre that accompanies this book for links to more information on the European Court of Justice, including the ECJ's own website: www.oxfordtextbooks.co.uk/orc/bache3e/

Chapter 24
Organized Interests

Chapter Overview

The term 'interest group' is used to describe a range of organizations outside of the formal institutions that seek to influence decision making. They provide a link between state actors and the rest of society, sometimes termed 'civil society'. Within the political systems of member states, interest-group activity is long established and it has increased considerably in the European Union (EU) arena since the launch of the single-market programme in the mid-1980s.

This chapter looks first at the general growth of interest-group activity at the European level, before analysing the types of group that try to influence EU policy making and the forms of representation open to interests. The resources that interest groups bring to the task are considered, as is how these resources gain the groups access to institutional actors. The chapter then looks at the strategies and tactics that groups use to try to influence the different institutions. Lastly, it looks at the issue of regulating interest-group access to the institutions.

[E]asy access to the European institutions and the dependence of those institutions on interest groups have allowed certain interests to have a substantial say in the European policy process ...

(Eising 2003: 205)

The Growth of Interest-Group Activity at the EU Level

Interest-group activity aimed at EU decision makers has grown spectacularly, particularly from the launch of the single-market programme in the mid-1980s. By the end of the 1990s, Mazey and Richardson (1999: 105) could speak of 'a dense European lobbying system ... which now exhibits many of the features of interest group intermediation systems long familiar in Western Europe'. Finding precise statistics on this growth is more difficult, but Commission figures suggested that, in the mid-1990s, there were around 3,000 interest groups active in Brussels, with around 10,000 individuals involved in the lobbying industry (Greenwood 1997: 3). More recent figures related to the number of lobbyists need to be treated with some caution (Greenwood

2007: 11). For instance, in 2005, the then Commissioner for Administrative Affairs, Siim Kallas, who was seeking to regulate lobbyists (see below), quoted the figure of 15,000, although the definition of lobbyists that was utilized and the evidence for the figure are not clear. By contrast, in April 2006, the European Parliament (EP) had issued 4,435 passes to lobbyists in connection with access to the buildings. However, as Greenwood noted (2007: 11), this figure is likely to be an underestimate because, for example, not all lobbyists register for a pass. Kallas reported in 2005 that 2,600 interest groups were operating at EU level (quoted in Greenwood 2007: 12).

For many organized interests, the development of direct representation at the EU level is in addition to their continuing attempts to influence national governments as part of their overall strategy to shape EU policy. However, the Brussels end of the strategy is increasingly important. Factors that contribute to this include:

- the growing policy competence of the EU;
- changes in the formal rules of decision making;
- the receptiveness of EU officials to interest-group representations;
- the 'snowballing' effect of groups following the lead of others, so as not to risk being disadvantaged;
- the Commission's support for a wider engagement of European civil society, particularly in the period following its 2001 White Paper on Governance, in which it committed itself to trying to ensure that the policy process was not biased towards certain interests (European Commission 2001a).

In line with the maxim that 'where power goes, interest groups follow', the increasing powers of EU institutions is an important reason for the rapid growth in interest-group activity at the European level. Whereas in the early years, the coal and steel industries and agriculture were the sectors most affected by the setting up of the European Communities (EC), there are now very few policy sectors that do not have an EU dimension (see Chapter 25).

Increased competences have been accompanied by changes in the rules of decision making (Chapter 19, pp. 236–43). The switch within the Council of Ministers to **qualified majority voting (QMV)** for most policy sectors makes it less sensible to lobby only at the national level, because a single state no longer has a veto over legislative proposals where this applies. There has also been a shift of power within the policy-making process to the EP, while the Commission's key role as initiator of legislation remains.

The EU provides relatively easy access for those seeking to influence decision making, which provides 'part of the explanation for the intensity of participation in the process by so wide a range of political and economic actors' (Wallace and Young 1997: 250). There are several advantages for policy makers of good relations with interest groups:

> Put simply, it is very difficult to make effective public policy without the *specialized expertise* which interest groups possess. Moreover, their cooperation in the *implementation* of public policy is a prime condition for implementation success. Finally, from the bureaucratic perspective, the mobilization of a constituency of *support* is vital to the long-term survival of bureaucracies.
>
> (Mazey and Richardson 1999: 106)

The importance of organized interests to policy makers, particularly in the complex emerging system of the EU, means that many groups find themselves greeted by an open door when they seek discussions in Brussels.

Although no one can be sure of the benefits of lobbying activities in Brussels, the fear of missing out has become a motivating factor for EU-level activity. Once some groups start to shift their activity to Brussels, a momentum builds up that carries other groups along with it. Mazey and Richardson (1999: 107) suggested that 'rather like bees around a honey pot, interest groups are attached to regulatory institutions in swarms. Once one set of groups begins to exploit incentives and opportunity structures at the European level, others are bound to follow; they cannot afford to be left out, whatever the cost'. Brussels has acquired the reputation of being 'an insider's town' (Greenwood 1997: 55; 2003: 2), in which those who do not have an established presence operate at a disadvantage.

Types of Interest Group

Interest groups that operate in Brussels can be classified under seven headings (Mazey and Richardson 1999: 108), as follows.

(1) *European associations* (for example, the Association of Petrochemicals Producers of Europe, the World Wildlife Fund for Nature—European Policy Unit)

(2) *National associations* (for example, the Confederation of British Industry, the Federation of Swedish Industry)

(3) *Individual firms* (for example, British Airways, Ford Motor Company)

(4) *Lobbying consultancy firms* (for example, European Public Policy Advisers)

(5) *Public bodies* (for example, regional governments and local authorities)

(6) *Ad hoc coalitions for single issues* (for example, the European Campaign on Biotechnology Patents, the Software Action Group for Europe)

(7) *Organizations of experts and epistemic communities* (for example, the European Heart Network, the Federation of Veterinarians of Europe).

Each of these seven types of organization has grown in the past two decades.

Different types of organization can represent any given set of interests at the same time. Business interests provide a good example. Business representation in Brussels takes the form of individual companies, collective national organizations (such as the Confederation of British Industry), and collective European organizations. The last category includes BUSINESSEUROPE, which brings together national business associations (and was known until January 2007 as the Union of Industrial and Employers' Confederations, or UNICE), and the European Round Table of Industrialists (ERT), which is made up of chief executives of major firms. The ERT was particularly active in moves to launch the single-market programme in the mid-1980s (see Chapter 27, p. 397). In addition, firms individually or collectively might employ lobbying consultancy firms to advance their case.

Business interests were represented in Brussels from the establishment of the European Economic Community in 1958. The creation of the Common Agricultural

Policy (CAP) stimulated a growth of interest groups from that sector in the 1960s. Following the logic that activity by one set of interests stimulates competing interests into similar activity, there is now a wide range of groups that act as countervailing forces to business lobbying in Brussels. Trade unions, consumer groups, and environmentalists are examples of countervailing forces to business interests, although these groups were late to the game and only really became prominent in the 1990s. (For brief portraits of five European interest organizations, see Insight 24.1.) The other type of group that has exploded in numbers in Brussels is the lobbying consultancy firm, which sells its expertise and contacts to a range of clients.

Insight 24.1 Illustrations of EU-Level Interest Groups

BUSINESSEUROPE can trace its origins back to the establishment in 1958 of the Union of Industrial and Employers' Confederations of the European Community (UNICE). It changed its name in 2007. BUSINESSEUROPE is a 'horizontal' body reflecting industrialists' and employers' groups. Specific industries have their own organizations. It has forty member federations from thirty-four countries, including Turkey and Iceland. It has around forty-five staff in Brussels, and its member organizations, such as the British Confederation of British Industry, have offices nearby. Website: **http://www.businesseurope.eu/**

The **European Round Table of Industrialists** was established in April 1983 when a group of leading European business leaders from companies such as Fiat, Philips, and Volvo met to form an organization to promote Europe's industrial competitiveness. It now comprises some forty-five chief executives and chairmen of major European multinational companies from eighteen countries. It 'advocates policies, at both national and European levels, which help create conditions necessary to improve European growth and jobs'. It has a small secretariat in Brussels. Website: **http://www.ert.be/**

The **European Trade Union Confederation (ETUC)** styles itself as 'the voice of European workers'. The ETUC can trace its origins back to the 1950s, but only took on its current title in 1973. Owing to competing trade union organizations in some member states (Christian, socialist, communist), it was only by the 1990s that the ETUC took on its broad representative character of today. It comprises eighty-two national trade union confederations from thirty-six European countries and twelve industry federations (such as the European Metalworkers' Federation). It works for a European social model comprising sustainable economic growth, full employment, and social protection. Its secretariat is in Brussels and has approximately 50 staff. Website: **http://www.etuc.org/**

The **Committee of Professional Agricultural Organizations (COPA)** and the **General Confederation of Agricultural Co-operatives (COGECA)** are the key interest groups relating to the farming sector. Set up in 1958 and 1959 respectively, they have a shared secretariat of over fifty staff, based in Brussels. COPA comprises farmers' unions from the member states, whilst COGECA's membership is of member states' agricultural co-operative associations. COPA-COGECA has a large number of working parties on different agricultural products: from eggs and poultry to wine. Website: **http://www.copa-cogeca.be/**

The **European Women's Lobby** was created in 1990. It aims to promote women's rights and equality between women and men in the European Union. It has member organizations in all twenty-seven member states and in three candidate countries. It has a small secretariat in Brussels. Website: **http://www.womenlobby.org/**

Source: All information sourced from the respective websites.

Forms of Interest Representation

Several forms of interest representation coexist in the EU:

- the full institutionalization of representation through the European Economic and Social Committee (EESC);
- the semi-institutionalized 'social dialogue';
- a **pluralist** system based on competitive lobbying;
- informally institutionalized policy networks;
- legal representation.

The EESC has its origins in the **'corporatist'** institutions that were set up between the wars in Germany (the Economic Council) and France (the *Conseil Economique et Social*), and which were created or recreated in five of the six original member states after the war, Germany being the exception. The EESC has not proven to be a particularly effective institution (Chapter 19, pp. 234–5), and when new forms of institutionalized relations between government, business, and trade unions were tried in several member states during the 1970s, attempts to replicate them at the EU level did not involve this institution. Instead, the Ministers of Social Affairs and Economic and Financial Affairs organized a series of tripartite conferences bringing together European business and trade union organizations in an arrangement that is often referred to as **neo-corporatism**. The tripartite conferences met six times in 1978 to discuss issues such as employment, inflation, wage restraint, fiscal policy, vocational training, and measures to increase productivity. The business groups were reluctant participants, though, and by the end of 1978, the European Trade Union Confederation (ETUC) had withdrawn from the process because of lack of progress.

The idea was revived by Jacques Delors when he became President of the Commission. In 1985, an approach was made to both ETUC and UNICE to open a 'social dialogue' to flank the momentum towards the single market. Delors suggested that if the idea were accepted, the Commission would refrain from introducing further social legislation, and would instead let it emerge out of the dialogue. Initially, two working parties were set up: on employment policies and on new technology and work. They met at the chateau of Val Duchesse outside Brussels, and the dialogue therefore became known as the 'Val Duchesse process'.

From the outset, there were difficulties about the status and functioning of the social dialogue, which was incorporated into the Social Protocol of the Maastricht Treaty. It was agreed that where the social partners could negotiate agreement on any aspect of social legislation, that agreement would automatically be accepted by the Commission and formulated as a proposal to the Council of Ministers, with the expectation that it would become part of the social legislation of the EC—although it would not apply to Britain, which at that time had an opt-out from the Social Protocol. The first piece of legislation to be agreed in this way, in 1995, concerned paid parental leave. However, subsequent progress was limited. The lack of enthusiasm of UNICE and its member organizations for EU-level neo-corporatism reflected the fact that business interests are in a stronger position to get their views heard under the alternative, pluralist system of interest representation.

A pluralist approach to lobbying suggests that interest groups operate in a more open and competitive political process. This pluralist approach is generally associated with lobbying in the United States. However, there are clear differences between lobbying in the EU and in the United States. As Cornelia Woll puts it (2006: 461), 'According to most studies, lobbying in the US is much more direct and aggressive than in the EU, where lobbyists take a more subtle and consensus-oriented approach'. Pluralism tends to be characterized by the dominance of large firms, putting them in an advantageous position to become core members of any emerging policy networks. In theory, this pluralist system could be just a temporary stage in the evolution of interest representation. Once the EU system settles down, it could move to a greater informal institutionalization based on policy networks (see Chapter 2, pp. 28–33), which has already occurred in some of the more established policy sectors, such as agriculture.

Overall, the relationship between organized interests and the EU wavers between pluralism and informal institutionalization. As evidence of the latter, the Commission maintains partnership arrangements with interest groups, as Greenwood points out (2007: 5). Accordingly, several Commission Directorates-General (DGs) have contact groups for 'civil dialogue', including the DGs responsible for Development, Trade, the Environment, and Employment and Social Affairs. The Commission has encouraged the establishment of some interest groups, such as, in 1990, the European Women's Lobby (Greenwood 2003: 223). It also has financial resources to promote the work of civil society groups, helping to ensure that 'asymmetries between different types of interests are less extreme than might otherwise be the case' (Greenwood 2007: 18).

Finally, although it constitutes a very different activity from lobbying, for certain categories of interest group, targeting the European Court of Justice (ECJ) has been a particularly fruitful activity. Mazey and Richardson (1999: 115) noted that '[w]omen's and environmental groups (and also trade unions) have been adept in securing favourable ECJ decisions which have been just as, if not more, effective than bringing about change in EU policy via other means'. Here, 'whistleblowing' activity of groups in highlighting non-compliance with EU decisions by member states has been prominent.

Resources

The extent to which groups command resources of varying types is crucial to understanding their relative influence. The control of key resources is an important factor in deciding whether a group will secure 'insider status' with policy makers or remain outside the core process.

Greenwood (1997: 18–20) identified eight types of resource as important to interest groups (Insight 24.2). When it comes to such resources, size matters: larger organizations are generally better resourced than smaller ones. At the level of individual firms, big-business interests possess far more of the resources that are needed to operate effectively than do small-business interests. For example, large firms will often have their own public relations departments, which means that they are better equipped to present their views than smaller firms. Also, the complexity and multi-level nature of EU decision making puts a premium on being able to deploy sufficient personnel to cover all possible access points.

> **Insight 24.2 Resources Available to Interest Groups**
>
> - Information and expertise
> - Economic muscle
> - Status
> - Power in implementation
> - The organization of the interest into a non-competitive format
> - Coherent organization with representative outlets able to make decisions with ease and alacrity
> - The ability to help the overloaded Commission with carrying out policies
> - The ability of a group to influence its members

The diffuse character of the Brussels process within and between institutions means that to be a participant often requires covering several access points in order to find the most useful one. Small groups, and small firms, thus find it much harder to engage than the better resourced organizations or firms.

(Wallace and Young 1997: 244)

Only large individual firms or other particularly well-resourced interest groups are able to pursue their own information gathering and lobbying without joining forces with other actors. To become more effective, smaller organizations have to pool resources. Kohler-Koch (1997: 58) provided the example of business: 'Large firms find it easy to become privileged interlocutors of the political-administrative system, thanks to their economic importance, while small and medium-sized firms rely more heavily on their collective force.' However, while there are resource advantages in separate interests coming together, such combinations of interests increase the risk that they will encounter problems of collective action: the interests aggregated within a combined group may find it difficult to agree among themselves about priorities and tactics.

This disparity in material resources does not necessarily mean that large individual firms have the best access to the policy-making process, though. Bouwen (2002; 2004a; 2004b) argued that the degree of access that an interest group can achieve to any of the EU's institutions depends on its ability to offer each institution the type of information that it most needs to perform efficiently its functions within the decision-making system. He identified three types of information that are important in differing degrees to the various EU institutions:

- expert knowledge;
- knowledge of the needs and concerns of actors in the relevant sector across Europe;
- knowledge of the specific concerns of national actors in the relevant sector.

Expert knowledge is essential for the institution to understand the technical working of the context into which the legislation is an intervention. It results in legislation that is better adapted to its purpose, and is therefore likely to work better. Information about the needs and concerns of actors in the relevant sector, both across Europe as a whole and in specific national contexts, enhances the legitimacy of the decision-making process, because a wide range of affected actors will feel that they have been listened to, and this ought to contribute to their compliance with the legislation and therefore to the chances of successful implementation.

Different types of interest group possess these different types of information in varying degrees. Interests that pursue their own lobbying—which will most often be large firms, because they have the resources to do so—are very good at providing expert information. European and national associations are less efficient at providing expert information, but they are very good at providing information on the concerns of actors across Europe in the case of European organizations, and on the concerns of national actors in the case of national associations. On the basis of this theoretical analysis, Bouwen (2002) drew up a number of hypotheses about the degree of access that different types of group would have to the different institutions of the EU. These are reviewed in the next section.

Organized Interests and the Institutional Actors

The Commission

For a number of reasons, the Commission is an important target for interest groups:

- it has a central role in setting the agenda;
- all proposals have to pass through it;
- it is there that the detail of proposals is decided;
- it is receptive to approaches from interest groups.

The Commission's agenda-setting role is of particular importance to interest groups. If they want to get particular issues placed on the agenda of the EU, the Commission is a good place to start lobbying. Alternatively, if they want to prevent measures from coming onto or rising up the agenda, influence in the Commission is vital. All policy proposals 'have to pass through the Commission gateway and are subject to detailed *processing* at that institutional site' (Mazey and Richardson 1999: 112). This means that the Commission is an important channel to monitor. It also means that it is the primary place for influencing the detail of proposals, which is often what concerns interest groups.

The Commission is widely recognized as being receptive to interest-group representations. This is not least because the Commission's limited human resources make it more dependent than other institutions on the information and expertise that interest groups can offer. Bouwen (2002: 379) argued that, in terms of the three types of knowledge that he had identified, the Commission needed expert knowledge most, to allow it to construct viable legislation that successfully addressed the problem and was most likely to be implemented successfully. Second, it required information on the concerns of actors across Europe in order to boost both its own legitimacy and that of the specific piece of legislation. It needed information on the concerns of specific groups of national actors only in so far as it proved necessary for it to broker a deal within the Council of Ministers between differing national preferences.

Mapping the Commission's demand for each type of information against the supply from different types of actor, Bouwen (2002: 382) hypothesized that large individual firms, which could provide good-quality expert knowledge efficiently, would have the best access to the Commission, followed by European associations, which could provide reliable information on the concerns of the sector across Europe. While national associations would enjoy the lowest level of access during the crucial drafting stage of legislation, at the later stages of the passage of the legislation through the Council of Ministers, they might well find that their particular expertise on the concerns of national actors was sought by the Commission. However, subsequent research indicated that European associations actually had the best access to the Commission, despite the fact that they were 'often considered to be internally divided, poorly resourced and unable to respond quickly to Commission requests for information' (Bouwen 2004a: 355). Large firms were close behind in second place, while national associations were far behind.

This finding was not predicted in Bouwen's original model of access to the Commission, but it was consistent with the observation of Greenwood (1997: 4) that the Commission preferred interaction with Euro-groups where possible:

> Places on its advisory committees are handed out to Euro groups first. Drafts of directives and other policy initiatives are often given to European business sector associations to comment on. Although single-firm representations to the Commission are heard, the firm concerned is usually told that the Commission would wish to explore the issue further by talking to the interest group concerned in order to ensure that it gets a more representative opinion.

Kohler-Koch (1997: 53) noted further that the Commission 'has actively promoted the organization of the less represented social interests in order to achieve more balanced participation'. It has also sought alliances with influential groups to strengthen its position vis-à-vis the Council in the EU system. Authoritative and representative interest groups can provide the unelected Commission with legitimacy in its arguments with the Council. As noted earlier, it has justified this position in connection with its 2001 White Paper on Governance, and the wish to avoid large groups becoming overly dominant in lobbying.

The Council of Ministers

The authority of the Council makes it an important target for interest groups. Yet in reality there is little opportunity for them to lobby either the European Council or the Council of Ministers directly. These institutions meet behind closed doors and, generally, groups do not have direct access. Because its members are supported by national administrations and permanent officials in Brussels, the Council has less need for the information resources of interest groups than does the Commission, and is thus less receptive to approaches. The consequence is that most lobbying of the Council is indirect rather than direct.

To influence the Council indirectly, groups seek contact with individual national governments. Initially, of course, they will try to influence their own national government—but as understanding of the EU policy process has grown, interest groups' lobbying techniques have become more sophisticated, and interest groups in one member state may now seek to influence governments in other member states. Which governments matter will vary with the issue. For obvious reasons, the member state holding the Council presidency will be a particular target.

Although lobbying national governments is only an indirect way of influencing EU affairs, it is a process that is familiar to most interest groups. It is, as Greenwood (2003: 39) argued, an arena 'where established policy networks and dependency relationships operate which can equally well be used for the purposes of EU representation as for the governance of domestic affairs'. Moreover, for those groups that do not have the necessary resources to lobby EU institutions, the national route may remain the only real option. However, the value of lobbying individual governments has declined with the extension of QMV in the Council. Even where a group has successfully persuaded a government of its case, under QMV, it is far from certain that the government will be able to assist, assuming it is persuaded of the lobbyists' case in the first place. As such, 'it is one thing to argue that the majority of groups still rely on the national opportunity structures, but quite another to conclude that this is an efficacious form of behaviour. It is no accident that large firms appear to show a growing preference for Euro-level lobbying' (Mazey and Richardson 1999: 119).

Bouwen (2002: 381) noted that, at the ministerial level, the Council is the most intergovernmental of the institutions—but at the level of the officials involved in the preparation of the ministerial meetings, there is also a considerable degree of supranationalism. In terms of his model, the governments of member states primarily need information on the needs and concerns of their own state's actors in the policy sector, so that they can formulate their national preferences on any legislation. However, at the level of officials, there is considerable concern for the impact of legislation on the European market as a whole, as well as the narrower focus on national interests, so the expert committees might well be open to representations from European associations. Expert knowledge is less needed from outside sources, as there is plenty available from national officials who staff the committees that consider the proposed legislation.

On this basis, Bouwen (2002: 382) expected national associations, together with large national firms that constituted 'national champions', to have the best access to the Council of Ministers via the national route. European associations were expected to have some access via the European route, with large individual firms (except 'national champions' who gained access through the national route) having the least access. These hypotheses were largely supported by the subsequent research (Bouwen 2004a). The best access was for national associations, closely followed by large firms that were national champions. Other large firms and European associations had very much less access.

The European Parliament

Despite the fact that the EP traditionally had less influence over decision making than either the Council or the Commission, it has always attracted considerable attention from interest groups. This is largely because of its long-standing advisory role, which has been viewed as an indirect route to influencing the other institutions. Moreover, members of the European Parliament (MEPs) are relatively accessible. In particular, those with a constituency interest in an issue will be the focus of attention.

More generally, the EP is seen as a 'natural ally' for groups lobbying on behalf of consumers, the environment, and a range of human rights including women's and children's rights. This is 'not because MEPs necessarily favour their demands, but because their interests match. MEPs are eager to take up those issues which attract a broad public interest and are grateful for any external support which mobilizes public attention, because this will increase their political weight in the decision-making process' (Kohler-Koch 1997: 55–6). In addition to representations to individual MEPs, they can also be targeted collectively through the numerous inter-groups that bring together MEPs with similar interests in a relatively formal arena.

As the logic of interest-group activity suggests, lobbying around EP plenary sessions and committee meetings has increased with the enhancement of Parliament's powers in the various Treaty reforms from the Single European Act (SEA) to the Lisbon Treaty. For example, in 2010, the EU's draft Capital Requirements Directive 3 was going through the legislative process under the co-decision process. With a range of controversial issues including bankers' remuneration in the draft legislation, it was no surprise that the full firepower of the banking lobby was directed at the EP and members of its Economic and Monetary Affairs Committee.

Like the Commission, the EP lacks the national administrative support that is available to the members of the Council. Bouwen (2002) argued that while the EP does rely on interest groups for expert knowledge to some extent, it initially has a much greater need for information on the concerns of the relevant actors in the sector across Europe, to alert it to impending legislation that might not meet the needs and interests of the European market as a whole. If it seeks to amend legislation in detail, it will also need expert knowledge. On the other hand, individual MEPs need information on the concerns of their own national actors in the relevant sector to alert them to legislation that might be damaging to their own constituents.

On this basis, Bouwen (2002: 382) expected European associations to have the best access to the EP as an institution, because they could provide the initial and crucial information on the likely impact of impending legislation on the sector at the European level. National associations were expected to have a lower level of access, but might well be able to gain access via the national route, through the offices of MEPs. Large firms were expected to have the lowest level of access. These hypotheses were again supported by subsequent research: European associations had the best access to the EP, closely followed by national associations, with individual large firms a long way behind (Bouwen 2004b: 492).

Strategies and Tactics

The strategies and tactics of interest groups will vary depending on the targeted decision maker and/or the issue concerned. There is no magic formula for success in lobbying. There are, however, tried-and-tested practices that suggest that some approaches are better than others. Greenwood (1997: 8) offered some advice for lobbying Brussels

Insight 24.3 How to Lobby in Brussels

- Have a clear strategy.
- Develop long-term relations with authorities. Establish a track record as a provider of useful, accurate, well-researched information.
- Find out who is drafting an item and make your representations early.
- Prepare well for meetings. Beware of using hired hands to present cases where their knowledge of your issue will inevitably be limited.
- Present with brevity and clarity.
- Be aware of all sides of the argument. Keep it low-key; do not over-lobby. Appreciate the limits of what can be achieved.
- Keep all viable channels of communication open.
- Know the system, and get to know the points of entry to the decision-making process.
- Remain vigilant.

Source: Greenwood (1997: 8)

(Insight 24.3). Much of this advice amounts to good common sense. Policy makers are often under great pressure, and even those who respond to interest-group approaches need to feel this is a good investment of their time. Those interests that are professional in their approach, that keep to the point and do not waste time, and that have realistic expectations of the policy process are likely to develop the best relationships with decision makers.

This advice also indicates clearly the importance of timing in the lobbying process. For many groups, making representations early is vital, particularly in relation to policy formation. As Greenwood noted (1997: 8): 'If you have not been able to influence the Commission draft proposal you have probably lost the case.' Related to this is the need to maintain ongoing relationships with Brussels policy makers to ensure that there is a good flow of information so that issues can be identified quickly. Ongoing relations are also important in responding to issues, in that '[i]f you need to start forming a relationship when there is a problem it is probably too late' (Greenwood 1997: 8).

Moreover, the impact of lobbying is affected by the extent to which the views of an interest group 'chime with the emerging prevailing wisdoms of policy and with the quest of European policy makers (including those from national governments) for a form of legitimation for their proposed actions' (Wallace and Young 1997: 245–6). Even interests that are effective in every way advocated by Greenwood may well find that their efforts are without success if they advocate views that are out of line with the views of key decision makers.

As any card player knows, skill in playing the hand that you have been dealt can allow you to win even when your opponents have better cards. There are limits, though, to how far effective strategy and tactics can equalize the disparity of resources. As argued above, attempts by other interests to combine resources may reduce the effectiveness with which they can be deployed, because of tensions within the coalition about priorities. Also, big business has the financial resource to buy the expertise that it needs to take the maximum advantage of its already strong hand. Perhaps it is in order to gain some insight into how to play their hand more effectively that smaller players turn to Brussels-based consultancy firms, despite their apparently poor record in gaining access to the institutional actors.

There is one other strategic approach open to interests that fail to achieve insider status: they can, in effect, turn over the gaming table by politicizing the issue. Pluralist lobbying usually is most effective when it takes place out of the view of the public, and well away from the political debate. Similarly, policy communities are cosy relationships between organized interests and officials. Politicians are sometimes included in these relationships, but are usually peripheral to them. The policy community can get on with the business of making public policy without interference so long as the issues do not attract the notice of the politicians or the public. In either case, if the profile of the issue is raised above the political threshold, then the nature of the process changes. The strategy of excluded groups with interests in the field is therefore to seek access by politicizing issues. As issues become politicized, they disrupt the exclusive relationships between public agencies and insider interests (Greenwood 1997: 23).

The adoption of such disruptive techniques may be more common in the EU context than is sometimes supposed. Research by Jan Beyers (2004) rejected the idea that the technocratic nature of decision-making processes in the EU meant that interest groups would avoid public activism. Beyers (2004: 211) found that, although the institutional supply of access favoured specific interests, the EU contained important institutional opportunities for other ('diffuse') interests that aimed to expand the scope of political conflict or signal policy concerns by using 'public political strategies'. Finally, those interest groups that normally have insider status may 'go nuclear' on an issue as a matter of last resort. Farmers' interest groups have assumed the highest profile with this tactic. For instance, in May 2009, in a protest against milk quotas, farmers blocked streets in the European quarter of Brussels with their tractors during a meeting of the Council of Agriculture Ministers.

Regulating Lobbying

Concerns about the transparency of the lobbying process have raised questions as to whether access to policy makers should be regulated. This issue was already debated in the 1990s (Bache and George 2006: 345–6). More recently, in 2005, Commissioner Siim Kallas launched the European Transparency Initiative as a way of trying to raise trust in the lobbying process (Eising and Lehringer 2010: 195–6). This approach was consistent with the Commission's 2001 White Paper on Governance. It culminated in the Commission establishing a register for lobbyists. The EP, by contrast, is sceptical of having 'accredited organizations' on the grounds that this can be bureaucratic (Greenwood 2007: 4). In addition, it opposes the Commission's efforts to cultivate legitimacy through engaging with the relevant interest groups on the basis that this conflicts with the wider representation of citizens by the EP and national parliaments (Eising and Lehringer 2010: 196).

The Commission's register of interest representatives became voluntary in March 2007, replacing an earlier database, CONECCS (Consultation, the European Commission and Civil Society), which had listed those civil-society organizations that were being consulted in a formal or structured manner (Richardson 2007: 237).

Efforts have been made to align the new register with that of the EP. The Commission's list numbered 2,830 in June 2010, as compared with 1,883 registered under the EP's scheme, which grants buildings access to those registered, and is therefore not strictly comparable (see **http://europa.eu/lobbyists/interest_representative_registers/ index_en.html**).

CONCLUSION

This chapter raises issues connected with two of the themes identified in the opening section of the book. The first is the theme of supranational versus intergovernmental interpretations of the nature of the EU. The second is the theme of how best to ensure the EU's legitimacy and combat the democratic deficit.

Interest-group activity may provide a litmus test for the degree to which the **supranational institutions** of the EU exercise independent influence over the policy process. If interest groups transfer their lobbying activities away from national governments to Brussels, this may be taken as an indication that the EU is a supranational organization. However, such a conclusion has to be modified in the light of arguments and evidence presented in this chapter. First, the increased level of interest-group activity in Brussels has not replaced activity at the national level, but has generally supplemented it: lobbying tends to follow a multi-level approach. Second, although groups must have some reason to expend financial resources on establishing a presence in Brussels, this does not mean that the reasons are well founded: they may simply be afraid of missing out on something. There is a point at which the sight of other groups swarming to Brussels will lead groups to follow, on the assumption that there must be something worth pursuing, even if there is not.

Once located in Brussels, groups will not all be equally effective in influencing the supranational institutions (the EP and the Commission; the intergovernmental Council of Ministers being less amenable to lobbying). Most studies suggest that business interests are more influential than other interests, such as organized labour, consumers, or environmental groups. Within the category of business interests, large firms are more influential than small firms. Whether this relative influence matters, of course, depends on the answer to the question of how much independent influence the supranational institutions have over policy outcomes. If they do have some influence, and if it is true that big-business interests have the most influence over the supranational institutions, then this could provide one explanation for the observation that the policies that emanate from Brussels tend to be pro-business and in line with an Anglo-Saxon model of capitalism. For their parts, and in different ways, the Commission and the EP seek to ensure that a wide range of interests are heard in the policy process.

On the other hand, the domination of the process by big-business interests may not be as clear as several writers suggest. Beyers (2004) showed that interests that feel themselves excluded can make their voice heard by politicizing the process, while the research undertaken by Bowen (2002; 2004a; 2004b) indicated that business interests do not have the privileged access to the institutions that is often asserted. It should also be noted, though, that formal access is not the same as effective influence: from a critical political economy perspective (Chapter 3), it could be argued that big business can exercise a structural power over decisions by influencing what Wallace and Young (1997: 245–6) called the 'prevailing wisdoms of policy'.

The second theme highlighted by the chapter is that engagement with interest groups is an important way for the EU institutions to obtain legitimacy at the input stage of policy making. It is particularly clear that the Commission is dependent on the expertise of interest groups, thereby legitimating its work. There have been attempts to advance this type of interaction as a new form of governance, characterized by the Commission's engagement with civil society (see Smismans 2007 for a justification based on 'reflexive deliberative polyarchy'). However, it is questionable whether this interaction offers a solution to the EU's democratic deficit. Moreover, if lobbying lacks transparency, its legitimacy is called into question. Attempts to regulate lobbyists' access to the institutions has been the response to this concern.

KEY POINTS

The Growth of Interest-Group Activity at the EU Level

- Interest-group activity in Brussels has increased greatly since the mid-1980s.
- Factors in this growth are: the growing policy competence of the EU; the perception of a shifting balance of institutional power in Brussels, most notably in favour of the EP; the receptiveness of EU officials to interest-group representations; and the 'snowballing' effect of groups following the lead of others so as not to risk being disadvantaged.

Types of Interest Group

- There are several different types of interest organization active in Brussels.
- Business interests were the first to locate in Brussels, and still account for the largest number of groups.
- Interest groups representing workers, consumers, environmental interests, and other parts of civil society have become increasingly active.

Forms of Interest Representation

- Five forms of interest representation coexist in the EU: 'corporatist'; 'neo-corporatist'; pluralist; informally institutionalized policy networks; and legal representation.
- Of these five, pluralism and informal institutionalization predominate.

Resources

- The most effective interest groups in a pluralist system are generally those that control key resources such as information and expertise, economic muscle, and status.
- Small organizations can pool resources, but they may then find problems in agreeing on priorities and tactics.
- The three types of information sought by the institutions are expert knowledge, information on the needs and concerns of actors in the relevant sector across Europe, and information on the needs and concerns of national actors in the sector.

Organized Interests and the Institutional Actors

- For some EU actors, interest groups are an important source of information and legitimation and, as such, are enthusiastically consulted.
- The Commission is in need of the expert knowledge that big-business interests can often provide most effectively, but it has also sought to cultivate links with European-level associations and to promote less-represented social interests.
- The Council is less reliant on organized interests than other institutions and, as such, is less open to approaches. Much lobbying of the Council is indirect, through individual national governments.

345

- The EP is a key target for organized interests, particularly following the growth of its powers since the mid-1990s. MEPs are thought to be particularly sympathetic to representations on issues of broad public interest.

Strategies and Tactics

- Effective strategies and tactics can increase the influence even of interest groups with limited resources at their disposal.

- It is possible to identify good practice in lobbying. Developing good ongoing relationships with policy makers and careful timing of interventions are important.

- To be influential, groups generally need to be in tune with the prevailing thinking of policy makers.

- Groups that find it difficult to gain access to the institutions often seek to politicize issues.

Regulating Lobbying

- Both the Commission and the EP have sought to regulate lobbyists' access.

FURTHER READING

For a thorough and comprehensive review of organized interests in the EU, see **J. Greenwood**, *Interest Representation in the European Union*, 2nd edn (Basingstoke: Palgrave Macmillan, 2007). In addition to considering interest group strategies, resources, and channels of influence, this book includes separate chapters on some of the major interests, including business, labour, and territorial interests.

Two valuable collections of essays on interest groups are **D. Coen and J. Richardson (eds)**, *Lobbying the European Union: Institutions, Actors, and Issues* (Oxford: Oxford University Press, 2009), and **J. Beyers, R. Eising, and W. Maloney (eds)**, *Interest Group Politics in Europe: Lessons from EU Studies and Comparative Politics* (Abingdon: Routledge, 2009). The latter volume comprises articles published in a special issue of *West European Politics*, 31 (2008): 1103–302. A useful analysis of how some interests are privileged over others in their relations with the EU is offered in **R. Balme and D. Chabanet**, *European Governance and Democracy: Power and Protest in the European Union* (New York: Rowman and Littlefield, 2008). For a study that has a more normative position, suggesting that deliberative democracy in the EU can compensate for the democratic deficit, see **J. Steffek, C. Kissling and P. Nanz (eds)**, *Civil Society Participation in European and Global Governance: A Cure for the Democratic Deficit?* (Basingstoke: Palgrave, 2008).

 online resource centre

Visit the Online Resource Centre that accompanies this book for links to more information on organized interests:
www.oxfordtextbooks.co.uk/orc/bache3e/

Part Four
Policies

So many policy sectors now have a European Union (EU) dimension that it is difficult to provide comprehensive coverage, especially within the confines of a general textbook in which the policies are just one part of the overall book. Essentially, the choice that we had to make was between coverage in breadth or in depth. We settled for depth, although we have expanded the breadth of the coverage since the second edition with new chapters on environmental policy and on the creation of an area of freedom, security, and justice.

Each of the nine chapters in Part Four of the book provides a detailed account and analysis of the development of one of the major areas of EU policy. They are 'major' both in the sense that these policy sectors have been central to the development of the EU, and that they have attracted a good deal of scholarly attention and generated academic debate. The exception is Chapter 25, which outlines the main patterns of policy making, and gives an overview of those policies that do not receive separate chapters to themselves.

Agriculture and *cohesion policy* between them account for over three-quarters of EU spending. In addition, agriculture was the first common policy of the EC and therefore has a central place in the history of what is now the EU. Early theories of European integration were built around the agricultural policy on the assumption that it would form the model for future common policies. When it did not, the explanations of why the predicted developments had not happened helped to advance theory further. Cohesion policies (such as regional development) have taken an increasing share of the budget of the EU, now around one-third of all spending. This policy sector has been at the forefront of experiments with innovative programmes and modes of governance. It was here that the partnership principle was first developed for EU policies, and here that there has been the clearest evidence of multi-level governance in operation. Inevitably, therefore, the study of the policy sector has become an important arena of theoretical endeavour.

Creating a common market has been a central objective of the process of European integration since the signing of the Treaty of Rome (EEC) in 1957. Moreover, the project to complete the *single market* in the mid-1980s revived the faltering process of European integration, and attempts to understand the success of the single-market programme, and the spillover from it to other common policies, generated a parallel revival of theoretical endeavour.

The most significant spillover was from the single market to the creation of a single currency. *Economic and monetary union* has been around as an objective since the Hague Summit in 1969 (Chapter 10, p. 135). It had proved both controversial and elusive, so there was inevitably a degree of scepticism when attempts were made to use the momentum from the single-market programme to move to a single currency. This time, though, the effort succeeded, although without the participation of all of the member states. As with the single market, the success generated heated academic debates about the explanation. At the same time, the economic and political strains that the sceptics had believed would prevent the formation of the single currency put the new system under pressure almost from the outset, providing the sceptics with ammunition to continue their academic critique.

In the twenty-first century, the physical safety and security of its citizens has become of greater concern to the EU in line with a greater emphasis on these aspects of policy in the domestic politics of the member states, and in the light of the greater uncertainty of an international context marked by threats from pollution and climate change and from organized crime. Protecting citizens from these threats is increasingly difficult for individual national governments acting alone. Pooling sovereignty at the level of the EU offers the possibility of more effective action. As a result, both *environmental policy* and the creation of an *area of freedom, security, and justice* have become more important policy areas since the previous editions of this book appeared, and so each has been given a chapter of its own in this edition.

While all EU policies have an external dimension, the two policy sectors mentioned in the previous paragraph operate very close to the interface between the internal and external aspects of policy. External relations proper have two aspects: economic and political. Although not constituting the totality of the EU's external economic relations, *trade and development aid* together form the most important part of that aspect of external relations, and have also been the subject of academic analysis from a wide variety of different theoretical perspectives. Each involves a political aspect as well as an economic, but external political relations in the traditional sense of foreign and (military) security policy come under the general heading of the *Common Foreign and Security Policy* of the EU.

Finally, the process of *enlargement* is one whereby external relations are transformed into internal relations. In addition, this process has profound implications for the operation and nature of the EU as a whole, while the promise of accession is an important incentive allowing the EU to bring about changes in the politics and governance of neighbouring states.

Chapter 25

Policies and Policy Making in the European Union

Chapter Overview

Starting in 1958 with policies on internal tariffs, agriculture, and overseas development, the European Community/European Union (EC/EU) has gradually acquired competencies in more and more areas of policy. A complex system of policy making has emerged to deal with these responsibilities. This chapter reviews the main patterns of policy making, and looks at those policies that have not been given separate chapters to themselves in the rest of this section of the book.

[B]oth member states and supranational institutions 'matter' in EU policy-making, but their respective roles and influence remains highly variable across different modes of EU policy-making.

(Pollack 2005: 46)

In July 1988, in a speech to the European Parliament (EP), Jacques Delors predicted that, 'In ten years, 80 per cent of economic legislation—and perhaps tax and social legislation—will be directed from the Community' (European Parliament 1988: 140). The prediction infuriated the British Prime Minister of the day, Margaret Thatcher, yet twenty years later the range of EU activity had increased to such an extent that the Europa website listed an EU competency in some thirty-one policy areas (Table 25.1). The Lisbon Treaty provided some additional competencies in the areas of space, tourism, sport, civil protection, and administrative co-operation; it recast others in areas such as energy and environment; it also spelt out the balance of different competencies between the Union and the member states (Table 25.2).

These policy areas vary in significance, which means that they have received very different levels of attention in academic studies. Several of the most significant policy areas, both from a practical and from an academic viewpoint, are considered in separate chapters in this section of the book. Others are considered in more cursory form in this chapter. They in turn are divided into policy areas that are relatively minor or derivative and others that could have justified separate chapters had space been unlimited.

Table 25.1 Policy Competencies of the European Union

Agriculture	Employment and Social Affairs	Humanitarian Aid
Audiovisual and Media	Energy	Human Rights
Budget	Enlargement	Information Society
Competition	Enterprise	Internal Market
Consumers	Environment	Justice and Home Affairs
Culture	External Relations	Public Health
Customs	External Trade	Regional Policy
Development	Fight against Fraud	Research and Innovation
Economic and Monetary	Fisheries & Maritime Affairs	Taxation
Affairs	Food Safety	Transport
Education, Training, Youth	Foreign and Security Policy	

Source: **http://ec.europa.eu**, © European Union, 1995–2010

Before turning to the policies, though, the chapter looks at how the European policy agenda is formed, and at the main patterns of policy making that have emerged to handle that agenda. Much of this material recaps what has already been said in the section on the institutions, so it will be briefly covered here with cross-references to the relevant sections of Part Three where appropriate.

The European Policy Agenda

What is meant by 'the policy agenda'? The domestic policy agenda for governments is comprised of issues that pose problems demanding solutions. Some of these issues arise from domestic political pressures, either from interest groups or from public opinion, or both. Others arise from the international environment, such as security concerns or the effects of the globalization of production on economic interests. These two sources of inputs can interact. International events can raise an issue up the domestic political agenda, which is what happened with environmental policy in the 1970s (see Chapter 30). Disasters such as oil tankers polluting seas and shores, and accidents at nuclear power stations elsewhere in the world, increased public awareness in Europe of the potential environmental consequences of industrialization in the 1970s, and made it easier for domestic environmental pressure groups to recruit new members and to draw attention to long-term environmental damage, such as the effects of acid rain on the Scandinavian and German forests.

How do such issues find their way onto the EU agenda, rather than remain domestic issues? Sometimes it is because there is an obvious functional logic to trying to solve the problem collectively. Even the British government, often hostile to the adoption of European solutions, recognized in the 1980s that the economic problems of Europe could only be effectively tackled by joint action to create a genuine single European market (see Chapter 27). Sometimes it is because the problem itself arises from *spillover* from other EU policies (see Chapter 1, pp. 9–10), and therefore demands a European

Table 25.2 The EU–Member State Balance of Policy Competences

Areas of exclusive competence

Customs union

Competition rules for the internal market

Monetary policy for those states in the eurozone

Conservation of marine biological resources under the Common Fisheries Policy

Common Commercial Policy

Where an international agreement is necessary to enable the Union to exercise its internal competence

Areas of shared competence

Internal market

Aspects of social policy

Economic, social, and territorial cohesion

Agriculture and fisheries (except marine conservation—see above)

Environment

Consumer protection

Transport

Trans-European networks

Energy

Area of freedom, security, and justice

Aspects of public health safety

Technological development and space

Development and humanitarian aid

Areas of policy co-ordination

Member states' economic policies

Member states' employment policies

Member states' social policies

Areas of supporting, co-ordinating, or supplementary action

Protection and improvement of human health

Industry

Culture

Tourism

Education, vocational training, youth, and sport

Civil protection

Administrative co-operation

The common foreign and security policy

The Union shall have competence ... to define and implement a common foreign and security policy, including the progressive framing of a common defence policy.

Source: Summarized from Articles 2A and 2B of the Treaty establishing the European Community as revised by the Lisbon Treaty (Official Journal of the European Union C 306, 17.12.2007: 46–8)

solution. The single European market led to a spate of cross-border mergers, some of which threatened to create monopolistic enterprises that would prevent the achievement of greater competition, which was the purpose of the single-market initiative. This put pressure on national governments to agree to regulation of mergers at European level (see below, pp. 359–60). Sometimes the pressure on governments from domestic interest groups is specifically for the transfer of regulation to the European level, as it was for the deregulation of national telecommunications (Chapter 27, Insight 27.2, p. 390). Sometimes some governments are receptive to European approaches to problems because it allows them to escape political unpopularity for the measures that are necessary. There was a strong element of this in the commitment of most EU member states to the creation of a single currency (see Chapter 28).

Within this complex picture, there are plenty of opportunities for an actor with a commitment to increased European integration to exploit the various pressures on governments. The usual suspect here is the European Commission, an institutional actor that owes its existence and importance to the process of European integration and therefore has every incentive to try to maximize the extent to which governments are prepared to transfer policies to the European level (Chapter 20, pp. 263–4). However, the actor that is responsible for definitively putting items on the EU policy agenda is the European Council. Indeed, all of the examples cited above arose from declarations by the European Council. While the Commission may exploit the circumstances to influence agenda setting, it does not set the agenda in terms of strategy and large-scale initiatives. Also, much of the shift of activity to the EU level is voluntary on the behalf of national governments, in search of collective solutions to problems that are increasingly difficult to resolve to the satisfaction of organized interests and public opinion domestically.

The EU Policy Process

Once an issue is accepted as a legitimate item on the policy agenda of the EU, a complex political and bureaucratic process is set in motion, which involves a plethora of actors. This used almost always to be based around the formal institutional procedures that are described in Chapter 19 (pp. 239–43), and it often still is, although other options have been used more frequently in recent years (see below, p. 355).

Although the details of the involvement of different institutional actors vary according to the procedure that is relevant to a particular policy area, all of the formal procedures begin with the Commission formulating a proposal for legislation. In doing this, the Commission normally consults widely. It will usually discuss the range of options with the most obviously relevant interest groups at an early stage. There is no point in coming up with proposals that stand no chance of being accepted by governments due to strong lobbying against them by interest groups at national level.

The Commission will also consult widely with technical experts in the field, either on an ad hoc basis or through its own complex of committees of experts. Just as there is no point in formulating proposals that interest groups will work hard to block, there is no benefit in pushing through legislation that will prove to be impossible to implement, a possibility that can be avoided by consulting experts. Finally, the Commission will sound out national government officials to discover the parameters within which it might prove possible to get an agreement in the Council of Ministers.

Of course, the Commission will receive conflicting opinions and advice when formulating its proposals, and will have to make judgments of its own between these viewpoints. There is sometimes an element here of the Commission being forced to go for the lowest common denominator in order to ensure that it can get some legislation through. This is most often likely to be the case where the policy area is a new one for the EU, when the premium for the Commission is to make a start on building an *acquis communautaire* that can form the basis for further advance at a later date. Often, though, the Commission will take risks in order to push a certain position. This can backfire, but in many cases the Commission has already ensured that it has allies, either among powerful interest groups or within the bureaucracies of national governments, who will back its proposals against opposition from elsewhere.

In preparing its proposals, the Commission will also often consult those members of the European Parliament (MEPs) who have a particular interest in a policy area, especially those who are members of the relevant specialist committee of the European Parliament (EP). It is sometimes assumed that the EP is inevitably an ally of the Commission, because it too is considered to be an institution with a vested interest in further European integration (Garrett and Tsebelis 1996; Tsebelis and Garrett 1996). However, the relationship between the EP and the Commission is much more complicated than that. MEPs have to respond to democratic pressure from their constituents, they face party-political pressures, and they are subject to lobbying from a wide variety of interest groups. Also, the EP has a vested interest in standing up to the Commission to prove its independence and importance.

Adding to the difficulties facing the Commission, other procedures have appeared for governments to pursue European solutions to their policy problems without delegating as much responsibility to the Commission. Less formal and more intergovernmental procedures were introduced in the form of what is known as the 'Open Method of Co-ordination' (OMC) (Chapter 15, p. 186). Also, in the Treaty on European Union (TEU), two new 'pillars' were created alongside the EC pillar (Chapter 19, pp. 226–7). These covered Justice and Home Affairs (JHA—see Chapter 31), and the Common Foreign and Security Policy (CFSP—Chapter 33). In neither of these pillars did the formal rules of the EC apply. They were explicitly 'intergovernmental' pillars, and although the Commission had a role to play, it did not have the sole right of initiative, as it did in the EC pillar. The Lisbon Treaty abolished this three-pillar structure, bringing what had been JHA—and was now known as the area of freedom, security, and justice (AFSJ)—largely under the 'normal legislative procedure' (what had previously been known as the co-decision procedure), although the CFSP remained subject to a different balance of institutional power.

Minor Policy Areas

To classify any areas of EU competence as 'minor' is likely to be controversial. Certainly they are not minor for the actors directly affected, and some of the areas so classified here actually have quite a high profile with the general public. However, the extension of EU competence to these policy areas did not have major implications for the development of European integration, and consequently they did not attract a great deal of academic attention or analysis.

These minor policy areas can be roughly divided into four groups: those that have some independent functional justification of their own; those that arise largely as a result of functional spillover from the single-market programme; those that are really about building a sense of European identity among the citizens; and those that arise from the commitment made at the Lisbon European Council in 2000 to make the EU into 'the most competitive knowledge-based economy in the world' by 2010. However, several of these policy areas show aspects of more than one of these types.

Those policies that arise from independent functional logics include fisheries, fraud, and some aspects of both public health and food safety. Those that arise largely as a result of spillover from the single European market include consumers, customs, taxation, and some aspects of both food safety and the information society. Those that arise from efforts to build a sense of European identity include culture and education. Those that arise directly from the Lisbon commitment include enterprise and many aspects of policy on the information society.

The Common Fisheries Policy (CFP)

The CFP arose from the need to regulate the exploitation of the EU's fish stocks. It originally also had the objective of encouraging the modernization of the less efficient national fishing fleets—but as depletion of fish stocks reached critical levels, the policy was reformulated in a comprehensive review in 2003, after which grants were available only to improve the safety and comfort of boats, not to provide them with the most modern equipment for taking as many fish out of the sea as possible.

Although the allocation of strict quotas to national fleets is invariably unpopular with the fishing industry, and every new allocation produces new predictions of the demise of fishing in one region or another, there is a clear functional logic to regulating fishing in EU waters. The alternative is either a new 'tragedy of the commons', in which every national fleet insists on taking as much as it can from the common pool until fish stocks collapse to unsustainable levels, or the emergence of national protectionism for coastal waters. The latter option is not feasible because of the overlap of coastal waters; even if the boundaries could be sorted out, fish would be unlikely to recognize them, so that one state's efforts to conserve stocks could be easily undermined by a neighbouring state's persistence in overfishing.

Fraud

Fraud against the EU started almost as soon as the first common policies emerged. The first positive common policy, agriculture, was the victim of some very elaborate schemes to obtain payments outside of the rules. Some farmers mis-stated the amount of land that they had under cultivation, and claimed subsidies for non-existent herds. Middlemen returned fraudulent figures for the quantities of produce that they held in storage. Export subsidies were claimed for grain that had never left the EU.

When the structural funds were expanded following the Southern enlargement in the 1980s (see Chapter 29, pp. 423–5), many figures for the costs of projects were artificially inflated, and some money simply disappeared. The existence of different rates of indirect taxes on goods such as cigarettes and alcohol within a frontier-free EU has led to big increases in the smuggling of such goods from countries with low tax rates for sale in countries with higher rates.

So, once the EU existed, fraud against it existed—and this clearly needed to be investigated centrally given that the perpetrators of the fraud often operated in several different states. Today, there is a European Anti-Fraud Office (OLAF) that operates within the Commission, but with a special status to ensure its independence.

Public Health and Food Safety

Public health policy has several aspects, one of which is the control of communicable diseases. In a world in which people travel extensively, diseases quickly cross national boundaries. This is especially true in an area without frontiers, such as the EU. Although the outbreak of severe acute respiratory syndrome (SARS) in 2003 did not affect Europe as badly as it did other parts of the world, it did show up the inadequacy of the EU's existing system of exchange of information between national public health authorities. As a direct result, it was agreed to set up a European Centre for Disease Prevention and Control, based in Sweden, which would take the leading role in co-ordinating efforts to combat the spread of disease and responding to threats of bio-terrorism.

This aspect of public health policy is a function that is more efficiently performed at a European level than at the national level, and is therefore directly justified by functional logic, as are harmonized regulations on the use, storage, and distribution of blood products, and on ensuring access to health care for citizens of one member state while they are resident in another member state. Much the same arguments about the appropriate functional scale of policy making apply to food safety, especially where trade in food products crosses national boundaries, as it does in the single European market.

The creation of a single European market (see Chapter 27) gave the biggest boost to European integration since the creation of the European Economic Community (EEC), not only because of what it meant for producers and consumers directly, but also because of the spillover effects. These included strengthening the independent functional logic of regulating food safety at a European level, which already existed but was enhanced by the need to ensure that consumers were not wary of buying food from other member states because they were worried about whether it was safe to eat. Similarly, the need to remove the real or imagined concerns of consumers about the safety of manufactured products, and about their ability to claim their rights in the event of the failure of a product bought from another member state, created a spill-over to the need for an EU-wide policy on consumer protection and consumer rights.

Customs

By creating a single European market, the EU paved the way for a geographical area without internal border controls. With the exception of the United Kingdom, which insisted on maintaining its border controls with the rest of the EU (and, by default, the Republic of Ireland, which has long-standing special travel arrangements with the

UK, and therefore cannot unilaterally abandon border checks on arrivals from within the EU without forfeiting those privileges), anyone entering the EU, and any goods entering, can thereafter travel freely within the area. This has meant that customs and immigration officials now operate mainly on the external borders of the EU to control the arrival of people and goods from outside of the EU. Under these circumstances, it is considered appropriate that the EU has a role in the co-ordination of the work of national customs services, and the harmonization of the training of customs officials. (Immigration is covered in Chapter 31.)

The Information Society

For producers, the need to ensure a level playing field of opportunity led to moves to open up cross-national competition in telecommunications (Chapter 27, Insight 27.2, pp. 390–1), which was the beginning of an EU policy on the information society. Once national regulation of telecommunications had been swept away, it became necessary to re-regulate the industry at the European level. Mostly, though, this policy arose in pursuit of the commitment made by the heads of governments at Lisbon in 2000, to transform the EU into 'the most competitive knowledge-based economy in the world by 2010'. This led directly to the '*e*Europe' programme, which set ambitious targets such as ensuring that all businesses, schools, and universities of EU members had broadband access to the Internet by 2005, with further targets for enabling new members to catch up. Facilitating broadband access for remote and rural areas also became a major priority of the Regional and Social Funds.

Building a European Identity

A few of the minor policy areas date back to an earlier commitment to try to build a stronger sense of European identity among the members of the EC/EU. Although the cultural dimension to European integration was only formally recognized in the TEU in 1992, attempts to build a stronger European cultural profile date back at least to 1985 when the practice began of naming one or more cities annually as the 'European capital of culture'. The funding of the capital of culture and of other initiatives to develop artistic and literary creation, to develop heritage sites, and to stimulate intercultural dialogue come under a budget head known as 'Culture 2000'.

The Executive Agency for Education, Training, and Youth oversees the administration of one of the main programmes that had its origins as part of the programme for building a European identity, but has now outgrown those origins to become an important part of education policy throughout the EU. The Lifelong Learning Programme (LLP) is the successor to programmes such as Socrates, an umbrella programme that supported exchanges of university students and staff, the development of teaching materials, and the building of trans-European educational networks. The main elements of the LLP are:

- Grundtvig for adult learners and their teachers;
- Comenius, for schools;
- Erasmus for higher education;
- Leonardo da Vinci for vocational training.

While formal EU competence over education policies generally has been strictly limited by national governments, the Commission has been an active participant in pan-European initiatives on higher education that fall under the heading of the 'Bologna process' (see Corbett 2005; Bache 2006). Initiated by the Bologna Declaration, which was signed by Ministers of Education from twenty-nine European states in 1999, the process aims to create a European higher education area by making degree standards more comparable throughout Europe. It has achieved a considerable modification of national degree programmes and quality standards, and has done so through the use of the OMC, despite scepticism in some quarters of the capacity of the OMC to bring about such fundamental changes.

Major Policy Areas

As well as these minor policy areas, there are several major policy areas for which it is not possible to include full chapters in this book. These are policies that have considerable practical significance in their own right, and that have attracted a certain amount of academic attention as well. They are: competition; employment and social policy; energy; research; and transport. Like the minor policy areas, most of these can be justified either through independent functional arguments, as spillover from the single European market, or as part of efforts to build a sense of European identity. The academic analyses also allow us to say more about the political logic behind these policies.

Competition

Competition policy has been called the 'first common policy' of the EC/EU (McGowan and Wilks 1995). Yet, though some elements of competition policy did exist prior to the adoption of the single-market programme, it was considerably enhanced as a direct spillover from the single market. As McGowan and Cini (1999: 177) pointed out, competition policy is a necessary adjunct to the single European market because if large firms were to react to the opening of national markets by adopting anti-competitive practices, such as collusion through cartels, or mergers to create effective European monopolies, the aim of the single market—to increase efficiency and benefit consumers by enhancing competition—would be frustrated. To counter such anti-competitive practices, EU competition policy has four main aspects: antitrust and cartels; merger control; state aids; and liberalization.

Antitrust activity is aimed at preventing cartels. The Commission investigates reports of collusion between producers, for example to fix prices, and penalizes through fines those companies found guilty of acting in restraint of competition. This is necessary to prevent large producers from colluding to stop new producers from breaking into the market, or to maintain profits at artificially high levels by not passing on cost savings to consumers.

Merger control is a centralized system for approving mergers that have Europe-wide implications. Unlike the Treaty of Paris, the Treaty of Rome contained no provisions for merger control. Various attempts by the Commission to persuade the member states to redress this omission failed, until the single-market programme led to a big

359

increase in the number of cross-border mergers (McGowan and Cini 1999: 178–9). Concern about the possible emergence of monopolistic market conditions put the issue firmly on the agenda.

It was pushed to the top of the agenda by the ruling of the European Court of Justice (ECJ) in the *Philip Morris* case (1987) that the power to prevent market domination through mergers could be inferred from other Articles of the Treaty. This introduced a major element of uncertainty into the calculations of industry about how extensive the inferred powers of the Commission might be, and this uncertainty led in turn to demands from big companies for the member states to adopt clear and explicit legislation defining those limits. The Council of Ministers responded by indicating to the Commission in November 1987 that, despite having rejected four previous proposals, it would now welcome a draft merger regulation. The proposal led to protracted debates and negotiations, but the regulation was eventually adopted in December 1989 and became effective in September 1990 (McGowan and Cini 1999: 180). Under the regulation adopted, a proposed merger must be cleared by the Commission if the merged company would have a turnover within the EU in excess of €250 million, and a worldwide turnover of more than €5 billion, unless more than two-thirds of the turnover would be within one country, in which case the merger is subject to national scrutiny.

The Commission has considerable autonomy in merger control. Proposed mergers are considered by a merger task force within the Directorate-General for Competition (previously DG IV). Merger control is very political because it raises issues such as whether large European companies should be allowed to emerge to act as 'European champions' in global competition with companies from the United States and Japan. This is the position particularly of French governments, and contrasts with the position of the British, Dutch, and other governments that the most important issue is the preservation of competition in the European market. Under the guidance of a series of Commissioners who have shown a strong commitment to the free-market interpretation (Leon Brittan, Karel van Miert, Mario Monti, Neelie Kroes), the Directorate-General has moved in that direction, but all rulings have to be approved by the full College of Commissioners, and here the outcome is not always certain as political considerations can intervene.

Politics is even more at the forefront of policy on state aids, which involves the Commission investigating instances in which the government of a member state grants any of its own companies subsidies, loans, tax breaks, loan guarantees, or preferential purchase deals on goods and services, to ensure that this is not giving those companies an unfair competitive advantage. As Michael P. Smith (1998: 58) pointed out, the difference between merger control and state aids is that, in the latter, the Commission is confronting governments directly. Autonomous powers were granted to the Commission at an early stage in the history of the EEC, because there was a widespread wish among governments to remove distortions to competition in the **common market**, and it was obvious that an impartial arbitrator was needed. The powers granted, though, proved to give the Commission more autonomy than envisaged.

Were Member States given the choice today, they would probably not delegate the same powers to the Commission as they did 40 years ago.

(Smith 1998: 76)

However, rolling back those powers would require a revision of the Treaty, and could jeopardize the success of the single market.

Pursuing competition cases has always been a time-consuming process, and the Directorate-General for Competition has long felt under-resourced and under pressure. With the prospect of further enlargement of the EU, the Directorate-General moved to involve national competition authorities more in the enforcement of EU competition law. This move was formally implemented in 2003 through a Council Regulation known as the 'Modernization Regulation' (1/2003). Since then, the Commission has become more of a co-ordinator within a formally constituted European Competition Network of national competition authorities, leaving its own expert staff to concentrate on particularly complex cases, especially those that have extensive cross-national implications and those that are most politically sensitive.

Employment and Social Policy

There has always been a social dimension to the EC/EU. The Treaty of Rome, generally a laissez-faire document, contained mention of the need to achieve social cohesion, to improve health and safety at work, to facilitate the free movement of labour, to promote equality between men and women in the workplace, to harmonize social security provision, and to promote a social dialogue between management and workers. However, the change of name for this policy sector to 'employment and social policy' is indicative of a shift in the priorities, which in turn may be indicative of how far the Anglo-Saxon model of capitalism and changing economic circumstances have shifted thinking within the EU as a whole.

Originally, EC social policy was predominantly about the protection of workers. Although a large part of the European Social Fund (ESF) has always been used to retrain workers, the emphasis of the social policy Articles of the Treaty of Rome was much more on creating a level playing field of competition by imposing on all producers the same levels of protection for employees as applied in the most regulated markets. An example of this is gender equality, which was given its own Article of the Treaty of Rome (originally Article 119, now Article 157 TFEU) because France had extensive domestic legislation on equal pay between men and women before the EEC was set up, and wanted to ensure that the competitiveness of French companies was not damaged by this in comparison with other member states.

After the common market had been established, some of the first pieces of social legislation to be passed concerned the equal rights of women and men in work-related matters. The Equal Pay Directive of 1975 imposed a legal requirement of equal pay for equal work; the Equal Treatment Directive of 1976 made discrimination illegal in access to employment and training and in respect to rights concerning dismissal; and the Social Security Directive of 1978 required equal treatment in access to state benefits. All of these were rights that were already embodied in French domestic legislation, and the other member states were under intense pressure from trade unions and women's groups to adopt them at European level. That pressure was increased by the ECJ with its rulings in equality cases such as *Defrenne* (1978), in which it stated that although Article 119 (EEC) dealt explicitly with equal pay between men and women, the Article clearly established the principle of elimination of discrimination between men and women in the workplace as a fundamental principle of Community law.

Other than in legislation on gender equality, social policy had made little progress by the mid-1980s. Jacques Delors tried to revive it by arguing that the single market needed a social dimension if it were to be acceptable to those who would initially lose out. Yet the member states were prepared to make only health and safety in the workplace subject to **qualified majority voting (QMV)** in the Single European Act (SEA). Although the opposition of the British Conservative government to social policy was the usual explanation for this lack of progress, it was very convenient for other governments to hide behind the British veto.

Delors's argument pointed most obviously to the need for some element of redistributive social expenditure controlled at the EU level, to redress the large divergences in prosperity that existed between different social groups. The only significant element of such redistributive expenditure that did exist already—other than for specific groups of workers, such as for farmers through the CAP—was the European Regional Development Fund (see Chapter 29). Expenditure on redressing regional disparities did increase considerably as a result of the SEA, and again as a result of the TEU.

However, no large-scale social programme emerged as a complement to the SEA. Not only were there financial limits to what the richer member states would pay as compensation for the single-market programme, but governments also generally remain sensitive to the transfer of policy competencies in this domain. In addition, the variety of national types of welfare provision among the member states has made even harmonization of policy impossibly complicated (Majone 1993: 160–1).

In one area, though, Delors did lay the foundations for what at one stage began to look like a promising approach to extending the social dimension. Soon after becoming President of the Commission, he instituted a 'social dialogue' with representatives of employers and employees at the European level. In 1985, Delors approached both the Union of Industries in the European Community (UNICE) and the European Trade Union Confederation (ETUC) to propose an ongoing negotiation on social legislation. He suggested that if the idea were accepted, the Commission would refrain from introducing further items of social legislation, and would instead let them emerge out of the dialogue. Initially, two working parties were set up: on employment policies and on new technology at work. The meetings took place at the chateau of Val Duchesse outside Brussels, and were therefore known as 'the Val Duchesse process'.

A fundamental difference of opinion soon emerged between UNICE and ETUC. The employers wanted the discussions to lead to publications but not legislation; the unions wanted them to result in legislation. The first of the two working parties produced an anodyne report, based on the lowest common denominator of what the two sides could agree, while the second one failed to arrive at an agreed report of any sort.

Following this false start, the Commission made an attempt to revive the process in January 1989. At a meeting in Brussels, it was agreed to set up a steering group to sustain the momentum of the process, and to extend the dialogue to all areas covered in the 'Social Charter' that had just been agreed by the heads of government. Although it had no great achievements to its name, the social dialogue—involving UNICE, ETUC, and also the European Centre of Public Enterprises (CEEP)—was incorporated into the Social Protocol of the TEU, and became part of the Social Chapter of the Treaty after the British Labour government signed up to the Protocol at Amsterdam in 1997.

Under the terms of this 'social agreement', the Commission is obliged to consult the 'social partners' on proposed legislation under the Social Chapter twice: first on the principle and then on the content of the draft legislation. At either stage, the social partners may inform the Commission that they wish to initiate discussions to reach a collective agreement. This effectively stops the formal procedure for at least nine months. If a collective agreement is reached in that time, the partners can ask the Commission to present it to the Council of Ministers for formal approval, which is normally expected to be given, so that their agreement then becomes law.

This institutionalization of the social dialogue appeared for a time to offer what Wendon (1998: 343) called 'alternative venues' for the Commission to pursue integrative measures. Strøby Jensen (2000: 86), using neofunctionalist concepts, talked about 'institutional-legalistic' spillover, a similar idea whereby once the institutional basis for the social dialogue was established, it provided a forum for Commission activism. In practice, though, the legislative achievements of the social agreement were very limited. The first item that was taken under the new procedure, on European Works Councils, could not be agreed, although legislation was subsequently adopted under the normal procedures in September 1994 (Falkner 2000: 707–8). This was at a time when the British government was still not a signatory to the Social Protocol, and was therefore not involved in the discussions in the Council of Ministers. That deprived UNICE of its generally most reliable ally. The message that if it failed to reach agreement with ETUC, it might find unwelcome legislation being pushed through anyway, encouraged UNICE to be somewhat more co-operative. Subsequently, directives were adopted through the new procedure on parental leave (December 1995, adopted by Council in June 1996), and two on 'atypical work' in 1999—one on the rights of part-time workers and one on the rights of workers on fixed-term contracts (Falkner 2000: 709–11). By 1999, though, this method had already been overtaken by a change of emphasis away from protecting the rights of workers towards providing opportunities for work for the unemployed, and by the introduction of the OMC into employment and social policy.

Persistent unemployment throughout the EU led to the introduction in the Amsterdam Treaty of a new Title on Employment, which called for a 'co-ordinated strategy for employment'. A special 'jobs summit' was held in Luxembourg in November 1997 at which a strategy was agreed that became the model for what the later (2000) Lisbon European Council was to entitle the OMC. The Luxembourg process involves agreement on a common set of European targets, with member states drawing up what were originally called National Action Plans for Employment (NAPs), and subsequently became National Reform Programmes (NRPs). The NRPs are then submitted to the Commission and Council for scrutiny, and recommendations may be made. The Commission then produces an annual report on the performance of member states and of the EU as a whole in achieving its objectives, and targets may be adjusted accordingly (Adnett 2001: 353–9).

Although no member state is obliged to adopt a particular approach to achieving its objectives, the emphasis on emulating best practice has led to moves to free labour markets of restrictions and provide training for the unemployed: an approach more in line with the Anglo-Saxon model of capitalism than with the various continental models that have traditionally put more emphasis on protecting the rights of those in work. On the other hand, Adnett (2001: 360) reported that there was little evidence of a convergence of national policies, and that indeed, in some areas, there was evidence of increasing diversity.

Following the Lisbon European Council (2000), the OMC was also applied to social policy as more traditionally understood in the EU. At Lisbon, member states committed themselves to draw up National Action Plans to combat poverty and social exclusion, to devise indicators for assessing progress, and to develop mechanisms for ensuring the achievement of objectives in these fields (Hodson and Maher 2001: 726, Table 1). This commitment underlines the argument of Borras and Jacobsson (2004: 190) that the Lisbon Strategy addresses *both* competitiveness and social cohesion. As they went on to emphasize, though, the outcome of adopting the OMC would change in the nature of the social dimension, which 'had arrived at a stalemate' because 'more EU rights would have invariably undermined the socio-economic agreements and social contracts upon which each national welfare arrangement has been historically built ... There was simply no political support for the further transfer of legal competencies to the EU in these areas' (Borras and Jacobsson 2004: 190).

In the area of employment and social policy, the OMC produced progress where the traditional method of European legislation was severely hindered by the lack of any consensus over priorities, and where the prospect of more such legislation risked further damaging the legitimacy of the EU. The result was to change the nature of the policy sector, both the content of policy outputs and the process. The influence of the EP and the ECJ was weakened by their effective and formal exclusion from the OMC. Although the OMC did not similarly weaken the Commission (Borras and Jacobsson 2004: 198), it did change the nature of the game, and sidelined the institutional forum centred on the social dialogue that was identified by Wendon (1998) and Strøby Jensen (2000). This in turn led to the suggestion that the adoption of the OMC put the states in control of the design and implementation of EU social policies, marginalizing both the Commission and the social partners (Edquist 2006; Gold et al. 2007).

Energy

Energy is an area in which policy objectives have changed as a result of changing circumstances. For a long time, the main objective of energy policy for the Commission was the liberalization of national markets, which were dominated by monopolistic national suppliers. This resulted in high energy costs, which damaged the global competitiveness of European manufacturers. The situation came to the fore in the aftermath of the single-market programme, with the Commission acting as a **policy entrepreneur** to cultivate spillover. This story is told in a later chapter (Chapter 27, Insight 27.3, p. 392).

Once the principle had been established that national energy markets would be opened up to competition from other member states, the potential existed to shift other aspects of energy policy to the EU level. In 2004, the Commission identified problems concerning the high level of dependence of the EU on fossil fuels and on imported sources of energy. Fossil fuels are finite, and burning them contributes to global warming. The supply of imported energy is liable to disruption from international crises, which can also increase prices quite dramatically. From these problems arises the need to develop co-ordinated programmes to save energy, to use it more efficiently, and to develop alternative sources.

In 2005, the European Council approved the development of a comprehensive European energy strategy, and in 2006, the Commission produced a Green Paper outlining such a strategy (European Commission 2006*a*). The first Commission proposals to implement this strategy were brought forward in January 2007, including the introduction of binding targets for each member state to switch to the use of renewable energy sources—biomass, hydro, wind, and solar—by 2020. These proposals were also accepted by the Council.

The Commission used concerns raised by wider global developments, particularly concern about the security implications of an over-reliance on energy from unstable parts of the world and about climate change, to expand its competencies beyond those concerned with opening the market to cover these other issues. Spillover from energy policy into transport and into research policy was also recognized by the Commission. Thus the transfer of energy supply from a national to a European market brought in its train the prospect of a whole set of new competencies for the EU. The Lisbon Treaty, Article 147, amended the wording of Title XXI of the TEU on energy policy to reflect these revised policy objectives, emphasizing security of supply and the need to achieve energy efficiency and energy saving in the context of environmental concerns.

Transport

A common transport policy was one of the Titles of the original Treaty. There is an obvious functional necessity for efficient cross-border transport, to make a reality of the ideal of a common market, and a functional logic to organizing it at the European level. Arising from this, the European Commission has responsibility for the planning and part-financing of trans-European networks (TENs) for different modes of transport. Despite several statements of support for the TENs, though, the member states have never been prepared to provide adequate funding, so that the programme is always lagging behind the aspirations.

Spillover from the single-market programme allowed the Commission to push through measures to open national transport markets to competition. The liberalization of air transport contributed to a reduction in fares and a consequent increase in passengers; the liberalization of rail transport, which began with the implementation of a first package of measures in March 2003, held out the prospect of opening 70–80 per cent of rail freight traffic over main lines to competition. In the road-haulage industry, internationally competitive firms had long argued against the principle of cabotage with respect to loads, a principle that had reserved to national transport firms the right to transport national goods. This had meant that lorries carrying goods from their own state to another member state had to return home empty, which was obviously uneconomical. It was possible to get agreement on the abolition of this principle once the single market was in operation.

As with other policy sectors, different problems were exacerbated by the opening of the markets, and these provided a continuing agenda for action by the Commission. Problems with road congestion, pollution, and the continuing fragmentation of some transport infrastructure were highlighted in a 2001 White Paper on Transport, which also set ambitious targets:

- to reduce road deaths;
- to improve the speed of freight trains by eliminating the causes of delay;
- to reduce flight delays by developing an integrated air-traffic control system;

- to regulate the allocation of airline landing slots;
- to promote investment in inland waterways;
- to improve maritime safety standards;
- to improve port services;
- to introduce integrated ticketing and baggage handling for mixed-mode journeys.

Through a combination of these measures, it was hoped to move the EU away from its heavy dependence on road transport, to eliminate some of the consequent congestion, and to reduce the consequent pollution. These objectives were explicitly linked by the Commission to the Lisbon Agenda for creating economic growth and jobs, and to the increasing concern for protection of the environment and reduction of carbon emissions.

A mid-term review in 2006 said that the plan should now concentrate on making railways more competitive, introducing a ports policy, developing transport systems making use of the latest technology, charging for infrastructure use, producing more biofuels, and finding ways in which to make towns and cities less congested.

Research

Although a European technological community had been part of the original vision of Jean Monnet, technological research was not included in the Treaty of Rome. The main reason was that the idea of developing 'national industrial champions' held strong sway in the 1950s, as it continued to through until the 1980s. Despite several periods of concern about the technological lead of the United States over Europe—for example, the furore sparked by Jean-Jacques Servan-Schreiber's book *The American Challenge* (Servan-Schreiber 1968)—attempts by the Commission to persuade member states to institute collaborative research programmes had little effect until the 1980s, when a major breakthrough occurred with the approval by the Council of Ministers in 1982 of the European Strategic Programme in Information Technology (ESPRIT).

The reasons for this breakthrough were similar to those that brought about the even bigger breakthrough of the single-market programme (Chapter 27, pp. 396–8). The weak recovery of Europe from the 1979 oil-price shock, in comparison with the vigorous recovery of the United States and Japan, led to much of talk of 'Eurosclerosis'. The policy of supporting national champions was clearly not working. In particular, the crucial electronics sectors in Europe were 'showing a poor performance in both capital and consumer goods' (Sharp 1991: 63). At the same time, national research budgets were under pressure because national budgets were being pushed into deficit by high unemployment, and the cost of research was increasing. It was increasingly apparent that the United States and Japan had a range and scale of research and technological-development programmes that no individual European state could afford to match (Peterson 1992: 231).

Those were the structural factors that made the 1982 breakthrough feasible. Agency was provided by Étienne Davignon, the EC's Commissioner for Industry from 1977 to 1985. Davignon responded to the concern about Europe's technological performance in electronics by convening the 'Big 12 Round Table' of leading European electrical and electronics firms. This organization provided the model for the later, more extensive, European Round Table of Industrialists. The consensus among the 'Big 12' was that EC-level support for research and development was essential if the European electronics industry were not to slip even further behind its competitors. This consensus was then pressed on national governments by the powerful large corporations (Sharp and Shearman 1987: 49). What made their lobbying even more effective was that Davignon had used his own network of contacts to ensure that the Round Table met not only at a technical level, but also at the level of chief executives:

> Until then the Commission had tended to work with research directors or their equivalents and initiatives had come unstuck because they had been unable to carry them higher up the hierarchy.

(Sharp 1991: 64)

Here, then, was a prime example of the Commission, in the form of Davignon, playing the role of a policy entrepreneur: identifying a problem, suggesting a solution at the European level, and creating then mobilizing a **transnational network** of producers to act as its allies in the private sector and to bring pressure to bear on governments to adopt the European solution.

Once the principle of centrally funded research was established in the field of electronics and information technology, other industries soon began to demand that they get similar support. There followed a whole series of 'Framework Programmes' that served to put the policy into practice. The EU's Seventh Framework Programme covering 2007–13 has a budget of €50.5 billion and covers a wide range of research areas, including:

- health;
- food, agriculture, and biotechnology;
- information and communication technologies;
- nanosciences and nanotechnologies;
- environment (including climate change);
- fusion energy—ITER;
- nuclear fission;
- transport (including aeronautics);
- security;
- space.

CONCLUSION

One of the first conclusions that leaps out from this brief review of the policy process and of various policy sectors is that there is no one consistent pattern of policy making. As suggested by governance and networks approaches (Chapter 2), different elements are important in different sectors and, as such, there is a need to disaggregate analysis of the policy process to understand these different patterns. At the same time, however, some patterns emerge.

The extent to which policies have either originated, or more often have accelerated, because of spillover from the single European market is clear. This emphasizes the central importance of the single-market programme, but also the continuing theoretical relevance of neofunctionalism (Chapter 1). The validity of neofunctionalism is also clear in the role played by the Commission in exploiting the spillover pressures to engineer transfers of competencies to the EU, often through forming alliances with interest groups. It fits well, too, with the way in which the deregulation of national markets in energy and transport led to the involvement of the EU in finding solutions to other problems in these sectors.

Yet introduction of the OMC into an increasing number of policy areas indicates the resilience of national sovereignty. It allows the governments to keep a tighter control over developments. It also adds weight to governance approaches that emphasize the increasing importance of informal modes of co-ordination rather than formal legislative initiatives.

KEY POINTS

- The policy competencies of the EC/EU have expanded considerably, although not all policies are of equal significance or have received equal academic attention.

The European Policy Agenda

- Policy agendas are composed of problems that governments face as a result of domestic political pressure and/or international developments.
- Issues on domestic policy agendas are pushed up to the EU level because of functional logic, because they arise from spillover from other EU policies, because domestic interest groups seek action at the EU level, or so that a government can escape domestic unpopularity for a necessary reform.
- The Commission is often able to exploit these circumstances to promote a European solution.
- The European Council is ultimately responsible for adding issues to the European agenda.

The EU Policy Process

- The formal process begins with the Commission drawing up proposals for legislation, at which stage it will consult widely with interest groups, technical experts, and national government officials. It will also consult MEPs.
- The TEU introduced two intergovernmental 'pillars' of the EU—CFSP and JHA—to which EC rules did not apply. The three-pillar structure was abolished by the Lisbon Treaty, although CFSP still has its own rules of procedure.
- OMC has been introduced into what was the EC pillar, giving the member states stronger control and excluding the EP and ECJ.

Minor Policy Areas

- Of the more minor policy areas, fisheries, fraud, and some aspects of both public health and food safety arise mainly from the functional logic of handling problems at the EU level.
- Policies on consumers, customs, taxation, and some aspects of both food safety and the information society arise predominantly from spillover from the single European market.
- Policies on culture and education look back to an earlier commitment to strengthen a sense of European identity.

- Policies on enterprise and many aspects of policy on the information society arise directly from the Lisbon commitment to make the EU the world's most competitive knowledge-based economy.

Major Policy Areas

- Competition policy developed largely through spillover from the common market and single market. It is an area in which the Commission has considerable autonomy, but in exercising its powers, it is often brought into conflict with individual national governments.
- Social policy was included in the original Treaty, but made little progress before the 1980s, and was boosted in the 1990s by a new emphasis on combating unemployment and the introduction of OMC into both employment and social policy.
- In the energy sector, spillover from the single market allowed the Commission to mobilize a coalition of industrial users of energy in favour of liberalization of national energy markets. Once an EU-wide energy market had been established in principle, it became logical to handle other problems, such as security of supply and environmental effects, at the EU level.
- A similar process operated for transport: spillover from the single market allowed the Commission to push through liberalization of national markets, and then other issues needed to be handled at the European level.
- Research policy started with the ESPRIT programme in the electronics and information technology sectors. The Commission exploited European concerns about US and Japanese advances in these sectors to pressurize governments to adopt an EC-wide programme of support for research.

FURTHER READING

The standard text on policy making in the EU is **H. Wallace, M. Pollack, and A. Young (eds)**, *Policy-Making in the European Union*, 6th edn (Oxford: Oxford University Press, 2010). Students should especially read the introductory chapters, written by the editors, but also the individual chapters on specific policies are the best possible starting point for following up on the other policies included in this chapter—competition, energy, research, social, and transport policy.

Because of its influence on later analysis of policy making, it is important to read **J. Peterson**, 'Decision-Making in the European Union: Towards a Framework for Analysis', *Journal of European Public Policy*, 2 (1995): 69–93.

On the OMC, there are two articles that, read consecutively, will give a good overall picture of the method and of its strengths and weaknesses: **D. Hodson and I. Maher**, 'The Open Method as a New Mode of Governance: The Case of Soft Economic Policy Co-ordination', *Journal of Common Market Studies*, 39 (2001): 719–46; and **S. Borras and K. Jacobsson**, 'The Open Method of Co-ordination and New Governance Patterns in the EU', *Journal of European Public Policy*, 11 (2004): 185–208.

 online resource centre **Visit the Online Resource Centre that accompanies this book for links to more information on European Union policy-making processes:** **www.oxfordtextbooks.co.uk/orc/bache3e/**

Chapter 26
Agriculture

Chapter Overview

The Common Agricultural Policy (CAP) was the first redistributive policy of the European Community (EC), and for many years the only one. The success of agriculture sustained the hopes of the advocates of integration during the 1960s, when it was seen as the start of a process that would lead to other common policies—but for a long time the other common policies did not appear. As a result, agriculture dominated payments from the common budget. Developed to ensure security of food supplies in the Community, the CAP proved highly expensive, with overproduction by farmers keen to maximize subsidies. Despite widespread criticism, the policy proved notoriously difficult to reform. Farmers' groups fiercely resisted change, and their importance in the domestic politics of key member states ensured that reform was slow and piecemeal. Only in the context of new internal and external pressures in the 1990s was significant change secured.

The Common Agricultural Policy (CAP) has long been of symbolic importance to the European integration process, and has been subject to calls for reform ever since the 1960s.

(Fouilleux 2007: 341)

History

Agriculture was one of only four common policies that had its own Title in the Treaty of Rome. The importance given to the sector owed a great deal to food shortages at the end of the Second World War. Governments agreed that it was important to ensure adequate supplies of food at reasonable prices. To achieve this, it was necessary to provide an adequate income to farmers, while taking measures to increase their productivity. All of the states involved in the original European Economic Community (EEC) were in agreement on these objectives.

France had a particular interest in agriculture. Small French farmers were politically important because they had the sympathy of the French people. On the other hand, France also had a lot of large and efficient farms. Part of the price that the French insisted on for their participation in the **common market** in industrial goods was the subsidization of the cost of maintaining their small farmers, plus the guarantee of a protected market for French agricultural exports.

Had the EC simply abolished restrictions on free trade in foodstuffs, the effect would have been to produce competition between member states to subsidize their own farmers. So free trade was not viable. Yet it was also recognized that the equalization of food prices was important for fair competition in industrial products. Higher food prices meant that workers demanded higher wages, thus raising industry's costs. To have a level playing field of competition between different national industrialists, cost differences arising from the effect of food prices needed to be limited.

Before reform in the 1980s, the CAP was a price-support system. Every year, national Ministers of Agriculture decided the level of prices for agricultural products that were covered by the CAP. These prices were ensured by the intervention of the Commission in the market to buy up enough of each product to maintain the agreed price. If prices subsequently rose above the agreed level, the produce that the Commission had purchased and placed into storage would be released onto the market to bring the price back down. In practice, though, this did not occur.

Prices were set at the level that would ensure the least efficient farmers in the EC an adequate income, which encouraged the more efficient, large-scale farmers to maximize their output, because the price was more than adequate to guarantee them a return on their investment. Thus surpluses in most products became permanent. The Commission's interventions in the market were all in one direction: to keep up prices by intervention buying. The amounts of produce in storage constantly grew and became an embarrassment, prompting press reports of 'food mountains' and 'wine lakes'. The cost of storage in itself became a significant burden on the Community budget.

The problems stemmed from the failure of agricultural policy itself to develop. What was commonly known as the CAP was, in effect, only a policy on agricultural price support. Sicco Mansholt, the Commissioner in charge of agriculture during Hallstein's presidency, saw a clear line of spillover from price support to the restructuring of European agriculture to create fewer, larger, more efficient farms. This would have allowed guaranteed prices to be reduced.

At the request of the Council of Ministers, Mansholt introduced proposals for such a restructuring in the late 1960s, but an economic recession in the 1970s led to resistance to the restructuring measures from those governments that had considerable agricultural populations.

Price settlements tended to remain high because of the political influence of farmers, which was everywhere considerable. At the same time, the high prices acted as a burden on the Community budget, and put a particular burden on the national budgets of West Germany and Britain, the two largest net contributors to the Community budget.

Failure to reform the CAP led to ever-larger surpluses of produce being kept in storage, and the cost of storage itself added to the budgetary burden. In an attempt to address at least this part of the cost, a decision was made in the course of the 1970s to encourage the export of the surpluses instead of storing them. As world market prices for all products covered by the CAP were consistently lower than the guaranteed internal prices, it was necessary for the EC to pay farmers the difference between the price that they received for the exports and the guaranteed price. Such export subsidies technically constitute what is known as the 'dumping' of products on world markets. They had the adverse effect of lowering world prices by adding to supply—but they also encouraged other agricultural producers to subsidize their own farmers so that they could compete with the EC farmers. This move from storage to export of surpluses was eventually to produce irresistible external pressure for reform of the CAP, although these pressures did not hit home until the 1980s.

Agriculture in the 1980s and 1990s

In the course of the 1980s and 1990s, the pressures built up for reform of the CAP (Insight 26.1). Together, these pressures did produce some reforms in 1984 and 1988, and a more radical reform in 1992.

In 1984, a system of quotas for dairy products was agreed. In 1988, agreement was reached on a complex package that put a legal limit on agricultural price support for 1988 and fixed future increases above that level at an annual maximum of 74 per cent of the increase in Community gross domestic product (GDP). If this limit were breached, there would be automatic price cuts for the relevant products in subsequent years until the ceilings ceased to be breached. Also, money was made available to encourage farmers to set aside arable land and to let it lie fallow (Butler 1993: 116–7).

Commissioner MacSharry introduced a further package of reform proposals in July 1991, and they were agreed with some modifications, and side-payments to sweeten the pill, in a very rapid ten months, by May 1992. Although known as the 'MacSharry

---

Insight 26.1 Pressures for CAP Reform in the 1990s

- Budget pressures, which had abated in the 1980s, again became significant as the United States allowed the value of the dollar to decline and reintroduced agricultural export subsidies of its own. This forced down world prices, and so increased the cost of export subsidies.

- The reunification of Germany brought into immediate membership of the EC considerable grain-producing areas, as well as extra dairy and beef livestock, adding to the problems of overproduction.

- The need to stabilize democracy and capitalism in the states of central and eastern Europe demanded that the west buy exports from them to allow them to obtain the hard currency necessary to buy from the west to re-equip their industries. These countries had few products in which they had any comparative advantage. Agricultural products were among the few. If the CAP had not prevented it, several of the states could have exported their agricultural goods to the EC.

- By 1992, the Uruguay Round of the GATT had reached a critical stage. In previous rounds of the GATT, agriculture had been raised as an issue, but had always been eventually left on one side because the participants did not want the overall package to collapse. This time, the fate of farmers was so serious that both the United States and the Cairns Group appeared to be prepared to collapse the deal unless it were included. Eventually in 1992, with the original deadlines for agreement already well past, the Cairns Group agreed to allow the United States to negotiate directly with the EC on agriculture.

reforms', they nevertheless bore the imprint also of President Delors and his *cabinet*. The package involved a sharp decrease in the prices for cereals and beef, to bring them more into line with world prices, linked to a move from supporting farmers through subsidies on production to direct support for rural incomes. More land was to be taken out of production altogether, with the farmers being compensated by direct payments; an early retirement scheme was introduced to encourage older farmers to cease production; and more environmentally friendly farming was encouraged, with the implication that this would lower yields (Ross 1995: 200).

Sceptics claimed that the reforms would not solve the budget problem, and in the short term would even increase the cost of the CAP. However, at the end of November 1993, MacSharry's successor, René Steichen, claimed that cereal production for 1993 was 16 million tonnes lower than it would have been without the reforms (*The Week in Europe*, 2 December 1993). More significantly, the reforms accepted for the first time that support for farmers could be separated from production.

To understand why it proved possible to agree these reforms, it is necessary to understand the pressures on policy makers. The main sources of pressure were the escalating cost of the CAP, enlargement, increasing concern about the environmental effects of intensive farming, and external pressures, particularly in the context of world trade negotiations.

The Cost of the CAP

Between 1974 and 1979, the cost of the CAP rose by 23 per cent, twice the rate of increase of incomes. It then stabilized between 1980 and 1982, but in 1983, the cost soared by 30 per cent, and the EC reached the ceiling of expenditure that could be covered from its own resources. Agreement to lift the limit had to be unanimous, and the British government would not agree to any increase without firm measures to curb the cost of the CAP. This led to the 1984 agreement on dairy quotas, and on a system of budgetary discipline whereby a maximum limit would be set to the size of the budget each year before the annual round of negotiations on agricultural prices. Ministers of Agriculture would therefore be negotiating within fixed parameters. Any budgetary overshoot would be clawed back in the following years.

In the event, this system did not work because there was no automatic mechanism for making the necessary adjustments to costs in the years following an overrun. Between 1985 and 1987, the cost of the CAP increased by 18 per cent per annum. Although the EC did not appear to face the immediate exhaustion of its financial resources as it had in 1984, by 1987 there was an estimated budgetary shortfall of 4 million to 5 million European currency units (ecus), which was covered by creative accountancy that simply pushed the problem forward in time.

So although some of the reforms in the 1980s marked significant departures from earlier policies, they 'failed to halt the relentless rise in the budget required for the CAP, and the reforms of 1992 became inevitable' (Colman 2007: 81).

Enlargement

The Southern enlargement (see Chapter 34, pp. 531–2) brought new demands on the budget that could only be met by either diverting money away from existing beneficiaries or expanding the size of the budget. This situation was compounded by the insistence of the Spanish, Portuguese, and Greek governments that they would not be able to participate in the freeing of the internal market of the EC by the end of 1992 unless the structural funds were substantially increased. At the London meeting of the European Council in December 1986, agreement was reached in principle on the doubling of the structural funds by 1993 (see Chapter 29, p. 425), thus requiring an increase in the resources of the EC. The first enlargement therefore added to the pressure for reform of the CAP to make room within the existing budget for these new items of expenditure.

With the collapse of communism at the end of the 1980s, Germany moved rapidly to reunification. In effect, this constituted an enlargement of the EC. The former East German territories included areas that were considerable agricultural producers, so threatening a big increase in the cost of the CAP.

Pressure on the EU to continue the process of reform of the CAP became greater as the former communist states of East-Central Europe began to press ever more strongly for full membership of the EU in the 1990s. After some initial reluctance, most member states came round to the realization that it would be necessary to grant membership to most of these states. Germany in particular became a strong advocate of Eastern enlargement. However, reports prepared by the Commission indicated that the existing CAP could not simply be applied to the applicant states without dramatic consequences for the budget of the EU.

> Extension of the Common Agricultural Policy in its present form to the acceding countries would create difficulties. Given existing price gaps between candidate countries and generally substantially higher CAP prices, and despite prospects for some narrowing of these gaps by the dates of accession, even gradual introduction of CAP prices would tend to stimulate surplus production, in particular in the livestock sector, thus adding to projected surpluses. World Trade Organization (WTO) constraints on subsidized exports would prevent the enlarged Union to sell its surpluses on third markets.
>
> (Quoted in Avery and Cameron 1998: 153)

Environmental Pressures

In the 1980s, there was growing concern about the environment in general, and about the effect of the CAP in particular (Lynggaard 2007: 300). The main beneficiaries of the CAP were large farmers who responded to the high prices by maximizing output. To do this, they pumped more and more fertilizer into the land, and hormones into animals, to improve yields. The rise of environmentalism provided a counter-weight to the general sympathy of European public opinion for farmers, and made it politically easier for governments to respond to the financial pressures with reform measures.

Sympathy for modern farming methods was further reduced in the late 1980s and early 1990s by the outbreak of a number of scares about the safety of food. Of these, the most serious was the epidemic of 'mad cow disease', or bovine spongiform encephalopathy (BSE), in the United Kingdom, which reached its height in 1992. Blame for this was put on intensive farming methods that ignored the welfare of animals.

The issue of food safety is not strictly an environmental concern, but it is closely related to and was associated with concerns about damage to the environment in the minds of the European public.

These problems became linked with the pressing issue of surpluses to produce a change in the perception of the CAP even amongst those institutions and groups most closely associated with it, so that 'by 1992, the conception that intensive farming is the source of both problems of agricultural surplus production and environmental depletion was institutionalized among all the central agents within the CAP' (Lynggaard 2007: 302).

External Pressures

External pressures proved a strong incentive for change in the CAP. The United States made the phasing out of agricultural subsidies a central part of its negotiating position for the Uruguay Round of the **General Agreement on Tariffs and Trade (GATT)** talks, which began in 1986. It was joined by the Cairns Group of fourteen agricultural-producing states, including Australia, Canada, New Zealand, and several Latin American states. All felt that they suffered from the dumping of the EC's agricultural exports onto world markets, which drove down prices and prevented them from selling some of their own production.

The 'MacSharry reforms' of 1992 allowed Ray MacSharry, the Commissioner for Agriculture, to negotiate a deal on agricultural trade that temporarily satisfied the United States and the Cairns Group, and meant that it was possible to conclude the Uruguay Round. That was not the end of the story, though. At the conclusion of the Uruguay Round, it was agreed to open a further round of trade talks at the end of 1999. It was clear that the compromises on agricultural trade reached in the Uruguay Round were provisional, and that agriculture would be a central element of the new round.

In June 1996, the British National Farmers' Union (NFU) produced a paper explaining why the EU would come under great pressure in these trade talks to reform the CAP further. At the end of the Uruguay Round, agreement had been reached to allow both the EU and the United States to continue to subsidize cereal and livestock farmers. These measures had, in the terminology of the agreement, been placed in a 'blue box'. This meant that the subsidies did distort production, but could be continued without legal challenge until 2003, provided that they were not increased. Another 'green box' was created, consisting of support for farmers that did not distort production. These included measures such as those that had already been introduced into the CAP by the MacSharry reforms: measures to take land out of production, or to encourage environmental protection. Since the agreement, the United States had unilaterally moved almost all of its support measures out of the blue box into the green box, leaving the EU alone in the blue box. Although the blue-box measures could be sustained until 2003, the EU would now be under tremendous pressure to reciprocate the unilateral US gesture (NFU 1996).

It was in this context that Franz Fischler, Agriculture Commissioner in the Santer Commission, produced a package of proposals for further reform in November 1995. These continued the pattern of the 1992 reforms, decoupling support for farmers from production and linking it to social and environmental objectives (European

375

Commission 1995). They were subsequently incorporated into the Commission document *Agenda 2000: For a Stronger and Wider Europe* (European Commission 1999*b*).

Agenda 2000 and the 2003 Reform

Agenda 2000 'consisted essentially of the Commission's recommendations for the Union's financial framework for the period 2000–06; the future development of the Union's policies, and in particular its two most important spending policies—the cohesion and structural funds, and the CAP; and the strategy for enlargement of the Union' (Avery and Cameron 1998: 101). On the CAP, it proposed large reductions in support prices and giving compensation to farmers in the form of direct payments, with a ceiling on the level of aid that any one individual could receive. Although explicitly linked to the Eastern enlargement in *Agenda 2000*, these reforms were in line with shifting support from the GATT 'blue box' to the 'green box'.

When negotiations began on the CAP proposals of *Agenda 2000* in February 1999, the French government predictably pressed for more limited reform. This position was supported by 30,000 farmers—mainly from France, Germany, and Belgium—protesting on the streets of Brussels, the biggest demonstration since those against the Mansholt reforms in 1971. After a temporary suspension of the negotiations, the Agriculture Ministers agreed on 11 March to cut cereal prices by 20 per cent, as proposed by the Commission, but to do so in two stages—half in 2000–01 and the other half in 2001–02. They agreed to lower milk prices by 15 per cent in line with the Commission's proposals, but only over three years starting in 2003, and dairy production quotas were actually raised slightly. They also agreed that beef prices should be cut by 20 per cent, but this was only two-thirds of the cut proposed by the Commission.

Fischler hailed the agreement as the most far-reaching reform of the CAP for forty years—but the states that had most strongly supported reform (Britain, Italy, Sweden, and Denmark) expressed their disappointment. They did not like the delays in implementing the cuts that had been forced through by France and Germany (which held the Presidency of the Council). They were to be even more disappointed following the Berlin European Council in March 1999, which was intended to approve the reform.

In Berlin, President Chirac of France simply refused to accept what the French Minister of Agriculture had negotiated. This reflected the fact that Chirac was a Conservative President who was forced to work with a Socialist government. He was blatantly playing domestic politics. However, so important was it to the German government to get an agreement during its presidency, and not to break publicly with France, that Chancellor Schröder eventually agreed to support a significant further dilution of the reform package. The dairy reforms were further delayed, and the cuts in cereal prices were scaled back from the compromise level reached by the Ministers of Agriculture. The other member states went along in return for side-payments: Spain and Greece got agreement to continuation of the Cohesion Fund (see Chapter 29, pp. 433–5); Britain got agreement to the continuation of the British budgetary rebate with only minor concessions.

The Agenda 2000 outcome was thus deeply compromised and must be judged a missed opportunity to reform the CAP.

(Lowe et al. 2002: 4)

But Commissioner Fischler did not give up. The 1999 reforms, although not as far-reaching as the Commission had wanted, did continue with the principle, first conceded in the MacSharry reforms, that the reduced production subsidies would be compensated by direct payments that were decoupled from production. In June 2001, a further reform in this direction was agreed as a way of helping small farmers who found the complexities of operating the multiple strands of the revised CAP just too burdensome. Under the Small Farmers' Scheme, farmers who received less than €1,250 in total from the CAP could opt to convert their payments into a single decoupled flat-rate payment based on a historical reference point (Daugbjerg 2009: 403). This reinforced the precedent of flat-rate decoupled payments that had been established as part of the 1999 reforms.

The shift to direct payments was also used to provide a solution to the problem of how to accommodate the very large farming sectors in the states of Central Europe that were negotiating for membership of the EU. It was clear that these farmers could not be offered production incentives equal to those available to farmers in the existing member states. Both the budgetary implications and the implications for agricultural surpluses would have been unbearable for the EU. Also, the administrative structures that needed to be put in place to implement the complex system of different payments would have stretched the capacities of the states and their farmers. Instead, in January 2002, the Commission proposed what it called the 'Simplified Approach' to calculating agricultural support in the new member states. The new member states would receive a flat-rate decoupled payment based on farm size, starting at 25 per cent of the average rate for the existing EU member states. This would be distributed to farmers by the state itself, using whatever criteria it deemed most relevant, so long as production subsidies were not involved.

Having established and then reinforced the principle of flat-rate decoupled payments, in July 2002, Fischler put forward a revised proposal for the full decoupling of agricultural subsidies from production in the existing EU by the end of 2004. He was helped by difficulties in the new Doha Round of WTO negotiations, which became bogged down at an early stage by disputes over agricultural subsidies.

Under these proposals, the amounts of money that each member state would receive would be the same as under the system that had been agreed at Berlin, but the money would be paid in a lump sum to the governments, which could then distribute between their farmers as they saw fit, so long as it was not paid in the form of a production subsidy. So, governments that did not wish to enter into a confrontation with their larger farmers, who received the bulk of the subsidies under the existing system, could simply pay the money out according to historic distributions; those that were keen to bring about a domestic restructuring of agricultural holdings could divide the money up differently. In either case, the payment would be linked to requirements for farmers to comply with EU-wide standards on environmental protection, food safety, and animal welfare. Fischler argued that the reforms would help the EU to meet the requirements of the Doha Round, and would at the same time integrate the new member states with the system of agricultural support operating in the rest of the EU. They also implied a degree of renationalization of the CAP.

After almost a year of debate, the Council of Agriculture Ministers reached a compromise at the end of June 2003. The essence of the Commission's proposals was adopted, although the shift to direct payments was deferred until 2005, and individual member states could apply for exceptions until 2007 to continue to subsidize production where there was a risk of farmers withdrawing from production altogether.

In 2008 there was an interim review of the state of the CAP, which went by the name of a 'health check'. Completed under the French presidency in the second half of 2008, the review agreed to shift money to rural development from 2009 and progressively to liberalize the dairy sector before the expiry of existing milk production quotas in 2015.

The Effect of Reform

Although it had been a long and sometimes frustrating series of negotiations, the cumulative effect on the CAP of the reform process that started in 1992 was to bring about a considerable shift in the pattern of support for farmers away from price support to direct support. By 2002–03, direct payments, or 'compensatory payments', accounted for 65 per cent of CAP support, and the June 2003 agreement meant that, by 2007, all support would be in this form. This, when combined with 'set aside' requirements, did have the effect of reducing the production surpluses that had plagued the system since it was set up, but it did nothing to redress the problem that the bulk of receipts from the CAP went to a small number of large farmers. In 2003, the OECD estimated that 70 per cent of CAP support still went to the richest 25 per cent of farms.

Large farmers had always benefited more than small farmers from the CAP because they were able to achieve higher yields. Thus, when payments were related to output, the larger and more efficient farmers pocketed the largest share. Direct payments were introduced under MacSharry to compensate farmers for the reduction in guaranteed prices towards world market prices. In order to minimize opposition to the changes, the direct payments were based on the size of farms. Farmers received payments linked to the number of hectares that they farmed. This reduced the incentive to maximize yields, which was the primary aim of the exercise. Production was further curtailed by making it a requirement of receiving the direct payments that 15 per cent of arable land be set aside and not used to produce crops. Similarly, meat producers were required to reduce the density of livestock per hectare in order to qualify for the direct payments. *Agenda 2000* extended the same principle further. It did nothing, though, to redirect subsidies from rich farmers to poor farmers. This political hot potato was effectively dropped into the laps of national governments by the June 2003 agreement to move to a 'single farm payment' that governments could distribute between different categories of farms as they chose.

The decoupling of subsidies from production gained the EU some credit in the Doha Round of trade negotiations, especially as the United States under the Bush Administration had moved in the opposite direction. The 2002 US Farm Trade Bill considerably increased subsidies to farmers, including direct production support. The situation that had prevailed between the United States and the EU when the Uruguay Round was concluded appeared to have been reversed, with the EU more virtuous than the United States on agricultural subsidies.

Explaining the CAP

Hardly surprisingly, intergovernmentalism (see Chapter 1, pp. 11–12) explains well the setting up of the CAP. Until the signing of the Treaties, there were no European institutional actors to take into account. The importance of agriculture has to be understood in terms of the perceived national interests of the six states that came together to form the EEC. It is often told as the story of how French agricultural interests made a deal with German industrial interests to produce an EEC founded on the twin pillars of the industrial common market and the guided price-support system of the CAP. This, though, is an oversimplification, and liberal intergovernmentalism, which looks at the domestic politics that produce the positions taken up by national governments in international negotiations, directs our attention to the importance of agriculture and of farmers in all of the member states.

Neofunctionalism (see Chapter 1, pp. 8–11) could only come into play once the EEC and the CAP existed, with institutional actors being formed at the European level, but several elements of neofunctionalism can be seen in the history of the CAP. Setting up a system of support for agriculture that was based on fixing the prices of commodities, in a context of mixed farming sizes, inevitably caused problems. The price level that was needed to keep inefficient small farmers in business was so high that it encouraged more efficient farmers to increase output to the maximum level. When combined with technological advances, this led to the food surpluses that became one of the biggest headaches of the EC. This outcome was not an unanticipated consequence of the CAP, though. It was foreseen by the Commission, and Sicco Mansholt tried to use it as a lever to get member states to take the next step, of rationalizing farm sizes. So this was a potential example of cultivated spillover. However, it did not work because the governments of the member states retreated from radical reform in the face of domestic political pressures, thus providing some support for the liberal intergovernmental critique of neofunctionalism (Chapter 1, pp. 12–14).

Neofunctionalism predicted also that the creation of a single common policy would set up spillover pressures for the adoption of other common policies. This did appear to be working in the 1970s, when frequent changes in the exchange rates of the currencies of the member states threatened to render the CAP unworkable. Again, though, the governments of the member states avoided the apparent implication that they would either have to fix their exchange rates or abandon the CAP, by improvising a solution based on 'green currencies', regulated by levies and rebates when produce crossed national boundaries. The spillover pressures certainly existed, but the governments proved able to resist them until they felt that they wanted to take the next step. Again, this seemed to vindicate intergovernmental analyses.

Ultimately, though, these ad hoc solutions were unstable. Neofunctionalism might be thought to have been vindicated when agreement between governments on the single-market programme, and the consequent removal of customs checks between states, forced the abandonment of the 'green currency' system. On the other hand, this was only made necessary by the intergovernmental decision to proceed with the removal of customs checks, and it was only made feasible by the adoption of the single currency, which again was the result of an independent decision by governments.

Turning to the theories of governance (see Chapter 2), the CAP appears at first sight to be a prime example of a sector in which supranational governance applies. Support for agriculture had been transferred from the national to the EC/EU level. Policy communities of national farmers' organizations and bureaucrats in national ministries of agriculture were apparently replaced by a European policy community of EU farmers' organizations and Commission officials in the Directorate-General for Agriculture. However, decisions both on fixing annual price levels and on the regulation and reform of the system remained firmly with national Ministers of Agriculture meeting in the Council of Ministers. The extent to which these Ministers became identified with the interests of their sector rather than with the interests of their governments is a question for empirical research, but examples of Ministers having to be overruled by the heads of government suggest that this particular Council may have developed a supranational tinge. More significantly, perhaps, the national bureaucrats in Agriculture Ministries remained involved, if for no other reason than that the actual implementation and administration of the policy remained at national level. The CAP may always, then, have been more accurately analysed as a system of multi-level governance rather than an example of supranational governance, and the reform process that was concluded in June 2003 enhanced the multi-level nature of the sector by restoring considerable discretion over the expenditure of CAP receipts to the national level.

That reform of the CAP became possible at all in the 1980s and 1990s has been explained through a variety of different theoretical perspectives.

Fouilleux (2007: 345), without using the term 'epistemic community' (see Chapter 2, pp. 32–3), adopted an explanation that invoked the importance of academic experts. She emphasized a learning process within the international agricultural policy community, a process that was sparked off by an exercise that the Organisation for Economic Co-operation and Development (OECD) initiated to review the agricultural policies of its member states. The responsible officials asked academics, mainly agricultural economists, to undertake a critique of existing policies, and, '[t]his process engendered a learning process within the international agricultural policy community, and induced a profound change in the way agricultural policy issues were defined'.

Moyer and Josling (1990) emphasized the weakening of the European agricultural policy community. The 1984 reforms were ineffective in restraining the growing cost of the CAP, because they were both too modest in their aims, and lacked effective enforcement mechanisms. This reflected two aspects of the reforms: first, that they were drawn up by an EC agricultural policy community that consisted of the Agriculture Directorate-General (DG VI) of the Commission, the European Agriculture Commissioner, and the representatives of farmers in the Committee of Professional Agricultural Organizations (COPA). These groups had developed close working relationships, and were unlikely to produce proposals that would seriously damage the interests of farmers, or reduce the importance of agriculture as an EC policy sector. Second, the proposals had to be agreed by the Council of Agriculture Ministers, most of whom were strongly influenced by national farmers' representatives.

By the time of the 1988 reforms, according to Moyer and Josling (1990: 86–7), the coalition against change had been weakened by the formation within the Commission of an inner circle. This inner circle consisted of the president, Jacques Delors, the Agriculture Commissioner between 1985 and 1989, Frans Andriessen, and the Budget Commissioner, Hening Christophersen. Delors's reason for supporting reform was the damage that failure to achieve it might do to the single-market programme: 'Delors had made the single European market something of a personal crusade and could not easily see this goal frustrated by agricultural stalemate' (Moyer and Josling 1990: 86). Under pressure from the Commission, which was prepared to take the Council of Ministers to the European Court of Justice if it did not agree a budget for 1988, a system of price stabilizers for agricultural produce was accepted in February 1988. That did not resolve the problems, though, and further reform was planned within the Commission during 1990.

The MacSharry reforms were the result of the same combination of internal and external pressures that had produced the 1988 reforms, but there is a vigorous academic debate about how important the different pressures were in producing the reforms. Rieger (2000: 193–6) argued that it was the mounting cost of the CAP that forced reform. Swinbank and Daugbjerg (2006) and Daugbjerg and Swinbank (2008) dismissed this argument and sided with Grant (1997: 196) in emphasizing the central importance of the international trade negotiations; indeed, according to Daugbjerg and Swinbank (2008: 637), this pressure 'had a decisive impact on the EU's decision to embark on CAP reform'.

Acceptance of his reform package allowed MacSharry to turn his attention to negotiating with the United States in the context of the GATT talks. Agreement was reached in December 1992, but the implications caused widespread protests from French farmers, and the Socialist government, faced with elections before the end of the year, chose not to reinforce its unpopularity by implementing the agreement. However, the Conservative government of Edouard Balladur, which was elected in March 1993, had little choice but to accept the agreement because of the implications for the French economy if the GATT round were not successful. France was the world's fourth largest exporter after the United States, Germany, and Japan, and it was the second largest exporter of services, with 10 per cent of total world trade (*Independent*, 7 November 1993). Theories of globalization (see Chapter 3, pp. 46–7) can easily be invoked to explain this outcome.

CONCLUSION

For three decades, from the late 1950s to the late 1980s, agricultural policy was absolutely central to both European integration and to academic attempts to understand the process. Then, at the end of the 1980s, a programme of reform began that rapidly moved the policy sector to the periphery of the EU. After many unsuccessful attempts to bring about reform, the CAP was beginning to look entrenched and immutable. Yet when reform began, it moved remarkably quickly. Within a few years, one of the pillars of European integration had been effectively dismantled, and the policy had been effectively renationalized.

Today, the CAP is no longer central to the politics of the EU. The extent to which successive reforms dismantled the supranational elements of the policy is indicated by the fact that, within the United Kingdom, agriculture is one of the policies that has been devolved from Westminster, and different spending priorities are pursued in England, Scotland, Wales, and Northern Ireland. This would have been inconceivable under the old CAP.

Although new policy areas have pushed agriculture out of its central role within the EU, the explanation for the evolution of the CAP remains an interesting historical and theoretical case study. The variety of explanations offered for the CAP's movement from pillar to peripheral policy covers a wide range of the theoretical perspectives identified in Part One of this book, and fully justifies the continued study of the sector.

KEY POINTS

History

- France made it a condition of its participation in the EEC that agricultural policy be a joint pillar alongside the common market in industrial goods.
- The policy that was set up was based on supporting the price of agricultural products so as to maintain the incomes of farmers.
- Prices were set through political bargaining, and tended to be high so as to give an adequate income to small, inefficient farmers, who were politically influential.
- The high prices encouraged large, efficient farmers to produce large surpluses.
- Storing the surpluses put a huge strain on the budget of the EC, and disposing of them through export subsidies attracted hostility from other agricultural-producing states.

Agriculture in the 1980s and 1990s

- Reforms were made in 1984, 1988, and 1992.
- The reforms were forced by the increasing budgetary cost of the CAP, enlargement, environmental pressures, and demands from other states in the context of world trade negotiations.

***Agenda 2000* and the 2003 Reform**

- Further reforms to the CAP were proposed in the context of the *Agenda 2000* budget negotiations, but they were watered down in intergovernmental bargaining between France and Germany.
- The principle of decoupling payments from production was accepted in the 1999 reforms, and was fully applied to the new member states of central and eastern Europe.
- Reforms were finally agreed in 2003 that continued the processes begun in 1992 of decoupling from production subsidies to farmers in the rest of the EU, and renationalizing the CAP.

Effect of Reform

- Decoupling subsidies from production allowed for better budgetary control and put the EU in a stronger position in world trade negotiations.
- The subsidies were only gradually extended to new member states in central and eastern Europe, thus preventing the feared sudden hike in budgetary costs.

Explaining CAP

- Intergovernmentalism and liberal intergovernmentalism explain the setting up of the CAP.

- Neofunctionalists expected spillover from the initial CAP both to lead to the reform of agriculture and to produce other common policies, but governments managed to resist these pressures for a long time.

- Arguments can be made for both supranational governance and multi-level governance as the best description of the CAP prior to the 1992 and 2003 reforms. After the 2003 reforms, the case for describing it as an example of multi-level governance is stronger.

- Various explanations have been given of the reform of the CAP, emphasizing the role of ideas, of policy communities, of internal pressures, and of external pressures.

FURTHER READING

On the difficulties and emerging prospects of reform of the CAP, in chronological order, see: **H. W. Moyer and T. E. Josling**, *Agricultural Policy Reform: Policy and Process in the EC and the USA* (Ames, 10: Iowa University Press, 1990); **A. Swinbank**, 'CAP Reform in 1992', *Journal of Common Market Studies*, 31 (1993): 359–72; **W. Grant**, 'The Limits of Common Agricultural Policy Reform and the Option of Renationalization', *Journal of European Public Policy*, 2 (1995): 1–18; **W. D. Coleman**, 'From Protected Development to Market Liberalism: Paradigm Change in Agriculture', *Journal of European Public Policy*, 5 (1998): 632–51; **P. Lowe, H. Buller, and N. Ward**, 'Setting the Next Agenda? British and French Approaches to the Second Pillar of the Common Agricultural Policy', *Journal of Rural Studies*, 18 (2002): 1–17; **C. Daugbjerg**, 'Sequencing in Public Policy: The Evolution of the CAP over a Decade', *Journal of European Public Policy*, 16 (2009): 395–411. For a more encompassing study, see **I. Garzon**, *Reforming the Common Agricultural Policy* (Basingstoke: Palgrave Macmillan, 2006).

Wyn Grant for many years ran an invaluable website on the CAP, which is still available in an archived version, and is now continued as a blog. Both are accessible via the Online Resource Centre.

 online resource centre Visit the Online Resource Centre that accompanies this text for links to more information on the development of the Common Agricultural Policy: www.oxfordtextbooks.co.uk/orc/bache3e/

Chapter 27
The Single Market

Chapter Overview

Although the European Union (EU) is much more than just a **common market**, the economic ideal of a common or single European market lies at its core. The aspiration to create a common market was fundamental in the decision in the mid-1950s to set up the European Economic Community (EEC). Thirty years later, the decision to institute a drive to achieve a single internal market by the end of 1992 was fundamental to the revival of European integration. It is hardly surprising, therefore, that analyses of the causes and consequences of these decisions have also been fundamental to theoretical debates about European integration.

This chapter looks at the original decision to create a common market, the patchy record of progress from the 1960s through to the 1980s, then at the moves to complete the internal market, what became known as the single-market programme, in the 1980s. It also reviews the development of internal-market policy and the record of implementation beyond 1992.

The single market programme marked a turning point in European integration.

(Young 2005: 93)

History

Article 9 of the Treaty of Rome (EEC) stated, 'The Community shall be based upon a **customs union**'; also, a substantial section of the Treaty was devoted to the free movement of persons, services, and capital (now Articles 45–66 TFEU). Together, these objectives constitute the construction of a single European market (SEM). Progress in achieving them has varied over time.

The decision to create a common market reflects two of the main motivations for setting up the EEC: to avoid any return to the national protectionism that had been economically disastrous for Europe between the world wars; and to promote economic expansion by creating a large internal market for European producers that would rival the large US market. The history of the decision is recounted in Chapter 7.

It was clear that the creation of a customs union would result in an uneven distribution of benefits and losses between the member states; although the precise distribution of those benefits and losses could not be predicted in advance, there were reasonable grounds for believing that West German industry might gain more than French industry would. That is why French negotiators were anxious to ensure that other commitments were made in the Treaty of Rome, to develop policies in areas in which their country could be expected to benefit more than West Germany, particularly agriculture. But the reason why the plunge was taken to create the EEC was that all six states expected their economies to be better off as a result of creating the internal market, even if some benefited more than others.

In 1960, the Council of Ministers took the decision to accelerate the original timetable for removing internal tariffs and quotas, and erecting a common external tariff, so that the common market would be completed by 1968 instead of 1970.

All seemed to be progressing smoothly, until, in July 1965, President de Gaulle withdrew France from all participation in the work of the Council of Ministers, plunging the European Community (EC) into crisis (Chapter 9, pp. 128–9). This 1965 crisis was to blame for taking much of the momentum out of the EC. However, de Gaulle did not stop the completion of the customs union, which was complete by July 1968. He did cause a delay, though, in the implementation of the rest of the Treaty. The wait turned out to be much longer than just for the retirement of de Gaulle. By the time that Pompidou became President of France, and adopted a more accommodative attitude to the EC, world economic circumstances had begun to shift away from the high growth of the 1950s and 1960s. By the time that the negotiation of the entry of Britain, Ireland, and Denmark had been completed at the start of 1972, clearing the way for a further deepening of the level of economic integration, the capitalist world was teetering on the brink of recession, and was soon to be pushed over the edge by the **Organization of Petroleum Exporting Countries (OPEC)** (Chapter 10, p. 133).

Throughout the '**stagflation**' years of the 1970s, further progress on the creation of a genuinely free internal market became almost impossible (Hodges and Wallace 1981; Hu 1981). Given the economic problems that they were experiencing, and the political problems that resulted, governments became particularly prone to short-termism, and sensitive to the protectionist impulses of domestic interest groups and public opinion. This was not a favourable environment for strengthening the internal market. Indeed, throughout the 1970s, there was a marked retreat from the common market by the member states. Unable to raise tariffs or quotas against imports from other members of the EC, governments became adept at finding different ways of reserving domestic markets for domestic producers. Non-tariff barriers (NTBs) proliferated.

These NTBs took a wide variety of different forms. Some, such as state aids to industry, were against the competition clauses of the EEC Treaty, and the Commission frequently took member states to the European Court of Justice (ECJ). However, the compliance of guilty states with the rulings of the ECJ was often tardy, and only effected once an alternative system for supplying the aid had been devised. The long process of investigation by the Commission, issuing of warnings, reporting to the ECJ, and waiting for the case to make its way to the top of the Court's increasingly long agenda, then had to begin all over again.

Other NTBs were more subtle. Particularly prevalent were national specifications on the safety of products, some of which were so restrictive that only nationally produced goods could meet them without modification to their basic design. Differing regulations could prevent a single manufacturer from producing on the

385

same production line for the whole EC market; in effect, the market was fragmented into a series of national markets again. Governments also used border customs formalities to make importing difficult, and only placed public contracts with national companies (Pelkmans and Winters 1988: 16–53).

Project 1992: Freeing the Internal Market

In the mid-1980s, the situation in the EC began to change rapidly, again in response to the changing international economic environment. In June 1984, at the Fontainebleau meeting of the European Council, two major steps were taken in breaking out of the *immobilisme* that had been afflicting the EC. First, agreement was reached on the long-running dispute over British contributions to the Community's budget; second, a committee was set up to look into the need for reform of the institutional structure and decision-making system of the EC.

At the beginning of 1985, a new Commission took office under the presidency of Jacques Delors, and in June 1985, Lord Cockfield, the British Commissioner for Trade and Industry, produced a White Paper on the freeing of the internal market from NTBs to trade in goods, services, people, and capital (European Commission 1985). This listed some 300 separate measures, later reduced to 279, covering the harmonization of technical standards, opening up **public procurement** to intra-EC competition, freeing capital movements, removing barriers to free trade in services, harmonizing rates of indirect taxation and excise duties, and removing physical frontier controls between member states (Insight 27.1). The list was accompanied by a timetable for completion.

At the Milan European Council in June 1985, the heads of government accepted the objectives of the White Paper and the timetable for its completion by the end of 1992. It was also agreed, against the protests of the British Prime Minister, Margaret Thatcher, to set up an intergovernmental conference (IGC) to consider what reforms of the decision-making process should accompany the initiative to free the market. The outcome of this IGC was the Single European Act (SEA), which was agreed by the heads of government at the Luxembourg European Council in December 1985, and eventually came into force, after ratification by national parliaments, in July 1987. It introduced **qualified majority voting (QMV)** into the Council of Ministers, but only for measures related to the freeing of the internal market, and even here certain areas—including the harmonization of indirect taxes and the removal of physical controls at borders—were excluded at British insistence.

Beyond 1992

The deadline of the end of 1992 was the target date for the Council of Ministers to agree all the 279 measures in the White Paper. To facilitate meeting the deadline, the Commission drew up a timetable for proposals to be made and to be agreed. As a result of this, over 95 per cent of the measures mentioned in the White Paper had been

Insight 27.1 The Commission's White Paper on Freeing the Internal Market

The White Paper provided no simple definition of what 'freeing the internal market' constituted, but it dealt with four 'freedoms':

- the free movement of goods;
- the free movement of services;
- the free movement of labour;
- the free movement of capital.

The aim of the White Paper was to remove physical barriers, fiscal barriers, and technical barriers to these four freedoms of movement.

The removal of physical barriers was dealt with by a series of proposed directives to end elaborate border checks on goods crossing from one EC member state to another, which were costly in themselves and caused long delays.

The removal of fiscal barriers was dealt with in a series of proposals to harmonize rates of VAT and excise duties.

'Technical barriers' was a portmanteau term covering a range of different things, including national standards for products, barriers to the free movement of capital, the free movement of labour, and public procurement rules.

National standards were dealt with by the adoption of the so-called 'new approach'. This was based on the principle enunciated by the ECJ in its judgment in the *Cassis de Dijon* case (Case 120/78, 1979). Ruling that the German government had acted illegally in preventing the sale of a French liqueur in Germany because its alcohol content was lower than specified in German law, the ECJ stated that any product that could legally be offered for sale in one member state should also be allowed to be offered for sale in every other member state. The only exceptions permitted to the principle were those imposed on health and safety grounds. In order to overcome this potential barrier, the Commission proposed that minimum health and safety standards for all products should be laid down by two European standards authorities, each of which is known by the initial letters of its name in French: CEN (the European Committee for Standardization), and CENELEC (the European Committee for Standardization of Electrical Products). If products met these minimum standards, they would be awarded a 'c.e.' mark, and could not legally be prevented from being put on sale in any member state.

Barriers to the free movement of capital had already started to disappear within the EC, and the White Paper simply proposed to complete this process through three directives covering cross-border securities transactions, commercial loans, and access to stock exchanges in other countries.

Barriers to the free movement of labour were to be tackled by directives covering the extension of rights of residence that already existed for workers, to citizens who were not active members of the labour force (students, retired people, the unemployed), and guaranteeing non-discrimination in access to social and welfare benefits. The Commission also undertook to prepare guidance and draft directives on the mutual recognition of professional and educational qualifications.

Public procurement referred to the purchasing policies of public authorities, which in most member states discriminated in favour of national suppliers and contractors. The aim was to open the largest contracts to competitive bidding by firms from across the EC.

agreed by the end of 1992 (Calingaert 1999: 157). This remarkable record of success, however, needs to be set against three further considerations, as follows.

- Council agreements have to be implemented; thus, agreement in the Council did not in itself mean that the single market was working. Before that stage would be reached, there were two further requirements: transposition and enforcement.
- The 5 per cent of the measures that had not been agreed included some of the most intractable and controversial in the White Paper.
- The White Paper did not cover some areas in which businesses wanted to see liberalization, because they were considered too controversial.

These difficulties post-1992 are reviewed below. It must be noted, though, that the single-market programme has overall been a considerable success, and that the momentum has been maintained despite the problems.

Transposition

Once a directive has been agreed by the Council of Ministers, it has to be transposed into the national laws of the member states. This process was slower in some states than in others, which meant that there were transposition problems ongoing more than a decade after the 1992 agreement. The Commission kept a running tally of the record of member states on transposition, and published the results annually as a league table. Concern about the low level of transposition overall, and particularly in certain member states, led to agreement in 2003 on an Internal Market Strategy that set the target for every state of keeping its 'implementation deficit' below 1.5 per cent. This meant that, at any one time, no state should have failed to transpose more than 1.5 per cent of all single-market directives that had been agreed at EU level. Some member states responded vigorously to the target. For example, Ireland more than halved its implementation deficit between May 2003 and January 2004 to get below 1.5 per cent. Other member states, however, responded less to the target. Although there was variation in the performance of member states, a small group of persistent offenders emerged, consisting of France, Germany, Greece, Italy, and Luxembourg. At the other end of the spectrum, Denmark, Spain, Finland, and Britain (in approximate order of merit) consistently kept within the target (European Commission 2004a).

Enforcement

Even when the member states have transposed internal market legislation, it still has to be enforced, and the record of national governments on this is very variable. The Commission has had to deal with a constant flow of complaints from member states about infringements of the rules by other member states, although the records of different states vary considerably. Two areas in which the record on enforcement is particularly bad are those products for which there are no harmonized EU standards, and public procurement.

Where there is no uniform EU standard for a product, internal-market regulations require national authorities to accept the standards of other member states. However, companies have often found their products being subjected to a battery of national test and certification requirements, especially in France and Germany. The British Department of Trade and Industry even set up its own Single Market Compliance Unit in the mid-1990s, to pursue cases in which British manufacturers felt they had been discriminated against in this way, and if necessary to report the offending state authorities to the Commission. Largely in response to the same problem, a network of national officials was established in 1997 in the hope that disputes might be resolved by negotiation rather than litigation. The network, called SOLVIT, did not prove very effective, but it was reformed following a Commission Communication on Effective Problem Solving (European Commission 2001b; 2002). This approach was in line with the general drift away from centralized supranational control towards decentralized international co-operation to solve problems. It is also in line with the recommendation of Metcalfe (1992) and others for the Commission to handle implementation by putting itself at the centre of networks of national implementers (Chapter 20, pp. 265–7).

Similar problems of non-recognition in the absence of harmonized standards arose in the services field, in which there was a marked reluctance to recognize the qualifications of individual workers, thus putting limits on the free movement of labour, and there were also barriers placed in the way of service companies operating across frontiers. In February 2004, Erkki Liikanen, the Commissioner for Enterprise and the Information Society, launched an initiative to set voluntary pan-European standards on training and quality assurance. The new standards would not be mandatory, but would be legally recognized across the EU. Firms taking up the standards would be able to ask for certification that they were in compliance. The hope was that the best firms and individuals would adopt the voluntary standards and, in doing so, raise the quality threshold. This would then make it more difficult for national authorities to find spurious grounds for excluding firms and individuals from other member states from their market. The system would cover firms and individuals offering a wide range of services, from funeral directors to language translators (*European Voice,* 26 February–3 March 2004).

On public procurement, eight directives were agreed by the end of 1993 that obliged all public authorities to advertise for tenders for public contracts worth over 5 million European currency units (ecus) in the *Official Journal* of the EC. Despite these directives, very few contracts were ever actually awarded to non-national firms, and there were a number of celebrated cases of governments blatantly flouting the rules. In 2004, the Commission was still complaining that many public administrations continued to award contracts without effective competition, and urged member states to tackle the problem, noting that a recent study had shown that public procurement costs could be as much as 34 per cent higher where EU rules were not applied (European Commission 2004a). Again, in the post-Maastricht political climate, the Commission was approaching the problem by exhortation rather than with threats of legal action. New legislation to improve the efficiency of public procurement procedures had meanwhile not been passed by the target date of the end of 2003.

Problem Areas

Some issues that were included in the White Paper proved particularly difficult for member states to agree on, and this is why only 95 per cent of the programme had been agreed by the end of 1992. Two that stand out are tax harmonization and company law. Arguably, agreement on both is necessary if there is to be a genuine single market in which companies can operate without regard to national boundaries. Without harmonization of taxes and a common company statute, companies that operate in several different states face a complex of regulations and paperwork.

Areas Omitted from the White Paper

Cockfield's White Paper made no mention of extending the single market to telecommunications. Although it did mention energy, this was subsequently dropped. Yet these were identified by businesses in the EU as two of the areas that most raised their costs of production in comparison with the United States. Other 'left-over' policy sectors were postal services and railways. They were all omitted from the 1992 Programme because they were sectors that had traditionally been in public ownership in the member states, and they had a public-service aspect to them. However, the Corfu European Council in June 1994 recognized that the extension of the internal market to telecommunications and energy was a priority action to raise European competitiveness. The Commission then tried, and to a certain extent succeeded, to liberalize these market sectors (Insights 27.2 and 27.3), although it was considerably more successful in the case of telecommunications than in the energy sectors, largely because energy was more highly politicized within member states and the pressure for change was not so great. With increased concern in the early twenty-first century about energy supplies and about the need to reduce carbon emissions, though, it became possible to build on the loose agreements reached earlier and a new package was agreed in late 2009.

Insight 27.2 The Liberalization of Telecommunications

Telecommunications in Europe was traditionally dominated by national monopoly suppliers—the post, telegraph, and telephone (PTT) public utilities. Attempts by the Commission to involve itself in the sector prior to 1982 proved fruitless. It was a sector dominated by national policy communities, which collaborated with each other at the international level to preserve the status quo.

An opportunity was opened for the Commission by the implications of deregulation of the telecommunications market in the United States in the early 1980s. This led to pressure from the government of the United States for the EC to open its markets for telecommunications equipment. AT&T, which had been forced to open up its domestic operations, was anxious to recoup lost revenue by moving into Europe, and IBM was looking to diversify into what promised to be an increasingly profitable market (Dang-Nguyen et al. 1993: 103).

The Commission (DG XIII) responded by commissioning a number of reports on how Europe was losing out to the United States following US deregulation. It used these to build a momentum in the same way that Delors and Cockfield used the Cecchini Report on the 'Costs of Non-Europe' (Cecchini et al. 1988) to build up momentum for the internal market. It also mobilized producer groups that had an interest in seeing an increase in the efficiency and a decrease in the cost of telecommunication services: the Union of Industrial and Employers' Confederations of Europe (UNICE), and the Information Technology User Group (INTUG).

Another element in the strategy was that the Commission tried to ride its project on the back of the single-market programme. Its discourse on telecommunications drew heavily on the 1992 Programme. Its approach assumed that a single market required a common infrastructure, of which telecommunications would be a part. Thus the creation of a European policy for telecommunications gathered momentum by association with the 1992 Programme (Fuchs 1994: 181).

Having established the legitimacy of a European policy for the sector, the Commission produced in 1987 a Green Paper on the *Development of the Common Market for Telecommunications, Services and Equipment*. This discussion document became the basis for the development of a policy in the sector much as the White Paper on the internal market had been the basis for the 1992 Programme. It advocated deregulation and increased competition, proposals that were consistent with developments in those member states that had begun to respond to the problem at national level, of which Britain was the leader.

The Green Paper advocated the separation of regulation of the sector from operation of the system, a reform that had already been introduced in Britain, France, and Germany; and the introduction of Open Network Provision (ONP), so that rival operators could compete using a common infrastructure. A concession to the PTTs was that they would remain in control of the provision of network services.

In 1988, the year after the publication of the Green Paper, the Directorate-General for Competition (DG IV) issued an administrative directive on the liberalization of the terminal-equipment market. The Commission argued that it had the right to act without specific approval by the Council of Ministers because it was acting in pursuance of Article 90 (3) of the Treaty of Rome (EEC) (now Article 86 of the Treaty on the European Community), under which the Commission is charged to ensure that special rights conferred on national companies by their governments do not prevent the completion of the common market. Although the Council of Ministers had approved the Green Paper—which listed liberalization of the market amongst its objectives—France, Belgium, Germany, and Italy took the Commission to the ECJ, alleging that it had exceeded its powers by not seeking the approval of the Council for the directive. In March 1991, the Court found in favour of the Commission.

Dang-Nguyen, Schneider, and Werle (1993: 108) interpreted this incident as evidence of a conflict between the interventionist philosophy of DG XIII and the free-market philosophy of DG IV, and stated that 'The Directive was issued by DG IV without consulting DG XIII'. However, given the internal procedures of the Commission on consultation of all DGs with an interest in a sector, it is difficult to see how this could have been the case. An alternative explanation is that the directive was another element in the strategy of the Commission as **policy entrepreneur**. In effect, DG IV was playing the 'hard cop' to DG XIII's 'soft cop'. Faced with the prospect of an enforced opening of telecommunications monopolies by DG IV's exploitation of Article 90 of the Treaty, the PTTs were more likely to co-operate with a negotiated process under the auspices of the Task Force.

With backing from the ECJ and assisted by strong pressure on national governments from the users of telecommunications, the Commission managed to secure the passage of a series of directives between 1992 and 2002, when a telecommunications regulatory package was agreed that came into effect in 2003. This set up a framework for national regulation. In late 2009, agreement was reached on further reform that would create EU-wide regulation of the sector.

Insight 27.3 The Liberalization of Energy Supply

According to Matlary (1997), a similar approach to that used in the case of telecommunications was used to push forward a common energy policy. Like telecommunications, the energy sectors were dominated by national monopolists, which most commonly were publicly owned. An open market in energy was originally part of the White Paper on the single market, but the opposition of national monopoly suppliers led to it being excluded. However, the Commission returned to the issue in 1989, making proposals for a phased dismantling of national monopolies over the electricity grids and gas supply networks. The linking of energy policy to the single-market programme was explicit. In April 1991, Sir Leon Brittan, the Commissioner for Competition Policy, said that there were two sectors that were vital to the internal market: telecommunications and energy.

It was unlikely that the national monopolists themselves would support liberalization moves, but the Commission was able to mobilize the support of large industrial users of energy, working through the existing institutionalized networks of UNICE and the ERT.

At the same time as the proposals for a phased dismantling of national monopolies were being negotiated, DG IV was stepping up its attacks on monopolistic practices using its powers under Article 90 of the EEC Treaty (now Article 86 of the Treaty on the European Community). As in the case of telecommunications, although the threat never became as explicit, the vested interests resisting integration were faced with a choice between a hard-line free-market approach from DG IV or a negotiated softer approach from another Directorate-General, in this case from the Directorate-General for Energy (DG XVII).

Negotiations in the Council of Ministers were protracted. The French government in particular was reluctant to end the monopoly of Electricité de France (EdF) over the distribution of electricity in France. It claimed that its primary concern was to protect the access of rural French domestic consumers to electricity at the same price as was available everywhere else in France. This was known as 'the public service argument'. However, it was also bowing to intense pressure from the Confederation Générale du Travail (CGT) trade union, which feared that liberalization would mean job losses.

Eventually, in June 1996, agreement was reached on a phased liberalization of electricity supply over six years, but it would only apply to large industrial users. The whole process of negotiation then had to be repeated to secure an agreement on liberalization of the market in gas supply, with the French government fighting as hard to protect the position of Gaz de France as it had to protect EdF. Eventually another compromise deal was reached in December 1997.

The Services Directive

Telecommunications and energy supply are specific examples of service industries, which as a whole proved to be much more difficult to liberalize than did trade in goods. By 2005, only 20 per cent of sales of services in the EU were traded across frontiers. This slow progress led the Lisbon European Council in March 2000 to request that the Commission produce an action plan to remove barriers. Liberalizing services was therefore part of the 'Lisbon Agenda' (Chapter 15, pp. 185–6; Chapter 25, p. 364). Following widespread consultations, in July 2002, its the Commission published its *Report on the State of the Internal Market for Services*. This was followed in January 2004 by a proposed Services Directive (Insight 27.4).

The Services Directive ran into vocal political opposition because it proposed to apply to services the 'country-of-origin principle' that had applied to trade in goods

Insight 27.4 What is the Scope of the Services Directive?

The Services Directive applies to the provision of a **wide range of services**—to private individuals and businesses—barring a few specific exceptions. For example, it covers:

- **distributive trades** (including retail and wholesale of goods and services);
- the activities of most **regulated professions** (such as legal and tax advisers, architects, engineers, accountants, surveyors);
- **construction** services and **crafts;**
- **business-related services** (such as office maintenance, management consultancy, event organization, debt recovery, advertising, and recruitment services);
- **tourism** services (e.g. travel agents);
- **leisure** services (e.g. sports centres and amusement parks);
- **installation** and **maintenance** of equipment;
- **information society** services (e.g. publishing—print and web, news agencies, computer programming);
- **accommodation** and **food** services (hotels, restaurants, and caterers);
- **training** and **education** services;
- **rentals** and **leasing** services (including car rental);
- **real estate** services;
- **household support** services (e.g. cleaning, gardening, and private nannies).

The Services Directive does not apply to the following services, which are explicitly excluded:

- **financial** services;
- **electronic communications** services with respect to matters covered by other community instruments;
- **transport** services falling into Title V of the EC Treaty;
- **healthcare** services provided by health professionals to patients to assess, maintain, or restore their state of health where those activities are reserved to a regulated health profession;
- **temporary work** agencies' services;
- **private security** services;
- **audiovisual** services;
- **gambling;**
- certain **social services** provided by the state, by providers mandated by the state, or by charities recognized as such by the state;
- services provided by **notaries** and **bailiffs** (appointed by an official act of government).

In any event, national rules and regulations relating to these excluded services have to comply with other rules of Community law, in particular with the freedom of establishment and the freedom to provide services as guaranteed in the Treaty on the Functioning of the European Union.

Source: Commission website: **http://ec.europa.eu/internal_market/services/services-dir/guides_en.htm#What_is_the_scope_of_the_Services_Directive_** (accessed May 2010); **http://ec.europa.eu**, © European Union, 1995–2010

since the *Cassis de Dijon* judgment of the ECJ in 1979 (see Chapter 23, p. 323). Under the *Cassis* judgment, if a good could be sold legally in one member state, it could be sold legally in any member state. This meant that where there were no EU-level standards for a product, it had only to meet the national standards of the state in which it was produced, and could then be legally exported to any other member state. Although it had caused some protest at the time, this principle had come to be accepted for trade in goods. The application of the same principle to trade in services, though, was not readily accepted.

For services, the country-of-origin principle meant that if the company that provided a service met the legal requirements of the member state in which it was based, it could offer the service in other member states. This implied, for example, that a British building firm could build a house in Germany using British workers whose terms and conditions of employment complied with British law, even if they did not comply with German law. From the outset, this alarmed both employers and trade unions in those member states that had the highest wages and conditions of service. The concern really became focused, though, in the aftermath of the 2004 enlargement. Whereas there might be a small difference in employment standards between Britain and Germany, the differences between the established member states and the new entrants were considerable. Fierce opposition was mounted to the directive in the run-up to the 2004 European Parliament (EP) elections, especially in Germany, France, and Sweden. In France, the directive was given the name 'the Frankenstein directive', a rather poor pun on the name of the Commissioner who introduced it, Frits Bolkestein, suggesting that the directive was a monstrous creation that would destroy jobs and social consensus.

When the new Commission took office in late 2004, the Services Directive became the responsibility of the new Irish Commissioner for the Internal Market, Charlie McCreevy. He quickly indicated that he would listen to the criticisms that had been voiced, and consider amending the directive. Some such action was considered prudent because the directive had become one of the issues around which discontent had crystallized in the French debate on the EU Constitution (Chapter 17, p. 207). President Chirac had called a referendum on whether to ratify the Constitution for 29 May 2005, but as polling day approached, opinion polls were showing a majority in favour of a 'no' vote. Those member states the governments of which favoured the Services Directive agreed to re-examine its provisions in an attempt to help Chirac to win his referendum. This did not mean that there were no underlying tensions: the new member states in particular were extremely keen to see the directive adopted in something like its existing form, as they expected to benefit considerably from it.

The directive was finally adopted on 12 December 2006, with a deadline for transposition into national legislation of 28 December 2009. At first reading, the EP removed the Commission's proposed country-of-origin principle. In its final form, the directive explicitly stated that its provisions did not affect national labour laws. The EP also excluded from the directive some of the most controversial services: broadcasting; postal services; audiovisual services; public transport; gambling; health care; and legal services. Legal services were later reinstated by the Council and were not removed again by the EP at second reading, so they are in the final version. On the other hand, the EP did successfully provide member states with a series of legally valid excuses for restricting activity by non-national companies, including national security, public health, and environmental protection.

Explaining the Single Market

There are four episodes in the story of the single market that have attracted attempts at explanation using theoretical perspectives: the original decision; the 1960 acceleration agreement; the successful initiative to complete the internal market by 1992; and the pattern of successes and failures in pursuit of this objective.

The Original Decision

The original commitment to create a common market is best explained using an inter-governmentalist framework (Chapter 1, pp. 11–14; Moravcsik 1998: 86–158). There might, though, be the possibility of constructing an explanation based on neofunctionalism (Chapter 1 pp. 8–11), stressing spillover from the European Coal and Steel Community (ECSC) (Chapter 8, pp. 116–20).

According to neofunctionalism, the success of the ECSC ought to have led other groups of producers to put pressure on their governments to extend the common market to their products so that they too could benefit. Yet there is no evidence that any national group of producers lobbied for the extension of the ECSC. So the experience of the creation of the EEC does not lend support to the neofunctionalist concept of political spillover.

There is also little evidence of supranational actors playing a key role in the original decision. Whereas the scheme for the European Atomic Energy Community (Euratom) emerged from the lobbying activities of Jean Monnet's Action Committee for the United States of Europe (Chapter 7, p. 108), the proposal for the EEC, although it was adopted by the Action Committee, originated with the Dutch government supported by the Belgian government, and was a revival of a scheme that they had long favoured and had implemented on a more limited scale between themselves in the form of the **Benelux economic union**. The initiative was taken by the political and administrative elites in small states, in pursuit of what they perceived as their national interest in being part of a larger economic grouping.

The Acceleration Agreement

Although the original decision to create a common market did not lend support to the neofunctionalist idea of spillover, the surprisingly rapid progress that was made in the 1960s towards achieving the common market did seem to do so. In particular, a decision taken by the Council of Ministers in 1960 to accelerate the original timetable for removing internal tariffs and quotas, and erecting a common external tariff, was celebrated by Leon Lindberg (1963: 167–205) as a graphic illustration of political spillover at work.

The EEC Treaty (Article 14) specified a precise timetable for the progressive reduction of internal tariffs. On the original schedule, it would have taken between eight and twelve years to get rid of all internal tariffs. This rather leisurely timetable reflected the concerns of some industrial groups about the problems of adjustment involved in ending national protection. However, once the Treaty was signed and it became obvious that the common market would become a reality, those same industrial interests responded to the changed situation facing them. Even before the Treaty came into operation on 1 January 1958, companies had begun to conclude cross-border agreements on co-operation, or to acquire franchised retail outlets for their products in other member states.

Corporate behaviour adjusted so rapidly to the prospect of the common market that companies became impatient to see the benefits of the deals concluded and of the new investments made. This led to pressure on national governments to accelerate the timetable. Remarkably, the strongest pressure came from French industrial interests, which had opposed the original scheme for a common market.

On 12 May 1960, the Council of Ministers agreed to a proposal from the Commission to accelerate progress on the removal of internal barriers to trade and the erection of a common external tariff, linked to the creation of the Common Agricultural Policy (CAP). Interest groups had only pressed for the common market to be accelerated. Progress was slow on agriculture; the negotiations had been dogged by disagreements over the level of support that ought to be given to farmers for different commodities. But the issues were clearly linked: progress on the CAP to accompany progress on the industrial common market had been part of the original deal embodied in the EEC Treaty.

In keeping the linkage between the two issues at the forefront of all of their proposals to the Council of Ministers, the Commission played a manipulative role that coincided with the view of neofunctionalism about the importance of central leadership. As described by Lindberg (1963: 167–205), the progress of the EEC between 1958 and 1965 involved the Commission utilizing a favourable situation to promote integration. Governments found themselves trapped between the growing demand from national interest groups that they carry through as rapidly as possible their commitment to create a common market, and the insistence of the Commission that this could only happen if the same governments were prepared to overrule the conflicting pressures on them from other groups and reach agreement on the setting of common minimum prices for agricultural products. It should be noted, though, that this interpretation has been contested by Andrew Moravcsik (1998: 159–237; see Chapter 9, p. 130)

The 1992 Programme

The decision to adopt the 1992 Programme provoked a fierce academic debate about the explanation. All voices in this debate agreed that structural factors favoured the single market. The differences concerned the role of supranational versus national actors.

The structural context was the sluggish recovery of the European economies from the post-1979 recession in comparison with the vigorous growth of the US and Japanese economies. In particular, the tide of direct foreign investment turned, so that, by the mid-1980s, there was a net flow of investment funds from western Europe to the United States. This augured badly both for the employment situation in Europe in the future, and for the ability of European industry to keep abreast of the technological developments that were revolutionizing production processes. European industrialists indicated that what would be most likely to encourage them to invest in Europe would be the creation of a genuine continental market such as that which they experienced in the United States. It was therefore in an attempt to revive investment and economic growth that governments embraced the single-market programme.

While there was scholarly agreement on this part of the explanation, disagreement came over which institutions were responsible for turning the concern with the competitiveness of the EC into a positive programme for action. From a position that was close to neofunctionalism, although missing the commitment to the key neofunctionalist concept of spillover, various analysts emphasized the role of the Commission and of supranational business interests. This analysis, though, was comprehensively contested by Andrew Moravcsik (1991).

According to Sandholtz and Zysman (1989: 96): 'The renewed drive for market unification can be explained only if theory takes into account the policy leadership of the Commission.' In their explanation, the Commission manipulated a conjunction of international events and domestic circumstances to push forward the process of European integration much as that neofunctionalists had expected it would back in the 1960s. It was seen as providing the essential leadership to exploit the prevailing international and domestic circumstances. In one of the earliest assessments of the single-market programme, Stanley Hoffmann (1989), who had been the main advocate of intergovernmentalism in the 1960s, emphasized the importance of Jacques Delors.

Before assuming office in January 1985, Delors spent much of the autumn of 1984 casting around for a 'big idea' that would provide a focus and an impetus for the incoming Commission (Grant 1994: 70). Institutional reform, monetary union, and defence co-operation were all considered, but eventually the completion of the single market was chosen. There were two main reasons for this decision. First, extensive consultations indicated that each of the other possibilities would be strongly resisted by the governments of some member states, but the opening up of the European market would command general support. Second, Delors believed that market integration would inevitably bring other important issues onto the agenda. For example, it would only be possible to pass all of the laws necessary to complete the single market if there were a reform of the decision-making process; in addition, movement towards a more integrated market would raise the question of monetary integration.

So, Delors was instrumental in giving the single-market objective a high priority, and he encouraged the members of the European Round Table of Industrialists (ERT) to bring pressure to bear on governments to support the single-market programme, so utilizing a **transnational network** to push forward the issue. He commissioned the Cecchini Report (Cecchini 1988) of leading European economists to put the weight of technical experts behind the project. The issue was already on the agenda, but Delors singled it out and pushed it to the top of that agenda. He acted as a policy entrepreneur, recognizing an opportunity to promote a policy that went with the grain of existing thinking, that would increase the level of integration between the member states, and that would put other integrative measures onto the agenda in its wake.

Sandholtz and Zysman (1989) also emphasized the role of supranational business interests in pushing the single market, mentioning particularly the role of the ERT. This, too, became almost accepted wisdom, with Cowles (1995) making the strongest statement of the importance of the role of the ERT.

Moravcsik (1991) contested this accepted wisdom. He considered two broad explanations for developments that furthered European integration: supranational institutionalism and intergovernmental institutionalism. His first category, supranational institutionalism, covered explanatory factors such as pressure from the EC institutions (primarily the EP and the ECJ), lobbying by transnational business interests, and political entrepreneurship by the Commission; it was therefore a model consistent with neo-functionalist theory. Moravcsik tested it against the empirical evidence relating to the SEA and found it wanting. He argued that the EP was largely ignored in the negotiation of the SEA; the transnational business groups came late to the single market, when the process was already well under way as a result of a consensus between governments on the need for reform; the Commission's White Paper on the single market was 'a response to a mandate from the member states' rather than an independent initiative from a policy entrepreneur (Moravcsik 1991: 45–8).

His second category, intergovernmental institutionalism, stressed bargains between states, marked by lowest-common-denominator bargaining and the protection of sovereignty. It was an example of what Keohane (1984) had described as the 'modified structural realist' explanation of the formation and maintenance of international regimes, but it took more account of domestic politics. Indeed, in his application of the model to the SEA, Moravcsik put a good deal of emphasis on domestic politics, and he ended his article with a plea for more work on this aspect of EC bargaining.

Bulmer (1998), summarizing the insights from research conducted and published by Armstrong and Bulmer (1998), argued that both neofunctionalist and intergovernmentalist accounts oversimplified the relationship between the actors. While Moravcsik was formally correct to stress that the Cockfield White Paper was a response to a request from the heads of government, the request came out of a European Council. Although the Commission is not a formal member of the European Council, it has 'insider status' at these meetings, and Delors was able to use his position at the table to press the case for the SEM.

For Bulmer, this privileged access, and the use made of it by Delors, illustrated the importance of institutional arrangements: an important aspect of the historical institutionalist approach. Other examples of the same phenomenon at work in the formulation of the SEM were the way in which the Italian presidency manipulated the institutional rules at Milan to call an IGC (Chapter 12, p. 153), and the paving of the way for the SEM by decisions of the ECJ, such as in the famous *Cassis de Dijon* ruling.

The Success of the Programme

Bulmer (1998) also provided an historical institutionalist explanation for the success of the 1992 Programme. Once it was launched, the single-market framework changed the context within which the EC operated. A new logic operated on governments holding the presidency; the ECJ became very important in interpreting the new commitments; and new norms were spread throughout the EC.

Once the single-market programme was accepted and publicized, governments holding the presidency found themselves under pressure to record a high rate of success on both the passage of directives and the transposition of directives into national legislation. A successful presidency was now judged partly on that record.

In every one of the six case studies looked at by Armstrong and Bulmer (1998), the role of the ECJ in handing down judgments on contested interpretations of the rules was significant. Given the clear and explicit commitment of the member states to the single-market programme, these judgments favoured free-market interpretations. For example:

> In air transport, the EC had played next to no regulatory role until the 1980s. The ECJ's ruling that existing bilateral regulatory arrangements were illegal, combined with the QMV introduced by the SEA, made liberalization inevitable and thus skewed things in favour of states advocating, and with expertise on, such a policy (the UK and the Netherlands).
>
> (Bulmer 1998: 380)

Alongside the intervention of the ECJ applying the new norms that had been incorporated into interpretation of existing EC law by the adoption of the single-market programme, the above quotation makes clear that the move to QMV in the Council of Ministers on single-market measures was also important to the success of liberalization in this sector.

From the perspective of historical institutionalism, the success of the single-market programme can be explained by the way in which the SEA changed the formal rules, and the adoption of the single-market programme changed the normative context within which those rules were operated. Although the full implications of the programme were far from apparent when it was adopted by the member states, its effect was to shift the initiative in the battle of economic ideas firmly in favour of the liberals.

CONCLUSION

Whether called the 'common market' or the 'single market', the concept of a geographical area free of artificial barriers to economic and commercial activity has always been central to the process of European integration. It has also been central to attempts to theorize the process. Some of the fiercest arguments have raged over the theoretical implications of developments in this policy sector.

By 2008, an imperfect single market was a reality. Helped by a global intellectual and policy orientation that favoured liberal economics, the norms of the single-market programme seemed to have become entrenched, and to be gradually wearing down the resistance of the ideas and interests that defended national protectionism of various types. All of this, though, was thrown into doubt by the global economic crisis that emerged during 2008. An alternative voice that expressed scepticism about whether liberalism had gone too far was being heard both within the EU and in the wider world. Whether it would lead to an attempt to retreat from the level of market integration that had been achieved, and whether that attempt could possibly be successful given that the single market had become the status quo over a wide range of economic activity, were open questions at the time of writing. If that reaction were to come about, the theoretical debates would no doubt be rejoined with vigour.

KEY POINTS

History

- The original decision to create a common market was one of the pillars on which the EEC was constructed.

- Progress towards this goal varied over time, with agreement to accelerate the timetable in the 1960s. By the 1980s, progress had stalled and was even going backwards with the proliferation of NTBs.

Project 1992

- In the mid-1980s, the governments of the member states adopted proposals from the Commission for the freeing of the internal market from NTBs by 1992, and this was linked to changes in the institutional rules.

Beyond 1992

- Despite a good record on passing directives to implement the 1992 Programme, both transposition of directives into national legislation and enforcement of the new rules were uneven between member states.
- Some policy sectors that were included in the 1992 Programme proved particularly difficult on which to get agreement, especially tax harmonization and company law.
- Other policy sectors were so controversial that they were not included in the original programme at all, especially telecommunications, energy, postal services, and railways.
- The liberalization of services generally proved difficult.

Explaining the Single Market

- Liberal intergovernmentalism effectively explains the original commitment to the common market.
- Agreement to accelerate progress on the common market in the mid-1960s was interpreted by Lindberg (1963) as support for neofunctionalism because of the role of the Commission and industrial interests, but this was later contested by Moravcsik (1998).
- Academic explanations of the acceptance of the 1992 Programme in the mid-1980s agreed on the importance of the global economic environment, but disagreed on the respective role of national governments, the Commission, and supranational interests.
- Historical institutionalism provides an explanation for the continued momentum of the single market, based on the institutionalization of new rules and norms.

FURTHER READING

The great debate between theorists about the single market began with **Wayne Sandholtz and John Zysman**, '1992: Recasting the European Bargain', *World Politics*, 42 (1989): 95–128; and continued with **Andrew Moravcsik**, 'Negotiating the Single European Act', *International Organization*, 45 (1991): 19–56. **Philip Budden** responded to Moravcsik's arguments from a **pluralist** perspective in his article, 'Observations on the Single European Act and the "Relaunch of Europe": A Less "Intergovernmental" Reading of the 1985 Intergovernmental Conference', *Journal of European Public Policy*, 9 (2002): 76–97. Another contribution worth reading is that by **Maria Green Cowles**, 'Setting the Agenda for a New Europe: The ERT and EC 1992', *Journal of Common Market Studies*, 33 (1995): 501–26. For a new institutionalist account, see **Kenneth Armstrong and Simon Bulmer**, *The Governance of the Single European Market* (Manchester: Manchester University Press, 1998).

On the case studies of telecommunications and energy, see **Peter Humphreys and Stephen Padgett**, 'Globalization, the European Union, and Domestic Governance in Telecoms and

Electricity', *Governance: An International Journal of Policy, Administration, and Institutions*, 19 (2006): 383–406.

On the controversial passage through the EP of the Services Directive, see **B. Lindberg**, 'Are Political Parties Controlling Legislative Decision-Making in the European Parliament? The Case of the Services Directive', *Journal of European Public Policy*, 15 (2008): 1184–204.

online resource centre

Visit the Online Resource Centre that accompanies this book for links to more information on the single market:
www.oxfordtextbooks.co.uk/orc/bache3e/

Chapter 28

Economic and Monetary Union

Chapter Overview

Economic and monetary union (EMU) first became an official objective of the European Community (EC) in 1969, but it was not achieved until thirty years later. This chapter examines the various attempts at EMU between 1969 and 1992, and the launch and subsequent progress of the single currency, the euro. It then looks at the interpretations and explanations that have been given by various academic commentators for the success of the latest attempt.

The euro and the ECB, while certainly dramatic developments, have not been overnight successes; rather EMU has deep roots in the history of European integration.

(McNamara 2005: 143)

Each element in the term 'economic union and monetary union' has a minimum definition and a maximum definition. The minimum definition of economic union is that states cease to follow completely independent economic policies and instead follow closely co-ordinated policies. The maximum definition of economic union is that economic policies are made centrally for all of the economies of the member states. The minimum definition of monetary union is that states maintain fixed exchange rates between their national currencies. The maximum definition of monetary union is the adoption of a single currency.

History

Economic and monetary union (EMU) first came to the fore as an objective of the EC in 1969 when the Commission produced the Barre Report. In December of the same year, the Hague Summit meeting of the EC heads of government made a commitment to the achievement of EMU 'by 1980'.

To make the commitment to EMU was one thing, but to agree how to do it was another. There were two broad approaches that were represented most clearly by the positions of the French and West German governments. The French government wanted a system for the mutual support of fixed exchange rates between national currencies. It argued that this in itself would produce economic convergence (Dyson 1994: 79–80). The West German government rejected that approach because it believed that it would involve using up West Germany's considerable foreign currency reserves to support the currencies of states that were following what the Germans saw as irresponsibly lax and inflationary economic policies. For West Germany, common economic policies had to come first—and they wanted their preference for monetary stability, rather than the growth-orientated policies of France, to be the basis of the common policies. At the time, the French position was described as 'monetarist', because it advocated monetary union ahead of economic union, while the German position was described as 'economist', because it advocated economic union ahead of monetary union (Tsoukalis 1977; Dyson 1994: 79–80).

The 'Snake'

This fundamental disagreement produced the compromise proposals of the Werner Committee in November 1970 (Chapter 10, pp. 137–8). Werner proposed that the co-ordination of economic policy and the narrowing of exchange-rate fluctuations should proceed in parallel. This arrangement for approximating the exchange rates of member currencies one to another became known as the 'snake in the tunnel' because each currency could move up and down ('snake' up and down) between a minimum and maximum value against other currencies in the system, which formed a floor and a ceiling of fluctuation (the tunnel).

Although the original 'snake' collapsed following the ending of the convertibility of the dollar in August 1971, it was reconstituted in April 1972, only to run into the same problems as its predecessor. Essentially, the problem was that some of the economies of the member states were very much weaker than that of the strongest, West Germany, and the Germans were not prepared to support the value of the currencies of the weaker economies. For example, in 1972, the German Federal Bank (Bundesbank) refused to intervene in the foreign exchanges to support the pound, with the consequence that speculation forced sterling out of the system.

By 1974, economic divergence was glaringly apparent in the EC, indicating that there were definite structural weaknesses in the economies of the peripheral states, including Britain. France sat delicately balanced on the edge between centre and periphery. These strains caused the complete collapse of the original EMU experiment after 1973.

The European Monetary System (EMS)

In October 1977, the Commission President Roy Jenkins took the initiative to revive EMU (Chapter 11, p. 143). It was taken up by the West German Chancellor Helmut Schmidt and the French President Valérie Giscard d'Estaing.

By this time, one of the main factors that had been a barrier to German enthusiasm for the original snake had been removed. Gradually, the governments of the other member states were coming round to accepting the West German economic priority of controlling inflation. Mainly this reassessment of policy was because of the acceleration of inflation following the 1973 oil-price rises. It was obvious that the economies that were having the least success in controlling inflation were also those with the highest rates of unemployment, and the poorest record on growth.

In December 1978, the Bremen European Council created the EMS. The central element was the exchange rate mechanism (ERM) for holding fluctuations in exchange rates within narrow bands. Accounting within the system was in a notional currency called the 'ecu', the value of which was an average of the values of the member currencies (Britain remained outside of the ERM, but sterling was included in the calculation of the value of the ecu). This system limited fluctuations in the values of the participating currencies for a number of years.

Origins of EMU

Moves to strengthen and extend the EMS were part of the programme of the Delors Commission from the outset. However, the issue really came into the forefront of debate in the aftermath of the decision to free the internal market by the end of 1992.

At the end of 1985, the Luxembourg European Council agreed on the terms of the Single European Act (SEA), including a commitment to monetary union. Further progress had to wait until the June 1988 Hanover European Council, which agreed to set up a committee of central bankers and technical experts, under the chairmanship of the President of the Commission, to prepare a report on the steps that needed to be taken to strengthen monetary co-operation. The report of this committee (Insight 28.1) was accepted by the June 1989 European Council meeting in Madrid. The momentum was sustained when the December 1989 European Council in Strasbourg agreed to set up an intergovernmental conference (IGC) to consider the institutional changes that would be necessary in order to move towards monetary union.

Monetary Union in the 1990s

The IGC on monetary union took as its negotiating text the report of the Delors Committee, which recommended that movement to monetary union should be to a timetable. This starting point still left plenty of significant details to be negotiated. Before the IGC began to meet in 1991, West Germany was reunified with East

---

Insight 28.1 The Delors Report

The 'Delors Report' proposed a three-stage progress to monetary union.

(1) The EC currencies that remained outside the exchange rate mechanism of the EMS (those of Britain, Greece, Portugal, and Spain) would join, and the wider band of fluctuation would disappear.

(2) Economic policy would be closely co-ordinated, the band of fluctuation of currencies within the EMS would be narrowed, and the governors of central banks would meet as a committee to prepare the ground for the institution of a European Monetary Co-operation Fund (EMCF).

(3) National currencies would be irrevocably locked together, and the ecu would become a real currency in its own right, administered by the EMCF.

Germany in October 1990. Germany entered the negotiations as clearly the largest state as well as the largest economy in the EC, putting it in a particularly strong negotiating position. Also in 1990, Britain joined the ERM.

Early in the IGC, there was a consensus that a monetary union would only be sustainable if it were underpinned by a considerable degree of economic convergence. The Treaty on European Union (TEU) provided five convergence criteria that would have to be met by any state before it could take part in the monetary union. Prospective members would have to have:

- a budget deficit of not more than 3 per cent of gross domestic product (GDP);
- a public debt of not more than 60 per cent of GDP;
- a level of inflation no more than 1.5 percentage points above the average level achieved by the three states with the lowest levels of inflation;
- interest rates that were no more than 2 per cent above the average level of the three states with the lowest levels;
- a record of respecting the normal fluctuation margins of the exchange rate mechanism for two years.

These criteria reflected the policy priorities of the German government in that they were all concerned with monetary stability.

Although the criteria were stringent, the Treaty did appear to leave room for some relaxation if states were moving in the right direction on all of the relevant indicators. At the same time, it was written into the Treaty that any state that did qualify would join the monetary union when it was set up, which would be in 1997 if possible, and not later than 1999. Only Britain was initially allowed to opt out of signing up for the monetary union in advance, although following the rejection of the Maastricht Treaty in the Danish referendum in June 1992, Denmark was granted a similar opt-out clause in a Protocol to the Treaty.

Putting Maastricht into Operation (1992–2002)

On 16 September 1992, Britain was forced out of the exchange rate mechanism by intensive speculation against the pound. The next day, the Italian lira also had to leave the mechanism. Then, in August 1993, the system came under so much pressure that it only survived by allowing the value of each national currency to fluctuate by 15 per cent either side of its notional value within the system. This was a very large margin of fluctuation for a system that was supposed to approximate to fixed rates of exchange.

One interpretation of these developments was that the member states were not ready for a single currency if they could not hold their exchange rates. Another interpretation was that the episode showed how important it was to move to a single currency so that speculators could not push the economies of the members apart. Certainly the problems deflected neither the French President, François Mitterrand, nor the German Chancellor, Helmut Kohl, from their commitment to monetary union.

405

It was not entirely clear, though, how much support the President and Chancellor had in their own countries. In France, high unemployment made the policy of tying the franc closely to the Deutschmark increasingly unpopular, and the country was paralysed by strikes in the later months of 1995, as the government tried to introduce policies that would allow it to meet the convergence criteria. In Germany, public opinion polls showed growing opposition to abandoning the Deutschmark, despite a conspiracy amongst the political elite to insist that the monetary union was the only course for the country. In November 1995, a poll published in *Die Woche* indicated that 61 per cent of the German people were opposed to the single currency (*Financial Times*, 11–12 November 1995).

Public scepticism about the single currency put the German government in an even stronger position in the bargaining about the detail of the arrangements. It could always argue that unless the German public was confident in the arrangements made, there would be no German participation, and therefore no single currency. In this way, Germany won all of the main arguments.

First, it was agreed that the European Central Bank (ECB) (Insight 28.2) would be located in Frankfurt; then, that the name of the new currency would not be the 'ecu', which the French preferred because it was the name of an old French coin, but the 'euro', because the German people did not have confidence in the existing ecu.

France put up a stronger fight on three other issues:

(1) the level of political control that would be exerted over the ECB;
(2) the rules that would govern budgetary policy after the start of the single currency;
(3) the identity of the first President of the ECB.

On the level of political control, the German government insisted that the ECB should be as independent as it was possible to make it. This was the only way that the German people would have confidence that the single currency would be run on a sound basis. The French government never accepted this: it wanted the ECB to be answerable to national governments.

This fundamental philosophical clash also underlay the differences between the two governments on the terms of the budgetary rules that would apply after the start of the single currency. The German government wanted the Maastricht convergence criterion for budget deficits—that budget deficits should not exceed 3 per cent of GDP—to become permanent. It also wanted a system to penalize states that overshot

---

Insight 28.2 The European Central Bank

The TEU set up a European Central Bank (ECB) charged with conducting the monetary policy of the eurozone. Its governing council consists of an Executive Board plus the governors of the national central banks. The Executive Board consists of a President, a Vice-President, plus four other members. They are appointed by common accord of the member states for a non-renewable term of eight years, and must be 'of recognized standing and professional experience in monetary and banking matters' (TEU A. 283(2)).

this target, and proposed a fine that would be automatic. The French government argued that the fine should be discretionary, and that the Finance Ministers should decide the issue in the light of prevailing economic circumstances.

At the Dublin European Council in December 1996, it was agreed that states that ran a deficit in excess of 3 per cent of GDP would be fined, but the fine would be automatically waived if GDP had fallen by more than 2 per cent in the previous year. If GDP had fallen by less than 2 per cent, but by more than 0.75 per cent, the Finance Ministers would have discretion to decide whether a fine should be imposed. This compromise allowed everyone to claim that they had won, but the fundamental principle was that of the German government.

When a new Socialist government was elected in France in June 1997, it made clear that it was unhappy with the stability pact that had been agreed at Dublin. At the Amsterdam European Council in June 1997, it was agreed that the stability pact would be supplemented by a growth and employment pact, and this was written into the Treaty. However, the terms of the employment pact did not involve any commitments to new EU expenditure, nor were they particularly interventionist in nature. The member states committed themselves: to review their tax and benefits systems to see whether there were any measures that were disincentives to job creation that could be removed; to pursue measures to make their labour markets more flexible; and to institute programmes of education and training to improve the employability of the workforce.

Over the five months following Amsterdam, national plans of action were drawn up. These were debated at a special 'jobs summit' in Luxembourg in November 1997, and adjustments were made to co-ordinate the measures. Nevertheless, the outcome at Amsterdam on monetary union has to be seen primarily as a success for the German government. The French government accepted the stability pact in return for much less than the employment chapter that it had originally wanted to be written into the Treaty.

Having lost the major arguments on EMU to Germany, the French government made an issue of the identity of the first president of the ECB. In May 1998, at a special European Council meeting in Brussels that had been called to launch the single currency, the French President, now Jacques Chirac, refused to accept the nomination of the Dutchman Wim Duisenberg as the first President of the ECB. Duisenberg had been the President of the forerunner of the ECB, the European Monetary Institute, and was the first choice of the clear majority of member states, including Germany. Eventually, in order to satisfy the French President, Duisenberg apparently agreed to step down halfway through his term of office to allow the Governor of the Banque de France, Jean-Claude Trichet, to take his place (*Financial Times*, 4 May 1998). However, Duisenberg subsequently told the European Parliament (EP) that he had not made such a precise commitment on when he would retire, and that he would decide when was the time for him to go (*Financial Times*, 8 May 1998).

The launch of the single currency was only slightly marred by this political controversy, and the financial markets reacted calmly to the shenanigans. The euro formally came into existence on 1 January 1999 with eleven members. Only Greece in the end was excluded by the convergence criteria. Britain, Denmark, and Sweden met the criteria, but excluded themselves. Britain and Denmark were allowed to do this under the terms of their 'opt-outs'. Sweden was able to claim on a technicality that it had not

407

> **Table 28.1 Membership of the EMS and the Single Currency**
>
> | | |
> |---|---|
> | 1979 | Start of EMS. Joined by Belgium, Denmark, France, Germany, Ireland, Italy, Luxembourg, and the Netherlands (all of the then member states of the EC except Britain) |
> | 1986 | Portugal and Spain joined the EC and the EMS |
> | 1989 | Spain joined the ERM |
> | 1990 | Britain and Portugal joined the ERM |
> | 1992 | Britain and Italy forced out of the ERM |
> | 1996 | Italy re-enter the ERM and Finland joined |
> | 1998 | Greece joined EMS and the ERM |
> | 1999 | Austria, Belgium, Finland, France, Germany, Ireland, Italy, Luxembourg, the Netherlands, Portugal, Spain formed the eurozone. Denmark and Greece joined a revised ERM-2 |
> | 2001 | Greece joined the euro |
> | 2002 | Introduction of euro notes and coins |
> | 2004 | Estonia, Lithuania, and Slovenia joined ERM-2 |
> | 2005 | Cyprus, Latvia, and Malta joined ERM-2; rules of eurozone Stability Pact revised |
> | 2007 | Slovenia joined the euro |
> | 2008 | Cyprus and Malta joined the euro |
> | 2009 | Slovakia joined the euro |

fulfilled the conditions because it had not been a member of the ERM for two years prior to the launch of the euro. Denmark and Greece joined a revised ERM-2 that was set up at the same time as the launch of the single currency, but which retained the wide 15 per cent fluctuation band. Britain and Sweden chose not to join ERM-2.

The ERM-2 continues to operate as, in effect, a training area for future members of the single currency, in which they are obliged to adopt good habits of economic management. The 1984 enlargement committed all of the new member states to becoming members of the single currency, but they were required to fulfil the convergence criteria before being allowed in, and had to be members of the ERM-2 for two years. Slovenia, Cyprus, Malta, and Slovakia have since joined the euro (Table 28.1).

The Single Currency in Operation

The Eurogroup

Because decisions on matters relating to the monetary union needed to be taken by the governments of the participating states, in 1998, an informal 'Euro Group' was set up consisting of the eurozone Finance Ministers, each accompanied by one economic official, together with representatives of the ECB and the Economic and Financial

Committee of EU officials. It meets ten to twelve times a year, usually on the evening before the formal sessions of the ECOFIN meeting of the Council of Ministers. It elects a President for two years, and it is the presidency that issues the invitations, prepares the agenda and afterwards circulates an informal memorandum of the most important points discussed and agreed.

As it is an informal body, the meetings of the Euro Group are not publicly minuted or subject to open scrutiny. Yet its importance has grown, thereby emptying the formal ECOFIN meetings of real decision-making power (Glover 2007: 710; Puetter 2006: 1).

Problems of Monetary Union

Although the single currency came into existence more smoothly than many economists predicted, it soon ran into difficulties. The external value of the euro fell steadily against the US dollar, and the 'eurozone' itself began to exhibit some of the problems of having a single interest rate for such a diverse economic area. National economies on the fringes of the zone, particularly those of Spain and Ireland, began to experience the symptoms of repressed inflation, with rapidly rising property prices and shortages of labour. At the same time, the core economies of Germany and France were experiencing sluggish growth, and a majority of states within the eurozone experienced lower rates of growth and higher unemployment than the economies of those EU member states—Britain, Denmark, and Sweden—that remained outside the single currency.

Against this background, it was perhaps unsurprising that the Danish people rejected membership of the euro in a referendum in September 2000, the British government concluded in June 2003 that the time was not right to make an application to join, and the Swedish people followed the Danish example in September 2003.

Redefining the Stability and Growth Pact

While Britain and Sweden were in the process of deciding that they did not want to be part of the eurozone, serious disputes broke out among the member states that were in the single currency over the application of the stability and growth pact. The pact effectively made the Maastricht convergence criteria permanent requirements for the participating states. In particular, they were expected to keep their budget deficits below 3 per cent of GDP. This proved very difficult to achieve in the context of low growth, teetering on the brink of recession. Although agreement was reached on making both Portugal and Ireland come into line when they breached the spending limits, by 2003, the states in the dock were the two giants of the eurozone: France and Germany.

France was already in breach of the deficit limit, and in receipt of a warning from the Commission, which monitored compliance, when presidential and parliamentary elections were held in May/June 2002. During the two election campaigns, President Chirac made pledges that meant it would be impossible for the new government to remain within the 3 per cent deficit limit. When challenged about this after the elections, the new French Prime Minister, Jean-Pierre Raffarin, asserted that, while the pact ought to be observed, 'France is not a run-of-the-mill country' (*Financial Times*, 8 January 2004). This implied that although Portugal and Ireland might be expected to abide by the rules, France was too important to be told what to do.

Such an attitude no doubt played well within France, where the EU was unpopular because of attempts by the Commission to get the government to abide by its commitments under the single-market programme on issues such as state aids and market access. It did not play so well, though, elsewhere within the EU, especially among smaller states that had grown concerned about the way in which the Franco-German alliance was steamrollering through decisions on other matters, such as agricultural reform.

At the same time the German government was also failing to keep its budget deficit within the 3 per cent limit. In February 2002, the Commission proposed issuing an 'early warning' to Germany over its rising deficit, but political manoeuvring led the Finance Ministers to reject the proposal. Although it exerted diplomatic pressure to avert the embarrassment of a formal warning in an election year, the German government did implement advice from the Commission on how to avoid exceeding the deficit limit, but it was still in breach of the limit in 2003 when it drew up its budget plans for 2004.

These budget proposals included a package of tax cuts that the German government believed were necessary to sweeten the structural economic reforms that the Commission had also been urging it to adopt for some time. The tax cuts, taken in the context both of the budget as a whole and of projections for rates of economic growth, implied that Germany would exceed the 3 per cent limit again in 2004. In this light, Pedro Solbes, the Commissioner for Monetary Affairs, warned in May 2003 that it might prove necessary to implement sanctions against Germany.

In November 2003, the eurozone Finance Ministers discussed a formal proposal from the Commission that sanctions be applied against both France and Germany unless they took steps to reduce their budget deficit for 2004 below the 3 per cent limit. Once it became obvious that there was no majority for the Commission's proposal, the Italian presidency proposed a suspension of the sanctions, and this was accepted by a majority vote. With this decision, the stability pact in effect ceased to exist as a mandatory set of rules for fiscal discipline and became no more than a set of guidelines on policy to national governments.

Yet neither Germany nor France ever challenged the principle of the pact, and in an attempt to minimize the damage that their action might cause, both agreed voluntarily to try to reduce spending for 2004: Germany by 0.6 per cent, which was only marginally less than the 0.8 per cent on which Solbes had tried to insist; France, less credibly, by 0.8 per cent. This seemed to make it clear that the principle at stake was not the need for fiscal discipline, but who was in charge: national governments or the European Commission.

That principle was also the reason for the decision of the European Commission, in January 2004, to take the Council to the European Court of Justice (ECJ) under Article 230 (previously 173) of the Treaty. The decision was taken by a majority vote in a badly divided College—but the view prevailed that it was the duty of the Commission in its role as guardian of the Treaty to test the legality of the act. In July 2004, the ECJ ruled that the Council had acted illegally in suspending the pact's mechanism for sanctioning member states, but affirmed that responsibility for making the member states observe budgetary discipline lay with the Council, not the Commission (*Financial Times*, 14 July 2004).

In March 2005, the stability pact was revised to relax the conditions under which a 3 per cent deficit would not be considered 'excessive', and the timetable for correcting an excessive deficit was stretched. In future, a member state exceeding the 3 per cent deficit can argue that it is doing so legitimately if it is trying through its excess expenditure to achieve European goals or to 'foster international solidarity', both of which are very broad objectives. Correction of an excessive deficit will in future require a reduction by 0.5 per cent per annum subject to full correction within five years, as opposed to the previous requirement to make the correction in one year.

Euro Notes and Coins

The other main development in monetary union after 1999 was the introduction of euro notes and coins on 1 January 2002. Between 1999 and 2002, the euro officially existed as an international currency, but national currencies continued to be used for domestic purposes. The replacement of the national currencies with the euro notes and coins was a significant development because it gave physical form to the new currency for ordinary citizens of the eurozone, and made it a part of their daily lives. The creation of a single currency in physical form provided an important symbol of European integration and for some signalled an important step towards the development of a European identity (Risse 2003).

The Eurozone Crisis 2010

In 2008–09, the capitalist world experienced a major financial crisis. At first, the euro itself seemed to be relatively unaffected, although individual member states of the eurozone, such as Spain and Ireland, experienced difficulties as property prices collapsed. Then, in October 2009, a general election in Greece produced a change of government. The outgoing New Democracy government had called the election early seeking a mandate to handle a looming financial crisis. When the new Socialist government took office, it revealed that the fiscal position of the state was far worse than the previous government had admitted.

It soon became apparent that Greek government statistics had concealed the true extent of the national budget deficit, which was far in excess of the 3 per cent of GDP allowed under the rules of the eurozone. In December 2009, two of the leading agencies that rate national creditworthiness downgraded Greece by one grade from A minus to BBB plus. This made financial markets reluctant to buy Greek government debt, and the spread on interest rates between Greek and German bonds began to widen, until by January 2010 it had reached 4 per cent. This was despite a show of intent by the Greek government to tighten government finances by cutting expenditure and increasing taxes, a move that provoked street demonstrations and strikes.

In February 2010, EU leaders met to consider whether Greece should be given assistance to allow it to cover its existing debts. As the cost of borrowing money on the international markets became steadily higher for the Greek government, there was a risk of it having to default on some of its debts, which could have led to a serious collapse in the value of the euro. Yet there was strong resistance in Germany to what was seen as a bailout for a country that had been profligate in its fiscal management, and German Chancellor Angela Merkel stated that it was for Greece to get itself out of the mess that it was in.

By April, though, it was apparent that the markets had decided Greece was incapable of rescuing itself, and belatedly the other members of the eurozone agreed a €30 billion rescue package. This turned out to be too little and too late, even after the **International Monetary Fund (IMF)** offered to put up another €15 billion. Spreads between the interest rates on Greek and German government bonds reached 4.69 per cent after the package was agreed, and one credit agency slashed Greece's rating even further to BB plus.

At the beginning of May 2010, a €110 billion package was agreed by eurozone Finance Ministers, comprising €80 billion from the other fifteen euro states at 5 per cent interest, well below what Greece would have to pay on financial markets, with the rest being provided by the IMF. Greece had to accept a €30 billion package of spending cuts and tax increases to reduce its budget deficit by 5 percentage points in 2010 and a further 4 percentage points in 2011. Agreement was also reached on a further general facility of €750 billion that would be available to other eurozone states that might find themselves under pressure.

The measures were unpopular in both Greece and Germany. In Greece, street protests were renewed, and three bank employees were killed when anarchists set light to the bank in which they worked. In Germany, the government suffered a setback when it lost a Land election in North Rhine-Westphalia and thereby its majority in the Bundesrat, the upper house of the federal parliament.

France had long pressed for monetary union to be backed by economic governance for the eurozone. Germany had resisted such a move, fearing that it would inevitably involve German bailouts for weaker national economies. Herman Van Rompuy, the President of the European Council, was charged with finding a more effective way of controlling the debt of weaker states by autumn 2010. However, the divide between the French and German positions looked difficult to reconcile, even though a solution would be critical to the very future of the eurozone. Thus, by the summer of 2010, it looked as though the EU had reached one of those periodic crises when it would either move to closer unity or start to unravel.

Explaining EMU

Academics have vigorously debated both why the decision to adopt a single currency was finally made, and why the particular form of monetary union was agreed. Among supranationalist explanations that have been debated have been spillover, the role of the Commission, and the role of central bankers as an epistemic community. Among intergovernmental explanations have been some that have stressed geo-political factors, and some that have stressed domestic economic factors. International factors form the background to both supranational and intergovernmental explanations.

Spillover

It could be argued, as it was argued by the Commission, that pressure for monetary union came as spillover from the decision to free the internal market. Making a reality of the single market implied eliminating the fluctuations in exchange rates that were a source of interference with trade across national boundaries. However, Sandholtz

(1993: 20–22) rejected the argument that there was a clear functional spillover from the single market to a single currency. The reasoning behind it was contentious:

> Among economists, there is no consensus on the desirability of monetary integration, much less on its functional necessity.
>
> (Sandholtz 1993: 21)

However, he argued that there was clearly what others have called 'cultivated spillover'. This occurs when the Commission 'cultivates' pressure on the governments of member states to adopt further measures of integration (Chapter 1, p. 10).

The Role of the Commission

The Commission used 1992 as an argument to press for a single currency, and it met with a receptive audience among the public, business, and political elites because the success of the single-market programme had provided a favourable environment. Tsoukalis (1996: 293) reinforced this argument. He suggested a strategic approach by the Commission that resembled that identified in Chapter 27 (p. 397) as the approach of the **policy entrepreneur**.

In terms of decision making, the negotiation on EMU during the Maastricht IGC bore considerable resemblance to earlier European initiatives and especially the one that had led previously to the adoption of the single-market programme. The gradual build-up of momentum, the steady expansion of the political base of support through coalition building, and the isolation of opponents were combined with an effective marketing campaign orchestrated by the Commission and addressed primarily towards opinion leaders and the business community. Central bankers were closely involved early on, notably through their participation in the Delors Committee, which produced the report on EMU. Later, they played an active role in the drafting of the relevant articles of the Treaty. Arguments about functional spillover were also successfully mixed with high politics and the appeal to 'Eurosentiment'—a recipe that had proved quite successful in the past.

Central Bankers as an Epistemic Community

Verdun (1999: 317) identified the central bankers as an 'epistemic community' in this process (see Chapter 2, pp. 32–3). They all agreed that the aim of monetary policy was to achieve price stability. They all agreed that to achieve this, monetary policies had to be freed from political influence. They all supported a supranational regulatory agent in the form of the European System of Central Banks (ESCB). She also argued (Verdun 1999: 320) that the Delors Committee itself fulfilled the four main requirements laid down by Haas (1992) for an epistemic community:

(1) a shared set of normative beliefs—that monetary union would benefit the EC;

(2) a shared set of causal beliefs—on the causes of inflation, on the importance of stable exchange rates, that the dominance of European monetary policy by the Bundesbank was unsatisfactory, that it was undesirable to have economic policy centrally directed;

413

(3) shared notions of validity;

(4) a common policy enterprise.

Verdun appeared to accept the intergovernmentalist view of the dynamics of monetary union, arguing that the member states invoked the assistance of this epistemic community in order to legitimate policy decisions that they wished to take. An alternative interpretation is to see Delors' use of the epistemic communities as entirely in line with the way in which he had used the epistemic community of economists in the form of the Cecchini Report to push forward the single-market programme (Chapter 27, p. 397).

Kaelberer (2003) agreed that the central bankers exhibited the characteristics of an epistemic community, but he warned against overstating either the extent to which they functioned as such a community during the EMU process, or the extent of their influence.

> The internal functioning of the Delors Committee and the central banking community did not fully correspond to the ideal of an epistemic community. While consensus was certainly widespread, it was not complete. Moreover, the functioning of the group of central bankers was quite hierarchical. This hierarchy was not the result of epistemic criteria but rather structural positions.

(Kaelberer 2003: 371)

There was a lack of consensus between the central bankers on how to approach monetary union, with the old division between the French monetarist and the German economist positions re-emerging (see above, pp. 402–3). The French central bank argued for rapid movement to a single currency, which would automatically bring about convergence in economic performance, while the Bundesbank insisted that monetary union must be preceded by economic convergence, with the onus on the governments of the states that wished to participate to meet the convergence criteria. Each position was backed by solid academic arguments, but the lack of consensus weakens the argument that the central bankers functioned as an epistemic community (Kaelberer 2003: 371–2).

The dispute was not resolved by consensus, either, as it should have been had the central bankers been operating fully as an epistemic community. According to Kaelberer (2003: 372), the President of the Bundesbank, Karl-Otto Pöhl, was not held in particularly high regard for his technical competence among the group of European central bankers. Rather than being resolved on the balance of technical arguments, or 'epistemic' criteria, the disagreement was resolved in favour of German policy priorities because of the political strength of the Bundesbank within the Delors Committee. Contrary to the definition of an epistemic community, there was a clear hierarchy within the Committee because of the strong bargaining position held by the Germans.

Kaelberer (2003: 375) also made the point that the influence of the central bankers on the transition to a single currency was limited by the fact that the Delors Committee was charged only to study how to achieve monetary union, not whether there should be a monetary union. The central bankers, who had not been supportive of the idea of a single currency, were 'trapped' into the process by governments that had already made the fundamental decision for political reasons. In this respect, Kaelberer (2003) agreed with Verdun (1999) in adopting an intergovernmentalist view of the dynamics of European monetary integration.

Intergovernmentalist Explanations

Acceptance of the explanation that both Kaelberer and Verdun appeared to offer would involve stressing the wish of national governments to transfer decision making on monetary policy to central institutions. This would allow the governments to disclaim responsibility for some of the unpopular economic measures that might be necessary to maintain competitiveness in the single market. Votes are closely correlated to the sense of economic well-being of the population of a state, and this has been a powerful factor encouraging parties in office to bow to protectionist demands that they may know not to be in the long-term national interest. If governments were increasingly losing their room to influence the short-term performance of the national economy, it would clearly be in their interest to make this as obvious as possible to the electorate. The EU could then be blamed for adverse economic fortunes.

Linked to this argument are concerns about the credibility of anti-inflationary commitments. Sandholtz (1993: 34–6) argued that the commitment of some governments to combating inflation was in doubt because of their previous record on this issue, and because of the political obstacles in the way of carrying through the necessary policies. In this context, a government might welcome having its hands tied by commitments to the EC/EU:

> monetary union would provide price stability for governments that would be unable, for domestic political reasons, to achieve it on their own.

(Sandholtz 1993: 35)

This hypothesis might explain why German preferences prevailed on the issues of the independence of the ECB and the constitutional commitment that the ECB should aim for price stability above other goals. Whatever other governments' public protestations that they found the German preferences too restrictive, in private they welcomed the opportunity to be tied into policies that they believed to be right, but did not believe that they could persuade their electorates to support. In states in which the general value of the EU was never in doubt, this technique could be used without undermining the legitimacy of EU membership itself. In other states, the outcome of the monetary union negotiations contributed to undermining the legitimacy of the EU.

Another explanation for EMU starts from the experience that member states had of the EMS. Sandholtz (1993: 27–30) noted that the EMS was working well, but that there was growing discontent in France and elsewhere with the way in which decisions on interest rates were made by the Bundesbank in the light of conditions only in West Germany, and these were then transmitted throughout the EMS member states because of the need to keep all currencies aligned in a context of open capital markets. This was the main motivation for the French government, in a paper circulated in January

1988, proposing to move beyond the EMS to a single currency. Sandholtz (1993: 30) argued, though, that this explanation ignored the possibility that a greater say for the other members of the EMS could be achieved by reforms to the system. The goal of a greater voice for France and for other countries in EC monetary policy could have been achieved by other means and did not require movement toward EMU.

This objection was met in part by the argument of Cameron (1997), who identified three asymmetries in the EMS that were unwelcome to France and other participants. First, there was the asymmetry of influence in making decisions on interest rates, which has already been noted above. Second, there was an asymmetry in adjustment costs, which fell particularly heavily on the weak-currency states. If the exchange rate of a weak-currency country threatened to fall below the range of its parity, it was expected to take the necessary action to support its currency. Failure to maintain the parity could lead to a devaluation, which would again place adjustment costs on the weak-currency state by feeding inflationary tendencies. Third, there was an asymmetry in the impact on the prosperity of strong-currency and weak-currency states. If realignments could be avoided (and they became less frequent the longer the system lasted), states that had higher levels of inflation would find that their exports were becoming relatively less competitive. States with lower rates of inflation would find their exports becoming steadily more competitive. This is how West Germany came to run large surpluses with all of its main EC trading partners. To these, Loedel (1998) added a fourth asymmetry: in international monetary influence. It was with West Germany that the United States conducted such dialogue as it held with Europe on international monetary matters. Other members of the EMS had no say in such monetary diplomacy.

On this argument, then, the experience of the EMS led member states other than West Germany to want to transfer control of monetary policy from the national to the European level. As things stood under the EMS, the German central bank had effective control over the monetary policy of other member states. While reform of the exchange rate mechanism might have tackled this problem, there were other disadvantages to the system that made movement to full monetary union preferable.

It is clear, though, that the asymmetries in the EMS do not explain why West Germany supported the single currency. After all, it was a system that favoured German interests. Here, Sandholtz (1993: 31–4) invoked West German foreign policy aims. The West German Foreign Minister, Hans Dietrich Genscher, who initially welcomed the French proposal, had a long record of wanting to balance West German policy to the east with strengthening its links within the EC. In the context of the accelerating collapse of communism in eastern and central Europe, this aim came to be shared by Chancellor Kohl. The issue also became linked to German reunification. In late 1989, Kohl produced a ten-point plan for German unification. Shortly afterwards, the EC states agreed to convene the IGC on EMU in 1990. Sandholtz suggested that this decision was precipitated by the concern of France and other neighbours of Germany that the reunified German state would lose interest in the EC, and might even become nationalist again. Such a danger became a theme of speeches given by Helmut Kohl in defence of the single currency. He repeatedly associated the single currency with European integration, and European integration with the avoidance of war in Europe. The single currency was an essential step on the way to political union, which in turn was essential to peace and stability.

In contrast, Moravcsik (1998: 381) was dismissive of the explanation based on German reunification because, he maintained, the timing was wrong. Firm commitments by France and West Germany to move decisively forward with EMU—and opposition by Britain to that goal—predated the fall of the Berlin Wall and remained unchanged after unification was completed in August 1990. On the other hand, Moravcsik did allow that, in this decision, the influence of the commitment of both Kohl and Genscher to European integration could not be dismissed:

> Genscher and Kohl appear to have been strongly predisposed toward integration, even in advance of a clear economic justification for it.

(Moravcsik 1998: 403)

At the same time, he argued that there was a German economic interest in monetary integration. The steady appreciation of the Deutschmark against other currencies was reducing the competitiveness of German exports, and merging it into a wider European currency offered the opportunity to dampen down this trend. Concerns about currency appreciation intensified in the 1990s in the face of the large costs of reunification and the collapse of the ERM in 1992 (Moravcsik 1998: 392).

Kaltenthaler (2002) attempted to cut through the dichotomy between explanations of German policy that stressed geo-political factors and those that stressed economic interests by distinguishing three distinct groups of actors who influenced German policy on monetary union whenever it was proposed. The first group was a 'foreign policy coalition', consisting of the Foreign Ministry and the Chancellor's office. The second group was a 'monetary stability coalition' of state actors with responsibility for financial and monetary policy, consisting primarily of the Finance Ministry and the Bundesbank. The third group consisted of societal actors, predominantly bankers and industrialists operating through organizations such as the Federation of German Banks (BDB), the Federation of German Industry (BDI), and the German Chambers of Commerce (DIHT). There was always a tension between these actors. The foreign policy coalition had the primary aim of 'embedding Germany in western institutions' (Kaltenthaler 2002: 70), and was particularly concerned to maintain the key diplomatic relationship with France. The monetary stability coalition, as the name implies, was concerned to ensure that domestic monetary stability was maintained. Which of these coalitions had the greater success in influencing policy was largely determined by their ability to attract the support of the third group, the societal actors (Kaltenthaler 2002: 72–3).

When the French government, dissatisfied with the asymmetrical operation of the EMS, first proposed moving to full monetary union in early 1988, the immediate reaction of the West German government was cool. This reaction reflected the combined opposition of the monetary stability coalition and the societal interests, which saw the French proposal as a device to gain control of German monetary policy and move it away from its emphasis on price stability. Chancellor Kohl and Foreign Minister Genscher both supported the proposal for geo-strategic reasons, to shore up the alliance with France. The balance of power shifted, though, with the fall of the Berlin Wall and the prospect of reunification. The banking and industrial interests saw tremendous prospects for expansion into East Germany, and therefore very much favoured reunification. France, though, held a veto over reunification, because it was one of the four powers that had occupied Germany after the war (together with Britain, the United States, and the Soviet Union), and the agreement of all four was needed for reunification to proceed.

Kaltenthaler (2002: 80) disagreed with Moravcsik (1998) that reunification was unimportant in explaining the commitment to monetary union, but whereas Sandholtz (1993) emphasized the strategic thinking behind the decision—that Kohl and Genscher wanted to reassure France and the other EU member states that it was still committed to the EU—Kaltenthaler emphasized the politics behind the decision. The foreign policy coalition won the support of the societal interests when it seemed as though monetary union was the price that would have to be paid to get France to agree to reunification. However, in the IGC, the monetary stability coalition was able to dictate the terms of monetary union because, on the principle of monetary stability, it still had the backing of the societal interests.

Turning from Germany back to more general explanations of monetary union, Sandholtz (1993: 23–7) argued that key domestic interest groups came to support the single currency. The 1992 Programme led to a big increase in cross-border mergers, which increased the constituency of firms that would benefit from the disappearance of currency-exchange costs. However, he acknowledged that the business support came after the single currency had become the leading project of the member states, so that it could not be used as the explanation for the commitment, although it could help to explain why the commitment was carried through against all obstacles.

Public opinion was generally pro-EC in the aftermath of the successful agreement on the 1992 single-market programme, but it also could not be seen as a cause of the commitment to the single currency; rather it was a permissive factor in most member states. Later, when it came to ratification of the Maastricht Treaty, less enthusiastic public opinion became an obstacle to carrying through the commitment.

International Pressures

Pressures for monetary union from the global system were present at several stages in the story. The debate about the impact of the collapse of communism has been reviewed above. In addition, from at least the early 1980s on, there was continuing and growing concern about the extent to which the United States was prepared to use the still-dominant position of the dollar in the international monetary system to benefit the US domestic economy. Large fluctuations in the value of the dollar threw off course the economic and budgetary plans of the EC, and gave it a strong incentive to develop a single European currency that could displace the dollar from its position of pre-eminence in the international system, which it continued to hold more by default than because of the strength of the currency.

CONCLUSION

Economic and monetary union raises many of the issues that are consistent themes of this book. The debate between supranational and intergovernmental interpretations of the nature of European integration rages as fiercely here as it does for the single-market programme, and the creation of another independent **supranational institution**, the ECB, feeds the argument between the same positions about the nature of the EU and its institutions. The form of monetary union that has been adopted gives another twist to the erosion of different national models of capitalism, and in doing so further helps to undermine the legitimacy of the EU.

The previous history of attempts to achieve EMU clearly indicated that the attempt at the end of the 1980s would have to face up to the difficult issue of the form that the monetary union would take. French and German views on the matter had long differed. France favoured institutional arrangements that would put the ECB directly under the guidance and ultimate control of the governments of the member states. West Germany favoured an independent central bank, not because the West German government wanted to increase the degree of supranationalism inherent in the EC's institutional architecture, but because the West German post-war tradition was that the value of the currency should not be subject to political interference, but should be determined by an independent bank. The Bundesbank had always been fiercely independent of the federal government in West Germany, and the confidence of the West German people in the new currency would be vitally dependent on similar arrangements applying to the ECB. The German view prevailed, with the result that the degree of supranationalism of the EU may have been increased, even if that was not the intention.

Institutionalizing this anti-inflation priority undermined the ability of other member states to protect employment at the risk of higher inflation. This was a fundamental part of the models of capitalism that operated in France, Italy, and elsewhere in the EU. The removal of another policy instrument from the toolkit of national governments risked undermining the legitimacy of the EU when recession cost jobs and the government could not respond effectively.

In effect, the existing system is only a monetary union, not an economic and monetary union. Economic policy is still set by the member states separately, albeit within guidelines laid down by the stability and growth pact. The economic crisis of 2008–09 led to a revival of demands from the French in particular for the strengthening of the political aspects of the system. However, it is difficult to see how the economic government of the eurozone would work, given the continuing policy differences between the governments of the member states and the unwillingness of the larger states to accept external instruction on how to conduct their economic affairs. Also, the ECB is more independent than almost any other central bank in the world. Even if it were to face a unified political grouping, its constitution would render it almost impervious to political instruction.

KEY POINTS

History

- In 1969, the Hague Summit committed the EC to achieve 'EMU by 1980'.

- There was tension over EMU between Germany and France. Germany made anti-inflationary policies the priority; France made economic growth the priority even at the risk of higher inflation.

- This disagreement led to the compromise proposals of the Werner Committee for closer co-ordination of economic policy accompanied by tying together the exchange rates of member states within narrow margins of fluctuations (the 'snake in the tunnel').

- The snake was ultimately broken by a combination of divergence in the economic performance of the members and the US policy of allowing the dollar to devalue.

- In the period following the 1973 oil crisis, other member states began to follow Germany's lead in supporting a low-inflation policy. This removed a major barrier to greater currency co-operation.

- In October 1977, the Commission President, Roy Jenkins, called for a new attempt at EMU. This initiative was supported by German Chancellor Schmidt and French President Giscard d'Estaing.
- In December 1978, the Bremen European Council created the EMS.

Origins of EMU

- In 1988, the Hanover European Council set up the Delors Committee to report on the steps needed to strengthen monetary co-operation in the light of the single market.
- An IGC in 1991 set a timetable for completion of monetary union, which would be not later than January 1999.
- The Maastricht Treaty (1991) set stringent criteria to ensure the convergence of member state economies prior to participation in monetary union.
- Only Britain was initially allowed to opt out of signing up for the monetary union in advance. Following the rejection of the Maastricht Treaty in the Danish referendum in June 1992, Denmark was granted a similar opt-out.

Putting Maastricht into Operation (1992–2002)

- Germany won all of the main arguments over the details of the monetary union, including the name of the single currency, the criteria that would guide its operation, the location of the ECB, and the identity of its first governor.
- The euro was launched in January 1999. Only Britain, Denmark, and Sweden declined to take part, while Greece failed to meet the qualifying criteria.
- Denmark and Greece joined a revised ERM-2. Later members of the EU were required to be members of this system for two years before being allowed into the euro.

The Single Currency in Operation

- A Euro Group was set up by the members of the single currency, and it has now assumed considerable importance, weakening the main Ecofin.
- Soon after it started, the euro ran into problems. Its value fell against the dollar, and the out-lying economies experienced inflation at the same time as the core economies experienced recession.
- The economies that remained outside of the eurozone experienced high levels of growth. Between September 2000 and September 2003, Britain, Denmark, and Sweden all decided not to apply for entry. On the other hand, the new member states of the EU all wanted to join EMU as soon as possible.
- Euro notes and coins were introduced at the start of 2002.
- When France and Germany breached the rules of the stability pact in 2002–03, they refused to accept censure from the Commission. In March 2005, the mandatory system for enforcing budgetary discipline was replaced by a more flexible set of guidelines.

Explanations of EMU

- Supranationalist explanations have included spillover, the role of the Commission, and the role of central bankers as an epistemic community.
- Intergovernmental explanations have stressed geo-political factors and domestic economic factors.
- International factors form the background to both supranational and intergovernmental explanations.

FURTHER READING

The essential starting point for further reading is **D. R. Cameron**, 'Economic and Monetary Union: Underlying Imperatives and Third-Stage Dilemmas', *Journal of European Public Policy*, 4 (1997): 455–85, which examines why the member states perceived EMU to be in their national interest, and considers some of the practical problems involved in operating a single currency. **W. Sandholtz**, 'Choosing Union: Monetary Politics and Maastricht', *International Organization*, 47 (1993): 1–39, reviews the history of the decision on monetary union, and analyses it in the light of theoretical perspectives, including neofunctionalism and intergovernmentalism. Unsurprisingly, the intergovernmental viewpoint is best represented by **A. Moravcsik**, *The Choice for Europe: Social Purpose and State Power from Messina to Maastricht* (London: UCL Press, 1998), 379–471. An excellent, detailed history is provided by **K. Dyson and K. Featherstone**, *The Road to Maastricht: Negotiating Economic and Monetary Union* (Oxford: Oxford University Press, 1999). Two more recent books that provide valuable insights are **M. Chang**, *Monetary Integration in the European Union* (Basingstoke: Palgrave Macmillan, 2009), and **D. Marsh**, *The Euro: The Politics of the New Global Currency* (New Haven, CT, and London: Yale University Press, 2009).

 online resource centre **Visit the Online Resource Centre that accompanies this book for links to more information on economic and monetary union, including the website of the European Central Bank: www.oxfordtextbooks.co.uk/orc/bache3e/**

Chapter 29
Cohesion Policy

Chapter Overview

In its narrow sense, cohesion policy can be understood as the governing principles of various funding instruments aimed at addressing social and economic inequalities in the European Union (EU). More broadly, it can be seen to have political goals connected to the development of a just society. Its origins lie in the development of EU regional policy, which began only in the 1970s, despite long-standing awareness of significant regional disparities. From modest beginnings in 1975, the policy field has expanded to account for over a third of the European Community (EC) budget. This chapter traces key developments and highlights shifts in the intergovernmental-supranational nature of policy control in the sector that first gave rise to the notion of multi-level governance (MLG).

The increasing involvement of the European Union in the development of European regions is one of the clearest examples of transnational policy cooperation...

(Adshead 2002: 7)

What is today known as EU cohesion policy had its origins in EC regional policy (Insight 29.1). Yet, despite evidence of wide disparities between Europe's regions, the Treaty of Rome made no specific commitment to the creation of a Community regional policy. It was not until 1975 that a European regional fund was created and 1988 before a coherent supranational policy emerged. Up to this point, national governments prevented a more effective supranational approach and the regional policy process was viewed as a 'virtual paragon of intergovernmentalism' (McAleavey 1992: 3). From 1988, control of the policy fluctuated between the Commission and member governments over time, issue, and policy stages. As a result, academic study of the field has been dominated by the intergovernmental–supranational debate (see Chapter 1).

History

While the Treaty of Rome made no specific commitment to the creation of a Community regional policy, it did provide a more general objective of promoting throughout the Community 'a harmonious development of economic activities, a continuous and balanced expansion' (Article 2). The Preamble to the Treaty also made reference to 'reducing the differences between the various regions and the backwardness of the less favoured regions' (Swift 1978: 10). At this stage, it was not clear whether these disparities would be addressed through member state or Community regional policies, or a combination of both. For almost two decades, the responsibility for regional policy remained with the member states, but wide disparities between EC regions persisted.

The Creation of a European Regional Policy

Agreement to create the European Regional Development Fund (ERDF) at the Paris Summit of 1972 reflected the increased salience of the issue of regional disparities in the context of the impending enlargement to include Britain, Denmark, and Ireland. The British government in particular pushed for the fund, being in need of something tangible to persuade a reluctant public and Parliament of the benefits of European Economic Community (EEC) membership. The other influential factors in the creation for the ERDF were a push toward economic and monetary union (EMU) provided by the Werner Report of 1970, and Commission plans to control member states' aid to industries (Bache 1998: 36–7).

From the decision in principle to create the ERDF, taken in 1972, it was a difficult journey to final agreement two years later, which came only when the Irish and Italian governments threatened to boycott the Paris Summit of 1974 unless they were promised progress on the matter. The size of the initial fund—1.3 billion European units of account (EUAs)—disappointed the ' *demandeur*' member states, but was nonetheless seen as an important breakthrough. It would provide up to half of the cost of development projects in eligible regions, with the remaining cost met from domestic sources. This principle of co-financing was to ensure domestic commitment to projects and has remained a fixture of the regional policy (and cohesion policy).

The new ERDF was distributed according to national quotas thrashed out by governments, rather than according to objective Community criteria. Each government demanded a quota, even though this meant that relatively prosperous regions in wealthier member states received funding at the expense of poorer regions elsewhere (see Table 29.1).

Governments also dominated policy implementation. In particular, they were reluctant to accept the additionality requirement that 'the Fund's assistance should not lead Member States to reduce their own regional development efforts but should complement these efforts' (European Commission 1975). On this issue, the British government was particularly difficult (Wallace 1977; Bache 1998). Resistance to this rare supranational principle of regional policy continued even when the Commission became more powerful to act after 1988, and the struggle over this issue became an important barometer in the intergovernmental–supranational debate.

The additionality requirement apart, there was little supranational influence over the principles of regional policy before the 1988 reform. There were some experiments with non-quota programmes after the review of 1979, and experiments with multi-annual programmes after 1984, which proved to be important forerunners of later policies. Generally, though, national governments shaped the broad contours of the policy and managed its effects, while supranational actors had only marginal influence. Moreover, there were no significant cross-sectoral or multi-level policy networks that were important to the later development of multi-level governance.

Table 29.1 ERDF National Quotas (1975)

	Percentage (%)
Belgium	1.5
Denmark	1.3
France	15.0
Germany	6.4
Ireland	6.0
Italy	40.0
Luxembourg	0.1
Netherlands	1.7
United Kingdom	28.0
Total	100.0

Note: Ireland was also to receive a further six MUA taken proportionally from the other countries, with the exception of Italy.

Source: Preston (1984: 75)

The Emergence of Cohesion Policy

Two important developments provided the political and economic context for the major reform of EU regional funding that came into effect on 1 January 1989: the enlargement of the Community to include Portugal and Spain in 1985; and the push towards greater economic and social cohesion given expression in the Single European Act (SEA) of 1986.

The accession of Spain and Portugal meant a considerable widening of regional disparities in the EU, leading to a doubling of the population of regions with a per capita gross domestic product (GDP) of less than 50 per cent of the Community average (European Commission 1989: 9). This in itself required an increase in regional allocations. Southern enlargement (Greece, Spain, and Portugal) was also important in prompting the introduction of a new type of regional development programme in 1985, the Integrated Mediterranean Programmes (IMPs). The IMPs experimented with principles of multi-annual programming and partnership that proved important to later reforms.

Moves to complete the internal market in the mid-1980s led to talk of a 'Golden Triangle' connecting the prosperous parts of the Community that would benefit most from the single market. In response to the concerns of the poorer regions, Article 130A of the SEA (now Article 187 TFEU) set out the need to strengthen 'economic and social cohesion' within the EC, in particular through 'reducing disparities between the various regions and the backwardness of the least-favoured regions' (European Commission 1989: 11).

The term *cohesion*, developed within the Commission as the counterpart of the moves to completing the internal market, had a dual meaning:

> It summarized a novel policy rationale to deal more effectively with the old problem of regional economic disparities, but it also held a political promise to involve subnational actors more openly in European decision-making ... subnational mobilization was crucial to its success.

(Hooghe 1996*b*: 89)

The 1988 Reform

The ERDF, the European Social Fund (ESF), and the European Agricultural Guarantee and Guidance Fund (EAGGF), referred to collectively as the 'structural funds', were central to cohesion policy. Article 130D of the SEA (now Article 161 TEC) called for a reform of these three funds, through a Framework Regulation on their tasks, their effectiveness, 'and on co-ordination of their activities between themselves and with the operations of the **European Investment Bank (EIB)** and other financial instruments' (European Commission 1989: 11). The Brussels European Council of February 1988 agreed the draft Regulations in principle and also agreed to a doubling of structural fund allocations by 1993. Approximately 9 per cent of the structural fund budget would be allocated through Community Initiative (CI) programmes, for which the Commission had greatest influence over both design and implementation. The final details were agreed in three main regulations that came into effect on 1 January 1989.

Insight 29.2 Principles Guiding the Operation of the Structural Funds

- **Concentration:** of the funds on the areas of greatest need as defined by the accompanying objectives (see Insight 29.3, p. 427).
- **Programming:** multi-annual programmes would be the norm for all funding, to ease the Commission's administrative burden and promote a more coherent approach.
- **Partnership:** partnerships would be established to oversee the administration of the funds and would require the formal involvement of local and regional actors for the first time.
- **Additionality:** the additionality requirement would be strengthened by a new regulation and by the greater involvement of the Commission and local and regional actors in the new partnership arrangements.

The operation of the funds would be guided by four complementary principles—concentration, partnership, programming, and additionality (Insight 29.2)—which were essentially those that the Commission had advocated throughout the development of regional policy. The share of funding received by each member state is detailed in Table 29.3 (p. 431).

Following the principle of *concentration*, several 'Objectives' were defined on the basis of which eligibility for funds would be determined (Insight 29.3). Despite the creation of new Objectives with detailed criteria for eligibility, the decisions on which regions (and thus which member states) received assistance under both Objectives 1 and 2 were either taken by or heavily influenced by member states.

Programming: After more than a decade of trying, the Commission finally secured Council support for multi-annual programmes for all structural funding. This switch promised more coherence in formulating strategies for regional development and brought greater certainty to the spending process. Objective 1 regions received programme funding for five years and Objective 2 regions for three years.

Programming followed a three-stage process. First, after full consultation with the sub-national implementers, national governments submitted regional development plans to the Commission. Each of these identified regional problems, set out a strategy indicating priorities, and provided an estimate of required funding. Second, the Commission incorporated member states' views in Community Support Frameworks (CSFs) that prioritized spending, outlined the forms of assistance, and provided a financial plan. Third, detailed operational programmes were agreed by the partners to provide the basis on which they would implement the objectives of the CSFs. These would identify appropriate measures, beneficiaries, and costings. Beyond this, each programme was monitored and assessed to ascertain whether money had been spent appropriately (European Commission 1989).

Partnership: The principle of partnership formed part of the Commission's view of regional policy from the 1970s (McAleavey 1995: 167). However, early Commission attempts to involve sub-national authorities in the making of regional policy received a mixed response. In Britain, for example, the 1984 reform agreement on this had

---

Insight 29.3 Priority Objectives of the 1988 Reform

Following the principle of concentration, structural fund expenditure was focused on five objectives, three with an explicit regional dimension (Objectives 1, 2, and 5a). The bulk of spending was focused on the most disadvantaged regions eligible under Objective 1 (approximately 65 per cent of total structural fund allocations).

- **Objective 1:** promoting the development of 'less developed regions', i.e. those with per capita GDP of less than, or close to, 75 per cent of the Community average under 'special circumstances' (ERDF, ESF, and EAGGF—Guidance Section).
- **Objective 2:** converting the regions seriously affected by industrial decline (ERDF, ESF).
- **Objective 3:** combating long-term unemployment—assisting people aged over 25, unemployed for over a year (ESF).
- **Objective 4:** assisting the occupational integration of young people, i.e. people below the age of 25 (ESF).
- **Objective 5:** (a) accelerating the adjustment of agricultural structures (EAGGF—Guidance Section); (b) promoting the development of rural areas (EAGGF—Guidance Section, ESF, ERDF).

In addition to the 'mainstream' structural funds allocated according to the five objectives, approximately 9 per cent of the ERDF budget was retained for 'Community Initiatives' (CIs). These were programmes devised by the Commission to meet outstanding regional needs. As with the non-quota and Community programmes, such as RESIDER (steel areas) and RENAVAL (shipping and shipbuilding areas), CI programmes would primarily address the needs of particular categories of regions, such as those suffering from the decline of a dominant industry.

---

little impact on a government, 'reluctant to allow local authorities much say in the preparation of the non-quota programmes ...' (Mawson, Martins, and Gibney 1985: 49). The partnership principle of the 1988 reform made the consultation of appropriate local and regional authorities a formal requirement for the first time. In addition to addressing the broader goal of cohesion, it was an attempt to make regional policy more effective by engaging in policy making those actors closest to the problems and priorities of targeted regions.

Additionality: The 1988 reform provided the Commission with an opportunity to strengthen its position for securing additionality. The final wording on additionality agreed by the Council stated:

> In establishing and implementing the Community Support Frameworks the Commission and the member states shall ensure that the increase in the appropriations for the (structural) funds ... has a genuine additional impact in the regions concerned and results in at least an equivalent increase in the total volume of official or similar (Community and national) structural aid in the member states concerned, taking into account the macro-economic circumstances ...

(Article 9 of Regulation 253/88 EEC)

The 1993 Reform

The funding agreements reached in 1988 ran until 1993, when a further review of the policy took place. The general thrust of the 1993 reform was towards continuity rather than radical change, with the principles and structures of the 1988 reform remaining largely intact. Yet the political and economic context in which the 1993 reform took place was very different from that of 1988, and so, consequently, was the scope for advancing Commission preferences.

While enlargement again formed part of the context, negotiations to include Austria, Finland, and Sweden were relatively straightforward. The new members posed no major sectoral problems for the EU. In terms of regional policy, this enlargement involved three concessions: part of Austria gained Objective 1 status; a new Objective 6 status was created for sparsely populated areas; and EC competition rules were adapted to accommodate the subsidy practices of the Nordic states (Wishlade 1996: 57). However, the crucial factor in shaping the context of the 1993 reform was the signing of the Treaty on European Union (TEU) at Maastricht in December 1991.

The TEU upgraded the importance of regional policy in the context of further moves towards closer economic and political union. Yet the period between the Maastricht European Council and the 1993 reform of the structural funds was marked by a change in the political and economic climate. In particular, 'growing unemployment and other economic difficulties within some northern member states heightened concerns about the costs and the cost-effectiveness of Community policies' (Wishlade 1996: 48).

By the time of the Edinburgh European Council in December 1992, 'agreement on the future Community budget (providing funding for the commitments entered into at Maastricht) was the most critical item requiring decision' (Bachtler and Michie 1994: 790). The compromise that was reached included an increase in the structural funds' budget to 27.4 billion European currency units (ecus) by 1999, virtually doubling the amount previously allocated. The context of monetary union was crucial in securing this increase, with the loss of national control of exchange rates increasing pressure for additional compensatory funds.

Following the budgetary envelope agreed at Edinburgh, the Commission's proposals for the 1993 reform were framed within the principles of concentration, partnership, programming, and additionality set out in the 1988 reform. The main proposals related to eligibility criteria, programming periods, and administrative arrangements.

Provisions of the 1993 Reform

The Commission's initial proposals for the 1993 reform were intended to address member states' concerns over the operation of the funds after 1988. Despite this, the member governments 'proceeded to change the substance of the Commission's proposals in several nontrivial ways to respond to concerns about the distribution of funds, efficiency, and member state control of the funds' operation' (Pollack 1995: 381). Thus, while the major principles adopted in the 1988 reform were maintained, governments secured important modifications to some of these principles.

The principle of concentration continued attempts to focus aid on the areas of greatest need. To do this, some amendments were made to the existing priority objectives (Insight 29.4). More controversial was the designation of, eligible areas. A number of governments pressed for, and secured the inclusion of, regions that did not meet the objective Community criteria. More generally, governments pressed their claims for a share of the total fund allocations. In particular, the Irish government claimed to have been promised a 13.5 per cent share of allocations at the Edinburgh European Council of December 1992 in return for concessions on allocations to the new Cohesion Fund. The Irish government threatened to veto the 1993 reform agreement if this promise was not honoured, which ultimately it was (Pollack 1995: 381–2).

In addition to conflicts over redistributive matters, the Council also amended the Commission's proposed administrative arrangements. Four issues were important (Pollack 1995: 382–3), as follows.

(1) Provisions for the monitoring and assessment of structural fund operations were strengthened, largely at the insistence of the British government.

(2) Member states were given a more important role in the designation of Objective 2 and 5b regions. Here, the governments of France, Germany and Britain were most influential.

Insight 29.4 Priority Objectives of the 1993 Reform

Objectives 1 and 2 were not changed from 1988. Objectives 3 and 4 were merged to create a new Objective 3. This aimed at 'facilitating the integration ... of those threatened with exclusion from the labour market' (European Commission 1993b: 11). The new Objective 4 was designed to give effect to new tasks laid down in the Maastricht Treaty to 'facilitate workers' adaptation to industrial changes and to changes in production systems' (European Commission 1993b: 11). Objective 5a maintained its initial goal of accelerating the adjustment of agricultural structures as part of the CAP reform, but a new fund was added to assist the fisheries: the FIFG. Problems arising from the decline in fishing and fish-processing activities would also be addressed through Objectives 1, 2, and 5b. Objective 5b changed slightly from the 'development of rural areas' to the 'development and structural adjustment of rural areas' (European Commission 1993b: 11). Objective 6 status was added to the list.

- **Objective 1:** promoting the development of 'less developed regions' (ERDF, ESF, and EAGGF—Guidance Section).
- **Objective 2:** converting the regions seriously affected by industrial decline (ERDF, ESF).
- **Objective 3:** combating long-term unemployment and promoting entry into the labour market (ESF).
- **Objective 4:** facilitating the adaptation of workers to industrial change (ESF).
- **Objective 5:** (a) accelerating the adjustment of agricultural and fisheries structures (EAGGF—Guidance Section, FIFG); (b) promoting rural development and structural adjustment (EAGGF—Guidance Section, ESF, ERDF).
- **Objective 6:** developing sparsely populated Nordic areas (ERDF, ESF, EAGGF—Guidance Section).

(3) The Council made amendments to the Commission's proposed wording on additionality, adding that it should take account of 'a number of specific economic circumstances, namely privatizations, an unusual level of public structural expenditure undertaken in the previous programming period and business cycles in the national economy'. This allowed member states to reduce spending on domestic structural measures without contravening the additionality requirement.

(4) The Council insisted on the creation of a Management Committee to facilitate greater national government control over CI programmes.

The Cohesion Fund

During the negotiations over the Maastricht Treaty, the Spanish government argued for a new compensatory mechanism additional to the structural funds. Spain was worried that otherwise it would be a net contributor to the Community budget by 1993. While the Spanish government did not get a compensatory financial instrument, it did secure the support of the other poorer member states—Portugal, Greece, and Ireland—in arguing for additional resources to compensate for regional disparities. Ultimately, faced with the threat of veto from the Spanish government, the Council agreed to establish a new Cohesion Fund (Morata and Munoz 1996: 215), with allocations of approximately 16 billion ecus for the period 1993–99 (European Commission 1996a: 147).

The Cohesion Fund provided broadly equal amounts for environmental improvements and transport infrastructure. It was targeted at member states with a GDP of less than 90 per cent of the Community average, not at specific regions. It would support up to 85 per cent of the costs of projects, a higher intervention rate than with any of the structural funds. As with the structural funds, the Cohesion Fund—and the interim instrument established before the Fund came into operation—was subject to indicative allocations: Greece, 16–20 per cent; Spain, 52–58 per cent; Portugal, 16–20 per cent; and Ireland, 7–10 per cent (Scott 1995: 38) (Tables 29.2 and 29.3).

Table 29.2 Cohesion Fund Allocations 1994–99 (estimated)

	%	ECU m (1994 prices)
Spain	55	7950
Greece	18	2602
Portugal	18	2601
Ireland	9	1301
	100	14454

Source: Commission (1996a: 147); **http://ec.europa.eu**, © European Union, 1995–2010

Table 29.3 Scale of Structural Intervention (including Cohesion Fund and Community Initiatives) 1994–99 (Allocations for 1989–93 in Parentheses)

	% Share of EU aid	EU aid as % of national GDP
Austria	1.13 (0)	0.19 (0)
Belgium	1.25 (1.18)	0.18 (0.11)
Denmark	0.50 (0.59)	0.11 (0.08)
Germany	12.97 (11.46)	0.21 (0.13)
Greece	10.58 (12.51)	3.67 (2.65)
Finland	1.19 (0)	0.40 (0)
France	8.92 (9.46)	0.22 (0.14)
Ireland	4.42 (6.68)	2.82 (2.66)
Italy	12.92 (16.0)	0.42 (0.27)
Luxembourg	0.06 (0.10)	0.15 (0.17)
Netherlands	1.56 (1.11)	0.15 (0.07)
Portugal	10.53 (12.9)	3.98 (3.07)
Spain	25.30 (20.57)	1.74 (0.75)
Sweden	0.93 (0)	0.37 (0)
United Kingdom	7.75 (7.27)	0.25 (0.13)

Source: Calculated from figures in Commission (1996*a*: 144); **http://ec.europa.eu**, © European Union, 1995–2010

Key principles guiding the structural funds did not apply to the operation of the Cohesion Fund. As Scott (1995: 39) noted: 'In the first instance, nowhere in the interim instrument or in the European Council guidelines regarding the main elements of the forthcoming Cohesion Fund Regulation is there any reference to the concept of partnership.' Instead, decisions on the projects (*not* programmes) to be funded would be made by the Commission in agreement with the 'member state' concerned. In terms of additionality, the Preamble to the Interim Regulation stipulated that member states should not 'decrease their investment efforts in the field of environmental protection and transport infrastructure', but the more tightly defined principle of additionality included in the structural fund regulations did not apply.

While the relaxed requirements on additionality and partnership for the Cohesion Fund left the implementation of these principles to the discretion of member states, this had to be understood in the context of moves towards monetary union that required severe constraints on public expenditure. In this context, governments were left with considerable discretion over how Cohesion Fund allocations would be spent. In particular, insistence on additionality would have created serious tension with the objective of reducing public expenditure in the 'Cohesion Four' countries.

The 1999 Reform

Negotiations over policy reforms for the post-2000 period took place in the context of negotiations to enlarge the EU to include central and eastern European (CEE) countries, and of a majority of member states joining the single currency.

Enlargement to include up to ten CEE countries, with an average GDP per capita typically at around one-third of the existing EU average, required a change to the existing structural fund criteria. Under the Structural Fund Regulations for 1994–99, the entire territories of the CEE countries would have qualified for Objective 1 and Cohesion Fund assistance. Applying the existing funding criteria to only Poland, Hungary, the Czech Republic, and Slovakia would have increased the total cost of the funds from 27.4 billion ecus to approximately 48 billion ecus.

Somehow, the Commission's proposals for reform had to strike a balance between the demands of existing member states and the need to facilitate enlargement. The context did not favour Commission advances on the principles of regional policy. In addition to the challenges of proposed enlargement, EMU was framing a mood of uncertainty within member states, creating a political atmosphere against further integration.

Commission Proposals

In March 1998, the Commission presented its proposed regulations for governing the structural funds for the period 2000–06. The proposed reform was centred on three priorities: greater concentration; decentralized and simplified implementation; and a strengthening of efficiency and control set against a background of budgetary discipline (European Commission 1998a: 2).

The Commission proposed to maintain the four governing principles of the structural funds—partnership, concentration, additionality, and programming. The partnership principle would be reformed so that the responsibilities of each of the partners would be defined more clearly to improve implementation, and a fifth principle—'efficiency'—was proposed to reassure people that public money allocated to the structural funds was well used. These proposals were relatively modest and in some areas hinted at a further renationalization of the funds.

The Commission signalled its intention to take a lesser role in the day-to-day management of the funds. This meant withdrawing its officials from involvement in partnership activities below the level of programme monitoring committees. Commission officials emphasized, though, that that programme monitoring committees would take on a more strategic role than previously. In addition, the Commission proposed retaining 10 per cent of the structural funds as a 'performance reserve' for it to allocate during the programme period to those regions spending funds most effectively.

The proposed enlargement of the EU focused the Commission's efforts on concentrating the funds on a smaller proportion of the existing EU's population. While existing member states accepted the need for concentration in principle, agreeing which areas would be affected by greater concentration in 1999 was difficult in practice. Moreover, the proposed Regulations suggested that, in addition to determining

Objective 1 areas, the Council would have more control over the designation of Objective 2 areas.

The convergence criteria for monetary union established at Maastricht had provided a loose interpretation of the additionality requirement after the 1993 reform. While the Commission's proposal for 'negotiated additionality', if accepted, appeared to be an improvement on this, its success would depend in large part on what the Commission would be able to negotiate with member states, most of which were about to experience the first challenges of monetary union to their national budgetary policies. The Commission proposed taking a specific indicator of additionality for each objective to facilitate more effective monitoring.

Programming remained a relatively uncontroversial principle of structural funding. One proposal for improvement was to reduce the three-stage programming process to two stages, except for very large allocations.

Partnership remained at the core of Commission thinking and its proposals for 1999 strengthened the principle by increasing the emphasis on involving the social partners, environmental agencies, and other non-governmental organizations that had a role in social and economic development.

The need to reduce the number of CIs to simplify procedures and reduce duplicative structures was accepted by the Commission. While CIs were to be reduced to three in number, this would mean more resources for each remaining CI.

Provisions of the 1999 Reform

The General Affairs Council formally adopted the new Structural Fund and Cohesion Fund Regulations in June 1999, following political agreement at the Berlin European Council in March and approval by the European Parliament in May. Financial allocations to the structural funds were €195 billion over the period 2000–06, with a further €18 billion provided for the Cohesion Fund. In addition, €7.28 billion was set aside for pre-accession structural assistance to applicant states. Total funding under these measures remained at 0.46 per cent of the EU's gross national product (GNP) over the period. Allocations by member state and by Objective are outlined in Table 29.4.

The guiding principles proposed by the Commission were accepted. On *concentration*, this meant that the number of structural fund Objectives was reduced from six to three (Insight 29.5). Also, as proposed by the Commission, the number of CIs was substantially reduced from the existing thirteen. The Commission had proposed retaining three Initiatives:

- Interreg (cross-border, transnational, and inter-regional co-operation);
- Leader (rural development);
- Equal (tackling discrimination in the labour market).

However, at the insistence of the European Parliament, a fourth programme was retained:

- Urban (to regenerate inner cities).

Table 29.4 Structural Funds: Breakdown by Member State for the Period 2000–06 (in €m at 1999 Prices)

Member state	Obj. 1	Transitional support for former Obj. 1 areas	Obj. 2 for former Obj. 2 and 5(b) areas	Transitional instrument (outside Obj. 1 areas)	Obj. 3	Fisheries	Total
Austria	261	0	587	102	528	4	1473
Belgium	0	625	368	65	737	34	1829
Denmark	0	0	156	27	365	197	745
Finland	913	0	459	30	403	31	1836
France	3254	551	5437	613	4540	225	14620
Germany	19229	729	2984	526	4581	107	28156
Greece	20961	0	0	0	0	0	0
Ireland[a]	1315	1773	0	0	0	0	3088
Italy	21935	187	2145	377	3744	96	28484
Luxembourg	0	0	34	6	38	0	78
Netherlands	0	123	676	119	1686	31	2635
Portugal	16124	2905	0	0	0	0	19029
Spain	37744	352	2553	98	2140	200	43087
Sweden[b]	722	0	354	52	720	60	1908
UK[a]	5805	1166	3989	706	4568	121	15635
EU15[c]	127543	8411	19733	2721	24050	1106	183564

Note: [a]Including Peace (2000–04), [b]Including the special programme for Swedish coastal zones. [c]EU totals for all fifteen member states.

Source: Inforegio Newsletter No. 65, June 1999, pp. 3–4; **http://ec.europa.eu**, © European Union, 1995–2010

> ### Insight 29.5 Priority Objectives of the 1999 Reform
>
> - **Objective 1:** would continue to assist the least-developed regions, defined as those with a GDP per capita at 75 per cent or less of the EU average over the previous three years. Henceforth, this criterion would be strictly enforced. In addition, the new Objective 1 included the regions that previously qualified under Objective 6, which were the sparsely populated regions of Finland and Sweden.
>
> - **Objective 2:** the changes to designation here were more significant. The existing Objectives 2 and 5b were merged into the new Objective 2, which thus covered 'areas undergoing socioeconomic change in the industrial and service sectors, declining rural areas, urban areas in difficulty and depressed areas dependent on fisheries' (Wishlade 1999: 39). Also significant was that Objective 2 would be concentrated on no more than 18 per cent of the EU population, with the safety-net mechanism ensuring that no member state's Objective 2 population would be less than two-thirds of its coverage under the 1994–99 programme period.
>
> - **Objective 3:** would apply across the EU, except for Objective 1 regions, and would assist in modernizing systems of education, training, and employment.

The *programming* process was retained, with the Commission adopting a more strategic role and delegating greater responsibility to domestic actors for the day-to-day implementation and monitoring of programmes. The reworded *partnership* principle required the involvement of organizations that reflected the 'need to promote equality between men and women and sustainable development through the integration of environmental protection and improvement requirements' (OJ L161, 26/6/99: 12). The principle of *additionality* was maintained, although its verification would depend on baseline figures of domestic spending that member states would play a key role in determining. Finally, in line with the principle of *efficiency*, a performance reserve was agreed by member states. However, this was limited to 4 per cent of each member state's share of funding, rather than the 10 per cent that the Commission had proposed.

The 1999 reform signalled a general acceptance that, after the 2004 enlargement, the bulk of funding would have to be redirected towards the new CEE member states. To help them to prepare for accession, a number of pre-accession instruments were put in place. The Instrument for Structural Policies Pre-Accession (ISPA) provided funding for transport and environmental projects, the Special Accession Programme for Agricultural and Rural Development (Sapard) provided assistance for agriculture and rural development, while the Poland and Hungary: Aid for Economic Restructuring programme (Phare) aimed to strengthen economic and social cohesion and administrative and institutional capacity. These three programmes would be worth €3 billion a year in the pre-accession period, and Phare alone would continue for the period 2004–06 at the rate of €1.6 billion. In this period, Bulgaria and Romania (which would join in 2007) would also be eligible for this funding. In addition, the new member states would be eligible to claim up to €21.8 billion of structural funding in the period 2004–06 (European Commission 2004*b*: xxii–xxiii).

The 2006 Reform

The context of this reform was shaped by the effects of the 2004 enlargement and by the Lisbon Agenda (Chapter 15, pp. 185–6, and Chapter 17, pp. 206–7), which accorded cohesion policy an important role.

The 2004 enlargement led to a doubling of socio-economic disparities in the EU and a decrease in the average GDP of the EU by 12.5 per cent, emphasizing the need for significant financial transfers between member states. The Lisbon Agenda prioritized growth, jobs, and competitiveness, which threatened to compromise the previous emphasis on decentralization and partnership (Andreou 2007). However, it was clear that the multi-level governance dimension of cohesion policy was linked positively to this agenda by the Commissioner for Regional Policy:

> Cohesion policy's very specific system of governance, involving all relevant partners in the region, is as important as the financial contribution. The emphasis we have on partnership in fact allows us to do two things: First of all, it allows us to increase understanding of what the Lisbon ... agenda is all about. Secondly it ensures that all the stakeholders involved realise that there is an enormous synergy between their interest in regional development and the EU interest in competitiveness.
>
> (Hübner 2004: 1)

The Commission set out its proposals for the structural funds for the period 2006–13 in its Third Report on Economic and Social Cohesion (European Commission 2004*b*). It argued that the three existing Objectives (1, 2, and 3) should be replaced by three new priorities:

- convergence—supporting growth and job creation in the least-developed member states and regions (Cohesion Fund; ERDF; ESF);
- regional competitiveness and employment—anticipating and promoting change (ERDF; ESF);
- European territorial co-operation—promoting the harmonious and balanced development of the Union territory (ERDF).

The *convergence* priority would cover those regions with a per capita GDP of less than 75 per cent of the Community average (previously covered by Objective 1) and would account for approximately 78 per cent of the structural fund budget. The *competitiveness* priority, effectively replacing Objectives 2 and 3, would have two strands: regional programmes to promote the attractiveness and competitiveness of industrial, urban, and rural areas; and national programmes to promote full employment, quality, and productivity at work, and social inclusion. The *co-operation* priority would build on experience of Interreg, to promote co-operation on issues at cross-border, transnational, and inter-regional level. Interreg, along with the other CI programmes (Equal, Leader, and Urban) would no longer exist separately, but their strengths would be incorporated into the new mainstream programmes. For example, in relation to Urban, the Commission proposed that there be a sub-delegation of responsibilities to city authorities (European Commission 2004*b*: xxxii). Finally, the Commission proposed that the EAGGF and Financial Instrument for Fisheries Guidance (FIFG) be removed from the structural fund programmes and be incorporated into mainstream policies for agriculture and fisheries.

In terms of the long-standing principles, it suggested that while the *programming* approach had increased planning capabilities, there had also been increasing concerns over the complexity of the programming process. *Partnership* was seen as a success that was increasingly inclusive and leading to more effective policies. *Concentration* was seen to have increased, but there was still concern that resources were being spread too thinly. Finally, the Commission suggested that *additionality* had been 'largely respected' in Objective 1 regions, but that verifying it for Objective 2 and 3 programmes had proved more difficult (European Commission 2004*b*: xxii). In response, the Commission proposed a simplification of the programming approach, offered member states greater responsibility for ensuring additionality, sought to strengthen the partnership requirement, argued for increased concentration of resources on the less prosperous member states, and placed a greater emphasis on performance.

As with previous reforms, the Commission proposals signalled the beginning of a bargaining process. A number of states, led by Britain, argued that there should be an end to the financial transfers to the richest member states. This would reduce the gross contributions to the EU budget of the richer states, which would then use the savings for their own regional policy purposes: a partial renationalization of EU regional policy. This proposal was eventually resisted by the Commission with support from an alliance of the southern member states. However, the Commission's concession was to repackage Objectives 2 and 3 as the 'regional competitiveness and employment' objective, which was linked to the goals of the Lisbon Agenda and which gave member states more discretion on how it could be used. This concession, while giving member states responsibility over area designation, also allowed the Commission to retain its influence over cohesion policy in the new member states (Bachtler and Mendez 2007: 545).

Provisions of the Reform

The 2006 reform led to a simplification in the architecture of cohesion policy for the 2007–13 period (Insight 29.6).

The three new objectives—convergence, regional competitiveness and employment, and European territorial co-operation—incorporated the previous Objectives 1 and 2, and also the CIs Interreg, Equal, and Urban. The Cohesion Fund became part of cohesion policy proper through being included in the convergence objective. The EAGGF and the Leader programme were replaced by the European Agricultural Fund for Rural Development (EAFRD) and the FIFG became the European Fisheries Fund (EFF). Both the EAFRD and EFF were given their own legal basis and were no longer part of cohesion policy (European Commission 2007*a*: 11). The overall cohesion policy budget for the 2007–13 period was €347 billion, 81.5 per cent of which would be spent in the 'convergence' regions.

The key principles again remained intact, with some amendments. A new corrective mechanism was introduced for instances in which the additionality principle might not be respected, and the principle of partnership was widened to say that 'any appropriate organization' can participate in negotiations relating to the use of the structural funds. The principle of *proportionality* was introduced to modulate the obligations

437

Insight 29.6 Objectives and General Rules of the 2006 Reform

The Cohesion Policy Architecture

2000–06		→	2007–13	
Objectives **Community Initiatives** **Cohesion Fund**	**Financial Instruments**	→	**Objectives**	**Financial Instruments**
Objective 1 Regions lagging behind in development terms	ERDF ESF EAGGF— Guarantee EAGGF— Guidance FIFG	→	Convergence	ERDF ESF Cohesion Fund
Cohesion Fund	Cohesion Fund			
Objective 2 Economic and social conversion zones	ERDF ESF	→	Regional competitiveness and employment	ERDF ESF
Objective 3 Training systems and employment policies	ESF			
Interreg III	ERDF	→	European territorial co-operation	ERDF
URBAN II (*)	ERDF			
EQUAL (*)	ESF			
Leader +	EAGGF— Guidance			
Rural development and restructuring of the fishing sector beyond Objective 1	EAGGF— Guarantee FIFG			
Four Objectives **Four Community initiatives** **Cohesion Fund**	**Six instruments**		**Three objectives**	**Three instruments**

(*) In 2007–13, Urban II and Equal will be part of the convergence objective, as well as of the regional competitiveness and employment objective.

Source: European Commission 2007a: 10; **http://ec.europa.eu**, © European Union, 1995–2010

Table 29.5 Indicative Allocation by Member State, 2007–13 (2007 Prices, in €m)

	Convergence			Regional competitiveness and employment		European territorial co-operation	Total
	Cohesion Fund	Convergence	Phasing-out	Phasing-in	Regional competitiveness and employment		
Austria			177		1027	257	1461
Belgium			638		1425	194	2258
Bulgaria	2283	4391				179	6853
Cyprus	213			399		28	640
Czech Republic	8819	17064			419	389	26692
Denmark					510	103	613
Estonia	1152	2252				52	3456
Finland				545	1051	120	1716
France		3191			10257	872	14319
Germany		11864	4215		9409	851	26340
Greece	3697	9420	6458	635		210	20420
Hungary	8642	14248		2031		386	25307
Ireland				458	293	151	901
Italy		21211	430	972	5353	846	28812
Latvia	1540	2991				90	4620
Lithuania	2305	4470				109	6885

continued

439

Table 29.5 (*Continued*)

	Convergence			Regional competitiveness and employment			
	Cohesion Fund	Convergence	Phasing-out	Phasing-in	Regional competitiveness and employment	European territorial co-operation	Total
Luxembourg					50	15	65
Malta	284	556				15	855
Netherlands					1660	247	1907
Poland	22176	44377				731	67284
Portugal	3060	17133	280	448	490	99	21511
Romania	6552	12661				455	19668
Slovakia	3899	7013			449	227	11588
Slovenia	1412	2689				104	4205
Spain	3543	21054	1583	4955	3522	559	35217
Sweden					1626	265	1891
United Kingdom		2738	174	965	6014	722	10613
Inter-regional/ Network co-operation						455	455
Technical Assistance							868
Total	**69578**	**199322**	**13955**	**11409**	**43556**	**8723**	**347410**

Source: European Commission (2007a: 25); **http://ec.europa.eu**, © European Union, 1995–2010

attributed to member states contingent on the total amount of expenditure of an operational programme (European Commission 2007a: 27).

A new strategic approach was adopted that introduced the national strategic reference framework (NSRF) as a new programming instrument that would provide a single overall vision of strategy at the level of each member state. This would be prepared by national governments in consultation with domestic partners and in dialogue with the Commission. The CSFs relating to Objective 1 and the single programming documents related to Objectives 2 and 3 would be cancelled so that operational programmes would be the only programming and management tool. These would be more strategic than in the past, with priorities rather than actions being detailed, thus giving member states greater autonomy over the details of implementation (European Commission 2007a: 33). This rationalization of the programming process was a response to the demands of member states, particularly those receiving relatively small amounts of structural funding, the complaints of which about bureaucracy had led to tension with the Commission in the 2000–06 period (Bachtler and Mendez 2007: 554).

Outside of the framework of cohesion policy, a new Instrument for Pre-Accession (IPA) was introduced in January 2007. IPA brought together all of the existing pre-accession instruments (including ISPA, Phare, and Sapard) into a single framework. This new instrument covered the candidate states (Croatia, the Former Yugoslav Republic of Macedonia, and Turkey) and the potential candidate states (Albania, Bosnia and Herzegovina, Montenegro, and Serbia—including Kosovo). IPA has five components; (1) transition assistance and institution building; (2) cross-border co-operation; (3) regional development; (4) human resources development; and (5) rural development (European Commission 2007c: 1). The latter three components are precursors to structural funding and involve preparing candidate countries for developing the necessary institutional capacity to be able to manage them effectively post-accession. This was seen as a weakness of the previous pre-accession instruments. Under IPA, the relevant components ((3) and (4)) would thus be administered along the same lines as the structural funds, with programming activities involving the relevant stakeholders.

Explaining Cohesion Policy

Two of the theoretical debates that have been identified in this book as central to the development of the study of the EU have been particularly relevant in this policy sector: first, the intergovernmental–supranational debate about the nature of the EU (Chapter 1); and second, the debate about whether European integration has produced a system of multi-level governance (Chapter 2).

The Intergovernmentalist–Supranationalist Debate

There is academic consensus that the major decisions on the creation of regional policy were taken by the heads of government, in particular at the summits in Paris in 1972 and 1974 and in Copenhagen in 1973. The Commission's influence over initial allocations and policy guidelines was at first limited, although the Commission was important in keeping the issue of regional policy alive in the difficult circumstances of the 1960s and early 1970s. Yet while the eventual establishment of the ERDF in 1975 owed a great deal to the Commission's persistence, intergovernmental politics ensured that it fell some way short of the redistributive policy instrument that the Commission sought.

While some member states sought to limit the increase in the fund allocations in the 1988 reform, the doubling of allocations owed much to the commitment of larger member states to the single-market programme. Although the funds did continue to benefit regions in the more prosperous member states, the main impact of the doubling of the funds was to transfer resources from Belgium, Denmark, Germany, France, and the Netherlands to Greece, Spain, Ireland, Italy, and Portugal, with the impact on Britain largely neutral (Marks 1992: 194).

Pollack (1995) argued that agreement to major reform in 1988 could be explained by changes in the preferences of the various member states—in particular net contributors such as Britain, France, and Germany—and as a result of the accession of Greece, Spain, and Portugal. The preferences of the net contributors changed in three ways. First, with the Iberian enlargement, the proportion of structural funds received by the 'big three' member states decreased significantly. This meant that, for these governments, 'the idea of greater Commission oversight seemed less like an intrusion into the internal affairs of one's own state, where EC spending was minimal, and more like a necessary oversight of the poor member states where the bulk of EC money was being spent' (Pollack 1995: 372). Second, the Iberian enlargement made France, like Britain and Germany, a net contributor to the EC budget, thus giving the 'big three' governments a common interest in the efficient use of the structural funds. Third, the spiralling costs of both the Common Agricultural Policy (CAP) and the structural funds made the level and efficiency of EC spending a 'political issue' of increasing concern to the governments of France, Germany, and Britain in the 1980s (Pollack 1995: 372).

In terms of the budgetary envelope agreed in 1988, an intergovernmentalist interpretation found favour amongst most commentators. The more prosperous member states strongly supported the completion of the single market and wanted this market extending to include Spain and Portugal. In this context, the doubling of the structural funds was accepted by the likely paymaster governments as a 'side-payment to Ireland and the Southern nations' in exchange for their political support on other issues (Moravcsik 1991: 62). Although not contesting this fundamental argument, Marks (1992: 198) conceptualized the side-payment argument as an illustration of *forced spillover*, 'in which the prospect of a breakthrough in one arena created intense pressure for innovation in others', thereby linking it to neofunctionalist analysis, and giving it a more supranationalist spin.

Consensus between scholars over other aspects of the 1988 reform is harder to find. For example, Hooghe (1996*b*: 100) argued that the Commission emerged 'as the pivotal actor in designing the regulations' through its 'monopoly of initiative'. An example was the inclusion of the partnership principle in the regulations, which was the major innovation of the 1988 reform. In contrast, Pollack (1995) suggested that this shift was a response to pressure from national governments to secure 'value for money' in the funds' administration.

While the context of the 1988 reform gave the Commission considerable scope for advancing its policy preferences, the 1993 reform represented a reassertion of control by the member governments in key areas. A good example was additionality. The tenacity with which the Commission had sought the implementation of additionality after 1988 was met by governments effectively diluting the requirement in 1993. Indeed, given the convergence criteria for monetary union agreed at Maastricht, for the Commission to pursue genuine additionality at this time would have been difficult: while additionality required member states to demonstrate additional public expenditure, the Maastricht convergence criteria limited domestic public spending.

Other changes in 1993 also reflected the reassertion of government preferences. While the partnership principle was confirmed, governments remained in control of the designation of 'appropriate partners'. The creation of a Management Committee to oversee CIs curtailed Commission discretion. In a high-profile conflict over the implementation of additionality after 1988, the Commission had used its control over the content, coverage, and timing of CIs to undermine the British government's arguments in defence of its approach to implementation (Bache 1999). The 1993 changes meant that this would be more difficult for the Commission to do in future.

In summary, the 1993 reform provided a measure of how the relative influence of actors fluctuated over a short period of time. The context had changed dramatically in the five years after the 1988 reform, leading to a shift in the balance of political resources away from the Commission towards the Council, which was reflected in the 1993 outcome.

As previously, the budgetary envelope for the 1999 reform of the structural funds was decided at Council level. In addition to limiting total allocations, member states secured safety-net mechanisms and transitional arrangements to protect their assisted regions from a sudden and dramatic reduction of funding. Moreover, the reduction of the proposed performance reserve from 10 per cent to 4 per cent was accompanied by provisions for member states' involvement with the Commission in determining the allocation of this reserve to regions that were performing well.

While the partnership principle was maintained, and its requirements made more precise, the selection of partners remained with governments. The additionality principle was also retained, but the new regulations did not suggest that member states' compliance would be any easier for the Commission to ensure. The reduction in the number of CIs, and of financial allocations to them, limited the Commission's scope for autonomy and innovation somewhat, although in its proposals the Commission had acknowledged the need for such a reduction. Institutional politics aside, CIs had been subject to criticism from a broad range of actors who deemed some programmes to be unnecessarily bureaucratic.

If the 1999 reform was not simply a renationalization of the structural funds, a number of changes from the Commission's initial proposals reflected the preferences of governments. Perhaps more significantly, in the context of proposed enlargement, the Commission's initial proposals were themselves relatively modest. Yet the Commission retained a key role in the process: for example, over issues of eligibility, programming, allocating the performance reserve, and in the design and implementation of CIs. Moreover, the key principles guiding the operation of the funds essentially remained those developed by the Commission.

443

In relation to the 2006 reform, Andreou (2007: 26) suggested that 'the compromise achieved by member states ... bears much more resemblance to the financially restrictive approach of the net payers, than to the original Commission proposal supported by the less prosperous member states'. Bruszt (2008: 616) argued that:

> the new EU regulations for the 2007–13 planning period did not alter the 'renationalizing' tendencies of the SF [Structural Funds] policies significantly. For the time being, the Commission does not seem to be interested in re-kindling its pro-regional activism of the 1990s

Instead, the priority was on ensuring the effective absorption of the funds, which often meant the development of central capacity.

However, as Bachtler and Mendez (2007: 551) suggested, it is important not to see cohesion policy negotiations purely in terms of the Commission versus the member states: while negotiations on some issues have been adversarial, on others there has been more collaboration and consensus. Related to this point, power relations between the Commission and member states should not necessarily be conceived in zero-sum terms, in which for one party to gain the other must lose. Instead, there is evidence of positive-sum outcomes, in which both parties achieve more of their goals. Moreover, Bachtler and Mendez (2007) suggested that claims over the renationalization of cohesion policy, while valid in some respects, were less convincing when applied to the development of the principles of concentration and programming, where the Commission's influence has been greater than acknowledged in much of the literature.

Multi-Level Governance

Much of the conceptual debate around cohesion policy has focused on the domestic effects of implementation and in particular the implementation of the partnership principle, which has been at the forefront of research on multi-level governance (MLG) (Chapter 2).

Hooghe (1996a) co-ordinated an early cross-national study on the effects of the 1988 reform principles on 'territorial restructuring' within eight member states. The study found that the implementation of the partnership principle varied considerably across member states. Actors at different levels—national, sub-national, and supranational—controlled different resources in different member states, influencing their ability to shape policy implementation within the framework set by EU-level agreements. In centralized member states, where central government actively sought to play a gatekeeper role over the political impact of the new arrangements, such as in Britain, it met with considerable success. Here, sub-national actors were mobilized, but not necessarily empowered. In more decentralized member states, sub-national authorities—normally regional governments—were better placed to take advantage of the opportunities provided by the partnership requirement. Later research (Kelleher et al. 1999) confirmed this pattern of differentiated MLG emerging through EU cohesion policy.

As funding has shifted towards CEE states, so has much of the academic research. Moreover, while research continues to discuss features of MLG, it often does so within the framework of Europeanization (Chapter 4). The role of the Commission in advancing MLG has been brought under particular scrutiny in this literature.

While the Commission initially sought to advance regionalization in CEE states, inspired by ideals of MLG, as accession grew closer, its position shifted to ensuring that the funds were absorbed on time, even if this meant that they were managed centrally through national ministries (Leonardi 2005: 164; Marcou 2002: 25). A study of the Czech Republic, Estonia, Hungary, Poland, and Slovenia identified national government 'gatekeepers' as generally 'firmly in control' of sub-national actors, who were able to participate in, but not significantly influence, the policy process (Bailey and De Propris 2002). Research on Estonia, Hungary, Poland, and Slovenia emphasized the importance of institutional traditions in each state in shaping the degree of regionalization emerging (Hughes, Sasse, and Gordon 2004; 2005), echoing the findings of earlier research on the EU15 (Hooghe 1996).

Two studies provided a mixed picture of the impact of cohesion policy on regionalization in the CEE states. Bachtler and McMaster (2008: 420–1) identified 'several points to support the contention that the role of regions has increased in terms of their legitimacy, institutional capacity and stability', but also suggested that 'the limitations and barriers to regional participation in the funds currently outweighs the opportunities'. Their bottom line was to challenge the idea that structural funds necessarily lead to stronger regions. Bruszt (2008) explained how the Commission's turn to (re)entralization for administering funds in the pre-accession period was resisted in some states, and thus features of MLG emerged. Here, the governance changes were explained in historical institutionalist terms as 'layering': 'the emergence of change on the margins, implying local rule transformation within a basically unchanged institution that does not challenge the dominant characteristics of the mode of governance' (Bruszt 2008: 620).

The study by Bache (2008) of the EU25 considered the impact of cohesion policy on Type I and Type II MLG (Chapter 2, p. 35). It identified a trend towards MLG across Europe, although this remained uneven. Moreover, the study indicated that while this trend was generally not due to states' engagement with the EU, it was not possible to understand the nature and pace of the changes taking place without reference to the EU and its cohesion policy. However, the effects of EU cohesion policy seemed more pronounced on Type II MLG than on Type I, with ad hoc functionally specific governance arrangements emerging at various territorial levels as a direct response. For the most part, this Europeanization effect was driven by rational responses to EU financial incentives, although there was also evidence that deeper learning could take place in the longer term, characterized by the voluntary adoption of EU practices in the domestic sphere.

More recently, research has begun on the impact of cohesion policy and the related pre-accession instruments—and particularly the relevant components of IPA—on governance in the candidate states of south-east Europe. Here, the prospects for EU-induced cohesion policy are enhanced by the increased alignment of pre-accession funding with structural fund requirements, but are reduced by the problems of limited governance capacities at both national and sub-national levels, leading to the Commission again emphasizing centralized implementation of funding, at least in the first phase (Bache 2010).

CONCLUSION

Judgements of the economic impact of EU cohesion policy often cast doubt on its effectiveness in addressing disparities between territories and social groups. However, it is arguably the political impact of the funds that has been of most significance. While the degree to which cohesion policy has reshaped governance and politics in recipient states should not be overstated, there has been increasing participation and dialogue between actors located in different sectors and at different territorial levels. While this effect may have peaked in the EU15, it continues to be important in the CEE states, and promises to be influential in the current wave of applicants.

KEY POINTS

History

- EC regional policy first emerged in the 1970s.
- Member states' governments dominated the policy process and there was no major movement towards the creation of a supranational policy.
- Enlargement and the single market programme provided the context for a major reform of the structural funds in 1988, which doubled financial allocations, strengthened the additionality principle, and introduced the principle of partnership.
- The 1993 reform maintained the guiding principles established in 1988, although aspects of the reform reflected a reassertion of member states' control.
- The Cohesion Fund was established as an additional compensatory instrument for the poorer member states.
- Proposed enlargement and completion of monetary union provided the context for the 1999 reform, which retained the principles of additionality, concentration, partnership, and programming while adding the principle of efficiency.
- A number of pre-accession instruments were introduced to prepare candidate states for membership.
- The context of the 2006 reform was the 2004 enlargement and the Lisbon agenda.
- The reform led to a simplification of the architecture of cohesion policy.
- IPA replaced previous pre-accession instruments, and components of this instrument mirrored administrative arrangements for the structural funds to prepare candidates states more effectively for accession.

Explaining Cohesion Policy

- The intergovernmental–supranational debate has been central to theorizing EU-level decision making over cohesion policy.
- The respective influence of key actors has fluctuated over time and across issues, and there is debate over the extent to which there has been a reassertion of government control over EU-level decision making since the 1988 reform.
- The concept of MLG is closely related to cohesion policy, particularly in understanding developments at the implementation stage, although there is significant variation in the degree of MLG evident across the EU.

FURTHER READING

Two books provide an overview of key developments in cohesion policy, while also contributing original case studies and analysis. **I. Bache**, *Europeanization and Multilevel Governance: Cohesion Policy in Britain and the European Union and Britain* (Lanham, MD: Rowman and Littlefield, 2008) brings together two of the main conceptual concerns in the field, with a detailed case study of the domestic effects of cohesion policy in Britain, and summary case studies of seven other states of the EU 15 and three from central and eastern Europe. **R. Leonardi**, *Cohesion Policy in the European Union* (Basingstoke: Palgrave Macmillan, 2005) takes an interdisciplinary approach to highlight the socio-economic as well as political impact of cohesion policy, drawing on a case study of Italy and of the ten new member states of the 2004 enlargement.

A number of articles and chapters have contributed to the conceptual debates around inter-governmentalism, supranationalism, and MLG. **G. Marks** developed his arguments about MLG from his analysis of the 1988 reform of the structural funds and subsequent disputes over implementation in 'Structural Policy and Multi-Level Governance in the EC', in **A. Cafruny and G. Rosenthal (eds)**, *The State of the European Community, vol. 2: The Maastricht Debates and Beyond* (Boulder, CO, and Harlow: Lynne Rienner and Longman, 1993), 391–410. **M. Pollack**, 'Regional Actors in an Intergovernmental Play: The Making and Implementation of EC Structural Policy', in **C. Rhodes and S. Mazey (eds)**, *The State of the European Union, vol. 3: Building a European Polity?* (Boulder, CO, and Harlow: Lynne Rienner and Longman, 1995), 361–90, reflects on both the 1988 and 1993 reforms and provides an essentially intergovernmental response to the arguments of Marks. **I. Bache**, 'The Extended Gatekeeper: Central Government and the Implementation of EC Regional Policy in the UK', *Journal of European Public Policy,* 6 (1999): 28–45, emphasizes the important contribution of policy implementation in shaping outcomes and informing conceptual debate.

More recently, **J. Bachtler and C. Mendez** critique the renationalization thesis applied to cohesion policy in 'Who Governs EU Cohesion Policy? Deconstructing the Reforms of the Structural Funds', *Journal of Common Market Studies,* 24 (2007): 535–64; **J. Bachtler and I. McMaster** look at regionalization effects in central and eastern Europe in 'EU Cohesion Policy and the Role of the Regions: Investigating the Influence of Structural Funds in the New Member States', *Environment and Planning C,* 28 (2008): 398–427, as does **L. Bruszt**, 'Multi-Level Governance: The Eastern Versions—Emerging Patterns of Developmental Governance in the New Member States', *Regional and Federal Studies,* 18 (2008): 607–27. Finally, the special issue of the *Journal of Southeast European and Black Sea Studies* (2010) 10(1) is dedicated to the subject of 'Cohesion Policy and Multi-Level Governance in South East Europe', drawing on case studies of established, new, and prospective member states.

 online resource centre

Visit the Online Resource Centre that accompanies this book for links to more information on European regional and structural policies, including the website of the Commission's Directorate-General for Regional Policy: www.oxfordtextbooks.co.uk/orc/bache3e/

Chapter 30
Environmental Policy

Vasilis Leontitsis

Chapter Overview

When the European Communities were established, environmental issues were low on the political agenda. However, they increasingly became more prominent at both national and European levels, and there is now a comprehensive environmental policy at the European Union (EU) level. Nowadays, environmental considerations are supposed to inform all aspects of EU policies, and notions such as sustainability have become increasingly important within EU discourse. The EU has experimented with new environmental policy instruments and has attempted to become a major player at the global level. However, implementation deficits have raised concerns over its ability to solve environmental problems successfully, whereas at the international level, its leading role has been compromised by its inability to reform its policies towards greater sustainability.

Completely unanticipated in 1957, environmental policy had moved from silence to salience within thirty years.

(Weale 1999*b*: 40)

The environment is a relatively new policy area of the European Union. It was not officially created until 1973, and it did not acquire a sound legal basis in the Treaties until the Single European Act (SEA) in 1987. However, it has seen dramatic expansion and assumed increasing importance within the EU. This chapter gives a brief historical account of the policy, examines recent developments, and discusses some of the major issues of current concern. Finally, the policy's evolution is discussed drawing on the theories presented in Part One of this book.

History

In the founding Treaties, there was no reference to the environment. The European Communities were established on economic grounds, and economic logic dictated the direction of European integration. Even at the national level, there were no coherent environmental policies in most member states during that period, so there was no pressure to co-ordinate policy measures at the Community level, other than to avoid trade distortions.

The situation changed drastically in the 1960s, when a series of environmental disasters and a better understanding of the consequences of unchecked economic development led to increased public consciousness of environmental issues. Environmental values found their way into the radicalized politics of the late 1960s and the green movement gained in salience in western European countries, especially in Germany. The 1972 United Nations Conference on the Human Environment, held in Stockholm, further increased awareness of environmental issues. As a response, several European countries tightened environmental regulation within their own territories. However, although environmental concerns had started to influence the domestic politics of some member states, there was not much activity in the European Economic Community (EEC). Until 1973, environmental measures taken at the Community level were few and far between (Table 30.1).

Prior to the Single European Act

Increased environmental measures at the national level posed a serious threat to the **common market**. There was always a danger that some of the member states would use environmental regulation to discriminate against products imported from other member states. Additionally, countries with high environmental standards were afraid of losing competitiveness to others with laxer environmental regulations. Finally, politicians acknowledged that pollution knows no boundaries and some environmental issues would be better tackled at the supranational level. Hence, the conditions were ripe for co-ordinated action to be taken at Community level.

At the Paris European Summit in 1972, the leaders of the member states stressed the importance of protecting the environment and urged the Community institutions to draw up an environmental action programme. The Commission took up the challenge and drafted the first European Environmental Action Programme (EAP) in 1973. Additionally, a small unit was created in the Commission responsible for the environment, and a dedicated committee was established in the European Parliament (EP). If

---

Table 30.1 Environmental Measures Taken Prior to 1973

- Directive 59/221 on ionizing radiation (amended with Directives 62/1633 and 66/45)
- Directive 67/548 on the classification, packaging, and labelling of dangerous substances (amended with Directive 71/144)
- Directive 70/157 on noise from vehicle exhaust systems
- Directive 70/220 on carbon monoxide and hydrocarbon emissions from road vehicles
- Directive 72/306 on emissions from diesel-engined vehicles

Source: Based on McCormick (2001: 45) (**http://www.palgrave.com/politics/eu/legislation_1958.asp**)

the years prior to that date represent the pre-history of the EU environmental policy, 1973 marks the beginning of its history proper.

The First EAP covered the years from 1973 until 1976. It was followed by the Second (1977–81) and Third (1982–86) EAPs. These environmental programmes did not contain any binding legal provisions. However, they did put in place a number of general principles that continue to guide environmental action in the EU. Among others, they stated that prevention is better than cure (the 'preventative principle'), that polluters should pay for the environmental damage that they cause (the 'polluter pays principle'), and that environmental damage should be combated at its source (McCormick 2001: 48–9; Lenschow 2005: 306–7).

However, the Commission still lacked explicit Treaty provisions on which to base its environmental initiatives. Throughout this period, it had to rely either on Article 100 (now Article 115 TFEU) on the approximation of laws affecting the common market, or the so-called 'catch-all' Article 235 (now Article 352 TFEU), which allowed for some action to be taken in areas that were not mentioned in the Treaties but where it was deemed necessary for the achievement of the main Community objectives. In both cases, unanimity was required in the Council of Ministers.

Irrespective of those legal complications, environmental legislation continued to accumulate during this period. According to Burchell and Lightfoot (2001: 36), 120 directives, twenty-seven decisions, and fourteen regulations were adopted between 1973 and 1985. This was mainly due to the leadership exhibited by the European Commission, supported by the rulings of the European Court of Justice (ECJ). Additionally, the role of member states with high environmental standards was pivotal in pushing for the adoption of some of their policies at the EU level. Nevertheless, the lack of specific environmental provisions in the initial treaties hindered the Commission in its efforts to promote environmental legislation and resulted in a 'piecemeal and reactive' environmental policy at the Community level (McCormick 2001: 55).

From the Single European Act (SEA) to the Treaty of Maastricht

The SEA gave environmental policy the Treaty base that it had previously lacked. The SEA inserted a new Environment Title into the Treaties (Articles 130R–T; now Articles 191–3 TFEU). Hence, environmental protection formally became part of the competences of the Community. The fundamental environmental principles adopted in the EAPs were confirmed. Furthermore, it was stated that '[e]nvironmental protection requirements shall be a component of the Community's other policies' (Article 130R; now Article 191). This sought to promote a more integrated approach when dealing with the environment at the Community level. Additionally, the right of individual member states to put in place environmental legislation stricter than that in other member states was recognized (Article 130T; now Article 193 TFEU). One more Article related to the environment was inserted in the Treaties: Article 100a (now Article 114 TFEU) explicitly provided for the adoption of environmental legislation at the Community level when the creation of the single market was otherwise affected.

When Articles 130R–T were utilized, unanimity was required in the Council, together with consultation with the EP. On the other hand, when Article 100a was used, the new co-operation procedure was followed together with **qualified majority voting (QMV)** in the Council. Hence, there were two different procedures that could be followed depending on whether a piece of environmental legislation was connected to the single market. This caused some confusion, and led to treaty-based games between actors. The Commission attempted to use Article 100a in most of its dealings, in order to bypass the hurdle of unanimity in the Council of Ministers, but it was legally challenged on a number of occasions (Burchell and Lightfoot 2001: 38). All in all, the new provisions did clarify the right of the Community to act in the sphere of the environment, but the two different policy-making procedures caused complications.

Nevertheless, European Community (EC) environmental policy continued growing, boosted by its formal recognition in the SEA. The Fourth EAP was adopted for the years 1987–92 and a European Environment Agency (EEA) was established. The EEA was founded in 1990, but disagreements about its location meant that its official opening was delayed until 1993. It was eventually located in Copenhagen, with a remit to collect and disseminate information.

At the global level, the publication of the Brundtland Report in 1987, with its gloomy observations on the effects of current patterns of economic development and its prompting towards sustainability, increased awareness of environmental issues. This gave a further push towards a more proactive environmental policy at the EC level, where the role of certain actors in promoting environmental regulation was critical.

In the early 1980s, the Commission unit on the environment was upgraded into a Directorate-General (DG), which, although small compared to other DGs, pursued environmental issues with great determination. The partial application of QMV in the Council of Ministers gave the Commission more leeway in its efforts to increase EC-wide environmental standards. During that period, the Commission acted as a successful **policy entrepreneur**, promoting ambitious and far-reaching legislation, such as the Directive on Environmental Information and the Habitats Directive. However, it continued to be torn between an economic and an environmental logic that were to some extent incompatible.

The *Danish Bottle* case (Case 302/86) was a characteristic example. The Danish government had introduced legislation that required all soft-drink and beer bottles to be recyclable. This would have caused increased costs for the producers and would particularly have affected exporters to the Danish market. The Commission reacted by taking the Danish government to the ECJ, arguing that such a measure constituted a trade barrier. In the end, the ECJ ruled in favour of Denmark, insisting that environmental protection was of such importance for the Community that, under certain circumstances, it could even justify measures that distorted trade. The significance of the decision was that, for the first time, the environment was put on an equal footing with the common market. The decision also showed the limits of the Commission's role as a promoter of environmental legislation and the continuing important role of the ECJ in solidifying the EC's environmental policy. The Court was willing 'to adjust a simple integrationist approach to the specific requirements of a common environmental policy' (Koppen 1993, quoted in Jordan 1999*a*: 9).

Finally, some member states continued pushing for more European-wide environmental regulation. Leading states on environmental issues attempted to upload environmental measures to the European level. In the case of acid rain, for example, the role of Germany was critical. Alarmed at the damage caused to its forests by acid rain, and responding to national pressures, Germany adopted laws on the reduction of sulphur dioxide (SO_2) at the national level in 1983. However, the fear of loss of competitiveness, alongside the understanding that acidification was a trans-boundary issue, led to

451

pressures for action to be taken at the EU level. As a result, the Large Combustion Plant Directive was adopted mirroring the relevant German legislation (Sbragia 1996).

From the Treaty of Maastricht to the Treaty of Amsterdam and Beyond

The 1993 Maastricht Treaty increased further the visibility of environmental policy in the Treaties. The environment was now listed in the opening Articles as a major goal of the EU, alongside the other major goals of an economic nature. In terms of processes, QMV was extended to almost all areas of environmental policy, but unanimity was retained in sensitive areas such as town and country planning, taxation, and energy choices (Article 130S; now Article 192 TFEU). The new co-decision policy-making procedure was adopted for all measures related to the common market, increasing the powers of the EP. On the other hand, co-operation was reserved for most, but not all, matters related to Article 130S. Hence, albeit to a lesser extent, the complicated and confusing policy-making procedures persisted.

The Amsterdam Treaty confirmed the mainstreaming of environmental policy by inserting the goal of sustainable development and environmental protection into the preamble of the Treaties. Additionally, it provided for the integration of environmental policies into all other policies of the EU. The co-decision procedure became the norm regardless of whether a piece of legislation was concerned with the internal market. Thus, the duality in policy processes that had persisted for more than a decade was finally eliminated and the role of the EP increased. However, unanimity was kept for the most controversial issues.

The Fifth EAP (1993–2000) was a major step towards a more coherent EU environmental policy. First, it continued the marked shift towards a more integrated approach when dealing with environmental issues. Unlike its predecessors, it focused on the sources of pollution rather than the elements being polluted. Hence, it dealt with different economic sectors, such as agriculture, energy, and transportation. Second, it put an emphasis on so-called new environmental policy instruments (NEPIs), such as eco-taxes and eco-labels. NEPIs offered the possibility of more flexibility in the instrument used (for a more detailed analysis, see the next section). Third, the Fifth EAP set concrete environmental objectives to be achieved in the medium term and in the long term. Finally, it introduced the principle of 'shared responsibility', aimed at involving an increased number of actors in the policy-making and implementation processes (European Commission 1992). All in all, the Fifth EAP continued the trend towards more sophisticated environmental governance at EU level.

Fears that the accession of Greece, Spain, and Portugal in the 1980s would negatively affect the level of environmental regulation in the Community failed to materialize in practice. Environmental legislation in those countries was strengthened alongside the general level of environmental regulation at the European level (Schreurs 2004). Moreover, the accession in the 1990s of Austria, Sweden, and Finland, countries with very high environmental standards, helped to further solidify the EU environmental policy and strengthened the pro-environment camp within the Council of Ministers (Liefferink and Andersen 1998). Those countries took the initiative on several occasions when they held the presidency of the Council of Ministers and helped to increase environmental standards within the EU.

Within thirty years, the EU's environmental policy had, to return to the opening quotation from Weale (1999*b*: 40), 'moved from silence to salience'. However, there had been a change in emphasis about when it was right to act at the EU level. The introduction of the principle of **subsidiarity** into the Treaties meant that the Union had to justify to what extent it could deal with environmental issues better than the member states and sub-national authorities. More emphasis was now put on better implementation and the integration of environmental considerations into other EU policies (Haigh 1999). The role of the member states, the Commission, and the ECJ remained important—but a growing role was now reserved for the EP and environmental lobbying groups in Brussels. The policy landscape had become more complex.

Recent Developments

The Lisbon Treaty reaffirmed the trend to greater consolidation. Although it mentioned the issue of climate change for the first time, it left most environmental provisions unchanged (Benson and Jordan 2008). The environment was explicitly mentioned as a policy area in which both the member states and the EU shared competence, whereas the list of sensitive matters requiring unanimity in the Council remained intact.

EU environmental policy has now reached a mature stage. Since the core of EU environmental legislation has already been put in place, producing new legislation has decreased in importance. Instead, four major issues have gained prominence: environmental policy integration; addressing the implementation deficit of EU environmental legislation; the possible use of NEPIs; and the role of the EU as an actor in the global arena.

Environmental Policy Integration

Starting in the 1970s, the environment progressively moved from the periphery to the centre of EU policy making. Nevertheless, awareness grew that, regardless of the progress that had been achieved, for EU environmental policy to be successful, all other policies had to support its aims. Although, during the 1990s, there were some efforts to 'green' the structural and agricultural policies (Lenschow 1999), a more general strategy for environmental policy integration (EPI) was deemed necessary (Jordan et al. 2008).

At the Cardiff European Council in June 1998, it was decided that the different sectoral Councils would present specific strategies aimed at incorporating environmental considerations into their respective policy areas. This became known as the 'Cardiff Process'. At the summit, three sectoral Councils were invited to submit their strategy plans: Agriculture, Transport, and Energy. Six months later, the Development, Industry, and Single Market Councils were asked to participate in the process, followed by the General Affairs, Economic and Finance, and Fisheries Councils.

However, the Cardiff Process soon faltered. A Commission report in 2004 admitted that '[i]t may be concluded that the Cardiff Process has produced mixed results'

453

(European Commission 2004*c*: 31). The same report identified several weaknesses in the process, such as lack of priority areas, implementation deficiencies, a great variation in quality among the different strategies, and lack of commitment on behalf of the sectoral Councils (ibid.). Even more importantly, the Commission's attention had moved towards the adoption of a new Sustainable Development Strategy (see below). According to Jordan and Schout (2006: 73):

> By late 2002, the production of new strategies and/or updating of existing ones had all but ceased, and the entire process began to move into the shadow of the newly emerging Lisbon process on social and economic reform.

In the late 1990s, stagnant economic conditions and high unemployment in Europe forced the EU governments to pay more attention to the economy. Hence, at the Lisbon European Council in March 2000, the Lisbon Agenda was put in place promising to make Europe 'the most dynamic and competitive knowledge-based economy in the world'. (On the Lisbon Agenda, see Chapter 15, pp. 185–6.)

The Lisbon Agenda initially contained two pillars: an economic one and a social one. The environment was not given a privileged position. However, under the influence of the Swedish presidency, a third, environmental pillar was added at the Gothenburg European Council in June 2001. In Gothenburg, the leaders of the member states decided on a European Sustainable Development Strategy (SDS), in order to 'green' the Lisbon Agenda. An external dimension was added to the existing SDS in the following year. Finally, the whole strategy was reviewed and revised during 2005–06, attempting to improve its outcomes. SDS has now become the central strategy in EU efforts to 'green' its policies at the expense of the Cardiff Process.

Sustainable development by definition has a horizontal quality, since it aims at inserting environmental considerations into the heart of policy making. Hence, EPI is an integral part of it. However, the EU has retained both the Cardiff Process, which addresses EPI, and the SDS, which addresses sustainability (Jordan et al. 2008: 165), whereas the Sixth EAP, which covers the years from 2002 to 2012, addresses similar issues. The multiplicity of strategies and the confusion that they have caused have hampered the goal of EPI. The new century has brought with it a more focused approach emphasizing EPI, but at the same time the EU lacks an overarching plan on how to achieve it.

The tension between environmental and economic goals has not been resolved. The initial adoption of a two-pillar Lisbon strategy clearly shows that economic considerations seemed to be more important than environmental concerns. Even after Gothenburg, questions persist about the extent to which the environment remains an issue isolated from the economy, or is a fundamental principle underpinning the other pillars. In theory, EPI has become mainstream within EU discourse, but in practice it has found it difficult to penetrate successfully the economic foundations of the European project.

Implementation Deficit

Although EU environmental policy has evolved over the years, there are huge implementation deficits, making the environment one of the worst-performing policy areas in the EU. From the 1980s onwards, it became clear that implementation in the

454

environmental field was a serious problem that could potentially lead to policy underachievement. The Fourth EAP devoted a whole section to implementation and the issue has retained a high profile ever since.

Implementation can be understood either in legal or in practical terms. The former refers to the extent that there has been transposition of EU legislation into national laws, whereas the latter refers to whether a law has been implemented in practice (Weale et al. 2000: 297–8). Since the Commission is chronically understaffed and under-resourced, it has found it easier to focus more on the legal than on the practical implementation deficit.

Problems with the legal aspect of implementation are exacerbated because most EU environmental legislation comes in the form of directives. (For the main types of EU legislation, see Chapter 19, p. 244.) Since directives are not directly applicable in the member states, national governments are responsible for translating them into national laws. Hence, problems arise when a member state does not take the appropriate action. Additionally, the member states and sub-national authorities are responsible for the practical implementation of those laws inside their territory. Consequently, the EU institutions, as in many other policy areas, are in the peculiar position of adopting environmental measures that are to be applied and enforced by national and sub-national authorities.

The Commission is formally responsible for overseeing the implementation of EU legislation, commensurate with its role as 'the guardian of the Treaties'. Since the Environment DG lacks the necessary resources to perform this role effectively, it depends to a great extent on the complaints procedure to be notified of infringements of the law. Non-governmental organizations (NGOs), the general public, governments, parliaments, and corporations can all file a complaint with the Commission when there is incomplete implementation of an environmental law by a member state. The role of the Commission is to investigate the complaint and, if the complaint holds, begin infringement proceedings against the member state. This can ultimately lead to a referral to the ECJ.

Until recently, the ECJ lacked the 'teeth' to enforce its verdicts on the member states. However, since the Treaty of Maastricht, the Commission can request the ECJ to fine member states that have failed to comply with previous Court decisions (Article 171; now Article 260 TFEU). The Commission was quick to threaten the use of the amended Article in a number of cases. Greece was the first member state to be convicted to pay a fine because of non-compliance with a previous Court decision (Chapter 23, p. 324).

Greece had already been found guilty of the maintenance of an illegal landfill site at Kouroupitos in the prefecture of Chania, Crete. However, the government failed to close the site as requested and so was referred back to the Court by the Commission. The ECJ, in a seminal decision, obliged Greece to pay €20,000 daily until it stopped the operation of the landfill (Case C-387/97). Since then, the Article has been used several times, albeit cautiously, and has helped in the enforcement of EU environmental legislation.

The Commission has adopted a number of strategies to increase the efficiency of environmental law and subsequently reduce the implementation deficit. Hence, it has opted for a simplification and codification of the existing regulations (European Commission 2007b: 14). Additionally, it has adopted a bottom-up approach when dealing with implementation issues. It has thus opted for wider consultation with a number of environmental-policy actors during the early stages of policy making, in order to enhance legitimacy and acquire the highest level of agreement with its proposals. In the Sixth EAP, for example, one reads that:

> The thematic strategies [adopted in the Sixth EAP] should be developed and implemented in close consultation with the relevant parties, such as NGOs, industry, other social partners and public authorities, while ensuring, as appropriate, consultation of Candidate Countries in the process.
>
> (European Commission 2001c: Article 4.3)

It has also been proposed that the EEA could be transformed into the implementation watchdog of EU environmental policy (Burchell and Lightfoot 2001: 77). However, the member states have been eager to protect themselves from such an outcome. An EEA that attempts to impose legal and practical implementation on the member states might prove to be a nuisance. Hence, the EEA not only currently lacks such powers, but it also relies on the member states to gather the environmental data necessary for its operation.

Despite the debate on better implementation of the adopted legislation, problems remain. Moreover, the recent enlargement to states from central and eastern Europe, with weak bureaucracies and acute environmental problems, could well increase the implementation deficit. One way in which to decrease the burden of implementation, at least in principle, is by using more flexible policy instruments. The next section analyses the attempts that have been made to turn away from command-and-control measures and towards more market-oriented approaches.

From Regulation to New Environmental Policy Instruments (NEPIs)

The discussion on NEPIs is not new. They have been used in the past by several member states experimenting with new ideas. Even at the EU level, with the Fifth EAP, there was a clear turn towards NEPIs. Until then, the old command-and-control approach was prevalent. According to Golub (1998: 2):

> ... [Command-and-control] is characterised by direct regulation: the government prescribes uniform environmental standards across large regions, mandates the abatement methods required to meet such standards, licenses production sites which adopt the required methods, and assures compliance through monitoring and sanctions.

Although the command-and-control approach has been widely used since the early years of environmental policy in both the EU and the member states, it has been criticized as economically inefficient, as inherently undemocratic, and above all as inflexible and ineffective (Golub 1998; Jordan et al. 2003). Instead, the NEPIs have been proposed as a better way of achieving environmental policy goals. They consist of market-based tools, such as eco-taxes, subsidies, and tradeable permits, and non-market-based instruments, such as voluntary agreements, eco-labels, and eco-audits. (For a full presentation of the different kinds of NEPIs, see Golub 1998 and Jordan et al. 2003.)

The Commission has been willing to experiment with some NEPIs, but not always with great success. For example, in the early 1990s, it attempted to introduce a carbon tax, but its efforts were successfully resisted by the UK and other member states. The unanimity hurdle in the Council, which still applies for taxation measures, was too difficult to overcome. In the end, in 2003, a rather minimal outcome was achieved: a modest directive allowing for the harmonization of energy taxes across the EU.

Another ambitious market-based measure, the EU carbon emissions trading scheme (ETS) (Insight 30.1), has met with more success. The scheme was initiated in 2005, in order to reduce carbon dioxide (CO_2) emissions and help to combat climate change. Its first phase lasted for two years and was severely criticized for the over-allocation of permits. Too many carbon permits were issued, causing their price to collapse (Ellerman and Buchner 2007: 78). The second trading period commenced in 2008 and efforts have been made to rectify the scheme's deficiencies. Despite the criticisms, the EU ETS has been the first, and so far the only, such trading programme to operate on a large, supranational scale.

NEPIs have received criticism from other quarters. Radical ecologists disagree with green consumerism measures, such as the endorsement of eco-labels, because they justify and promote consumption instead of reducing it (Dobson 2007: 120–1). Moreover, a considerable number of radical ecologists and academics remain sceptical about market-based measures, since they see capitalism as part of the problem rather than the solution (Eckersley 1993). The most important criticism remains that their increased use has not always led to the positive results initially anticipated.

Despite this, the Commission remains enthusiastic about NEPIs. In recent reports, it has praised market-based instruments and their positive effects (European Commission 2005*b*; European Commission 2005*c*; European Commission 2007*b*). Hence, it has made it a priority to promote the use of market-based instruments 'for the flexibility they offer in meeting sustainable development objectives' (European Commission 2000*b*: 16).

Insight 30.1 The EU Carbon Emissions Trading Scheme (ETS)

The EU carbon emissions trading scheme is the main tool used by the EU to combat climate change. It is a 'cap and trade' scheme, which means that it sets an overall emissions cap, but it also allows trade to take place among the companies within the system. Each member state drafts a National Allocation Plan (NAP) according to its international obligations to reduce carbon emissions. A NAP not only determines the total number of allowances that each country is permitted to allocate, but it also contains a detailed plan on how many allowances each company that participates in the scheme receives. An allowance is equal to a tonne of CO_2 emissions. The companies that pollute less than permitted can sell their allowances to other companies that exceed their emission permits. Thus, a carbon market is created that, in theory, rewards the companies that make efforts to reduce emissions and penalizes companies that do not.

At the time of writing, the EU ETS was being revised. From January 2013 onwards, more than half of the carbon allowances will be auctioned rather than allocated. Additionally, there will be no NAPs. Instead, the system will be managed centrally at the EU level, whereas more industry sectors and more greenhouse gases will be included in the scheme.

It is important to remember, though, that despite the recent popularity of NEPIs, the old command-and-control measures still constitute the bulk of EU environmental legislation (Holzinger et al. 2006). Jordan (1999*a*: 15) claimed that, at the time of writing, 'Regulation shows no sign of being totally eclipsed by alternative tools'. The same observation holds today. A mixed bag of both traditional and new policy instruments is in use and this is likely to continue well into the future.

The EU as a Global Actor

The environmental role of the EU has recently increased at the global level. The EU has managed to play a leading part in international environmental conferences and broker global agreements on crucial environmental issues, such as climate change. Nevertheless, this new role has not come about easily. The EU had to develop the institutional capacity to perform such a task and also acquire the legitimacy, both at home and in the international arena, to operate as an international actor.

Sbragia and Damro (1999: 55) traced the origins of the EU's international presence in the early 1970s. In this period, the member states started signing a series of environmental agreements that threatened to derail the creation of the common market. The Commission felt the need to expand its competences in the field in order to protect the goal of economic integration in Europe. Additionally, the ECJ's *European Road Transport Agreement (ERTA)* ruling of 1971 acknowledged that when the EEC is given the right to legislate in a policy area, it is automatically given external competences in that area.

With the acquisition in the SEA of formal environmental powers within the EC, the European Commission became more assertive on the world scene. Hence, when the 1985 Vienna Convention and the 1987 Montreal Protocol on the ozone layer were signed, the EC succeeded in becoming a signatory. The United States and other countries initially reacted badly to that, but the dispute was finally resolved when both the member states and the EC became contracting parties (Sbragia and Damro 1999: 57). From then onwards, the joint participation of both the EC/EU and the member states in world environmental conferences became the norm. In the following years, the EC/EU emerged as an important global player in international environmental negotiations, such as the world summits on sustainable development in 1992 in Rio de Janeiro and in 2002 in Johannesburg (Lightfoot and Burchell 2005).

However, the single most important issue in which the EU has shown a leadership role has been that of climate change. Starting in the early 1990s, it became accepted that action should be taken to reduce emissions of greenhouse gases in order to combat climate change. As the debate on the greenhouse effect was gradually pushed higher up the environmental agenda, the EU managed to solidify its position as a world leader due to its ability to strike a burden-sharing agreement among its member states, and the unwillingness of the United States to commit to binding reductions in emissions.

The Council initially agreed in 1997 that, although the EU as a whole was committed to reduce the emission of greenhouse gases, the poorest member states should be allowed to increase their emissions, with the increase being offset by bigger decreases in the most developed countries. In the 1997 Kyoto Protocol, the EU agreed to reduce its emissions of greenhouse gases by 8 per cent from their 1990 levels by 2008–12. The final, post-negotiation, burden-sharing agreement saw Greece, Portugal, Spain, and

Ireland being allocated an increase of more than 10 per cent and countries such as Germany, Denmark, and Luxembourg accepting reductions higher than 20 per cent (Table 30.2). The ability of the member states to distribute the burden of the Kyoto Protocol between themselves showed the degree of solidarity within the EU. Alongside the reluctance of the United States to ratify the agreement, it gave the EU the necessary credibility to lead the talks on climate change.

Regardless of those successes in making an impact in the international environmental arena, the external dimension of the EU remains precarious. There is still great confusion regarding 'who speaks on behalf of the EU'. A rule of thumb is that the Commission speaks for the EU in all areas in which it has exclusive competence, and the Council when there is mixed competence (Sbragia and Damro 1999: 55). In practice, the situation is much more complicated. First, there is rivalry within the Commission about who is to take the lead in global negotiations, especially when complicated issues are discussed that relate to a number of different DGs (Lightfoot and Burchell 2005). Second, there are grey areas about when the Commission or the Council is to take the lead, although co-ordination processes have been improved. Finally, questions arise about the stance of the member states in the negotiations and to what extent they follow the line adopted by the EU.

Table 30.2 Burden-Sharing Agreement among Member States Regarding the EU Kyoto Emission Target

Country	Emissions reductions (Base year: 1990)
EC	−8%
Luxembourg	−28%
Denmark	−21%
Germany	−21%
Austria	−13%
United Kingdom	−12.5%
Belgium	−7.5%
Italy	−6.5%
Netherlands	−6%
France	0
Finland	0
Sweden	+4%
Ireland	+13%
Spain	+15%
Greece	+25%
Portugal	+27%

Source: Directive 2002/ 358/EC, **http://ec.europa.eu**, © European Union, 1995–2010

The United Nations (UN) Conference on Climate Change in Copenhagen in late 2009 was a setback to the EU's attempts to play a leading role in international discussions on the issue. The conference was marked by a greater willingness of the United States to play an active role on the issue, and cast doubts on whether the EU had secured for itself a leading role on global environmental issues.

Explaining EU Environmental Policy

The rapid expansion and increasing importance of EU environmental policy make it an interesting test case for theorizing. Why was the policy created in the first place and what has been the motor behind its apparently impressive expansion? This section discusses the contrasting explanations of the policy's creation and evolution offered by different theoretical perspectives.

There are not many pure intergovernmentalist analyses (Chapter 1, pp. 11–14) of EU environmental policy (Lenschow 2007). This is not surprising taking into account the strong role that the EU institutions have played. Intergovernmentalist accounts put emphasis on the role of the member states in advancing or containing environmental policy. They explain its emergence as a rational decision made by the member states aimed at decreasing the possible negative consequences of environmental competition. Thus, the member states initially delegated power to the EC institutions in the environmental field, in order to protect the goal of the common market, which was beneficial to all of them.

One should expect lowest-common-denominator (LCD) outcomes to have prevailed, at least during the initial period when unanimity applied in the Council of Ministers. However, as Lenschow (2007: 415) points out, 'the rather remarkable expansion of the field did not usually come at the price of LCD decisions'. If LCD were to have been the case, the poor countries of the south would have dictated the pace of environmental policy evolution. Rather, these countries had to increase considerably their environmental standards, converging upwards with the other member states.

Intergovernmentalists would also stress that, even after the SEA, unanimity has been retained for the most important issues, such as energy use and taxation. Although QMV was progressively expanded, a cluster of these core issues has remained untouched. Long negotiations prior to the Amsterdam and Nice Treaties did not succeed in expanding QMV to those areas. The member states retained the initiative where it matters. The case of the failed carbon tax proposal is a good example. As noted above, the Commission did try in the 1990s to advance the idea of an EU-wide energy tax, but was defeated in the Council of Ministers. So, while the member states have chosen to concede some powers on environmental issues, they have kept control in the most important cases.

Although intergovernmentalism has been used only rarely in its pure form, state-centric explanations have been widely used by scholars (Sbragia 1996; Liefferink and Andersen 1998). According to such analyses, there are two major camps of countries within the EU on environmental policy: the leaders and the laggards. Denmark, the Netherlands, Germany, Austria, Sweden, and Finland are generally considered as leading countries in promoting legislation, whereas Greece, Portugal, Ireland, and

Spain—together with the new member states—are considered to put obstacles in the way of the adoption of tougher environmental measures. It is the pull and push between these two camps that has contributed the most towards the evolution of EU environmental policy.

However, a model that crudely divides the member states into opposing camps is far too simplistic. Börzel (2000) demonstrated that there is no clear-cut divide between the rich north and the poor south in promoting and implementing environmental legislation. Hence, although the state-centric, pull–push model is parsimonious and gives a robust explanation of the policy, it could lead to oversimplifications.

A member state might resist a policy measure not because it is an environmental laggard, but rather because this measure does not relate to either its regulatory policy tradition or to the relevant policy measures that it has adopted at home. It has thus been proposed that what primarily matters is the extent of 'fit' or 'misfit' between the domestic environmental policies of a member state and environmental policies at the EU level (Risse et al. 2001). In order to minimize the costs of EU environmental policy, the member states attempt to upload their own environmental policies to the EU level (Börzel 2002). This has often caused regulatory competition among them (Héritier et al. 1996; Sbragia 2000).

The UK, for example, has recently managed to increase its influence over the policy-making process (Héritier et al. 1996; Sbragia 2000). This state has traditionally conceived environmental policy in a different way from the leading states of central and northern Europe, Germany in particular (Sbragia 1996: 250–3). So long as Germany had the lead in influencing EU legislation, Britain was perceived as a laggard. However, since the 1990s, the UK has shown a more proactive role, uploading elements of its own regulatory model (Jordan 2002; 2006). As a result, the initial role of the two countries has been reversed, with Germany having difficulties in transposing a number of environmental directives into national laws (Sbragia 2000).

The literature has also looked at the role that the new member states have played in EU environmental policy and the impact of accession. Schreurs (2004) attempted to offer a broad account on how past accessions affected the EU environmental policy-making process. Liefferink and Andersen (1998) looked at the way in which Finland, Sweden, and Austria influenced environmental policy after they became full members. Finally, there has been a recent surge in publications focusing on the member states of central and eastern Europe (Jehlicka and Tickle 2004; Carmin and VanDeveer 2004).

Neofunctionalist analyses (Chapter 1, pp. 8–11) stress the importance of spillover effects following the creation of the common market to explain the emergence and evolution of environmental policy. The argument here is that the environmental measures that several member states took from the late 1960s onwards threatened to derail the goal of economic integration (Zito 1999). The environmental issues that affected the smooth functioning of the common market had to be tackled at the EC level. Once a distinct environmental policy was created, it could not be contained by national governments. Unanimity was progressively replaced by QMV, and the role of the EP increased, whereas environmental issues not relevant to the common market were finally brought within the EU policy-making remit. Weale (1999*b*: 40) described the expansion of environmental policy as integration by stealth and argued that it could 'be regarded as a textbook illustration of the [Monnet] method at work'. (On the Monnet method, see Chapter 1, p. 7.)

The strength of this theoretical perspective lies in its ability to accommodate more fully the role of the EU institutions. According to neofunctionalism, the European Commission was quick to respond to the European Council's calls for environmental measures. It thus exploited the window of opportunity that opened at the beginning of the 1970s to promote the idea of an EC environmental policy. Throughout the following years, the Commission showed policy entrepreneurship in advancing important legislation. This could explain some far-reaching directives, such as the Drinking and Bathing Water Directives. Neither drinking water nor bathing water is directly relevant to the common market, nor do they have any obvious supranational justification. Indeed, one could argue that both are sub-national goods. In that sense, there was cultivated spillover promoted by the Commission that advanced European integration in this policy area.

The ECJ's role has also been pivotal (Koppen 1993). It supported the Commission throughout the years in its struggles with the Council of Ministers. In some cases, such as the *Danish Bottle* and the *Kouroupitos* cases (see above), it showed clear signs of environmental leadership. Finally, the EP, which many observers consider to be the 'greenest' of the EU institutions, has increased in importance, especially since the SEA. In most instances, the co-decision procedure has given the EP increased powers, which it has used to advance a green agenda.

However, while the Commission has been of paramount importance in promoting EU environmental policy, closer scrutiny reveals that, as a result of its inherent internal divisions, it has not always been in favour of unconditional policy expansion. There is great competition between the economic DGs (Trade, Competition) and the much smaller Environment DG. The Commission does not always support green legislation, since the Environment DG sometimes fails to gain broader support within the College of Commissioners. The *Danish Bottle* case reveals that the Commission has sometimes adopted points of view that are less environmentally friendly. Its role has not always been expansionist. Finally, even when the Commission has attempted to increase the level of environmental legislation, the member states have, in some cases, managed to contain its ambitions. So for instances such as the failed energy tax, intergovernmentalism gives a more persuasive account.

Neofunctionalism has been strongly criticized for adopting a linear view of progress (Zito 1999: 21; Lenschow 2007: 416). It seems to assume a progressive strengthening of EU environmental policy and expects a decreasing input from the member states as the policy advances. Reality does not support these predictions. For example, the Nice and Lisbon Treaties hardly changed anything in their provisions concerning the environment. In addition, although the Cardiff Process promised to integrate the environment into other EU policies within a few years, it faltered. The Lisbon Agenda showed that the perennial clash between the environment and the economy had not been resolved and that there was always a possibility of a setback in environmental policy if other, more pressing, matters demanded the attention of the EU leaders.

Governance theories (see Chapter 2) have difficulty explaining the origins of the policy, since their main focus is on day-to-day politics. Nevertheless, they give a rather more detailed account of the present situation and the complexity surrounding it. They can accommodate a whole range of new actors that play an increasing role in EU environmental affairs, such as NGOs or epistemic communities (Chapter 2, pp. 32–3), without denying the continuing importance of both the member states and the EU institutions. According to governance theories, the evolution of EU environmental policy cannot be explained unless we take into consideration the fact that the EU has evolved to become a polity in its own right. New tools, borrowed from domestic and comparative politics, are thus necessary, since thinking in the traditional terms derived from international relations cannot adequately capture this fundamental change.

The policy networks theoretical perspective (Chapter 2, pp. 29–31) attempts to trace and analyse networks that are created by a cluster of actors participating in the development and execution of EU environmental policy. This perspective pays particular attention to pooled resources, alliances formed, and bargaining within networks. It also assumes that the hierarchical model of government has given way to a more fluid and complex model of governance. One could observe the increasing reliance of the EU on the creation and stirring of policy networks. Jordan and Schout (2006: 21) argued that 'the EU has decided to rely more heavily on networked governance to tackle wicked policy issues such as environmental coordination'. The increasing use of the Open Method of Co-ordination and the Cardiff Process are two good examples of that turn (Chapter 15, p. 186).

New institutionalism (Chapter 2, pp. 22–7) puts emphasis on institutions and their ability to restrict and/or shape actors' preferences. Rational choice institutionalism, in particular, focuses on the inter-institutional and intra-institutional power games developed during the policy-making process. It deals with the way in which institutional reforms have changed the rules of the game and have restricted or enabled actors. Unlike neofunctionalism, it does not subscribe to the irreversibility of European integration, nor does it expect the EU institutions to be pro-integration and policy expansionist in all instances. Rather it focuses on the fragmentation within the Commission and the Council, the fight for more power among the EU institutions, and the power games between the member states and the institutions at the EU level (Jordan 1999b). Strategic thinking by rational actors is at the heart of its explanatory framework.

The environment is a policy area in which practitioners are faced with a great level of uncertainty. Hence, the epistemic communities approach (Chapter 2, pp. 32–3) could be used to explain some of the policy shifts that have been observed during recent years. Acid rain, ozone depletion, and climate change are complicated phenomena that the politicians have had difficulty in grasping. Practitioners have turned to environmental experts to increase their information on the causes of these phenomena and how to combat them. Thus, through the channel of epistemic communities, ideas have been diffused and environmental policies reshaped.

A very good example of the influence of epistemic communities is the issue of climate change. The broad agreement among environment experts that there is a strong causal relationship between climate change and the level of greenhouse gases was decisive in pushing measures to reduce CO_2 onto the policy agenda. Moreover, not only did policy experts dictate what gases had to be reduced, but they also helped to shape the policy schemes for this to happen: namely, the creation of the carbon emission trading scheme. Their influence was fundamental in providing technical expertise and changing the broader framework within which EU environmental policy functioned.

There is no one theory that can completely explain the origins and evolution of EU environmental policy in its entirety. Different perspectives shed light on different aspects. Intergovernmentalism, and state-centred theories generally, give an insightful account of the way in which member states influence policy. Neofunctionalism accommodates the importance of the EU institutions in advancing the policy. Finally, governance theories have explained successfully the day-to-day politics, the multiplicity of actors, and their interconnections.

One way in which to deal with this problem is to combine theoretical perspectives, aiming at a more holistic theoretical explanation. Weale et al. (2000: 45), for example, claimed that both a neofunctionalist and an intergovernmentalist logic can be traced in the way in which the EU's environmental policy system was created. As Zito (1999: 33) pointed out, combining theoretical perspectives may lack parsimony, but it does provide a way of explaining task expansion in the absence of an adequate single theory.

CONCLUSION

The environment is a good example of how a peripheral policy area can, in a matter of a few years, become important in the EU. However, although the policy has expanded greatly, the future remains unclear. Despite the progress that the EU has made in tackling environmental problems, it has found it difficult to reconcile the competing policy objectives of economic development and environmental protection. The notions of sustainable development and EPI could provide the links to bridge the gap between these two competing policies, but the full incorporation of environmental principles into the core of EU decision making remains to be seen. Additionally, a number of other matters that are discussed in this chapter—such as making more use of NEPIs, addressing the perennial implementation deficit, and acquiring a global role in environmental politics—demand further attention. All of these issues, alongside the effects of the recent enlargement and, above all, the mounting world environmental problems, will set the EU environmental agenda well into the future.

KEY POINTS

History

- The initial Treaties did not contain any environmental provisions.
- 1973 marked the beginnings of environmental policy at Community level.
- The SEA formalized EC environmental policy.
- The Treaty of Maastricht increased the visibility of the environment in the Treaties.

Recent Developments

- Recently, the area of focus has moved from producing new legislation to greening all other EU policies, improving implementation records, using new, more flexible policy instruments, and increasing the ability of the EU to act as an international environmental actor.
- Although EPI has improved, there are problems deriving from the multiplicity of actions and the lack of an overarching strategy.
- The implementation record for environmental policy is one of the worst in the EU. Although efforts have been made to address the implementation deficit, success has been limited.

- The EU has started experimenting with NEPIs, although the old command-and-control instruments remain in use.

- The EU has attempted to increase its international role on environmental issues, although issues remain concerning who is to speak on behalf of the EU and to what extent the EU can achieve the environmental goals that it has set for itself.

Explaining Environmental Policy

- No individual theory or approach can adequately explain the origins and evolution of EU environmental policy.

- Intergovernmentalism captures best the influence of certain member states in advancing the case for EU policy.

- Neofunctionalism explains the active role that the Commission, the ECJ, and the EP have played in shaping the content of environmental policy.

- The new governance theories are better equipped to explain the multiplicity of actors currently taking part in EU environmental policy and the fluidity of the current policy environment.

FURTHER READING

For an excellent overview of the EU environmental policy, see **J. McCormick,** *Environmental Policy in the European Union* (Basingstoke: Palgrave, 2001), and **J. Burchell and S. Lightfoot,** *The Greening of the European Union? Examining the EU's Environmental Credentials* (London and New York: Sheffield Academic Press, 2001). On EPI, see **Andrew Jordan et al.,** 'The European Union', in *Innovation in Environmental Policy? Integrating the Environment for Sustainability* (Edward Elgar: Cheltenham, 2008), 159–79. Additionally, the collection of seven articles published in the special themed issue of *Environment and Planning C: Government and Policy,* 17 (1999), entitled 'European Union Environmental Policy at 25', shed light on all major issues of the EU environmental policy ranging from theory to issues related to the use of NEPIs, implementation concerns, and the rise of the EU as a global actor in this policy area.

 online resource centre

Visit the Online Resource Centre that accompanies this book for links to more information on environmental policy:
www.oxfordtextbooks.co.uk/orc/bache3e/

465

Chapter 31

Freedom, Security, and Justice

Chapter Overview

The policy activity of the European Union (EU) in Justice and Home Affairs (JHA) was given formal recognition in the 1992 Treaty on European Union (TEU). Through subsequent reforms, latterly the implementation of the Lisbon Treaty, the policy has been recast around creating an area of freedom, security, and justice (AFSJ). This chapter initially explores the emergence and growth of JHA policy in the EU, and the Treaty reforms that led to the emphasis on creating an AFSJ. It looks at the institutions and policies related to the AFSJ. Finally, it explores the debates and interpretations that have been offered for the policy area's dynamics. A key feature of this policy area's evolution has been the use of 'laboratories' outside the EU and of EU measures that have not involved all of the member states.

[T]he AFSJ has become the site of some of the most intensive integration activity. Furthermore, despite a decade of effort to put the Area in place, there is no sign that the energies that have been devoted to its achievement thus far are starting to flag ...

(Baker 2009: 834)

Freedom, security, and justice are areas that have traditionally been understood as the core responsibilities of the nation state. It is an indication of the wide-ranging nature of the integration process that these policy areas have come under the EU's umbrella. Introduced principally by the Maastricht Treaty of 1992, the policy area initially was termed Justice and Home Affairs (JHA) and was located in its own pillar of the EU. However, the Amsterdam Treaty moved immigration and asylum policy to pillar one as part of an aim to create an area of freedom, security, and justice (AFSJ). The AFSJ was greatly enhanced by the Lisbon Treaty, which ended the separate existence of the third pillar and also consolidated police and judicial co-operation into the AFSJ. Reflecting this move, this chapter is entitled 'Freedom, Security, and Justice', although the early part is framed in terms of JHA. The policy area has matured even if it remains contested because of the way in which it strikes at national sovereignty. The AFSJ has developed its own governance arrangements, including a range of agencies. A key characteristic of JHA and AFSJ has been the use of differentiated integration, whereby not all member states participate in all of the arrangements.

The chapter explores the history, culminating in the AFSJ becoming the overarching policy framework under the Lisbon Treaty. It considers the AFSJ's institutional character and policy content. Finally, it explores the key explanations and debates relating to this policy area. In light of its dynamism since 1993, it is no exaggeration to describe this policy area as the 'new frontier' of European integration.

History

Early Co-operation: Before the Treaty on European Union

The founding Treaties of the 1950s made few provisions relating to what has emerged since the 1990s. The commitment to the free movement of persons and specifically of workers was notable (Article 48 EEC Treaty). However, this provision only became significant with the developing momentum in the mid-1980s to create the single market (see Chapter 27). Other very limited rights bestowed on individuals in the early decades of integration were economic- and market-related. Even with the fragmented policy initiatives of the 1980s, there was no indication of the scope that the AFSJ would take in the EU of today (see Insight 31.1).

Until the 1990s, the driving forces behind co-operation lacked real salience. In consequence, the policy responses resembled a patchwork. Accordingly, one of the key characteristics in this early period, and still relevant today, was the use of a 'laboratory' approach to the policy area (Monar 2001: 748–52). Co-operation thus took place in

---

Insight 31.1 The Scope of the Area of Freedom Security and Justice

The main areas are:

- free movement of persons;
- immigration and asylum;
- judicial co-operation in civil and criminal matters;
- police and customs co-operation;
- combating organized crime;
- combating terrorism;
- combating drugs;
- combating human trafficking;
- fundamental rights;
- citizenship;
- combating discrimination (including racism and xenophobia);
- external—or enlargement-related—aspects of the above.

Full details of the policy measures in force are obtainable at the Commission's webpage: **http://ec.europa.eu/justice_home/fsj/intro/fsj_intro_en.htm**; **http://ec.europa.eu**, © European Union, 1995–2010

different forums and was not confined to the European Community (EC)/EU. Three particular 'laboratories' undertook experiments that prepared the ground for the rapid policy advances of the 1990s. These were the Council of Europe, 'Trevi', and the Schengen group.

The Council of Europe's texts on extradition, mutual legal assistance in criminal matters, the international validity of criminal judgments, and the transfer of sentenced persons—some dating back to the late 1950s—were to become central to JHA co-operation between EU member states. Indeed, they have become part of the *acquis* that applicant states are required to adopt before they can become new members (Monar 2001: 749). Perhaps more importantly, though, through co-operation in the Council of Europe, the traditionally parochial outlook of interior ministries began to be broken down. National officials gained experience of working co-operatively with their counterparts in other European states. Awareness was raised of national sensitivities and peculiarities, and of the problems involved in co-operation. 'Trevi' was a loose form of co-operation within the European political co-operation (EPC) machinery (see Chapter 33). It was therefore an intergovernmental process comprising EC member governments. Trevi was set up in 1975 as a response to increasing terrorist activity in Europe, but was later extended to the fight against drugs trafficking and organized crime. It also provided the experience of working together that paved the way for more structured co-operation once the Treaty on European Union (TEU) was put into effect in 1993. The work of Trevi was particularly influential for the development within JHA of Europol (the European Police Office) (see below).

The third 'laboratory' is comprised of the 'Schengen group' of member states that agreed to eliminate internal border controls. This initiative can be traced back to Franco-German efforts in 1984 to include some components of JHA activity in what became the Single European Act (SEA). It became clear that one of the core components—the lifting of passport controls to accompany the opening of the single market—was not acceptable to Britain, Ireland, and Denmark. In consequence, the Schengen group emerged as a laboratory for developing a passport-free zone (see Insight 31.2). The implications of removing passport controls proved to be more far-reaching than envisaged and the scope of JHA co-operation widened to include compensatory control measures.

The Schengen 'laboratory' undertook valuable work that paved the way for JHA agreements on asylum and policies, extradition, and police co-operation. It also created

Insight 31.2 The Schengen Area

The name 'Schengen' comes from a small town in Luxembourg located at the border with both Germany and France. The signing of the Schengen Agreement on 14 June 1985 took place on board the pleasure boat *Princesse Marie-Astrid*, moored in the river Moselle, which, at Schengen, forms the boundary between Luxembourg and Germany. Initial members were France, Germany, Belgium, Luxembourg, and the Netherlands. The Agreement's implementing arrangements were agreed in 1990 through the Schengen Convention. The term Schengen is still utilized to denote the area comprising those states that have given up border controls with each other (see Figure 31.1).

a 'culture of co-operation' (Monar 2001: 752) and laid the basis for the **transnational networks** of police and judicial authorities that are essential to the successful implementation of JHA measures. The EU's Amsterdam Treaty (1997) incorporated policy agreed under the Schengen provisions into the EU Treaties, giving it a new legal personality.

One consequence of the Schengen arrangements was the need to start work on complementary external measures. The Dublin Convention, signed in 1990 and coming into force in 1997, was designed to stop asylum seekers making more than one application to enter the EU, trying to find the easiest point of access: a tactic known as 'asylum shopping'. Unlike with the Schengen arrangements, however, Britain, Ireland, and Denmark chose to participate. In 2003, the convention was revised and subsequently became known as the Dublin Regulation.

Policy Dynamics and JHA Structures under the Treaty on European Union

How did the policy co-operation in these laboratories culminate in the creation of the JHA 'pillar' within the EU, as agreed at Maastricht in 1991? A number of overlapping dynamics were at play and became irresistible during the negotiation of the TEU. First of all, the Treaty was negotiated when European integration had attained a new level of dynamism from the SEA and creation of the single market. Giving JHA prominence in the new Treaty was part of this dynamic and was championed by the German Chancellor, Helmut Kohl. At the same time, specific consequences of the single market, with its removal of border controls, gave new urgency to intensified co-operation in order to provide alternative means of control over illegal immigration and cross-border criminality. Free movement of goods could facilitate smuggling, especially of goods such as cigarettes that attracted very different levels of tax in different parts of the EU. Free movement of people could allow criminals to commit a crime in one member state and retreat to another to evade detection and capture. Free movement of capital could facilitate financial crime, including the 'laundering' of money obtained from criminal activities. Also, individuals and businesses who took advantage of the single market to buy or sell in other member states found it difficult and prohibitively expensive to gain access to another state's system of justice if things went wrong. These potential threats necessitated a collective policy response.

A third dynamic arose from the interaction between globalization and the redefinition of notions of security. While the single market raised the scope for cross-border criminality, this was part of a larger-scale phenomenon. The end of the Cold War dramatically increased the opportunity for international crime and cross-border migration from the former communist states, although the scale of the threat was not as great as some of the predictions (Geddes 2006: 453). Economic migrants and asylum-seekers were drawn to EU states. The civil wars in former Yugoslavia led to increases in asylum applications. Subsequently, the threat from terrorism took on especial salience with the Al-Qaeda '9/11' terrorist attacks in the United States in September 2001 and subsequent bombings in Madrid (March 2004) and London (July 2005). These actions produced further rapid escalation in JHA policy making within the EU. Alongside these developments, the growth of the Internet has introduced new challenges associated with 'cyber crime'.

The new global challenges were intrinsically linked to a redefined security agenda. Traditionally, security was seen as how states guaranteed their defence in military terms: as part of foreign policy in a state-centred system of international relations. However, this understanding has been challenged on two fronts. First, security has come to be understood in different ways: for instance, as societal security (Waever 1996). Issues such as cross-border criminality or illegal immigration have taken on greater importance on the political agenda. Second, the international concern with terrorism after 9/11 has emphasized the role of non-state actors, such as Al-Qaeda or its sympathizers, in internal security. Thus security has established itself as a key theme in *home* affairs policy—or to use the academic terminology, home affairs policies have become 'securitized'.

A final dynamic for JHA policy came from a small number of states that, recognizing such dynamics, advocated the development of the EU's capacity to address the new internal security agenda. Foremost amongst these was Germany, the member state with the largest number of borders with different states: a situation exacerbated by the opening up of frontiers to its east with end of the Cold War. At the same time, its relatively liberal asylum policy was attracting increasing number of applicants. The Kohl government sought to utilize the EU as an argument for making its asylum rules more restrictive and thus justifying the necessary domestic reforms.

These stimuli were making the case for EU responsibility stronger. The laboratories discussed earlier and a growing number of other intergovernmental agreements were creating multiple (and messy) institutional arrangements. According to Jörg Monar, interior and justice ministry officials, the police, and the customs authorities gradually came to realize that they were 'increasingly sitting in "the same boat" as regards a broad range of issues' (2001: 754). There was therefore a strong logic to providing a common EU framework for the policy responses.

The agreement reached in the Maastricht Treaty was to create a separate intergovernmental 'third pillar' within which JHA co-operation could be developed. The Treaty identified many of the main areas detailed in Insight 31.1. However, the institutional arrangements proved far from satisfactory. During the Maastricht negotiations, a majority of states had unsuccessfully favoured integrating JHA policy into EC business, but failed to agree on how to achieve this. At the same time, states such as Britain were insistent on not giving authority to the European Commission and other supranational bodies, notably the Court of Justice. Consequently, the institutional arrangements in the third pillar were a compromise.

The JHA Council and the Commission shared the right to initiate policy. Much of the detailed work was undertaken under the auspices of three steering groups, which reflected sub-areas of JHA work: asylum and immigration; police and customs co-operation (the busiest); and judicial co-operation in civil and judicial matters (den Boer and Wallace 2000: 502–3). Officials from different national agencies, including customs and the police, as well as the judicial authorities, worked more intensively than in the past, leading to changes in their working practices as well as those of interior and justice ministries. Some non-governmental organizations concerned with human rights and asylum issues began to emerge at EU level in response to the EU's new powers.

The main policy-making difficulty, however, was that JHA showed the pitfalls of an intergovernmental system. Decision making was slow and unwieldy; decisions, if taken, tended towards the lowest common denominator. In addition, the visibility of

JHA decision making was low and parliamentary control virtually non-existent. Dissatisfaction led to pressure for institutional reform, which came about with the 1997 Amsterdam Treaty.

The Reforms of the Amsterdam Treaty

The Amsterdam Treaty brought about a number of significant changes to JHA policy. Of central importance was the new overarching mission to create an AFSJ (see Insight 31.3). This terminology was used in order to present the reforms as a major new programme in integration that, according to the Amsterdam Treaty, 'would provide citizens with a high degree of safety'. The AFSJ therefore sought to engage with the European public on the emerging new security agenda. Once again, the new arrangements represented a compromise between the different member governments in the Treaty negotiations (for details, see den Boer and Wallace 2000: 513). The **Benelux** states were amongst the most supportive of communitarization of JHA policy into the first pillar. Britain, by contrast, was opposed.

The most important institutional change was the transfer of visa, asylum, and immigration policies to the first pillar. The policy provisions went hand in hand with new decision-making rules: namely, **qualified majority voting (QMV)** in the Council. These rules in fact only came into operation from January 2005, by which time much legislation was agreed, but on the basis of unanimity. Pillar three remained, but with a narrower set of JHA responsibilities: namely, police and judicial co-operation in criminal matters (PJCCM).

At a relatively late stage in the negotiations leading to the Amsterdam Treaty, several states proposed the incorporation of the Schengen system into the EU. The Dutch government, which held the presidency of the Council in the first half of 1997, was extremely influential in securing this outcome. However, the exact 'outcome' was not entirely clear for some time because 'there was indeed no definitive or agreed text of the Schengen *acquis*' (den Boer and Wallace 2000: 514). Hence a major immediate task in JHA policy making once the Amsterdam Treaty came into force in May 1999 was to actually catalogue the accumulated decisions taken within the Schengen 'laboratory'. This task was made complex by the fact that some of the decisions and associated policy instruments were matters for the first pillar and others for the third pillar.

What was at first clearer about the incorporation of the Schengen provisions into the EU was that the British and Irish governments had negotiated opt-outs in view of

---

Insight 31.3 The Key Changes to JHA in the Amsterdam Treaty

- Visa, asylum and immigration policies were 'communitarized'—that is, transferred from the third pillar to the first pillar.
- The residual responsibilities in the third pillar were confined to police and judicial co-operation in criminal matters (PJCCM), although provisions were enhanced.
- The Schengen conventions and associated decisions within that framework were to be transferred to the responsibility of the EU.

their non-participation in the Schengen system. These opt-outs, it should be noted, stemmed primarily from UK governments' preference to maintain passport controls, a position usually justified by reference to the country's island status. In order to maintain its common travel area with the UK, Ireland maintained a similar opt-out. Denmark's participation in the Schengen zone had by this time increased, since the 1995 enlargement had brought in other states within the Nordic passport area. In effect, the Nordic passport area became part of the Schengen zone, the rules of which consequently were extended to Iceland and Norway.

The Area of Freedom Security and Justice (AFSJ): From Amsterdam to Nice

The ambition to develop the AFSJ as a new 'project' for the EU bore fruit. The European Commission began to build up its policy capacity, reflecting its enhanced powers of initiative arising from the Amsterdam Treaty. It reorganized its existing task force, creating in October 1999 a fully fledged Directorate-General (Directorate-General for Justice, Freedom, and Security). The European Parliament was given consultation rights on first pillar JHA decision making during the transition period. It increased its policy engagement and strengthened its committee, eventually called the Civil Liberties, Justice, and Home Affairs Committee. The European Court of Justice for the first time obtained some very restricted powers in relation to first-pillar JHA policy. Finally, the Council of Ministers also underwent some reorganization. Since JHA policy was located in two separate pillars of the EU, two separate committee structures were established under the authority of the Justice and Home Affairs Council. A final key institutional development arose from the engagement of the heads of government. In October 1999, the European Council, meeting in Tampere (Finland), was devoted to the development of the AFSJ. It agreed on a substantial programme of work for the period ahead and set in train a pattern of five-yearly programmes underpinned by scorecards and other mechanisms to ensure that momentum would be maintained. The Hague Programme (2004) and the Stockholm Programme (2009) were agreed subsequently by the European Council to maintain the policy momentum.

The Treaty of Nice made less fundamental changes to JHA. QMV was extended to limited parts of judicial co-operation as well as to anti-discrimination measures and matters relating to refugees. The first two of these were also to be covered by the co-decision process, thus making small inroads into a policy area in which the European Parliament (EP) had historically lacked real powers. With one exception, the other main JHA-related changes arising from the Treaty of Nice were general institutional reforms, prepared for the forthcoming enlargement (see Chapter 19). The exception was the Charter of Fundamental Rights of the European Union. The Charter comprised six chapters spelling out a set of principles. They covered dignity (for example, the right to life and the prohibition of the death penalty); freedoms; equality; solidarity; citizens' rights; and justice. The British government was opposed to the Charter of Fundamental Rights being given legal status as part of the Treaty of Nice. Consequently, the Charter was 'solemnly proclaimed' at Nice in December 2000. For the time being, its status was to be political, but then subject to discussion as part of the subsequent constitutional debate.

The Lisbon Treaty

The Lisbon Treaty brought about some fundamental institutional reforms to JHA policy (Duff 2009: 95–102; Kietz and Parkes 2008) (see Insight 31.4). The first point to note is the new, upgraded commitment that:

> The Union shall offer its citizens an area of freedom, security and justice without internal frontiers, in which the free movement of persons is ensured in conjunction with appropriate measures with respect to external border controls, asylum, immigration and the prevention and combating of crime.

(Article 3 TEU)

Symbolically, this objective was located ahead of such priorities as the single market and the single currency. In addition, the abolition of the three-pillar system meant that those parts of JHA that remained in the third pillar—namely PJCCM—were brought into the '**Union method**' (see Chapter 19). The 'third pillar' was abolished and incorporated in a single part (or 'Title') of the Treaty on the Functioning of the European Union (TFEU) on the AFSJ. Thus the whole of JHA policy in principle moves back to a single pattern of policy making: one in which the Treaty provides for QMV in the Council, co-decision rights for the EP and, with some restrictions, the jurisdiction of the European Court of Justice (ECJ). The work of agencies—notably Europol and Eurojust (see below)—was brought under closer parliamentary scrutiny.

In fact, the situation is a bit more complicated than this. At first glance, it appears as if the whole of JHA policy, including PJCCM, is now conducted within a supranational framework. However, a number of exceptional arrangements are written into the Treaties and reflect the fact that the member governments were unwilling to give up their powers quite so easily:

- the Commission continues to be denied the exclusive right of initiative, since a quarter of the member states may also launch initiatives;
- the European Council is given the powers to set the strategic guidelines of policy (such as it has done with the five-yearly programmes, latterly the 2009 Stockholm Programme);

Insight 31.4 The Key Changes to the AFSJ in the Lisbon Treaty

- Abolition of the third pillar and transfer of police and judicial co-operation (PJCCM) into a new chapter within the TFEU's provisions on the AFSJ
- All proposals in the AFSJ to be adopted by the 'Union method', but with five-year transitional rules for PJCCM as well as various other exceptional policy-making rules
- EU Charter on Fundamental Rights becomes legally binding, but with special provisions weakening its application in the UK, Poland, and the Czech Republic
- New opt-out provisions for the UK, Ireland, and Denmark

- an 'emergency brake' procedure has been introduced into PJCCM whereby a member state can declare a matter to be of national interest through appeal to the European Council;
- PJCCM is only fully subject to the Union method after a five-year transition period and there are some special exceptions because member states wished to limit the possible impacts on their systems of criminal justice;
- Britain, Ireland, and Denmark have secured new opt-outs from PJCCM.

These changes are of considerable importance, but the full effects will not be seen until 2015, when the transitional arrangements end for PJCCM. At that point, the Commission will gain powers to launch infringement proceedings on PJCCM, an area in which policy implementation by the member states has been patchy (Duff 2008: 99). The ECJ will assume much greater importance as well. In February 2010, the EP made first use of new powers under the Lisbon Treaty to reject, on civil liberties grounds, a counter-terrorist agreement between the EU and the United States to exchange data on bank transfer payments.

The Area of Freedom, Security, and Justice

Before exploring the specific policy areas that the AFSJ is by now addressing, it is worth drawing attention to other emergent institutional trends. A number of data systems, agencies, and networks have emerged as mechanisms to put the AFSJ into practice. In many ways, these resemble wider trends in political practice, whether in the EU or in member states, particularly the delegation of new policy tasks to expert bodies, and the use of new technology to tackle policy challenges. As illustrations, we look at the Schengen Information System, Europol, Eurojust, and Frontex.

Schengen Information System

The Schengen Convention provided for a multinational database for the use of immigration, border control, police, and judicial authorities in any of the Schengen member states. This database is called the Schengen Information System (SIS). It is a key policy instrument put in place to accompany removal of border and passport controls. Another policy instrument is the 'Schengen visa', which allows the holder to visit—in the absence of border controls—any of twenty-five states (see Figure 31.1). The SIS is therefore an important instrument linking together participants' databases in order to facilitate JHA co-operation (see Insight 31.3).

As can be seen from examples in Insight 31.5, the SIS can be used in a range of situations. It is operationalized by so-called SIRENE bureaux. Located in each of the Schengen states, these bureaux deal with a Supplementary Information Request at the National Entry (SIRENE): the data-checking process that may lead to a 'hit', as outlined in Insight 31.3. In 2000, the UK successfully secured agreement from Schengen states to participate in all of the Schengen *acquis* provisions concerning criminal law and policing (but excluding cross-border hot pursuit by police officers). As a consequence, the UK is able in theory to participate in the SIS, but the government chose to defer until the launch of a larger-capacity database system known as SIS II. Like

Figure 31.1 Member State Participation in the Schengen Zone 2010

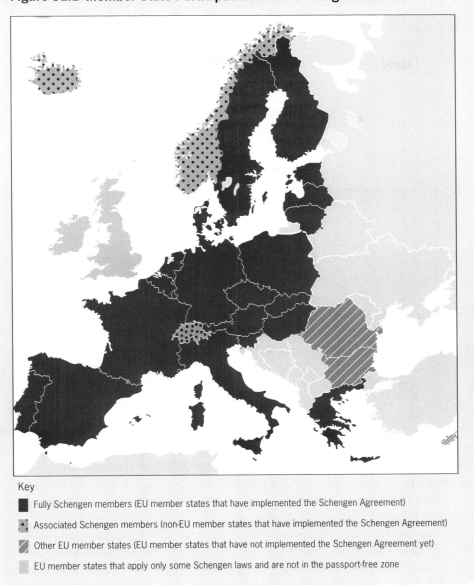

Key

■ Fully Schengen members (EU member states that have implemented the Schengen Agreement)

▨ Associated Schengen members (non-EU member states that have implemented the Schengen Agreement)

▨ Other EU member states (EU member states that have not implemented the Schengen Agreement yet)

▨ EU member states that apply only some Schengen laws and are not in the passport-free zone

many large-scale computer projects, it has been running behind schedule. The UK would in any case remain excluded from *immigration data* within the SIS for as long as it retains its opt-out from Schengen provisions on passport controls (House of Lords 2007: 11). Ireland is in a similar situation to the UK, having secured agreement on the same basis in 2002.

A separate database exists in relation to the asylum regime under the Dublin Regulation. Known as EURODAC, this Commission-run database is designed to identify whether an asylum applicant or a foreign national found illegally present within a

> ### Insight 31.5 Examples of the Schengen Information System in Operation
>
> - A consulate of one of the Schengen states is considering an application for a short-term visa, which would be valid for visiting all Schengen states (a 'Schengen visa') and checks the database. The consequence of a 'hit' on the SIS is that, in principle, the visa application must be refused. A new Visa Information System is to deal with such issues from late 2010.
> - A person in police custody is the subject of an extradition request or a European Arrest Warrant (EAW), which is listed in the SIS. A 'hit' would usually result in the arrest of the fugitive and the exchange of further documentation so that the process of extraditing or surrendering the fugitive can get under way.
> - A police officer checks the SIS to see whether a vehicle with foreign licence plates is listed as a stolen vehicle in an alert in the SIS. A 'hit' on the stolen vehicle would trigger bilateral contacts between the national authority that made the hit and the national authority that issued the alert.
>
> *Source:* House of Lords (2007: 10)

member state has previously claimed asylum in another member state, or whether an asylum applicant entered the Union territory unlawfully. All twenty-seven member states plus Norway, Iceland, and Switzerland—the signatories to the Dublin Regulation—participate in EURODAC.

Europol, Eurojust, and Frontex

Europol, Eurojust, and Frontex (see Table 31.1) are three key agencies in charge of particular aspects of the AFSJ (on agencies more generally, see Lavenex 2010: 467–70; also Table 31.2). They aim to facilitate co-operation between member-state agencies in different areas of policy that are all of centrality to achieving the AFSJ. Each has grown in size and been allocated new tasks as policy has developed in the face of new threats and as confidence has developed between domestic agencies, such as the police.

All three agencies have developed an 'external face' as part of their work, reflecting the way in which thinking about policy has evolved. Europol and Eurojust work closely with European neighbours, such as Norway and Switzerland, but also with counterparts elsewhere, such as in the United States. Frontex's co-operation with third countries tends to focus on states that are major transit points for illegal immigrants or are the ultimate sources of the migration flows. An examination of Frontex's work programme gives an indication of the focal points of its operations (Frontex 2009). These are the perceived weak spots in the EU's frontiers: the EU's external land borders in south-eastern Europe and the western Balkans and with Ukraine; the sea borders in the Atlantic and the Western Mediterranean; and air borders at major international gateways. All of these are recognized routes for illegal immigration and, in the case of land and sea routes, for people-smuggling.

One distinctive feature of Frontex is that it can mount operations by providing short-notice assistance where a security threat emerges, for example through its 'Rapid

Table 31.1 Europol, Eurojust, and Frontex

Agency	Europol	Eurojust	Frontex
Responsibility	European law enforcement agency	EU's judicial co-operation unit	Securing the external borders of the EU
Date of establishment (decision; operational)	1992; 1999	1999; 2002	2004; 2005
Location	The Hague, Netherlands	The Hague, Netherlands	Warsaw, Poland
Mode of operation	Facilitates bilateral exchange of information between all member state police forces	Facilitates co-operation between investigating and prosecuting authorities in the member states; exchange of personal data and judicial information	Exchange of information and co-operation between member states' border guards, customs, and police
Policy remit	Combating international crime: motor vehicle crime; organized crime; drug trafficking; illicit immigration networks; terrorism; forgery of money (counterfeiting of the euro); trafficking in human beings; and money laundering	Largely as for Europol	Integration of member states' national border security systems to deal with threats at the EU's external frontier Tasks include immigration, repatriation, surveillance, border checks, and risk analysis
Staffing/structure	Approx. 600 staff, including over 100 police liaison officers from the member states	27 'national members', typically senior judges or public prosecutors (one per member state)	250 central staff; 450 border guards ready for deployment to a 'hot spot'

Border Intervention Teams' (known in Frontex jargon as 'RABITs'). Frontex also has aircraft, helicopters, and patrol vessels at its disposal. For example, from 2007, Frontex sea patrols have monitored areas in which large numbers of illegal immigrants were arriving by sea: notably, the Canary Islands, Malta, and Italy. Quite apart from the immigration dimension, many migrants were making a perilous sea journey in overcrowded or scarcely seaworthy boats. RABITs are deployed when sudden influxes of illegal migrants challenge the capacity of a particular state, and draw upon the standby team of about 450 border guards.

AFSJ Policy Measures

Many of the policy activities entailed by the AFSJ can be identified from examining the evolution of JHA co-operation as well as looking at some of its executive agencies. However, it is worth summarizing them as well as including some of the policy work that has not yet been discussed (see Table 31.2).

Free movement of persons enshrines the right of all EU citizens to travel freely around the member states of the EU and to settle anywhere within the EU. This provision means that no special requirements are needed other than a valid travel document to enter the member state concerned. The same principle is extended to Norway, Iceland, and Liechtenstein (as member states of the European Economic Area; see Chapter 34, p. 539) and to Switzerland on the basis of a bilateral accord. For the Schengen zone states (see above), internal border checks have been abolished. Their abolition has been accompanied by harmonized controls at the external frontiers of the Schengen zone. The SIS offers controls designed to compensate for the loss of border checks. In addition, it facilitates operation of the common policy on short-stay visas for third-country nationals.

The EU member states have committed themselves to a common *immigration and asylum* policy. Large numbers of legal and illegal migrants, as well as asylum seekers, have sought to come to the EU. Asylum is granted to a person who fears persecution for reasons of race, religion, nationality, membership of a particular social group, or

---

Table 31.2 An Overview of the AFSJ

Policy area	EU-level agencies or other bodies involved	'Pioneer groupings'
Free movement	None directly	Schengen zone, including Schengen Information System
Immigration and asylum	Frontex, European Asylum Support Office	Prüm Convention
Judicial co-operation in civil and criminal matters	Eurojust, European Judicial Network	
Police and customs co-operation	Europol, European Police Chiefs' Task Force, European Police College (CEPOL)	Schengen provisions, Prüm Convention
Combating organized crime	Europol, Eurojust	
Combating terrorism	Europol, Eurojust, European Police Chiefs' Task Force	
Combating the drugs trade	Europol, Eurojust	
Combating human trafficking	Europol, Eurojust, Frontex	
Fundamental rights and anti-discrimination	Fundamental Rights Agency	

political opinion and should be in conformity with the international standards set by the **Geneva Convention**. The EU aims to have a fully harmonized system in which applicants for asylum would receive equivalent treatment across member states. Work continues on creating this common system under the 2009–12 Stockholm Programme. At the end of 2009, it was agreed to set up a European Asylum Support Office in 2010, to be located in Malta. Its role is to facilitate co-operation among member states in the implementation of the EU's common asylum system.

The work on immigration is complex. It entails: spelling out who may legally enter the EU, for example as an economic migrant; monitoring illegal immigration and developing an action plan against it; and encouraging policies to enable integration of legitimate immigrants within member states. In May 2009, the EU adopted a so-called 'blue card' visa system to attract young, highly skilled workers to Europe in areas in which their skills are needed. The scheme drew on the US green card system, but the colour was changed to reflect the EU flag. The card will give the recipients a specified set of rights. Danish, British, and Irish opt-outs apply. However, the member states control a key component: determining the numbers of economic migrants who will be allowed to enter their country.

Judicial co-operation in civil and criminal matters has not proceeded as rapidly as with asylum and immigration. Member governments have taken longer to recognize the EU's role in justice matters: hence the intergovernmental processes of the third pillar until implementation of the Lisbon Treaty. Member states have agreed to 'approximate' the definition of, and the level of sanctions for, specific types of offence, in particular those with transnational aspects. Second, mutual recognition of decisions taken by judges in other member states is set to become the cornerstone of judicial co-operation in criminal matters. Finally, the EU is starting to be perceived as an international actor in judicial co-operation.

It was particularly in this part of policy that new momentum was gained following the 11 September 2001 bombings in the United States. This culminated in the best-known development, the European Arrest Warrant (EAW), which has replaced conventional extradition between member states with a judicial procedure (Baker 2009: 842). The broad recognition is that in areas in which cross-border crime takes place it is possible for criminals to exploit differences in criminal justice systems to their advantage. Areas in which the EU has identified this problem as requiring action extend beyond terrorism to include international trafficking (for example, of illegal immigrants or child pornography), financial crime (for example, money laundering), cyber crime, environmental crime, and racism and xenophobia. This area required more intensive work and its transfer to the Union method under the Lisbon Treaty was designed to this end.

Similar principles underpin action in civil law, except that it is usually in recognition of the rights of citizens and companies. For instance, greater mobility has increased the number of international marriages/partnerships and these may result in the need for access to another member state's system of justice, such as over child custody, when a relationship breaks down. Similarly, the increase in cross-border commerce results in the need for access to justice beyond the 'home' member state. As with co-operation on criminal matters, policy making has taken on a new legislative character following implementation of the Lisbon Treaty. The European Judicial Network, which has set up national contact points in each of the member states, is a means of facilitating judicial co-operation and access to justice in other member states. Eurojust is the agency enabling co-operation between prosecuting authorities in the member states.

Police and customs co-operation has become increasingly necessary as a result of European integration itself but also because of globalization and the securitization of home affairs. Police co-operation concentrates on crime prevention, as well as specific tasks on terrorism and combating hooliganism at sport events. Operational co-operation of police forces is the task of Europol, while the European Police Chiefs' Task Force provides a top-level arena for discussion between police forces. CEPOL (the European Police College) was set up as an EU agency in 2005. Its task is to bring together senior police officers from across the EU in a network designed to enable cross-border co-operation in the fight against crime and promoting public security and law and order. It does so specifically by organizing training activities and presenting research findings. Its base is in Bramshill, England, but its activities are held on an EU-wide basis.

More intensive police co-operation can take place under the auspices of Schengen, including the 'hot pursuit' by police authorities of suspected criminals into the territory of a neighbouring Schengen state. Such measures are a logical consequence of removing border controls, otherwise escape across borders would obstruct criminal justice. Nevertheless, 'hot pursuit' is a clear departure from traditional notions of national sovereignty. It also necessitates a strong degree of trust between police forces, possibly including joint patrols or investigation teams in border regions, as well as a likely need for language training. Customs administrations of the member states also contribute to the fight against cross-border crime through the prevention, detection, investigation, and prosecution of illegal movement of goods, the trafficking of prohibited goods, money laundering, and so on.

Combating organized crime, terrorism, drugs, and human trafficking represent four areas of intensive co-operation in which member state police and customs authorities play a key role. In each area, a programme and/or strategy has been agreed. For instance, the fight against organized crime became part of a (Vienna) action plan in 1999; an EU strategy ('the Millennium Strategy') was launched in 2000 and it featured strongly in The Hague Programme of 2004. The fight against terrorism has numerous component parts, but focused around prevention, protection, prosecution, and response. Detailed measures include: analysis of radicalization and disrupting terrorist-related flows of money (prevention); countering chemical and biological threats (protection); information exchange between law-enforcement agencies and retention of telecommunications data (prosecution); and improving 'consequence management' (response). An action plan and strategy exist for combating drugs, together with numerous specific measures.

As can be seen from the above, internal security looms large in many of the EU's policy measures. However, there is more to the 'freedom' component of the AFSJ than free movement. A key contribution comes in the form of the protection of *fundamental rights*, which is closely linked with action taken to *combat discrimination*, such as racism and xenophobia. Another related area is the EU's action on children's rights. These components of AFSJ are not strongly connected with the more security-focused policy activities.

The EU's role in assuring fundamental rights has been far from straightforward. On the one hand, a core of fundamental rights is associated with the 1950 European Convention on Human Rights. The Convention, which all member states have signed, is attached to the Council of Europe (the quite separate European organization, based in Strasbourg; see Chapter 5, p. 84). Under Article 6 TEU, the EU is committed to adhere to its principles. Indeed, following the Lisbon Treaty, the EU is to accede to the Convention in its own right (see Insight 31.6). Principles of non-discrimination were agreed in the Amsterdam Treaty enabling the EU to 'combat discrimination based on sex, racial or ethnic origin, religion or belief, disability, age or sexual orientation' (now in Article 19 TFEU). On the other hand, as Joseph Weiler (1999: 102) notes, 'the definition of fundamental human rights often differs from polity to polity'. Consequently, a few member states have been concerned about the development of the EU's profile on fundamental rights, whilst there have also been substantive issues arising from the jurisprudence of the ECJ.

The most obvious example of the former relates to the UK's unwillingness to allow the Charter of Fundamental Rights of the EU to be given legal status in the Nice Treaty. This issue became contentious again during the protracted negotiations leading to ratification of the Lisbon Treaty. Consequently, whilst the Charter of Fundamental Rights now has the same legal status as the Treaties, its text is still not included in them. Further, the UK, Poland, and the Czech Republic have obtained assurances in Protocols to the Lisbon Treaty that make exceptions to the 'justiciability' of the Charter (in other words, the ability to invoke the Charter in domestic courts). Historically, the German Constitutional Court challenged the primacy of European law until it embodied a set of fundamental rights.

The granting of legal status to the EU Charter of Fundamental Rights, as well as the Lisbon Treaty's provision for the EU to accede to the European Court of Human Rights (ECHR), should place the EU's commitments on these matters beyond doubt. In March

---

Insight 31.6 The EU and Fundamental Rights

(1) The Union recognizes the rights, freedoms, and principles set out in the Charter of Fundamental Rights of the European Union of 7 December 2000, as adapted at Strasbourg, on 12 December 2007, which shall have the same legal value as the Treaties.

The provisions of the Charter shall not extend in any way the competences of the Union as defined in the Treaties.

The rights, freedoms, and principles in the Charter shall be interpreted in accordance with the general provisions in Title VII of the Charter governing its interpretation and application and with due regard to the explanations referred to in the Charter, that set out the sources of those provisions.

(2) The Union shall accede to the European Convention for the Protection of Human Rights and Fundamental Freedoms. Such accession shall not affect the Union's competences as defined in the Treaties.

(3) Fundamental rights, as guaranteed by the European Convention for the Protection of Human Rights and Fundamental Freedoms and as they result from the constitutional traditions common to the Member States, shall constitute general principles of the Union's law.

Source: Article 6 TEU

2007, the EU's Fundamental Rights Agency was established to: collect information and data; provide advice to the European Union and its member states; and promote dialogue with civil society to raise public awareness of fundamental rights. It built on the work of the European Monitoring Centre on Racism and Xenophobia, but the remit was widened to reflect the EU's explicit concern with fundamental rights after 2000.

The EU's engagement with children's rights is underpinned by the Fundamental Charter and a strategy has been developed over recent years. During the negotiation of Romanian accession to the EU, concern was expressed about children's rights in state-run orphanages and improvements were demanded as part of the accession process. This undoubtedly had a feedback effect on internal provisions within the EU and a number of measures have ensued. In its strategic objectives for 2005–09, the Commission (European Commission 2005: 9) stated: 'A particular priority must be effective protection of the rights of children, both against economic exploitation and all forms of abuse, with the Union acting as a beacon to the rest of the world.' A further area in which the EU has taken action on citizen's rights relates to data protection.

Citizenship is the final area of rights-related policy on the part of the EU. The Maastricht Treaty initiated the notion of EU citizenship, which supplements rather than replaces national citizenship of a member state. By developing fundamental rights in EU law and in political declarations, as outlined above, the objective is to flesh out what it means to be an EU citizen. The four specific citizenship rights provided for in the Maastricht Treaty are set out in Insight 31.7.

All of the above have an *enlargement-related* dimension. Accession states have to meet the EU's human rights requirements to secure entry, as the case of children's rights in Romania shows. Equally, they need to demonstrate that they can meet EU standards on such matters as secure external frontiers, standards of justice, and policing systems. Financial assistance and training programmes have been available to accession states to help them to adapt to the *acquis communautaire* in JHA/AFSJ policy.

Insight 31.7 Citizenship of the EU

Citizens of the Union shall enjoy the rights and be subject to the duties provided for in the Treaties. They shall have, inter alia:

(a) the right to move and reside freely within the territory of the Member States;

(b) the right to vote and to stand as candidates in elections to the European Parliament and in municipal elections in their Member State of residence, under the same conditions as nationals of that State;

(c) the right to enjoy, in the territory of a third country in which the Member State of which they are nationals is not represented, the protection of the diplomatic and consular authorities of any Member State on the same conditions as the nationals of that State;

(d) the right to petition the European Parliament, to apply to the European Ombudsman, and to address the institutions and advisory bodies of the Union in any of the Treaty languages and to obtain a reply in the same language.

Source: Article 20 TFEU

Finally, many of the security measures outlined above have an *external dimension* beyond enlargement (Lavenex 2010: 474–5). In this sense, the AFSJ has given a new dimension to the EU's foreign policy. Some of these external activities have already been outlined: the liaison of Europol and Eurojust with US authorities in combating terrorism, for example, and of Frontex with states from which there are significant flows of illegal immigrants. Initially developed in a somewhat ad hoc manner, the Hague Programme called for the development of a strategic approach covering all external aspects of the AFSJ. The document—*A Strategy for the External Dimension of JHA: Global Freedom, Security and Justice*—was adopted by the Council in December 2005 (Council of the EU 2005). It is worth noting the priorities set for 2005–06 by way of illustration of the external dimension of the AFSJ:

- strengthening counter-terrorism co-operation with North Africa;
- improving co-operation on organized crime, corruption, illegal immigration, and counter-terrorism, between the EU, Western Balkans, and relevant countries in the European Neighbourhood;
- increasing EU support to combating drug production in and trafficking from Afghanistan, including transit routes;
- increasing and enhancing dialogue and co-operation on migration issues with countries of origin and transit in Africa;
- implementing with Russia the 'Common Space' of freedom, security, and justice.

These measures added to an existing transatlantic dialogue on security matters with the United States and Canada, work with the Western Balkans on building up institutions to guarantee the rule of law, and developing links with India and China. In addition, there have been strong efforts to integrate the external dimension of the AFSJ with other aspects of the EU's foreign and security policy.

Andrew Geddes (2008: 170–85) outlined the evolution of the external dimension of immigration and asylum policy and highlighted two phases of development. Its initial concern was with enlargement (ahead of the 2004 and 2007 expansions). In a second phase, policy attention shifted to the European 'neighbourhood': an arc of states bounding the EU from Belarus on the north-eastern flank to Morocco on the southern one. In order to try to discourage illegal immigration, various measures have been taken: information campaigns in the sending states; financial aid to try to improve economic conditions in the sending states; the creation of a 'return fund' to repatriate illegal immigrants; and financial support for the integration of third-country nationals in the EU. As Geddes (2008: 184) notes, while it was straightforward to obtain the co-operation of accession states, since the incentive of membership was clear enough, the EU's leverage on other countries addressed by the external dimension of asylum and immigration policy is both reduced and very variable between states.

Explaining the AFSJ

Because of its relatively recent emergence, overarching analytical explanations of the dynamics of JHA/AFSJ policy are not as developed as for other policy sectors. In addition, it is a diverse policy area and brings together scholars of migration studies, criminologists, lawyers, security specialists, and others, but they do not necessarily engage in common debates.

Neofunctionalist accounts, such as exist, emphasize a functional spillover between the lifting of border controls as part of the single-market project (see Boswell 2010: 281–2; Geddes 2006: 455–6). However, there do seem to be some limits to this explanation. Important early developments took place in the Schengen Agreement and not the EU. The murky procedures gave little scope for interest groups to pursue 'political spillover', never mind 'cultivated spillover' from central institutions, since they were absent from Schengen arrangements until communitarization in the late-1990s. A more plausible interpretation in terms of 'institutionalizing European space' is offered by Turnbull and Sandholtz (2001), emphasizing the early (functional) spillover but linking it to external factors (the end of the Cold War) and the advocacy role of Helmut Kohl. However, this analysis only covers the period to mid-1995.

An alternative account of policy dynamics is offered by Virginie Guiraudon (2000). It draws on the public policy literature on 'venue-shopping' and applies it to immigration policy. It is argued that interior and justice ministries sought to escape domestic controls from their respective domestic justice and rights regimes. Anticipating further migratory flows arising from greater openness of borders, they sought increased control through developing new policy arenas with an institutional setting in which their interests would be strengthened. This explanation looks plausible both for the EU and for the 'laboratories' such as Schengen. However, it does not sit well with the way in which it was German Chancellor Kohl and French President Mitterrand who advocated lifting passport controls. They had to put pressure on their interior ministries, who dragged their feet in the early period (Bulmer 2010). Venue-shopping becomes a much more persuasive argument for subsequent developments. The venue-shopping account acknowledges the spillover effects of neo-functionalism but places national actors in a prominent role. However, it does not correspond to intergovernmentalism because the venue-shopping account is about particular ministries trying to escape domestic control, and is thus more differentiated. It aligns better with the broader EU policy pattern identified by Helen Wallace (2005: 87), and termed 'intensive transgovernmentalism'.

A more orthodox intergovernmentalist account of policy appears to have some importance, given that member governments retained the key decisional powers for a significant period (see also Lavenex 2010: 466–7). Moreover, the continued insistence by the UK on retaining border checks is consistent with an emphasis on national government gatekeeping. However, this position has become less plausible since the communitarization of immigration and asylum policy after Amsterdam and of PJCCM after Lisbon. Multi-level governance has some limited application, but only in those states where policies relating to freedom, security, and justice straddle different levels of governance: notably, in a federal system such as Germany or devolved systems such as Spain or the UK. In Britain, to take a specific instance, the distinctive system of Scots law has to be taken into account in judicial co-operation.

Finally, a persuasive interpretation has been offered by Stephan Stetter (2000). While he acknowledged that spillover effects from the single market and from migratory pressures had some explanatory value, he suggested that 'they do not explain the specific institutions and methods which have been established at the EU level to deal with this policy area' (Stetter 2000: 81). Instead, his explanation builds on regulation and **principal–agent theories**. His argument, which is applied to immigration policy, is that the early efforts at international intergovernmental co-operation were not effective. Putting the Schengen and Dublin Conventions *into effect* was protracted. Consequently, the EU's third pillar offered a potential escape from this problem but the member governments constantly had to balance the potentially more efficient nature of delegated policy against the possible loss of domestic control. For most member states, the third pillar was ineffective as a solution to migration policy problems owing to the lack of clear objectives, timetable, and the weak legal instruments. This failure therefore led to the member states communitarizing the policy subject to a five-year transition period in which the Commission was effectively 'on probation' to ensure that control of policy was not being lost. It had become clear, as Stetter (2000: 96) puts it, that 'only Community instruments and methods could provide a guarantee that [the Amsterdam Treaty's AFSJ] objectives could be achieved'. Hence key regulatory authority has been delegated to EU institutions—in line with principal–agent theory—to tackle the shortcomings of the original, intergovernmental policy framework.

Following the Lisbon Treaty, this pattern of communitarization was repeated for the remainder of the third pillar. Furthermore, the delegation of authority moved beyond the Commission to the array of agencies described above (Table 31.1). These developments appear to strengthen Stetter's interpretation.

The breadth and diversity of the policy are having the effect of fragmenting its study (Boswell 2010: 278). This situation is especially unfortunate in light of the policy area having been reassembled by the Lisbon Treaty into the AFSJ. A number of other policy debates are therefore worth reviewing.

An early debate emerged from the tension that exists in the area of free movement and immigration/asylum. This tension centres on the reduction of the *internal* controls on intra-EU migration and the heightening of controls towards third-country nationals. In particular, refugee rights seemed to suffer. A debate ensued about whether the EU was becoming 'fortress Europe', although the terminology was criticized by some as misleading since large numbers of visitors enter the EU, as do legal migrants especially where skills are lacking (see Geddes 2008: 28–31).

The 'fortress Europe' debate was supplanted by a wider debate on 'securitization', which can be applied not only to immigration but also to the AFSJ in general (Boswell 2010: 280). The debate here is whether policy is becoming dominated by security concerns to the cost of freedom and especially justice. Exponents of the securitization literature emphasize how experts in home affairs have played upon popular insecurity to extend new controls, such as over immigration (see, for instance, Huysmans 2006). There is undoubtedly a tension between freedom and justice, on the one hand, and security, on the other, in AFSJ policy generally (see Baker 2009). It is not confined to academic debates, either. Thus, the operation of the 2010 team of Commissioners is worth monitoring. One Commissioner (Viviane Reding) was given responsibility for Justice, Fundamental Rights, and Citizenship; another (Cecilia Malmström) was made responsible for Home Affairs. Hence the former, whose portfolio is more freedom-oriented, faces another Commissioner with a more security-oriented one.

A third tension exists between a common EU approach and the practice of so-called 'pioneer groups' moving ahead more quickly. The Schengen laboratory is the most obvious example. However, there are other illustrations. An inner group of, initially, five member states (France, Germany, Italy, Spain, and the UK) has acted as agenda-setter within JHA/AFSJ policy. This grouping—a French initiative—was expanded to six (the 'G6') with the 2004 enlargement by including Poland. A further example more along the lines of Schengen is the Prüm Convention. Initiated by the German government, the convention was designed to facilitate the exchange of data (including access to other signatories' DNA databases) for crime prevention and prosecution purposes. Signed by seven EU states on 27 May 2005, it seemed designed to circumvent the cumbersome nature of JHA policy making, in which unanimity prevailed. However, it included explicit provision for later adoption by the EU, which duly occurred, albeit with some controversial provisions excluded, in the 2007 German presidency. As Daniela Kietz and Andreas Maurer (2007) put it:

> Modes of cooperation like Prüm can . . . be interpreted as the result of the core group of national internal security actors, which dominate proceedings, [seeking] to enlarge their room for manoeuvre and retain control over policy-making by minimising the influence of the supranational institutions, national veto-players and also other member states.

In view of the strengthened powers of the Commission and the EP on PJCCM arising from the Lisbon Treaty, it becomes clear what is at stake with such pioneer groups. Are they a way of facilitating policy making in an EU of twenty-seven, in which gaining unanimity (until 2015) is difficult to achieve, especially with the new emergency brake procedure? Or are they a way of bypassing parliamentary scrutiny and the Commission's concern with justice and liberty as a means of advancing a security-focused policy agenda?

CONCLUSION

The development of the AFSJ has been a very significant development in European integration. Starting from modest beginnings and in large part outside the EC itself, the policy area was established as an intergovernmental pillar and then communitarized over a staged process. The development is striking given that JHA—not least the issue of border control—have traditionally been seen as key powers of the nation state. It is not surprising that these areas of policy did not reach the EU agenda until after many others. However, it is also clear that there was some linkage arising from the dismantling of barriers to trade as part of the single market.

The analysis of JHA/AFSJ policy in general terms has largely not been oriented around the theoretical debates examined in this volume. Nevertheless, it is clear that these debates are relevant, since policy dynamics have tended to be either functional or political. Member governments have been extremely reluctant to delegate their sovereign powers unless there is a clear demonstration that an issue cannot be addressed without co-operation amongst the EU states. UK governments have been especially hesitant; passport controls seem to hold a symbolic importance, even though they were not needed for travel to/from Ireland. Despite these concerns, the delegation of tasks to the EU has accelerated. The evidence is clear from: the strengthening of the Commission; the use of the co-decision process in the EP; the growing powers of the

ECJ; the emergence of AFSJ-related interest groups such as refugee non-governmental organizations (NGOs); the importance of groups of experts such as the European Police Chiefs' Task Force; and the growth of EU agencies.

To be sure, there remain deficiencies in putting policies into action, especially in PJCCM. And it should be pointed out the EU has no authority to intervene in the internal security of its member states. Nevertheless, driven in large part by new security challenges, the pace of change has been quite rapid. Although progress to creating the AFSJ has often been criticized as slow, when developments are looked at from a wider perspective—for instance, through comparison with foreign and security policy, which can be traced back to 1970—it becomes clear that significant steps have been taken. The Stockholm Programme, agreed at the European Council in December 2009, and the implementation of the Lisbon Treaty provisions, also in December 2009, suggested the dynamism was not going to let up. Nevertheless, action at the EU level is largely dependent on implementation by member state authorities. This aspect is likely to come increasingly under the spotlight.

KEY POINTS

History

- JHA was not envisaged in the founding Treaties.
- The initial steps in co-operation were taken in diverse forums ('laboratories'), such as the Council of Europe, Trevi, and Schengen.
- The free movement of goods and people under the SEA increased the number of problems that demanded a collective policy response.
- Globalization and changes in the international system posed new security threats. Security became more widely defined and more politically salient.
- In the TEU, JHA was made a 'third pillar' of the EU. The institutional arrangements were a compromise between those who wanted closer co-operation and those who wanted to retain more national control.
- The Amsterdam Treaty committed the EU to creating an area of freedom, security, and justice. Visa, asylum, and immigration policies were transferred to the first pillar and came under QMV. Pillar 3 became PJCCM. Schengen was incorporated into the EU.
- At Nice in 2000, the heads of government solemnly declared their commitment to a Charter of Fundamental Rights.

Lisbon Treaty

- Lisbon abolished the third pillar and incorporated PJCCM into a Title on the Area of Freedom, Security, and Justice.
- In line with broader trends in public administration, new policy tasks have been delegated to expert bodies and new technology has been deployed.
- Important institutional developments include the Schengen Information System, Europol, Eurojust, and Frontex.

Area of Freedom, Security, and Justice

- Creating an AFSJ is now a central objective of the EU.

- The AFSJ involves: free movement of persons; common immigration and asylum policies; judicial co-operation in civil and criminal matters; police and customs co-operation; combating organized crime, terrorism, drugs, and human trafficking; the protection of fundamental rights; action to avoid unjust discrimination; and citizenship.

- Many of these activities have implications for the enlargement process and have a wider international dimension.

Explaining the AFSJ

- Neofunctionalist explanations of JHA stress spillover, but its explanatory value is limited.

- Related analyses invoke the concepts of 'institutionalizing European space' and 'venue-shopping'.

- Intergovernmental explanations were plausible for early developments, but less so with the communitarization of key JHA policies.

- Regulatory analysis and principal–agent theory have also been used to explain aspects of JHA.

- JHA is very broad in scope and has been studied independently by scholars from different disciplines, leading to fragmentation.

- Debates have emerged about 'fortress Europe', 'securitization', and the future role of 'pioneer groups'.

FURTHER READING

Useful analysis of the evolution of this policy area is offered by: **S. Lavenex**, 'Justice and Home Affairs: Communitarization with Hesitation', in **H. Wallace, M. Pollack, and A. Young (eds)**, *Policy-Making in the European Union*, 6th edn (Oxford: Oxford University Press, 2010), 458–77; **J. Monar**, 'The Dynamics of Justice and Home Affairs: Laboratories, Driving Factors and Costs', *Journal of Common Market Studies*, 39 (2001): 747–64; and **U. Uçarer**, 'Justice and Home Affairs', in **M. Cini and N. Pérez-Solórzano Borragán (eds)**, *European Union Politics*, 3rd edn (Oxford: Oxford University Press, 2010), 306–23.

For reviews of the dynamics of the policy area, see: **C. Boswell**, 'Justice and Home Affairs', in **M. Egan, N. Nugent, and W. Paterson (eds)**, *Research Agendas in EU Studies: Stalking the Elephant* (Basingstoke: Palgrave Macmillan, 2010), 278–304; and **A. Geddes**, 'The Politics of European Union Domestic Order', in **K. E. Jørgensen, M. Pollack, and B. Rosamond (eds)**, *Handbook of European Union Politics* (London: Sage Publications, 2006), 449–62. A useful summary of annual policy developments is provided by **Jörg Monar** in the *Journal of Common Market Studies'* special Annual Review edition: for example, 'Justice and Home Affairs', *Journal of Common Market Studies: Annual Review*, 47 (2009): 151–70.

 online resource centre

Visit the Online Resource Centre that accompanies this book for links to more information on Justice and Home Affairs: www.oxfordtextbooks.co.uk/orc.bache3e/

Chapter 32
Trade and Development Aid

Chapter Overview

Up to now, this part of the book has dealt primarily with the internal policies of the European Union (EU). In this chapter and the next, the focus shifts to policies that concern the relations of the EU with the rest of the world. This chapter looks at the external trade relations of the EU in the context of the wider framework of global trade agreements, and at its policies on development aid, particularly with the African, Caribbean, and Pacific (ACP) states. It also looks at the combination of trade and aid policies towards the near neighbours of the EU in the rest of Europe and in North Africa. From this examination of policy, it becomes clear that too sharp a distinction cannot be drawn between economic and political aspects of the external relations of the EU.

Free trade and preferential trade agreements are a major element in EU foreign policy and are at the forefront of EU policy towards developing countries and neighbouring countries in Europe.

(Brenton and Manchin 2002: 1)

History

From the outset, the European Economic Community (EEC) aimed to become a major international economic actor. Its main pattern of bilateral and multilateral trade relations was structured through the international institutions that were set up after the Second World War to promote the emergence of the post-war trading system. It also pursued an active policy of cultivating special relations with former European colonies, which sometimes provided a tension with its commitments under the wider trading arrangements. More recently, the EU became concerned to use economic and trade instruments to help to stabilize the economies of its near neighbours in other parts of Europe and in North Africa.

The International Context for EU Policy

When the EEC came into existence, international economic relations were governed by the agreements reached at negotiations in **Bretton Woods**, New Hampshire, in 1944. These agreements set up several institutions designed to help an international economic system to emerge. At the heart of the structure was a monetary system nominally based on gold, but in practice with the US dollar as the anchor. To assist the development of states' economies, the **International Bank for Reconstruction and Development (IBRD)**, or **World Bank**, was created. To help states that got into temporary difficulties with their balance of payments, the **International Monetary Fund (IMF)** was set up. There was also intended to be an International Trade Organization (ITO), to facilitate the gradual introduction of global free trade agreements, and to regulate trade disputes between states. However, the US Congress would not agree to the ITO, so instead a series of intergovernmental negotiations were initiated, known as the **General Agreement on Tariffs and Trade (GATT)**.

One important feature of the GATT framework was that the EEC, after its formation, had a single representative. This followed from the commitment in the Treaty of Rome to have a common commercial policy that was solely a Community competence (Article 113, now Article 207 TFEU).

Within the GATT framework, a key concept was that of 'most favoured nation' (MFN) treatment. This meant that states would not negotiate more favourable deals with some partners than they were prepared to offer to all of the participants in GATT. Exceptions were allowed to the rule, though, and the EEC received special dispensation from the MFN principle to allow it to dismantle tariffs on internal trade between the member states, because there was provision in the rules to allow the creation of **customs unions** and **free trade areas** that might speed up the process of dismantling barriers to free trade globally. Another area in which the EEC concluded preferential trading deals was in relation to the former colonies of the member states. There were also special agreements with prospective future members of the EEC. These arrangements were not uncontroversial, though, and they became more liable to challenge when the GATT was superseded by the World Trade Organization (WTO) in 1995.

The GATT was a weak organization. It was never intended to stand alone, and only became the arbiter of international trade relations because the ITO failed to appear. Although the GATT had a procedure for resolving disputes, it was easy for a state that was losing a case to block a ruling against it. The arrangements began to collapse in the late 1970s and 1980s with the growth of protectionism in the face of a global economic downturn. In response, GATT launched a marathon round of trade negotiations in 1986, known as the Uruguay Round. The negotiations were scheduled to be completed by 1990, but stretched out until 1994. The difficulty of reaching agreement, and the prospect of having to enforce a much more complex package of arrangements, led to the creation of the WTO, a far stronger body than GATT.

Development Policy

One area of considerable concern to the original EEC was its relations with ex-colonies. When the Treaty of Rome was signed in 1957, the vast majority of independent countries that eventually became the ACP group remained the responsibility of colonial powers. In 1956, France, which of the original EEC member states had the largest number of colonies, requested that its overseas territories be granted associated status with the proposed EEC.

Relations were initially dealt with in an Implementing Convention, which was replaced in July 1963 by the Yaoundé Convention, named after the capital of Cameroon, where it was signed. Both these instruments had the objective of gradually moving towards a free trade area between the EEC and the former French colonies, and there was a European Development Fund (EDF) for the purpose of granting EC financial aid to the associated countries and territories to promote their social and economic development (Frey-Wouters 1980: 14).

Neither the Implementing Convention nor the Yaoundé agreements marked a serious attempt to break with the traditional pattern of relations between Europe and the developing world. A. H. Jamal, a former Tanzanian Minister of Communications, described the Yaoundé Convention as providing 'an institutional dependence on the part of some African countries on one particular metropolitan power—France' (Jamal 1979: 134), and the EDFs under the Implementing Convention and Yaoundé were described by another commentator as 'basically a device to offload the costs of French colonial mercantilism on the EEC in return for other EEC states receiving access to their markets and sources of supply' (Green 1976: 50).

Many hoped that the first Lomé agreement would mark a turning point in these relations. Lomé was negotiated in the early 1970s as a result of the accession of Britain to the EC. Like France, Britain was a former imperial power, and the addition of its former colonies brought to forty-six the number of associated states. The Lomé agreement was received by the ACP states more enthusiastically than its predecessors had been. As one observer put it:

> When Lomé 1 was signed, both sides claimed that it was qualitatively different from anything that had gone before; a contract between equal partners and a step towards a New International Economic Order.

(Stevens 1984: 1)

Revised Lomé agreements were reached in the late 1970s and the 1980s. In most respects, the terms of the subsequent Lomé Conventions were disappointing. Although aid was increased in each agreement, it was not by enough to take account of the combined effects of increases in inflation and in population. When inflation and population growth were taken into account, the period leading up to Lomé 3 (1976–85) saw a fall in European Community (EC) real *per capita* transfers to ACP states of 40 per cent (Hewitt 1989: 291).

In the period 1980–87, Africa's *per capita* gross domestic product (GDP) fell by an average of 2.6 per cent and its returns on investment were substantially down (Glaser 1990: 26). This meant that, on top of the unfulfilled hopes of various aid schemes, many ACP countries were under intense pressure to repay loans. By 1983, the IMF and the World Bank were implementing stabilization and structural adjustment programmes in those countries, and the EC response to ACP problems had to be implemented in close co-ordination with these institutions. This situation placed the IMF in the driving seat 'with its own short-run conditions overwhelming those of all the other partners' (Hewitt 1989: 296).

Thus, by the late 1980s, ACP states believed that Lomé seriously neglected their main concerns: the impossibility of servicing debt; and the increasing demands of the World Bank and the IMF for changes in economic and social policies. By the early 1990s, to these concerns were added concerns over the effect of the completion of the single European market and over the aid demands on the EC from the former Communist countries of eastern Europe.

Relations with Near Neighbours

With the collapse of communism, the EU faced the problem of instability among its near neighbours. At the end of the Cold War, the EC signed technical co-operation agreements with the central and eastern European countries (CEECs). These were subsequently replaced with 'Europe Agreements': Association Agreements that fell short of envisaging full membership. Then, in June 1993, the Copenhagen European Council accepted the legitimacy of the aspirations of the newly independent states to become members. On 1 May 2004, eight CEECs—the Czech Republic, Estonia, Hungary, Latvia, Lithuania, Poland, Slovakia, and Slovenia, together with Cyprus and Malta—became members of the EU. In 2007, Bulgaria and Romania also became members.

In the Balkans, as part of its stability pact for south-eastern Europe, the EU agreed a Memorandum of Understanding (MoU) on Trade Liberalization and Facilitation with Albania, Bosnia and Herzegovina, Croatia, the Federal Republic of Yugoslavia (Serbia and Montenegro), and the former Yugoslav Republic of Macedonia. This was the first stage in what became known as the Stabilization and Association Process (SAP). The next stage was that once states were considered to have made sufficient progress in political and economic reform, and in building administrative capacity, they would be offered a Stabilization and Association Agreement (SAA) with the EU, to help them to prepare for possible full membership.

While the governments of France and the southern member states could see the arguments for enlargement to the east, and even accepted them, they were concerned that the problems of the Mediterranean, which affected them more than did instability in the east, would be relegated to a secondary issue. Instability in North Africa, particularly a civil war in Algeria, was already having an impact on them in the form of refugees, and in threats to their companies' investments in the region.

Their concern that attention would be diverted from the problems of the Mediterranean was recognized by the German government when it held the presidency of the EU in the second half of 1994. Agreement was reached at the Essen meeting of the European Council in December 1994 to launch an initiative on North Africa and the Middle East. This assumed more tangible form during 1995 under the successive French and Spanish presidencies, culminating in a major conference in Barcelona on 23–29 November 1995 involving the EU member states, the Maghreb states (Algeria, Morocco, and Tunisia), Israel, Jordan, Lebanon, Syria, Turkey, Cyprus, and Malta. From this emerged the Euro-Med Partnership Agreement (see below).

External Trade Policy

The EU is the world's largest trading entity. In 2006, it accounted for 17.1 per cent of global trade in goods (Table 32.1), and it regularly accounts for around 20 per cent of total world trade, including services (Table 32.2). This makes trade policy central to its external activities.

The Common Commercial Policy

In the negotiation of multilateral and bilateral trade agreements, the EU operates under the rules of its own common commercial policy. Article 207 TFEU gives the EU exclusive competence in commercial policy, including external trade negotiations. However, this is an EU competence, which is not the same as a Commission competence. Before it can even enter into trade negotiations, the Commission has to get the agreement of the Council of Ministers on a negotiating mandate. The negotiations are then to be conducted 'in consultation with a special committee appointed by the Council' (Article 207(3) TFEU). Because the corresponding Article in the Treaty of Rome was numbered 113, this Committee was originally known as the Article 113 Committee. Following the renumbering of the Treaty Articles that took effect in 1999, until the coming into force of the Lisbon Treaty in December 2009, the Committee was known as the Article 133 Committee. It consists of senior civil servants of the member states who monitor the position taken by the Commission at every stage of trade negotiations to ensure that it is in line with the negotiating mandate laid down by the Council of Ministers. The senior committee meets monthly throughout the year, and there are weekly meetings of deputies. Once an agreement has been reached in the negotiations, it has to be ratified by the member states meeting in full Council, using **qualified majority voting (QMV)**.

For a long time, not only was the Commission bound by the mandate and closely monitored in trade negotiations, but also the EC/EU did not even have formal full competence except for trade in goods. Until the Lisbon Treaty, trade in services and in intellectual products were not included. Originally, this was because they were not the subjects of trade negotiations when the Treaty of Rome was drawn up. In 1994, the European Court of Justice (ECJ) ruled that the EU did not have sole competence in negotiations on such matters, but shared the competence with the member states. In

---

Table 32.1 Global Trade in Goods 2006

European Union	17.1%
United States	16.0%
China	9.6%
Japan	6.6%
Others	50.6%

Source: **http://ec.europa.eu**, © European Union, 1995–2010

Table 32.2 **EU 15/25 World Market Share 1996–2004, in Value and Volume Terms**

Value terms

Exporter	1996	2004
EU25	19.8	21.0
EU15	18.8	20.3

Volume terms

Exporter	1996	2004
EU25	19.2	17.5
EU15	18.6	16.7

Source: Adapted from European Commission (2008: Table 1, p. 11); **http://ec.europa.eu**, © European Union, 1995–2010

September 1996, the Commission asked the Council of Ministers to extend its remit to these sectors, but met with a cool response.

Young (2000: 101) suggested three considerations that made the member states, and especially the larger of them, reluctant to extend competence in these new trade issues to the EU: the new issues are more sensitive domestically than trade in services; some member states do not trust the Commission to represent their interests in these areas; and if competence were ceded to the EU, where common agreement was blocked by a coalition of unwilling member states, there would be no possibility of those states that wanted to go further in liberalizing such areas concluding agreements independently of the EU.

In the Treaty of Amsterdam, the member states inserted a clause that allowed them to give the Commission full negotiating responsibility in these sectors for specific future negotiations, without further change to the Treaties, but only if they were unanimous in agreeing to do so. Eventually, they were defined as areas of exclusive EU competence in the Lisbon Treaty, but unanimity remains the voting rule in the Council for agreements in the field of trade in services and the commercial aspects of intellectual property 'where such agreements include provisions for which unanimity is required for the adoption of internal rules', and in the field of trade in cultural and audiovisual services 'where these agreements risk prejudicing the Union's cultural and linguistic diversity' (Article 207(4) TFEU).

Another set of instruments of the common commercial policy are those designed to protect the EU from unfair trade practices by non-members. These instruments include restrictions that can be imposed where non-members are suspected of dumping produce on the EU market at less than the cost of production, and similar measures to counter unfair subsidies. On these sorts of issue, though, the EU prefers, wherever possible, to work through the WTO.

It is not always easy for the member states to reach common positions on external trade policy. For example, in 1997, there was internal dispute over the imposition of anti-dumping measures against imports of unbleached cotton cloth. (Insight 32.1). The divisions between member states in this case illustrated two aspects of the difficulty in reaching common positions: there was a straight division on the basis of national economic interest, and a more general issue about free trade versus managed trade. Among the EU 15 (that is, prior to the Eastern enlargement), generally the northern member states were more in favour of liberalization, while suspicions of market opening were felt most strongly in the southern member states. France has had particular difficulties with the idea of unmanaged global free trade.

Despite such difficulties, the thrust of EC commercial policy has been consistently in the direction of free trade. In the Doha Round of trade negotiations, which began in 2001, the EU's negotiating position with respect to traditional trade policy was described by Young (2007: 798) as 'aggressive, with a heavy emphasis on increasing market access in non-agricultural products, … rather than a preoccupation with protecting European industrial sectors'.

Disputes within the World Trade Organization

Partly because of the increased complexity of the rules, and partly because of the advent of more effective machinery, recourse to dispute panels has increased considerably under the WTO, averaging forty disputes a year as compared to six per year under the GATT procedures (McQueen 1998: 436). This has affected the EU because of increased challenges to its practices, particularly from the United States.

Since the WTO began operation in January 1995, the United States and the EU have struggled to dominate the procedures and the agenda, or at least to ensure that the other does not dominate. Each side has brought complaints against the other.

In 1998, a fierce dispute blew up over the EU's banana regime (Insight 32.2), and in 1999, two issues arose about the application of biotechnology to agricultural produce (Insight 32.3). In 1998, the EU launched its own WTO appeal against the foreign sales corporation (FSC) provisions of US tax law (Insight 32.4).

The result of these moves and counter-moves was that the United States and the EU entered the twenty-first century each armed with the right to impose WTO-approved

495

Insight 32.2 The WTO Dispute over the EU Banana Regime

This was part of the Lomé Agreements with former French and British colonies. It gave preferential access to the EU market for bananas grown in those Caribbean and Pacific states that were parties to the agreement. The United States objected to the discrimination against bananas produced in Latin America, mainly by US-owned companies. Eventually, in April 1999, the WTO did authorize the imposition of sanctions by the United States, although at a much-reduced level from those originally proposed. The whole issue generated a surprising amount of bitterness and heat considering that it concerned a product that was grown in neither the EU nor the United States. It was eventually settled in December 2009 by an agreement under which the EU would reduce its tariffs on imported bananas progressively over seven years, and the United States and banana-producing countries from Latin America agreed to drop litigation against the EU.

---

sanctions on the other. Further tensions emerged over accusations and counter-accusations of illegal subsidies by both sides to their major producers of civil aircraft (Airbus and Boeing). The whole situation held the potential to develop into a trade war, which would have benefited neither party. Perhaps because of the awareness of both sides of the potential for damage to themselves as well as to the global trading system, restraint has been shown in the application of sanctions.

Insight 32.3 Two WTO Disputes over the Application of Biotechnology to Foodstuffs

In 1999, the United States won a complaint to the WTO against a ban by the EU on the import of hormone-treated beef. The ban reflected the strong prejudice of EU consumers against meat that contained hormones, and was first imposed in 1987. The United States maintained that this action was against WTO rules because there was no scientific evidence that there was any risk to human health from eating such meat. The EU insisted that it wanted to complete its own scientific tests before agreeing to lift the ban. Early in 1999, the WTO ruled against the EU, and the United States said that it would impose retaliatory sanctions unless the ban was lifted, but the EU refused to lift the ban in the face of intense consumer opposition. It did offer to allow the import of hormone-treated beef if it was clearly labelled as such, but the United States rejected this compromise because it said that the labelling itself implied that there was something wrong with the beef.

Also in 1999, the EU placed an effective moratorium on the granting of licences for genetically modified (GM) crops. This move was attacked by the United States as imposing a non-tariff barrier on agricultural trade. In 2001, the Commission proposed to introduce rules on the labelling of foodstuffs that contained GM crops, and a requirement that the origins of foodstuffs be traceable back to the crops from which they were produced. The United States considered these to be unreasonable requirements that would probably be impossible to implement, and would certainly be very costly, eliminating any advantage that US farmers gained from adopting the new technology, and requested a WTO panel on the issue.

Insight 32.4 The WTO Dispute over the US Foreign Sales Corporation Tax Provisions

The FSC came into effect in 1984, and allowed US corporations to claim exemption on between 15 and 30 per cent of their earnings from exports. The EU maintained that this amounted to an export subsidy in breach of WTO rules. The United States considered that the appeal was simply EU retaliation against its appeals on bananas and beef, pointing out that it had taken the EU fourteen years to get round to protesting about the FSC, and that there was no evidence of pressure on the Commission from European businesses for the complaint to be made at this time (Ahearn 2002: 4). However, in October 1999, a WTO disputes panel found in favour of the EU, and the United States was told to come into compliance with its WTO obligations by October 2000. In November 2000, the FSC was repealed and replaced by the Extraterritorial Income (ERI) provisions. This allowed tax breaks up to the same amount to US corporations on all foreign earnings, including their earnings from foreign investments. By extending the provision beyond export earnings in this way, Congress hoped to redefine the tax provision. Predictably, the EU appealed and the WTO ruled against the ERI, and against the counter-appeal from the Bush Administration (Ahearn 2002: 5). In August 2002, the WTO disputes panel ruled that the EU could impose up to US$4 billion of sanctions in retaliation.

Relations with the African, Caribbean, and Pacific States

The original ACP states were all former colonies of one or other of the member states of the EU, although as the Lomé Convention was regularly updated, other states that had never been colonies of EU members joined. When the Cotonou Agreement was signed in June 2000, more ACP states joined, bringing the total to eighty (Table 32.3, p. 498).

The Cotonou Agreement

Negotiations on what became Cotonou followed a Commission 'Green Paper' highlighting the ongoing problems of ACP countries (European Commission 1996c). The Green Paper identified two main reasons why the Lomé pattern could not continue, as follows.

- The preferences under Lomé were becoming less valuable as the liberalization of global trade proceeded; this was evidenced by a decline in the ACP share of the EU market.

- Lomé was incompatible with WTO rules. Although various waivers had been granted, the rules were quite clear. Article 1 of the WTO Charter requires participants not to discriminate between other WTO members in trade concessions. Exceptions are allowed to this rule for less developed countries (LDCs), but the concessions must apply to all LDCs. There were two problems about the compatibility of Lomé with these WTO rules: first, many of the ACP states covered by Lomé were not classified as LDCs by the WTO; second, there were nine LDCs that were not included in Lomé.

Table 32.3 The ACP States

African States

Angola, Benin, Botswana, Burkina Faso, Burundi, Cameroon, Cape Verde, Central African Republic, Chad, Comoros, Congo (Republic of), Congo (Democratic Republic of), Djibouti, Equatorial Guinea, Eritrea, Ethiopia, Gabon, Gambia, Ghana, Guinea, Guinea-Bissau, Ivory Coast, Kenya, Lesotho, Liberia, Madagascar, Malawi, Mali, Mauritania, Mauritius, Mozambique, Namibia, Niger, Nigeria, Rwanda, Sao Tome and Principe, Senegal, Seychelles, Sierra Leone, Somalia, South Africa, Sudan, Swaziland, Tanzania, Togo, Uganda, Zaire, Zambia, Zimbabwe

Caribbean States

Antigua and Barbuda, Bahamas, Barbados, Belize, Cuba, Dominica, Dominican Republic, Grenada, Guyana, Haiti, Jamaica, St Kitts and Nevis, St Lucia, St Vincent and the Grenadines, Suriname, Trinidad and Tobago

Pacific States

Cook Islands, Federated States of Micronesia, Fiji, Kiribati, Marshall Islands, Nauru, Niue, Palau, Papua New Guinea, Solomon Islands, Timor-Leste, Tonga, Tuvalu, Vanuatu, Western Samoa.

In response to these problems with the existing arrangements, the Commission proposed dividing the ACP states into LDCs, which could choose to continue to receive non-reciprocal trade concessions that would also be offered to the nine LDC states that had previously been excluded, and the non-LDCs, which would be offered Economic Partnership Agreements (EPAs). The EPAs would involve reciprocity, so the ACP states would have to offer free access to EU goods. To be WTO-compatible, they would also have to cover 'substantially all' trade, which was generally interpreted as 90 per cent of products, so agricultural produce that had been excluded from Lomé to protect areas that were adjudged 'sensitive' by EU member states would have to be included. The EU agreed that it would conclude such agreements either with individual states or regional groupings, but indicated a strong preference for Regional Economic Partnership Agreements (REPAs).

The Cotonou agreement covered a twenty-year period, allowing for a revision every five years. Financial allocations would also be made on a five-yearly basis. Amendments to the agreement would be decided by a joint ACP–EC Council of Ministers, which would normally meet on an annual basis. The agreement placed emphasis on dialogue between the EU and recipient states. Clarity was given to the partnership principle, so that it would 'encourage the integration of all sectors of society, including the private sector and civil society organisations' (European Commission 2000: Article 2). In the first five-year period, the Agreement provided 13.5 billion European currency units (ecus) for development projects. Other objectives included: the encouragement of equality between men and women at every level—political, social, and economic—and the promotion of sustainable management of the environment and of natural resources. The most significant change from Lomé, though, was the gradual replacement of the system of trade preferences by a series of new economic partnerships based on the progressive and reciprocal removal of trade barriers (European Commission 2000: Ch. 2, Articles 36–8).

Relations with Near Neighbours

As the EU does not cover the whole of Europe, various economic arrangements have been made with other European states, and special relationships have also been cultivated with the states on the other side of the Mediterranean Sea. The most important reason for the conclusion of these agreements has been to provide a degree of stability amongst the near neighbours of the EU.

Relations with Other European States

Because many European states wish to become members of the EU, Association Agreements have been traditionally the most common type of arrangement. They are in effect pre-accession agreements with states that want to become full members of the EU. The agreements involve a variety of trade concessions by the EU, with partial reciprocation by the other parties. One of the earliest such agreements was with Turkey in 1973. In recognition of the disappointment of Turkey at not being treated as a candidate for membership of the EU in the enlargement round that ended in 2004, in 1996, the Association Agreement with it was extended into a special customs union.

The Euro-Med Agreements

Following on from the 1995 Barcelona Conference, the EU developed the concept of a Euro-Mediterranean ('Euro-Med') Partnership. Essential components of the concept were Euro-Med Association Agreements. These were bilateral agreements that varied in detail, but had certain common features, including:

- political dialogue;
- respect for human rights and democracy;
- WTO-compatible free trade, to be implemented in stages over twelve years;
- provisions relating to intellectual property, services, **public procurement**, competition rules, state aids, and monopolies;
- economic co-operation;
- co-operation on social affairs and migration;
- cultural co-operation.

The process was relaunched as the Union for the Mediterranean at the Paris Summit for the Mediterranean in July 2008, and new objectives were added to those above:

- the de-pollution of the Mediterranean Sea;
- the establishment of maritime and land highways;
- civil protection initiatives to combat natural and man-made disasters;
- a Mediterranean solar energy plan;
- the inauguration of the Euro-Mediterranean University in Slovenia;
- the Mediterranean Business Development Initiative focusing on small and medium-sized enterprises.

In 2009, there were seventeen non-EU states involved in the process: Albania; Algeria; Bosnia and Herzegovina; Croatia; Egypt; Israel; Jordan; Lebanon; Libya; Mauritania; Monaco; Montenegro; Morocco; the Occupied Palestinian Territories; Syria; Tunisia; Turkey.

The European Neighbourhood Policy

In 2004, the relations of the EU with neighbouring states were brought together under the European Neighbourhood Policy (ENP). Its objectives were: to share the benefits of the 2004 enlargement with neighbouring countries without offering the perspective of membership, and so to prevent the emergence of stark dividing lines between EU and non-EU states; and to build security in the area surrounding the EU. Although the ENP is not a purely economic arrangement, the provision of financial assistance and economic co-operation, including access for the neighbouring states to the EU's internal market, are central to its operation.

The neighbouring countries covered by the ENP are those to the south and to the east. To the south, the ENP incorporates the Euro-Med Agreements and embraces all of the states that were already part of that process. To the east, it covers Armenia, Azerbaijan, Belarus, Georgia, Moldova, and the Ukraine. It does not cover states to the east that already have a prospect of membership—Turkey, and the Western Balkan states of Croatia, Serbia, Montenegro, Bosnia-Herzegovina, Albania, and the former Yugoslav Republic of Macedonia. Nor does it cover Russia, although it has been agreed between the EU and Russia that their mutual relations will be developed in consistency with the ENP, and Russia will benefit from the European Neighbourhood and Partnership Instrument (ENPI).

In line with the objective of avoiding stark dividing lines between the EU and its neighbours, it was intended from the outset that the ENPI would have a specific focus on cross-border co-operation and intra-regional co-operation. The principles used in the management of the ENPI are those that were pioneered in the management of the structural funds for regional development in the EU: multi-annual programming, partnership, and co-financing (Chapter 29, pp. 426–7).

Throughout the political and economic dialogue with neighbouring states, the emphasis has been on the development of the rule of law, good governance, respect for human rights—including minority rights—the promotion of good-neighbourly relations, and the principles of the market economy and sustainable development.

Explaining Trade and Development Aid Policies

Theoretical explanations of the external trade and development aid policies of the EU have focused on the politics of formulating a common commercial policy and on the relations of the EU with the ACP states. In both cases, use has been made of the idea of a 'multi-level game', derived from Robert Putnam's concept of a 'two-level game', combined with insights from institutionalist approaches. In the case of relations with the ACP states, there is also an alternative set of explanations based on neo-Marxian frameworks of analysis.

Explaining External Trade Policy

Explanations of the external trade policy of the EU have not generally supported supranational theories, although given the qualms of France and some of the other member states about policies of liberalization, the idea of the Commission playing an autonomous role can be put forward. Most analyses, though, adopt an approach based on the idea of a multi-level game, to which has been added an institutionalist perspective.

One possible explanation of the trade policy of the EU is that the Commission is able to play a role as an autonomous actor (Damro 2007). On this view, divisions within the EU between member states, combined with the need for the Council to approve trade agreements by a qualified majority rather than unanimity, opened up an opportunity for active and committed Commission leadership to influence the direction of policy. Such leadership was provided by a succession of Trade Commissioners, all of whom favoured trade liberalization. In the Santer Commission, Sir Leon Brittan held the portfolio from 1994 to 1999, and set a strong free-trade agenda; he was followed by Pascal Lamy (1994–2009), who, despite his French nationality, continued to push the EU in the same direction during the Prodi Commission, as did his successor in the Barroso Commission, Peter Mandelson (2004–08).

This does not mean that there were no differences in emphasis between the Commissioners. Meunier (2007a) looked at the differences between the 'managed globalization' favoured by Lamy and the position of his successor, Mandelson, as expressed in the 2006 communication *Global Europe: Competing in the World* (European Commission 2006b). 'Managed globalization' made multilateralism the central doctrine of EU trade policy, and linked trade to political objectives such as social justice and sustainable development. 'Global Europe' argued that the central objective of EU trade policy should be to open markets abroad for European companies. The shift of emphasis involved a downgrading of the political adjuncts to trade negotiations and a retreat from the commitment to multilateralism. Although multilateralism was still to be afforded primacy, an informal moratorium on bilateral agreements until the end of the Doha Round, which Lamy had introduced, was abandoned.

Meunier (2007a) noted that neither the adoption of the approach of managed globalization nor the shift to that of 'Global Europe' involved a new mandate from the member states. This seemed to indicate a degree of autonomy of the Commission in making EU policy on external trade. However, little evidence was found to sustain the argument that the Commission had a significant autonomous effect on the policy. Indeed, the shift from managed globalization to 'Global Europe' could plausibly be presented as a reassessment in the light of changing circumstances. The autonomy of the Commission was judged to be limited to reframing and repackaging the interests of the member states, and perhaps tweaking them at the margins (Meunier 2007a: 922).

Intergovernmental explanations have centred on the idea of trade negotiations as a multi-level game. Putnam (1988) described the making of foreign policy for a state as a 'two-level game'. Moravcsik (1991; 1993; 1998) incorporated this insight into his theorizations of the nature of the relationship between the EC/EU and its member states (Chapter 1, p. 13). At one level, the government of each member state has to find a position that will satisfy the balance of pressures in its domestic political arena. It then has to play a game at the level of negotiations with the other member states to try to achieve an agreement that falls within the parameters of what is acceptable domestically.

However, the position in EC trade negotiations is even more complex. The nature of the relationship between the member states, the Commission, and the trade partners means that it is a three-level, rather than a two-level, game (Collinson 1999). The three levels are as follows.

(1) The government of each of the member states has to find a negotiating position that reflects its own domestic constraints.

(2) All of the governments then have to negotiate around these positions in determining together the negotiating mandate for the Commission in the wider trade talks.

(3) The Commission then has to negotiate in the wider talks within the tight parameters of this mandate.

If it is necessary to go beyond these parameters to reach a deal, the Commission has to refer back to its constituency in the Council, and the members of that constituency (the governments of the member states) have to refer back to their domestic constituencies.

Matters are made even more difficult by the multi-issue nature of trade talks. It has already been suggested that when the Treaty of Rome was drawn up, certain issues that are central to contemporary world trade were not considered to be part of the agenda. Trade in the 1950s was predominantly in goods. Today, there is growing trade in services and intellectual property. Foreign direct investment has also grown rapidly and become a matter of concern, with some governments wishing to regulate it and others wishing to embed international rules that ban national discrimination against foreign investment. In addition, agriculture, which was effectively excluded from the earliest rounds of GATT negotiations by a tacit agreement between the participants, has become a central issue.

Young and Peterson (2006) added even more complexity by pointing to the emergence of a new trade agenda that is no longer concerned with restrictions that occur at the border of national economies, but increasingly involves attempts to harmonize or regulate national domestic rules that affect trade, such as state subsidies, and technical barriers to trade.

Young (2000) had earlier advocated supplementing liberal intergovernmental analysis of trade policy with an institutionalist approach. According to this analysis, the three-level game is structured by the institutionalization of the policy sector. Young (2007) used such an approach in an analysis of the EU's positions in the Doha Round, in which the EU was argued to have taken a more liberal position on traditional trade issues than it did on the newer issues. This variation Young explained by examining the different institutionalization of political forces within each set of issues.

On the traditional trade issues, the range of actors was generally limited to national and EU-level officials and companies within the EU that were directly affected, either because they competed with imports and sought protection, or because they were export-oriented and sought the opening of markets in other countries even at the cost of dismantling EU protection. Within this limited policy arena, a growing acceptance among officials that free trade offered the best prospects for high levels of economic growth, combined with the increasing dominance of the export-oriented firms, ensured that since at least the mid-1980s the EU became more committed to trade liberalization.

Because the newer 'deep trade' agenda involves 'behind-the-border' issues, such as the adverse trade effects of national rules, state subsidies, and public procurement, a different range of actors is involved. As well as trade officials, non-trade departments both of the Commission and the national governments have central roles, and they are less likely to share the acceptance of the benefits of free trade that forms the ideational context for policy making among trade officials. National governments are more central actors at the EU level because the policies covered involve them directly, as with subsidies that they pay or public contracts that they award, in both cases for domestic reasons. Also, the sorts of issue covered by the new agenda have much wider direct political implications within states. This is particularly true of the 'social trade' agenda, which affects such issues as measures to protect the environment or consumers. Here, both politicians and campaigning interest groups, such as environmental groups and consumer groups, have an incentive to become active within the policy-making process. For all of these reasons, it is much less likely that the EU will end up with a liberalization agenda on these issues than it is for traditional trade issues.

Relations with the ACP States

Using another adaptation of the two-level game model, Forwood (2001), going against treatments of Cotonou as a radical restructuring of Lomé, argued that a closer examination of the negotiations showed 'that the ability of the negotiators to rise to the challenges facing EU–ACP relations was compromised by the complexities of international negotiations' (Forwood 2001: 424).

Member states of the EU took up different positions on the proposals in the Commission's Green Paper. France wanted to continue with the principles of Lomé to maintain the special relationship with the ACP states. It also opposed adjustments to the relationship that might lead to the ending of agricultural exemptions. Germany wanted to see an end to Lomé, which it considered to be a 'colonial relic'. It was most supportive of the proposals in the Green Paper. Denmark, Sweden, and the Netherlands were primarily concerned to protect the interests of the LDCs. They wanted to see the nine LDCs that were excluded from Lomé brought into the new arrangements. They were also concerned about the Commission's idea of REPAs because they believed that they would benefit the non-LDC members of the ACP group at the expense of the LDCs. Britain shared this suspicion of the idea of REPAs, but like France wanted to maintain a special relationship with the ACP states as a whole (Forwood 2001: 428–9).

The result of these divided views was a compromise mandate for the Commission to take into the negotiations with the ACP states: the continuation of a special relationship would be available, but those ACP states that were unwilling to continue with the relationship would be offered EPAs, either on an individual basis or as REPAs (Forwood 2001: 431).

During the negotiations with the ACP states, the Commission's hand was weakened by the collapse of the WTO trade talks in Seattle in December 1999. This focused attention on the position of developing countries, making it more difficult for the EU to force through any agreement with which the ACP states were unhappy and about which they might complain publicly, thereby damaging the international image of the EU. It also demonstrated that the developing countries still had the ability to throw a spanner in the works of global liberalization (Forwood 2001: 437), particularly in the context of growing public dissatisfaction with the perceived inequities of global trading arrangements. The principal reason, though, that Forwood (2001: 438) invoked for an outcome that is here characterized as one in which 'all the features of Lomé have fundamentally been rolled over into the new Convention' was the historical institutionalist idea of 'path dependence' (Chapter 2, p. 25). In the case of Lomé, it was explained thus:

> The legacy of 25 years of Lomé was such that negotiators were not able merely to wipe the slate clean and start afresh. This legacy is more than a legal commitment, but also a moral and political obligation of the EU Member States towards the ACP countries.

(Forwood 2001: 434)

Forwood was working within theoretical frameworks that are familiar within European studies. In distinct contrast to the analysis produced by this approach, utilizing multi-level games and historical institutionalism (Chapter 2, pp. 24–6) are analyses utilizing neo-Marxian frameworks (Chapter 3, pp. 47–50), which illustrates well the value of a multi-theoretical perspective such as is advocated throughout this book.

There is a long tradition of analysing the relations between the EEC/EC/EU and the ACP states in neo-Marxian terms of dependency and neo-colonialism (for example, Galtung 1976). This tradition was continued in critiques of the Commission's arguments for moving from the Lomé pattern to that eventually adopted in Cotonou, but the emphasis was much more on the Gramscian concept of the hegemony of ideas.

Gibb (2000: 477–8) argued that the Commission, in its Green Paper, had presented the requirements of the WTO as an insuperable barrier to continuation of Lomé, but in reality the WTO system was one that the EU had itself been fully involved in installing. An alternative to changing the Lomé principles to make them compatible with the WTO would have been to change the WTO rules to make them compatible with the Lomé principles. Some ACP delegations had suggested that the EU and ACP jointly argue for the acceptance by the WTO of a new category of free trade agreement, a 'soft' or 'low' agreement, that would not be subject to the same stringent requirements as were implied by existing WTO rules. The EU chose not even to raise this issue during the Millennium Round trade negotiations. The conclusion was that, '[t]he WTO is ... at the centre of the post-Lomé negotiations because the EU placed it there. And it placed it there because it is in its own best interests to do so' (Gibb 2000: 478).

Other assessments of the new agreement included one by Hurt (2003) that was similar to the critique by Gibb (2000) of the Commission's pre-Cotonou position, although it went further by analysing the aid provisions as well as the trade provisions of the agreement. It drew attention to the similarity of principles underpinning Cotonou to the principles of other institutions of international economic management, including not only the WTO but also the IMF and the World Bank. This similarity was attributed to the dominance of neoliberal ideas, which served the interests of powerful actors within the developed world.

> The current neoliberal hegemony of ideas sits broadly compatibly with the self-interests of political élites and the outward-orientated fraction of the capitalist class within the EU member states.

(Hurt 2003: 174)

This assessment treated the EU as a unified entity that responded to the interests of the dominant political elites and 'the outward-orientated fraction of the capitalist class'. It also appeared to assume that the final agreement reached at Cotonou represented a clear victory for the more radical ideas for reform of Lomé that the Commission had put forward.

Relations with Near Neighbours

It should be possible to extend all of the analyses of Cotonou to other bilateral trade agreements that the EU has reached, such as the Euro-Med Agreements, or the ENP. Garson (1997) offered an analysis of the Euro-Med Agreements that showed clear similarities to those of Cotonou.

He argued that the Agreements represented a challenge for both parties, but particularly for the Mediterranean partner states. Compared with the position of Greece, Spain, and Portugal when they opened their markets to free trade with the then EC in the 1970s, most of the new Mediterranean partners of the EU were at a lower stage of economic development in the early twenty-first century. They had inadequate economic and financial structures to attract foreign capital, serious administrative shortcomings, and a lack of educational and training institutions to teach new skills as technology changed. In the medium term, they could expect to see negative effects from free trade with the EU. Lowering customs duties would reduce government revenues, requiring higher domestic taxes. Their trade deficits would probably deteriorate because imports would grow faster than exports, and this could trigger devaluations of their currencies. It was also unlikely that there would be any immediate decline in unemployment or poverty. The benefits would only appear in the long term. If foreign direct investment could be attracted, that would give workers in the partner states access to higher levels of knowledge and skills, leading to higher productivity, which would in turn attract further foreign investment. More jobs would be created, and wages would rise.

Despite these warnings about short-term and medium-term risks, the Mediterranean partner states were prepared to accept the terms of the arrangements offered them by the EU. It is instructive to compare these terms overall—not just the economic terms—with those offered to the EU's ACP partner states when the Cotonou Agreement was negotiated in the late 1990s, at about the same time as the Euro-Med Agreements were being negotiated. The similarity of the approach suggests that the analyses of the EU's changing relationship with the ACP states might also have some applicability to the Euro-Med Agreements. In particular, the arguments of Gibb (2000) and Hurt (2003) on the hegemony of neoliberal ideas that benefited the dominant capitalist class within the EU, would seem to be directly relevant.

CONCLUSION

Examination of the external economic relations of the EU brings to the fore several of the theoretical themes that have appeared throughout this book: the tension between nationalism and supranationalism; the complexities of bargaining within multiple international forums; and the role of dominant ideas across different forums. It also shows the impossibility of clearly separating internal and external policies, and economic and political issues.

The complex decision-making rules for the common commercial policy demonstrate the dangers of any oversimplification of the relationship between intergovernmentalism and supranationalism. The Commission clearly plays an important role, and has a certain autonomy over the conduct of trade negotiations under the Articles of the original Treaty dealing with the common commercial policy. The member states have always been influential, though. They have to agree the negotiating mandate within which the Commission works, and they have to secure sufficient domestic support before their representatives dare vote for the ratification of the agreements, which acts as a further constraint on the Commission's room for making deals. This complexity is well captured by the theoretical concept of the multi-level game, especially when supplemented by an institutionalist analysis that takes into account variations in the constellations of actors, established practices, and ideational contexts of the different issue areas.

Analyses of the Lomé and Cotonou Agreements have tended to give more emphasis to the role of ideas. The same ideas—open free trade, democratic institutions, good governance, partnership between state and non-state institutions, respect for the environment—that increasingly informed development policy towards the ACP states were incorporated into agreements reached with the EU's near neighbours.

Many of the objectives listed above and built into the external agreements are clearly not economic in any narrow definition of the term, and would usually be considered political. Thus the division between the economic and the political cannot be drawn too starkly. Nevertheless, the external political relations of the EU are usually distinguished from the external relations examined in this chapter, not least because they are operated under different institutional arrangements. They are the subject of the next chapter.

KEY POINTS

History

- When the EEC was set up in the 1950s, world economic relations were governed by the 1944 Bretton Woods agreements. Trade relations were governed by the GATT.

- A key principle of the GATT was MFN: that members had to offer to all other member states terms of trade as favourable as the best terms they offered to any other state. The EEC gained exemption from MFN for the internal **common market** and for its relations with former colonies of EEC members.

- Relations with the former colonies initially continued their dependence on France in particular. When Britain joined the EEC, the Lomé Convention provided the ACP states with a fairer deal.

- Following the collapse of communism in eastern Europe, the EU concluded special trade and aid agreements with the CEECs in an attempt to ensure the stability of its near neighbours. For the same reason, special agreements were reached with the states of the southern Mediterranean.

External Trade Policy

- Trade negotiations are conducted by the Commission on behalf of the EU as a whole, working to a mandate agreed by the Council of Ministers and supervised by a Committee of national representatives.
- Until the Lisbon Treaty came into force, trade in services and intellectual products were not automatically covered by this arrangement: the governments of the member states had to agree ahead of each round of negotiations to allow the Commission authority in these areas.
- Under the terms of the Lisbon Treaty, trade in services and intellectual products are an EU competence, but unanimity remains the voting rule where sensitive domestic issues are concerned.
- The Commission has the power to impose duties and other restrictions on imports of goods to the EU where dumping or unfair subsidies are suspected.
- Member states are often divided over trade issues both by conflicting economic interests and by their general attitude to free trade.
- Since the introduction of the WTO, the EU has been involved in a series of trade disputes, mainly with the United States.

Relations with the African, Caribbean, and Pacific States

- Prior to 1975, relations between the EEC and the former colonies of the member states were governed by the Implementing Convention and (from 1963) the Yaoundé Conventions, which essentially maintained the relationship of dependence of the developing countries on the European states, but spread the costs within the EEC between the member states, despite most of the dependencies being former French colonies.
- Between 1975 and 2000, the relations of the EC/EU with the ACP states were governed by the Lomé Conventions. The terms of Lomé were more favourable to the ACP states, reflecting the international economic circumstances in which they were negotiated in the 1970s.
- By the end of the 1990s, when Lomé was renegotiated, it was clear that its terms were incompatible with the rules of the WTO in several respects.
- A new agreement was signed in 2000 in Cotonou, Benin. The Lomé system of trade preferences was replaced by a series of new economic partnerships based on the progressive and reciprocal removal of trade barriers. There was also a new emphasis on political, social, and environmental issues.

Relations with Near Neighbours

- Relations with other European states have most commonly been Association Agreements leading to eventual full membership. Since the collapse of communism, a variety of other agreements have been devised that stop short of offering a perspective on membership.
- The Euro-Med Agreements involve not only southern European non-member states, but also the states of North Africa on the other side of the Mediterranean.
- The European Neighbourhood Policy covers both the European partners in the Euro-Med Agreements and European states further east that were part of the former Soviet Union. The aim of the policy is to prevent the emergence of stark dividing lines between EU and non-EU

states by offering many of the advantages of association to states that do not have a prospect of membership.

Explaining Trade and Development Aid Policies

- Shared responsibility for trade negotiations produces a complex pattern of bargaining that has been characterized as a 'three-level game'.

- Such rational choice analyses of trade negotiations have been supplemented by institutional analysis.

- Both types of analysis have also been applied to relations with the ACP states.

- An alternative approach sees Cotonou as evidence of the dominance of neoliberal ideas within the EU.

FURTHER READING

The most comprehensive review of the external trade policy of the EU is provided by **S. Meunier**, *Trading Voices: The European Union in International Commercial Negotiations* (Princeton, NJ: Princeton University Press, 2007).

The common commercial policy of the EU is analysed as a multi-level game in **S. Collinson**, '"Issue Systems", "Multi-Level Games" and the Analysis of the EU's External Commercial and Associated Policies: A Research Agenda', *Journal of European Public Policy*, 6 (1999): 206–24. The increasing complexity of trade policy is well set out in **A. R. Young and J. Peterson**, 'The EU and the New Trade Politics', *Journal of European Public Policy*, 13 (2006): 795–814.

M. Carbone, *The European Union and International Development: The Politics of Foreign Aid* (Abingdon: Routledge, 2007) develops an analytical model to explain the role of the Commission and of the member states in this area of decision making, and **A. Mold (ed.)**, *EU Development Policy in a Changing World: Challenges for the 21st Century* (Amsterdam: Amsterdam University Press, 2007) discusses the impact of wider developments, including the 2004 and 2007 enlargements, on the EU's foreign policy agenda and development policy.

 online resource centre **Visit the Online Resource Centre that accompanies this book for links to more information on the external economic relations of the EU, including the website of the relevant Directorates-General of the Commission: www.oxfordtextbooks.co.uk/orc/bache3e/**

Chapter 33

Common Foreign and Security Policy

Chapter Overview

External political relations were always handled outside of the European Community (EC) framework, and initially were outside of the Treaty framework altogether. From 1993 to 2009, they formed the second pillar of the European Union (EU), on Common Foreign and Security Policy (CFSP) (the Lisbon Treaty abolished the three pillars). Although CFSP was officially an intergovernmental pillar, the Commission came to play an important role, and informally there were some similarities between the way in which the CFSP pillar operated and the way in which the EC pillar operated, even though the formal rules were different. Serious attempts were made to strengthen the security and defence aspects of the CFSP in the face of the threats that faced the EU from instability in its neighbouring territories. Explaining the development of close co-operation in areas of 'high policy' poses a challenge for theories of the EU.

There has been a dramatic increase in the EU's external relations 'output', but this has not always matched expectations that the EU will act decisively, consistently, and influentially in international relations.

(Smith 2003: 244)

History

Prior to the Lisbon Treaty taking effect in December 2009, the external economic relations of the EC with the rest of the world were covered by the Treaty establishing the European Community (TEC), and generally came under the competencies of the Commission—but the member states also separately developed machinery for formulating common positions on political issues of foreign policy. This initially developed outside of the framework of the Treaties under the name of European Political Co-operation (EPC). It entered the Treaties as Title III of the Single European Act (SEA) in July 1987, although still on an intergovernmental basis. Title V of the Treaty on European Union (TEU) set up a Common Foreign and Security Policy (CFSP) as the second pillar of the EU, and some additions were made to the machinery of the CFSP in the Amsterdam Treaty. In the late 1990s, efforts were made to establish a European Security and Defence Policy (ESDP), and this was brought into the EU by the Nice Treaty, which came into effect at the start of 2003.

European Political Co-operation (EPC)

EPC was suggested by French President Pompidou at the Hague Summit in 1969, but was seen at the time as little more than a sop to his Gaullist supporters. Few participants or observers thought that it would amount to anything, because it closely resembled the Fouchet Plan, which had already been rejected (Chapter 9, Insight 9.2, p. 128), and because it proposed co-operation in the field of 'high politics' as defined by Hoffmann (1964; 1966), an area in which national interests would be expected to get in the way of common action (Chapter 1, pp. 11–12). Nevertheless, the initiative led to the setting up of a committee under the chairmanship of the Belgian Étienne Davignon, and its report—the Davignon or Luxembourg Report—recommending increased co-operation on international political issues, was adopted by Foreign Ministers meeting in Luxembourg in October 1970.

The machinery of EPC consisted mainly of regular meetings to co-ordinate national stances to particular areas of the world, or to particular issues. Foreign Ministers met at least twice a year, but in practice much more often. Immediately below the ministerial level, Foreign Office political directors met, on the original plan every three months, but in practice monthly. In addition to the meetings of Foreign Ministers and political directors, other institutional innovations were the COREU (*correspondance Européenne*) telex link, and Working Groups on a range of policy and geographical issues. COREU allowed officials in the Foreign Ministries of member states to communicate with each other as frequently as they wished on a confidential line. By the mid-1970s, the Foreign Offices of member states were exchanging an average of 4,800 confidential telexes a year in an intensive process of consultation (Smith 2004: 107). By the time that the EPC was superseded by CFSP in the Maastricht Treaty, there were more than twenty quasi-permanent Working Groups (Smith 2004: 105). To ease problems in the six-monthly transition between presidencies, from 1976, the rules of procedure that had emerged were codified in a document known as the *coutumier* (the French for 'custom').

Until 1987, EPC had no secretariat to provide administrative back-up. This was provided by whichever member state held the presidency of the Council at the time, imposing additional strain on the state holding the presidency, and also working against proper continuity across changes of presidency. Disappointment at the failure of the EC to respond effectively to the Iranian crisis in 1979 led to a review of EPC—the London Report—that recommended improved procedures for use in a crisis, and the creation of a small permanent Secretariat. These recommendations were adopted in October 1981, and led directly to the creation in the SEA of a small Secretariat, situated in Brussels.

EPC was originally set up as a parallel process to that of economic integration within the EC, but the two became closely linked. The distinction between matters proper to EPC and EC matters was rigidly maintained in the early years of the operation of EPC at the insistence of the French. This reached the heights of absurdity in November 1973, when the Foreign Ministers of the then nine member states met in Copenhagen one morning under the heading of EPC, and then flew to Brussels to meet in the afternoon of the same day as the EC Council of Ministers.

The rigid separation finally broke down with the opening of the 'Euro-Arab dialogue' in 1974. This was a structured series of regular meetings between representatives of the EC and representatives of the Arab states, prompted by the oil crisis of 1973–74. The Arab participants in the talks insisted on maintaining a clear linkage between trade and political questions, which forced the EC to fudge the lines of demarcation on its side. Once the artificial distinction had broken down here, it soon became less evident elsewhere in the external relations of the EC.

Once the EPC/EC distinction had been eroded, the Commission, originally excluded from meetings under the machinery of EPC, had to be admitted. One of the most compelling reasons for involving the Commission was that it proved difficult to do anything other than make declarations under EPC without having the use of the normal instruments of foreign policy. As military capabilities were unlikely to be made available to EPC, the obvious 'soft' weapon to use was economic sanctions, together with economic rewards such as loans. These economic instruments fell under the competencies of the EC, and were administered by the Commission. In theory, national economic mechanisms could have been used to back-up EPC declarations, but this would have been less efficient than using centralized EC mechanisms, and might have worked against EC external economic policies.

After it began to be involved in EPC meetings, the Commission came to play a significant co-ordinating role between EPC and the Council of Ministers. This arose for two reasons: the lack of an EPC Secretariat until 1987; and the fact that Foreign Offices tended to send different people to the two different categories of meeting, while the Commission, with a considerably smaller staff upon which to draw, usually sent the same people. Where questions arose that overlapped the two forums, the Commission representatives were the most likely to spot the overlap and to be able to guide a meeting away from making decisions that were incompatible with those already made elsewhere.

Another development was that, for reasons of democratic legitimacy, reports on EPC started to be made to the European Parliament (EP). The reports were originally made only to the Parliament's Political Affairs Committee, but subsequently they came to be made in a full plenary session, usually as part of the same statement on progress in Community affairs that was made by the Foreign Minister of the state holding the Council presidency. Members of the EP were allowed to question the Minister about EPC matters as well as about more strictly Community matters.

Procedurally, then, EPC made big strides in the course of the 1970s, and became intertwined with the institutions and procedures of the EC. These advances were then formalized in the SEA in 1985–86. The SEA gave EPC a written basis for the first time, but the Articles relating to it were not subject to judicial interpretation by the European Court of Justice (ECJ).

Although EPC was at one time described as an example of 'procedure substituting for policy' (Wallace and Allen 1977), it had several substantive successes. For example, the member states achieved a high degree of unity in the United Nations (UN), voting together on a majority of resolutions in the General Assembly, and developing a reputation for being the most cohesive group there at a time when group diplomacy was becoming much more common.

Perhaps even more impressively, EPC formulated a common position on the Middle East. This in itself was quite an achievement, given that prior to EPC there had been wide divergences in the extent of sympathy for Israel and for the Arab states in different member states. Reaching an agreed position allowed the EC, through the Euro–Arab dialogue, to pursue its clear interest in improving trade with the Arab **Organization of the Petroleum Exporting Countries (OPEC)** states in the 1970s. In June 1980, this common policy culminated in the Venice Declaration, which went further than the United States was prepared to go in recognizing the right of the Palestinians to a homeland.

The then nine member states were also extremely successful in formulating a common position at the Conference on Security and Co-operation in Europe (CSCE) in Helsinki in 1975, and at the follow-up conferences in Belgrade in 1977, and Madrid in 1982–83. Indeed, the whole CSCE process was an initiative of the EC states. Again, the common position adopted by the EC ran somewhat contrary to the position of the United States. The Americans regarded the Helsinki process with some suspicion because they thought it risked legitimating Communist rule in eastern Europe. In January 1995, the CSCE took on more permanent form as the Organization for Security and Co-operation in Europe (OSCE).

Admittedly, there were also failures. It proved difficult to find a joint position on the invasion of Afghanistan by the Soviet Union in December 1979. The British government argued strongly for following the lead of the United States in boycotting the Olympic games in Moscow, while the French in particular were not prepared to do so, and the West German government was unhappy at the way in which the United States used the issue to heighten East–West tension. On balance, though, there were more successes than there were failures, and it could at least be argued that these successes helped the procedure to develop as much as vice versa.

At the beginning of the 1990s, the EC failed to respond adequately to two separate international crises. The first was in the Persian Gulf, where Iraq invaded its neighbour Kuwait in August 1990. The second was in Yugoslavia, where fighting broke out in June 1991 between the former Yugoslav army and Croat and Slovenian separatist forces. In both cases, the immediate response of the EC was positive, but as the crises developed, differing national interests paralysed the process of political co-operation, and the United States ended up having to take the lead in resolving both.

The Common Foreign and Security Policy (CFSP) and European Security and Defence Policy (ESDP)

While it was struggling to deal with crises in the Gulf and former Yugoslavia, the EC was also transforming itself into the EU. The intergovernmental conference (IGC) on political union, which began in January 1991, had the future evolution of EPC as a central item on its agenda. The more radical agenda, supported by Commission

President Jacques Delors and by the German government, was to bring EPC into the framework of the EC, with the Commission perhaps not having the sole right of initiative but being centrally involved, and **qualified majority voting (QMV)** applying to decisions in the Council of Ministers. Security and defence would be added to the remit of this new mechanism for a common foreign policy. The opposite pole was marked out by the British, who argued against QMV on issues that were central to the sovereignty of the member states, and were particularly concerned that any moves to establish a common policy for security and defence should not undermine the NATO alliance.

The two voices in this debate drew opposite conclusions from events in the Gulf. Both sides agreed that the failure of the EC to respond effectively to the crisis indicated how far there still was to travel to a common policy. However, whereas Delors told the EP that the ineffective response indicated the urgency of pushing forward to political union (*Debates of the European Parliament*, 23 January 1991, 3–398/139), British Prime Minister John Major told the House of Commons that this failure clearly indicated that Europe was not ready for a common policy (Hansard, 22 January 1991, col. 162).

In a compromise between these two positions, a three-pillar structure was adopted at Maastricht, with the CFSP and Justice and Home Affairs (JHA) forming intergovernmental pillars of the new EU alongside the EC pillar. Majority voting in the second pillar was restricted to the implementation measures needed to carry through decisions of principle that would have to be taken by consensus, and even then the QMV would only apply if all states were to agree to accept it in a particular case. There were some other enhancements of EPC, including moving the old EPC secretariat into the Council Secretariat and giving it a larger staff and budget. Overall, though, the TEU really represented a victory for the minimalist position on the CFSP.

The tragedy in former Yugoslavia did have a beneficial effect in bringing France and Britain closer together on security and defence. The common experience of operating under UN auspices in Bosnia led to increased co-operation on the ground, which spread into the creation of a joint air-force command unit. Nevertheless, when in 1998 a further crisis occurred in the Kosovo province of Serbia, the EU again proved unequal to the task of making a rapid response. It was NATO that undertook a bombing campaign against Serbia to force it to retreat from the persecution of the ethnic Albanians in Kosovo. The United States spearheaded the NATO effort.

The failure of the EU to act in Kosovo provided the impetus for a move to extend CFSP to security and defence. In December 1998, at a bilateral Franco–British summit in Saint-Malo, France, French President Jacques Chirac and British Prime Minister Tony Blair jointly announced their support for an ESDP. A year later, the Helsinki European Council announced what was called the 'headline goal' of creating by the end of 2003 a European Rapid Reaction Force of 50,000 to 60,000 troops, plus naval and air back-up, that could be sustained in the field for up to one year. In March 2000, the institutions of the ESDP began provisional operation: a political and security committee, known by its French acronym COPS (standing for *Comité Politique et de Sécurité*); a military committee; and the basis for a joint military command structure.

The Amsterdam Treaty had already made some modifications to the CFSP, particularly in creating the post of High Representative, the holder of which would be the first point of contact for CFSP matters. In November 1999, it was agreed to appoint the then NATO Secretary-General, Javier Solana, to this post. The Commission had argued that the post should go to one of the Commissioners, but the heads of government decided to make it a position within the Council framework, thus storing up potential for problems in the co-ordination of the work of the two institutions.

Amendments to the TEU at Amsterdam drew a distinction between, on the one hand, deciding the principles and general guidelines of the CFSP, and common strategies in pursuit of these, and on the other, the adoption of joint actions, common positions, and implementing decisions. The first category of decision had to be unanimous; QMV could decide the second. Also, a member state could abstain in a vote and make a formal declaration that it would not be bound by the vote. This would allow the EU as a whole to be committed to the decision, but not the individual abstaining state, which would only be obliged not to act in any way that would conflict with the pursuit of the action by the EU.

Amsterdam also incorporated the so-called 'Petersberg Tasks' into the EU. In June 1992, the Western European Union (WEU) Petersberg Declaration had said that member states would allocate armed forces to peace-keeping and humanitarian tasks in Europe (on the WEU see Insight 7.1, p. 108 and Insight 33.1, below). This had committed only the members of WEU, but the 1997 Amsterdam Treaty committed all EU member states to the tasks. ESDP was officially brought into the TEU by amendments made in the 2000 Nice Treaty, which took effect at the start of 2003.

Further amendment was made to the institutions of the CFSP in the Lisbon Treaty. First, the three-pillar structure was abolished, and CFSP became an integral part of an EU that now had a consolidated legal personality. However, this does not mean that CFSP has become regular EU business: it is still 'subject to specific rules and procedures' (Article 24(1) TEU).

Insight 33.1   The Revival of Western European Union (WEU)

WEU was set up in 1954 following the collapse of the Pleven Plan for a European Defence Community (Chapter 7, Insight 7.1, p. 108). The original members were Belgium, France, Luxembourg, the Netherlands, Britain, West Germany, and Italy. Portugal and Spain became members in 1990 and Greece in 1995, bringing the membership to ten.

By the 1980s, WEU had apparently become moribund, but proposals to revive it as a vehicle for co-ordinating European positions were made by the Belgian and French governments in 1984.

Prior to the Gulf War of 1990, WEU co-ordinated mine-sweeping operations in the Persian Gulf, which had been mined during the Iran–Iraq war. It was therefore in a strong position to provide a co-ordination mechanism for the member states involved in the Gulf War, which it did, and continued with mine-sweeping operations afterwards.

WEU co-operated with NATO to monitor the embargo against former Yugoslavia in 1993, providing a joint naval task force. It also helped to enforce the sanctions on the Danube, providing patrol boats, vehicles, and personnel to work alongside the national agencies of Bulgaria, Hungary, and Romania. From 1994 to 1996, the WEU provided a police contingent to the EU administration in Mostar in Bosnia-Herzegovina, to assist in the setting up of a Bosnian–Croat joint police force.

These activities, which prefigured the Missions later undertaken by the EU under its ESDP (below), continued with a police mission in Albania from 1997 to 2001, a Demining Assistance Commission to Croatia in 1999, and a General Security Surveillance Mission in Kosovo in 1998–99.

To facilitate closer co-ordination, in 1992 the WEU secretariat was moved from London to Brussels, where both the European Commission and NATO headquarters were located. In 1999 Javier Solana, the EU High Representative for the CFSP, was appointed Secretary-General of WEU as well.

Following the effective transfer of its crisis-management functions to the EU, the WEU now consists of a small Secretariat with only residual functions related to preparing and preserving archives, and administering pension and other staff liabilities. Until the Lisbon Treaty came into effect, it could be argued that the Brussels Treaty still formed the basis of a mutual defence pact between the ten member states, but Lisbon amended the TEU so as to envisage a possible future common defence under Article 42, which says that should a member state experience armed aggression on its own territory, the other states shall assist it by all means in their power.

Second, the 'High Representative for the Common Foreign and Security Policy' became the 'High Representative of the Union for Foreign Affairs and Security Policy'. This was more than a change of name. Whereas the original post was combined with that of Secretary-General of the Council, and there was a separate Commissioner for External Relations, the new post carried with it the position of a Vice-President of the European Commission, and the incumbent was to chair all meetings of the Council of Foreign Ministers, thus making it a position that straddled both institutions, and acted as a bridge between external economic relations and the CFSP/ESDP. The Lisbon Treaty also established an External Action Service to assist the High Representative, to be formed by staff drawn from the external relations departments of the Council and Commission, with provision for additional staff to be seconded from the national diplomatic services of the member states. At the Brussels European Council in September 2009, the heads of government agreed to appoint Baroness Catherine Ashton, until then the Commissioner for Trade, to the post with effect from the Treaty coming into force on 1 December 2009, the appointment being subject to ratification by the EP.

CFSP and ESDP in Action

The start of CFSP did not suggest a great leap forward in either the capabilities or the ambitions of the EU. The first actions undertaken were modest, and were all in areas that built on EPC. Monitors were sent to observe the elections in Russia in December 1993; humanitarian aid for Bosnia was co-ordinated; and a new political framework was developed for aid to the West Bank and Gaza. Subsequently observers were sent to monitor the first non-racial elections in South Africa, and the EU played an active role in the preparations for elections in the Palestinian homeland.

A more ambitious proposal, which originated with French Prime Minister Edouard Balladur, came to fruition in March 1995, when fifty-two states from western and eastern Europe signed a stability pact binding themselves to be good neighbours, and to respect the rights of minorities. Although there were several flaws in the pact, especially the exclusion for one reason or another of all of the Yugoslav successor states, the pattern was adopted later in the year by the Spanish presidency to develop a regional pact for the Mediterranean, in the face of growing concern in southern Europe about Islamic fundamentalism in the Arab world and about illegal immigration from there.

When the 2001 terrorist attack on the United States took place, the EU, as in previous crises, initially reacted positively and decisively. Within 36 hours, declarations in support of the United States had been made by the Commission President, the Commissioner for External Relations, the Special Representative for Foreign Affairs, and the General Affairs Council. The Commission rapidly tabled proposals for a European Arrest Warrant, and agreement on this was reached in December, despite reservations by Italy (Hill 2004: 145–7). Overall, in the 'war against terror', despite the problems of operating across all three pillars of the Maastricht structure, the EU responded with 'an unforeseeable speed, range and flexibility' (Hill 2004: 150).

Solidarity was also maintained during the subsequent US campaign in Afghanistan to unseat the Taliban government. The one part of the early response that did not reinforce CFSP was the apparent wish of Britain, France, and Germany to act independently of the EU as a whole. Blair, Chirac, and Schröder met to discuss their responses to September 11 ahead of the Ghent European Council in October 2001, and intended to do so again in London in early November. On the latter occasion, though, the insistent protests of other member states led to a widening of the invitation, with the result that the meeting was also attended by Italy, Spain, and the Netherlands, by the Belgian presidency, and by the High Representative, Javier Solana. Although the instinct of the leaders of the three large states had not been to work through CFSP, the outcome showed that this was difficult for them to do against the wishes of others.

Problems really began, though, with the identification of an 'axis of evil' by US President George W. Bush in his 2002 State of the Union speech. Three states were identified as part of this axis: Iraq, Iran, and North Korea. The EU was working diplomatically to bring Iran back into full participation in the international community, and had managed to persuade Tehran to associate itself with the 'war against terror', and not to object to the invasion of Afghanistan. Bush's public condemnation was a setback for these efforts of the EU to build a constructive relationship with Iran. Similarly, the reference to North Korea set alarm bells ringing in Brussels because the EU was following a policy of functional engagement of the North Korean regime in the hope of tempting it out of isolation. Again, the bellicose tone of President Bush did not contribute to the success of this effort. In the case of Iraq, the EU was not following a strategy of its own, but the general view of member states was that the existing UN policy was working: the use of military air patrols to contain Saddam Hussein's reach, together with economic sanctions, and the offer of easing sanctions to lever compliant behaviour.

Of its 'axis of evil' states, it was Iraq that the United States chose to tackle first, and this precipitated a serious split within the EU. In the build-up to the eventual invasion, France and Germany led a small group of states that opposed any military action, while Britain, Spain, and Italy were the leading supporters of a larger group (if the accession states are included) that backed the US action. In March 2003, France publicly declared that it would veto any resolution in support of military action against Iraq that might be presented by the United States and Britain to the UN Security Council. This led to a bitter verbal attack on France by Tony Blair in the House of Commons on 18 March 2003.

As Howorth (2003: 179–80) made clear, the tensions had started to rise before this. Blair's response to the attacks on New York had been to reaffirm Britain's attachment to NATO. When the Spanish presidency attempted to reorient the European Rapid Reaction Force to turn it into a weapon that could be used against terrorism, Blair opposed the change, arguing that the war against terror should be handled through NATO. He subsequently supported a US proposal to the November 2002 NATO Summit in Prague for a NATO Response Force to react to terrorist incidents, and in April 2003, he was critical of the French position of rivalry with the United States, which he contrasted with the British position of partnership.

Following the invasion of Iraq by a US-led coalition backed by Britain in March 2003, Franco–British relations were at a very low ebb, and the prospects for ESDP looked poor. Yet Howorth (2003: 187) reported that there were signs at the end of 2003 of both sides trying to improve matters. In August, at a meeting of European states in Rome, a clash was expected over whether ESDP needed its own planning headquarters, which France insisted it must have, or whether the EU should develop a permanent planning cell within the Supreme Allied Headquarters Europe (SHAPE) of NATO. But the clash did not happen: the meeting agreed that both developments would be useful, and that they would complement one another. Then, in September, Blair agreed in principle that the EU should have the joint planning capacity to conduct operations without the involvement of NATO, a concession that appeared to alarm the United States. So, the signs were that the British wanted to facilitate the relaunch of the ESDP.

There were also three successful international operations under ESDP in the course of 2003 (Allen and Smith 2004: 97). In March, an EU force replaced the NATO force in the former Yugoslav Republic of Macedonia, a move that had been scheduled for 2002 but had been delayed by Greek objections. In the middle of the year, there was a successful EU intervention to restore order in the Republic of Congo. Then, in December, the European Council agreed to provide a replacement for the NATO stabilization force in Bosnia.

In 2006, the EU provided military forces to help to ensure the security necessary for the holding of elections in the Republic of Congo, and in 2008, it deployed 3,000 troops as part of a joint EU–UN force to protect refugee camps in Chad and the Central African Republic. Following the war between Russia and Georgia in 2008, the EU provided a mission to monitor the ceasefire. Also, in 2008, it sent a naval force to help deter piracy off the coast of Somalia. In addition to these operations involving mainly the armed forces, a number of operations involving police personnel and civilians were undertaken in places as diverse as Kosovo, Palestine, and Afghanistan. These were concerned with providing training and expertise to support local police forces and judicial institutions. Altogether, by the start of 2010, some twenty-four missions had been undertaken (Table 33.1).

Table 33.1 ESDP Missions up to February 2010

Name of mission	Start date	End date	Purpose
EU Somalia Training Mission	2010	2011	To strengthen the Somali security sector by providing military training for Somali recruits
EUNAVFOR Somalia	2008		To combat piracy off the Somali coast
EU SSR Guinea-Bissau	2008		To provide advice and assistance on reform of the security sector in Guinea-Bissau
EUPOL RD Congo	2007		To provide training to the police in the Democratic Republic of Congo
EUSEC RD Congo	2005		To provide advice and assistance to strengthen the security sector in the Democratic Republic of Congo
ARTEMIS DRC	2003	2003	To contribute to the stabilization of security conditions and improvement of the humanitarian situation in the Great Lakes region of the Democratic Republic of Congo. Time-limited military operation
EUFOR RD Congo	2006	2006	To provide sufficiently stable conditions for elections to take place in the Democratic Republic of Congo. Time-limited military operation
EUPOL Kinshasa	2005	2007	To monitor and advise on the setting up of the Integrated Police Unit of the Congolese National Police and to ensure that it met international standards of best practice
EU Support to AMIS (Darfur)	2005	2007	To provide support to the African Union's Mission to Darfur, Sudan
EUFOR TCHAD/RCA	2008	2009	To protect civilians and facilitate the delivery of humanitarian aid in eastern Chad and the north-east of the Central African Republic
ALTHEA BiH	2004	ongoing	To contribute to a stable security situation in Bosnia and Herzegovina
EUPM BiH	2003	ongoing	To establish sustainable policing arrangements in Bosnia and Herzegovina through monitoring, mentoring, and inspection activities
EULEX Kosovo	2008	ongoing	To assist the Kosovo authorities in establishing the rule of law

(continued)

Table 33.1 (*Continued*)

Name of mission	Start date	End date	Purpose
CONCORDIA/ FYROM	2003	2003	To contribute to ensuring a stable security environment for the establishment of the former Yugoslav Republic of Macedonia
EU PAT	2005	2005	To provide training and support for the development of the police service in the former Yugoslav Republic of Macedonia. Followed up on PROXIMA
PROXIMA / FYROM	2003	2005	To assist the police in the former Yugoslav Republic of Macedonia by providing monitoring, mentoring, and advice, and to provide specific assistance in the fight against organized crime
EUPOL Afghanistan	2007	ongoing	To contribute to the establishment of sustainable and effective civilian policing arrangements in Afghanistan
EUMM Georgia	2008	ongoing	To contribute to stability in Georgia and the surrounding region, and to monitor the security situation
EUJUSTLEX Iraq	2005	ongoing	To provide training to senior Iraqi judiciary, police, and prison officers
EUBAM Rafah	2005	ongoing	To monitor the implementation of the 2005 Agreement between Israel and the Palestinian Authority on movement through the Rafa crossing (Gaza)
EUPOL COPPS/ Palestinian Territories	2005		To provide support to the Palestinian Authority to establish sustainable and effective policing arrangements
EUJUST/Themis Georgia	2004	2005	To advise the Georgian authorities on tackling urgent challenges within the criminal justice system and assist in the reform process
Aceh Monitoring Mission—AMM	2005	2006	To monitor implementation of the 2005 peace agreement between the Indonesian government and the Free Aceh Movement
EUBAM Moldova and Ukraine	2005	ongoing	To improve the capacity of Moldovan and Ukrainian border and customs services to prevent and detect smuggling, human trafficking, and customs fraud

Source: **http://ec.europa.eu**, © European Union, 1995–2010

Explaining CFSP and ESDP

Until recently, explanations of political co-operation were rather weakly linked to theory. There were many detailed empirical accounts, some of the best written by practitioners, but although all such accounts are inevitably underpinned by theoretical assumptions, these were rarely made explicit. Most discussion was around the idea of the 'capability–expectations' gap, which was a valid concept, but was explicitly not intended as an explanatory theory (Hill 1993: 306), and which therefore did not address the central question of why political co-operation took place at all.

Perhaps the difficulty was that the academic community that initially emerged around political co-operation was dominated by 'realists' who started their analysis from the assumption that national interest was the sole motivating force of national foreign policy. As Glarbo (1999: 634) observed, although realist analyses differed from one another in detail, they all held to the common core proposition 'that the interests of single European nation states will eternally block integration within the high politics realms of foreign, security and defence policy'. Where common policies were devised, this would be explained by the coincidence of converging national interests; more often, such common positions were dismissed as trivial. Only with the deployment of social constructivist and other similar perspectives to the understanding of political co-operation did the debate become more theoretically sophisticated.

The Capability–Expectations Gap

Between the agreement of the TEU and its final ratification, Christopher Hill (1993) produced an assessment of political co-operation in which he developed a concept that was to become widely used in the subsequent literature: the 'capability–expectations gap'. Hill (1993: 309) cast doubt on whether the EC should be conceived as an actor in international affairs. It lacked autonomy, and was not distinct from other actors: notably, the member states. Many foreign-policy practitioners external to the EC, and some internal practitioners, too, had mistaken the EC for an actor. The mistake arose because the EC did have a distinct international 'presence'.

To mistake it for an actor, though, was to raise expectations of what it could achieve. It was expected to perform certain functions in the international system, such as acting as a counter-weight to the dominance of the United States. Yet the EC lacked the capability to meet these expectations. It lacked the resources, and the instruments—but also, because it was not an actor, it lacked the ability to reach agreement internally (Hill 1993: 310–15). This was why the capability–expectations gap existed, and Hill (1993: 315) believed that the gap had only been increased by the SEA and the TEU, which suggested advances in the international activity of the EC/EU that it was incapable of making.

In a review of the factors that have strengthened the 'actorness' of the EU since Hill's 1993 assessment, and those that continued to weaken it, Krotz (2009) argued that the EU was still a long way from being an international actor, although the forces making for actorness were strengthening and those working against it might be weakening, opening up the possibility of 'a fully grown high-politics actor Europe on the world stage', but not for some decades ahead.

Theoretical Explanations of Political Co-operation

Ginsberg (1989) made an early attempt to apply theory systematically to the explanation of political co-operation, examining seven theoretical perspectives on EC activity in the field of foreign policy. The first four he termed 'classical perspectives': the national interest perspective; the elite actor perspective; the domestic politics perspective; and the bureaucratic politics perspective. The remaining three he called 'alternative perspectives': integration logic; interdependence logic; and 'self-styled' logic.

Ginsberg argued that the national interest perspective was better at explaining the breakdown of joint action than it was at explaining why joint action sometimes occurred. The elite-actor perspective, he argued, could work either way: elite actors could favour or oppose political co-operation. A domestic politics perspective offered little theoretical leverage because there was very little input from domestic politics into foreign policy generally, and especially not into the elite-dominated process of EPC. While bureaucratic politics was neither really accepted nor dismissed (Ginsberg 1989: 17–19), integration theories he believed provided some explanatory leverage: the creation of EPC was 'in part an example of neofunctionalist spillover' (Ginsberg 1989: 25) because one of the main drivers of the process was the need for a political complement to the economic policies of the EC. Interdependence theories put the focus on the external environment, and saw EPC as an attempt 'to reduce the adverse costs of global interdependence by deliberately co-ordinating joint policy actions' (Ginsberg 1989: 31). However, while interdependence might be a background condition that could stimulate integration, Ginsberg did not believe that it could explain the why and where of it.

His own favoured perspective in the book was the 'self-styled' logic, a synthesis of elements from all of the other perspectives, which took the EC and the member states seriously as actors responding to their environment. This eclectic approach was not, however, taken up by other contributors to the debate, which tended to fall into the same pattern of division as the wider debates about European integration.

Glarbo (1999) put forward two alternatives to realist approaches. The first was that important developments in political co-operation can only be understood as the outcome not only of national interest, but also of a growing level of communication between national officials. The second was that, contrary to realist analyses, integration *had* occurred within the field of political co-operation; it was a form of social integration stemming from the communication processes that the institutions of EPC and CFSP had set up.

Prior to the launch of EPC in 1970, there was relatively little routine communication between national foreign policy elites, although some regularized interaction between national elites involved in defence issues had begun through NATO and the WEU. Under these conditions of little cross-national interaction, the national diplomatic actors held national images of the international system and of the foreign policies of other states, including those of their EC partners. They also defined the national interest in a way that was determined by these images and by purely national social interactions. The start of EPC soon began to change that. Perceptions began to change after 1970, when implementation of the Luxembourg Report led to the creation of new structures through which national actors came into institutionalized contact with their counterparts from other member states.

The period between the Luxembourg Report and the Copenhagen Report in 1973 saw the improvisation of institutional developments to put flesh on the Luxembourg Report's skeletal framework of institutions, which was necessary to make EPC work. The whole structure of schedules for meetings of Ministers and the political committee, the setting up of the group of correspondents, the working groups, and the involvement of national permanent representations, ambassadors, etc. was developed incrementally, then formalized in the Copenhagen Report. The process did not stop there, though, but continued after the Copenhagen Report. In 1974, in response to divisions between member states over the Middle East and energy policy, the 'Gymnich formula' was devised whereby Foreign Ministers met informally without a fixed agenda and without the involvement of large numbers of officials. The name came from the venue of the first meeting: Schloss Gymnich in Germany. So successful did the formula prove that the procedure was institutionalized as meetings twice a year.

During the early years of EPC, the focus was almost entirely on two issues: relations with the communist world and those with the Middle East. On the first, the member states together devised the idea of the CSCE, which started as a one-off conference in 1975, but through the follow-up conferences became institutionalized as a means of fostering functional links between eastern and western Europe. The process was never enthusiastically supported by the United States, and eventually was prevented from bearing fruit by the decision of the Reagan Administration to pursue confrontational policies with the Soviet Union that ultimately brought about the collapse of the communist system. Nevertheless, CSCE is generally considered to be a success of the EPC, and it generated the OSCE, which was helpful in picking up some of the pieces left after the destruction wrought by the United States. In the Middle East, also, the member states came to define a common position that was distinct from that of the United States.

Realists explained CSCE as trivial, and the Middle East as a coincidence of national interests. Glarbo (1999: 643–4) explained them as the emergence of a process of discovering a European identity. From these early endeavours to find a common policy emerged what is often referred to as the 'co-ordination reflex', a habit of co-ordinating responses to the international environment not as a means of achieving national objectives, but as 'the done thing'.

The 'continuous communicative process' (Glarbo 1999: 644) that the EPC set going shifted the perceptions of the actors. They became sensitive to the constraints on the other actors, and tried to accommodate them. A code of conduct emerged whereby actors tried not to surprise their partners with faits accomplis. They also came to define the national interest differently, taking account of the emerging *acquis politique*, the accumulation of decisions and policy positions adopted through the EPC process. These developments were recognized by the actors, who were quite prepared to acknowledge in interviews with academics that their national practices had been modified as a result of participation in EPC, and who themselves contributed in surprisingly large numbers to the literature on the process, thereby coming to 'participate in the epistemic community surrounding this field' (Glarbo 1999: 659). In public statements, the advantages of EPC were presented in terms of how the process served national interests, but only because this was the language that was expected and understood by the wider public.

In a series of articles, Michael E. Smith (1999; 2000; 2001; 2003; 2004) developed a theoretical perspective on political co-operation that drew on the insights of social constructivism and historical institutionalism. In this perspective, while the process of political co-operation began as an intergovernmental bargain, once the process was under way, it took on a different aspect.

It is an analysis that has echoes of neofunctionalism, which also accepted that the spillover process only began after the EC had been set up by intergovernmental agreement. (It should be noted, though, that in the earliest of the articles listed above—Smith 1999: 305—an alternative analysis is suggested, that EPC could be the result of functional spillover 'to augment the expanding economic policies of the EC in the face of its first enlargement'. This echoes the analysis of Ginsberg 1989: 25 as reported above.)

There were three linked elements in the transition from intergovernmentalism to a new system that went beyond intergovernmentalism to take on some of the features of supranational governance. In decreasing order of importance, these were: the development of transgovernmental relations; the development and codification of EPC rules; and the forging of links with EC actors, especially the Commission (Smith 1999: 309–10).

The initial bargain was part of the deal that allowed French President Pompidou to agree to British entry to the EC. In return for lifting the veto that had been imposed by his predecessor—President de Gaulle—Pompidou got agreement to a funding scheme for the Common Agricultural Policy that would benefit France, and to the setting up of a system of political co-operation that resembled the scheme that de Gaulle had advocated in the Fouchet Plan. Initial negotiations within EPC were conducted on the basis of existing national positions, so that, in its early years, EPC looked like classic intergovernmentalism—but this did not last. The intensive interaction between national representatives that was implicit in the idea of political co-operation constituted a system of transgovernmental relations in which these discrete national positions began to be modified (Smith 2004: 114–22).

Gradually also a system of norms and unwritten rules of behaviour began to emerge (compare the analysis in Glarbo, 1999). The norms emphasized the importance of communication and consultation on foreign policy issues. They also included a firm understanding that discussions were confidential, and that they would proceed on the basis of consensus, not voting nor veto. In addition, reserved domains in areas of particular sensitivity to one or more states were accepted without requiring justification. All of this made it much easier for discussion to take place without any national representation feeling threatened by having entered into the engagement, and facilitated the building of trust between the participants. Out of this trust, and the constant process of discussion, emerged a socialization of participants, which led naturally to the gradual displacement of instrumental rationality by social rationality: the replacement of a bargaining approach by a problem-solving approach (Smith 2004).

The second aspect of the movement of EPC away from intergovernmentalism was the development and codification of EPC rules. This process, which can be described as the 'institutionalization' of EPC, has already been described above (pp. 510–11). The increasingly rich institutional structure provided the forum for intensive interaction between officials from different levels in national Foreign Ministries. The **transgovernmental network** of diplomats and technical experts was thus extended and deepened. Such intensive interaction could not but influence the attitudes of professional diplomatic actors, and through them the process of defining the national interest (compare here the process described in Chapter 21, pp. 282–5). It fed back into national institutional structures, too. Political co-operation required the creation of new posts to serve it. This led to the expansion of national diplomatic services, and a reorientation of internal structures, sometimes amounting to complete reorganizations (Smith 2000: 619–23).

The third element in the transformation of EPC was the forging of links with EC institutions, especially the Commission. The reasons for involving the Commission and the EP in political co-operation have been outlined above (p. 511). Eventually, the role of the Commission in ensuring the consistency of EPC and EC actions was codified in the SEA (Smith 2001: 90). From this point on, the involvement of the Commission in political co-operation was not only customary, but it was also mandatory. The EP was allowed a minor role for reasons of democratic legitimacy, although the ECJ was kept at arm's length from CFSP.

Explaining ESDP

Can this analysis also be applied to ESDP? Certainly the initiation of the security and defence dimension to CFSP has to be explained in terms of intergovernmental politics. In this case, coinciding national interests, one of the realist/intergovernmental explanations for political co-operation, has to be given a dominant role. The experience of the crises in the Gulf, in Bosnia, and in Kosovo all pointed up the weakness of the EU. From the French point of view, awareness of the gap that had opened up between US and European military capabilities, and especially the dependence of the French armed forces on the United States for reconnaissance and for transport of equipment, pushed towards closer collaboration with NATO in the short term because it was obvious that there was no immediate prospect of these vital gaps being filled by France without an unsustainable increase in military expenditure. In the longer term, the gaps might be filled by collaboration between European states, but clearly the co-operation of the British would be essential given that Britain was the other main military power in the EU. From the British point of view, the rapprochement between France and NATO was encouraging, and, in the wake of the two Balkan crises, the United States began to pressure the Europeans to get their act together so that they could make a bigger contribution to policing their own hinterland.

It is possible, though, that other factors were at work. Howorth (2004) identified an 'epistemic community' that had formed around the issue of defence. He argued that one of the facilitating factors in the determination of Britain and France to take forward the project of ESDP in 2001 was 'the close-knit epistemic community of senior officials in London and Paris who, from the early 1990s onwards, had gradually developed a common mindset around the necessity and legitimacy of ESDP' (Howorth 2003: 175).

Whatever the contribution of these pre-existing transgovernmental links to the start of the ESDP, once collaboration began, the same process identified by Michael E. Smith for political co-operation generally, and outlined above, could be expected to take place. CFSP had been kept firmly under the control of national Foreign Offices. National Ministries of Defence were not given a role. This changed with the ESDP initiatives. New transgovernmental links started to be built between officials of national Ministries of Defence, and between military personnel. Some links already existed, of course, because of co-operation in NATO and the WEU, although the links were less intense for France, which was outside of the NATO command structure, and for those EU member states that were not members of NATO or WEU.

Because it was in its early stages when events changed everything in September 2001, the ESDP process of socialization was particularly prone to be disrupted. In the summer of 2001, the pre-existing alliance of like-minded officials identified by Howorth (2004) had already been disrupted by a major reshuffle of responsibilities in London. The new officials came into office just before the strategic priorities of the government were reordered by the events of 11 September. They were therefore less committed to the ESDP when the political direction changed (Howorth 2003: 177–8). However, by this time, the institutional structure of ESDP was already in place, so the process of intensive interaction of officials was going to continue. As Smith (1999) argued, socialization and institutionalization interact with one another. The processes are still new when compared with the parallel CFSP processes for non-military co-operation on foreign policy, and so are particularly vulnerable to being blown off course by events. They operate at a slow pace, beneath the level of current affairs—but once institutionalized, they can be expected to continue, and eventually to have an impact on the way in which national leaders perceive events and respond to them.

CONCLUSION

European co-operation on the political aspects of external relations arose partly out of necessity and partly out of the ambitions of some EC member states, particularly France, to use the EC as a platform to exert greater global influence than any one European state could exercise acting alone. It expanded partly as a result of the process itself generating its own momentum, and partly through the member states trying to learn the lessons of their failures to deal adequately with a series of international crises.

The necessity for EPC came from the inextricable tangling of external economic and external political relations. For the EC to maximize its economic influence, it had to have a coherent relationship between the economic and the political. From an early stage, other states expected the EC to behave as a single unified actor on the world stage, placing a burden of expectation on the member states for which they were partly responsible because they spoke of European integration in terms that represented aspirations rather than realities.

For successive French governments, EPC represented a vehicle for France's global ambitions to be realized. That would only work, though, were France to be driving the vehicle. Also, France's keenness on using the greater weight given to it from having the backing of the other member states did not extend to wanting to see any erosion of national sovereignty. In short, France wanted to keep control of the whole process itself. This was just about feasible so long as France and Germany were the dominant states in a small EC, and so long as German governments were more anxious to maintain the alliance with the French than to assert their own country's status in the world. It became much more problematic once Britain became a member. Although the British agreed with the French in not wanting to see an erosion of national sovereignty, they disagreed on many substantive aspects of international diplomacy, including particularly the relationship of the EC/EU to the United States.

By this time, though, EPC had taken on something of a life of its own. The practice of collaboration between national foreign ministries led to a habit of consultation that eroded stark national positions on issues that did not become overtly politicized. Major crises proved difficult for the Europeans to handle jointly because they had a high domestic profile and senior politicians took control of the decisions. Between crises, though, a web of procedures and a growing *acquis* of joint positions were imperceptibly eroding the separate national foreign policies and slowly putting a European policy in their place.

Paradoxically, the crises themselves contributed to furthering EPC. Each time the EC/EU failed to act decisively in a crisis, each time the United States was able to take the lead or had to do so because of European failings, there was a round of soul-searching and attempts to make future co-operation more effective. This produced the transition from EPC to CFSP and the efforts to create an ESDP. While the 'capability–expectations' gap remained, the weight of international expectations acted as a spur to continued efforts to increase capabilities. The creation of the role of High Representative in the Amsterdam Treaty, and the extension of the role and responsibilities of this post in the Lisbon Treaty, were indicative of a desire to reduce the gap by increasing the 'actorness' of the EU, while the appointment of Catherine Ashton, who was inexperienced in international affairs and not well known outside of Brussels and the community of trade officials, perhaps indicated a continuing reluctance of the larger member states to lose any control over foreign and security policy.

KEY POINTS

History

- European political co-operation (EPC) was set up in 1970. It consisted of regular meetings of Foreign Ministers and of senior Foreign Office officials to try to co-ordinate national foreign policies.

- EPC was incorporated into the Treaties for the first time with the SEA, which also created a small EPC secretariat.

- Initially, the Commission was excluded from meetings of Foreign Ministers under EPC, but gradually the role of the Commission increased.

- EPC had several substantive successes to its name: achieving a high degree of unified voting at the UN; conducting an effective 'Euro–Arab dialogue'; and launching and sustaining the CSCE process.

- Failures of EPC occurred in responding to the invasion of Afghanistan by the USSR in December 1979, over the Gulf Crisis in 1990–91, and over successive crises in former Yugoslavia.

The Common Foreign and Security Policy (CFSP) and European Security and Defence Policy (ESDP)

- In the run-up to Maastricht, the Commission and the Germans argued for EPC to come under EC rules (including QMV) and to include security and defence issues; the British opposed this, stressing the intergovernmental nature of EPC and the central role of NATO in defence.

- The TEU made CFSP a separate pillar of the EU from the EC; QMV was restricted to implementation of agreed measures, and could only be used if all participants agreed.

- In 1998–99, as a reaction to the failure of the EU to respond effectively to the crisis in Kosovo, the first steps were taken towards the ESDP. The institutions of ESDP began work in 2000. It was incorporated into the EU by the Nice Treaty.

- The Treaty of Amsterdam created the post of High Representative for CFSP, which was later extended in the Lisbon Treaty to the High Representative for Foreign Affairs and Security Policy. Lisbon also created the European External Action Service.

CFSP and ESDP in Action

- Initial actions under CFSP were modest and built on EPC; subsequently stability pacts for Europe and for the Mediterranean extended the scope of activity.

- The terrorist attacks in the United States in September 2001 caused a series of setbacks to the progress that had been made on the ESDP. Initial support for the United States began to waver in the light of the Bush Administration's identification of an 'axis of evil'. The invasion of Iraq led to an open rift, especially between Britain, which supported the US action, and France and Germany, which condemned it.

- Despite these setbacks, by the end of 2009, ESDP had undertaken some twenty-two crisis-management missions.

Explaining CFSP and ESDP

- Hill (1993) identified a 'capability–expectations gap' in the international activities of the EC, which he expected would only increase when it became the EU.

- Realists assumed that political co-operation would never amount to more than trivial actions or would only achieve success where national interests coincided.

- Social constructivist perspectives emphasize the extent to which social interaction between foreign policy practitioners has led to a changing of their perspectives and the emergence of a common outlook.

- Historical institutionalist perspectives add to the constructivist analysis the insight that pragmatic institutional developments build in 'path dependence' for the process, making it difficult to reverse.

- The process that brought about the approximation of general foreign policy positions may now be repeated for security and defence policy.

FURTHER READING

A clear introduction to the complexity of the European Union's external relations is provided by **Karen Smith**, *European Union Foreign Policy in a Changing World* (Cambridge: Polity Press, 2008). Also very useful is **C. Hill and M. Smith (eds)**, *International Relations and the European Union* (Oxford: Oxford University Press, 2005), with a second edition due in 2011.

Given its importance to so many later contributions, and the frequency with which the central idea is misunderstood or misused, an article that should certainly be read is **C. Hill**, 'The Capability–Expectations Gap, or Conceptualising Europe's International Role', *Journal of Common Market Studies*, 31 (1993): 305–28; the analysis can then be followed up by looking at *Hill, The Actors in Europe's Foreign Policy* (London: Routledge, 1996), and 'Closing the Capability–Expectations Gap', in **J. Peterson and H. Sjursen (eds)**, *A Common Foreign Policy for Europe? Competing Visions of the CFSP* (London: Routledge, 1998), 18–38. A more recent review of the factors that have increased the 'actorness' of the EU, and those that continue to weaken it is provided in **U. Krotz**, 'Momentum and Impediments: Why Europe Won't Emerge as a Full Political Actor on the World Stage Soon', *JCMS: Journal of Common Market Studies*, 47 (2009): 555–78.

A useful assessment of the progress made by the ESDP can be found in **A. Menon**, 'Empowering Paradise: The ESDP at Ten', *International Affairs*, 85 (2010): 227–46.

online resource centre

Visit the Online Resource Centre that accompanies this book for links to more information on the Common Foreign and Security Policy, including to the website of the relevant Directorate-General of the Commission: www.oxfordtextbooks.co.uk/orc/bache3e/

Chapter 34
Enlargement

Chapter Overview

Starting with six member states originally, the European Community (EC)/European Union (EU) has grown through successive enlargements—from six to nine, then ten, twelve, fifteen, twenty-five, and now twenty-seven. This chapter looks at each of the main enlargement rounds in turn, outlining what happened and what the effect was on the EC/EU, and at the outstanding applications that are still under consideration, paying particular attention to the application of Turkey, which has proved extremely divisive between member states within the EU. A procedure emerged over the six rounds of enlargement that is being applied to the present applications, and this is explained. Academic explanations of why the various applications for membership were made, and why they were accepted by the EC/EU, are reviewed.

The enlargement of the European Union is a key political process both for the organization itself and the international relations of Europe in general.

(Schimmelfennig and Sedelmeier 2002: 500)

In the original Treaties, membership of the European Communities was held open to all European states, but the procedure was not specified in detail. When the success of the enterprise of integration led to requests for membership from other states, the Commission had to develop a procedure, to which it has added incrementally over the six rounds of enlargement. Each enlargement round has had a profound effect on the nature of the EC/EU itself. Academic studies have raised questions about why applications have been made, why they have been accepted, and what effect enlargements have had on the EU.

History

The EC/EU has preferred to negotiate enlargements with groups of states together. This has produced six distinct rounds of enlargement (Table 34.1), starting in 1973 when Britain, Denmark, and Ireland became members.

Table 34.1 Enlargements of the EEC/EC/EU

Year	1973	1981	1986	1995	2004	2007
New members	Denmark, Ireland, UK	Greece	Portugal, Spain	Austria, Finland, Sweden	Cyprus, Czech Republic, Estonia, Hungary, Latvia, Lithuania, Malta, Poland, Slovakia, Slovenia	Bulgaria, Romania

Source: **http://ec.europa.eu**, © European Union, 1995–2010

The second enlargement was in 1981, when Greece became a member, and the third was in 1986, when Portugal and Spain joined. For analytical purposes, the second and third enlargements are often treated as a single 'Southern enlargement', as they were undertaken for similar reasons and involved similar issues.

The fourth enlargement was that of 1995, which admitted Austria, Finland, and Sweden. Because the applicants (including Norway, which rejected membership in a referendum) were the leading members of the European Free Trade Association (EFTA) (Insight 34.1), this is usually referred to as 'the EFTA enlargement'.

The fifth and sixth enlargements, in 2004 and 2007, are often referred to collectively as 'the Eastern enlargement' because most of the new entrants were former

---

Insight 34.1 EFTA at the End of the 1980s

The European Free Trade Association (EFTA) was set up in 1959 and entered into force in January 1960. It was a response to the setting up of the European Economic Community (EEC) in 1958. The original members of EFTA were Austria, Britain, Denmark, Norway, Portugal, Sweden, and Switzerland.

By the late 1980s, EFTA consisted of seven states of varying size.

Country	Population (000s)
Sweden	8,640
Austria	7,820
Switzerland	6,790
Finland	5,030
Norway	4,260
Iceland	256
Liechtenstein	30

- The economies of the EFTA states had been linked with those of the EC since the 1970s by a series of bilateral free trade agreements.

- By the end of the 1980s, EFTA was economically closely integrated with the EC.

- The EC did 25 per cent of its trade with EFTA, a higher proportion than with the United States, while the EFTA states sent 56 per cent of their exports to the EC, and bought 60 per cent of their imports from the EC.

communist states in central and eastern Europe. Strictly speaking, this name is inaccurate, because two of the entrants in 2004—Cyprus and Malta—were Mediterranean island states.

The First Enlargement

In August 1961, Britain, Denmark, and Ireland applied for membership of the EC. In April 1962, Norway also applied. The key applicant here was Britain. The other applicants were highly dependent on their economic links with Britain, which were fostered through their membership of EFTA. None of these states could afford to risk the loss of trade with their biggest customer that might result from Britain going into the European Economic Community (EEC) while they remained outside.

Negotiations went on throughout 1962, until in January 1963, President de Gaulle of France unilaterally announced that France was not prepared to accept British membership. As any member state could veto entry, and as the other applications were dependent on British entry, the enlargement round collapsed.

In May 1967, Britain, Denmark, and Ireland applied again, and Norway joined the second application in July. This time, negotiations did not even get under way: France blocked agreement on opening negotiations in December 1967. Following the replacement of de Gaulle by Georges Pompidou as French President in 1969, a summit meeting at The Hague agreed on a package of measures to 'relaunch Europe' that included opening negotiations with the applicants, the 1967 applications of which remained on the table (Chapter 10, p. 136). On 1 January 1973, Britain, Denmark, and Ireland became members of the EC. Norway negotiated terms of entry, but the Norwegian people rejected membership in a subsequent referendum in 1972.

The impact of the first enlargement on the EC was profound. In terms of bargaining games, not only did the total number of member states increase by 50 per cent, but there was also another 'big state' among the new members—Britain—which changed the coalition dynamics that had previously been dominated by France and West Germany. In terms of the sense of self-identity of the EC, the admission of two states—Britain and Denmark—that were sceptical of the 'European ideal' made it much more difficult to find a common discourse to conceptualize the mission of the organization.

The Southern Enlargements

As explained above, the second and third enlargements of the EC are often treated as a single 'Southern' enlargement. Greece became a member state in January 1981, and Spain and Portugal in January 1986. In all cases, political considerations overrode economic in the decision to enlarge.

All three of the states concerned had just emerged from periods of dictatorship, and the desire to consolidate democracy and guard against a resurgence of authoritarianism featured strongly in the reasons for the applications and the reasons for their acceptance. It was assumed that EC membership, conditional on democratic government, would help to achieve that. The impact of this enlargement on the EC/EU was in its way as great as that of the first enlargement. Again, it changed the bargaining dynamics of the organization. The three new members shifted the orientation of the EC to the south, and the membership of Greece and Spain ensured that there would be a stronger Mediterranean dimension to policy. In political co-operation, the influence of Spain and Portugal led to a greater emphasis on relations with Latin America. Perhaps most significantly in the short run, Spain, with the support of the other new entrants, took the lead in demanding larger structural funds (Chapter 29, p. 442) and soon showed itself adept at playing the EC negotiating game to get them.

On the other hand, Greece's membership had some less positive consequences. Its long-standing disputes with Turkey proved an embarrassment to the EC/EU on more than one occasion, and spilled over into a hard line on Cyprus. Also, its position on the edge of the Balkans meant that Greece had sensitivities in the region that were difficult for other EU members to understand. These became particularly pertinent in the early 1990s following the break-up of Yugoslavia (see Chapter 15, pp. 184–5).

The EFTA Enlargement

In the early 1990s, several member states of EFTA enquired about membership. At first, they were offered a form of close association that fell short of full membership. Subsequently, though, they lodged formal applications, and eventually Austria, Finland, and Sweden became members of the EU on 1 January 1995. Norway again rejected membership in a referendum in 1994, after terms of entry had been agreed.

Because the new members were wealthy, were already culturally aligned with the prevailing values of the existing member states, and had been closely associated with the EC prior to their membership, the effects of this enlargement were smaller than those of any other enlargement.

One effect was the emergence of a Nordic bloc within the Council of Ministers. From 1995, Denmark received support from Sweden and Finland for positions on issues such as environmental protection and human rights that it had long defended, and the Nordic states combined to press the membership claims of the Baltic states (Estonia, Latvia, and Lithuania) in the Eastern enlargement round. Austria joined the Nordic states in reinforcing the coalition of member states for which environmental protection was a significant issue. Because the new members were all net contributors to the budget, their presence reinforced the coalition in favour of reform of the budgetary rules.

The 'Eastern' Enlargement

With the collapse of communism in 1989, the EC was faced with a large number of potential new members, all of which expressed an aspiration to join. The first response was to conclude 'Europe Agreements', Association Agreements that fell short of envisaging full membership. Then in June 1993 the Copenhagen European Council accepted the legitimacy of the aspirations of the newly independent states to become members, and laid down criteria that they would have to fulfil in order for their applications to be considered. Applications came in rapidly from ten central and eastern European countries (CEECs) plus Cyprus, Malta, and Turkey (Table 34.2).

In December 1997, the Luxembourg European Council agreed that negotiations should open with five of these states—the Czech Republic, Estonia, Hungary, Poland, and Slovenia—plus Cyprus (Malta had withdrawn its application), but hold back on the five others. In December 1999, the Helsinki European Council agreed to open

Table 34.2 Association Agreements and Accession Applications

State	Date of Association Agreement	Date of Accession Application
Bulgaria	March 1993	December 1995
Cyprus	December 1972	July 1990
Czech Republic	October 1993	January 1996
Estonia	June 1995	November 1995
Hungary	December 1991	March 1994
Latvia	June 1995	October 1995
Lithuania	June 1995	October 1995
Malta	December 1970	July 1990
Poland	December 1991	April 1994
Romania	February 1993	June 1995
Slovakia	October 1993	June 1995
Slovenia	June 1996	June 1996

Source: Europa website: **http://europa.eu.int/scadplus/leg/en/lvb/e40001.htm; http://ec.europa.eu**, © European Union, 1995–2010

negotiations with the remaining five CEECs, plus Malta, which had resubmitted its application. On 1 May 2004, eight CEECs—the Czech Republic, Estonia, Hungary, Latvia, Lithuania, Poland, Slovakia, and Slovenia—plus Cyprus and Malta, became members of the EU.

The two outstanding applications from former eastern European communist states were from Bulgaria and Romania. Starting from a lower base of both economic development and legal stability than the other applicants, they took longer to satisfy the basic criteria, but both became members in 2007.

The effects of this enlargement were profound. In order to be ready to take as many as twelve new members, the EU had to deal with some difficult issues requiring reforms of both policies and institutions. Two policy issues were particularly crucial to the prospects for enlargement: agriculture (Chapter 26, pp. 376–8) and the structural funds (Chapter 29, pp. 436–4). In both cases, the existing member states that were beneficiaries from the funds proved very reluctant to surrender their benefits to facilitate enlargement. The institutional questions were those that were already apparent at the time of the EFTA enlargement: the weighting of votes under **qualified majority voting (QMV)**, and the size of the blocking minority; the abandonment of the national veto in more policy sectors; and the size of the Commission.

Further Applications

With the completion of the Eastern enlargement, the EU faced the question of how far it would continue to expand geographically. There was no shortage of prospective applicants. There was the prospect of applications from the Yugoslav successor states, and expressions of interest from successor states of the former Soviet Union and even from several North African states. Above all, there was the pressing issue of Turkish membership.

Most of the successor states to the former Yugoslavia were not expected to be ready to make applications for some time, but in March 2003, Croatia applied for membership, and was granted candidate status in June; then, in March 2004, so did the former Yugoslav Republic of Macedonia. In April 2004, the Commission recommended the opening of negotiations with Croatia, which had made remarkable progress in a short time on both the political and economic fronts, and accession negotiations began in October 2005. The former Yugoslav Republic of Macedonia was granted candidate status in December 2005. Montenegro applied for membership in December 2008, Albania in April 2009, and Serbia in December 2009.

Beyond them lay states that had formerly been part of the Soviet Union itself: Armenia, Azerbaijan, Georgia, Moldova, and Ukraine. After June 2004, the borders of the enlarged EU abutted these states, but there was little prospect that they would be accepted as applicants. In May 2004, Günter Verheugen appeared to rule it out when he said (*Financial Times*, 13 May 2004): 'Membership is not on the agenda for these countries. Full stop.' His statement applied also to North African states such as Morocco and Tunisia that had expressed an interest in eventual membership. Clearly, these latter states were not European, which allowed membership to be ruled out. Nothing was so clear about the application from Turkey.

Turkey had been an applicant for membership for longer than any of the states that gained entry in 2004. An Association Agreement envisaging eventual membership had been signed in 1963. It had been suspended in 1970 and again in 1980, following military takeovers of power, but reinstated following elections and a return to civilian government in 1973 and again in 1983. In 1987, Turkey lodged its first formal application for membership of the EU. Two years later, the EU responded by saying that no further enlargement was envisaged in the foreseeable future. In 1995, a **customs union** agreement was signed, the first time that such an agreement had not been part of a process of accession. Then in 1997 came the Luxembourg European Council and the decision to move forward with various applications, but excluding Turkey. Two years later, the Helsinki European Council reversed this decision and recognized Turkey as an applicant, although without setting a date for the start of membership negotiations. Negotiations did eventually begin in October 2005, at the same time as those for Croatia.

Following the financial crisis of 2008–09, in which Icelandic banks suffered badly, the Icelandic parliament, the Althingi, narrowly voted (by thirty-three votes to twenty-eight with two abstentions) to apply for EU membership. The Prime Minister, Johanna Sigurdardottir, indicated that she would also like to see Iceland adopt the euro as soon as possible. Iceland was granted candidate status in June 2010.

The Enlargement Procedure

Over the course of the five rounds of enlargement, a procedure has gradually evolved. Each of the enlargements has added something to this emerging approach.

When a potential applicant approaches the EU, the first step is for the European Council to consider whether the application is acceptable in principle. If it is, then the Commission produces an official Opinion on the application. This consists of a report on the economic and political position of the applicant state, and a recommendation on whether to proceed to negotiations immediately, or whether to delay. Usually, the recommendation to delay is to give the applicant time to strengthen its claim to be ready for membership. If so, then a plan of action is produced to facilitate this, which will normally involve an Association Agreement or the strengthening of existing agreements.

If the decision of the European Council is to proceed with the application immediately, it will set a date for the opening of negotiations. The Commission will then convene meetings of various sectoral groups of experts to work out the detail of the EU's negotiating position. Negotiations then commence with the applicant(s). These are handled on a day-to-day basis by the groups of experts, often by correspondence rather than in formal meetings. They are co-ordinated by the Commission, and overseen by the Council of Foreign Ministers.

When agreement has been reached by the expert working groups in all sectors, and have been pronounced acceptable by the Foreign Ministers, the terms are passed to the European Council for formal approval. Assuming that approval is given, an Accession Treaty is drawn up with each applicant state. The Accession Treaty then has to be ratified by the European Parliament on the side of the EU, and by either the national parliament of the applicant state, or by referendum depending on the constitutional procedures of each state.

The practice that was established at the time of the first enlargement was that the existing member states would sort out arrangements that suited them before the new members were admitted. The corollary of this was French insistence that accession for the new members could only be on the basis of acceptance of the complete *acquis communautaire* (Preston 1995: 452). This was to ensure that Britain did not try to slip out of the uncomfortable budgetary position into which the French believed that it had manoeuvred it. The implicit understanding that there was a deal in operation here explains the strength of French (and German) resistance to subsequent British demands for a correction of the budgetary imbalance.

The main contribution that the Southern enlargement made to the principles on which future enlargements would be conducted, was the precedent set for the acceptance of applications for geo-strategic and political reasons even where the economic conditions were not ideal. This was relevant to the applications from a range of CEECs following the collapse of communism in 1989. Although the economies of these states were not strong, the need to ensure their political stability was; the 1975 Council decision to override the Commission's Opinion on Greece, and later to wave aside doubts about the economic preparedness of Portugal for membership for similar political reasons, created a precedent to do the same for these new applicants.

The EFTA enlargement did not produce any new principles, but in the negotiation of the Eastern enlargement, formal criteria were laid down for the first time. These criteria arose from concern about the preparedness of the former communist states for membership, and because they were agreed at the June 1993 Copenhagen European Council, they are known as the Copenhagen criteria (1993). They are:

- a political criterion—that an applicant must have stable institutions, guaranteeing democracy, the rule of law, human rights, and the protection of minorities;

- an economic criterion—that an applicant must have a functioning market economy and the capacity to cope with competitive pressures within the single market of the EU;
- a criterion relating to the *acquis communautaire*—that an applicant must be able to take on the obligations of membership, including adherence to the aims of political, economic, and monetary union.

Although these were originally criteria for the acceptance of applications, they have also came to structure the negotiations on membership, and were applied in the negotiations with subsequent applicants. The criteria owed much to the consensus in other international organizations such as the **International Monetary Fund (IMF)** and **World Bank** on the conditions under which assistance would be given to states requesting it.

As a postscript to the procedure for joining the EU, it should be noted that, until the Treaty of Lisbon entered into force in December 2009, there was no procedure for leaving the EU. Greenland, which had joined as part of Denmark in 1973, held a referendum on membership after it gained home rule in 1979, which produced a vote to leave. A special Treaty, the Greenland Treaty of 1984, had to be drawn up to facilitate this. The Lisbon Treaty amended the Treaty on European Union to include a new Article 50, which says:

A Member State which decides to withdraw [from the Union] shall notify the European Council of its intention . . . The Union shall negotiate and conclude an agreement with that State, setting out the arrangements for its withdrawal . . .

Explaining Enlargement

Schimmelfennig and Sedelmeier (2002) produced a typology of the academic literature on enlargement, classifying it according to the research focus along four dimensions:

- the enlargement policies of the applicants;
- the enlargement policies of the existing member states;
- the enlargement policies of the EU;
- the impact of enlargement.

Structuring existing studies along these dimensions, Schimmelfennig and Sedelmeier (2002: 523–4) were able to conclude that:

- the bulk of the analytical studies were on the last two enlargements;
- the analyses of the EFTA enlargement focused primarily on their first dimension—questioning why the EFTA states applied for membership;
- the analyses of the Eastern enlargement focused primarily on their second and third dimensions—questioning why the applications were accepted, and on what conditions the applicants were offered membership.

Schimmelfennig and Sedelmeier (2002: 508–15) also divided existing studies of enlargement according to whether they emphasized interests or ideas in their analysis. They referred to these as 'rationalist' and 'constructivist' institutionalism (see Chapters 2 and 3).

In what follows, the variation of the degree of explanation offered for the various enlargements and for the various elements identified by Schimmelfennig and Sedelmeier (2002) reflects the paucity or richness of the published analyses.

Explanations of the First Enlargement

It is generally agreed that to understand why the applicant states of the first enlargement decided to seek entry, it is primarily necessary to consider the reasons for the British application. The other applicants were so tightly bound economically to Britain that they could not afford to stay outside the EC if Britain went in. There were two main factors behind the British application: economic and geo-strategic.

Sluggish economic growth in Britain in the late 1950s was increasingly blamed by economists both inside and outside government on the pattern of trade. Britain at the end of the 1950s still did a high proportion of its trade with the countries of its former Empire, now voluntarily grouped together as the Commonwealth—but the fastest growth in trade was between industrialized countries. This was reflected in the high rates of growth within the newly formed EEC. The success of the EEC surprised British policy makers, and led to efforts in the late 1950s to conclude a free trade agreement with the six. When this failed, an application for British entry for economic reasons began to be taken seriously. For Moravcsik (1998: 164), such economic reasons were paramount: 'The British membership bid was ... aimed primarily at the advancement of enduring British commercial interests.'

Political considerations started to point in the same direction when de Gaulle began to dominate the EEC, and became especially influential when he made proposals for political co-operation in the Fouchet Plan (Insight 9.2, p. 128). British concern centred on the known hostility of de Gaulle to US hegemony in the capitalist world. Fouchet contained reference to co-operation on defence, but no reference to NATO. Because it was a central doctrine of British defence policy that the United States must be allowed to exercise leadership of the western defence effort through NATO, Fouchet set alarm bells ringing in London. It did the same in Washington. Camps (1964: 336) recorded that the British government came under increasing pressure from the United States to join the EEC so as to act as a counterweight to French influence, and she believed that this was 'a very important—perhaps the controlling—element in Macmillan's decision to apply'. The same perception seems to have been one of the significant factors in de Gaulle's decision to block enlargement throughout the 1960s.

Initially, the EC member states other than France were interested in British membership for predominantly political reasons. They saw Britain as a future counterweight to French domination of the EC. Concern on this issue was particularly strong where political co-operation was involved. As Ludlow (1997) made clear, the negotiations on British accession in the early 1960s were implicitly linked to the parallel negotiations on the Fouchet Plan. When de Gaulle vetoed British entry, the Fouchet negotiations collapsed (Chapter 9, pp. 127–8). The reason why France finally accepted the British application in 1972 was primarily economic. The post-war economic boom

537

faltered in the late 1960s and British entry offered the prospect of giving a boost to the EC economies. The change of French President cleared the way.

Explanations of the Southern Enlargement

As suggested above (p. 531), the reasons for the applications of Greece, Portugal, and Spain have not generally been considered problematic. Each emerged from a period of right-wing dictatorship in the course of the 1970s, and the democratic government of each was anxious to embed the democratic constitution by tying in the state to the EC. It seemed equally clear that the existing member states were prepared to accept the applications for essentially the same reason: to stabilize their own southern flank. This assumption that there was no problem to be explained worked against detailed research on issues that were investigated for other enlargements.

Explanations of the EFTA Enlargement

The EFTA enlargement was the first to be systematically analysed in the literature. As Schimmelfennig and Sedelmeier (2002: 517) put it: 'The key question pursued is: why did the EFTA countries, after a long period of deliberate nonmembership in the European Community (EC), develop an interest in closer ties with, and membership of, the EC at the beginning of the 1990s?'

At the beginning of the 1980s, the European economies generally experienced an economic downturn. In response to the downturn, the EC launched the '1992 Project' to create the single European market. In the course of the 1980s, the member states of EFTA became concerned about the impact on investment in their economies of the EC's decision to create the single internal market. Export-oriented businesses in the EFTA states experienced difficulties in selling to the EU, with the result that increasingly businesses wanted to be inside the single market, and investment began to flow in that direction. Even large national companies of the EFTA states, such as Volvo of Sweden, were locating their investments inside the EC and not in the EFTA countries. This led the EFTA states to enquire about closer links with the EC, despite the unpopularity of the idea of membership inside some of the states concerned.

The other factor that affected the decision was the end of the Cold War. Events in 1989 removed one of the main objections of opponents of membership within the EFTA states. Austria, Finland, and Sweden were all neutral during the Cold War, and there had been doubts about whether membership of an organization that was developing a Common Foreign and Security Policy was compatible with neutrality. The end of the Cold War called into question the meaning of neutrality, and effectively dissipated the doubts on that score.

Sweden is the most studied of the cases from this enlargement. It illustrates well why analysts have considered their main problem to be explaining the reasons for the EFTA states' applications. Sweden was an exemplar of a social-democratic **neo-corporatist** type of state, and its social-democratic governments had previously rejected membership of the EC on the grounds that the free-market orientation of the organization would jeopardize the Swedish model of capitalism. Yet in 1991 a social-democratic government applied for membership at just the time that the EC was taking a major step in a neo-liberal direction with the single-market programme (Bieler 2002: 576): why?

Ingebritsen (1998) offered a rational choice explanation for the decision, in the mould of liberal intergovernmentalism. She concentrated on the leading industrial sectors, which in Sweden were export-oriented. The largest firms were also transnational, and in the course of the 1980s began to transfer production abroad. Swedish governments were already concerned about the country's lack of competitiveness, and the internal-market programme offered a means of injecting more competitiveness into the economy. So the combination of the push factor of the loss of investment and the pull factor of achieving domestic economic objectives through taking on external commitments (hand-tying) made the choice for membership of the internal market rational for the Swedish government.

At first, the EFTA states were offered membership of a new organization called the European Economic Area (EEA) (Insight 34.2). The Swedish government tried this approach, but it was abandoned in favour of an application for full membership because it did not satisfy the large Swedish manufacturers and did not stop the outward flow of **investment capital**. Essentially, the same analysis was applied to Finland, where the economy was also dominated by capital-intensive manufacturing exporters.

Fioretos (1997) offered a similar analysis. Essentially, Fioretos (1997) argued that globalization had increased the power of corporations in the domestic arena and allowed them to force governments onto paths of policy that they—the corporations—preferred. Like Ingebritsen (1998), Fioretos (1997) offered a rationalist analysis that was compatible with liberal intergovernmentalism.

Liberal intergovernmentalism analyses European integration as an example of a two-level game, in which the first stage is the formation of preferences (Chapter 1,

---

Insight 34.2 The European Economic Area

When the EFTA states first enquired about membership of the EC, the reaction from the Commission was to suggest an alternative. In January 1989, Commission President Delors proposed the idea of the European Economic Space (EES), which was later renamed the European Economic Area (EEA). This would give the EFTA states membership of the single market without them becoming full members of the EC. For the governments of the EFTA states, the EEA had the advantage that it might be easier than full membership of the EC to sell to their electorates. The disadvantage was that they would have no voice in the ongoing negotiation of the regulation of the single market. They would be obliged to accept agreements reached in their absence.

The EEA Agreement was signed between the then seven member states of EFTA and the then twelve member states of the EC in May 1992. Switzerland rejected membership in a referendum held in December 1992. The EEA entered into force for the remaining EFTA states on 1 January 1994, but one year later its membership on the EFTA side was reduced again when the accession to the EU of Austria, Finland, and Sweden took effect on 1 January 1995. This left Iceland, Norway, and (after 1 May 1995) Liechtenstein.

The EFTA members of the EEA enjoy the benefits of membership of the single market, but they have to adopt the law of the EU on social policy, consumer protection, the environment, and company law without having any formal voice in the making of those laws. They also have to contribute to the costs of maintaining the single market, including the social costs, but receive no money themselves from the various EU funds.

p. 13). At this stage: 'Groups articulate preferences; governments aggregate them' (Moravcsik 1993: 483).

This is exactly the relationship theorized by Fioretos (1997). In response to the economic downturn of the 1980s, Swedish firms took advantage of growing globalization to became transnational. This strengthened their hand in domestic bargaining with government because they had a much stronger option to exit the game than previously—that is, if they did not get their way, they could close down production in Sweden and switch it elsewhere. The firms were kept in Sweden in the 1980s by a series of devaluations that kept the krona at a competitive exchange rate with the economies of the EC, which were the main markets for Swedish manufactured products. This strategy could not be pursued indefinitely, though, and increasingly investment capital did leave Sweden for EC locations that offered lower costs of production and lower transport costs because of greater proximity to the market. Weakened in the domestic bargaining game by the greater ease with which capital could relocate, the Swedish social democrats had to pursue membership of the single market, which meant membership of the EC once it became clear that the EEA was an unsatisfactory compromise for Swedish firms.

Bieler (2000; 2002) offered a neo-Gramscian analysis (see Chapter 3, p. 50) that gave more emphasis to the role of ideas. Sweden was compared with Austria. Whereas the transnational sectors were the primary economic actors in Sweden, in Austria, the dominant economic sector was not transnational. It consisted of internationally oriented national firms, which were dependent on exports to the EC but did not have the production facilities outside their own country that the larger Swedish firms had acquired during the 1980s. This sector dominated the Austrian Federation of Industrialists.

In order to convince the Austrian government to apply for membership, the Federation had to overcome political opposition. So it undertook what Bieler (2002: 583) called a 'hegemonic project'. This involved issuing a series of studies that not only advanced a strong version of the neo-liberal economic argument, but also dealt with the constitutional implications of membership and the issue of what it implied for Austria's post-war neutrality. These arguments then fed into internal debates within the two main political parties—the Social Democratic Party and the People's Party. Although they encountered opposition from representatives of the economic sectors that had been sheltered from foreign competition by the state, and from representatives of the public sector, they eventually won over the leadership of both parties, thus setting the course for the application. By the time of the Austrian referendum in June 1994, a new orthodoxy had emerged around membership, thus ensuring a comfortable 'yes' vote by 66.6 per cent to 33.4 per cent.

In Sweden, Bieler (2002: 586–7) argued that the transnational corporations did not need to build a hegemonic project in favour of membership because they had the option of exit. Instead, they brutally spelt out the implications of not joining: notably, in a series of advertisements in national newspapers in the run-up to the 1994 general election (Fioretos 1997: 316). Swedish membership was pushed most strongly by the Ministry of Finance and the Prime Ministers' Office, and Bieler (2002: 585) argued that this showed that 'neo-liberal restructuring had become … internalized within the Swedish form of state in view of domestic economic recession'. In other words, the Swedish government was looking for a long-term means of solving the country's chronic economic problems, and had accepted the ideological claims of neo-liberalism to provide the only such solution. It was therefore trying to tie its own hands by joining the EC, which would provide an external buttress against resistance to the dismantling of the welfare state and neo-corporatist institutions of Sweden.

The initial response of the EU was to offer the prospective applicants a form of relationship that fell short of full membership. This position was then abandoned, and the applications for full membership accepted. So why the change of attitude?

At the time of the initial approach from the EFTA states, the EC was trying to process the legislation that was needed to make a reality of the internal market. It was also looking to the next stage in the process. To prevent another round of enlargement dominating the attention of the organization, and possibly deflecting the course of the spillover from the single market to the single currency, Delors proposed the creation of a European Economic Space. This later became the EEA (Insight 34.2).

The EEA negotiations were successfully concluded in 1991, and a Treaty was signed in 1992—but it became increasingly apparent that businesses were simply not prepared to accept that members of the EEA would be full members of the single market. Investment flows did not revert to previous patterns. The EEA suffered a further blow to its credibility when the Swiss people rejected membership of it in a referendum in December 1992. The government of Austria had already applied for full membership of the EC in July 1989, and Finland, Norway, and Sweden did likewise between July 1991 and November 1992.

By this time, the prospect had emerged of an eventual Eastern enlargement to embrace states that were economically considerably less developed than the existing member states. The EFTA applicants were wealthy, and potential net contributors to a common budget that would come under much greater pressure if the CEECs were eventually accepted. So, the EFTA applications were accepted.

Explanations of the Eastern Enlargement

As with the membership applications of Greece, Portugal, and Spain in the 1970s, the wish of the former communist states to become members of the EU has hardly been considered problematic. The states that had emerged from Soviet domination wanted to cement their status as Europeans, and to foreclose any possibility of being drawn back into the Russian sphere of influence. From this point of view, membership of NATO was the more important objective, but membership of the EU was also a guarantee, albeit weaker. The former communist states also saw EU membership as essential to their future economic success, and it fitted with a widespread desire to reaffirm a European identity.

Bieler (2002: 588–9) applied neo-Gramscian concepts to the analysis of why the applications by the former communist states were made. He suggested that the decision to apply was taken by what he called 'cadre élites within state institutions'. These elites had taken advantage of the collapse of the previous regimes to take power and to introduce programmes of neo-liberal reconstruction, supported by external forces. When the restructuring programmes precipitated big falls in gross domestic product (GDP), the legitimacy of the elites and of their reform programmes were jeopardized. EU membership was pursued as a buttress against resistance and reversion to anti-capitalist politicians and policies. It was sold to the populations of the CEECs as a historical 'return to Europe'. However, the volatility of society and politics in the CEECs ruled out the construction of a pro-EU historical bloc organized around a hegemonic project such as Bieler (2002: 582–5) had identified in Austria. Instead, the process in the CEECs was what Gramsci had described as a 'passive revolution', led from above by the state elites. This had implications for the commitment of socio-economic actors to the project.

The immediate reaction of the EC to the collapse of communism was to offer the Europe Agreements, which did not make a commitment to eventual membership. In explanation of this, Friis (1998) pointed out that the collapse of communism came quickly and was not anticipated. The immediate response of the EC to developments focused on the implications of the rapid moves to reunify Germany (Friis 1998: 323). The European Commission had to deal with the prospect of a sudden increase in the territory of the EC, and the adaptation of common policies to the addition of another 17 million people with a GDP per head well below the EC average. Attention inevitably focused on these issues until they were resolved.

Second, the negotiation of the EFTA enlargement was still at an early stage in 1989. Indeed, the EC was still following a policy of trying to persuade the EFTA applicants to become part of the single market without becoming members of the EC—that is, the EEA negotiations. As with German reunification, this issue had to be settled before serious attention could be given to the position of the CEECs. Also, it would have been surprising had the CEECs been given a perspective of membership before negotiations had opened on the applications of the prior EFTA applicants. The deal offered in the original Europe Agreements was similar to that on offer to the EFTA states at that stage: membership of the single market without membership of the EC.

Third, the EC was in 1989 about to embark on the process of agreeing to a monetary union. The Delors Report was published April 1989, before Hungary cut the first hole in the iron curtain by throwing open its borders to the west in May. The Madrid European Council in June 1989 agreed to set up an intergovernmental conference (IGC) to consider the Treaty changes needed to allow monetary union, and to set a date for the start of stage one of the process outlined in the Delors Report. This process may have been accelerated by the events in central and eastern Europe, but essentially it was a separate process that had already begun, and another one that occupied the attention of the member states and the Commission.

Between 1990 and 1995, the three pressing issues identified above were all cleared out of the way. Formal reunification of Germany took place on 3 October 1990. The TEU, setting out the timetable and conditions for monetary union, was agreed at the Maastricht European Council in December 1991, and formally signed by Foreign Ministers in February 1992. Terms of entry for Austria, Finland, and Sweden were agreed in the early hours of 1 March 1994. Once these issues were resolved, removing what Friis (1998: 333) described as 'the negative spillover from internal negotiating tables', there was the possibility of contemplating further enlargement.

The persistence of the CEECs in pressing for entry to the EC/EU was strengthened by the acceptance of the EC that the EEA scheme was not going to work for the EFTA applicants. It would have been difficult to convince the CEECs that membership of the single market without membership of the EU would be any more successful or acceptable for them once the argument had been conceded for the EFTA applicants. It would have looked simply as though the EC/EU was prepared to accept prosperous member states and not those most in need of support.

Security considerations became more urgent in the context of growing instability in Russia (Friis and Murphy 1999: 220). The USSR broke apart rapidly between August and December 1991. It formally ceased to exist on 31 December 1991. The Russian state that emerged after many of the former Soviet republics had proclaimed independence was an insecure place in which nationalist voices received a hearing from the population, and in turn the governments under President Boris Yeltsin came under pressure to talk tough with 'the near abroad'. In these circumstances, the concern of the CEECs for security from an aggressive Russia led to increased demands for membership of both the EC and NATO. These two issues became intertwined. The United States was concerned not to expand NATO membership too precipitately for fear of alarming Russia, so it put pressure on the EC to offer membership as a sort of second-order guarantee of independence to the states most affected. There was particular pressure on the EC to offer membership to the three Baltic states—Estonia, Latvia, and Lithuania—because they were too close to Russia to make NATO membership feasible, but they were also too close to Russia for comfort given the rising nationalist sentiment there. Although it was never likely that the EC would accede directly to any such demand from the United States, it had to show that it was prepared to move some way to contributing to the stabilization of eastern Europe. Also, as Yugoslavia began to disintegrate on the very doorstep of the EC, concerns about security grew in the member states themselves.

The prevarication on whether to proceed with all twelve applications together or whether to prioritize some of the applicants reflected the different stakes that different member states had in the enlargement. Germany was particularly keen to see early enlargement to take in at least its closest neighbours: Poland, Hungary, and the Czech Republic. This was both for security and economic reasons. The security reasons are obvious: reunification rendered Germany once more a central European state itself; and instability in neighbouring states was highly undesirable. The economic motivations reflected the traditional economic links between Germany and its central European neighbours. France, on the other hand, had less of a stake in either consideration, as it had no contiguous land frontier with the central European states, and had fewer economic links. For France and the other Mediterranean member states, there was a real risk that Eastern enlargement would reduce their influence in the EU, shifting the centre of gravity away from them towards Germany. The French government was therefore more prepared to take a leisurely approach, whereas the German government wanted as few obstacles as possible placed in the way of early accession for its favoured candidates.

The European Commission's motivation in proposing to proceed with only some of the applications reflected particularly its concerns about its limited resources. The process of accession is long and complex, and can tie up a lot of the available resources of the Commission. Member states have never been prepared to provide all of the extra resources necessary to allow it to perform efficiently the task set for it, and there was no indication that they would do so on this occasion.

Acceptance of the Commission's proposal to limit the number of applicants with which accession negotiations would begin reflected a temporary meeting of minds between Germany and France. The link to NATO enlargement, and the pressure that the EU had come under from the United States to proceed rapidly on a broad front, made it very attractive for France to agree to a more limited start, to show that the EU was not going to be pushed around by the United States.

The change of tactic at Helsinki, to open negotiations with the remaining applicants, reflected a number of changed circumstances. First, the CEECs that had not been placed in the first group had become increasingly restive about their treatment. Second, the pressure from the United States had receded as the security threat posed by Russia appeared also to recede. Third, the change of heart in Malta opened the prospect to France, Spain, Portugal, Italy, and Greece of having another Mediterranean small state in the first group of members to offset the influx of small and medium-sized CEECs. Of the second six, Malta was the most equipped to catch up with some of the first six applicants and get membership early.

Bieler (2002: 590) also offered an analysis of why the applications were accepted. He identified the key to the acceptance of the applications as the support given after 1997 by the European Round Table of Industrialists (ERT). Bieler maintained that the ERT was recruited as an ally by the Commission, but was willingly recruited because many of the transnational corporations that made up the membership of the ERT had invested heavily in the CEECs and therefore had an interest in consolidating the conditions for profitable production there.

Turkey

Turkey's application for membership of the EU is linked to the attempts of an elite in Turkey, persistently since the early part of the twentieth century, to establish it as a western country. The explanation for Turkey's application therefore lies in its past to some degree.

After the end of the First World War and the collapse of the Ottoman Empire, the modern state of Turkey emerged from a prolonged civil war in which the new nationalists defeated the Sultan. The radicals, led by Mustafa Kemal Atatürk, defeated the more conservative of the nationalist forces and established a republic. The reformists then set about a process of westernizing and modernizing Turkey. This involved legislation to abolish Islamic law and Islamic modes of dress, to institute a new Civil Code modelled on the Swiss example, and to introduce the Roman alphabet (Ahmad 2001: 850; McLaren 2000: 118).

When private business interests failed to respond to the reforms by investing in the modernization of the economy, and in the wake of the world economic crisis of 1930, an ideology of 'Kemalism' was developed that involved the state carrying out economic modernization from the top. The armed forces became associated with this process, setting themselves up as the guardians of the secular state. This role was consolidated after the Second World War, as a semi-modernized Turkey stuttered and staggered away from statism towards democracy. The struggles between the classes that benefited from modernization and those that suffered produced political crises that led to military interventions in 1960 and 1970 (Ahmad 2001: 850–1).

In neo-Gramscian terms, the 1959 application for associate membership of the EC, and the post-dictatorship enquiry about full membership, were attempts by the socio-economic classes that benefited from modernization to consolidate that direction for the economy. In constructivist terms, it was about strengthening the contested identity of Turkey as a western, European nation rather than as an eastern, Muslim nation.

The decision in the 1960s to conclude an Association Agreement with Turkey envisaging eventual membership can be explained in geo-strategic terms. Turkey had just emerged from a period of military rule, and the political scene was volatile. The predominant strategic concern of the period was the Cold War, and Turkey stood on the cusp of the communist world. It was important for the capitalist states to shore up this flank of NATO, and to do that it was important to strengthen the democratic forces that favoured a western and capitalist orientation for the state. The danger was not so much a communist takeover, as that Turkey would lurch into deeper and deeper crises of instability and become an unreliable ally.

Further military intervention in 1970 indicated that this tactic had not worked, and led to the suspension of the Association Agreement. The restoration of democracy in 1973 reactivated the agreement, but tensions between the neo-fascist right and the extreme left precipitated a further military intervention in 1980. Democracy was restored in 1983, but it was not until 1987 that Turkey was sufficiently stable for a formal application to the EU to be a credible move.

Müftüler-Bac and McLaren (2003) analysed the reasons for the decision of the EU to exclude Turkey from the list of prospective members in 1997, and for the change of position in 1999. They considered this to be a puzzle because nothing significant had changed in Turkey in the intervening period. In solving the problem, they adopted an intergovernmental perspective, arguing that the explanation lay in the changing preferences of the governments of existing member states, which in turn reflected their national interests.

Different member states had championed the applications of different candidate states, and that was for self-interested reasons. Germany had championed the Czech Republic, Hungary, and Poland because stability in those states was essential to German security, but also because of a sense of historical obligation for wrongs committed by previous German regimes. The Nordic states—initially Denmark alone, but with the support of Sweden and Finland once they became members—championed the applications of the Baltic states, with which they had ties of geography and history. France championed Romania because of long-standing cultural links, and as a partial counter-balance to the extra influence that the membership of the Central European states would give to Germany.

Turkey not only had no champion among the existing member states, but in Greece, it had an adversary. Germany also had grave doubts about the acceptability of Turkish entry. The ability of Greece to exercise a veto over moves towards Turkish membership, and the opposition of Germany to any such moves, explained the omission of Turkey from the list of candidates in 1997. By the end of 1999, though, both of these opponents had changed position.

In late 1999, there was a dramatic improvement in relations between Greece and Turkey. Müftüler-Bac and McLaren (2003) offer four explanations for this:

- Theo Pangalos, a long-standing adversary of Turkey, was replaced by the far more pragmatic and accommodating George Papandreou as Greece's Foreign Minister;

545

- a terrible earthquake in Turkey in August 1999 produced a wave of sympathy among the Greek public, and emergency assistance from the Greek government;
- in trying to gain membership of the European single currency, the Greek government was struggling to cut its budget deficit, and a relaxation of tensions with Turkey offered the prospect of significant savings on defence expenditure;
- Greece was using up a lot of political capital within the EU in causing trouble for the others over Turkey, political capital that it needed to conserve if it was not to lose out in areas such as receipts from the structural funds following the Eastern enlargement.

There was also a change in the German position between 1997 and 1999. For the German government of Helmut Kohl, the main objection to Turkish membership, which was often unspoken, was a concern that it was not culturally compatible with the image that the CDU/CSU held of Europe: in other words, Turkey was not Christian. This was also a view held by other Christian Democrat politicians from outside of Germany. The change of position in Germany came about as a result of the replacement of the CDU–CSU government in 1998 with an SPD–Green government under Gerhard Schröder. Müftüler-Bac and McLaren (2003: 23–4) represented the issue for the new government as one of domestic politics: the need to integrate the large Turkish minority more securely into German society.

So complete was the change in the German position that, at the June 1999 Cologne European Council, at the end of the German presidency, Schröder formally proposed that the Luxembourg decision on Turkey be reversed. The move proved premature: the change of Greece's position still lay in the months ahead, Italy had just been involved in a diplomatic row with Turkey over its refusal to extradite a Kurdish nationalist leader, and Sweden expressed serious reservations about the human rights situation in Turkey. Nevertheless, the conversion of Germany meant that Turkey now had the advocate that it had lacked in 1997.

As well as marking out clearly the changed position of Germany, the Cologne European Council was also significant because of the adoption of a new approach to enlargement negotiations. Previously, the EU had tried to negotiate enlargement with groups of candidates together. At Cologne, the 'principle of differentiation' was adopted. Essentially, this meant that, in future, the EU would negotiate with states individually without any target for completion of the negotiations, and the Commission would monitor progress and regularly update the member states on when different states might be ready to join. This change of policy was recognition that there was growing discontent in the CEECs that were not in the 'top six' group that had been identified in Luxembourg, discontent that might hinder and even reverse the progress of reform. The Kosovo conflict was then in full crisis as a reminder of the consequences of not moving swiftly to ensure stability. The decision also marked the wish of the heads of government to reward Bulgaria and Romania for their support of NATO in Kosovo. Once it has been taken, though, it became more feasible for negotiations with Turkey to begin, and much more difficult to oppose them.

To continue the story beyond where Müftüler-Bac and McLaren (2003) left it: in November 2002, the election of a new government changed the situation in Turkey. The Justice and Development Party (AKP), which now came into office, was an Islamic party, but not a traditionalist or fundamentalist party. It was committed to pursuing the westernization of Turkey, the goal of the secular republic since Atatürk. This made it difficult for the military, the self-appointed guardians of the legacy of Atatürk, to intervene as they had in the past to overturn the democratic process on the grounds that the principles of the republic were being betrayed.

Under the premiership of Recep Tayyip Erdogan, the AKP vigorously set about trying to satisfy the political prerequisites to a successful Turkish bid for membership of the EU. Within the space of little over a year, the new government made sufficient change in the political and legal systems to attract a warm commendation from the Commission in its 2003 Report on Turkey's Progress towards Accession. Although a great deal remained to be done, the first steps to removing the blockage had been taken in earnest. The pressure that Erdogan exerted on the Turkish Cypriot government to accept a settlement of the division of the island also helped to win over Greece, and to win Turkey friends in other quarters.

Britain, always sympathetic to Turkey's claims, became a strong advocate of its cause. In the aftermath of a spate of terrorist bombings in Ankara in November 2003, the British Foreign Secretary, Jack Straw, called for Turkish membership 'as soon as possible', and the Europe Minister, Denis MacShane, said, 'Europe is incomplete without Turkey' (Foreign and Commonwealth Office 2004). The dominant reason for British support was geo-strategic. Turkey occupied a geographical position between the EU and the Middle East. It bordered Iran, Iraq, and Syria. It had a majority of Muslims among its population, at a time when the EU was increasingly being accused of a bias against Muslims. A stable and western-oriented Turkey was therefore an important strategic goal for the west, and the best way of ensuring the stability and western orientation of Turkey was to admit it to the EU.

Continuing opposition to Turkey's membership of the EU emerged particularly in France. The prospect was not made more attractive by the strong public support for Turkish membership expressed by the United States. When US President Bush, in Ankara for a NATO summit, called for Turkey to be admitted to the EU, French President Chirac said that he should mind his own business. Nevertheless, Chirac was prepared to go along with the German wish to see negotiations open with Turkey. Erdogan also helped to win the French vote during a diplomatic tour in the summer of 2004 by arriving in Paris with an order from the Turkish state airline for thirty-six Airbus airliners, and an agreement on co-operation on developing nuclear energy.

By 2008, though, the prospects for Turkish membership were looking bleak. With the Christian Democrats back in office in Germany, the German position had moved against Turkish membership. When the former French President Valéry Giscard d'Estaing said in an interview with the *Le Monde* in November 2002 that allowing Turkey into the EU would mean 'the end of the European Union', he was widely seen as articulating a belief that was held by politicians in most of the EU's member states.

Wimmel (2009) examined the reaction to this interview in the 'quality press' of France, Germany, and Britain. He found that the French and German coverage across both conservative and liberal newspapers was more sympathetic to Giscard's position, and less sympathetic towards Turkey's entry, than was the position of the British press. He linked this to 'different visions of Europe's finality' (Wimmel 2009: 224), meaning that the French and Germans had a different conception of what the EU was about and where it ought to be going than prevailed in Britain. In particular, the British vision of the EU has always seen it as a common or single market with the addition of limited

547

co-operation on foreign policy, defence, and security issues. Britain has also embraced a multi-cultural society domestically, and cultural diversity is viewed as a good thing for Europe as a whole. While German and French visions of 'Europe's finality' differed between the different political camps in each country, both conservatives and liberals were concerned about the supposed contradiction between widening and deepening of the EU, arguing that extending the boundaries to embrace as large a state as Turkey would set back attempts to consolidate the policies and identity of the existing EU. Conservatives also worried about the cultural differences between Christian Europe and Muslim Turkey. So the whole issue of Turkish membership crystallized divergent visions of the enterprise of European integration.

CONCLUSION

It was surely never envisaged by the founders of the European Coal and Steel Community (ECSC) and the EEC that these organizations of six states would expand over the next half century to a membership of twenty-seven, with more applicants waiting to join. The reasons for this expansion have been much debated, both as to why the applications were made and why they were accepted, but they come down to some mix of economic and political considerations.

How to handle the negotiations with candidate countries, the actual policy of how to do enlargement, has evolved over time, each enlargement adding to the *acquis*. The effects of the enlargements have been varied, and are difficult to estimate because of the absence of any evidence about how the EC/EU would have developed without the new members. All of these aspects of enlargement have been addressed by different authors, but the coverage is uneven, leaving plenty of room for further research.

Partly this is because the study of the EU has grown more sophisticated over time. There is nothing to stop analysis of earlier enlargements being revised in the light of later theoretical concepts, but this tends not to happen. An exception is Moravcsik (1998), who analysed the first enlargement using the concepts of liberal intergovernmentalism. There is scope for the application of other approaches, particularly constructivist and neo-Gramscian approaches, to this enlargement, and for the application of both, plus rationalist approaches, to the Southern enlargement.

There is also still plenty of work to be done on applying theory systematically to the Eastern enlargement. For example, because the issue of why the CEECs applied for membership has not been seen as a problem, it has not received much sustained analytical attention. As Schimmelfennig and Sedelmeier (2002: 524) argued, this makes it difficult for comparisons to be drawn with previous enlargements, even with the EFTA enlargement, which has been extensively analysed, but which analysis has focused particularly on the issue of why the new applicants chose to apply. There is also room for a more systematic application of theory to the analysis of the Turkish application, and to those of the states of former Yugoslavia.

KEY POINTS

History

- There have been six rounds of enlargement.
- The first enlargement brought into the EC two states, Britain and Denmark, that were sceptical about European integration.

- The second and third enlargements are often treated together as a 'Southern enlargement'. It gave the EC a stronger Mediterranean orientation, and raised the profile of Latin America in external relations. Greece's membership caused some problems for relations with other states in the Balkans.
- As a result of the fourth enlargement, environmental protection became more important, the coalition in favour of budgetary reform was strengthened, and a Nordic bloc was formed.
- The fifth and sixth enlargements are often treated together as an 'Eastern enlargement'. It forced reform of the institutions and of key policies.
- In 2010, Croatia, the former Yugoslav Republic of Macedonia, Turkey, and Iceland had candidate status. Montenegro, Albania, and Serbia had also applied.

The Enlargement Procedure

- A procedure has been developed over the six rounds of application.
- Once an application has been approved by the European Council, the Commission prepares an Opinion. Negotiations proceed in sectoral groups. Agreed terms have to be ratified by the Council of Foreign Ministers and the European Council.
- Existing member states try to sort out problems that might be caused by the new members before the enlargement is completed.
- The Southern enlargement set a precedent for member states to overrule an unfavourable Commission Opinion on political grounds.
- The Eastern enlargement led to a set of criteria for membership that have come to structure negotiations with applicants.

Explaining Enlargement

- The first enlargement was driven by both economic and geo-strategic considerations.
- The EFTA enlargement was a response to the success of the single-market programme.
- The Eastern enlargement was a result of a wish to consolidate democracy and capitalism in the former communist states.
- Turkey's application was part of the Kemalist programme to modernize the state and economy. Its difficult history reflects the opposition of Greece, and the doubts of Germany and France.

FURTHER READING

Comprehensive coverage of the first four enlargements is contained in **C. Preston**, *Enlargement and European Integration in the European Union* (London: Routledge, 1997). It contains sections on the accession process for each new member state and information on other applications. It considers the effects of enlargement on each member state, on the EU's policies and on the structure and processes of the EU. A complete narrative of how those enlargement negotiations developed, with copious quotations from official documentation, is provided in **G. Avery and F. Cameron**, *The Enlargement of the European Union* (Sheffield: Sheffield Academic Press, 1998).

For analyses using conditionality and Europeanization interpretations, see **F. Schimmelfennig and U. Sedelmeier (eds)**, *The Europeanization of Central and Eastern Europe* (Ithaca, NY: Cornell University Press, 2005), and **H. Grabbe**, *The EU's Transformative Power: Europeanization Through Conditionality in Central and Eastern Europe* (Basingstoke: Palgrave Macmillan, 2005).

For a full neo-Gramscian analysis, the conscientious student will look at **A. Bieler**, *Globalization and Enlargement of the European Union: Austrian and Swedish Social Forces in the Struggle over Membership* (London: Routledge, 2000), although others may find enough information in **Bieler**'s later article, 'The Struggle over EU Enlargement: A Historical Materialist Analysis of European Integration', *Journal of European Public Policy*, 9 (2002): 575–97. This analysis can be usefully compared with that of **C. Ingebritsen**, *The Nordic States and European Unity* (Ithaca, NY: Cornell University Press, 1998).

online resource centre

Visit the Online Resource Centre that accompanies this book for links to more information on the enlargement of the EU, including the website of the relevant Directorate-General of the Commission: www.oxfordtextbooks.co.uk/orc/bache3e/

References

Adnett, N. (2001), 'Modernizing the European Social Model: Developing the Guidelines'. *Journal of Common Market Studies*, 39: 353–64.

Adshead, M. (2002), *Developing European Regions? Comparative Governance, Policy Networks and European Integration*. Aldershot: Ashgate.

Ahearn, R. (2002), 'US–European Union Trade Relations: Issues and Policy Challenges'. *CRS Issue Brief for Congress*. (http://fpc.state.gov/documents/organization/9546.pdf).

Ahmad, F. (2001), 'Turkey', in J. Krieger (ed.), *The Oxford Companion to the Politics of the World* (2nd edn), New York: Oxford University Press, 850–1.

Aldcroft, D. H. (1978), *The European Economy, 1914–1970*. London: Croom Helm.

Allen, D. and Smith, M. (1998), 'External Policy Developments'. *Journal of Common Market Studies: The European Union, 1997, Annual Review of Activities*: 69–91.

_____ and _____ (2004), 'External Policy Developments'. *Journal of Common Market Studies: The European Union, 2003, Annual Review of Activities*: 95–112.

Alter, K. (1996), 'The European Court's Political Power'. *West European Politics*, 19: 458–87.

_____ (1998), 'Who Are the "Masters of the Treaty"? European Governments and the European Court of Justice'. *International Organization*, 52: 121–47.

_____ (2001), *Establishing the Supremacy of European Law: The Making of an International Rule of Law in Europe*. Oxford: Oxford University Press.

Amoore, L., Dodgson, R., Gills, B. K., Langley, P., Marshall, D., and Watson, I. (1997), 'Overturning "Globalisation": Resisting the Technological, Reclaiming the "Political"'. *New Political Economy*, 2: 179–95.

Anderson, J. (2002), 'Globalization and Europeanization: A Conceptual and Theoretical Overview'. Paper prepared for the conference on 'Germany and Europe: A Europeanized Germany?', ESRC Future Governance Programme, The British Academy, London, May 9–10.

_____ (2003), 'Europeanization in Context: Concept and Theory', in K. Dyson and K. Goetz (eds), *Germany, Europe and the Politics of Constraint*. Oxford: Oxford University Press, 37–54.

_____ (2009), 'Policy with Politics in the EU: Can You Get There from Here?'. *Comparative European Politics*, 7: 374–83.

Andreou, G. (2007), 'The New EU Cohesion Policy: Enlargement, "Lisbonisation" and the Challenge of Diversity'. *EU CONSENT Annual State of the Art Report, Second Year*. Athens: Hellenic Foundation for European and Foreign Policy (ELIAMEP).

Armstrong, H. (1989), 'Community Regional Policy', in J. Lodge (ed.), *The European Community and the Challenge of the Future*. London: Pinter, 167–85.

Armstrong, K. and Bulmer, S. (1998), *The Governance of the Single European Market*. Manchester: Manchester University Press.

Aspinwall, M. (1998), 'Collective Attraction: The New Political Game in Brussels', in J. Greenwood and M. Aspinwall (eds), *Collective Action in the European Union: Interests and the New Politics of Associability*. London and New York: Routledge, 196–213.

_____ and Greenwood, J. (1998), 'Conceptualising Collective Action in the European Union: An Introduction', in J. Greenwood and M. Aspinwall (eds), *Collective Action in the European Union: Interests and the New Politics of Associability*. London and New York: Routledge, 1–30.

Avery, G. and Cameron, F. (1998), *The Enlargement of the European Union*. Sheffield: Sheffield Academic Press / University Association for Contemporary European Studies.

Bache, I. (1995), 'Additionality and the Politics of EU Regional Policy Making', *Political Economy Research Centre Working Papers*, no. 2. Sheffield: Political Economy Research Centre, University of Sheffield.

_____ (1996), *EU Regional Policy: Has the UK Government Succeeded in Playing the Gatekeeper Role over the Domestic Impact of the European Regional Development Fund?*. PhD thesis, University of Sheffield.

_____ (1998), *The Politics of European Union Regional Policy: Multi-Level Governance or Flexible Gatekeeping?*. Sheffield: Sheffield Academic Press/University Association for Contemporary European Studies.

_____ (1999), 'The Extended Gatekeeper: Central Government and the Implementation of EC Regional Policy in the UK'. *Journal of European Public Policy*, 6: 28–45.

_____ (2004), 'Multi-Level Governance and EU Regional Policy', in I. Bache and M. Flinders (eds), *Multi-Level Governance*. Oxford: Oxford University Press, 165–78.

_____ (2006), 'The Europeanization of Higher Education: Markets, Learning or Politics?'. *Journal of Common Market Studies*, 44: 231–48.

_____ (2008), *Europeanization and Multi-Level Governance: Cohesion Policy in the European Union and Britain*. Lanham: Rowman and Littlefield.

_____ (2010), 'Europeanization and Multi-Level Governance'. *Journal of Southeast European and Black Sea Studies,* 10: 1–12.

_____ and Bristow, G. (2003), 'Devolution and the Core Executive: The Struggle for European Funds'. *British Journal of Politics and International Relations*, 5: 405–27.

_____ and Chapman, R. (2008), 'Democracy through Multi-Level Governance? The Implementation of the Structural Funds in South Yorkshire'. *Governance*, 21: 397–418.

_____ and Flinders, M. (2004), 'Conclusions and Implications', in I. Bache and M. Flinders (eds), *Multi-Level Governance*. Oxford: Oxford University Press, 195–206.

_____ and George, S. (2006), *Politics in the European Union* (2nd edn). Oxford: Oxford University Press.

_____, George, S., and Rhodes, R. A. W. (1996), 'Cohesion Policy and Subnational Authorities in the UK', in L. Hooghe (ed.), *Cohesion Policy and European Integration*. Oxford: Oxford University Press, 294–319.

_____ and Jones, R. (2000), 'Has EU Regional Policy Empowered the Regions? A Study of Spain and the United Kingdom'. *Regional and Federal Studies*, 10: 1–20.

_____ and Jordan, A. (2004), 'Britain in Europe and Europe in Britain: The Europeanization of British Politics?'. Paper presented at the ESRC/UACES Conference on *The Europeanization of British Politics?*, Sheffield, 16 July.

_____ and _____ (2006a), 'Europeanization and Domestic Change', in I. Bache and A. Jordan (eds), *The Europeanization of British Politics,* Basingstoke: Palgrave Macmillan, 17–36.

_____ and _____ (eds) (2006b), *The Europeanization of British Politics*. Basingstoke: Palgrave Macmillan.

_____ and Marshall, A. (2004), 'Europeanisation and Domestic Change: A Governance Approach to Institutional Adaptation in Britain'. *Europeanisation Online Papers*, No. 5/2004, Queen's University Belfast. (http://www.qub.ac.uk/schools/SchoolofPoliticsInternationalStudiesandPhilosophy/Research/PaperSeries/EuropeanisationPapers/).

_____ and Olsson, J. (2001), 'Legitimacy through Partnership? EU Policy Diffusion in Britain and Sweden'. *Scandinavian Political Studies*, 24: 215–37.

Bachtler, J. and McMaster, I. (2008), 'EU Cohesion Policy and the Role of the Regions: Investigating the Influence of Structural Funds in the New Member States'. *Environment and Planning C: Government and Policy*, 26: 398–427.

_____ and Mendez, C. (2010), 'Who Governs EU Cohesion Policy? Deconstructing the Reforms of the Structural Funds'. *JCMS: Journal of Common Market Studies*, 24: 535–64.

_____ and Michie, R. (1994), 'Strengthening Economic and Social Cohesion? The Revision of the Structural Funds'. *Regional Studies*, 28: 789–96.

Bailey, D. and De Propris, L. (2002), 'EU Structural Funds, Regional Capabilities and Enlargement: Towards Multi-Level Governance?'. *Journal of European Integration*, 24: 303–24.

Baker, E. (2009), 'The European Union's "Area of Freedom, Security and (Criminal) Justice" Ten Years On'. *The Criminal Law Review*, 12: 833–50.

Barber, L. (1995), 'The Men Who Run Europe'. *Financial Times: Weekend FT*, 11/12 March: I–II.

Barroso, J. (2009), 'State of the Union: Delivering a "Europe of Results" in a Harsh Economic Climate'. *Journal of Common Market Studies*, Annual Review, 57: 7–16.

Barysch, K. (2003), 'Germany: The Sick Man of Europe?'. *Centre for European Reform Policy Brief*. London: CER.

Baun, M. J. (1996), 'The Maastricht Treaty as High Politics: Germany, France and European Integration'. *Political Science Quarterly*, 110: 605–24.

Beach, D. (2005), *The Dynamics of European Integration: Why and When Institutions Matter*. Basingstoke: Palgrave Macmillan.

Beetham, D. and Lord, C. (1998), *Legitimacy and the European Union*. London and New York: Longman.

Benson, D. and Jordan, A. (2008), 'A Grand Bargain or an "Incomplete Contract"? European Union Environmental Policy after the Lisbon Treaty'. *European Energy and Environmental Law Review*, 17: 280–90.

Benz, A. (2003), 'Compounded Representation in Multi-Level Governance', in B. Kohler-Koch (ed.), *Linking EU and National Governance*. Oxford: Oxford University Press, 82–110.

Beyers, J. (2004), 'Voice and Access: Political Practices of European Interest Associations'. *European Union Politics*, 5: 211–40.

____ and Dierickx, G. (1998), 'The Working Groups of the Council of the European Union: Supranational or Intergovernmental Negotiations?'. *Journal of Common Market Studies*, 36: 289–317.

Bieler, A. (2000), *Globalization and Enlargement of the European Union: Austrian and Swedish Social Forces in the Struggle over Membership*. London: Routledge.

____ (2002), 'The Struggle over EU Enlargement: A Historical Materialist Analysis of European Integration'. *Journal of European Public Policy*, 9: 575–97.

Birch, A. (2001), *Concepts and Theories of Modern Democracy* (2nd edn). London and New York: Routledge.

Blair, A. (2002), 'Adapting to Europe'. *Journal of European Public Policy*, 9: 841–56.

Boltho, A. (1982), *The European Economy: Growth and Crisis*. Oxford: Oxford University Press.

Bomberg, E. and Peterson, J. (2000), 'Policy Transfer and Europeanization'. *Europeanisation Online Papers*, No. 2/2000. Queen's University, Belfast. (http://www.qub.ac.uk/schools/SchoolofPoliticsInternationalStudiesand Philosophy/Research/PaperSeries/EuropeanisationPapers/).

____ Cram, L., and Martin, D. (2003), 'The EU's Institutions', in E. Bomberg and A. Stubb (eds), *The European Union: How Does it Work?*. Oxford: Oxford University Press, 43–68.

Bonefeld, W. (2001), *Politics of Europe: Monetary Union and Class*. Basingstoke: Palgrave.

Borras, S. and Jacobsson, K. (2004), 'The Open Method of Co-ordination and New Governance Patterns in the EU'. *Journal of European Public Policy*, 11: 185–208.

Börzel, T. (1998), 'Organizing Babylon: On the Different Conceptions of Policy Networks'. *Public Administration*, 76: 253–73.

____ (2000), 'Why There is no "Southern Problem". On Environmental Leaders and Laggards in the European Union'. *Journal of European Public Policy*, 7: 141–62.

____ (2002), 'Pace-Setting, Foot-Dragging, and Fence-Sitting: Member State Responses to Europeanization'. *Journal of Common Market Studies* 40: 193–214.

____ (2010), 'Why Lisbon Won't Do the Trick'. *EUSA Review*, 23 (1): 4–7 (European Union Studies Association, USA). (http://www.eustudies.org/publicationsreviewwinter10.php).

____ and Risse, T. (2000), 'When Europe Hits Home: Europeanization and Domestic Change'. *European Integration Online Papers (EioP)* 4:15. (http://eiop.or.at/eiop/texte/2000–015a.htm).

____ and ____ (2003), 'Conceptualising the Domestic Impact of Europe', in K. Featherstone and C. Radaelli (eds), *The Politics of Europeanization*. Oxford: Oxford University Press, 57–82.

____ and ____ (2007), 'The Domestic Impact of European Union Politics', in K.E. Jørgensen, M. Pollack, and B. Rosamond (eds), *Handbook of European Union Politics*. London: Sage, 483–504.

Boswell, C. (2010), 'Justice and Home Affairs', in M. Egan, N. Nugent, and W. Paterson (eds), *Research Agendas in EU Studies: Stalking the Elephant*. Basingstoke: Palgrave Macmillan, 278–304.

Bourne, A. (2003), 'The Impact of European Integration on Regional Power'. *Journal of Common Market Studies*, 41: 597–620.

Bouwen, P. (2002), 'Corporate Lobbying in the European Union: The Logic of Access'. *Journal of European Public Policy*, 9: 365–90.

____ (2004a), 'Exchanging Access Goods for Access: A Comparative Study of Business Lobbying in the European Union Institutions'. *European Journal of Political Research*, 43: 337–69.

____ (2004b), 'The Logic of Access to the European Parliament: Business Lobbying in the Committee on Economic and Monetary Affairs'. *Journal of Common Market Studies*, 42: 473–95.

Bowler, S. and Farrell, D. (1995), 'The Organizing of the European Parliament: Committees, Specialization and Co-ordination'. *British Journal of Political Science*, 25: 219–43.

Branch, A. P. and Øhrgaard, J. C. (1999), 'Trapped in the Supranational–Intergovernmental Dichotomy: A Response to Stone Sweet and Sandholtz'. *Journal of European Public Policy*, 6: 123–43.

Brenton, P. and Manchin, M. (2002), 'Making EU Trade Agreements Work: The Role of Rules of Origin'. *CEPS Working Document no. 183*. Brussels: Centre for European Studies.

Breslin, S., Hughes, C., Phillips, N., and Rosamond, B. (eds) (2002), *New Regionalism in the Global Economy: Theories and Cases*. London: Routledge.

Bromley, S. (2001), 'Conclusion: What is the European Union?', in S. Bromley (ed.), *Governing the European Union*. London: Sage, 287–303.

Bruszt, L. (2008), 'Multi-level Governance: The Eastern Versions—Emerging Patterns of Developmental Governance in the New Member States'. *Regional and Federal Studies*, 18: 5, 607–27.

Buller, J. (1995), 'Britain as an Awkward Partner: Reassessing Britain's Relations with the EU'. *Politics*, 15: 33–42.

_____ and Gamble, A. (2002), 'Conceptualising Europeanization'. *Public Policy and Administration*, 17: 4–24.

Bulmer, S. (1983), 'Domestic Politics and European Policy-Making'. *Journal of Common Market Studies*, 21: 349–63.

_____ (1993), 'The Governance of the European Union: A New Institutionalist Approach'. *Journal of Public Policy*, 13: 351–80.

_____ (1998), 'New Institutionalism and the Governance of the Single European Market'. *Journal of European Public Policy*, 5: 365–86.

_____ (2007), 'Theorizing Europeanization', in P. Graziano and M. Vink (eds), *Europeanization: New Research Agendas*. Basingstoke: Palgrave Macmillan, 46–58.

_____ (2009), 'Institutional and Policy Analysis in the European Union: From the Treaty of Rome to the Present', in D. Phinnemore and A. Warleigh-Lack (eds), *Reflections on European Integration: 50 Years of the Treaty of Rome*. Basingstoke: Palgrave Macmillan, 109–24.

_____ (2010), 'Germany: From Launching the EU 'Constitutional Debate to Salvaging a Treaty', in M. Carbone (ed.), *National Politics and European Integration: From the Constitution to the Lisbon Treaty*. Cheltenham, UK, and Northampton, MA: Edward Elgar, 51–70.

_____ (forthcoming), 'Shop till you Drop? The German Executive as Venue-Shopper in Justice and Home Affairs?', in P. Bendel, A. Ette, and R. Parkes (eds), *The Politics of Control*. Berlin and London: Lit Verlag.

_____ and Burch, M. (1998), 'Organising for Europe: Whitehall, the British State and the European Union'. *Public Administration*, 76 (4): 601–28.

_____ and _____ (2000), 'The Europeanisation of British Central Government', in R. A. W. Rhodes (ed.), *Transforming British Government, Volume 1: Changing Institutions*. London: Macmillan, 46–62.

_____ and _____ (2009), *The Europeanisation of Whitehall: UK Central Government and the European Union*. Manchester: Manchester University Press.

_____ and Paterson, W. (2010), 'Germany and the European Union: From "Tamed Power" to Normalized Power?'. *International Affairs*, 86: 1051–73.

_____ and Radaelli, C. (2004), 'The Europeanisation of National Policy?'. *Europeanisation Online Papers,* No. 1/2004, Queen's University, Belfast. (http://www.qub.ac.uk/schools/SchoolofPoliticsInternationalStudiesandPhilosophy/Research/PaperSeries/EuropeanisationPapers/).

_____ and _____ (2005), 'The Europeanisation of National Policy', in S. Bulmer and C. Lequesne (eds), *The Member States of the European Union*. Oxford: Oxford University Press, 338–59.

_____ and Wessels, W. (1987), *The European Council: Decision-Making in European Politics*. Basingstoke: Macmillan.

_____, Dolowitz, D., Humphreys, P., and Padgett, S. (2007), *Policy Transfer in European Union Governance: Regulating the Utilities*. Abingdon: Routledge.

Burch, M. and Gomez, R. (2003), 'Europeanization and the English Regions'. Paper presented to the ESRC Seminar Series/UACES Study Group on the Europeanization of British Politics and Policy-Making, Sheffield, 2 May.

Burchell, J. and Lightfoot, S. (2001), *The Greening of the European Union? Examining the EU's Environmental Credentials*. London and New York: Sheffield Academic Press.

Burley, A-M. and Mattli, W. (1993), 'Europe Before the Court: A Political Theory of Legal Integration'. *International Organization*, 47: 41–76.

Burns, C. (2002), 'The European Parliament', in A. Warleigh (ed.), *Understanding European Union Institutions*. London: Routledge, 61–80.

_____ (2004), 'Co-decision and the European Commission: A Study of Declining Influence?'. *Journal of European Public Policy*, 11: 1–18.

Butler, F. (1993), 'The EC's Common Agricultural Policy', in J. Lodge (ed.), *The European Community and the Challenge of the Future* (2nd edn). London: Pinter, 112–30.

Butt Philip, A. (1983), 'Pressure Groups and Policy-Making in the European Community', in J. Lodge (ed.), *Institutions and Policies of the European Community*. London: Pinter, 21–6.

_____ (1992), 'British Pressure Groups and the European Community', in S. George (ed.), *Britain and the European Community: The Politics of Semi-Detachment*. Oxford: Clarendon Press, 149–71.

Cafruny, A. and Ryner, M. (2009), 'Critical Political Economy', in A. Wiener and

T. Diez (eds), *European Integration Theory* (2nd edn). Oxford: Oxford University Press, 221–40.

Calingaert, M. (1999), 'Creating a European Market', in L. Cram, D. Dinan, and N. Nugent (eds), *Developments in the European Union*. Basingstoke and London: Macmillan, 153–73.

Cameron, D. R. (1992), 'The 1992 Initiative: Causes and Consequences', in A. Sbragia (ed.), *Euro-Politics: Institutions and Policymaking in the 'New' European Community*. Washington DC: Brookings Institution, 23–74.

_____ (1997), 'Economic and Monetary Union: Underlying Imperatives and Third-Stage Dilemmas', *Journal of European Public Policy*, 4: 455–85.

Camps, M. (1964), *Britain and the European Community 1955–1963*. London: Oxford University Press.

_____ (1967), *European Unification in the Sixties: From the Veto to the Crisis*. London: Oxford University Press.

Caporaso, J. (1998), 'Regional Integration Theory: Understanding our Past and Anticipating our Future'. *Journal of European Public Policy*, 5: 1–16.

_____ (1999), 'Toward a Normal Science of Regional Integration'. *Journal of European Public Policy*, 6: 160–4.

_____ and Keeler, J. T. S. (1995), 'The European Union and Regional Integration Theory', in C. Rhodes and S. Mazey (eds), *The State of the European Union Vol. 3: Building a European Polity?*. Boulder, CO, and Harlow, Essex: Lynne Rienner and Longman, 29–62.

Carbone, M. (2007), *The European Union and International Development: The Politics of Foreign Aid*. Abingdon: Routledge.

_____ (2010), 'Conclusion: Preference Formation, Inter-State Bargaining and the Treaty of Lisbon', in M. Carbone (ed.), *National Politics and European Integration: From the Constitution to the Lisbon Treaty*. Cheltenham, UK, and Northampton, MA: Edward Elgar, 215–32.

Carchedi, G. (2001), *For Another Europe: A Class Analysis of European Economic Integration*. London: Verso.

Carmin, J. and VanDeveer, S. D. (2004), 'Enlarging EU Environments: Central and Eastern Europe from Transition to Accession'. *Environmental Politics*, 13: 3–24.

Carrubba, C. J. (2003), 'The European Court of Justice, Democracy, and Enlargement'. *European Union Politics*, 4: 75–100.

Cecchini, P. (1988), *The European Challenge 1992: The Benefits of a Single Market*. Aldershot: Gower.

Centre for European Policy Studies (1990), *1989 Annual Conference Proceedings, vol. 1: The Single Market and Economic and Monetary Union*. Brussels: CEPS.

Centre for Urban and Regional Development Studies (CURDS) (1997), 'Written Evidence', in House of Lords (1997), *Reducing Disparities within the European Union: The Effectiveness of the Structural and Cohesion Funds, Volume 2—Evidence*. Select Committee on the European Communities, Session 1996–97, 11th Report. London: HMSO, 52–62.

Chalmers, D., Davies, G., and Monti, G. (2010), *European Union Law* (2nd edn). Cambridge: Cambridge University Press.

Checkel, J. (2007), 'Constructivism and EU Politics', in K.E. Jørgensen, M. Pollack, and B. Rosamond (eds), *Handbook of European Union Politics*. London: Sage, 57–76.

Christiansen, T. (1996), 'A Maturing Bureaucracy? The Role of the Commission in the Policy Process', in J. Richardson (ed.), *European Union: Power and Policy-Making*. London: Routledge, 79–95.

_____ (2010), 'The EU Reform Process: From the European Constitution to the Lisbon Treaty', in M. Carbone (ed.), *National Politics and European Integration: From the Constitution to the Lisbon Treaty*. Cheltenham, UK, and Northampton, MA: Edward Elgar, 16–33.

_____, Jørgensen, K.E., and Wiener, A. (1999), 'The Social Construction of Europe'. *Journal of European Public Policy*, 6: 528–44.

Chryssochoou, D. (2007), 'Democracy and the European Polity', in M. Cini (ed.), *European Union Politics* (2nd edn). Oxford: Oxford University Press, 359–74.

Church, C. and Phinnemore, D. (2010), 'From the Constitutional Treaty to the Treaty of Lisbon', in M. Cini and N. Perez-Solórzano Borragán (eds), *European Union Politics* (3rd edn). Oxford: Oxford University Press, 48–68.

Cini, M. (1996), *The European Commission: Leadership, Organisation and Culture in the EU Administration*. Manchester: Manchester University Press.

_____ and McGowan, L.(1998), *Competition Policy in the European Union*. Basingstoke and London: Macmillan.

Cocks, P. (1980), 'Towards a Marxist Theory of European Integration'. *International Organization*, 31: 1–40.

Coleman, W. D. (1998), 'From Protected Development to Market Liberalism: Paradigm Change in Agriculture'. *Journal of European Public Policy*, 5: 632–51.

Collinson, S. (1999), '"Issue Systems", "Multi-Level Games" and the Analysis of the EU's External Commercial and Associated Policies:

A Research Agenda'. *Journal of European Public Policy*, 6: 206–24.

Colman, D. (2007), 'The Common Agricultural Policy', in M. Artis and F. Nixson (eds), *The Economics of the European Union: Policy and Analysis* (4th edn). Oxford: Oxford University Press, 77–104.

Committee of the Regions (2009), *The Committee of the Regions White Paper on Multi-Level Governance*. CdR 89/2009 fin FR/EXT/RS/GW/ym/ms. Brussels: Committee of the Regions.

Coombes, D. (1970), *Politics and Bureaucracy in the European Community*. London: Allen & Unwin.

Copsey, N. and Haughton, T. (2009), 'The Gathering Storm: A Drama in Two Acts'. *Journal of Common Market Studies, Annual Review,* 57: 1–5.

Corbett, A. (2005), *Universities and the Europe of Knowledge: Ideas, Institutions and Policy Entrepreneurship in European Union Higher Education Policy*. Basingstoke: Palgrave.

Corbett, R. (1993), *The Treaty of Maastricht*. London: Longman.

_____ (2000), 'Academic Modelling of the Codecision Procedure'. *European Union Politics,* 1: 373–81.

_____, Jacobs, F., and Shackleton, M. (1995), *The European Parliament* (3rd edn). London: Catermill.

_____, _____, and _____ (2003), 'The European Parliament at Fifty: A View from the Inside'. *Journal of Common Market Studies,* 41: 353–73.

Cornish, P. and Edwards, G. (2001), 'Beyond the EU/NATO Dichotomy: The Beginnings of a European Strategic Culture'. *International Affairs,* 77: 587–95.

Council of the EU (2005), *A Strategy for the External Dimension of JHA: Global Freedom, Security and Justice*. 14366/3/05 REV 3. Brussels: General Secretariat of the Council, 30 November.

_____ (2009a), *List of Council Preparatory Bodies*. Document 11602/09. Brussels: General Secretariat of the Council, 30 June.

_____ (2009b), *Draft 18-Month Programme of the Council*. 16771/09. Brussels: General Secretariat of the Council of the EU, 27 November.

Cowles, M. G. (1995), 'Setting the Agenda for a New Europe: The ERT and EC 1992'. *Journal of Common Market Studies,* 33: 501–26.

_____ (2003), 'Non-State Actors and False Dichotomies: Reviewing IR/IPE Approaches to European Integration'. *Journal of European Public Policy,* 10: 102–20.

_____, Caporaso, J., and Risse, T. (eds) (2001), *Transforming Europe: Europeanization and Domestic Change*. Ithaca, NY, and London: Cornell University Press.

Cox, R. (1981), 'Social Forces, States and World Orders: Beyond International Relations Theory'. *Millennium: Journal of International Studies,* 10: 126–55.

_____, with Sinclair, T. (1996), *Approaches to World Order*. Cambridge: Cambridge University Press.

Cram, L. (1996), 'Integration Theory and the Study of the European Policy Process', in J. Richardson (ed.), *European Union: Power and Policy-Making*. London: Routledge, 40–58.

_____ (1997), *Policy Making in the EU: Conceptual Lenses and the Integration Process*. London and New York: Routledge.

_____ (2001), 'Whither the Commission? Reform, Renewal and the Issue–Attention Cycle'. *Journal of European Public Policy,* 8: 770–86.

Crombez, C. (1996) 'Legislative Procedures in the European Community'. *British Journal of Political Science,* 26: 199–228.

_____ (1997), 'The Co-decision Procedure in the European Union'. *Legislative Studies Quarterly,* 22: 97–119.

_____ (2000), 'Understanding the EU Legislative Process: Co-decision—Towards a Bicameral European Union'. *European Union Politics,* 1: 363–8.

_____ (2001), 'The Treaty of Amsterdam and the Codecision Procedure', in G. Schneider and M. Aspinwall (eds), *The Rules of Integration: Institutionalist Approaches to the Study of Europe*. Manchester: Manchester University Press, 101–22.

Daddow, O. J. (2004), *Britain and Europe since 1945: Historiographical Perspectives on European Integration*. Manchester: Manchester University Press.

Damro, C. (2007), 'EU Delegation and Agency in International Trade Negotiations: A Cautionary Comparison'. *Journal of Common Market Studies,* 45: 883–903.

Dang-Nguyen, G., Schneider, V., and Werle, R. (1993), 'Networks in European Policy-Making: Europeification of Telecommunications Policy', in S. S. Andersen and K. A. Eliassen (eds), *Making Policy in Europe: Europeification of National Policy-Making*. London: Sage, 93–114.

Daugbjerg, C. (2009), 'Sequencing in Public Policy: The Evolution of the CAP over a Decade'. *Journal of European Public Policy,* 16: 395–411.

_____ and Swinbank, A. (2007), 'The Politics of CAP Reform: Trade Negotiations, Institutional

Settings and Blame Avoidance'. *Journal of Common Market Studies*, 45: 293–312.

____ and ____ (2008), 'Curbing Agricultural Exceptionalism: The EU's Response to External Challenge'. *World Economy*, 31: 631–52.

DeBardeleben, J. and Hurrelmann, A. (eds) (2007) *Democratic Dilemmas of Multilevel Governance: Legitimacy, Representation and Accountability in the European Union*. Basingstoke: Palgrave Macmillan.

De Búrca, G. (1998), 'The Principle of Subsidiarity and the Court of Justice as a Political Actor'. *Journal of Common Market Studies*, 36: 217–315.

Dedman, M. (2010), *The Origins and Development of the European Union 1945–2008* (2nd edn). London: Routledge.

De Gucht, K. (2003), 'The European Commission: Countdown to Extinction?'. *European Integration*, 25: 165–8.

Dell, E. (1995), *The Schuman Plan and the British Abdication of Leadership in Europe*. Oxford: Clarendon Press.

den Boer, M. and Wallace, W. (2000), 'Justice and Home Affairs: Integration through Incrementalism?', in H. Wallace and W. Wallace (eds), *Policy-Making in the European Union* (4th edn). Oxford: Oxford University Press, 493–519.

de Schoutheete, P. (2002), 'The European Council', in J. Peterson and M. Shackleton (eds), *The Institutions of the European Union*. Oxford: Oxford University Press, 21–46.

Deutsch, K. (1953), *Nationalism and Social Communication: An Inquiry into the Foundations of Nationality*. Cambridge, MA: MIT Press.

____, Burrell, S. A., Kann, R. A., Lee Jr., M., Lichterman, M., Lindgren, R. E., Loewenheim, F. L., and van Wagenen, R. W. (1957), *Political Community and the North Atlantic Area: International Organization in the Light of Historical Experience*. Princeton, NJ: Princeton University Press.

Devuyst, Y. (1999), 'The Community-Method After Amsterdam'. *Journal of Common Market Studies*, 37: 109–20.

Diebold Jr, W. (1959), *The Schuman Plan: A Study in Economic Cooperation, 1950–1959*. New York: Praeger.

Dimitrakopoulos, D. (2004), *The Changing European Commission*. Manchester: Manchester University Press.

Dinan, D. (1994), *Ever Closer Union? An Introduction to the European Community*. London: Macmillan.

____ (2004), 'The Road to Enlargement', in M. Cowles and D. Dinan (eds), *Developments in the European Union*. Basingstoke: Palgrave Macmillan, 7–24.

Dobson, A. (2007), *Green Political Thought* (4th edn). London and New York: Routledge.

Dougan, M. (2008), 'The Treaty of Lisbon 2007: Winning Minds not Hearts'. *Common Market Law Review*, 45: 617–701.

Duchêne, F. (1994), *Jean Monnet: The First Statesman of Interdependence*. New York and London: W.W. Norton & Company.

Duff, A. (2009), *Saving the European Union. The Logic of the Lisbon Treaty*. London: Shoehorn Media.

Dyson, K. (1994), *Elusive Union: The Process of Economic and Monetary Union in Europe*. Harlow: Longman.

____ and Featherstone, K. (1999), *The Road to Maastricht: Negotiating Economic and Monetary Union*. Oxford: Oxford University Press.

____ and Goetz, K. (2002), 'Germany and Europe: Beyond Congruence'. Paper given to the British Academy Conference, 'Germany and Europe: A Europeanised Germany?' London, 11 March.

Eckersley, R. (1993), 'Free Market Environmentalism: Friend or Foe?'. *Environmental Politics*, 2: 1–19.

Edquist, K. (2006), 'EU Social Policy Governance: Advocating Activism or Servicing States?'. *Journal of European Public Policy,* 13: 500–18.

Edwards, G. and Pijpers, A. (1997), *The Politics of European Treaty Reform: The 1996 Intergovernmental Conference and Beyond*. London and Washington, DC: Pinter.

____ and Spence, D. (eds) (1994), *The European Commission*. Harlow: Longman.

Egeberg, M. (2003), 'The European Commission', in M. Cini (ed.), *European Union Politics*. Oxford: Oxford University Press, 131–47.

____ (2006), *Multilevel Union Administration: The Transformation of Executive Politics in Europe*. Basingstoke: Palgrave Macmillan.

____ (2010), 'The European Commission', in M. Cini and N. Perez-Solórzano Borragán (eds), *European Union Politics* (3rd edn). Oxford: Oxford University Press, 125–40.

Ehin, P. (2008), 'Competing Models of EU Legitimacy: The Test of Popular Expectations'. *Journal of Common Market Studies,* 46: 619–40.

Eising, R. (2003), 'Interest Groups in the European Union', in M. Cini (ed.), *European Union Politics*. Oxford: Oxford University Press, 192–210.

____ and Lehringer, S. (2010), 'Interest Groups and the European Union', in M. Cini and N. Pérez-Solórzano-Borragán (eds), *European Union Politics* (3rd edn). Oxford: Oxford University Press, 189–206.

557

Ellerman, D. A. and Buchner, B. K. (2007), 'The European Union Emissions Trading Scheme: Origins, Allocation and Early Results'. *Review of Environmental Economics and Policy*, 1: 66–87.

Ellina, C. (2003), *Promoting Women's Rights: The Politics of Gender in the European Union*. New York: Routledge.

Eriksen, E. and Fossum, J. (2002), 'Democracy through Strong Publics in the European Union'. *Journal of Common Market Studies*, 40: 401–24.

Etzioni, A. (2004), 'The EU as Test Case of Halfway Supranationality'. *EUSA Review*, 17: 1–3.

Eurobarometer (2004a), *Eurobarometer Spring 2004: Public Opinion in the European Union*. EB61. Luxembourg: Eurostat.

_____ (2004b), *Eurobarometer Autumn 2004: Public Opinion in the European Union*. EB62. Luxembourg: Eurostat.

Europa (2010), 'The EU at a Glance: The History of the European Union'. (http://europa.eu/abc/history/) (accessed 15.07.10).

European Commission (1973), 'Report on the Regional Problems in the Enlarged Community'. Presented to the Council on 4 May. *Bulletin of the European Communities 6, Supplement 8/73*. Brussels: European Communities.

_____ (1975), 'Preamble' to Regulation (EEC) No. 724/75 of 18 March 1975 establishing a European Regional Development Fund. *Official Journal*, L73, 21/3/75. Brussels: European Commission.

_____ (1985), *Completing the Internal Market*. COM (85)310. Brussels: European Community.

_____ (1989), *Guide to the Reform of the Community's Structural Funds*. Brussels/Luxembourg: European Communities.

_____ (1992), *Towards Sustainability: A European Community Programme of Policy and Action in Relation to the Environment and Sustainable Development*. COM (1992) 23 final. Brussels: Commission of the European Communities.

_____ (1993a), *The Council's Common Position on the Revision of the Structural Fund Regulations*. Communication from the Commission to the European Parliament. SEC (93) final. Brussels: European Communities.

_____ (1993b), *Community Structural Funds 1994–99, Revised Regulations and Comments*. Brussels/Luxembourg: European Communities.

_____ (1995), *The Agricultural Situation in the European Union*. Brussels and Luxembourg: European Communities.

_____ (1996a), *First Report on Economic and Social Cohesion*. Brussels and Luxembourg: European Commission.

_____ (1996b), *Social and Economic Inclusion through Regional Development: The Community Economic Development Priority in European Structural Funds in Great Britain*. Brussels: European Commission.

_____ (1996c), *Green Paper on Relations between the European Union and the ACP Countries on the Eve of the 21st Century: Challenges and Options for a new Partnership*. Brussels: European Commission.

_____ (1997), *Agenda 2000: For a Stronger and Wider Union*. Brussels: European Commission.

_____ (1998a), 'Proposed Regulations Governing the Reform of the Structural Funds 2000–2006 (preliminary version)'. 18 March. *Inforegio*.

_____ (1998b), *Reform of the Structural Funds, Explanatory Memorandum*. Brussels: European Commission.

_____ (1999a), *The Amsterdam Treaty: A Comprehensive Guide*. Brussels/Luxembourg: European Communities.

_____ (1999b), *Agenda 2000: For a Stronger and Wider Europe*. Brussels/Luxembourg: European Communities.

_____ (2000), 'Partnership Agreement between the African, Caribbean and Pacific Group of States of the One Part, and the European Community and its Member States of the Other Part, signed in Cotonou, Benin on 23 June, 2000'.

_____ (2001a), *European Governance: A White Paper*. COM (2001) 428 final, 25 July.

_____ (2001b), *Communication on Effective Problem Solving in the Internal Market*. COM (2001) 702.

_____ (2001c), *Environment 2010: Our Future, Our Choice. Sixth Community Environment Action Programme*. COM (2001) 31 final. Brussels: Commission of the European Communities.

_____ (2002), *Action Plan for a Single Market*. IP/02/1110. Brussels: Commission of the European Communities.

_____ (2003), *Internal Market Strategy: Priorities 2003–6*. COM (2003) 238. Brussels: Commission of the European Communities.

_____ (2004a), *First Report on the Implementation of the Internal Market Strategy 2003–2006*. COM (2004) 22 final. Brussels: Commission of the European Communities.

_____ (2004b), 'A New Partnership for Cohesion: Convergence, Competitiveness, Cooperation'. *Third Report on Economic and Social Cohesion*. Luxembourg: European Communities.

_____ (2004c), *Commission Working Document. Integrating Environmental Considerations into Other Policy Areas: A Stocktaking of the Cardiff Process*. COM (2004) 394 final. Brussels: Commission of the European Communities.

_____ (2005a), _Second Implementation Report of the Internal Market Strategy 2003–2006_. COM (2005) 11 final. Brussels: Commission of the European Communities.

_____ (2005b), _Communication from the Commission to the Council and the European Parliament: The 2005 Review of the EU Sustainable Development Strategy—Initial Stocktaking and Future Orientations_. COM (2005) 37 final. Brussels: Commission of the European Communities.

_____ (2005c), _Communication from the Commission to the Council and the European Parliament: On the Review of the Sustainable Development Strategy—A Platform for Action_. COM (2005) 658 final. Brussels: Commission of the European Communities.

_____ (2005d), _Strategic Objectives 2005–2009 Europe 2010: A Partnership for European Renewal, Prosperity, Solidarity and Security_. Communication from the President in agreement with Vice-President Wallström. COM (2005) 12 final.

_____ (2006a), _A European Strategy for Sustainable, Competitive and Secure Energy_. Brussels: European Union.

_____ (2006b), _Global Europe: Competing in the World_. Brussels: European Commission.

_____ (2007a), _Cohesion Policy 2007–13: Commentaries and Official Texts_. Luxembourg: Office for Official Publications of the European Communities.

_____ (2007b), _Communication from the Commission to the European Parliament, the Council, the European Economic and Social Committee and the Committee of the Regions on the Mid-Term Review of the Sixth Community Environment Action Programme_. COM (2007) 225 final. Brussels: Commission of the European Communities.

_____ (2007c) _Financial Instruments and EU Enlargement Projects_. Brussels: DG Enlargement. (http://ec.europa.eu/enlargement/financialassistance/indexen.htm).

_____ (2008), _Global Europe: EU Performance in the Global Economy_. Brussels: European Commission Directorate General for Trade.

European Council (2009), 'European Council Decision of 1 December 2009 Adopting its Rules of Procedure'. 2009/882/EU. _Official Journal of the European Union_, L315/51, 2 December.

European Parliament (1988), _Official Journal of the European Communities: Annex—Debates of the European Parliament_, 1988–9, no. 2–367.

European Union (2005), _From the ECSC to the Constitution: Treaty of Maastricht on European Union_. Brussels: Europa.

Eurostat (1980), 'Gross Domestic Product at Market Prices: Regional Indicators'. _Basic Statistics of the Community_ (various editions). Luxembourg: European Communities.

Evans, A. (1999), _The EU Structural Funds_. Oxford: Oxford University Press.

_____ (2003) 'The Europeanization of Business Interest Representation: UK and French Firms Compared'. _Comparative European Politics_, 1: 313–4.

Fairbrass, J. (2006), 'Organized Interests and Interest Politics', in I. Bache and A. Jordan (eds), _The Europeanisation of British Politics?_. Basingstoke: Palgrave, 135–51

Faist, T. and Ette, A. (2007), _The Europeanization of National Policies and Politics of Immigration: Between Autonomy and the European Union_. Basingstoke: Palgrave Macmillan.

Falkner, G. (2000), 'The Council or the Social Partners? EC Social Policy between Diplomacy and Collective Bargaining'. _Journal of European Public Policy_, 7: 705–24.

Farrell, H. and Héritier, A. (2003), 'Formal and Informal Institutions under Codecision: Continuous Constitution-Building in Europe'. _Governance_, 16: 577–600.

Featherstone, K. (1994), 'Jean Monnet and the "Democratic Deficit" in the European Union'. _Journal of Common Market Studies_, 32: 149–70.

_____ (2003), 'Introduction: In the Name of "Europe"', in K. Featherstone and C. Radaelli (eds), _The Politics of Europeanization_. Oxford: Oxford University Press, 3–26.

_____ and Papadimitriou, D. (2008), _The Limits of Europeanization: Policy Conflict and Reform Capacity in Greece_. Basingstoke: Palgrave Macmillan.

Fioretos, K-O. (1997), 'The Anatomy of Autonomy: Interdependence, Domestic Balances of Power, and European Integration'. _Review of International Studies_, 23: 293–320.

Follesdal, A. and Hix, S. (2006), 'Why There is a Democratic Deficit in the EU: A Response to Majone and Moravcsik'. _Journal of Common Market Studies_, 44: 533–62.

Foreign and Commonwealth Office (1996), _A Partnership of Nations_. Cm 3181. London: HMSO.

_____ (2004), 'Turkey and the EU'. _Enlargement Update_, Spring 2004. London: HMSO. (http://www.europe.gov.uk/enlargement).

Forster, A. (1998), 'Britain and the Negotiation of the Maastricht Treaty: A Critique of Liberal Intergovernmentalism'. _Journal of Common Market Studies_, 36: 347–67.

Forsyth, M. G., Keens-Soper, H. M. A., and Savigear, P. (eds) (1970), *The Theory of International Relations: Selected Texts from Gentili to Treitschke*. London: George Allen & Unwin.

Forwood, G. (2001), 'The Road to Cotonou: Negotiating a Successor to Lomé'. *Journal of Common Market Studies*, 39: 423–42.

Fouilleux, E. (2007), 'The Common Agricultural Policy', in M. Cini (ed.), *European Union Politics* (2nd edn). Oxford: Oxford University Press, 340–55.

Franchino, F. (2007), *The Powers of the Union: Delegation in the EU*. Cambridge: Cambridge University Press.

Freestone, D. (1983), 'The European Court of Justice', in J. Lodge (ed.), *Institutions and Policies of the European Community*. London: Pinter, 45–53.

Frey-Wouters, E. (1980), *The EC and the Third World: The Lomé Convention and its Impact*. New York: Praeger.

Friis, L. (1998), 'Approaching the "Third Half" of EU Grand Bargaining: The Post-Negotiation Phase of the "Europe Agreement Game"'. *Journal of European Public Policy*, 5: 322–38.

_____ and Murphy, A. (1999), 'The European Union and Central and Eastern Europe: Governance and Boundaries'. *Journal of Common Market Studies*, 37: 211–32.

Frontex (2009), *Programme of Work 2009*. Warsaw: Frontex. (http://www.frontex.europa.eu/gfx/frontex/files/justyna/programmeofwork2009final.pdf).

Fuchs, G. (1994), 'Policy-Making in a System of Multi-Level Governance: The Commission of the European Community and the Restructuring of the Telecommunications Sector'. *Journal of European Public Policy*, 1: 177–94.

Fursdon, E. (1980), *The European Defence Community: A History*. London: Macmillan.

Galtung, J. (1976), 'The Lomé Convention and Neo-Capitalism'. *African Review*, 6: 33–42.

Gamble, A. and Payne, A. (eds) (1996), *Regionalism and World Order*. Basingstoke and London: Macmillan.

Garrett, G. (1992), 'International Cooperation and Institutional Choice: The European Community's Internal Market'. *International Organization*, 46: 533–60.

_____ (1995), 'The Politics of Legal Integration in the European Union'. *International Organization*, 49: 171–81.

_____ and Tsebelis, G. (1996), 'An Institutional Critique of Intergovernmentalism'. *International Organization*, 50: 269–99.

_____ and Weingast, B. (1993), 'Ideas, Interests and Institutions: Constructing the European Community's Internal Market', in J. Goldstein and R. Keohane (eds), *Ideas and Foreign Policy*. Ithaca, NY: Cornell University Press, 173–206.

_____, Keleman, R. D., and Schultz, H. (1998), 'The European Court of Justice, National Governments, and Legal Integration in the European Union'. *International Organization*, 52: 149–76.

Garson, J.-P. (1997), 'Opening Mediterranean Trade and Migration'. *OECD Observer*, 209: 21–24. (http://www.oecd.org/dataoecd/36/2/1908464.pdf).

Geddes, A. (2006), 'The Politics of European Union Domestic Order', in K. E. Jørgensen, M. Pollack, and B. Rosamond (eds), *Handbook of European Union Politics*. London: Sage Publications, 449–62.

_____ (2008), *Immigration and European Integration: Beyond Fortress Europe* (2nd edn). Manchester: Manchester University Press.

George, S. (1989), 'Nationalism, Liberalism and the National Interest: Britain, France, and the European Community'. *Strathclyde Papers on Government and Politics*, no. 67. Glasgow: University of Strathclyde.

_____ (1994), 'Supranational Actors and Domestic Politics: Integration Theory Reconsidered in the Light of the Single European Act and Maastricht'. *Sheffield Papers in International Studies*, no. 22. Sheffield: University of Sheffield.

_____ (1996a), *Politics and Policy in the European Community* (3rd edn). Oxford: Oxford University Press.

_____ (1996b), 'The European Union: approaches from international relations', in H. Kassim and A. Menon (eds), *The European Union and National Industrial Policy*. London and New York: Routledge, 11–25.

_____ (1998), *An Awkward Partner: Britain in the European Community* (3rd edn). Oxford: Oxford University Press.

_____ (2004), 'Multi-Level Governance and the European Union', in I. Bache and M. Flinders (eds), *Multi-Level Governance*. Oxford: Oxford University Press, 107–26.

Gibb, R. (2000), 'Post- Lomé: The European Union and the South'. *Third World Quarterly*, 21: 457–81.

Gilbert, M. (2008), 'Narrating the Process: Questioning the Progressive Story of European Integration'. *Journal of Common Market Studies*, 46: 641–62.

Gillingham, J. (1991a), *Coal, Steel, and the Rebirth of Europe, 1945–1955*. Cambridge: Cambridge University Press.

_____ (1991b), 'Jean Monnet and the European Coal and Steel Community: A Preliminary

Appraisal', in D. Brinkley and C. Hackett (eds), *Jean Monnet: The Path to European Unity*. Basingstoke and London: Macmillan, 129–62.

Ginsberg, R. H. (1989), *Foreign Policy Actions of the European Community: The Politics of Scale*. Boulder, CO: Lynne Rienner.

_____ (1994), 'The European Union's Common Foreign and Security Policy: An Outsider's Retrospective on the First Year'. *ECSA Newsletter*. Pittsburgh, PA: European Community Studies Association.

Giordano, B. (2004), 'The Future of EU Regional Policy after 2006: Lots More Water to go under the Bridge'. *Regions*, 252: 19–22.

Glarbo, K. (1999), 'Restructuring the CFSP of the EU'. *Journal of European Public Policy*, 6: 634–51.

Glaser, T. (1990), 'EEC/ACP Cooperation: The Historical Perspective'. *The Courier*, 120, March/April.

_____ and Hix, S. (2000), 'Europeanised Politics? European Integration and National Political Systems'. *West European Politics*, 23: 94–120.

Glover, M. (2007), 'Review' [of Puetter (2006)]. *Parliamentary Affairs*, 60: 709–15.

Goetz, K. (2000), 'European Integration and National Executives: A Cause in Search of an Effect?'. *West European Politics*, 23: 211–31.

Gold, M., Cressey, P., and Leonard, E. (2007), 'Whatever Happened to Social Dialogue? From Partnership to Managerialism in the EU Employment Agenda'. *European Journal of Industrial Relations*, 13: 7–25.

Golub, J. (1998), 'New Instruments for Environmental Policy in the EU: Introduction and Overview', in J. Golub (ed.), *New Instruments for Environmental Policy in the EU*. London and New York: Routledge, 1–29.

Grabbe, H. (2001), 'How Does Europeanization Affect CEE Governance? Conditionality, Diffusion and Diversity'. *Journal of European Public Policy*, 8: 1013–31.

_____ (2003), 'Europeanization Goes East: Power and Uncertainty in the EU Accession Process', in K. Featherstone and C. Radaelli (eds), *The Politics of Europeanization*. Oxford: Oxford University Press, 303–27.

Grant, C. (1994), *Delors: Inside the House that Jacques Built*. London: Nicholas Brealey Publishing.

Grant, W. (1993), 'Pressure Groups and the European Community: An Overview', in S. Mazey and J. Richardson (eds), *Lobbying in the European Union*. Oxford: Oxford University Press, 27–46.

_____ (1995), 'The Limits of Common Agricultural Policy Reform and the Option of

Denationalization'. *Journal of European Public Policy*, 2: 1–18.

_____ (1997), *The Common Agricultural Policy*. Basingstoke and London: Macmillan.

Green, R.H. (1976), 'The Lomé Convention: Updated Dependence or Departure towards Collective Self-Reliance?'. *African Review*, 6: 43–54.

Greenwood, J. (1997), *Representing Interests in the European Union*. Basingstoke and London: Macmillan.

_____ (2003), *Interest Representation in the European Union*. Basingstoke: Palgrave Macmillan, 2003.

_____ (2007), *Interest Representation in the European Union* (2nd edn). Basingstoke: Palgrave Macmillan.

_____, Levy, R., and Stewart, R. (1995), 'The European Union Structural Fund Allocations: "Lobbying to Win" or Recycling the Budget?'. *European Urban and Regional Studies*, 2: 317–38.

Gualini, E. (2003), 'Challenges to Multi-Level Governance: Contradictions and Conflicts in the Europeanization of Italian Regional Policy'. *Journal of European Public Policy*, 10: 616–36.

Guiraudon, V. (2000), 'European Integration and Migration Policy: Vertical Policy-Making as Venue-Shopping'. *Journal of Common Market Studies*, 38: 251–71.

Guyomarch, A., Machin, H., and Ritchie, E. (1998), *France in the European Union*. Basingstoke: Macmillan.

Haas, E. B. (1958), *The Uniting of Europe: Political, Social and Economic Forces 1950–57*. London: Library of World Affairs.

_____ (1968), *The Uniting of Europe: Political, Social and Economic Forces, 1950–1957* (2nd edn). Stanford, CA: Stanford University Press.

_____ (1970), 'The Study of Regional Integration: Reflections on the Joy and Anguish of Pretheorizing'. *International Organization*, 24: 607–46.

_____ (2001), 'Does Constructivism Subsume Neo-functionalism?', in T. Christiansen, K.E. Jørgensen, and A. Wiener (eds), *The Social Construction of Europe*. London: Sage: 22–31.

Haas, P. (1992), 'Introduction: Epistemic Communities and International Policy Coordination'. *International Organization*, 46: 1–35.

Hagemann, S. and De Clerck-Sachsse, J. (2007), 'Old Rules, New Game: Decision-Making in the Council of Ministers after the 2004 Enlargement'. Special Report. Brussels: Centre for European Policy Studies, March.

561

____ and Hoyland, B. (2008), 'Parties in the Council?'. *Journal of European Public Policy*, 15: 1205–21.

Haigh, N. (1999), 'European Union Environmental Policy at 25: Retrospect and Prospect'. *Environment and Planning C: Government and Policy*. 17: 109–12.

Hall, P. (1990), 'The State and the Market', in P. Hall, J. Hayward, and H. Machin (eds), *Developments in French Politics*. Basingstoke and London: Macmillan, 171–87.

____ (2003), 'Institutions and the Evolution of European Democracy', in J. Hayward and A. Menon (eds), *Governing Europe*. Oxford: Oxford University Press, 1–14.

____ and Taylor, R. (1996), 'Political Science and the Three New Institutionalisms'. *Political Studies,* 44: 936–57.

Hallstein, W. (1962), *United Europe: Challenge and Opportunity*. Cambridge, MA, and London: Harvard University Press and Oxford University Press.

Halstead, J. (1982), *The Development of the European Regional Fund since 1972*. PhD thesis, University of Bath.

Hanf, K. and Soetendorp, B. (eds) (1998), *Adapting to European Integration: Small States and the European Union*. London: Longman.

Hantrais, L. (2000), *Gendered Policies in Europe: Reconciling Employment and Family Life*. Basingstoke: Macmillan.

Harmsen, R. (1999), 'The Europeanization of National Administrations: A Comparative Study of France and the Netherlands'. *Governance*, 12: 81–113.

Harrison, R. (1974), *Europe in Question*. London: George Allen & Unwin.

Hay, C. and Rosamond, B. (2002), 'Globalization, European Integration and the Discursive Construction of Economic Imperatives'. *Journal of European Public Policy*, 9: 147–67.

Hayes-Renshaw, F. and Wallace, H. (1997), *The Council of Ministers*. Basingstoke: Macmillan.

____ and ____ (2006), *The Council of Ministers* (2nd edn). Basingstoke: Palgrave Macmillan.

____, Lequesne, C., and Mayor Lopez, P. (1989), 'The Permanent Representations of the Member States to the European Communities'. *Journal of Common Market Studies*, 28: 121–37.

Heisbourg, F. (2000), 'Europe's Strategic Ambitions: The Limits of Ambiguity'. *Survival*, 42: 5–15.

Hennessy, P. (1991), 'Public Servant of a New World Order'. *Independent*, 14 October.

Héritier, A. (2007), *Explaining Institutional Change in Europe*. Oxford: Oxford University Press.

____, Kerwer, D., Knill, C., Lehmkuhl, D., Teutsch, M., and Douillet, A.-C. (2001), *Differential Europe: The European Union Impact on National Policymaking*. Lanham, MD: Rowman and Littlefield.

____, Knill, C., and Mingers, S. (1996), *Ringing the Changes in Europe: Regulatory Competition and Redefinition of the State—Britain, France, Germany*. Berlin: Walter de Gruyter.

Hewitt, A. (1989), 'ACP and the Developing World', in J. Lodge (ed.), *The European Community and the Challenge of the Future*. London: Pinter, 285–300.

Hill, C. (1993), 'The Capability–Expectations Gap, or Conceptualising Europe's International Role'. *Journal of Common Market Studies*, 31: 305–28.

____ (1996), *The Actors in Europe's Foreign Policy*. London: Routledge.

____ (1998), 'Closing the Capability–Expectations Gap', in J. Peterson and H. Sjursen (eds), *A Common Foreign Policy for Europe?: Competing Visions of the CFSP*. London: Routledge, 18–38.

____ (2004), 'Renationalizing or Regrouping? EU Foreign Policy Since 11 September 2001'. *Journal of Common Market Studies*, 42: 143–63.

Hirst, P. and Thompson, G. (1996), *Globalization in Question: The International Economy and the Possibilities of Governance*. Cambridge: Polity Press.

Hix, S. (1994), 'The Study of the European Community: The Challenge to Comparative Politics'. *West European Politics*, 17: 1–30.

____ (1999), *The Political System of the European Union*. Basingstoke and London: Macmillan.

____ (2000), 'How MEPs Vote'. Briefing note 1/00, ESRC 'One Europe or Several?' Programme. London: ESRC.

____ (2006), 'Democracy, Parties and Elections'. (http://www.lse-students.ac.uk/HIX/working%20Papers/06-Democracy.pdf).

____ (2008), 'Towards a Partisan Theory of EU Politics'. *Journal of European Public Policy*, 15: 1254–65.

____ and Goetz, K. (2000), 'Introduction: European Integration and National Political Systems'. *West European Politics*, 23: 1–26.

____ and Lord, C. (1997), *Political Parties in the European Union*. Basingstoke and London: Macmillan.

____ and Marsh, M. (2007), 'Punishment or Protest? Understanding European Parliament Elections'. *The Journal of Politics*, 69: 495–510.

____, Kreppel, A., and Noury, A. (2003), 'The Party System in the European Parliament: Collusive or Competitive?'. *Journal of Common Market Studies*, 41: 309–31.

____, Noury, A., and Roland, G. (2005), 'Power to the Parties: Cohesion and Competition in the European Parliament, 1979–2001'. *British Journal of Political Science*, 35: 209–34.

____, Raunio, T., and Scully, R. (2003), 'Fifty Years On: Research on the European Parliament'. *Journal of Common Market Studies*, 41: 191–202.

Hodges, M. and Wallace, W. (eds) (1981), *Economic Divergence in the European Community*. London: Butterworth.

Hodson, D. and Maher, I. (2001), 'The Open Method as a New Mode of Governance: The Case of Soft Economic Policy Co-ordination'. *Journal of Common Market Studies*, 39: 719–46.

Hoffmann, S. (1964), 'The European Process at Atlantic Crosspurposes'. *Journal of Common Market Studies*, 3: 85–101.

____ (1966), 'Obstinate or Obsolete? The Fate of the Nation State and the Case of Western Europe'. *Daedalus*, 95: 862–915.

____ (1982), 'Reflections on the Nation-State in Western Europe Today'. *Journal of Common Market Studies*, 21: 21–37.

____ (1989), 'The European Community and 1992'. *Foreign Affairs*, 68: 27–47.

Holland, S. (1980), *Uncommon Market*. Basingstoke and London: Macmillan.

Holzinger, K., Knill, C., and Schäfer, A. (2006), 'Rhetoric or Reality? "New Governance" in EU Environmental Policy'. *European Law Journal*, 12: 403–20.

Hooghe, L. (1996*a*), 'Introduction: Reconciling EU-Wide Policy and National Diversity', in L. Hooghe (ed.), *Cohesion Policy and European Integration*. Oxford: Oxford University Press, 1–26.

____ (1996*b*), 'Building a Europe with the Regions: The Changing Role of the European Commission', in L. Hooghe (ed.), *Cohesion Policy and European Integration*. Oxford: Oxford University Press: 89–128.

____ (1998), 'EU Cohesion Policy and Competing Models of Capitalism'. *Journal of Common Market Studies*, 36: 457–77.

____ and Marks, G. (2003), 'Unravelling the Central State, but How?'. *American Political Science Review*, 97: 233–43.

____ and ____ (2004), 'Contrasting Visions of Multi-Level Governance', in I. Bache and M. Flinders (eds), *Multi-Level Governance*. Oxford: Oxford University Press, 15–30.

____ and ____ (2008), 'A Postfunctionalist Theory of European Integration: From Permissive Consensus to Constraining Dissensus'. *British Journal of Political Science*, 39: 1–23.

Hoskyns, C. (1996), *Integrating Gender: Women, Law and Politics in the European Union*. London: Verso.

____ (2004), 'Gender Perspectives', in A. Wiener and T. Diez (eds), *European Integration Theory*. Oxford: Oxford University Press, 217–36.

House of Lords (1997), 'Reducing Disparities within the European Union: The Effectiveness of the Structural and Cohesion Funds, Volume 2—Evidence'. *Select Committee on the European Communities, Session 1996–97, 11th Report*. London: HMSO.

____ (2007), European Union Committee. *Schengen Information System II (SIS II)*, 9th Report of Session 2006–07. London: HMSO.

Howell, K. (2003), 'The Europeanization of British Financial Services'. Paper presented to the ESRC Seminar Series/UACES Study Group on the Europeanization of British Politics and Policy-Making, Sheffield, 2 May.

Howorth, J. (2003), 'France, Britain and the Euro-Atlantic Crisis'. *Survival*, 45: 173–92.

____ (2004), 'The Role of Discourse, Ideas and Epistemic Communities in the Forging of ESDP'. *West European Politics*, 27: 211–34.

Hu, Y. (1981), *Europe under Stress*. London: Butterworth.

Hübner, D. (2004), *Lisbon and Cohesion Policy: Complementary Objectives*. Speech by the member of the European Commission responsible for Regional Policy. UNICE Competitiveness Day, Brussels, 9 December. (http://europa.eu/rapid/pressReleasesAction.do?reference=SPEECH/04/535) (accessed 01.10.09).

Hughes, J., Sasse, G., and Gordon, C. (2004), 'Conditionality and Compliance in the EU's Eastward Enlargement'. *Journal of Common Market Studies,* 42: 523–51.

____, ____, and ____ (2005), *Europeanization and Regionalization in the EU's Enlargement to Central and Eastern Europe: The Myth of Conditionality*. Basingstoke: Palgrave Macmillan.

Humphreys, P. and Padgett, S. (2006), 'Globalization, the European Union, and Domestic Governance in Telecoms and Electricity'. *Governance*, 19: 383–406.

Hurt, S. R. (2003), 'Co-operation and Coercion? The Cotonou Agreement between the European Union and ACP States and the End of the Lomé Convention'. *Third World Quarterly*, 24: 161–76.

Hussain, N., with Hudson, G. and Whitman, R. (2005), 'Referendums on the EU Constitutional Treaty: The State of Play'. Chatham House European Programme, *Briefing Paper EP BP 05/02*. London: Chatham House.

Hutton, W. (2005), 'My Problem with Europe'. *Observer*, 5 June: 18–19.

Huysmans, J. (2006), *The Politics of Insecurity. Fear, Migration and Asylum in the EU*. London: Routledge.

Ingebritsen, C. (1998), *The Nordic States and European Unity*. Ithaca, NY: Cornell University Press.

Jachtenfuchs, M. (2001), 'The Governance Approach to European Integration'. *Journal of Common Market Studies*, 39: 245–64.

____ and Kohler-Koch, B. (2004), 'Governance and Institutional Development', in A. Wiener and T. Diez (eds), *European Integration Theory*. Oxford: Oxford University Press, 97–115.

Jacobs, F. and Corbett, R. (1990), *The European Parliament*. Harlow: Longman.

Jamal, A.H. (1979), 'Preparing for Lomé Two'. *Third World Quarterly*, 1: 134–40.

Jehlicka, P. and Tickle, A. (2004), 'Environmental Implications of Eastern Enlargement: The End of Progressive EU Environmental Policy?'. *Environmental Politics*, 13: 77–95.

Jenkins, R. (1977), 'Europe's Present Challenge and Future Opportunity: The First Jean Monnet Lecture delivered at the European University Institute, Florence, 27 October 1977'. *Bulletin of the European Communities Supplement 10/77*: 6–14.

____ (1989), *European Diary, 1977–1981*. London: Collins.

Jordan, A. (1999*a*), 'Editorial Introduction: The Construction of a Multilevel Environment Governance System'. *Environment and Planning C: Government and Policy*, 17: 1–17.

____ (1999*b*), 'The Implementation of EU environmental Policy: A Policy Problem without a Political Solution?'. *Environment and Planning C: Government and Policy*, 17: 69–90.

____ (2002), 'Decarbonising the UK: A "Radical Agenda" from the Cabinet Office?'. *Political Quarterly*, 73: 344–52.

____ (2006), 'Environmental Policy', in I. Bache and A. Jordan (eds), *The Europeanization of British Politics*. Basingstoke: Palgrave, 231–47.

____ and Liefferink, D. (eds) (2004), *Environmental Policy in Europe: The Europeanization of National Environmental Policy*. London: Routledge.

____ and Schout, A. (2006), *The Coordination of the European Union: Exploring the Capacities of Networked Governance*. Oxford: Oxford University Press.

____, ____, and Unfried, M. (2008), 'The European Union', in A. J. Jordan and A. Lenschow (eds), *Innovation in Environmental Policy?*

Integrating the Environment for Sustainability. Cheltenham: Edward Elgar, 159–79.

____, Wurzel, R. K. W., and Zito, A. R. (2003), '"New" Instruments of Environmental Governance: Patterns and Pathways of Change'. *Environmental Politics*, 12: 1–24.

Judge, D. and Earnshaw, D. (2002), 'The European Parliament and the Commission Crisis: A New Assertiveness?'. *Governance*, 15: 345–74.

____ and ____ (2008), *The European Parliament* (2nd edn). Basingstoke: Palgrave Macmillan.

____, ____, and Cowan, N. (1994), 'Ripples or Waves: The European Parliament in the European Community Policy Process'. *Journal of European Public Policy*, 1: 27–52.

Kaelberer, M. (2003), 'Knowledge, Power and Monetary Bargaining: Central Bankers and the Creation of Monetary Union in Europe'. *Journal of European Public Policy*, 10: 365–79.

Kaltenthaler, K. (2002), 'German Interests in European Monetary Integration'. *Journal of Common Market Studies*, 40: 69–87.

Kapsis, I. (2010), 'The Courts of the European Union', in M. Cini and N. Pérez-Solórzano-Borragán (eds), *European Union Politics* (3rd edn). Oxford: Oxford University Press, 176–88.

Kasack, C. (2004), 'The Legislative Impact of the European Parliament under the Revised Co-decision Procedure: Environmental, Public Health and Consumer Protection Policies'. *European Union Politics*, 5: 241–60.

Kassim, H. (1994), 'Policy Networks, Networks and European Union Policy Making: A Sceptical View'. *West European Politics*, 17: 15–27.

____ (2003), 'Meeting the Demands of EU Membership: The Europeanization of National Administrative Systems', in K. Featherstone and C. Radaelli (eds), *The Politics of Europeanization*. Oxford: Oxford University Press, 83–111.

____ (2008), '"Mission Impossible", but Mission Accomplished: The Kinnock Reforms and the European Commission'. *Journal of European Public Policy*, 15: 648–68.

Katz, R. (2000), 'Models of Democracy: Elite Attitudes and the Democratic Deficit in the European Union'. Paper prepared for the workshop 'Competing Conceptions of Democracy in the Practice of Politics', European Consortium for Political Research Joint Sessions of Workshops, Copenhagen, 14–19 April.

Katzenstein, P. (1996), *The Culture of National Security*. New York: Columbia University Press.

Kelleher, J., Batterbury, S., and Stern, E. (1999), *The Thematic Evaluation of the Partnership Principle: Final Synthesis Report*. London: Tavistock Institute.

Keohane, R. (1984), *After Hegemony: Co-operation and Discord in the World Political Economy*. Princeton, NJ: Princeton University Press.

—— (1989), 'Neoliberal Institutionalism: A Perspective on World Politics', in R. Keohane (ed.), *International Institutions and State Power*. Boulder, CO, San Francisco, CA, and Oxford: Westview Press, 1–20.

—— and Nye, J. S., Jr (1977), *Power and Interdependence: World Politics in Transition*. Boston, MA: Little, Brown.

Kerr, Lord J. (2004), 'Plenary Session: The 2003–2004 Grand Bargain'. Presentation at 'Towards a European Constitution', a conference organized by the Federal Trust and the University Association of Contemporary European Studies, Goodenough College, London, 1–2 July.

Kietz, D. and Maurer, A. (2007), 'Fragmentation and De-Democratisation of European Justice and Home Affairs? The Consequences of the Prüm Avant-Garde'. Paper given at the European Union Studies Association 11th Biannual Conference, 17–19 May, Montreal.

—— and Parkes, R. (2008), 'Justiz- und Innenpolitik nach dem Lisabonner Vertrag'. Diskussionspapier, Stiftung Wissenschaft und Politik, 13 May. (http://www.swp-berlin.org/common/getdocument.php?assetid=5000).

—— and von Ondarza, N. (2010), 'Wilkommen in der Lissabonner Wirklichkeit'. *SWP-Aktuell*, 29, March. Berlin: Stiftung Wissenschaft und Politik.

Knill, C. (2001), *The Europeanization of National Administrations: Patterns of Institutional Change and Persistence*. Cambridge: Cambridge University Press.

—— and Lenschow, A. (1998), 'Coping with Europe: The Impact of British and German Administrations on the Implementation of EU Environmental Policy'. *Journal of European Public Policy*, 5: 595–614.

Kohler-Koch, B. (1996) 'Catching up with Change: The Transformation of Governance in the European Union'. *Journal of European Public Policy*, 3: 359–380.

—— (1997), 'Organized Interests in European Integration: The Evolution of a New Type of Governance?', in H. Wallace and A. R. Young (eds), *Participation and Policy-Making in the European Union*. Oxford: Clarendon Press, 42–68.

—— and Eising, R. (eds) (1999), *The Transformation of European Governance*. London: Routledge.

—— and Rittberger, B. (2006), 'The "Governance Turn" in EU Studies'. *Journal of Common Market Studies: Annual Review*, 44: 27–49.

—— and —— (2007), *Debating the Democratic Legitimacy of the European Union*. Lanham, MD: Rowman and Littlefield.

Koppen, I. (1993), 'The Role of the European Court of Justice', in D. Liefferink, P. Lowe, and A. P. J. Mol (eds), *European Integration and Environmental Policy*. London: Belhaven Press, 126–49.

Kreher, A. (1997), 'Agencies in the European Community: A Step towards Administrative Integration in Europe'. *Journal of European Public Policy*, 4: 225–45.

Kreppel, A. (2000), 'Rules, Ideology and Coalition Formation in the European Parliament: Past, Present and Future'. *European Union Politics*, 1: 340–62.

—— (2002), *The European Parliament and Supranational Party System: A Study in Institutional Development*. Cambridge: Cambridge University Press.

—— (2003), 'Necessary but not Sufficient: Understanding the Impact of Treaty Reform on the Internal Development of the European Parliament'. *Journal of European Public Policy*, 10: 884–911.

Kronsell, A. (2005), 'Gender, Power and European Integration Theory'. *Journal of European Public Policy*, 12: 1022–40.

Krotz, U. (2009), 'Momentum and Impediments: Why Europe Won't Emerge as a Full Political Actor on the World Stage Soon'. *JCMS: Journal of Common Market Studies*, 47: 555–78.

Kuper, R. (1998), *The Politics of the European Court of Justice*. London: Kogan Page.

Ladrech, R. (1994), 'Europeanization of Domestic Politics and Institutions: The Case of France'. *Journal of Common Market Studies*, 32(1): 69–88.

Laffan, B. (1983), 'Policy Implementation in the European Community: The European Social Fund as a Case Study'. *Journal of Common Market Studies*, 21: 389–408.

—— (1992), *Integration and Co-operation in Europe*. London and New York: UACES/Routledge.

—— (1997a), *The Finances of the European Union*. Basingstoke and London: Macmillan.

—— (1997b), 'From Policy Entrepreneur to Policy Manager: The Challenge Facing the European Commission'. *Journal of European Public Policy*, 4: 422–38.

Laqueur, W. (1972), *Europe Since Hitler*. Harmondsworth: Penguin.

Laurent, P.-H. and Maresceau, M. (eds) (1998), *The State of the European Union, Vol. 4: Deepening and Widening*. Boulder, CO, and London: Lynne Rienner.

Laursen, F. and Vanhoonacker, S. (eds) (1992), *The Intergovernmental Conference on Political Union*. Maastricht: European Institute of Public Administration/Nijhoff.

_____ and _____ (eds) (1995), *The Ratification of the Maastricht Treaty: Issues, Debates and Future Implications*. Maastricht: European Institute of Public Administration/Nijhoff.

Lavenex, S. (2010), 'Justice and Home Affairs: Communitarization with Hesitation', in H. Wallace, M. Pollack, and A. Young (eds), *Policy-Making in the European Union* (6th edn). Oxford: Oxford University Press, 458–77.

Lenschow, A. (1999), 'The Greening of the EU: The Common Agricultural Policy and the Structural Funds'. *Environment and Planning C: Government and Policy*, 17: 91–108.

_____ (2005), 'Environmental Policy: Contending Dynamics of Policy Change', in H. Wallace, W. Wallace, and M. A. Pollack (eds), *Policy-Making in the European Union* (5th edn). Oxford: Oxford University Press, 305–27.

_____ (2007), 'Environmental Policy in the European Union: Bridging Policy, Politics and Polity Dimensions', in K. E. Jørgensen, M. Pollack, and B. Rosamond (eds), *Handbook of European Union Politics*. London: Sage, 413–31.

Leonardi, R. (2005), *Cohesion Policy in the European Union: The Building of Europe*. Basingstoke: Palgrave Macmillan.

Levitt M. and Lord, C. (2000), *The Political Economy of Monetary Union*. Basingstoke and London: Macmillan.

Lewis, J. (1998), 'Is the "Hard Bargaining" Image of the Council Misleading? The Committee of Permanent Representatives and the Local Elections Directive'. *Journal of Common Market Studies*, 36: 479–504.

_____ (2000), 'The Methods of Community in EU Decision-Making and Administrative Rivalry in the Council's Infrastructure'. *Journal of European Public Policy*, 7: 261–89.

_____ (2003a), 'Informal Integration and the Supranational Construction of the Council'. *Journal of European Public Policy*, 10: 996–1019.

_____ (2003b), 'The Council of the European Union', in M. Cini (ed.), *European Union Politics*. Oxford: Oxford University Press, 148–65.

_____ (2010), 'The Council of the European Union', in M. Cini and N. Pérez-Solózano Borragán (eds), *European Union Politics* (3rd edn). Oxford: Oxford University Press, 141–61.

Liefferink, D. and Andersen, M. S. (1998), 'Strategies of the "Green" Member States in EU Environmental Policy-Making'. *Journal of European Public Policy*, 5: 254–70.

Lightfoot, S. and Burchell, J. (2005), 'The European Union and the World Summit on Sustainable Development: Normative Power Europe in Action?'. *Journal of Common Market Studies*, 43: 75–95.

Lindberg, B. (2008), 'Are Political Parties Controlling Legislative Decision-Making in the European Parliament? The Case of the Services Directive'. *Journal of European Public Policy*, 15: 1184–1204.

_____, Rasmussen, A., and Warntjen, A. (2008), 'Party Politics as Usual? The Role of Political Parties in EU Legislative Decision-Making'. *Journal of European Public Policy*, 15: 1107–26.

Lindberg, L. (1963), *The Political Dynamics of European Economic Integration*. Stanford, CA, and London: Stanford University Press and Oxford University Press.

_____ (1966), 'Integration as a Source of Stress on the European Community System'. *International Organization*, 20: 233–65.

Locher, B. and Prügl, E. (2009), 'Gender and European Integration', in A. Wiener and T. Diez (eds), *European Integration Theory* (2nd edn). Oxford: Oxford University Press, 181–97.

Lodge, J. (1990), 'Ten Years of an Elected Parliament', in J. Lodge (ed.), *The 1989 Election of the European Parliament*. Basingstoke and London: Macmillan, 1–36.

_____ (1994), 'The European Parliament and the Authority-Democracy Crisis', in P-H. Laurent (ed.), *The European Community: To Maastricht and Beyond*. Special edition of *The Annals of the American Academy of Political and Social Science*, January: 69–83.

Loedel, P. H. (1998), 'Enhancing Europe's International Monetary Power: The Drive Toward a Single Currency', in P-H. Laurent and M. Maresceau (eds), *The State of the European Union, Vol. 4: Deepening and Widening*. Boulder, CO, and London: Lynne Rienner, 243–61.

Lord C. (1998), *Democracy in the European Union*. Sheffield: Sheffield Academic Press/University Association for Contemporary European Studies.

_____ (2001), ' Democracy and Democratization in the European Union', in S. Bromley (ed.), *Governing the European Union*. London: Sage, 165–90.

_____ and Harris, E. (2006), *Democracy in the New Europe*. Basingstoke: Palgrave Macmillan.

_____ and Magnette, P. (2004), '*E Pluribus Unum*? Creative Disagreement about Legitimacy in the EU'. *Journal of Common Market Studies*, 42: 183–202.

Lowe, P., Buller, H., and Ward. N. (2002), 'Setting the Next Agenda? British and French Approaches to the Second Pillar of the

Common Agricultural Policy'. *Journal of Rural Studies*, 18: 1–17.

Ludlow, P. (Peter) (1991), 'The European Commission', in R. Keohane and S. Hoffmann (eds), *The New European Community: Decisionmaking and Institutional Change*. Boulder, CO, San Francisco, CA, and Oxford: Westview Press, 85–132.

Ludlow, P. (Piers) (1997), *Dealing with Britain: The Six and the First UK Application to the EEC*. Cambridge: Cambridge University Press.

Lynggaard, K. (2007), 'The Institutional Construction of a Policy Field: A Discursive Institutional Perspective on Change within the Common Agricultural Policy'. *Journal of European Public Policy*, 14: 293–312.

McAleavey, P. (1992), 'The Politics of European Regional Development Policy: The European Commission's RECHAR Initiative and the Concept of Additionality'. *Strathclyde Papers on Government and Politics*, no. 88. Glasgow: University of Strathclyde.

_____ (1993), 'The Politics of the European Regional Development Policy: Additionality in the Scottish Coalfields'. *Regional Politics and Policy*, 3: 88–107.

_____ (1995), *Policy Implementation as Incomplete Contracting: The European Regional Development Fund*. PhD thesis. Florence: European University Institute.

McAllister, R. (2010), *European Union: An Historical and Political Survey*. (2nd edn). London: Routledge.

McCormick, J. (2001), *Environmental Policy in the European Union*. Basingstoke: Palgrave.

McGowan, L. and Cini, M. (1999), 'Discretion and Politicization in EU Competition Policy: The Case of Merger Control'. *Governance*, 12: 175–200.

_____ and Wilks, S. (1995), 'The First Supranational Policy in the European Union: Competition Policy'. *European Journal of Political Research*, 28: 141–69.

McLaren, L. M. (2000), 'Turkey's Eventual Membership of the EU: Turkish Elite Perspectives on the Issue'. *Journal of Common Market Studies*, 38: 117–29.

McLaughlin, A. M. and Greenwood, J. (1995), 'The Management of Interest Representation in the European Union'. *Journal of Common Market Studies*, 33: 149–65.

McNamara, K. (2005), 'Economic and Monetary Union', in H. Wallace, W. Wallace, and M. Pollack (eds), *Policy-Making in the European Union* (5th edn). Oxford: Oxford University Press, 141–60.

McQueen, M. (1998), 'Lomé versus Free Trade Agreements: The Dilemma Facing the ACP Countries'. *World Economy*, 21: 421–43.

Mair, P. (2004), 'The Europeanization Dimension'. *Journal of European Public Policy*, 11: 337–48.

Majone, G. (1993), 'The European Community Between Social Policy and Social Regulation'. *Journal of Common Market Studies*, 31: 153–70.

_____ (1996), *Regulating Europe*. London: Routledge.

_____ (1998), 'Europe's "Democratic Deficit": The Question of Standards'. *European Law Journal*, 4: 5–28.

_____ (2001), 'Two Logics of Delegation: Agency and Fiduciary Relations in EU Governance'. *European Union Politics*, 2: 103–22.

_____ (2002), 'The European Commission: The Limits of Centralization and the Perils of Parliamentarization'. *Governance*, 15: 375–92.

Mamadouh, V. and Raunio, T. (2003), 'The Committee System: Powers, Appointments and Report Allocation'. *Journal of Common Market Studies*, 41: 333–51.

Mancini, G. F. (1991), 'The Making of a Constitution for Europe', in R. Keohane and S. Hoffmann (eds), *The New European Community: Decisionmaking and Institutional Change*. Boulder, CO, San Francisco, CO, and Oxford: Westview Press, 177–94.

Mandel, E. (1968), *Die EWG und die Konkurrenz Europa–Amerika*. Frankfurt/M: Europäische Verlagsanstalt.

Manners, I. (2007), 'Another Europe is Possible', in K.E. Jørgensen, M. Pollack, and B. Rosamond (eds), *Handbook of European Union Politics*. London: Sage, 77–95.

March, J. G. and Olsen, J. (1984), 'The New Institutionalism: Organizational Factors in Political Life'. *American Political Science Review*, 78: 734–49.

_____ and _____ (1989), *Rediscovering Institutions: The Organizational Basis of Politics*. New York and London: Free Press.

_____ and _____ (1996), 'Institutional Perspectives on Political Institutions'. *Governance*, 9: 247–64.

Marcou, G. (ed.) (2002), *Regionalization for Development and Accession to the European Union: A Comparative Perspective*. Budapest: Local Government and Public Service Reform Initiative.

Marks, G. (1992), 'Structural Policy in the European Community', in A. Sbragia (ed.), *Euro-Politics: Institutions and Policymaking in the 'New' European Community*. Washington, DC: Brookings Institution, 191–224.

_____ (1993), 'Structural Policy and Multilevel Governance in the EC', in A. Cafruny and G. Rosenthal (eds), *The State of the European Community, Vol. 2: The Maastricht Debates and Beyond*. Boulder, CO, and Harlow: Lynne Rienner and Longman, 391–410.

_____ (1996a), 'Exploring and Explaining Variation in EU Cohesion Policy', in L. Hooghe (ed.), *Cohesion Policy and European Integration*. Oxford: Oxford University Press, 388–422.

_____ (1996b), 'An Actor Centred Approach to Multilevel Governance'. Paper presented at the American Political Science Association meeting, San Francisco, CA, 29 August–1 September.

_____ and Hooghe, L. (2004), 'Contrasting Visions of Multi-Level Governance', in I. Bache and M. Flinders (eds), *Multi-Level Governance*. Oxford: Oxford University Press, 15–30.

_____, _____, and Blank, K. (1996), 'European Integration from the 1980s: State-Centric v Multi-Level Governance'. *Journal of Common Market Studies*, 34: 341–78.

Marsh, D. and Rhodes, R. A. W. (1992), 'Policy Communities and Issue Networks: Beyond Typology', in D. Marsh and R. A. W. Rhodes (eds), *Policy Networks in British Government*. Oxford: Oxford University Press, 249–68.

Marshall, A. (2005), 'Europeanization at the Urban Level: Local Actors, Institutions and the Dynamics of Multi-Level Interaction'. *Journal of European Public Policy*, 12: 668–86.

Matlary, J. H. (1993), *Towards Understanding Integration: An Analysis of the Role of the State in EC Energy Policy*. PhD thesis. Oslo: University of Oslo.

_____ (1997), *Energy Policy in the European Union*. Basingstoke and London: Macmillan.

Mattila, M. (2008), 'Voting and Coalitions in the Council after the Enlargement', in D. Naurin and H. Wallace (eds), *Unveiling the Council of the European Union: Games Governments Play in Brussels*. Basingstoke: Palgrave Macmillan, 23–35.

Mattli, W. and Slaughter, A-M. (1985), 'Law and Politics in the EU: A Reply to Garrett'. *International Organization*, 49: 183–90.

_____ and _____ (1998), 'Revisiting the European Court of Justice'. *International Organization*, 52: 177–209.

Mawson, J., Martins, M., and Gibney, J. (1985), 'The Development of the European Community Regional Policy', in M. Keating and B. Jones (eds), *Regions in the European Community*. Oxford: Clarendon Press, 20–59.

Mayne, R. (1991), 'Gray Eminence', in D. Brinkley and C. Hackett (eds), *Jean Monnet: The Path to European Unity*. Basingstoke and London: Macmillan, 114–28.

Mazey, S. (1992), 'Conception and Evolution of the High Authority's Administrative Services (1952–1956): From Supranational Principles to Multinational Practices', in E. V. Heyen (ed.), *Yearbook of European Administrative History 4: Early European Community Administration*. Baden-Baden: Nomos, 31–47.

_____ and Richardson, J. (1999), 'Interests', in L. Cram, D. Dinan, and N. Nugent (eds), *Developments in the European Union*. Basingstoke and London: Macmillan, 105–29.

Menon, A. (2003), 'Conclusion: Governing Europe', in J. Hayward and A. Menon (eds), *Governing Europe*. Oxford: Oxford University Press, 413–22.

_____ (2004), 'The Foreign and Security Policies of the European Union', in M. Cowles and D. Dinan (eds), *Developments in the European Union*. Basingstoke: Palgrave Macmillan, 221–36.

_____ (2010), 'Empowering Paradise: The ESDP at Ten'. *International Affairs*, 85: 227–46.

Mény, Y. (2003), 'From Popular Dissatisfaction to Populism: Democracy, Constitutionalisation, and Corruption', in J. Hayward and A. Menon (eds), *Governing Europe*. Oxford: Oxford University Press, 250–63.

_____, Muller, P., and Quermonne, J.-L. (1996), 'Introduction', in Y. Mény, P. Muller, and J.-L. Quermonne (eds), *Adjusting to Europe: The Impact of the European Union on National Institutions and Policies*. London: Routledge, 1–24.

Metcalfe, L. (1992), 'Can the Commission Manage Europe?'. *Australian Journal of Public Administration*, 51: 117–30.

_____ (2000), 'Reforming the Commission: Will Organizational Efficiency Produce Effective Governance?'. *Journal of Common Market Studies*, 38: 817–41.

Meunier, S. (2007a), 'Managing Globalization? The EU in International Trade Negotiations'. *Journal of Common Market Studies*, 45: 905–26.

_____ (2007b), *Trading Voices: The European Union in International Commercial Negotiations*. Princeton, NJ: Princeton University Press.

Middlemas, K. (1995), *Orchestrating Europe: The Informal Politics of European Union, 1973–1995*. London: Fontana.

Milward, A. S. (1984), *The Reconstruction of Western Europe, 1945–51*. London: Routledge.

_____ (1992), *The European Rescue of the Nation State*. London: Routledge.

Mitrany, D. (1943), *A Working Peace System*. London: Royal Institute of International Affairs.

_____ (1966), 'The Prospect of Integration: Federal or Functional'. *Journal of Common Market Studies*, 4: 119–49.

Mold, A. (ed.) (2007), *EU Development Policy in a Changing World: Challenges for the 21st Century*. Amsterdam: Amsterdam University Press.

Monar, J. (2001), 'The Dynamics of Justice and Home Affairs: Laboratories, Driving Factors and Costs'. *Journal of Common Market Studies*, 39: 747–64.

_____ (2009), 'Justice and Home Affairs'. *Journal of Common Market Studies: Annual Review*, 47: 151–70.

Monnet, J. (1962), 'A Ferment of Change'. *Journal of Common Market Studies*, 1: 203–11.

Morata, F. and Munoz, X. (1996), 'Vying for European Funds: Territorial Restructuring in Spain', in L. Hooghe (ed.), *Cohesion Policy and European Integration*. Oxford: Oxford University Press, 195–214.

Moravcsik, A. (1991), 'Negotiating the Single European Act'. *International Organization*, 45: 19–56.

_____ (1993), 'Preferences and Power in the European Community: A Liberal Intergovernmentalist Approach'. *Journal of Common Market Studies*, 31: 473–524.

_____ (1994), 'Why the European Community Strengthens the State: Domestic Politics and International Cooperation'. Working Paper Series No. 52, Center for European Studies, Harvard University.

_____ (1995), 'Liberal Intergovernmentalism and Integration: A Rejoinder'. *Journal of Common Market Studies*, 33: 611–28.

_____ (1998), *The Choice for Europe: Social Purpose and State Power from Messina to Maastricht*. Ithaca, NY, and London: Cornell University Press and UCL Press.

_____ (2002), 'In Defence of the "Democratic Deficit": Reassessing Legitimacy in the European Union'. *Journal of Common Market Studies*, 40: 603–24.

_____ (2004), 'Plenary Session: The 2003–2004 Grand Bargain'. Presentation at 'Towards a European Constitution', a conference organized by the Federal Trust and the University Association of Contemporary European Studies, Goodenough College, London, 1–2 July.

_____ and Nicolaïdes, K. (1999), 'Explaining the Treaty of Amsterdam: Interests, Influences, Institutions'. *Journal of Common Market Studies*, 37: 59–85.

_____ and Schimmelfennig, F. (2009), 'Liberal Intergovernmentalism', in A. Wiener and T. Diez (eds), *European Integration Theory* (2nd edn). Oxford: Oxford University Press, 67–87.

_____ and Vachudova, M. (2002), 'Bargaining Among Unequals: Enlargement and the Future of European Integration'. *EUSA Review*, 15: 1, 3–5.

_____ and _____ (2003), 'National Interests, State Power, EU Enlargement'. *European Politics and Societies*, 17: 42–57.

Moser, P. (1996) 'The European Parliament as a Conditional Agenda Setter: What Are the Conditions? A Critique of Tsebelis (1994)'. *American Political Science Review*, 90: 834–8.

_____ (1997), 'A Theory of the Conditional Influence of the European Parliament in the Cooperation Procedure'. *Public Choice*, 91: 333–50.

Moxon-Browne, E. (1993), 'Social Europe', in J. Lodge (ed.), *The European Community and the Challenge of the Future* (2nd edn). London: Pinter, 152–62.

Moyer, H. W. and Josling, T. E. (1990), *Agricultural Policy Reform: Politics and Process in the EC and the USA*. Ames, IO: Iowa State University Press.

Müftüler-Bac, M. and McLaren, L.M. (2003), 'Enlargement Preferences and Policy-Making in the European Union: Impacts on Turkey'. *Journal of European Integration*, 25: 17–30.

Mutimer, D. (1994), 'Theories of Political Integration', in H. Michelmann and P. Soldatos (eds), *European Integration: Theories and Approaches*. London and Lanham, MD: University Press of America, 13–42.

Nanetti, R. (1996), 'EU Cohesion and Territorial Restructuring in the Member States', in L. Hooghe (ed.), *Cohesion Policy and European Integration*. Oxford: Oxford University Press, 59–88.

National Farmers' Union (1996), *Briefing: 1996 US Farm Bill*. London: NFU.

Niemann, A. (2006), *Explaining Decisions in the European Union*. Cambridge: Cambridge University Press.

_____ and Schmitter, P. (2009), 'Neofunctionalism', in A. Wiener and T. Diez (eds), *European Integration Theory* (2nd edn). Oxford: Oxford University Press, 45–66.

Nugent, N. (1995), 'The leadership capacity of the European Commission'. *Journal of European Public Policy*, 2: 603–23.

_____ (1999), *The Government and Politics of the European Union* (4th edn). Basingstoke and London: Macmillan.

569

_____ (2004), 'Previous Enlargement Rounds', in N. Nugent (ed.), *European Union Enlargement*. Basingstoke and New York: Palgrave Macmillan, 10–33.

Nuttall, S. (1994), 'Keynote Article: The EC and Yugoslavia—*Deus ex Machina* or *Machina Sine Deo*?', in N. Nugent (ed.), *The European Union 1993: Annual Review of Activities*. Oxford: Blackwell, 11–24.

O'Brennan J. (2008), *The European Union and the Western Balkans: Stability and Europeanization through Enlargement*. Abingdon: Routledge.

Olsen, J. (2002), 'The Many Faces of Europeanization'. *Journal of Common Market Studies*, 40: 921–52.

_____ (2003), 'Europeanization', in M. Cini (ed.), *European Union Politics*. Oxford: Oxford University Press, 333–48.

Olsson, J. (2003), 'Democracy Paradoxes in Multi-Level Governance'. *Journal of European Public Policy*, 10: 283–300.

Organisation for Economic Co-operation and Development (1970), *Economic Outlook* (July): 1, Table 1.

Payne, A. (2000), 'Globalization and Modes of Regionalist Governance', in J. Pierre (ed.), *Debating Governance*. Oxford: Oxford University Press, 201–18.

Pearce, N. and Paxton, W. (eds) (2005), *Social Justice: Building a Fairer Britain*. London: Institute for Public Policy Research.

Pech, L. (2003), 'The Solution to the "Democratic Deficit": A New Type of Governance for the European Union?'. *Journal of European Integration*, 25: 131–50.

Pelkmans, J. (1994), 'The Significance of EC-1992', in P-H. Laurent (ed.), *The European Community: To Maastricht and Beyond*. Special edition of *The Annals of the American Academy of Political and Social Science*, January: 94–111.

_____ and Winters, L. A. (1988), *Europe's Domestic Market*. London: Routledge.

Peters, B. G. (1992), 'Bureaucratic Politics and the Institutions of the European Community', in A. Sbragia (ed.), *Euro-Politics: Institutions and Policymaking in the 'New' European Community*. Washington, DC: Brookings Institution, 75–122.

_____ (1997), 'The Commission and Implementation in the European Union: Is There an Implementation Deficit and Why?', in N. Nugent (ed.), *At the Heart of the Union: Studies of the European Commission*. Basingstoke and London: Macmillan, 187–202.

_____ and Pierre, J. (2004), 'Multi-Level Governance and Democracy: A Faustian Bargain?', in I. Bache and M. Flinders (eds), *Multi-Level Governance*. Oxford: Oxford University Press, 75–89.

Peterson, J. (1991), 'Technology Policy in Europe: Explaining the Framework Programme in Theory and Practice'. *Journal of Common Market Studies*, 31: 473–524.

_____ (1992), 'The European Technology Community: Policy Networks in a Supranational Setting', in D. Marsh and R. A. W. Rhodes (eds), *Policy Networks in British Government*. Oxford: Oxford University Press, 226–48.

_____ (1995a), 'Policy Networks and European Union Policy Making: A Reply to Kassim'. *West European Politics*, 18: 389–407.

_____ (1995b), 'Decision-Making in the European Union: Towards a Framework for Analysis'. *Journal of European Public Policy*, 2: 69–93.

_____ (1995c), 'European Union Research Policy: The Politics of Expertise', in M. Rhodes and S. Mazey (eds), *The State of the European Union, Vol. 3: Building a European Polity?*. Boulder, CO, and Harlow: Lynne Rienner and Longman, 391–412.

_____ (1997), 'The European Union: Pooled Sovereignty, Divided Accountability'. *Political Studies*, 45: 559–78.

_____ (2004), 'Policy Networks', in A. Wiener and T. Diez (eds), *European Integration Theory*. Oxford: Oxford University Press, 117–36.

_____ (2009), 'Policy Networks', in A. Wiener and T. Diez (eds), *European Integration Theory* (2nd edn). Oxford: Oxford University Press, 105–24.

_____ and Bomberg, E. (1993), 'Decision Making in the European Union: A Policy Networks Approach'. Paper prepared for presentation to the annual conference of the UK Political Studies Association, Leicester, 20–22 April.

Philippart, E. and Edwards, G. (1999), 'The Provisions on Closer Co-operation in the Treaty of Amsterdam'. *Journal of Common Market Studies*, 37: 87–108.

Phinnemore, D. (2003), 'Towards European Union', in M. Cini (ed.), *European Union Politics*. Oxford: Oxford University Press, 46–64.

_____ (2010), 'The European Union: Establishment and Development', in M. Cini and N. Perez-Solórzano Borragán (eds), *European Union Politics* (3rd edn). Oxford: Oxford University Press, 32–47.

Pierson, P. (1996), 'The Path to European Integration: A Historical Institutionalist Analysis'. *Comparative Political Studies*, 29: 123–63.

_____ (1998), 'The Path to European Integration: A Historical Institutionalist Analysis', in W. Sandholtz and A. Stone Sweet (eds), *European*

Integration and Supranational Governance. Oxford: Oxford University Press, 27–58.

Pollack, M. (1995), 'Regional Actors in an Intergovernmental Play: The Making and Implementation of EC Structural Policy', in C. Rhodes and S. Mazey (eds), *The State of the European Union, Vol. 3: Building a European Polity?*. Boulder, CO, and Harlow: Lynne Rienner and Longman, 361–90.

——— (1996), 'The New Institutionalism and EC Governance: The Promise and Limits of Institutional Analysis'. *Governance*, 9: 429–58.

——— (1997), 'The Commission as an Agent', in N. Nugent (ed.), *At the Heart of the Union: Studies of the European Commission.* Basingstoke and London: Macmillan, 109–28.

——— (2001), 'International Relations Theory and European Integration'. *Journal of Common Market Studies*, 39: 221–44.

——— (2003), *The Engines of European Integration: Delegation, Agency and Agenda Setting in the EU.* Oxford: Oxford University Press.

——— (2004), 'The New Institutionalisms and European Integration', in A. Wiener and T. Diez (eds), *European Integration Theory.* Oxford: Oxford University Press, 137–56.

——— (2005), Theorizing EU Policy-Making', in H. Wallace, W. Wallace, and M. A. Pollack (eds), *Policy-Making in the European Union* (5th edn). Oxford: Oxford University Press, 13–48.

——— and Hafner-Burton, E. (2000), 'Mainstreaming Gender in the European Union'. *Journal of European Public Policy*, 7: 432–56.

Porter, B. (1983), *Britain, Europe and the World, 1850–1982: Delusions of Grandeur.* London: Allen & Unwin.

Poulantzas, N. (1974), 'Internationalisation of Capitalist Relations and the Nation State'. *Economy and Society*, 2: 45–79.

Preston, C. (1983), 'Additional to What? Does the UK Government Cheat on the European Regional Development Fund?'. *Politics*, 3: 20–6.

——— (1984), *The Politics of Implementation: The European Community Regional Development Fund and European Community Regional Aid to the UK 1975–81.* PhD thesis. Colchester: University of Essex.

——— (1995), 'Obstacles to EU Enlargement: The Classical Community Method and the Prospects for a Wider Europe'. *Journal of Common Market Studies*, 33: 451–63.

——— (1997), *Enlargement and Integration in the European Union.* London: Routledge.

Puchala, D. (1975), 'Domestic Politics and Regional Harmonization in the European Communities'. *World Politics*, XXVII: 496–520.

Puetter, U. (2006), *The Eurogroup: How a Secretive Circle of Finance Ministers Shape Economic Governance.* Manchester: Manchester University Press.

Putnam, R. (1988), 'Diplomacy and Domestic Politics: The Logic of Two-Level Games'. *International Organization*, 42: 427–60.

——— (1993), *Making Democracy Work: Civic Traditions in Modern Italy.* Princeton, NJ: Princeton University Press.

Radaelli, C. (2000), 'Whither Europeanization? Concept Stretching and Substantive Change'. *European Integration Online Papers* 4(8), (http://papers.ssrn.com).

——— (2004), 'Europeanisation: Solution or Problem?'. Paper presented to the ESRC/UACES Conference on the *Europeanization of British Politics*, Sheffield Town Hall, 16 July.

——— (2006), 'Europeanization: Solution or Problem?', in M. Cini and A. Bourne (eds), *Palgrave Advances in European Studies.* Basingstoke: Palgrave Macmillan, 56–76.

Ramussen, H. (1986), *On Law and Policy in the European Court of Justice: A Comparative Study in Judicial Politics.* Dordrecht: Martinus Nijhoff.

Rattinger, H. (1994), 'Public Attitudes Towards European Integration in Germany after Maastricht: Inventory and Typology'. *Journal of Common Market Studies*, 32: 525–40.

Raunio, T. (2007), 'Political Parties in the European Union', in K. E. Jørgensen, M. Pollack, and B. Rosamond (eds), *Handbook of European Politics.* London: Sage Publications, 247–62.

Reif, K. and Schmitt, H. (1980), 'Nine Second-Order National Elections: A Conceptual Framework for the Analysis of European Election Results'. *European Journal of Political Research*, 8: 3–45.

Rhodes, M. and van Apeldoorn, B. (1997), 'Capitalism versus Capitalism in Western Europe', in M. Rhodes, P. Heywood, and V. Wright (eds), *Developments in West European Politics.* Basingstoke and London: Macmillan, 171–89.

Rhodes, R. A. W. (1981), *Control and Power in Central–Local Relations.* Aldershot: Gower.

——— (1986), *The National World of Local Government.* London: Allen and Unwin.

——— (1988), *Beyond Westminster and Whitehall: The Sub-Central Governments of Britain.* London: Unwin Hyman.

——— (1995), *The New Governance: Governing without Government.* London: ESRC/RSA.

———, Bache, I., and George, S. (1996), 'Policy Networks and Policy-Making in the European

Union: A Critical Appraisal', in L. Hooghe (ed.), *Cohesion Policy and European Integration*. Oxford: Oxford University Press, 367–87.

Richardson, J. (1996), 'Actor-Based Models of National and EU Policy Making', in H. Kassim and A. Menon (eds), *The European Union and National Industrial Policy*. London and New York: Routledge, 26–51.

_____ (2007), 'Organized Interests in the European Union', in K. E. Jørgensen, M. Pollack, and B. Rosamond (eds), *Handbook of European Union Politics*. London: Sage Publications, 231–46.

Richardson, K. (1997), 'Introductory Foreword', in H. Wallace and A. R. Young (eds), *Participation and Policy-Making in the European Union*. Oxford: Clarendon Press, xvii–xxiv.

Rieger, E. (2000), 'The Common Agricultural Policy: Politics against Markets', in H. Wallace and W. Wallace (eds), *Policy-Making in the European Union* (4th edn). Oxford: Oxford University Press, 179–209.

Risse-Kappen, T. (1996), 'Exploring the Nature of the Beast: International Relations Theory and Comparative Policy Analysis Meet the European Union'. *Journal of Common Market Studies*, 34: 53–80.

Risse, T. (2003), 'The Euro between National and European Identity'. *Journal of European Public Policy*, 10: 487–505.

_____ (2004), 'Social Constructivism and European Integration', in A. Wiener and T. Diez (eds), *European Integration Theory*. Oxford: Oxford University Press, 159–76.

_____ (2009), 'Social Constructivism and European Integration', in A. Wiener and T. Diez (eds), *European Integration Theory* (2nd edn). Oxford: Oxford University Press, 144–60.

_____, Cowles, M. G., and Caporaso, J. (2001), 'Europeanization and Domestic Change: Introduction', in M. G. Cowles, J. Caporaso, and T. Risse (eds), *Transforming Europe: Europeanization and Domestic Change*. Ithaca, NY, and London: Cornell University Press, 1–20.

Rittberger, B. (2003), 'The Creation and Empowerment of the European Parliament'. *Journal of Common Market Studies*, 41: 203–25.

Rosamond, B. (1999), 'Discourses of Globalization and the Social Construction of European Identities'. *Journal of European Public Policy*, 6: 652–68.

_____ (2000), *Theories of European Integration*. Basingstoke and London: Macmillan.

_____ (2003), 'New Theories of European Integration', in M. Cini (ed.), *European Union Politics*. Oxford: Oxford University Press, 109–27.

Ross, G. (1995), *Jacques Delors and European Integration*. Cambridge: Polity Press.

Sabatier, P. (1988), 'An Advocacy Coalition Framework of Policy Change and the Role of Policy-Oriented Learning Therein'. *Policy Sciences*, 21: 129–68.

_____ (1998), 'The Advocacy Coalition Framework: Revisions and Relevance for Europe'. *Journal of European Public Policy*, 5: 98–130.

Sandholtz, W. (1993), 'Choosing Union: Monetary Politics and Maastricht'. *International Organization*, 47: 1–39.

_____ (1998), 'The Emergence of a Supranational Telecommunications Regime', in W. Sandholtz and A. Stone Sweet (eds), *European Integration and Supranational Governance*. Oxford: Oxford University Press, 134–63.

_____ and Stone Sweet, A. (1998), *European Integration and Supranational Governance*. Oxford: Oxford University Press.

_____ and Zysman, J. (1989), '1992: Recasting the European Bargain'. *World Politics*, 42: 95–128.

Sbragia, A. (1996), 'Environmental Policy: The "Push-Pull" of Policy-Making', in H. Wallace and W. Wallace (eds), *Policy-Making in the European Union* (3rd edn). Oxford: Oxford University Press, 235–55.

_____ (2000), 'Environmental Policy: Economic Constraints and External Pressures', in H. Wallace and W. Wallace (eds), *Policy-Making in the European Union* (4th edn). Oxford: Oxford University Press, 293–316.

_____ and Damro, C. (1999), 'The Changing Role of the European Union in International Environmental Politics: Institution Building and the Politics of Climate Change'. *Environment and Planning C: Government and Policy,* 17: 53–68.

Scarrow, S. (1997), 'Political Career Paths and the European Parliament'. *Legislative Studies Quarterly,* 22: 253–63.

Scharpf, F. (1989), 'The Joint-Decision Trap: Lessons from German Federalism and European Integration'. *Public Administration*, 66: 239–78.

_____ (1997) 'Economic Integration, Democracy and the Welfare State'. *Journal of European Public Policy* 4: 18–36.

_____ (1998), *Governing in Europe: Effective and Democratic?*. Oxford: Oxford University Press.

_____ (1999a), 'Review Section Symposium: The Choice for Europe—Social Purpose and State Power from Messina to Maastricht: Selecting Cases and Testing Hypotheses'. *Journal of European Public Policy*, 6: 164–8.

_____ (1999b), *Crisis and Choice in European Social Democracy*. Ithaca, NY: Cornell University Press.

_____ (2004), 'The European Democratic Deficit: Contested Definitions or Diverse Domains?'. *EUSA Review*, 17: 5–6.

Scheinman, L. (1967), 'Euratom: Nuclear Integration in Europe'. *International Conciliation*, no. 563.

Schimmelfennig, F. and Sedelmeier, U. (2002), 'Theorizing Enlargement: Research Focus, Hypotheses, and the State of Research'. *Journal of European Public Policy*, 9: 500–28.

____ and ____ (2004), 'Governance by Conditionality: EU Rule Transfer to the Candidate Countries of Central and Eastern Europe'. *Journal of European Public Policy*, 11: 661–79.

____ and ____ (eds) (2005), *The Europeanization of Central and Eastern Europe*. Ithaca, NY: Cornell University Press.

Schmidt, V. (2003), 'Democratic Legitimacy in a Regional State'. Paper prepared for presentation at the American Political Science Association National Meetings, Philadelphia PA, 28–31 August.

____ (2004), 'Democratic Challenges for the EU as "Regional State"'. *EUSA Review*, 17: 4–5.

____ (2006), *Democracy in Europe*. Oxford: Oxford University Press.

____ (2009) 'Explaining Democracy in Europe', *Comparative European Politics*, 7: 396–407.

Schmitt, H. and Thomasen, J. (eds) (1999), *Political Representation and Legitimacy in the European Union*. Oxford: Oxford University Press.

Schmitter, P. (1970), 'A Revised Theory of Regional Integration'. *International Organization*, 24: 836–68.

____ (1996), 'Examining the Present Euro-Polity with the Help of Past Theories', in G. Marks, F. Scharpf, P. Schmitter, and W. Streeck (eds), *Governance in the European Union*. London: Sage, 1–14.

____ (2000), *How to Democratize the European Union ... And Why Bother?*. Lanham, MD: Rowman and Littlefield.

____ (2004), 'The European Union is Not Democratic: So What?'. *EUSA Review*, 17: 3–4.

Schneider, G. and Seybold, C. (1997), 'Twelve Tongues, One Voice: An Evaluation of European Political Cooperation'. *European Journal of Political Research*, 31: 367–96.

Schreurs, M. (2004), 'Environmental Protection in an Expanding European Community: Lessons from Past Accessions'. *Environmental Politics*, 13: 27–51.

Scott, J. (1995), *Development Dilemmas in the European Community: Rethinking Regional Development Policy*. Buckingham and Philadelphia, PA: Open University Press.

____ (1998), 'Law, Legitimacy and EC Governance: Prospects for "Partnership"'. *Journal of Common Market Studies*, 36: 175–94.

Scott-Smith, G. (2003), 'Cultural Policy and Citizenship in the European Union: An Answer to the Legitimation Problem?', in A. Cafruny and G. Rosenthal (eds), *The State of the European Community, Vol. 2: The Maastricht Debates and Beyond*. Boulder, CO, and Harlow: Lynne Rienner and Longman, 261–84.

Scully, R.M. (1997a), 'The European Parliament and the Co-decision Procedure: A Reassessment'. *Journal of Legislative Studies*, 3: 58–73.

____ (1997b), 'The European Parliament and Co-decision: A Rejoinder to Tsebelis and Garrett'. *Journal of Legislative Studies*, 3: 93–103.

____ (2001), 'National Parties and European Parliamentarians: Developing and Testing an Institutionalist Theory'. *EPRG Working Paper*, no. 6, (http://www.lse.ac.uk/collections/EPRG/working-papers.htm).

Sedelmeier, U. and Young, A. (2008), 'Editorial: The EU in 2007—Development Without Drama, Progress Without Passion'. *Journal of Common Market Studies, Annual Review*, 46: 1–5.

Seers, D. and Vaitsos, C. (1980), *Integration and Unequal Development: The Experience of the EEC*. Basingstoke and London: Macmillan.

Servan-Schreiber, J-J. (1968), *The American Challenge*. Harmondsworth: Penguin.

Shackleton, M. and Raunio, T. (2003), 'Codecision since Amsterdam: A Laboratory for Institutional Innovation and Change'. *Journal of European Public Policy*, 10: 171–87.

Sharp, M. (1989), 'The Community and the New Technologies', in J. Lodge (ed.), *The European Community and the Challenge of the Future*. London: Pinter, 223–40.

____ (1991), 'The Single Market and European Technology Policies', in C. Freeman, M. Sharp, and W. Walker (eds), *Technology and the Future of Europe: Global Competition and the Environment in the 1990s*. London: Pinter Publishers, 59–76.

____ and Shearman, C. (1987), *European Technological Collaboration*. London: Royal Institute of International Affairs / Routledge and Kegan Paul.

Shonfield, A. (1969), *Modern Capitalism: The Changing Balance of Public and Private Power*. Oxford: Oxford University Press.

Smismans, S. (2007), 'How Political Theory Could Deal with the Role of Civil Society Organisations in European Governance: Reflexive Deliberative Polyarchy', in C. Ruzza and V. Della Sala (eds), *Governance and Civil Society in the European Union: Normative*

Perspectives. Manchester: Manchester University Press, 73–88.

Smith, A. (1992), 'National Identity and the Idea of European Unity'. *International Affairs*, 68: 55–76.

Smith, G. (2003), 'The Decline of Party', in J. Hayward and A. Menon (eds), *Governing Europe*. Oxford: Oxford University Press, 179–91.

Smith, H. (2002), 'The Politics of Regulated Liberalism: A Historical Materialist Approach to European Integration', in M. Rupert and H. Smith (eds), *Historical Materialism and Globalisation: Essays on Continuity and Change*. London: Routledge, 257–83.

Smith, J. (James) (2001), 'Cultural Aspects of Europeanization: The Case of the Scottish Office'. *Public Administration*, 79: 147–65.

Smith, J. (Julie) (1999), *Europe's Elected Parliament*. Sheffield: Sheffield Academic Press / University Association for Contemporary European Studies.

Smith, K. (2003), *European Union Foreign Policy in a Changing World*. Cambridge: Polity Press.

Smith, M. E. (1999), 'Rules, Transgovernmentalism, and the Expansion of European Political Cooperation', in W. Sandholtz and A. Stone Sweet (eds), *European Integration and Supranational Governance*. Oxford: Oxford University Press, 304–33.

_____ (2000), 'Conforming to Europe: The Domestic Impact of EU Foreign Policy Co-operation'. *Journal of European Public Policy*, 7: 613–31.

_____ (2001), 'Diplomacy by Decree: The Legalization of EU Foreign Policy'. *Journal of Common Market Studies*, 39: 79–104.

_____ (2003), 'The Framing of European Foreign and Security Policy: Towards a Post-Modern Policy Framework?'. *Journal of European Public Policy*, 10: 556–75.

_____ (2004) 'Institutionalization, Policy Adaptation and European Foreign Policy Cooperation'. *European Journal of International Relations*, 10: 95–136.

Smith, M. P. (1997), 'The Commission Made Me Do It: The European Commission as a Strategic Asset in Domestic Politics', in N. Nugent (ed.), *At the Heart of the Union: Studies of the European Commission*. Basingstoke and London: Macmillan, 167–86.

_____ (1998), 'Autonomy by the Rules: The European Commission and the Development of State Aid Policy'. *Journal of Common Market Studies*, 36: 55–78.

Spierenburg, D. and Poidevin, R. (1994), *The History of the High Authority of the European Coal and Steel Community: Supranationality in Action*. London: Weidenfeld.

Stein, E. (1981), 'Lawyers, Judges, and the Making of a Transnational Constitution'. *The American Journal of International Law*, 75: 1–27.

Stetter, S. (2000), 'Regulating Migration: Authority Delegation in Justice and Home Affairs'. *Journal of European Public Policy*, 7: 80–103.

Stevens, A. and Stevens, H. (2001), *Brussels Bureaucrats? The Administration of the European Union*. Basingstoke: Palgrave Macmillan.

Stevens, C. (1984), *The EEC and the Third World: A Survey, 4—Renegotiating Lomé*. London: Hodder and Stoughton.

_____ (2000), 'Trade with Developing Countries: Banana Skins and Turf Wars', in H. Wallace and W. Wallace (eds), *Policy-Making in the European Union* (4th edn). Oxford: Oxford University Press, 401–26.

Stone Sweet, A. and Sandholtz, W. (1997), 'European Integration and Supranational Governance'. *Journal of European Public Policy*, 4: 297–317.

_____, _____, and Fligstein, N. (eds) (2001), *The Institutionalization of Europe*. Oxford: Oxford University Press.

Strøby Jensen, C. (2000), 'Neofunctionalist Theories and the Development of European Social and Labour Market Policy'. *Journal of Common Market Studies*, 38: 71–92.

Swann, D. (1995), *The Economics of the Common Market: Integration in the European Union* (8th edn). Harmondsworth: Penguin.

Swift, M. (1978), 'A Regional Policy for Europe'. *Young Fabian Pamphlet 48*. London: Fabian Society.

Swinbank, A. and Daugbjerg, C. (2006), 'The 2003 CAP Reform: Accommodating WTO Pressures'. *Comparative European Politics*, 4: 47–64.

Taggart, P. (1998), 'A Touchstone of Dissent: Euroscepticism in Contemporary Western European Party Systems'. *European Journal of Political Research*, 33: 363–88.

Tait, R. (2009), 'Turkish Anger over Herman Van Rompuy Appointment'. *The Guardian*, 20 November.

Tallberg, J. (2003), 'The Agenda-Shaping Powers of the EU Council Presidency'. *Journal of European Public Policy*, 10: 1–19.

_____ and Johansson, K. M. (2008), 'Party Politics in the European Council'. *Journal of European Public Policy*, 15: 1222–42.

Tarrow, S. (2003), 'Contentious Politics in Western Europe and the United States', in J. Hayward and A. Menon (eds), *Governing Europe*. Oxford: Oxford University Press, 231–49.

Tofarides, M. (2003), *Urban Policy in the European Union: A Multi-Level Gatekeeper System.* Aldershot: Ashgate.

Tranholm-Mikkelsen, J. (1991), 'Neofunctionalism: Obstinate or Obsolete? A Reappraisal in the Light of the New Dynamism of the European Community'. *Millennium*, 20: 1–22.

Traynor, I. (2009), 'Europe has Shown it Wants to be a Supersize Switzerland'. *The Guardian*, 20 November.

Tsakaloyannis, P. (1981), 'The Greco–Turkish Dispute in the Light of Enlargement'. *Sussex European Papers no. 11: The Mediterranean Challenge VI.* Brighton: University of Sussex.

Tsakatika, M. (2007), 'Governance vs Politics: The European Union's "Constitutive Democratic Deficit"'. *Journal of European Public Policy*, 14: 867–85.

Tsebelis, G. and Garrett, G. (1996), 'Agenda Setting Power, Power Indices, and Decision Making in the European Union'. *International Review of Law and Economics*, 16: 345–61.

____ and ____ (2000), 'Legislative Politics in the European Union'. *European Union Politics*, 1: 9–36.

____ and ____ (2001), 'The Institutional Foundations of Intergovernmentalism and Supranationalism in the European Union'. *International Organization*, 55: 357–90.

Tsoukalis, L. (1977), *The Politics and Economics of European Monetary Integration.* London: Allen & Unwin.

____ (1996), 'Economic and Monetary Union: The Primacy of High Politics', in H. Wallace and W. Wallace (eds), *Policy-Making in the European Union* (3rd edn). Oxford: Oxford University Press, 279–99.

Turnbull, P. and Sandholtz, W. (2001), 'Policing and Immigration: The Creation of New Policy Spaces', in A. Stone Sweet, W. Sandholtz, and N. Fligstein (eds), *The Institutionalization of Europe.* Oxford: Oxford University Press, 194–220.

Uçarer, U. (2010), 'Justice and Home Affairs', in M. Cini and N. Pérez-Solórzano Borragán (eds), *European Union Politics* (3rd edn). Oxford: Oxford University Press, 306–23.

Urwin, D. W. (1985), *Western Europe since 1945: A Short Political History* (4th edn). London and New York: Longman.

____ (1995), *The Community of Europe: A History of European Integration since 1945* (2nd edn). New York: Longman.

van Apeldoorn, B., Overbeek, H., and Ryner, M. (2003), 'Theories of European Integration: A Critique', in A. Cafruny and M. Ryner (eds), *A Ruined Fortress? Neoliberal Hegemony and Transformation in Europe.* Lanham, MD: Rowman and Littlefield, 17–46.

van der Eijk, C. and Franklin, M. (1996), *Choosing Europe? The European Electorate and National Politics in the Face of Union.* Ann Arbor, MI: University of Michigan Press.

van der Veen, M. (2010), 'Ireland Votes "No", Then "Yes", Once More: The Lisbon Treaty Referenda'. *EUSA Review*, 23(1): 15–18. (European Union Studies Association, USA). (http://www.eustudies.org/publicationsreviewwinter10.php).

Verdun, A. (1999), 'The Role of the Delors Committee in the Creation of EMU: An Epistemic Community?'. *Journal of Common Market Studies*, 34: 531–48.

____ (2003), 'An American/European Divide in European Integration Studies: Bridging the Gap with International Political Economy'. *Journal of European Public Policy*, 10: 84–101.

Wæver, O. (1996), 'European Security Identities'. *Journal of Common Market Studies*, 34: 103–32.

Wagstyl, S. (2005), 'The Pull of the West: Why the Benefits Bestowed by Brussels have Come Early for the EU's Former Communist Countries'. *Financial Times*, 21 February.

Wallace, H. (1973), *National Governments and the European Communities.* London: Chatham House/PEP.

____ (1977), 'The Establishment of the Regional Development Fund: Common Policy or Pork Barrel?', in H. Wallace, W. Wallace, and C. Webb (eds), *Policy-Making in the European Communities.* London: John Wiley and Sons, 137–63.

____ (1983a), 'Negotiation, Conflict and Compromise: The Elusive Pursuit of Common Policies', in H. Wallace, W. Wallace, and C. Webb (eds), *Policy-Making in the European Communities* (2nd edn). London: John Wiley and Sons, 43–80.

____ (1983b), 'Distributional Politics: Dividing up the Community Cake', in H. Wallace, W. Wallace, and C. Webb (eds), *Policy-Making in the European Communities* (2nd edn). London: John Wiley and Sons, 81–113.

____ (1986), 'The British Presidency of the European Community's Council of Ministers'. *International Affairs*, 62: 583–99.

____ (1997), 'Introduction', in H. Wallace and A. R. Young (eds), *Participation and Policy-Making in the European Union.* Oxford: Clarendon Press, 1–16.

____ (1999), 'Piecing the Integration Jigsaw Together'. *Journal of European Public Policy*, 6: 155–79.

____ (2000a), 'Europeanisation and Globalisation: Complementary or Contradictory Trends?'. *New Political Economy*, 5: 369–82.

_____ (2000*b*), 'Flexibility: A Tool of Integration or a Restraint on Disintegration?', in K. Neunreither and A. Wiener (eds), *European Integration after Amsterdam: Institutional Dynamics and Prospects for Democracy*. Oxford: Oxford University Press, 175–91.

_____ (2005), 'An Institutional Anatomy and Five Policy Modes', in H. Wallace, W. Wallace, and M. Pollack (eds), *Policy-Making in the European Union* (5th edn). Oxford: Oxford University Press, 49–90.

_____ and Young, A. (1997), 'The Kaleidoscope of European Policy-Making: Shifting Patterns of Participation and Influence', in H. Wallace and A. R. Young (eds), *Participation and Policy-Making in the European Union*. Oxford: Clarendon Press, 235–50.

Wallace, W. and Allen, D. (1977), 'Political Co-operation: Procedure as Substitute for Policy', in H. Wallace, W. Wallace, and C. Webb (eds), *Policy-Making in the European Communities*. London: John Wiley and Sons, 227–48.

Warleigh, A. (2003) *Democracy in the European Union: Theory, Practice and Reform*, London: Sage.

_____ (2006), 'Conceptual Combinations: Multi-level Governance and Policy Networks', in M. Cini and A. Bourne (eds), *Palgrave Advances in European Union Studies*. Basingstoke: Palgrave Macmillan, 77–95.

Watson, R. (1998), 'Sweetening the Bitter Pill of Budget Consolidation'. *European Voice*, 26, March–April: 16.

Weale, A. (1997), 'Democratic Theory and the Constitutional Politics of the European Union'. *Journal of European Public Policy*, 4: 665–9.

_____ (1999*a*), *Democracy*. London: Macmillan.

_____ (1999*b*), 'European Environmental Policy by Stealth: The Dysfunctionality of Functionalism?'. *Environment and Planning C: Government and Policy*, 17: 37–51.

_____, Pridham, G., Cini, M., Konstadakopulos, D., Porter, M., and Flynn, B. (eds) (2000), *Environmental Governance in Europe: An Ever Closer Ecological Union?* Oxford: Oxford University Press.

Weiler, J. (1993), 'Journey to an Unknown Destination: A Retrospective and Prospective of the European Court of Justice in the Arena of Political Integration'. *Journal of Common Market Studies*, 31: 417–46.

_____ (1999), *The Constitution of Europe: 'Do the New Clothes have an Emperor' and other Essays on European Integration*. Cambridge: Cambridge University Press.

Wendon, B. (1998), 'The Commission as an Image-Venue Entrepreneur in EU Social Policy'. *Journal of European Public Policy*, 5: 339–53.

Wessels, W. (1991), 'The EC Council: The Community's Decision-Making Center', in R. Keohane and S. Hoffmann (eds), *The New European Community: Decisionmaking and Institutional Change*. Boulder, CO, San Francisco, CA, and Oxford: Westview Press, 133–54.

_____ (1996), 'Institutions of the EU System: Models of Explanation', in D. Rometsch, and W. Wessels (eds), *The European Union and Member States: Towards Institutional Fusion?*. Manchester: Manchester University Press, 20–36.

_____ and Rometsch, D. (1996), 'Conclusion: European Union and National Institutions', in D. Rometsch, and W. Wessels (eds), *The European Union and Member States: Towards Institutional Fusion?*. Manchester: Manchester University Press, 329–65.

Westlake, M. (1994), *The European Parliament: A Modern Guide*. London: Pinter.

_____ (1995), *The Council of the European Union*. London: Catermill.

Whitworth, S. (1994), *Feminism and International Relations*. London: Macmillan.

Wilks, S. and McGowan, L. (1995), 'Disarming the Commission: The Debate over a European Cartel Office'. *Journal of Common Market Studies*, 33: 259–73.

Wimmel, A. (2009), 'Beyond the Bosphorous? Comparing Public Discourses on Turkey's EU Application in the German, French and British Quality Press'. *Journal of Language and Politics*, 8: 223–43.

Wincott, D. (1995), 'Institutional Interaction and European Integration: Towards an Everyday Critique of Liberal Intergovernmentalism'. *Journal of Common Market Studies*, 33: 597–609.

Wise, M. and Croxford, G. (1988), 'The European Regional Development Fund: Community Ideals and National Realities'. *Political Geography Quarterly*, 7: 161–82.

Wishlade, F. (1996), 'EU Cohesion Policy: Facts, Figures, and Issues', in L. Hooghe (ed.), *Cohesion Policy and European Integration*. Oxford: Oxford University Press, 27–58.

Woll, C. (2006), 'Lobbying in the European Union: From *Sui Generis* to a Comparative Perspective'. *Journal of European Public Policy*, 13: 456–69.

Wright, V. (1990), 'The Administrative Machine: Old Problems and New Dilemmas', in P. Hall, J. Hayward, and H. Machin (eds), *Developments in French Politics*. Basingstoke and London: Macmillan, 114–32.

Wyles, J. (2007), 'Treaty Path Leads the EU Downhill'. *European Voice*, 11 October: 18–24.

Young, A. R. (2000), 'The Adaptation of European Foreign Economic Policy'. *Journal of Common Market Studies*, 38: 93–116.

_____ (2005), 'The Single Market', in H. Wallace, W. Wallace, and M. A. Pollack (eds), *Policy-Making in the European Union* (5th edn). Oxford: Oxford University Press, 93–112.

_____ (2007), 'Trade Politics Ain't What it Used to Be'. *Journal of Common Market Studies*, 45: 789–811.

_____ and Peterson, J. (2006), 'The EU and the New Trade Politics'. *Journal of European Public Policy*, 13: 795–814.

Young, H. (1998), *This Blessed Plot: Britain and Europe from Churchill to Blair*. London: Macmillan.

Young, J. W. (1993), *Britain and European Unity, 1945–92*. Basingstoke: Macmillan.

Zito, A. (1999), 'Task Expansion: A Theoretical Overview'. *Environment and Planning C: Government and Policy*, 17: 19–35.

Glossary

acquis communautaire Often abbreviated simply to *acquis*, this is a French phrase for which it is difficult to find a precise English translation. A French–English dictionary would define *acquis* as something like 'acquired knowledge' or 'accumulated experience', but the connotation in this phrase is much more like 'heritage'. The *acquis* is the body of laws, policies, and practices that have accumulated over the lifetime of the European Communities, and now the European Union. Any new member state joining the EU has to accept the *acquis* as part of its terms of entry. The adjective '*communautaire*', when applied to the *acquis* or to other nouns, means more than just 'of the (European) community'. It has connotations of something that is in sympathy with the co-operative spirit that informed the original European Community. The term '*communitaire*', which can be found all too frequently in texts on the European Union, is simply an incorrect piece of 'Franglais'.

balance of trade The difference between the exports and imports of a state, or other economic unit such as the EU.

Benelux This is an acronym made up of the first parts of the names of the member states: *Be*lgium; the *Ne*therlands; and *Lux*embourg. The governments of these three states adopted a **customs union** while in exile in London in 1944, and extended this to an **economic union** on 1 January 1948.

black box of the state The realist tradition in international relations assumed that relations between states could be understood without analysing the internal politics of the states. It was assumed that each state had a clear and abiding national interest, derived largely from its geographical position in the world and from strategic considerations such as the need to prevent neighbouring states from being able to dominate the region, and the need to defend any colonies and overseas territories that the state might possess. This national interest was assumed to be stronger than any differences between political parties within the country, so that changes of government would produce little lasting change in foreign policy. Therefore, the state could be treated as though it were a 'black box' into which the analyst need not peer.

Bretton Woods In 1944, a major economic conference was held at Bretton Woods in New Hampshire, USA. Agreement was reached on the basis of a post-war international economic and monetary system. The key principles were free trade and monetary stability. Monetary stability was to be achieved by tying the value of national currencies to the US dollar, which in turn was tied to the value of gold at the rate of US\$35 per ounce. The **International Monetary Fund (IMF)** was set up to assist in the establishment of the system, and to provide short-term and medium-term loans to states experiencing temporary problems with their balance of payments. The system lasted until 1971, when it collapsed because the United States was forced to devalue the dollar against gold. It was temporarily replaced by the **Smithsonian agreements**.

common market A **customs union**, but with the addition of free movement of factors of production, including capital and labour.

Community method The predominant form of decision making in the EU, based on a Commission proposal and co-decision with the European Parliament and Council of Ministers (via **QMV**). (See also **Union method**).

corporatism/corporatist The terms 'corporatist' and 'corporatism' comes from the Latin verb *corporare*, meaning 'to form into a body'. The process of forming individuals into collective bodies produces corporations, which are artificial persons created by individuals, who authorize the corporation to act on their behalf. Between the wars in Europe the idea of the 'corporate state' emerged, in which representation of the people would not be by geographical constituencies, but through vocational corporations of the employers and employees in each trade and industry. It was seen as an alternative 'third way' between capitalism and Communism. In practice, corporatism came to be most closely associated with the Fascist regime in Italy after 1928, and was widely imitated by other authoritarian regimes. This association discredited the term in the eyes of the Anglo-Saxon states, but the idea still held some resonance in Roman Catholic social thought, hence its revival, without the formal title of corporatism, in the post-war constitutions of some western European states.

customs union A **free trade area** that has a uniform set of rules on trade with the outside world.

dirigisme/dirigiste A French term that translates literally into English as 'directionism'. It is an economic doctrine that gives a central role to the state in the direction of economic development under capitalism. Typically, the state draws up a national economic plan that acts as a framework within which both state-sector and private-sector enterprises can co-ordinate their decisions on investments. The term 'indicative planning' is often used in English to suggest the same system.

economic union A **common market** with unified economic and monetary policies.

epistemology The theory of knowledge; about how knowledge is acquired and validated.

European Investment Bank (EIB) The EIB is an EU agency that is charged to provide capital at affordable rates to support projects that contribute to the integration, balanced development, and economic and social cohesion of the member states. It does this by raising funds itself on the capital markets, and then loaning the funds at favourable rates of interest to support projects that further these objectives. It also implements the financial components of

agreements under the European development aid policies.

Euro-sceptic(ism) Euro-scepticism indicates either qualified or unqualified opposition to the process of European integration.

free trade area Member states remove all tariff and quota barriers to trade between themselves, but retain independent trade policies with the outside world.

G20 A forum that brings together twenty major advanced and emerging economies to promote the financial stability of the world and to achieve sustainable economic growth and development. It was established in 1999.

General Agreement on Tariffs and Trade (GATT) The GATT was negotiated in 1947 and started operation on 1 January 1948. It consisted of a standing conference for the negotiation of tariff cuts, and an agreement that all such cuts would be multilateral, not bilateral. This was embodied in the principle of 'most favoured nation treatment' for all signatories of the agreement: any trade concession extended by one member to another had to be extended to all other members. It was originally intended that the GATT would be one part of an overarching International Trade Organization (ITO), but this proposal ran into resistance in the US Congress, and never received ratification. The GATT held eight rounds of multilateral trade negotiations, culminating in the Uruguay Round, which opened in Punte del Este, Uruguay, in 1986 and was not completed until 1994. It was this round that focused attention on the trade-distorting effects of the EU's Common Agricultural Policy. One of the agreements in the Uruguay Round was the creation of a new World Trade Organization (WTO), which began operation on 1 January 1995. Its functions are: to administer WTO trade agreements; to act as a forum for trade negotiations; to handle trade disputes; to monitor national trade policies; to provide technical assistance and training for developing countries; to co-operate with other international organizations. (*Source:* **http://www.wto.org/**)

Geneva Convention The Geneva Convention is the term used for a set of Treaties and protocols that set the standards in international law

579

for humanitarian rights during periods of war. There are, in fact, four conventions. They provide, amongst other things, a set of humanitarian standards for dealing with wounded fighters, prisoners of war, civilians, and medical or religious personnel.

International Monetary Fund (IMF) The IMF was set up in 1944: to promote international monetary co-operation; to facilitate the expansion and balanced growth of international trade; to promote stability in exchange rates; to assist in the establishment of a multilateral system of payments in respect of trade between member states; to contribute to the elimination of foreign exchange restrictions; to provide short-term and medium-term loans to states experiencing temporary balance of payments difficulties. (*Source:* **http://www.imf.org/external/about.htm**)

investment capital Refers to assets that are invested in a country in the form of factories, businesses, etc.

liquid capital Refers to assets that are placed into bank deposits or similar sources from which they may quickly be withdrawn and transferred elsewhere.

neo-corporatism/neo-corporatist In the 1970s, academics coined the term 'neo-corporatism' to describe a relationship between the state and organized economic interests that was less formal than **corporatism**, but nevertheless institutionalized patterns of consultation on policy between governments, business, and trade unions in several leading western European states.

ontology Refers to the nature of being; an underlying understanding of the world.

OPEC See **Organization of the Petroleum Exporting Countries**

ordinary legislative procedure (OLP) This term was introduced by the Lisbon Treaty to cover those instances in which the Council of Ministers may decide on legislation by **QMV**, while holding co-decision powers with the European Parliament. The terminology is designed to present this pattern as the default arrangement in EU decision making, while all other arrangements (unanimous voting in the Council and consent or consultation procedures in the EP) are termed 'special legislative procedures'.

Organization of the Petroleum Exporting Countries (OPEC) OPEC was created at a conference of petroleum-exporting states in Baghdad in 1960. The founder members were Iran, Iraq, Kuwait, Saudi Arabia, and Venezuela. They were later joined by eight other members: Qatar (1961); Indonesia (1962); Libya (1962); the United Arab Emirates (1967); Algeria (1969); Nigeria (1971); Ecuador (1973–92); and Gabon (1975–94). OPEC's objective is to co-ordinate and unify petroleum policies among member countries, in order to secure: fair and stable prices for petroleum producers; an efficient, economic and regular supply of petroleum to consuming nations; and a fair return on capital to those investing in the industry. (*Source:* **http://www.opec.org/opec**)

passerelle **clause** A *passerelle* clause permits a procedural reform to take place within the EU without the need for a full Treaty reform process. Typically, such a clause would allow the European Council to agree (unanimously) that a particular area of policy making can move from unanimity to **QMV** in the Council of Ministers. First provided for in the Amsterdam Treaty, the number of provisions was extended in the Lisbon Treaty, as well as the requirement for approval by national parliaments added. The first practical use of a *passerelle* provision came in 2004 when, following a five-year transition period after the implementation of the Amsterdam Treaty, the European Council unanimously agreed to move to introduce QMV rules in asylum and immigration policy.

pluralism/pluralist In a pluralist system, interest groups lobby the formal institutions to try to get their preferred legislative options. It is a competitive system of seeking influence, but although early pluralist theories suggested that there was a level playing field of competition, it is now generally accepted that some groups have greater resources than others, and so benefit more from this form of interest representation.

policy entrepreneur A policy actor who seeks to exploit favourable political conditions in order to promote a particular initiative or policy.

principal–agent theory A branch of rational choice theory that investigates the relationship between institutions that delegate tasks and authority (the principals) and the institutions to which they delegate (the agents). The main concern of principal–agent theory is to investigate the degree to which agents can 'cut slack' so as to achieve a degree of freedom from their principals, freedom that they can use to follow their own agendas rather than the agendas of the principals. Principal–agent theory has been widely used in the investigation of the degree of freedom available to federal agencies in the United States, and in discussion of the relationship of the European Commission to the governments of the member states.

public procurement Purchases of goods and services by governments or other public agencies for use in the public sector, covering everything from paper clips to major projects of civil engineering such as the construction of highways.

qualified majority voting (QMV) A system of voting practised in the Council of Ministers. Under QMV, each member state is given a weighting, which broadly reflects its population size. For a decision to be approved, it is necessary to reach the specific thresholds set down in the Treaties. The rules have been revised over time as a result of institutional reforms and reflecting successive increases in the number of member states. For details of the rules set down most recently, see Table 19.3 (p. 233). QMV applies to many areas of policy: see Table 19.2 (p. 232). QMV is distinct from unanimous voting. Under the latter, all member states must agree before a decision can be taken. Under QMV, by contrast, it is possible for one or a small number of states to be overruled in the Council.

regulated capitalism A form of capitalism that is characterized by government intervention to influence the shape of the economy. It is best understood in contrast to free-market capitalism, in which governments seek to allow markets to regulate themselves and determine the overall shape of the economy.

roll-call voting This is the term given to the formal record of voting in the European Parliament or other assemblies. It is often used by researchers to investigate patterns of behaviour on the part of individual elected politicians and the coherence of the party or party grouping to which they belong.

Smithsonian agreements In 1971, the **Bretton Woods** system of international payments, which had been set up at the end of the war, collapsed. It was replaced by a new set of agreements that were signed at the Smithsonian Institute in Washington, DC, in December 1971. Under these arrangements, the US dollar was substantially devalued against all other currencies, and the major central banks of all other states agreed to try to hold the value of their currencies in a range of fluctuation of 2.25 per cent either side of the US dollar, a maximum range of fluctuation of 4.5 per cent. This attempt to restore fixed exchange rates collapsed in March 1973 in the face of extreme speculative pressure, and the world then entered the era of floating exchange rates that we have today.

stagflation Economists used to believe that there was a trade-off between economic growth and inflation. Policies could either promote economic growth, at the price of higher inflation, or they could focus on restraining inflation at the cost of lower rates of economic growth. Governments made policy choices based on this assumption: some aimed for lower growth in return for low inflation; others preferred high rates of inflation in order to promote high rates of growth. However, following the oil crisis in 1973, the trade-off no longer seemed to work. States began to experience the worst of both worlds: stagnation with inflation, or 'stagflation' as it became known.

subsidiarity Subsidiarity is an ambiguous concept and is taken to mean different things by different political actors. For example, it is interpreted by the British government to mean that action should not be taken at the EU level unless it can be shown that the objectives of the action can be better achieved at that level than at the national level. This interpretation appears to be supported by the wording of Article 5 (formerly Article 3b) of the TEC. The German government interprets it more generally to mean that decisions should be taken at the lowest level of government at which they can be made effective. This implies a commitment to internal devolution of power within states. This interpretation appears to be supported by the wording of Article 1 (formerly Article A) of the TEU.

supranational institutions 'Supranational' literally means 'above the national'. A supranational institution is one that has power or influence going beyond that permitted to it by national governments. An international institution, in contrast, is one that results from the co-operation of national governments, and has no power beyond that permitted to it by those governments.

transgovernmental and transnational networks Links across national boundaries between interest groups and individuals outside of government (transnational) or between departments of national government and individuals working for governments (transgovernmental), which are not monitored or controlled by national foreign offices or other core departments of the executive.

Union method This term relates to mainstream EU business where the Commission typically has the power of initiative, the Council of Ministers and the EP decide on the legislation, and the Court of Justice holds authority as final arbiter on any disputes arising from the Treaties or EU legislation. Prior to implementation of the Lisbon Treaty, the equivalent term used in the academic literature was the **Community method**, which applied to the practices in the then European Community 'pillar' of the EU's former three-pillar architecture (see Chapter 19, p. 227). The Union method does not apply to foreign and security policy, which is treated on a more intergovernmental basis, and has no role for EU law and the Court of Justice, while the Commission and EP have significantly reduced importance.

variable-geometry Europe A method of differentiated integration that allows for a permanent separation between a group of member states that wish to co-operate more closely in a particular area and those that do not wish to do so.

World Bank (International Bank for Reconstruction and Development or IBRD) The IBRD was founded in 1944 to give loans to states to aid their economic recovery. It is now one of five closely associated institutions that together constitute the World Bank Group: the IBRD, which provides loans and development assistance to middle-income countries and creditworthy poorer countries; the International Development Association (IDA), which is focused on the poorest countries, providing them with interest-free loans and other services; the International Finance Corporation (IFC), which promotes growth in the developing world by financing private sector investments and providing technical assistance and advice to governments and businesses; the Multilateral Investment Guarantee Agency (MIGA), which helps to encourage foreign investment in developing countries by providing guarantees to foreign investors against loss caused by non-commercial risks; and the International Centre for Settlement of Investment Disputes (ICSID), which provides conciliation and arbitration facilities for the settlement of investment disputes between foreign investors and their host countries. (*Source:* **http://www.worldbank.org/**)

Abbreviations and Acronyms

AASM	Associated African States and Madagascar
ACP	African, Caribbean, and Pacific
AFSJ	area of freedom, security, and justice
AMIS	African Union Mission in Sudan
AKP	Justice and Development Party (Turkey)
APEC	Asia–Pacific Economic Co-operation
BBC	British Broadcasting Corporation
BDB	Bundesverband Deutscher Banken
BDI	Bundesverband der Deutschen Industrie
Benelux	Belgium, the Netherlands, and Luxembourg
BkartA	Bundeskartellamt (German Cartel Office)
BSE	bovine spongiform encephalopathy
CAP	Common Agricultural Policy
CBI	Confederation of British Industry
CdP	Commissariat du Plan (French Economic Planning Commission)
CDU	Christian Democratic Union (Germany)
CEE	central and eastern Europe
CEEC	Committee for European Economic Co-operation
CEECs	central and eastern European countries
CEEP	European Centre of Public Enterprises
CEN	European Committee for Standardization
CENELEC	European Committee for Electrotechnical Standardization
CEPOL	the European Police College
CEPS	Centre for European Policy Studies
CET	common external tariff
CFDT	Confédération Française Démocratique du Travail
CFP	Common Fisheries Policy
CFSP	Common Foreign and Security Policy

CGT	Confédération Générale du Travail
CI	Community Initiative
CJD	Creutzfeldt-Jakob disease
CJEU	Court of Justice of the European Union
CNPF	Conseil National du Patronat Français
COGECA	General Confederation of Agricultural Co-operatives
COPA	Committee of Professional Agricultural Organizations of the European Community
COPS	Comité Politique et de Sécurité (see also PSC)
CoR	Committee of the Regions and Local Authorities
COREPER	Committee of Permanent Representatives
COREU	Corréspondance Européenne (Telex link)
COSAC	Conference of European Affairs Committees of the Parliaments of the European Union
CSCE	Conference on Security and Co-operation in Europe
CSFs	Community Support Frameworks
CSU	Christian Social Union (Germany)
DDR	Deutsche Demokratische Republik (East Germany)
DG	Directorate-General
DIHT	Deutscher Industrie- und Handelskammertag
EAFRD	European Agricultural Fund for Rural Development
EAGGF	European Agricultural Guarantee and Guidance Fund
EAP	European Environmental Action Programme
EAW	European Arrest Warrant
EBRD	European Bank for Reconstruction and Development
EC	European Community
ECB	European Central Bank
ECHO	European Community Humanitarian Aid Office
ECHR	European Court of Human Rights
ECJ	European Court of Justice
ECO	European Cartel Office
ECOFIN	Economic and Financial Affairs Council
ECSC	European Coal and Steel Community
ecu	European currency unit
EDC	European Defence Community
EdF	Electricité de France
EDF	European Development Fund
EEA	(1) European Economic Area; (2) European Environment Agency
EEAS	European External Action Service

EEC	European Economic Community	
EES	European Economic Space	
EESC	European Economic and Social Committee	
EFC	Economic and Finance Committee	
EFF	European Fisheries Fund	
EFTA	European Free Trade Association	
EIB	European Investment Bank	
EMCF	European Monetary Co-operation Fund	
EMF	European Monetary Fund	
EMI	European Monetary Institute	
EMS	European Monetary System	
EMU	economic and monetary union	
ENP	European Neighbourhood Policy	
ENPI	European Neighbourhood and Partnership Instrument	
EP	European Parliament	
EPA	(1) European Parliamentary Assembly; (2) Economic Partnership Agreement	
EPC	(1) European Political Community (until 1952); (2) European political co-operation	
EPI	environmental policy integration	
EPP	European People's Party	
EPP-ED	European People's Party and European Democrats	
ERDF	European Regional Development Fund (see also RDF)	
ERI	Extraterritorial Income	
ERM	exchange rate mechanism	
ERP	European Recovery Programme ('Marshall Plan')	
ERT	European Round Table of Industrialists	
ERTA	European Road Transport Agreement	
ESC	Economic and Social Committee	
ESCB	European System of Central Banks	
ESDP	European Security and Defence Policy	
ESF	European Social Fund	
ESPRIT	European Strategic Programme for Research and Development in Information Technology	
ETS	emissions trading scheme	
ETUC	European Trade Union Confederation	
EU	European Union	
EUA	European Unit of Account	
EUF	European Union of Federalists	
EUMS	European Union's Military Staff	

EURACOM	European Action for Mining Communities
Euratom	European Atomic Energy Community
EUREKA	European Research Co-ordination Agency
EURODAC	EU-wide electronic system for the identification of asylum-seekers
Eurojust	EU's judicial co-operation unit
Europol	European Police Office
FDP	Free Democrat Party (Germany)
FIFG	Financial Instrument for Fisheries Guidance
FLN	National Liberation Front (Algeria)
FN	Front National (National Front, France)
Frontex	The European Agency for the Management of Operational Co-operation at the External Borders of the Member States of the European Union
FSC	foreign sales corporation
GAC	General Affairs Council
GAERC	General Affairs and External Relations Council
GATT	General Agreement on Tariffs and Trade
GDP	gross domestic product
GM	genetically modified
GNP	gross national product
HMSO	Her Majesty's Stationery Office
HRUFASP	High Representative of the Union for Foreign Affairs and Security Policy
IAR	International Authority for the Ruhr
IBRD	International Bank for Reconstruction and Development
ICSID	International Centre for Settlement of Investment Disputes
IDA	International Development Association
IFC	International Finance Corporation
IGC	intergovernmental conference
IMF	International Monetary Fund
IMPs	Integrated Mediterranean Programmes
INTUG	Information Technology User Group
IPA	Instrument for Pre-Accession
IPE	international political economy
IR	international relations
ISPA	Instrument for Structural Policies Pre-accession
ITO	International Trade Organization
JHA	Justice and Home Affairs
KFOR	Kosovo Force

LCD	lowest common denominator
LDC	less developed country
LI	liberal intergovernmentalism
LLP	Lifelong Learning Programme
MAFF	Ministry of Agriculture, Fisheries and Food (Britain)
MEP	member of the European Parliament
MFN	most favoured nation
MIGA	Multilateral Investment Guarantee Agency
MoU	Memorandum of Understanding
MP	member of Parliament (Britain)
MRP	Mouvement Républicain Populaire (France)
NAFTA	North American Free Trade Agreement
NAPs	(1) National Action Plans (for employment) (2) National Allocation Plans (for carbon emissions)
NATO	North Atlantic Treaty Organization
NEPI	new environmental policy instrument
NFU	National Farmers' Union (Britain)
NGOs	non-governmental organizations
NPD	National Democratic Party (Germany)
NRPs	National Reform Programmes
NSRF	national strategic reference framework
NTB	non-tariff barrier
NUM	National Union of Mineworkers (Britain)
OECD	Organisation for Economic Co-operation and Development
OEEC	Organisation for European Economic Co-operation
OJ	Official Journal
OLAF	European Anti-Fraud Office
OLP	ordinary legislative procedure
OMC	Open Method of Co-ordination
ONP	Open Network Provision
OPEC	Organization of Petroleum Exporting Countries
OSCE	Organization for Security and Co-operation in Europe
PASOK	Panhellenic Socialist Party (Greece)
PCP	Portuguese Communist Party
Phare	Poland–Hungary: Actions for Economic Reconstruction
PJCCM	police and judicial co-operation in criminal matters
PR	proportional representation

PS	Parti Socialiste (Socialist Party, France)
PSC	Political and Security Committee (see also COPS)
PSOE	Spanish Socialist Workers Party
PSP	Portuguese Socialist Party
PTTs	post, telegraph, and telephone companies
QMV	qualified majority voting
RABITs	Rapid Border Intervention Teams
RDF	Regional Development Fund
RENAVAL	Community Initiative programme for the conversion of shipbuilding areas
REPA	Regional Economic Partnership Agreement
RESIDER	Community Initiative programme for the conversion of steel areas
RPF	Rassemblement du Peuple Français (Gaullist Party, France)
RPR	Rassemblement pour la République
SAA	Stabilization and Association Agreement
SAP	Stabilization and Association Process
Sapard	Special Accession Programme for Agriculture and Rural Development
SARS	severe acute respiratory syndrome
SCA	Special Committee on Agriculture
SDP	Social Democratic Party (Britain)
SDS	sustainable development strategy
SEA	Single European Act
SEM	single European market
SHAPE	Supreme Headquarters Allied Powers Europe
SIRENE	Supplementary Information Request at the National Entry
SIS	Schengen Information System
SNA	sub-national authorities
SPD	Sozialdemokratische Partei Deutschlands (Social Democratic Party, Germany)
Stabex	System for the Stabilization for Export Earnings
TEC	Treaty Establishing the European Community
TENs	trans-European networks
TEU	Treaty on European Union
TFEU	Treaty on the Functioning of the European Union
UDF	Union pour la Démocratie Française
UK	United Kingdom
UKIP	UK Independence Party
UN	United Nations
UNICE	Union of Industrial and Employers' Confederations of Europe

US(A)	United States (of America)
USSR	Union of Soviet Socialist Republics
VAT	value added tax
WEU	Western European Union
WTO	World Trade Organization

Chronology

1940s

● **1945**

February Yalta Summit between the United States, the Soviet Union, and Britain. Agreed 'spheres of interest' in post-war Europe

May Surrender of Germany ends the war in Europe

September Surrender of Japan. End of the Second World War

● **1946**

September Civil war breaks out in Greece

September Winston Churchill's speech in Zurich in which he calls for a 'United States of Europe'

December European Union of Federalists (EUF) formed

● **1947**

February British government tells US administration that it cannot continue aid to Greece and Turkey

March Truman Doctrine announced in US Congress

March Treaty of Dunkirk signed by Britain and France

April Soviet walkout of Four-Power Council of Foreign Ministers

June Marshall Plan announced

July Committee for European Economic Co-operation (CEEC) set up

● **1948**

January Benelux states commence economic union

March Treaty of Brussels signed by Britain, France, and Benelux states

April Organization for European Economic Co-operation (OEEC) replaces CEEC

May European Congress in The Hague

● **1949**

April Federal Republic of Germany established

April North Atlantic Treaty signed in Washington, DC, setting up NATO

April International Authority for the Ruhr (IAR) established

May Council of Europe formed

1950s ● **1950**

May Schuman Plan for coal and steel announced (Schuman Declaration)

June Korean War begins

October Pleven Plan for a European Defence Community (EDC) launched

November Council of Europe adopts European Convention on Human Rights

● **1951**

April Treaty of Paris signed, establishing the European Coal and Steel Community (ECSC)

● **1952**

May European Defence Community (EDC) Treaty signed in Paris

July ECSC begins operation

● **1953**

March Draft Treaty for a European Political Community (EPC) adopted

September European Convention on Human Rights comes into force

● **1954**

August EDC Treaty rejected by French National Assembly (collapse of EPC)

October Treaty creating Western European Union (WEU) signed

November Monnet announces that he will not stand for a second term as President of the High Authority of the ECSC

● **1955**

April Spaak memorandum to ECSC states proposing an extension of sectoral integration

April Beyen memorandum on behalf of the Benelux states proposing a general common market

June Messina Conference agrees to set up Spaak Committee to consider future of integration

October Monnet sets up Action Committee for the United States of Europe

● **1956**

March Spaak Report published

May Governments agree Spaak Report

June Start of 'Messina negotiations' based on the Spaak Report

October USSR invades Hungary to put down anti-communist uprising

October Suez crisis: Israel, Britain, and France attack Egypt and occupy Port Said, but forced to withdraw their troops in the face of opposition from the United States

591

1950s

● **1957**

March Completion of 'Messina negotiations'

April Treaties of Rome (establishing the EEC and Euratom) signed

● **1958**

January EEC and Euratom begin operations: Walter Hallstein becomes the first President of the EEC Commission, Louis Armand the first President of the Euratom Commission

July CAP system of common prices agreed at Stresa Conference

● **1959**

January Customs duties within the EEC cut by 10 per cent

1960s

● **1960**

May Acceleration agreement on the common market and Common Agricultural Policy between six EC states

December Organisation for Economic Co-operation and Development (OECD) supersedes OEEC

● **1961**

February Paris Summit agrees to set up committee under Christian Fouchet to review co-operation

March Fouchet negotiations begin

July Association Agreement signed with Greece

August Britain, Denmark, and Ireland apply for membership of the EC

December Commission convenes first conference on European regional policy

● **1962**

April Norway applies to join the EEC

July CAP system of common prices agreed at Stresa Conference

December Nassau agreement between Macmillan and Kennedy

● **1963**

January De Gaulle announces his veto of British membership

July First Yaoundé Convention comes into effect

September Association Agreement signed with Turkey

● **1965**

April Merger Treaty signed, agreeing to merge the institutions of the ECSC, EEC, and Euratom

July Start of French boycott of the Council of Ministers

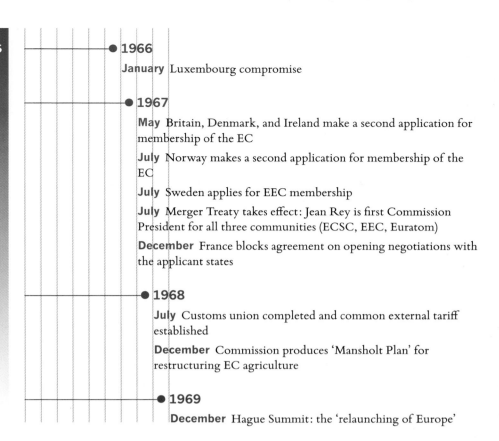

1960s

●1966

January Luxembourg compromise

●1967

May Britain, Denmark, and Ireland make a second application for membership of the EC

July Norway makes a second application for membership of the EC

July Sweden applies for EEC membership

July Merger Treaty takes effect: Jean Rey is first Commission President for all three communities (ECSC, EEC, Euratom)

December France blocks agreement on opening negotiations with the applicant states

●1968

July Customs union completed and common external tariff established

December Commission produces 'Mansholt Plan' for restructuring EC agriculture

●1969

December Hague Summit: the 'relaunching of Europe'

1970s **●1970**

June Membership negotiations begin with Britain, Ireland, Denmark, and Norway

July Franco Malfatti becomes President of the European Commission

October Davignon Report on European political co-operation

●1971

January Second Yaoundé Convention signed

February Werner Report on economic and monetary union

March Start of first attempt to move to monetary union with the joint floating of European currencies

March Farmers demonstrate in Brussels against Mansholt Plan. Council of Agricultural Ministers agrees a modified version of the Plan

August Ending of the convertibility of the US dollar into gold marks the collapse of the Bretton Woods international monetary system, closely followed by the collapse of the first experiment with European monetary union

December Smithsonian agreements on international monetary regime to replace Bretton Woods

●1972

January Completion of membership negotiations with Britain, Ireland, Denmark, and Norway; Accession Treaties signed

1970s

March Sicco Mansholt becomes President of the European Commission

March Start of the 'snake in the tunnel' system of EC monetary co-ordination

March European Parliament accepts Commission proposals for creation of EC regional policy

May Irish referendum in favour of EC membership

June British pound withdrawn from the 'snake in the tunnel'

September Norwegian referendum rejecting EC membership

October Danish referendum in favour of EC membership

October Paris Summit accepts the case for EC regional policy and requests the Commission to prepare a report on the issue

● **1973**

January François-Xavier Ortoli becomes Commission President

January First enlargement of EC from six to nine member states

February Italy forced to leave the 'snake'

May 'Thomson Report' on regional problems presented to the Council of Ministers

December OPEC oil crisis

● **1974**

January France forced to leave the 'snake'

July Turkish invasion of Cyprus

December Paris Summit: agrees to direct elections to the European Parliament, creation of the European Council, and the creation of the European Regional Development Fund (ERDF)

● **1975**

January ERDF comes into operation

February First Lomé Convention comes into effect

March First European Council meeting in Dublin

June British referendum agrees continued membership of EC

June Greek application for membership of EC

July France rejoins the 'snake'

August Signing of the 'Final Act' at the Conference on Security and Co-operation in Europe (CSCE) in Helsinki

● **1976**

January Commission Opinion on Greek application: not very favourable

April France leaves the 'snake' for the second time

July Opening of Greek accession negotiations

● **1977**

January Roy Jenkins becomes President of the European Commission

1970s

March Portuguese application for membership of the EC

July Spanish application for membership of the EC

October Jenkins lecture at the European University Institute, Florence: calls for a new attempt at monetary union

● **1978**

July Bremen European Council agrees to pursue proposal from Schmidt and Giscard for a 'zone of monetary stability in Europe'

October Opening of accession negotiations with Portugal

December Bremen European Council agrees to create the European Monetary System (EMS)

● **1979**

February Opening of accession negotiations with Spain

March EMS begins

May Greek Accession Treaty signed

June First direct elections to the European Parliament

June EC makes Venice Declaration recognizing the right of Palestinians to a homeland

November Dublin European Council: Prime Minister Thatcher demands a British budgetary rebate

December USSR invades Afghanistan

1980s ● 1980

March Second Lomé Convention comes into effect

June Venice Declaration of the EC member states on the situation in the Middle East

December Second stage of the EMS scheme postponed indefinitely

● **1981**

January Gaston Thorn becomes President of the European Commission

January Greece becomes a member of the EC

October London Report on European Political Co-operation (EPC) published

November Genscher-Colombo Plan calls for a new European Charter to replace the Treaties and form a constitution for the European Communities

● **1982**

June EMS currencies realigned; French socialist government agrees to reform its domestic economic policies and to retreat from its attempts to reflate the economy

● **1983**

January Stuttgart European Council signs Solemn Declaration on European Union

March Further realignment of EMS currencies

CHRONOLOGY

1980s

1984

February European Parliament approves draft Treaty on European Union

March System of quotas for dairy products agreed as part of reform of CAP

June Fontainebleau European Council: British budgetary dispute settled; Dooge Committee on institutional reform set up

June Elections to European Parliament

December Third Lomé Convention signed

1985

January Jacques Delors becomes President of the European Commission

February Brussels European Council: mandates Commission to produce a plan for the single European market

June Cockfield White Paper on the freeing of the internal market

June Portuguese and Spanish Accession Treaties signed

June Milan European Council: 1992 Programme agreed

December Single European Act agreed in principle by heads of government at Luxembourg European Council

1986

January Portugal and Spain join the EC

February Single European Act signed by Foreign Ministers in Luxembourg (nine states) and subsequently the Hague (the remaining three states)

1987

April Turkey applies for EC membership

July Single European Act comes into effect

1988

February Brussels European Council: agrees to a doubling of the structural funds; legal limit placed on increases in spending on agricultural support

June Hanover European Council: sets up the Delors Committee on monetary union

July Jacques Delors makes a speech to the EP in which he predicts that, in ten years' time, 80 per cent of economic legislation will be directed from Brussels; infuriates British Prime Minister Thatcher

September Margaret Thatcher's Bruges speech

1989

January Reformed structural funds, with new policy principles agreed during 1988, come into operation

1980s

January Start of revived 'social dialogue' between representatives of employers and trade unions

June Delors Report on monetary union; accepted by heads of government at Madrid European Council

June Elections to European Parliament

July German monetary union

July Austria applies for EC membership

September Start of collapse of communism in Eastern Europe

October Delors lectures to the College of Europe in Bruges

December Fourth Lomé Convention signed

December Strasbourg European Council sets up an intergovernmental conference (IGC) to consider institutional changes necessary for completing monetary union

1990s

1990

July Stage 1 of economic and monetary union begins

July Cyprus applies for EC membership

July Malta applies for EC membership

August Iraq invades Kuwait

October Reunification of Germany; five new Länder become part of the EC

1991

January Start of IGC on political union

June Start of conflict between federal Yugoslav army and Slovenian separatist forces

July Sweden applies for EC membership

July Agriculture Commissioner MacSharry introduces his proposals for reform of the CAP

November EC imposes sanctions on Yugoslavia

December Maastricht European Council: agrees principles of Treaty on European Union (TEU), and to set up a cohesion fund to assist Greece, Spain, Ireland, and Portugal

1992

January Badinter Commission gives support for recognition of Macedonia and qualified support for Croatian independence

February Maastricht Treaty on European Union signed

March Finland applies for EC membership

May Switzerland applies for EC membership

May MacSharry proposals for reform of CAP agreed by Agriculture Ministers

June Danish referendum rejects TEU

597

1990s

June WEU Petersberg Declaration commits member states to allocate armed forces to peace keeping and humanitarian tasks in Europe

September French referendum accepts TEU

September British forced to withdraw from exchange rate mechanism of EMS

November Norway applies for EC membership

November Blair House agreement between the EU and the USA on trade in agricultural goods: paves the way for the completion of the Uruguay Round of GATT negotiations

December Swiss referendum rejects membership of the European Economic Area: Swiss government withdraws application for membership of EC

December Edinburgh European Council agrees opt-out for Denmark from single currency

1993

May Second Danish referendum accepts TEU

August The ERM's 'narrow bands' have to be widened to 15 per cent to allow it to survive

November TEU comes into effect

December EU monitors observe Russian elections

1994

January Stage 2 of economic and monetary union begins

January Start of European Economic Area (EEA)

January Reforms of structural funds agreed during 1993 come into effect

February Greek government refuses the former Yugoslav Republic of Macedonia access to the port of Salonika

April Hungary applies for EU membership

April Poland applies for EU membership

June Austrian referendum in favour of EU membership

June Corfu European Council agrees to extend internal market to energy and telecommunications

June Elections to European Parliament

October Finnish referendum in favour of EU membership

November Swedish referendum in favour of EU membership

November Norwegian referendum rejects EU membership

1995

January Austria, Finland, and Sweden become members of the EU

January Jacques Santer becomes President of the European Commission

January World Trade Organization (WTO) begins to operate

January CSCE becomes the Organization for Security and Co-operation in Europe (OSCE)

March 'Stability Pact' signed by 52 states from western and eastern Europe in an attempt to stabilize the political and security situation in eastern Europe

June Romania applies for EU membership

June Slovak Republic applies for EU membership

October Latvia applies for EU membership

November Estonia applies for EU membership

November Barcelona Conference launches the process that leads to the 'Euro-Med' agreements between the EU and North African and other states bordering the Mediterranean

November Agriculture Commissioner Franz Fischler introduces his proposals for further reform of the CAP; they are subsequently incorporated into *Agenda 2000*

December Lithuania applies for EU membership

December Bulgaria applies for EU membership

December 'New Transatlantic Agenda' agreed between the EU and the USA

December Madrid European Council decides on 'euro' as the name for the single currency

1996

January Czech Republic applies for EU membership

June Slovenia applies for EU membership

March Intergovernmental conference to review TEU officially opens in Turin

September Commission requests that member states extend its mandate in international trade negotiations to cover trade in services; request is refused

December Dublin European Council agrees a 'stability pact' to support monetary union

1997

June Amsterdam European Council: agreement on terms of Treaty of Amsterdam, including to supplement the stability pact with a growth and employment pact
All EU member states commit to the 'Petersberg tasks' as agreed by WEU members in June 1992

July Publication of Commission's *Agenda 2000* on eastern enlargement and the reform of the CAP and structural funds

October Treaty of Amsterdam signed

November Special 'jobs summit' held in Luxembourg to work out the principles of the 'co-ordinated strategy for employment' agreed at Amsterdam in June; effectively the 'Luxembourg process' is the first example of the 'Open Method of Co-ordination' (OMC)

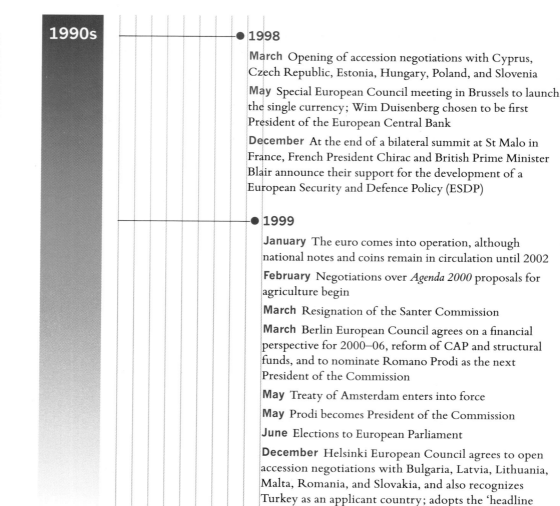

1990s

1998

March Opening of accession negotiations with Cyprus, Czech Republic, Estonia, Hungary, Poland, and Slovenia

May Special European Council meeting in Brussels to launch the single currency; Wim Duisenberg chosen to be first President of the European Central Bank

December At the end of a bilateral summit at St Malo in France, French President Chirac and British Prime Minister Blair announce their support for the development of a European Security and Defence Policy (ESDP)

1999

January The euro comes into operation, although national notes and coins remain in circulation until 2002

February Negotiations over *Agenda 2000* proposals for agriculture begin

March Resignation of the Santer Commission

March Berlin European Council agrees on a financial perspective for 2000–06, reform of CAP and structural funds, and to nominate Romano Prodi as the next President of the Commission

May Treaty of Amsterdam enters into force

May Prodi becomes President of the Commission

June Elections to European Parliament

December Helsinki European Council agrees to open accession negotiations with Bulgaria, Latvia, Lithuania, Malta, Romania, and Slovakia, and also recognizes Turkey as an applicant country; adopts the 'headline goal' of creating a European Rapid Reaction Force by the end of 2003

2000s

2000

March Institutions of ESDP begin provisional operation

March Special European Council held in Lisbon agrees to a new EU strategy on employment, economic reform, and social cohesion, and makes a commitment to turn the EU into 'the most competitive knowledge-based economy in the world' by 2010

June Signing of Cotonou Agreement as successor to Lomé

June Greece gains approval to join single currency

September Danish people vote to reject adoption of the euro

December Nice European Council agrees the Treaty of Nice and formally proclaims the Charter of Fundamental Rights of the European Union

2001

January Greece joins single currency

June Irish people vote to reject the Treaty of Nice

2000s

September Terrorist attacks in New York and Washington, DC

September European Council votes to support United States and to develop EU response following September 11 terrorist attacks

November In the face of protests from other member states, a planned trilateral meeting in London between Blair, Chirac, and Schmidt, to co-ordinate their countries' responses to the September terrorist attacks, has to be widened to include the EU High Representative for the CFSP, the Belgian Presidency of the Council, and the leaders of Italy, Spain, and the Netherlands

December Laeken European Council adopts the Declaration on the Future of the European Union, preparing the ground for a European Constitution

2002

January Citizens start using euro notes and coins in the twelve participating member states

February Convention on the Future of Europe begins its deliberations in Brussels, chaired by former French President Giscard d'Estaing

December US President Bush identifies an 'axis of evil' that includes Iraq

2003

February Treaty of Nice enters into force

March A coalition of states led by the United States and Britain invades Iraq; France and Germany condemn the invasion

March An EU force replaces the NATO stabilization force in the former Yugoslav Republic of Macedonia

April EP assents to the accession of ten new member states

June Agreement in Council of Ministers on final decoupling of agricultural payments from production

June Giscard d'Estaing presents draft EU Constitution to the European Council

September Swedish people vote to reject adoption of the euro

October Rome IGC convenes to consider draft EU Constitution

November Jean-Claude Trichet replaces Wim Duisenberg as President of the ECB

November Eurozone heads of government decide not to impose sanctions on France and Germany for breaching the rules of the stability pact

December Proposals of the Constitutional Convention presented to the European Council

2004

February Commission outlines its proposals for the operation of the structural funds in the period 2007–13

March Terrorist bombings in Madrid

April Adoption of an Internal Market Strategy to improve transposition of EU agreements into national law

May Ten new member states join the EU

601

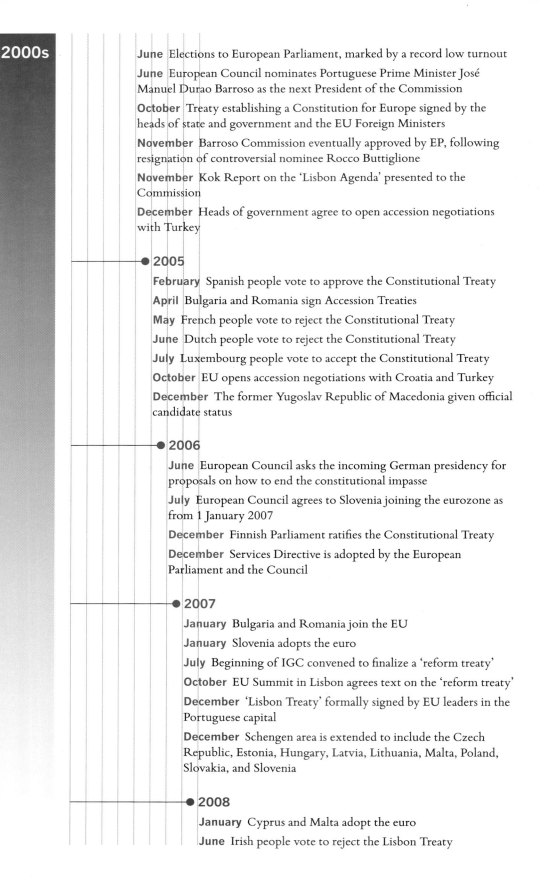

2000s

June Elections to European Parliament, marked by a record low turnout

June European Council nominates Portuguese Prime Minister José Manuel Durao Barroso as the next President of the Commission

October Treaty establishing a Constitution for Europe signed by the heads of state and government and the EU Foreign Ministers

November Barroso Commission eventually approved by EP, following resignation of controversial nominee Rocco Buttiglione

November Kok Report on the 'Lisbon Agenda' presented to the Commission

December Heads of government agree to open accession negotiations with Turkey

● **2005**

February Spanish people vote to approve the Constitutional Treaty

April Bulgaria and Romania sign Accession Treaties

May French people vote to reject the Constitutional Treaty

June Dutch people vote to reject the Constitutional Treaty

July Luxembourg people vote to accept the Constitutional Treaty

October EU opens accession negotiations with Croatia and Turkey

December The former Yugoslav Republic of Macedonia given official candidate status

● **2006**

June European Council asks the incoming German presidency for proposals on how to end the constitutional impasse

July European Council agrees to Slovenia joining the eurozone as from 1 January 2007

December Finnish Parliament ratifies the Constitutional Treaty

December Services Directive is adopted by the European Parliament and the Council

● **2007**

January Bulgaria and Romania join the EU

January Slovenia adopts the euro

July Beginning of IGC convened to finalize a 'reform treaty'

October EU Summit in Lisbon agrees text on the 'reform treaty'

December 'Lisbon Treaty' formally signed by EU leaders in the Portuguese capital

December Schengen area is extended to include the Czech Republic, Estonia, Hungary, Latvia, Lithuania, Malta, Poland, Slovakia, and Slovenia

● **2008**

January Cyprus and Malta adopt the euro

June Irish people vote to reject the Lisbon Treaty

2000s

June European Council urges other member states to continue with the ratification process for the Lisbon Treaty

August Military conflict breaks out between Georgia and Russia

September EU Summit condemns Russia's 'disproportionate reaction' in Georgia

December EU announces the creation of an 'eastern partnership' with six former Soviet states (Armenia, Azerbaijan, Belarus, Georgia, Moldova, and Ukraine)

December European Council gives Ireland reassurances over areas of concern in the Lisbon Treaty and the Irish government agrees to hold a new referendum by the end of 2009

December EU leaders agree to cut greenhouse gas emissions by 20 per cent by 2020

December Montenegro applies for EU membership

2009

January Slovakia adopts the euro

April Albania applies for EU membership

June European Parliament elections held

July Iceland applies for EU membership

September Heads of government appoint Herman Van Rompuy as first President of the European Council and nominate Baroness Catherine Ashton for the post of High Representative of the Union for Foreign Affairs and Security Policy

September European Parliament votes in favour of a second five-year term for Commission President Barroso

October Irish people vote to accept the Lisbon Treaty in a second referendum

December Lisbon Treaty comes into effect

December Serbia applies for EU membership

2010s

2010

February New Commission takes office headed by President Barroso

May EU and IMF agree financial package for Greece

June Iceland given official candidate status in June 2010

General Index

Diagrams are given in italics

607

SDS *see* European Sustainable Development Strategy
SEA *see* Single European Act 1987
Secretariat, the *274*, 310
Security and Co-operation in Europe (CSCE) 139, 174, 512, 522
Serbia 221, 534
services directive 392–4
severe acute respiratory syndrome (SARS) 357
SHAPE *see* Supreme Allied Headquarters Europe
single currency 160, 164, 179, 250, 420, *see also* Euro, the
Single European Act 1987 (SEA) 13, 24, 151, 153–8, 164, 177, 226, 231, 240, 275, 296, 299, 308, 341, 362, 386, 398, 404, 423, 425, 448–52, 458, 460, 464, 510, 512, 520, 524, 526
single European market (SEM) *see* single-market
single-market 261, 264, 352, 354, 356, 357, 359–61, 384–400, 442, 446
Single Market Compliance Unit (UK) 389
SIRENE bureaux 474
SIS *see* Schengen Information System
Slovakia 203, 219, 408, 432, 532–3
Slovenia 207, 209, 219, 408, 532–3
Small Farmers' Scheme 377
Smithsonian agreements 1971 138
'snake', the 137–8, 141, 403, 419
SNAs *see* sub-national authorities
Social Charter 159–61, 172, 362–3
social constructivism 312, 523 *see also* constructivism
Social Democratic Party (SPD) (Germany) 96, 135, 144, 147, 203
Social Protocol 335, 362–3
Social Security Directive (1978) 361
Socialist Group *see* Progressive Alliance of Socialists and Democrats
Socrates *see* Lifelong Learning Programme
SOLVIT 389
South Africa 515
South Korea 105
Soviet Union *see* USSR

Spaak Committee 111–12
Spain 11, 142, 144–5, 149, 173, 177, 182, 188, 193, 204, 217, 288, 322, 374, 376, 409, 425, 430, 442, 452, 458–61, 505, 517, 530–2, 538, 541
Spanish Socialist Workers' Party (PSOE) 204
SPD *see* Social Democratic Party (Germany)
Special Committee on Agriculture (SCA) 281, 283, 285
special 'jobs summit' (Luxembourg 1997) 363
spillover 9–10, 19, 412–13
 cultivated 9, 10, 19, 413
 exogenous 19
 functional 9–10, 19, 413
 geographical 10
 political 9, 19, 395
stability and growth pact 409–11
Stabilization and Association Agreement (SAA) 492
Stabilization and Association Process (SAP) 492
Stockholm Programme (2009) 472, 479, 487
Structural Fund Regulations (1994–99) 432–3, 435
structural funds 243, 374, 425–6, *431*, 432, *434*, 442–4
sub-national authorities (SNAs) 34
subsidiarity 164, 240–1, 248, 264, 324, 453
Suez Canal crisis 110, 114–15
supranationalism 7, 12–14, 14–19, 23–4, 54, 70, 89, 94, 98, 103, 117, 121–2, 124, 129–30, 135, 140, 149, 157, 220, 280, 288–9, 311, 328, 344, 383, 397–8, 412, 419
Supreme Allied Headquarters Europe (SHAPE) 517
Sustainable Development Strategy 454
Sweden 138, 173–4, 176, 182, 190, 198, 203, 376, 407–9, 420, 428, 452, 461, 503, 530, 532, 538–41, 545
Switzerland 476, 478, 541

T

Tampere Programme (2000) 279
tax harmonization 390
TEC *see* Treaty of the European Community
telecommunications 15, 390–2

TENs *see* trans-European networks
'territorial restructuring' 444
TFEU *see* Treaty on the Functioning of the European Union
thick trust 285
three-pillar structure 227, *227*, 368, 473, 479, 487, 514, 516
trade 490–508
trade and development aid 349
trans-European networks (TENs) 365
transgovernmentalism 9, 34, 484, 524–5
transnational networks 263, 397, 469
transnationalism 9, 16, 34, 38
transport 365–6
transposition 388
Treaties *226*
Treaties of Rome (1957) 13, 52, 108, 111–14, 119–20, 124–7, 134, 153, 212, 226–7, 229, 234, 253, 359, 361, 366, 370, 384, 490–1, 493, 502
Treaty of Amsterdam (1997) 24, 171, 174, 177–9, 182, 186, 187, 226–7, *232*, 243, 250, 265, 294, 296, 300, 309, 362, 363, 452–3, 466, 469, 471–2, 481, 487, 494, 510, 514, 526
Treaty of Brussels (1948) 107
Treaty of Dunkirk 88
Treaty of the European Community (1997) (TEC) 212, 227, 253, 509
Treaty on the Functioning of the European Union (TFEU) 213, 225–7, 240, 244, 246, 248, 250, 263, 324, 473, 513
Treaty of Lisbon (2009) 67, 75, 77, 108, 189, 197, 211–16, 218–21, 224, 226–9, 231, *232*, 233, 235–44, 246, 248, 250–4, 256, 258, 263–4, 269, 272–3, 275–6, 278, 280–2, 288, 290, 292, 295–6, 299, 309, 311–12, 315–16, 351, 355, 358, 363, 365, 366, 368, 436–7, 446, 453–4, 462, 473–4, 479, 481, 485–7, 493–4, 507, 514–15, 527, 536
Treaty of Luxembourg (1970) 297
Treaty of Nice (2001) 181, 189, 192, 195, 226–7, 233, 251, 258, 462, 472, 487, 510, 514, 527
Treaty on European Union (TEU) 13, 24, 159–61, 161–4, 165, 169–70, 174–6, 177–8,

Author Index

Diagrams are given in italics

615